THE ESSENTIAL CAPUTO

THE ESSENTIAL CAPUTO

Selected Writings

EDITED BY B. KEITH PUTT

Indiana University Press

This book is a publication of

Indiana University Press
Office of Scholarly Publishing
Herman B Wells Library 350
1320 East 10th Street
Bloomington,
Indiana 47405 USA

iupress.indiana.edu

The paper used in this publication meets the minimum requirements of the American National Standard for Information Sciences—Permanence of Paper for Printed Library Materials, ANSI Z39.48-1992.

MANUFACTURED IN THE UNITED STATES OF AMERICA

Library of Congress Cataloging-in-Publication Data

Names: Caputo, John D., author. | Putt, B. Keith, editor.
Title: The essential Caputo : selected writings / edited by B. Keith Putt.
Description: Bloomington : Indiana University Press, 2018. | Includes bibliographical references and index.
Identifiers: LCCN 2017044491 (print) | LCCN 2017048242 (ebook) | ISBN 9780253032232 (ebook) | ISBN 9780253032225 (hardcover : alk. paper) | ISBN 9780253032218 (pbk. : alk. paper)
Subjects: LCSH: Philosophy, American—20th century. | Philosophy, American—21st century. | Religion—Philosophy.
Classification: LCC B945.C141 (ebook) | LCC B945.C141 P88 2018 (print) | DDC 191—dc23
LC record available at https://lccn.loc.gov/2017044491

1 2 3 4 5 23 22 21 20 19 18

CONTENTS

ACKNOWLEDGMENTS

Joseph Shipley traces the genealogy of "acknowledgment" back to the Indo-European root "gn," which means both "to know" and "to beget." That explains why words such as "recognize" and "generate" derive from that exact same root. This dual etymology seems quite appropriate in the context of acknowledging the persons and organizations that have had dominant influences on the genesis of this Caputo reader. It does appear that professional courtesy would dictate that I recognize the people who genuinely contributed as sine quibus non to the "birth" of this project, those without whose support, insight, hard work, and official approval I could never have generated this bibliographical celebration of John D. Caputo's extensive scholarship.

Not surprisingly, my first expression of gratitude goes to Jack Caputo himself. As I note in my introductory chapter, for over a quarter of a century, Jack has been an esteemed and admired friend and a compelling and provocative intellectual influence; therefore, I thank him generally for the profound personal and professional impact he continues to have on who I am and what I do. More specifically, however, I want to thank him for allowing me to edit this reader. When Creston Davis, who has the distinction of being the original source of the idea of a Caputo reader, first asked Jack whom he would prefer to be the editor of such a text, he gave Creston my name. Consequently, had it not been for Jack's confidence that I could actually complete this project, my name would not be on the cover! I most definitely appreciate that confidence.

Next I want to recognize the contributions made by the excellent Indiana University Press editorial staff. First, Paige Rasmussen, assistant acquisitions editor, has done a superb job of handling all of the logistics involved in the submission process. She has kept me basically on schedule and always well-informed of the next step. Second, Julia Turner did an outstanding job copyediting the manuscript. She certainly ensured a more clean and readable volume. Last, but certainly not least, Dee Mortensen, editorial director, has made the entire publishing process far less painful and far more enjoyable just by contributing to it her professionalism, her creativity, and her insights. She is a good friend and, fortunately for me, a wise one.

The work of actually compiling the reader would not have been as successful had it not been for three other important people. I am certainly indebted to Mary Kate Young, my teaching assistant at Samford University, for her dependable and dedicated work on transferring all of the Caputo readings into PDF format. If she turns out to be as good a nurse as she was a readings copier, her patients will be extremely healthy! I also want to thank my other teaching assistant, Malee Galloway, for her excellent help in generating the volume's index. She kindly reassured me that the task was not the most tedious work she has ever done!

My deepest gratitude goes to my sweet wife, Dr. Sharon Putt, whom I genuinely adore. She put her own writing project aside for several weeks in order to help me do a close edit of the twenty-two essays that compose this reader. Had she not done so, I would most likely still be editing the chapters. I also want to thank her for her consistent but gentle nagging, always reminding me that I needed to stay at the computer and quit binge-watching Netflix.

Finally, I want to acknowledge the following publishers who graciously granted copyright permission to reprint the selections that compose this reader. Obviously, without their approval, this project would have been stillborn:

Chapter 3 "The Becoming Possible of the Impossible: An Interview with Jacques Derrida," in *A Passion for the Impossible: John D. Caputo in Focus*, ed. Mark Dooley, 21–33 (Albany: State University of New York Press, 2003). [©2003 State University of New York. All rights reserved.]

Chapter 4 "Meister Eckhart and the Later Heidegger, Part I," *Journal of the History of Philosophy* 12 (1974): 479–94. [©1974 Journal of the History of Philosophy, Inc. Reprinted with permission of Johns Hopkins University Press.]

Chapter 5 "Meister Eckhart and the Later Heidegger, Part II," *Journal of the History of Philosophy* 13 (1975): 61–80. [©1974 Journal of the History of Philosophy, Inc. Reprinted with permission of Johns Hopkins University Press.]

Chapter 6 "Heidegger's Dif-ference and the *Esse/Ens* Distinction in St. Thomas" *International Philosophical Quarterly* 20 (1980): 161–81.

Chapter 7 "Demythologizing Heidegger: *Alētheia* and the History of Being," *Review of Metaphysics* 41 (March 1988): 519–46.

Chapter 8 "Hermeneutics as the Recovery of Man" *Man and World* 15 (1982): 343–67. [With permission of Springer.]

Chapter 9 "Cold Hermeneutics: Heidegger and Derrida" *Journal of the British Society for Phenomenology* 17 (1986): 252–74.

Chapter 10 "On Not Knowing Who We Are: Madness, Hermeneutics and the Night of Truth in Foucault," in John D. Caputo, *More Radical Hermeneutics: On Not Knowing Who We Are*, 17–40 (Bloomington: Indiana University Press, 2000).

Chapter 11 "Beyond Aestheticism: Derrida's Responsible Anarchy," *Research in Phenomenology* 18 (1988): 59–73.

Chapter 12 "On Not Circumventing the Quasi-Transcendental: The Case of Derrida and Rorty," in *Working Through Derrida*, ed. Gary Madison, 147–69 (Evanston: Northwestern University Press, 1993).

Chapter 13 "Shedding Tears beyond Being: Derrida's Confession of Prayer," in *Augustine and Postmodernism: Confessions and Circumfession*, eds. John D. Caputo and Michael J. Scanlon, 95–114 (Bloomington: Indiana University Press, 2005).

Chapter 14 "The Good News about Alterity: Derrida and Theology," *Faith and Philosophy* 10 (1993): 453–70.

Chapter 15 "The Time of Giving and Forgiving/Edifying Divertissement No. 3," in John D. Caputo, *The Prayers and Tears of Jacques Derrida: Religion without Religion*, 160–88 (Bloomington: Indiana University Press, 1997).

Chapter 16 "Toward a Postmodern Theology of the Cross: Heidegger, Augustine, Derrida," in *Postmodern Philosophy and Christian Faith*, ed. Merold Westphal, 202–25 (Bloomington: Indiana University Press, 1999).

Chapter 17 "Jacques Derrida (1930–2004)," *Journal for Cultural and Religious Theory* 6 (December 2004): 6–9

Chapter 19 "In Search of a Sacred Anarchy: An Experiment in Danish Deconstruction," in *Calvin O. Schrag and the Task of Philosophy after Postmodernity*, eds. Martin Beck Matuštík and William L. McBride, 226–50 (Evanston: Northwestern University Press, 2002).

Chapter 20 "The Experience of God and the Axiology of the Impossible," in *The Experience of God: A Postmodern Response*, eds. Kevin Hart and Barbara E. Wall, 20–41 (New York: Fordham University Press, 2005).

Chapter 21 "Without Sovereignty, Without Being: Unconditionality, the Coming God and Derrida's Democracy to Come," *Journal for Cultural and Religious Theory* 4, no. 3 (August 2003): 9--26.

Chapter 22 "'Lazarus, Come Out': Rebirth and Resurrection," in John D. Caputo, *The Weakness of God: A Theology of the Event*, 236–58 (Bloomington: Indiana University Press, 2006).

Chapter 23 "A Prayer for the Impossible: A Catechumen's Guide to Deconstruction," in John D. Caputo, *What Would Jesus*

Deconstruct: The Good News of Postmodernism for the Church, 57–80 (Grand Rapids: Baker Academic, 2007). [©2007 Baker Academic, a division of Baker Publishing Group. Used by permission.]

Chapter 24 "God, Perhaps: The Fear of One Small Word," in John D. Caputo, *The Insistence of God: A Theology of Perhaps*, 3–23 (Bloomington: Indiana University Press, 2013).

THE ESSENTIAL CAPUTO

Part One

Radical Hermeneutics: Reflections

1
The Repetition of Sacred Anarchy: Risking a Reading of Radical Hermeneutics

B. KEITH PUTT

In February 1990, a good friend and I decided to journey to Conception Seminary in northwest Missouri in order to attend a conference on Catholic philosophy and deconstruction. Little did I realize how consequential those three days at that Benedictine monastery would be for me, personally and professionally. It was there and then that I first met and began to read John D. (Jack) Caputo. Jack initiated the weekend conference by delivering the first keynote address, a lecture entitled "Sacred Anarchy: Fragments of a Postmodern Ethics." Although I did not know it at the time, I later realized that the essay actually reprises various significant themes that he first articulates in the final chapter of his 1987 book, *Radical Hermeneutics*, themes that continue to direct his thought decades later. For example, "Sacred Anarchy" offers another commentary on his distinction between responsible postmodernism and irresponsible postmodernism, a distinction that comes in tandem with the tension that develops when the religious perspective confronts the tragic perspective with reference to the issue of suffering.[1] In *Radical Hermeneutics*, he raises the issue of how the religious perspective on suffering evokes a certain theology, a certain way of talking about God as always siding with those who suffer, with the victims of oppression, hunger, injustice, and disregard. For him, responsible postmodernism adopts the religious perspective and embraces, in one way or another and in one vocabulary or another, the theological position of joining God in the desire to alleviate the suffering of wounded flesh. This religio-theological sensitivity to the problem of suffering constitutes part of the mystery of existence—with "mystery" functioning as a legislating theme in that final chapter.

Just a year after the publication of *Radical Hermeneutics*, in the 1988 essay "Beyond Aestheticism: Derrida's Responsible Anarchy" (chapter 11 in this reader), Jack obviously transfers the adjective "responsible" from qualifying "postmodernism" to qualifying "anarchy" in order to maintain the ethical dynamic of his thought while simultaneously acknowledging the necessity for avoiding the hierarchical closure of any ersatz rational absolute. Then, two years later, "responsible" is itself replaced with "sacred" in the lecture "Sacred Anarchy," in which Jack amplifies aspects of "Beyond Aestheticism" and carries the themes of religion, suffering, God, and ethical responsibility into new directions. First, instead of contrasting responsible, religious postmodernism with irresponsible, tragic postmodernism, he writes as something of a contemporary Matthew Arnold and distinguishes between a Hebraic approach and a Hellenistic approach.[2] The latter approach he identifies with Martin Heidegger, who tends to write rather elitist texts about Greek temples and strong bodies; consequently, there appears to be little Heideggerian attention paid to the weakness of flesh and to the vulnerability of suffering. In contradistinction to this inattention, the Hebraic, or Jewish, perspective focuses significantly on the issue of the vulnerability of flesh—that is, that which can be wounded, torn, subjected to death, but also that which can be vulnerable to therapy, to healing, and to renewed life. Eventually, Jack personifies the Jewish perspective in a particular individual who is not quite Jewish and not quite Christian, someone whom he names Yeshua, preferring his Aramaic name to the more typical Christian name, Jesus. He contends that Yeshua reveals a certain ethical sensitivity to the weakness of flesh and to the need for the alleviation of suffering. In his declarations, his deeds, and even in his death, Yeshua manifests a morality that Jack terms an "ethics of the cross." In other words, Jack moves from the more general categories of mystery and God to a more specific analysis of the "sacred" under the factical rubric of Christianity.

Quite surprisingly, at least to me, Jack never published the complete text of "Sacred Anarchy: Fragments of a Postmodern Ethics." Of course, one may find brief references to the text in various publications, such as the 1993 volume entitled *Against Ethics*, where it makes up the substance of one of Magdalena de la Cruz's philosophical-lyrical discourses. Furthermore, one finds certain aspects of its content in Caputo's 1997 work *The Prayers and Tears of Jacques Derrida*. Still, the phrase "sacred anarchy" itself does not appear overtly in either book. That is not the case a decade later if one examines what could be called Caputo's "discovered trilogy."[3] Both the content of the keynote address and its title are found throughout *The Weakness of God* (2006), *The Insistence of God* (2013), and *The Folly of God* (2015). Both are also central to *What Would Jesus Deconstruct?* (2007) and *Hoping Against Hope* (2015). One might correctly claim, therefore, that all of these major works are creative extrapolations of what Jack lays out *in nuce* in "Sacred Anarchy." If so, then that keynote address may well be considered a textual synecdoche that encapsulates the primary motifs of Jack's literary production. I certainly interpret the essay as a uniquely compelling work for comprehending the nuances of Jack's thought over the past four decades. Not surprisingly, then, "Sacred Anarchy: Fragments of a Postmodern Ethics" has now been published as the fifteenth selection in the group of radical readings that compose this Caputo reader. I simply could not envision a Caputo reader without it.

THE POETICS OF RADICAL HERMENEUTICS

If you are reading this sentence, then you are, indeed, reading a Caputo reader—with "Caputo reader" functioning as a decidedly polysemic nominal phrase. Obviously, if you took the time to scan the table of contents before you turned to this introductory chapter, you would recognize the first meaning inherent in that overdetermined expression. This book is, indeed, a "Caputo reader" in the sense that it incorporates into one volume twenty-one full or partial texts—that is, "readings"—from the rather vast Caputoan corpus. The publication lying open before you may, therefore, be considered an anthology of selected works authored by Jack over a period of four decades, an anthology offering an easy guide for getting a "read" on his multidimensional philosophy. As an anthology, it collects or gathers together a representative assortment of texts that exemplify the continuities and discontinuities marking the evolution of various philosophical perspectives that he has typically denominated as "radical hermeneutics."

"Anthology" certainly operates here as an appropriate synonym for "reader," given that the term derives from the Greek *anthologia*, which literally means a "gathering of flowers," or a "bouquet." Quite often, the term refers bibliographically to a collection of "literary" flowers, that is to say, poems. Of course, Jack does not write poetry, at least not in the typical senses of that genre. Yet, if you do continue on and read some of the selections collected in this volume, you will discover, perhaps unexpectedly, that he does, indeed, write as a "poet." He creates (in the Greek, *poiein*) what he calls various "poetics"—ranging, for example, from the "poetics of obligation"[4] in 1993 to the "poetics of God" or "theopoetics"[5] in 2015. Scattered across the two decades separating those two expressions of poetics one may also find the "poetics of the impossible,"[6] the "poetics of the event,"[7] the "poetics of the cosmos" or "cosmopoetics,"[8] and the "poetics of the kingdom,"[9] just to name a few. Ironically, one might well conclude, after a broader reading of Caputo, that all of these "poetics" manifest various perspectives on what I would call a "poetics of the rose." Jack has consistently been a "cherubinic wanderer" preferring roses as the primary blossoms in his philosophical *anthologias*, specifically because they bloom *ohne warum*, *sans pourquoi*, "without why," thereby calling for a certain *Gelassenheit*, or "letting-be," that avoids the princely demands of the Principle of Sufficient Reason.[10] For this reason, he has developed his own unique philosophically poetic or poetically philosophical voice in order to speak constantly from and at the limits of metaphysical reason alone.[11]

Of course, one might infer from his article "Demythologizing Heidegger: *Alētheia* and the History of Being" (chapter 7 in this reader) that Jack's dismissal of the pretentious claims made by any recital of epic plots about definitive movements of capitalized words, such as Being, Spirit, Truth, Providence, or Destiny, manifests a genuine disdain for *muthos*, for the efficacy of narrative, or the poetic, or any symbolic genres of discourse. But such an inference would simply be mistaken. Jack only criticizes literary attempts that arrogantly presume to establish metanarratives privileging the one over the many, subsuming the plurality of subplots under some grand totalizing yarn that seeks to weave together a unified pattern having no loose ends. He believes, to the contrary, that a genuine poetics will emphasize the limits of such closed systems of thought, accentuate the porous nature of rational discourse, and celebrate the competitive profusion of multiple stories that demand the repetition of hermeneutics,[12] with "repetition," according to "Hermeneutics as the Recovery of Man" (chapter 8 in this reader) being a transformative asymptotic process of creative meaning.[13] He summarizes this position quite well in a recent expression of his "poetics" manifesto: "We defer all absolute knowledge, absolute concepts, absolute spirits; we call for adjourning the meeting of the Department of Absolute Knowledge, *sine die*. In the place of the pretensions of metaphysics we put an unpretentious poetics, the various and irreducibly plural ways we have of giving figure and form to our experience of the unconditional, of giving it narratival and pictorial form, in words and images, striking sayings and dramatic scenes."[14]

One can determine, from the above confession, that Jack's philosophical poetics inculcate both an aporetics and an apophatics. As one travels near the limits of metaphysics, one desires to move beyond those limits, yet discovers that such transcendence is impossible. One may never totally escape the flux of existence and the limitations and uncertainties that the flux ensures. Poetics, then, is always *un pas au-dela*, "a step (not) beyond,"[15] a movement—always a *kinesis*, never a *stasis*—that remains messianic, heading toward a destination always "to come." As a result, discourse remains within the embrace of the negative, wrestling constantly with the inability to articulate certainty and truth without tapping out and conceding to the functional ineffability of such articulations. Poetics, therefore, constantly speaks about how to avoid speaking, thereby remaining both apophatic and loquacious.

One encounters an early expression of the aporetic/apophatic nature of Jack's developing poetics simply by reading the first two selections in the current anthology, the two parts of "Meister Eckhart and the Later Heidegger." I consider it quite appropriate to begin a Caputo reader with textual evidence of the centrality of Christian mysticism and Meister Eckhart for his radical hermeneutics. During the forty years since the publication of these essays, he has continually extrapolated the critical implications of mystery and negative theology for developing an alternative discourse to the traditional philosophical language of foundationalism and its craving for certainty. Furthermore, the specific context of Eckhartian mysticism emphasizes the theological sensitivity that has consistently characterized his thought. Although he has openly been identified as a "theologian" only for the past decade or so, he has effectively been doing theology throughout his career. He concedes as much on a couple of occasions: first when he testifies that God has been "a lifelong task"[16] and second when he acknowledges "a weakness for theology."[17] One may well say of Caputo what he says of Heidegger, that he "has been interested in theological issues from the very beginning of his studies" and for decades has been "transforming the ideas and the language of the Western religious tradition."[18]

Ironically, Jack's obsession with theology leads to a certain subversion of Derrida, who early on in his work identifies the totalizing dynamic of metaphysics as specifically "theological," with "God" serving as the "transcendental signified" that ensures a closure to meaning and truth.[19] Jack, on the other hand, develops an understanding of "God" as precisely a name for the event that keeps reality open to mystery and preempts every attempt at reconstructing some type of Cartesian certainty. "God" names the ateleological interruptive spirit that acts as a quasi-transcendental for the continuation of poetics.[20] Poetics can now be theological (theopoetics) and religious in the more radical sense of the anonymity of the call to something impossible, something unprogrammable, something that respects ethical alterity, and something that deconstructs every status quo—for example, something like a poetics of the Kingdom of God. In the interest of full disclosure, therefore, I must now complete the quotation above referencing Jack's manifesto of poetics:

> In the place of the pretensions of metaphysics we put an unpretentious poetics, the various and irreducibly plural ways we have of giving figure and form to our experience of the unconditional, of giving it narratival and pictorial form, in words and images, striking sayings and dramatic scenes, *which is what we mean by a theopoetics of the folly of God. Religion is a song to the unconditional, a way to sing what lays claim to us unconditionally. But as to identifying what the unconditional is, if it is, we beg to be excused. This is a hermeneutics where nobody has the key, the code, the legendum* (emphasis added).[21]

For Jack, a "theopoetics of the folly of God" translates quite easily into a theology of the event, which is, in itself, a theology of the "perhaps." Indeed, he clearly distinguishes logic from poetics at this very point, insisting that "[l]ogic addresses the modally possible, whereas a poetics is always a grammar of the 'perhaps,' which is the prime modality of the event. . . . [I]n a poetics the possible belongs to the humble sphere of what Derrida calls the 'perhaps,' the *peut-être*. The *peut-être* threatens to irrupt from within and to disturb the conditions of *être*, supplying the dangerous perhaps of the possibility of the impossible that solicits us from afar."[22]

I allege that one may validly read Caputo's corpus as expressing several different, yet complementary, variants of poetics, each emerging in some manner out of two concepts, the "without" and the "perhaps." These two concepts are among Jack's favorite words. He uses, not just mentions, them constantly, whether in English, German, or French. From his dependence noted above on Angelus Silesius's *ohne warum*, "without why," concerning the rose's propensity to bloom with no concern for the Principle of Sufficient Reason to his glosses on Derrida's "religion without religion," where he speaks of faith as "*sans vision, sans verité, sans révelation*" or "*sans voir, sans avoir, sans savoir*," Jack is never without access to the "without."[23] Likewise, he consistently advocates the centrality of the "perhaps," here again utilizing the Derridean translation of that concept. Derrida does not define *peut-être* in its literal etymological sense of "may" (*peut*) "be" (*être*) but in the more active sense of "it may happen."[24] Derrida's paraphrase of *peut-être*, therefore, directly connects "perhaps" with the idea of the "event," another one of those ideas that Jack endorses throughout his corpus, especially with reference to his theology. He declares that the event just happens without why and without the compulsion of the preordained. It cannot be programmed or anticipated by the inexorability of logic, the necessity of causality, or the manipulation of individual or social sovereignty. It remains messianic, always "to come" in some absolute future that will have been but never is—one of the only "absolutes" that Jack allows![25] Consequently, the event subverts every dissimulation of totalized meaning, or hegemonic capital T truth, or reductionistic claim to certainty. In "On Not Knowing Who We Are" (chapter 10 in this reader), Jack refers to this condition using Foucault's phrase the "night of truth," which ultimately denies the "truth of truth."[26] Concomitantly, the event grounds only the ungrounded "perhaps," haunting it as a specter of undecidability that demands taking the risk of decision.[27]

Jack argues that this hauntology of the perhaps as "a principle *without* [emphasis added] principle, an anarchic and unmonarchical *arche*" inspires the "ability to sustain uncertainty and to venture into the unknown."[28] It establishes and conserves the constancy of several coefficients, including the "coefficient of uncertainty,"[29] the "coefficient of contingency,"[30] and the "coefficient of undecidability" itself.[31] These hauntological coefficients comprise a "spectral hermeneutics,"[32] which seeks to engage the flux of existence with a minimal metaphysics that respects the inherent pluralism and difference within reality and that rejects the presumption of a Platonic essentialism.[33] It recognizes and exploits the "irreducible depth and uncertainty in things . . . [the] indeterminacy built right into things" and keeps all traditions fluid and corrigible, operating in an "under-determined situation that requires judgment and human determination."[34] Furthermore, all of this comes to a unique, even if not singular, manifestation in a theology of the anarchic Kingdom of God, specifically a poetics of the Kingdom of God that informs a theopoetics of the name of "God" as a sacred "quasi-transcendental signifier" signifying the event that haunts the *sans* and the *peut-être*. As Jack confesses in "Shedding Tears beyond Being" (chapter 13 in this reader), the hauntological nature of poetics leaves us "awash in question," never knowing who we are, from whom the call originates, to whom we pray, or what we love when we love our God.[35]

Of course, granting the fundamental emphases on poetics, the "without," and the "perhaps" in Jack's thought does not certify one precise interpretation of his radical hermeneutics. As Paul Ricoeur so accurately indicates, one may never escape the conflict of interpretations that the essential plurivocity of texts demands.[36] Yet one should not expect anything less from a volume of "readings," since to "read" carries with it, at least etymologically, the potentiality of uncertainty, risk, and mystery. In the English semiotic pedigree of "to read," specifically in the German branch of the family tree, the root, *raten*, means both "to advise" and "to guess." This secondary meaning actually denotes a familial connection, therefore, between "read" and "riddle"; consequently, to read a text is to confront a riddle, to make a guess as to what the text may mean. Under the present circumstances, however, guessing and riddling are not inappropriate concepts when reading a Caputo reader, since the included selections manifest on numerous occasions that the uncertainty associated with these two terms permeates radical hermeneutics from its beginning. Again, Ricoeur contends that hermeneutics consistently relies on the strategy of the "wager" as a proper initiation into the process of interpretation.[37] Given his propensity to consort with secrets, uncertainties, the ubiquity of the "perhaps" and the "*non-savoir*," and the centrality of faith, Jack, too, might well agree that deciphering the riddles of radical hermeneutics requires reading to be a constant gambling on meanings.

Allow me, then, to put my money on the table, ante up, and play the hermeneutical game; that is, I wish to place a bet on a particular way of reading the enclosed readings, as well as of reading the entire Caputo corpus over the four decades of its development. Doing so undeniably insinuates another denotation to the nominal phrase "Caputo reader," because in proposing a variant reading of the texts, I confirm that I, too, am a "Caputo reader." As a result, I want to offer for your consideration my particular reading of Caputo that seeks to consolidate his works under the broader rubric of the essay that introduced me to him and inaugurated my reading of his work almost three decades ago—that is, "Sacred Anarchy: Fragments of a Postmodern Ethics." I hope to argue successfully that all of the intricacies of his philosophy of religion and philosophical theology, with their primary themes of poetics, the "without," and the "perhaps," coalesce around the provocative phrase "sacred anarchy." As I note above, the "perhaps" directly addresses the anarchic conditions of uncertainty and faith and the "without" derives directly from a sacred context, explicitly the context of Christian mysticism. Consequently, the phrase "sacred anarchy" appears to me to operate quite conspicuously as an axiological principle for deciphering Jack's intrinsic *vouloir dire* as an author.

Of course, I admit that there are other valid readings of Caputo and that other Caputo readers can gamble quite reasonably on alternative strategies for consolidating the complexities of his fertile thought. Furthermore, I admit that reading Jack through the lens of "sacred anarchy" as a "canon within the canon" may not be overtly evidenced by his own personal authorial intentionality. To be sure, just above I do humbly suggest that it is merely referencing an "intrinsic *vouloir dire*." Nonetheless, I do not consider my hermeneutical wager to be a fool's bet. I feel confident that a convincing case may be made for considering "sacred anarchy" to be a functionally viable principle for deciphering the nuances of the Caputoan corpus. The phrase intimates a proper textual adhesive that not only binds together the various radical readings that constitute this volume but also binds together the four decades of creative interpretations that embody Caputo's unique philosophical and theological voice. Accordingly, I will now make my wager, deal the cards, and wait to see if I hold a decent hand.

AN "ONTOLOGY" OF SACRED ANARCHY

Between the appearance of the phrase "sacred anarchy" in the keynote address in 1990 and its significant book-length use in *The Weakness of God* in 2006, one can find it as a titular legislating principle in a fascinating article entitled "In Search of a Sacred Anarchy: An Experiment in Danish Deconstruction" published in 2002 (chapter 19 in this reader). In this essay, Jack reprises a major concept that he addresses extensively in his "Edifying Divertissement No. 4" section of *The Prayers and Tears of Jacques Derrida*, specifically the concept of the Kingdom of God. I consider this 2002 article to be quite significant not only in summarizing the development of Jack's thought up to that time but also in telegraphing the future development of that thought over the next fifteen years. In this article, he overtly connects the idea of sacred anarchy with the idea of the Kingdom of God and, furthermore, connects Yeshua's "ethics of the cross" directly to the proclamation of that kingdom. He establishes this connection through the use of the deconstructive notion of *différance*, which, according to Derrida, has no relationship whatsoever to the idea of kingdom, except as its denial. *Différance* disallows any concept of rule or control, of any expression of *arché*—be it monarchical or hierarchical—and, therefore, "governs nothing, reigns over nothing, and nowhere exercises any authority."[38] Yet, Jack speculates transversely, "in the best spirit of deconstruction," whether one could, perhaps, entertain *de jure* "the possibility of a kingdom of the kingdomless, a kingdom of those who do not reign and have no power, an un-kingly, *an-archic* kingdom" [emphasis added].[39] Moreover, he believes that he finds just such a kingdom *de facto* in Jesus's proclamation of the Kingdom of God, a kingdom that functions as a subversive, interruptive, and deconstructive alternative to every status quo. It is, indeed, an anarchic kingdom predicated on the rule of a God who does not operate according to the coercive, oppressive, and dominating power of the world.

In order to identify the God manifested in Jesus's teachings on the kingdom, Jack remains "biblical" and relies on the theology of weakness developed by the Apostle Paul in his first epistle to the Corinthians. Paul insists that, according to the logic of the world, God is illogical and unruly, even to the point of madness. Given the criteria for power in the world, God is weak; given the criteria for rationality in the world, God is foolish; and given the criteria for what rises to the level of metaphysical being in the world, God constantly consorts with nothingness. Paul insists that the good news of the gospel consists in the grace and mercy manifested in both the weakness and the foolishness of God. Paul considers the anarchic power of the powerless God to be disruptive of all of the world's criteria, even going so far as to quote from the prophet Isaiah and claim that God "will destroy the wisdom of the wise."[40] Now, Jack loves this Pauline prophetic proclamation primarily because of the subsequent genealogy of the Greek word for "destroy." Paul uses the verb *appolumi*, a word that translates into Latin as the verb *destruere* and the noun *destruction*. Interestingly enough, Luther uses this term to describe his criticism of medieval scholasticism, and there is good evidence that Heidegger derives his use of *Destruktion* from Luther's usage. But, of course, Derrida develops his word *déconstruction* from Heidegger's *Destruktion*; consequently, one might well consider Paul as the nominal patriarch of deconstruction when he claims that God "deconstructs" the power and wisdom of the world through the weakness and foolishness of the "word (*logos*) of the cross (*stauros*)."[41]

At this point, one may confirm the development of Jack's "ethics of the cross" expressed in "Sacred Anarchy" into the "logic of the cross" expressed here in "In Search of a Sacred Anarchy." Furthermore, as one encounters the staurological inversive dynamic that serves throughout as a defining principle the Caputoan corpus for the deconstructive Kingdom of God, one may well retroject its origin here to this essay. For Jack, the theology of the weakness and foolishness of God expressed in the logic of the cross obviously contradicts the metaphysical theology of classical theism. God is not the omnipotent, omniscient, omnipresent, transcendent deity that personifies total presence or acts as a transcendental signified ensuring absolute knowledge and absolute meaning. The God revealed by Jesus is no super being who directs reality through determined acts of sovereignty that may be easily co-opted by arrogant human beings who baptize their own will to power as sanctioned by, or as expressions of, this metaphysically potent God. On the contrary, the Kingdom of God anarchically confounds such thought, disrupts those notions of power and prestige, and subordinates the principles of the world to the powerless power of the widows and orphans, the excommunicated and exiled, to the "least of these" with whom Jesus identifies. Here again Jack refers to Paul's material on the weakness of God, since in that discussion the apostle indicates that God confounds the being of the world by siding with all of those whom the world considers to be nobody and nothing. Paul refers to them as the *ta me onta*, literally "the ones without being."[42] Jack contends that in this context, God deconstructs the being of the world by identifying directly with these non-beings; that is, God withdraws "from the worldliness of the world, from the world's order of presence" and settles "into those pockets or recesses which are formed in the world by the little ones, the nothings and nobodies of the world."[43]

The dialectic of "withdrawal from" and "settling into" suggests the traditional concepts of God's transcendence and immanence, a dialectic that remains operative within the argument of "In Search of a Sacred Anarchy." In this essay, the Kingdom of God is not an issue of whether God exists or does not exist, but, instead, of "where" God exists and "how" God exists. Indeed, throughout most of his work, Jack has maintained an element of what, in "The Good News about Alterity" (chapter 14 in this reader), he calls deconstruction's "armed neutrality" regarding a presumed referentiality to the language of faith.[44] That is to say, deconstruction maintains a critical openness to apodictic statements concerning divine existence or nonexistence. Certainly here in this article, Jack does not hesitate to embrace the language of divine existence, proposing that God exists within the context of human existence as a critical and interruptive force calling into question structures of coercion and domination. He refers to this notion of divine existence as God's "insistence," a term that synonymizes with the paleonym "immanence."[45] He claims that one no longer needs to distinguish between God's separation from the world and God's connection to the world, because in the Kingdom of God as proclaimed by Jesus and glossed by the apostle Paul, God is located in medias res, always standing (*sistere*) in the midst of the nobodies who suffer because of the oppressive structures of the status quo. In other words, God's insistence discloses the immanent spirit of divine contradiction that seeks to subvert the world's oppressive powers.

The concept of the insistence of God becomes quite significant in Jack's later development of a theology of the event. Eventually, he moves the concept away from the issue of immanence and contrasts it to the idea of existence, a move that establishes the thesis of the second volume of his theological trilogy, *The Insistence of God*. God's insistence replaces the notion of existence and qualifies the anonymous call that summons individuals to engage in something of an *imago dei* and identify, too, with the "least of these" who have no voice or position in society. Clearly, the prominence of "insistence" in the development of Jack's radical theology of the event adds considerable cachet to the importance of the second overt treatment of "sacred anarchy" in 2002. According to my reading of the Caputoan corpus, "In Search of a Sacred Anarchy" is actually the first time that he uses the concept, and the fact that he does so in the context of how to comprehend the mystery of God's immanent response to the ethical issue of suffering further ensures the importance of that text. Indeed, when he next addresses this issue in 2006 in *The Weakness of God*, he does so basically by plagiarizing—I mean, "repeating"—this article![46]

One could argue that "In Search of a Sacred Anarchy" transitions Jack's thought from an "ethics of the cross" through the "logic of the cross" to what may be termed a "politics of the cross," since over the last decade and a half he has focused overtly on the ethico-political implications of "God" and of the Kingdom of God for a theology of the event as a pragmatic and prophetic transformation of the world. Not surprisingly, he has actually overtly developed his own version of a *theologia crucis*, a "theology of the cross," as is evidenced by his essay "Toward a Postmodern Theology of the Cross" (chapter 16 in this reader). Yet, I contend that even over the entire four decades of his radical hermeneutics, Jack has in various ways and under diverse vocabularies been stimulated both to discover and to invent deconstructive implications for a postsecular understanding of the interconnections between politics and theology. I want to suggest further that the phrase "sacred anarchy" may well be a successful rubric for prosecuting this development of the Caputo corpus from its inception to its most recent expressions. In offering this suggested reading, I propose two metonymic moves, from "anarchy" to "kingdom" and from "sacred" to "incarnation."

"Anarchy" directly addresses the notion of kingdom, since kingdom typically includes the issue of some kind of rule, *arché*, or established power structure. Anarchy, as the opposite of such a structure or the negation of any idea of such a structure, either denounces the viability of "kingdom" or transforms how that concept may be defined. Jack finds prescribed in Jesus's proclamation of the Kingdom of God as an unruly kingdom—a kingdom of weakness, of foolishness, of the madness of turned cheeks, of questionable searches for lost sheep, and of unending forgiveness—a decidedly redemptive transformation of the concept of kingdom. He contends that to appreciate the anarchical Kingdom of God, one must recognize hermeneutically that any discourse addressing that kingdom is always poetic, consisting not of constative statements of literal meaning but of metaphors, similes, hyperboles, and parables. In other words, "anarchy" drives him to "kingdom," and both terms drive him to engage in all of the strategies of poetics that I discuss earlier in this essay.

Most recently, Jack has referred to the poetics of the kingdom as instantiating a certain version of Hegelian *Vorstellungen* (representations), but a version that results from what he terms a "decapitated Hegel," one that does not operate as a medium through which one achieves the Concept, but as the only reality of the kingdom that one may encounter.[47] In other words, with reference to religious language about the kingdom, there are only *Vorstellungen*, only poetic representations of a Kingdom of God that can never be exhaustively realized. Jack refers to a *Vorstellung* as a "world-picture, a world-praxis, a world-formation, a world-creation, an event of *poiesis* . . . [or] a form of life" (emphasis added).[48] As such, the kingdom of God offers an alternative ontology, another way of interpreting and living in the world.

Jack's connection between *Vorstellungen* and poetics with reference to ontological exploration appears to have a certain affinity with Ricoeur's emphasis on the preconstructive, constructive, and reconstructive dynamics of imaginative language. Ricoeur declares throughout his work that discourse may contribute both "models of" and "models for" reality. He contends that through the productive imagination, human beings discover (models of) and invent (models for) order and purpose in existence. Through the creative processes (*poiesis*) of narrative, metaphor, and symbols, imaginative discourse reinterprets and refashions, Ricoeur would say "configures" and "reconfigures," human being-in-the-world.[49] This poetic procedure inevitably questions any extant situation by virtue of the fact that it consistently offers alternative ontologies that may attract readers to engage in imaginative variations of the ego in order to entice them to embrace the new reality.[50] This, to me, is clearly analogous to Jack's understanding of Jesus's kerygma of the kingdom. As a potent religious *Vorstellung* or imaginative reordering of a new life-world, Jesus's poetics of the kingdom challenges the status quo by offering to the imagination an alternative structuring of reality, a new form of being-in-the-world. As such, the poetics of the kingdom actually offers a new model *for* reality, thereby motivating the existential realization of the kingdom through the metamorphosis of social and political structures. In "'Lazarus, Come Out'" (chapter 22 in this reader), Jack identifies this metamorphic efficacy of the kingdom with the notion of metanoetics, from the Greek *metanoia*, meaning "change of mind" or "change of heart." This metanoetic potentiality operates as a poetic power that manifests the "phenomenological core of what theology calls a miracle."[51] The miracle of metanoetics, therefore, does not concern an event that countermands natural processes but manifests an unpredictable ethico-political alteration of human society stimulated by the poetic efficacy of symbolic, imaginative discourse.

Jack's understanding of the transfiguring potency of the Kingdom of God also broaches Kevin Hart's idea of the "basileic reduction," expressed in his recent book *Kingdoms of God*. According to Hart, and in agreement with Ricoeur, the parables of Jesus reveal the Kingdom (*basileia*) of God to be an alternative structure for patterning human existence. To do so, they necessarily place in a tensive relationship the different forms of life that qualify either living according to "worldly" standards of logic and power or living according to the kingdom principles of the rule of God, a distinction that mirrors Jack's differentiation between the "logic of the world" and the "logic of the cross." Hart refers to this conflictual differentiation as a "reduction" from the world to the kingdom, in other words, a "basileic reduction," whereby an alternative ontology appeals to the imagination of those who encounter, either orally or textually, Jesus's discourse on the Kingdom of God.[52] By making the reduction to the kingdom, one disengages the facticity of the natural attitude for power and prestige and engages in a phenomenology of the kingdom as an ironic and prophetic critique, even a subversion, of what passes as common human existence. Using a creative confusion of modes of perception, Hart contends that in the parables we "*see* the [kingdom] in *hearing* Jesus" (emphasis added). Yet, this "visible hearing," in a Ricoeurean sense, operates as an impetus to the imagination to reflect on the decision to enter that kingdom and literally change one's mode of existence to fit the new reality. As Hart states explicitly, whether the parables establish the Kingdom of God or not is a risk dependent on whether individuals decide "to live it out or keep on living as before." [53] This results in a constant "realized eschatology" of the kingdom as "already but not yet."[54]

So, too, in his poetics of the kingdom, Jack engages in a phenomenology of an alternative ontology, for as he admits in "The Experience of God and the Axiology of the Impossible" (chapter 20 in this reader), he seeks to work his way "back into the texture of the phenomenological structure of experience," which he insists demands consideration of "God."[55] To do so, he once again makes use of the concept of insistence in the later sense of contrasting it with existence instead of the earlier sense of considering it a supplement to immanence,[56] although, somewhat ironically, the idea of immanence is not fully preempted. He claims specifically that the Kingdom of God does not exist but only insists; that is, it is not some identifiable social or political reality but a call that issues forth from who knows where and from who knows whom and demands, without sovereignty, that one identifies with the widow and orphan, consoles those who are oppressed and treated unjustly, and responds graciously to those the world considers to be nobody. Yet, as I note above, Jack has most definitely read his Meister Eckhart, and, consequently, knows that acts of mercy, grace, and love are themselves the very instantiation of the Kingdom of God. In other words, the Kingdom of God does, indeed, exist in those very events of grace motivated by the call of obligation. For Jack, events such as these always occur, as he claims in "The Time of Giving and Forgiving" (chapter 15 in this reader), with a "kind of aleatory gratuitousness and anarchic abandon which lets something different come."[57] He later designates this aleatoric mercy the "nihilism of grace."[58] These events of aleatoric grace then establish a certain kingdom ontology, a "being" of the kingdom as disclosed in realistic acts of love.

To be sure, his poetics of the kingdom sounds remarkably similar to the principles of the Social Gospel, which should not be too surprising given that he conspicuously relies on this theological movement in his work of practical theology and ecclesiology, *What Would Jesus Deconstruct?*, a work that directly relates to Charles Sheldon's *In His Steps*, a classic text in the Social Gospel tradition. The influential "patriarch" of the movement, Walter Rauschenbusch, reminds his readers that Jesus encouraged his disciples to seek first the Kingdom of God, that is, not to reduce faith to a purely private spirituality but to affirm that the gospel intends to convert the social order.[59] In like manner, Jack rejects any interpretation of religion that considers faith to be a type of spiritual centripetal force that draws an individual into the singularity of her own piety instead of directing her centrifugally outward toward the ethical alterity of the other.[60] Furthermore, as the Social Gospel movement criticized any eschatological reduction of the Kingdom of God to some future reality having no ethical or political influence on current affairs, likewise, Jack, in his phenomenology of the kingdom, refuses to postpone its reality or influence to some future moment. Instead, he agrees with Hart and adopts a realized eschatology, recognizing that the Kingdom of God is always "already but not yet." In other words, whenever the acts of mercy and love prescribed by Jesus are embodied by individuals who seek to obey the kingdom *kerygma*, then the Kingdom of God does truly exist—but always anarchically.[61]

Still, the anarchy of the ethico-political Kingdom of God remains in some respect a "sacred" anarchy. Ian Ramsey, the influential twentieth-century philosopher of religious language, notes that in theological language, ordinary discourse is often made strange through the use of certain "qualifiers" or adjectives. For example, God is not merely "Other" but is "Wholly" Other, with "Wholly" directing alterity in a new direction. Correspondently, one could say that Jack depends on the same dynamics of adjectivizing. For him, it is not enough simply to posit the anarchy of the Kingdom of God; on the contrary, one must add the qualifier "sacred." Use of the qualifier "sacred," however, places one in an etymological process that allows the use of "sacrament," which, in turn, places one in a metonymic process that allows for the use of "incarnation." If a sacrament is indeed an empirical symbol or vehicle for grace, then there is an incarnational aspect to the sacrament, given that the particular sacramental vehicle or medium is an embodiment or material designation of something immaterial. Furthermore, of course, "incarnation," at least within the traditions of Christian theological language, necessarily provokes the idea of God's being made flesh. Consequently, Jack's use of "sacred anarchy" requires that one investigate not only the *Kingdom* of God but also the Kingdom of *God*. In other words, there can be no basileiology without an accompanying theology. Not surprisingly, therefore, one finds in Jack's developing thought not only a poetics of the kingdom but a poetics of God, a theological poetics that closely tracks with the basileic reduction and reprises the significance of a divine "insistence." Jack adjusts deconstruction's armed neutrality just a bit and contends that God does not exist. He rejects any metaphysical affirmation of an entitative deity, of any super being that exists ontologically as a willing, thinking, and acting singularity. He says of God precisely what he says of the kingdom—that God does not exist but *insists*. Jack argues that "God" names the insistent call of obligation, the anonymous motivation to engage in acts of charity, acts of liberation, and acts of healing. Only by understanding God as insisting and not as existing does he think one can adequately interpret the Pauline notion of the weakness of God.

Still, if Jack's poetics of God is commensurable with his poetics of the kingdom, then the productive inconsistency in the latter may be found in the former, specifically, that the nonexisting God does, indeed, exist, that is, in some manner, one can affirm a theological ontology that is not ontotheological! To be sure, Jack's insistence of God is not a total rejection of the existence of God, if by "existence" one means that God is incarnate in the very acts of mercy and love accomplished by human beings. It does mean, however, that God needs human beings in order to exist, in order to embody God in the very ethical and political activities that manifest the Kingdom of God in human society. This ethico-political incarnation of God genuinely defines Jack's poetics of God as a "Theopoetics," a "doing" of God. Jack is fond of borrowing Augustine's pragmatic definition of truth as not what is verified or established logically but as *facere veritatem*, what is done actively and ethically. Such a definition works well with reference to the Kingdom of God, for the truth of the kingdom is always expressed as what is done in obedience to the kingdom directives. Correlatively, one might say that the existence of God in the incarnate acts of mercy and grace is the result of a *facere deum*. As a result, one could see Jack's theopoetic notion of incarnation as analogously similar to Rudolf Bultmann's notion of resurrection. Bultmann rejects any historical or literal resuscitation of the body of Jesus; however, he does believe in a certain type of resurrection, specifically a kerygmatic resurrection. For Bultmann, Jesus is resurrected each time the gospel is proclaimed, which indicates that resurrection is a *Sprachereignis*, or speech event.[62] Likewise, Jack does not accept any literal or metaphysical reality to God as ontic, but he does accept that God "exists" in the acts of those who have responded to the call of obligation. The "existence" of God is, therefore, an *Ethikereignis*, or ethics event. In this way, Jack's perspective is quite similar to Paul's notion that the church is the body of Christ, a communal incarnation of the presence of God. The church, the *ecclesia*, those who have been "called (*kalein*) out (*ek*)," actually give material reality to the idea of "God" by becoming a social incarnation of the love of God in both the objective and subjective genitival senses of that phrase.

Nevertheless, the question always remains as to whether God exists or not, since God may or may not exist depending on how human beings respond to the call of the kingdom. This results in what Richard Kearney would term the "God-Who-May-Be." Kearney claims that "God neither is nor is not but may be."[63] He predicates this theological perspective on the revelation of the divine name to Moses in Exodus 3:14 where God discloses the Tetragrammaton, which for Kearney is not to be translated as the typical "I am who I am" but more properly "I am who I will be," thereby placing God's present existence as consistently promised in the future tense.[64] In other words, God "is" always as the one who "may be."[65] Similarly, Jack insists that the insistence of God ensures a futurity to God, which, in turn, leaves open the possible existence and nonexistence of God. God *is* always as the one who *May Be*, or as Jack expresses it in "Without Sovereignty, Without Being" (chapter 21 in this reader), God is always the one who is to come, the God who has no sovereign power but makes an "unconditional appeal,"[66] an appeal that Kearney would classify as an unconditional love to be "enfleshed" in the world by human beings.[67]

One should understand the "may be" of the God "to come" in the Derridean sense of *peut-être* discussed above, which means that the possibility of God's existence should be comprehended as messianic, as that which "may always happen." Furthermore, doing so connects the "God-Who-May-Be" with the idea of the "Divine Perhaps," to use a phrase from the Hebrew scripture scholar Terrence Fretheim.[68] One should not be surprised, therefore, that in "God, Perhaps" (chapter 24 in this reader), Jack dreams of "a new species of theologians, of theologians to come, theologians of the 'perhaps.'"[69] These would be theologians who conceive of God's existence as dependent on and, therefore, vulnerable to whether human beings actualize that promised divine existence through transformative ethical acts demanded of those who desire to live as citizens of the Kingdom of God. Consequently, both the Kingdom of God and God must be understood in the future perfect tense as that which will have been or, better still, as that which will have come or arrived. The ontology of the kingdom and of God, consequently, always remains a meontology, a (me)ontology of sacred anarchy.

The idea that the "being" of God depends on the acts of human beings once again connects Caputo with Kearney, specifically with the messianic connotations of the idea of the Sabbath. Kearney theorizes that God may well have actively fashioned human imagination and passively rested on the Sabbath day specifically in order to empower human beings to participate in and contribute to the ongoing process of creation.[70] Given this interpretation, one might conclude that the Sabbath has unmistakable poetic, ethical, and political implications. In the first book of Jack's trilogy, *The Weakness of God*, part Two of the text is entitled "The Kingdom of God: Sketches of a Sacred Anarchy" (not an inappropriate title!). This part properly begins with chapter 7, a significant sabbatical number, which is entitled "Metanoetics: The Seventh Day, or Making All Things New." In this chapter, Jack argues that the whole notion of the Sabbath is the notion of a time of healing and mending, of continuing to work on creation as unfinished, actually a time of *re*-creation. This sounds to me remarkably similar to Kearney's contention that in the first creation story, Elohim "rests" not because of some divine fatigue, but precisely in order to allow human beings to participate in the ongoing act of creation. Human beings become co-creators with God, which means that the Sabbath is an ongoing process dependent on the commitment and activity of human beings. This asymptotic sabbatarianism coordinates nicely with Jack's notion of the realized eschatology of both the kingdom and of God. The Kingdom of God will exist as long as human beings are engaged in acts of mercy; God will exist as long as human beings incarnate God in those very same acts. In other words, both the kingdom and God depend on the messianic and prophetic dynamics inherent in the process of sacred anarchy, which is, itself, unavoidably both ethical and political.

I contend that all of the implications of "sacred anarchy" point directly or indirectly to Jack's radical hermeneutics and radical theology as expressions of a nascent political theology. That thesis, then, is something of a side bet added to my primary wager that "sacred anarchy" adequately condenses the enclosed selected readings in this Caputo reader and also the entire movement, dare I say "flux," of Jack's forty years of prolific literary productivity. I, as a Caputo reader, read Caputo as having creatively and provocatively cultivated certain prolegomena toward producing a political theology with a decidedly Christian connotation, a political theology that incorporates deconstruction, ethics, religion, biblical hermeneutics, theology, phenomenology, and ecclesiology into a diverse, daring, and edifying, one might even say prophetically therapeutic, discourse on the mystery of existence. This mystery, this "essential" non-knowing that remains without certainty, but, perhaps, always with faith, demands our constant sensitivity to the insistent call to embody both "God" and the kingdom in our religio-political acts of sacred anarchy. Jack has not significantly developed the potentialities for an overt political theology that lie inherent in the inchoate references that characterize his "sacred anarchy." Perhaps that may well be the future direction of his thought as he moves into the fifth decade of his productivity. In other words, we may have to wait for a Caputoan political theology "to come," one deferred until another day. Yet such a "messianic" anticipation is not unexpected by us Caputo readers!

Obviously, all of this introductory chapter to the Caputo reader is merely my own hermeneutic of radical hermeneutics, simply one reading among a plurality of potential readings, merely a good-faith wager on the preeminence of sacred anarchy for unifying Jack's radical hermeneutics. You as another Caputo reader will, of course, develop your own interpretations as solutions to the riddle of how to read Caputo. But that is part of the *apologia* for this reader—to give you some raw material that you need to begin or to extend that hermeneutical enterprise. With this reader, then, the game is afoot; therefore, place your bets, enjoy the riddle, and have a good read.

NOTES

1. John D. Caputo, "Sacred Anarchy: Fragments of a Postmodern Ethics," unpublished manuscript, 9.
2. Matthew Arnold, *Culture and Anarchy* (Floyd, VA: SMK Books, 2015), chapter 4.
3. John D. Caputo, *The Folly of God: A Theology of the Unconditional* (Salem, OR: Polebridge Press, 2016), 4.
4. John D. Caputo, *Against Ethics: Contributions to a Poetics of Obligation with Constant Reference to Deconstruction* (Bloomington: Indiana University Press, 1993), 20–21.
5. Caputo, *Folly of God*, 93–96.
6. John D. Caputo, *The Weakness of God: A Theology of the Event* (Bloomington: Indiana University Press, 2006), 102.
7. Ibid., 4.
8. John D. Caputo, *The Insistence of God: A Theology of Perhaps* (Bloomington: Indiana University Press, 2013), 177.
9. John D. Caputo, *What Would Jesus Deconstruct? The Good News of Postmodernism for the Church* (Grand Rapids, MI: Baker Academic, 2007), 134–38.
10. Caputo has long relied on the connection between Heidegger's use of Angelus Silesius's poem *Cherubinic Wanderer*, in which the poet claims that the rose blossoms "without why," and Meister Eckhart's mystical claim that the soul, too, should live out the love of God

"without why." An early reference to this connection may be found in "Meister Eckhart and the Later Heidegger, Part Two" published in 1974 and included as the second reading in this current volume, while the latest reference may be found in *Hoping against Hope* published in 2015 (John D. Caputo, *Hoping against Hope: Confessions of a Postmodern Pilgrim* [Minneapolis: Fortress Press, 2015], 24–30).

11. Caputo, *Hoping against Hope*, 28–30.

12. John D. Caputo, "Demythologizing Heidegger: *Alētheia* and the History of Being" Review of Metaphysics 41 (March 1988), 541–42.

13. John D. Caputo, "Hermeneutics as the Recovery of Man," *Man and World* 15 (1982), 345.

14. Caputo, *Folly of God*, 104.

15. Jacques Derrida, *The Ear of the Other: Otobiography, Transference, Translation*, ed. Christie McDonald, trans. Peggy Kamuf (Lincoln: University of Nebraska Press, 1988), 19; Caputo, *What Would Jesus Deconstruct?*, 42–46.

16. John D. Caputo, "In Search of a Sacred Anarchy: An Experiment in Danish Deconstruction," in *Calvin O. Schrag and the Task of Philosophy after Postmodernity*, ed. Martin Beck Matuštík and William L. McBride (Evanston: Northwestern University Press, 2002), 230.

17. Caputo, *Weakness of God*, 1.

18. John D. Caputo, "Meister Eckhart and the Later Heidegger, Part II," *Journal of the History of Philosophy* 13 (1975): 79.

19. Jacques Derrida, *Positions*, trans. Alan Bass (Chicago: University of Chicago Press, 1981), 19–20. Cf. also Mark C. Taylor, *Erring: A Postmodern A/theology* (Chicago: University of Chicago Press, 1984), 105.

20. Caputo, *Weakness of God*, 9, 14. See also John D. Caputo, *Deconstruction in a Nutshell: A Conversation with Jacques Derrida* (New York: Fordham University Press, 1997), 173; John D. Caputo, *The Prayers and Tears of Jacques Derrida: Religion without Religion* (Bloomington: Indiana University Press, 1997), 287; John D. Caputo and Gianni Vattimo, *After the Death of God*, ed. Jeffrey W. Robbins (New York: Columbia University Press, 2007), 52, 64.

21. Caputo, *Folly of God*, 104–5.

22. Caputo, *Weakness of God*, 105.

23. Caputo, *Deconstruction in a Nutshell*, 166; John D. Caputo, *More Radical Hermeneutics: On Not Knowing Who We Are* (Bloomington: Indiana University Press, 2000), 263.

24. Jacques Derrida, "As If It Were Possible, 'Within Such Limits' . . ." in *Negotiations: Interventions and Interviews, 1971–2001*, ed. and trans. Elizabeth Rottenberg (Stanford: Stanford University Press, 2002), 344.

25. John D. Caputo, "The Return of Anti-Religion: From Radical Atheism to Radical Theology," *Journal of Cultural and Religious Theory* 11 (Spring 2011), 44–45; Caputo, *Deconstruction in a Nutshell*, 156.

26. John D. Caputo, "On Not Knowing Who We Are: Madness, Hermeneutics and the Night of Truth in Foucault," in *More Radical Hermeneutics*, 17.

27. Caputo, *Insistence of God*, 17, 31.

28. Ibid., 6, 8.

29. John D. Caputo, *On Religion* (New York: Routledge, 2001), 18–19.

30. Caputo, *More Radical Hermeneutics*, 253.

31. John D. Caputo, "Hauntological Hermeneutics and the Interpretation of Christian Faith: On Being Dead Equal before God," in *Hermeneutics at the Crossroads*, ed. Kevin J. Vanhoozer, James K. A. Smith, and Bruce Ellis Benson (Bloomington: Indiana University Press, 2006), 102.

32. Caputo and Vattimo, *After the Death of God*, 51.

33. Caputo, *Deconstruction in a Nutshell*, 101; John D. Caputo, *Radical Hermeneutics: Repetition, Deconstruction, and the Hermeneutic Project* (Bloomington: Indiana University Press, 1987), 273; and Caputo, *Against Ethics*, 93, 221.

34. Caputo, *More Radical Hermeneutics*, 198–99.

35. John D. Caputo, "Shedding Tears beyond Being," in *Augustine and Postmodernism: Confessions and Circumfession*, eds. John D. Caputo and Michael J. Scanlon (Bloomington: Indiana University Press, 2005), 110.

36. Paul Ricoeur, *Oneself as Another*, trans. Kathleen Blamey (Chicago: University of Chicago Press, 1992), 180.

37. Paul Ricoeur, *Interpretation Theory: Discourse and the Surplus of Meaning* (Fort Worth: Texas Christian University Press, 1976), 40.

38. Caputo, "In Search of a Sacred Anarchy," 227.

39. Ibid., 228.

40. 1 Corinthians 1:19.

41. Ibid., 1:18.

42. Ibid., 1:28.

43. Caputo, "In Search of a Sacred Anarchy," 238.

44. John D. Caputo, "The Good News about Alterity: Derrida and Theology," *Faith and Philosophy* 10 (1993): 463.

45. Caputo, "In Search of a Sacred Anarchy," 238.

46. Caputo, *Weakness of* God, 45.

47. Ibid., 92.

48. Ibid., 94.

49. Paul Ricoeur, "The Human Experience of Time and Narrative," in *A Ricoeur Reader: Reflection and Imagination*, ed. Mario J. Valdes (Toronto: University of Toronto Press, 1991), 115; Paul Ricoeur, "On Interpretation," in *From Text to Action: Essays in Hermeneutics*, vol. 2, trans. Kathleen Blamey and John B. Thompson (Evanston: Northwestern university Press, 1991), 6.

50. Paul Ricoeur, *Interpretation Theory: Discourse and the Surplus of Meaning* (Fort Worth: Texas Christian University Press, 1976), 40; Paul Ricoeur, "The Function of Fiction in Shaping Reality," in Valdes, *Ricoeur Reader*, 122–23.

51. John D. Caputo, "'Lazarus, Come Out': Rebirth and Resurrection," in *Weakness of God*, 240.

52. Kevin Hart, *Kingdoms of God* (Bloomington: Indiana University Press, 2014), 131–32.

53. Ibid., 153–54.

54. Kevin Hart, "The Kingdom and the Trinity," in *Religious Experience and the End of Metaphysics*, ed. Jeffrey Bloechl (Bloomington: Indiana University Press, 2003), 154.

55. John D. Caputo, "The Experience of God," in *The Experience of God: A Postmodern Response*, ed. Kevin Hart and Barbara E. Wall (New York: Fordham University Press, 2005), 21.

56. John D. Caputo, "God, Perhaps: The Fear of One Small Word," in *Insistence of God*, 1

57. John D. Caputo, "The Time of Giving and Forgiving/Edifying Divertissement No. 3," in *Prayers and Tears of Jacques Derrida*, 168.

58. Caputo, "God, Perhaps," 22.

59. Walter Rauschenbusch, *The Social Principles of Jesus* (New York: The Woman's Press, 1917), 74.

60. Caputo, *On Religion*, 34.

61. Caputo, *Weakness of* God, 52.

62. Rudolf Bultmann, *Kerygma and Myth* (New York: Harper & Row, 1953), 209.

63. Richard Kearney, *The God Who May Be: A Hermeneutics of Religion* (Bloomington: Indiana University Press, 2001), 1.

64. Ibid., 28.

65. Ibid., 22.

66. John D. Caputo, "Without Sovereignty, without Being: Unconditionality, the Coming God and Derrida's Democracy to Come," in *Religion and Violence in a Secular World*, ed. Clayton Crockett (Charlottesville: University of Virginia Press, 2006), 154.

67. Richard Kearney, *Debates in Continental Philosophy: Conversations with Contemporary Thinkers* (New York: Fordham University Press, 2004), 237.

68. Fretheim interprets God's relationship with Israel as one of spontaneity and reciprocal response. Scripture indicates in several passages (Ezekiel 12:1–3, Jeremiah 26:2–3, and Isaiah 47:12) that God leaves God's future actions open and uncertain awaiting Israel's response to the divine Word. Who God will be and what God will do, then, depend on the decisions made by God's people. *Perhaps* they will respond; *perhaps* they will repent; *perhaps* they will obey. Although God knows what God will do in reaction to the various particular responses that might come from Israel, God does not know which of those reactions will be actualized. Fretheim contends that "Israel's response[s] . . . contribute in a genuine way to the shaping not only of its own future, but to the future of God" (*The Suffering of God* [Philadelphia: Fortress Press, 1984], 45–47).

69. Caputo, "God, Perhaps," 3.

70. Richard Kearney, *The Wake of Imagination: Toward a Postmodern Culture* (London: Routledge, 1994), 50.

2
From Sacred Anarchy to Political Theology: An Interview with John D. Caputo

CLAYTON CROCKETT

CLAYTON CROCKETT (HEREAFTER CC): According to the editor B. Keith Putt, the notion of "sacred anarchy" is the hidden thread that animates your work from *Radical Hermeneutics* up to the present. Can you explain in your terms what you mean by sacred anarchy, and do you agree with Keith's insistence on the importance of this theme for your thought?

JOHN D. CAPUTO (HEREAFTER JDC): Let me say first of all that this is Keith's interpretation. It is his responsibility to demonstrate it, to carry it through. I am, structurally speaking, in no better position to comment upon it than Keith. In fact, he may be in the better position given that I am too close. In either case, I do not want to answer this question, or any other question you will pose, in such a way as to situate myself as having the secret. It is not as if Keith has made a guess at the secret code or secret word that governs these texts, whereas I am the one who knows the secret and can certify whether he is right, whether he has laid it bare. Despite the etymology of the word, the interpretation of the "author" is not authoritative. Anything I say here just creates more texts, more interpretation.

That being said, I found this a good interpretation. Radical hermeneutics means that interpretation goes all the way down, even to the roots. There are no un-interpreted facts of the matter, only more interpretations, each a function of its angle of entry. But that does not mean that just any interpretation will do. There are good interpretations and bad interpretations, creative ones and destructive ones, productive ones and merely reproductive ones, and each must make a case for itself. So I have thought from the first time I heard Keith say this—and he has been saying it for a long time—that this is a good interpretation. This is what struck him the very first time we met in 1990, and it has held up for a quarter of a century. What I like about the expression, which refers not to a hierarchy but to a hier*an*archy, is that the sacred is found in the transgression. It first occurred to me reading the kingdom of God sayings in the New Testament, sayings I had read many times before, of course. But this time I had deconstruction in the back of my mind. There the focus falls on the marginalized, the excluded, the outsider, even the outlaw, the rogue, which calls for a systematic reversal and displacement. So we have here an expression that condenses both biblical and deconstructive motifs, an expression that can be understood in terms of a well-known theoretical matrix like deconstruction, while also having an ethico-religious and biblical resonance. Even looking back at the very beginning of my scholarly work on Heidegger and Meister Eckhart, I was interested there in comparing two transgressions, the transgression of metaphysics by thinking that takes place in Heidegger and the sacred transgression of metaphysical theology that takes place in the mystics. So, yes, this is an economic formulation of a very great deal of what I am doing.

CC: So your understanding of radical hermeneutics means that you are not the sole or final authority on your work. How does radical hermeneutics become radical theology? And does radical theology retain for you all of these ideas about interpretation? Would you endorse either or both of the designations "radical hermeneutical theology" or "radical theological hermeneutics"?

JDC: I started using the word "radical" in *Radical Hermeneutics* (1987) long before I started thinking about radical theology, in order to theorize the difference between a Gadamerian hermeneutics and a more deconstructive one. Radical hermeneutics, I liked to say, holds the feet of hermeneutics to the fire of deconstruction and burns off the residual metaphysics of *Geist* that clings to Gadamer's idea of "tradition." I should add that my Gadamerian friends, like James Risser, assure me that this has already taken place in Gadamer himself. That is my "pyro-theology," to borrow a word from Peter Rollins and an image from Derrida's *Cinders*. For a long time, I resisted using the word theology at all, because I simply took it to mean either onto-theology or faith-based confessional theology, something out to arrest the play, until later on, under the prodding of Jeff Robbins, I came to reconsider that decision. Words always have contextual deployments, and there are good strategic reasons to reuse old words like theology, to redescribe them, to rethink them, which is what Derrida meant by paleonymy. So in the subtitle of *The Weakness of God*, I spoke of a "theology of the event," by which I meant what I, well, what Charlie Winquist, and you, and Jeff, and I—is there a Syracuse school here?!—among others nowadays call "radical theology." In her blurb for that book, Catherine Keller said I had come out of the closet as a theologian, which made me laugh. But as with everything Catherine says, there was a lot to it.

Looking back, I think now that *Radical Hermeneutics* was already a radical theology in this sense, and that is clear in the final chapter of the book. I have always been mad about religion—in both senses of the word mad! Radical theology is a form taken by radical hermeneutics, when the subject matter is God, the gods, the holy, religion. It stands in contrast to confessional theology. It is a modality, an inflection of radical hermeneutics—in just the way that we can radicalize our discourse about ethics, as I did in *Against Ethics*, or art, or science. Nowadays, I prefer the word "theopoetics," but we could use either of these expressions, "radical hermeneutical theology" or "radical theological hermeneutics," although they are both a bit of a mouthful. Either way, it should be clear that radical here does not have a foundational sense—a firm foundation, a *fundamentum inconcussum*—but a non-foundational sense. Radical means "shaking the foundations" of metaphysics, of the confessional theologies, exposing the "roots' (*radix*) as just a deeper layer of interpretation, rereading these structures more radically, poststructurally. Both the Scriptures and the tradition of confessional theology are matters for radical hermeneutical rereading. So in radical theology, the contingency and deconstructibility of the discourse of confessional theology, the instability and reinterpretability of its subject matter, are made to go all the way down. In radical theology, we confess, we "circum-fess," that whatever we mean by God or religion must be made to tremble. Think of how the impressive Neoplatonic architecture of the high Christology of the early Councils rests upon the shaky footings of a Jewish exorcist and healer from Nazareth largely lost in the fog of history. Better to say it is already trembling on its own and does not need us to intervene and "make" it tremble. Of course, none of this is or is meant to be negative. When we shake the roots, or let them shake, we are not destroying them. This is an affirmative operation that gives them a future of renewal and reinterpretability. We affirm the open-endedness of the subject matter, of words like justice or God, of what is being promised, of what is being recalled.

CC: You have been criticized by philosophers for being too enthusiastic for and insufficiently critical of religion.

JDC: I think that was most true of *The Prayers and Tears of Jacques Derrida*. There was a certain excitement of discovery in that book, which brought this criticism down upon me. I was identifying a religion without religion in Derrida—that was the breakthrough—as against Mark Taylor's claim, which then prevailed, that deconstruction is the hermeneutics of the death of God. But this required both differentiating this deconstructive religion from confessional religion and differentiating this religious deconstruction from earlier readings of deconstruction, and, in so doing, I may at times have been too enthusiastic. I was proposing a stumbling block to the theologians and a scandal to the deconstructionists. To the theologians I said that there is something to learn about religion and theology from Jacques Derrida. To both the deconstructionists and the critics of deconstruction, I said, to put it in Kierkegaardian terms, there is indeed an exception to the universal in deconstruction, which disturbs the business as usual of philosophy, but it is a religious, not an aesthetic, exception. It is not lower than the universal, but higher. I am willing to confess to a certain enthusiasm in this book, which left both camps unhappy. On the one hand, the philosophers wanted to hear nothing about Derrida's religion. David Wood, a friend of mine and a close reader of Derrida, invited me to Vanderbilt to present this thesis, and he introduced my talk by saying that "let us all hope Caputo is wrong!" On the other hand, many confessional theologians wanted to hear nothing of this religion without confessional religion and only heard hostility. One of them, a very well-known philosopher of religion, said to me, his nose piously pointed toward heaven, "I have nothing to learn about religion from Jacques Derrida!"

But while this book involved a radicalization of confessional religion, this is not the same as an attack. In fact, as you point out, I was also criticized from the other side. I was actually attacked by Martin Hägglund for defending traditional theism, which was no less a misunderstanding. The radicalization of Christianity is carried out in *The Weakness of God*, the successor book, which is about God and not Jacques Derrida—and contrary to some critics I have never confused the two(!)—where I undertake a deconstructive reading of Christian theology. I focused in particular on the first two chapters of First Corinthians (Part One) and of the kingdom of God sayings in the synoptic gospels (Part Two). This book even had a "Scriptural Index"! I tried in the most affirmative way to analyze the Christian "event," mainly in the Derridean sense, but not without reference to Deleuze's *Logic of Sense*, that tracks the deployment of the name of God in the New Testament. Of course, this affirmation is not an affirmation of orthodoxy, because orthodoxy is not an affirmation of truth for me. It is a standardization, a regulation, a strangulation of the truth, a prevention of the event. It is orthodoxy that is negative, that makes straight (*orthe*) the twists and turns of the truth. Too often it is an exercise in anti-hermeneutical calcification—whether of tradition (Catholicism) or of a text (Protestant literalism). It fears a more unsettling truth in Christianity, a more unprotected search for truth, and it is a failure of nerve when confronted with what a "text" or a "tradition" is. If this gives the orthodox scandal, that is as it should be. After all, that is exactly the effect Jesus had. This analysis was meant to be radical, but not to be negative, not an exercise in hostility to Christian texts and tradition, although that is all some people will hear. It was an affirmation of a more radical Christian experience, an attempt to get closer to it, to feel its pulse, to get down to its inner life, to get down in the dirt and dig into its roots (*radix*), without the mystifications and confusions of supernaturalism.

CC: What do you say to people who feel that you are attempting to destroy more traditional views of God, religion, and salvation? Doesn't this get at the fundamental misunderstanding of deconstruction, the assumption that it involves tearing down or breaking apart?

JDC: Yes, that is a familiar misunderstanding. A radicalization is not a simple destruction in the garden variety sense. It is a deconstruction, that is to say, a way to reinvent and reconfigure, to repeat, retrieve, and—in the case of religion—renew our understanding of God and of religion itself. Otherwise they will destroy themselves, with no help from us, which is what is happening to the mainstream denominations today. Radical theology does not destroy but tries to be faithful to the underlying event taking place in Christianity, to its form of life or mode of being-in-the- world, to conserve Christianity in its very infidelity to the varieties of orthodoxy, which it takes to be the real betrayal of the event. In part 2 of *The Insistence of God* I took pains to set this out, to describe a "chiasmic" intertwining of radical theology and confessional theology: on the one hand, the insistence of the event *in* the concrete confessional traditions; on the other hand, the historical traditions as expressions *of* the event, its realization, actualization, existence.

What we are calling radical theology is the radicalization *of* something, of an inherited historical tradition and of inherited texts. It is parasitical upon them.

Within the first fifteen minutes of listening to "radical" theologians, you can identify their genealogy. Radical theology does not critique from without (modernism) but inhabits from within (postmodernism). That is why, as a matter of fact, this radicalization takes place frequently enough *in* the confessional traditions themselves—whenever one of their theologians is excommunicated or fired from their teaching job it is because they have happened upon the event! I have a subscription to the *National Catholic Reporter*, and in almost every issue, I read about a breakout of radical theology in the Catholic Church, which is treated by the local bishop as a fire to be extinguished! Within certain limits, Pope Francis is trying to change this, but the change is slow and difficult. So without this chiasm, there is double trouble: On the one hand, confessional theology freezes over into dogma and terror. But, on the other hand, without it radical theology is left to be a free-floating exercise in a completely uprooted ahistorical discourse, speculative and academic in the worst sense, with no relation to concrete religious traditions. So in my case, because my legacy is Christian, this is a radicalization of Christian theology in particular. I have, after all, written three books—*The Weakness of God*, *The Folly of God*, and *Hoping against Hope*—whose titles are direct citations from St. Paul. Christianity is not the tradition I have chosen to work on but the tradition that has chosen to work on me. I do not have a Christian tradition; it has me.

CC: You have been writing more for a religious readership, in some ways tied to the "emergent" church, and yet your writings retain a rigorous philosophical conceptuality that, while not always at the surface, remains implicit in your work. Furthermore, even when your books were more explicitly philosophical, there were these playful flourishes and turns of phrase that exceed most stereotypical philosophical writings. How do you balance or reconcile the efforts to write for a less philosophically sophisticated readership while maintaining a deep engagement with the most cutting-edge expressions of Continental philosophy?

JDC: It's a bit of a high-wire act, but one that I enjoy—to find an idiom that is at once readable to a nonspecialist yet, at the same time, does not dilute the philosophical content. If I thought I was doing the latter, I would give it up at once. On the one hand, let's say the right hand, there are the works written for an academic audience and published by a university press, where all the standard protocols of academic refereeing are in place. On the other hand, the left hand, books aimed at a wider, literate but non-specialist audience. As you and I know, it takes a specialist to understand and assess the work of people like Heidegger and Derrida, but what they say, as we also know, is of such importance that it needs to get a wider airing. I think that is what we all do as undergraduate teachers and, in that sense, this other line of books represents a continuation of my teaching. If I were not a teacher, I think it would have been more difficult to do this. I have a friend who, having recently retired, got out his old roll books and counted up how many students he had taught over his career. I remember thinking that, were I to do that, I would add in how many books I have sold, as that is also part of my reach as a teacher. The work of the left hand is intended to light little fires, or to fan existing fires, in and on the edge of the confessional traditions, not to burn them down, but to ignite the event.

But I think you are making an important point here, that there is another twist to all this, that there is actually a continuity between the two lines of books. The strictly academic work is already transgressive; it does not at every point observe academic protocols. I would like to point out that this was not always true. Contemporary readers of mine would be surprised were they to go back to my first two books, *The Mystical Element in Heidegger's Thought* (1978) and *Heidegger and Aquinas* (1982)—and I don't think they do that very often. That is why I am very happy that Keith has included representative selections of my early work in this collection. There they would find a young scholar writing in a cold sober and completely academic style, no playful flourishes anywhere on the horizon. It had never crossed my mind in those days to do anything else.

CC: So then what happened?

JDC: I like to say that Derrida loosened my tongue, which happened first in *Radical Hermeneutics* (1987), particularly in the third part, where I first formulated my "research program." When we force young people on the job market today to lay out their research program, I smile discreetly and quietly think to myself that I had no idea of mine until I was in my midforties. Any answer I would have given to that question when I was a graduate student would have been wrong. The Marxists will say this change of style is economically determined, that it was cunning of me to wait until I was a tenured full professor and could afford to take some stylistic liberties without putting my job at risk! But truth to tell, before I took to heart the deep criticism of modernism and of normalization that was launched by the poststructuralists, Derrida first of all but not just Derrida, I was simply interested in proving myself according to the received protocols of the university. I was never tempted to do otherwise.

But in the third part of *Radical Hermeneutics*, I decided to write from my heart, or better put, to allow my heart to enter into my scholarly work, to do scholarly work with a heart. This was also part of a decision not simply to do exegetical-interpretive work, but to think out loud, in print, to seriously ask myself what I think and then to say it. The matter for thought (*die Sache des Denkens*), as Heidegger called it, is also a matter of the heart, of thinking with the heart. But if Derrida was the trigger for this change of style, the model was Kierkegaard. I have been a lifelong and loyal reader of Kierkegaard, from my first year in college, when I was still a member of a Catholic religious order. I mean the Kierkegaard of the pseudonymous works—not, I confess, of the "veronymous" works, which are just too "edifying" for me, too Lutheran, too world-weary. To cite the magnificent expression the pseudonyms deploy, "The comic is the incognito of the religious." That is my motto, the model of my writing—and that is the continuity between the two lines of books—I am always laughing through my tears.

CC: Who do you consider your primary audience today?

JDC: Ever since I retired in 2011—more economic determinism, no more need to produce refereed publications—I have consciously allowed my focus to shift to this wider audience. As I think about your question, I would say that the people I have most in mind today are not academics but thoughtful, literate readers who are seeking to become articulate about their philosophical and theological questions. Sometimes they will even take on formidable books. I even know one of them who is now reading *Of Grammatology*. They are not afraid! Sometimes they are pastors hanging on by their teeth to their faith. Sometimes they are people who have left the church, who are "recovering" evangelicals or Catholics or something. Many are people who have not left the church, which is very important, because that is the inside/outside, within/without model of deconstruction, inhabiting something from within and repeating it differently. I think here of John Skinner, a bit of a rogue Anglican priest and a follower of Bonhoeffer, who heads up a group called "New Monasticism." But either way they realize that they no longer believe what they are saying—or what they have been told—in church. But neither do they simply *dis*believe it. So they need new distinctions and another set of categories—neither belief nor disbelief, neither theism nor atheism, neither undiluted faith nor undiluted reason, neither the religious nor the secular. They believe, and they do not believe. They disbelieve, and they do not disbelieve. Either way, something is eating at them, which is the event.

They need, in short, the discursive resources of what has been called, with a word that I concede has been beaten senseless by overuse, the postmodern framework. By this I mean a style of thinking that undermines these stable categories and throws these rigid oppositions into confusion, in order to feel about in the dark for another more elemental form of life that cannot be contained in these boxes, that cannot be held captive by these rigid modernist prison yards. They need a way to think articulately about these matters of the heart. They reject the fraudulent claim of religious "authorities" who delude themselves, and try to delude us, with the fantasy that they have some inside information about matters of irreducible mystery, who are peddling the fiction that we can live forever if we just do what they say. In another life, such people would sell used cars. My ideal readers sense all this, but they need a vocabulary, so I think of myself as feeding them lines, like a *souffleur* who prompts the actors from offstage about their lines. I should add that I am trying to do this not only in my writing but also by way of public speaking engagements, of podcast lectures, and interviews on the Internet. I work a lot with Tripp Fuller and his Homebrewed Christianity website. I spoke at The Hatchery, the start-up in Los Angeles in which he is engaged with Spencer Burke. I work with Pete Rollins whenever I can, and I have spoken at all three of Phil Snider's "Subverting the Norm" conferences. These are wonderful people doing wonderful work. But again, this is a matter of emphasis. I still do strictly academic work—otherwise I would dry up, which some people have also recommended to me!

CC: Right. So in *The Insistence of God*, you develop this Derridean theology of "perhaps" as a resource to think about religion for a wider intellectual audience, but you also critically engage important contemporary philosophers. Can you say something about the newer figures in Continental philosophy you discuss there, like Quentin Meillassoux and what is sometimes called Speculative Realism, Speculative Materialism, or even Object-Oriented Ontology, in relation to more conventional French poststructuralism? What are the promises and pitfalls of these new approaches?

JDC: It says something, doesn't it, that we can refer to poststructuralism as "more conventional"?! Let me begin by saying that these newer trends represent a salutary challenge to contemporary Continental philosophy as it has evolved over the last fifty years, particularly in the USA. We have become so confident in our arguments against "scientific reductionism," which I think are very sound, that we have allowed ourselves to ignore what the sciences are telling us about the natural world, which is quite spectacular. So what is promising here is the challenge posed by these philosophers to refocus Continental philosophy on the natural sciences, not merely on the methodological questions that preoccupy philosophers but on the substantive results, instead of demonizing them. My most general (and polemical) theorem in this regard is that physics is all the metaphysics we will ever get. I am willing to go along with the new materialists and stipulate that metaphysics means an account of the way the world is "in itself," outside the "correlation." So I agree to accept the way that Meillassoux puts it. That means, as Derrida likes to put the same point, to think about the world "as if we were dead" or had never been born to begin with. Then I ask myself, is there anything we are saying now about the world that would survive our destruction, anything that would survive our death or not require our birth? And I think the answer is, yes, we can think *now* about how the world would be *then*, or how it was before we were born, only in the language of the mathematical sciences. The sun would not "rise" or "set" in such a world, and brooks would not "brood," but the laws of astronomy would still obtain. I am conceding, indeed, insisting, that the philosophers and theologians have nothing to add to this search, not as such. So I reject "speculative philosophy" as sheer speculation. If you want to know how the world looks without us, and you want to speculate about the origin of the universe long before we were on the scene or how it will be after we are gone, then you have to learn a great deal of mathematics and learn how to conduct experiments!

CC: Why isn't this a kind of scientific reductionism?

JDC: For two reasons. First, the enterprise in which the sciences are caught up is an infinite task. The more the scientists learn, the more mysterious, the more majestic, the cosmos becomes. That is why I say "all we will ever get," because even science is not going to get it all. I am amused by "religious people" who think that religion offers them a deal that will allow them to live forever. When confronted with someone who says there is no afterlife, they will say, "You mean, this is all there is?" That should make us smile. About this infinitely complex, majestic, and mysterious universe, they complain—is that all there is? As if they understood it and are disappointed. The religion of the afterlife is mythological and half-blasphemous, as Tillich says, and to that religion the atheism of the new realism is a proper theological response.

Secondly, we are *not* dead, not *yet*, and the most pressing challenge we face has to do with the quality and the texture of our life before death.

That is, it really does have to do with the "correlation," properly understood, meaning our relationship to the world, our place in the cosmos, our being-in-the-world-before-death, taking "before" in the double sense of preceding it chronologically, before it happens (*ante*), what came to be before me, and also of standing before (*apud*) it as before a judge. In a way, both the sciences and the humanities are all doing this, working on and in the correlation, all the time, but what we call philosophy and theology do it the most explicitly, "*ex professo*," as it were. So in *The Insistence of God*, I objected to Meillassoux's criticisms of the "correlation," at least in *After Finitude*, and I tried to show that he is criticizing a simulacrum of this work of phenomenology, one that a superficial reading of Husserl might seem to justify (but doesn't) and is completely avoided and explicitly rejected by every phenomenologist after Husserl. The "world" the post-Husserlians describe is the one that is already running, that long preceded us, in which we have arrived without asking for it! Truth is a relationship, and what interests phenomenology is the relation, *our* relation to the world, which does not reduce the world to a subjective projection of ours. We study an asymmetric relationship in which we human beings, whose being is being-in-the-world (Heidegger), can be reduced to our relationship to the world, but the world cannot be reduced to its relationship to us. The world is a non-totalizable mystery, prior to and older than us. Meillassoux has produced a ridiculous caricature of Continental philosophy, as if we were all "young earthers," and then concluded that we have adopted a ridiculous position. Only people who have not studied the texts of phenomenology carefully can be hoodwinked by this joke. But to forget the question of our *relation* to the world is to commit the comic mistake described by Kierkegaard—that the "speculative thinker forgets that he exists!" That is the truly ridiculous thing to do. That is the real joke.

But the preexistent "world" referred to in this expression is not the geocentric cosmos known to the ancient Greeks and the Scriptures, nor the simpler Copernican cosmos known to the Enlightenment, but the dazzling world of Einsteinian and quantum physics. The bit in Meillassoux that I quite agree with is his critique of "fideism," of the Kantianism of Continental philosophy, of the fear and trembling before the natural sciences. This is the lifelong debate I have had with my good friend Merold Westphal, for whom Continental philosophy plays the role of a postmodern Kant, where the idea is to deny knowledge to make room for faith. That reduces Continental philosophy to apologetics, building the levies of Continental philosophy high enough to hold off the rising tide of natural science and this in order to keep the powders of a traditional orthodox religion dry. But for a lot of us, Continental philosophy plays the role of Hegel, not Kant, and it conducts a much more searching critique of religion than the Kantians are willing to face up to. I don't know if you realize this, but this latter-day Hegelianism of mine I owe in no small part to you, when you invited me to contribute to a volume you edited entitled *Hegel and the Infinite*. The piece I wrote for you got me thinking about Hegel differently. Prior to that, I was content to repeat the postmodern critique of "absolute knowledge" in Hegel, and I had neglected to see how much I agreed with Hegel's analysis of religion as a *Vorstellung*, religion as an imaginative, pictorial, and symbolic representation of our living relation to the world. But I call my view a "headless Hegelianism," meaning that religion is a *Vorstellung* but one bereft of a *Begriff*. It is a symbol that lacks any "absolute knowledge" authorized to decode that symbol into hard conceptual knowledge. It is at best a *Vorstellung* of the "event," of the coming of what we cannot see coming.

CC: Is that why you speak of a "cosmo-poetics?"

JDC: Exactly. I like to joke that, if I were philosophizing under the influence of enough good beer—this would be a session sponsored by "Homebrewed Christianity" no doubt(!)—I would by the end of the evening declare myself a "panentheist." Panentheism is a lure for me. I think it is an intoxicating view. It is a song to the universe. I was speaking at a Tillich conference at Union Theological Seminary a little while ago where I heard a nice presentation of panentheism by Robert Corrington. He made panentheism turn on Scotus Eriugena's distinction between *natura naturans* and *natura naturata*, which he called an "ecstatic naturalism." Think of Tillich's ground of being as the ground of the glory of the natural world, the welling up and spilling over of the ground into the effulgent beauty and majesty of the world. I love all this. But I would add that this is a poem, while insisting that poems are exceedingly important. It does not succeed in being a metaphysics, a speculative account of the world "in itself," as if we were *dead*! It is the world we *live* in. That does not make it a subjectivizing projection of ours, which is Meillassoux's mistake. A true correlation is a real relation between two real *relata*. So we describe in an imaginative or non-objectifying language our real relation with a very real and overwhelming world, in exactly the same way that the heliotropism of a plant, which would not exist without the plant, is a very real relation and not a "subjective projection." So I would call it a "cosmo-poetics," a rich hermeneutic phenomenology of our being-in-the-world, which we also see in the work of Catherine Malabou.

If you want this cosmo-poetics to be a *metaphysics* of *natura naturans*, then you would have to add something that, at the risk of ruining a good story, is missing from this story—let us say a *natura de-naturata*. You would have to incorporate into this story the very real possibility that this song to life is a song to a transient and local phenomenon, to an isolated system, and that in the long run, as many, maybe even most, scientists today think, we are heading for heat death, for oblivion, for the utter dissipation and dissemination of the universe, which is expanding at an increasing rate of acceleration into entropic dissolution. Would that not spell the death of the God of panentheism? Is not this God mortal like the rest of us? I don't affirm this dogmatically, of course. I just say that it is a very real possibility and panentheistic metaphysics (a) cannot take account of it and wants to hear some other story and (b) has absolutely no resources to validate some other story, say, about endless universes, because, as a metaphysics, it is metaphysical "speculation." It entirely lacks the wherewithal to advance the cause of another story other than to offer it moral encouragement. If there is another story, it would be determined by mathematics and experimental evidence, and panentheism must wait, hat in hand, for the scientific results to come in.

But I would add that entropy does not result in nihilism. It does not make this life of ours meaningless. On the contrary, it makes our life all the more precious, a fleeting but priceless moment of life in a vast cosmos, and maybe there are others, too, in which we have had the mysterious good fortune to participate. That is what I call the "nihilism of grace."

CC: You just referred to Malabou. In addition to the Speculative Realists, you also discuss Malabou, Bruno Latour, and Slavoj Žižek in *The Insistence of God*. How do they fit into this picture?

JDC: I am closest of all to Catherine Malabou, because she has passed through the discipline of Hegel, Heidegger, and Derrida. She is in the avant-garde of contemporary Continental philosophy because of the way she works together phenomenological and poststructural theories with the actual work being done today in brain science, from which she borrows the word "plasticity." This is exactly the place that Continental philosophy should be today. I think "plasticity" is a felicitous way to speak of what is real without embracing what Heidegger and Derrida called the metaphysics of presence, of the substantial, the static. The plasticity of being means becoming, transformation, like the process philosophers. My only question here, as with the panentheists, is this: How prepared is Malabou's Hegel, and the plasticity of being, to deal with the death of God, the entropic one? To adopt her trope, could God, or the plasticity of being, step on a "plastic" explosive and get blown to bits? Once again, as opposed to Brassier, I do not assert entropic destruction dogmatically. I only say it is a leading hypothesis, and I ask how can this view accommodate it?

I very much admire Latour, but I think he has fallen into the wrong hands. I would try to wrest him free from the Speculative Realist camp. He himself bad mouths what I think is a completely phony account of phenomenology and seems to base his criticism of what he calls postmodernism upon the headlines he has read in the newspapers. But when he gets down to describing his views in an affirmative way, the result, as Don Ihde has shown, is to give what amounts to what can only be called a brilliant hermeneutical-phenomenological account, an antireductionist rendering, of how science conducts its business in the concrete. He is close to Michel Serres, whom I also greatly admire, and to the older tradition of French philosophy of science, which we Continental philosophers, with only a few exceptions, have been neglecting, which is the part that Meillassoux is getting right. This is a completely unverifiable thing to say, but I like to think that if Derrida had set out to work in the philosophy of science, in which he had some early interest—remember, his "Origin of Geometry" essay pursued the "scientific" side of Husserl and won the Jean Cavaillès prize—the result would not be unlike what Latour has done. In *Insistence*, I detail the overlap.

The case of my relationship with Žižek is quite complicated, and on this point I would strongly recommend Katharine Sarah Moody's book *Radical Christianity and Emerging Christianity*, which works it all out with great care. I think Katharine is completely right. We are all grateful to Slavoj for having provided philosophy with such a prominent voice in the public conversation. I invited him both to Villanova University and Syracuse University, and I enjoyed every minute of it. He's a Mensch. Philosophically, I think the critical remarks he directs against me in *The Monstrosity of Christ* are simply careless and done in haste; at one point, he thinks he is citing me when he is citing Vattimo! Generally, the rhetoric he directs against postmodernism is misguided, and his remarks about Derrida tend to be unguarded when they are not simply wrong. In my case, as Katharine shows, this all tends to occlude several points of agreement between us, e.g., about the weakness of God and the idea of a radical Christianity understood as a call to galvanize human responsibility for its own fate. I think his notion of the virtual Spirit, which only exists if we make it happen, is pretty much what I mean by the "insistence" of God, and I could not agree more with his analysis of the big Other and his critique of John Milbank. Politically, I would describe myself as a social democrat while he advocates an "austere socialist dictatorship," which I consider an appalling prospect but fortunately empty rhetoric, almost as senseless as the Bartleby conclusion to *The Parallax View*. No one pays any attention to this kind of empty academic bombast. Žižek is a good example of why I am so suspicious of "political theory." While I regard the notion of a "non-all" as an important contribution, I think the fundamental assumption of Žižek and Lacan, that desire is a lack, is completely wrong, a grim crypto-Calvinism, the depravity of all our faculties. I think desire is affirmative, that it issues in an ongoing production of the world, a forward repetition in the Kierkegaardian sense. After fifteen minutes of listening to psychoanalysis, I become a completely anti-Oedipus Deleuzian. Stylistically, I find Žižek tiring. I can only read that "such and such appears to be the case but the truth is completely the opposite" so many times before I nod off! Once in a while, perhaps, but on every page? Its strongest feature is that it is a cure for insomnia. Once again, Katharine has the patience and the balance to work all this out with more care than I do.

CC: You mentioned panentheism, which is also a favored term of process theologians. I think that you and Catherine Keller are doing the most creative and constructive work in theology right now. Can you explain where you differ from her theological perspective?

JDC: I am closer to the work of Catherine Keller than to anyone else working in our field. We are partners, kindred spirits. When I read her, I agree with everything. In addition to her creativity as a thinker, her writing draws upon an enormous multidisciplinary erudition, so I learn all sorts of things from her that that I never knew about. I first encountered her work—we hadn't yet met—when I was working on part one of *The Weakness of God*, where I argue against the agent God, omnipotence, and *creatio ex nihilo*. The first draft of my argument was based on the historical critical biblical literature—most of this stuff is an innovation of the speculative theologies and heresiologies of the second century CE. Then one day, unrequested, a complimentary copy of *Face of the Deep* arrived in the mail. It was an unexpected visitation, arriving like a knock on the door in the middle of the night. I could not believe my good fortune. It was a grace, and I consumed it immediately. *Face of the Deep* put a postmodern and theopoetic face on my skeletal argument, the historical critical argument, and breathed some life into it. She also forced me to consider more clearly the feminist implications of speaking of weakness. Catherine's criticism of the book was that, while this was a good lesson for men drunk with power, feminists have been told quite enough about embracing weakness. She pointed out that power can be understood otherwise, as sharing power and empowering the oppressed. Of course she was right. That encouraged me to sharpen the idea that the weakness of God—the delimitation of a Supreme Being and Omni-Problem Solver—corresponds to the intensification of human responsibility. It requires a corresponding strength to respond to the call, to answer what is calling in the name of God, with decisive action. The weak force of the event is not an abstraction but a call to action. That point was in danger of being occluded in *The Weakness of God*, and it is corrected in *The Insistence of God* by the emphasis put on the figure of Martha in that book.

So when Catherine speaks of chaos, multiplicity, affectivity, relationality, interdependence, or entanglement, I write everything down, all the while furiously nodding in assent. When she says she prefers the figure of the *tehom* to Tillich's "ground of being," I shout "hear, hear" and write in the margins, "see also the anonymity of the *il y a* and *es gibt*." When she proposes to think "ground" in proximity to the dirt of the earth, in a kind of geo-poetics, a play possible in English but not with the German *Grund*, I stand and applaud. It is the same instinct that led me to speak of Yeshua the earthman in *The Insistence of God*. When she calls this all theopoetics, again I agree. So the short answer to your question is, I agree with everything.

CC: You agree with everything?

JDC: Almost. I agree with everything, but I put a different spin on it or assign it a different status. Take the word "theopoetics." I don't mean a discourse on God's *poiesis*, on God as the poet of the universe, on the divine creativity, on the *natura naturans*, which is the metaphysical notion also found in Roland Faber, with whom Catherine has collaborated. I mean a creative discourse (*poiesis*) on God, so the poetics is lodged not on the side of God but on the side of our discourse. The poetics in theopoetics does not serve as a modifier of the *theos* but as a displacement of the *logos* in the word *theology*. For me, the name of God is the name of a call, one of the names under which the event of the call has been known to travel. It is the name of a chance for the future, of the possibility of *the* impossible, the name of something that is getting itself said and done in that name, and in all the beliefs and practices that cluster around that name—and all of this in the middle voice. Do not separate the caller from the call. Theopoetics is a radical hermeneutics of this call, a constellation of discursive resources—of metaphors and metonyms, of parables and paradoxes, and so on—that bring the call to words. Not only the call, of course, but the response, in words and deeds, since the name of God is the name of a deed.

So theopoetics inserts itself within a larger cosmopoetics, which describes our "entanglement" (Keller's word) with the cosmos, our experience of being-*in*-the-cosmos, or in-the-chaosmos. Not God-in-all or All-in-God, as in panentheism, but our being-*in*-the-all, which is, of course, a non-all. I prefer to save the word metaphysics for a view that takes a long cold hard look at the world as if we were dead or never born. But while we are alive, there are other demands on our time, for example, to give an account—let's say a radical hermeneutic ontology—of living in the midst of such a cosmos, of our chaosmotic, chiasmic entanglement with the cosmos. Cosmopoetics is a way to speak of the cosmos while we are still alive, whereas metaphysics is colder business. It takes up the features of the world that are not entangled with our life, that can do without us, that can be disentangled from us, that are disinterested in us. I am not trying to be Nietzsche, Camus, or Sartre. My cosmopoetics assumes a congeniality between our genesis and the cosmos. In bringing us forth, the cosmos has not produced a monster. We are not Sisyphus, a useless passion, a Lacanian lack, dragging through life with depraved Calvinistic faculties, or some Kierkegaardian creature grieving over its incommensurability with the universe, its heterogeneity with the finite. None of that. We are a bit of luck, of good fortune, a happy event, like a birth.

CC: Does your difference with Keller hinge on an evaluation of Whitehead's importance for philosophy and theology?

JDC: Yes, that is the hinge, the *cardo*, the cardinal point. First of all, let us recognize the family gathering of Whitehead, Deleuze, Leibniz, and Nicholas of Cusa, all metaphysicians, to a man (literally), which Catherine has arranged in her work, to which she also adds an interloper, Jacques Derrida, all gathered to raise a glass to Joyce's "chaosmos," that is, to the eventiveness of the universe. If I were invited to this party, I would show up early. Catherine would describe all this as a cosmology, and I would redescribe it as a cosmopoetics (or a radical hermeneutic) in just the way I would redescribe theology as theopoetics. It is always the *logos* that gives me pause, not the *cosmos* or the *theos*. Either way, the underlying idea is to provide for a groundless ground, an open-ended, intertwined, interdependent, unprogrammability in things. Catherine calls upon a process-metaphysics of space-time events, while I speak in a more descriptive way in terms of *différance*, of an unprogrammable spacing-timing, for which both of us find "nicknames" in the Scriptures in the *tohu-wa-bohu* and the *tehom* and in philosophy in Plato's *khora*. I have signaled my affinity to all this by saying in *Weakness* that in the analysis of the event, I am trying to run together both Deleuze and Derrida, both the out-breaking (*ex + venire*) of the underlying event, the explicating of the implicit, *and* the in-breaking (*in + venire*) of the in-coming of the event of the *tout autre*, so that something happens that is not implicit but a surprise. So you can see how much our views converge. In *Prayers and Tears*, by the way, I even imagine a conversation between Derrida and Nagarjuna on emergent codependence. There is literature on that.

But I worry that in Whitehead there is a strong metaphysical God, not the mortal god of theopoetics. So if there is a difference between us, it is found in the discursive status we accord to what we are saying, the same song in different keys—is this a cosmology (metaphysics) or cosmopoetics (hermeneutics)? Catherine thinks my reservations about metaphysics are too stiff-necked, too hard-headed, too inflexible, and that I have too "strong" a concept of metaphysics. If we can imagine power otherwise, can we not imagine metaphysics otherwise? Does metaphysics always have to mean the metaphysics of presence, of stable *ousia*, always "strong" metaphysics, an overbearing, overreaching grab for an overarching truth that crushes the unprogrammable event? Why not take this objection *to* metaphysics and make it an axiom *of* metaphysics, of another metaphysics, a metaphysics of the open-ended, unprogrammable? That is a fair point. Such a metaphysics would be neither an a priori, rationalist, dogmatic metaphysics characteristic of modernity, nor a metaphysical theology of a medieval sort. Instead, it would be an experimental, tentative, scientifically literate, revisable, and provisional metaphysics, not of being but of becoming. Tomorrow morning, we both agree, we may wake up to find that some PhD in physics, working in a patent office because she can't find a teaching job, has changed everything, and we must start over. So just as I say theopoetics is a "weak theology," why not say cosmo-poetics is a "weak metaphysics." Truth to tell, with such a description of metaphysics—and I have never said this before—I can make an uneasy peace. This would be another case of Derridean paleonymy, new wine in old skins, redeploying old words. I should add that in our conversations, Catherine points out that she herself does not describe her own work as metaphysics, that the word is too "masculinizing" for her—in the family gathering I mentioned, there were only men(!)—but that she learns a great deal from people like Whitehead who puts this word to good purpose. I can sign my name to that pact. Like Catherine, indeed like Heidegger, too, I think we never stop learning from great metaphysicians—like Aristotle and Hegel! They are geniuses of imagination—of imagining new vocabularies, says Rorty; of imagining worlds, says Heidegger. I would say, of imagining events.

CC: But you are still uneasy?

JDC: Yes, because I would still prefer to call it a hermeneutic ontology, or cosmo-poetics, meaning a way of giving words to the very basic and deeply lodged categories of our encounter or chiasmic intertwining with the world or, in Catherine's vocabulary, of our entanglement with the world. Partly it is an old allergy, a tick I have developed over the years, about this word. I started my career as a young Catholic and a serious student of the metaphysics of *ipsum esse per se subsistens* in Thomas Aquinas, but I was weaned away from this by Heidegger. I love the mystical theology of Meister Eckhart, but not the Neoplatonic metaphysics that backs it up. I love being seized by the unconditional in the radical theology of Paul Tillich, but not the metaphysics of German Idealism that backs it up. So I pause in fear and trembling before the speculative metaphysics of Whitehead. Plus, I do not want to give up the polemical punch packed in saying that physics is all the metaphysics we are going to get. Let us go back to what I just said about panentheism, to what I take to be at present the majoritarian opinion of the physicists, that we are headed for entropic dissipation, for a kind of metaphysical *nihil negativum*. If that is right—it is enough for me that it be admitted as a hypothesis, I do not assert it dogmatically—then what are we to say about the divine creativity? Is the divine lure luring us into oblivion? Does the divine eros spell *thanatos*? On this hypothesis, the cosmos is *dis*-entangling itself from itself at an increasingly accelerating rate of disentanglement. At some point, we would not be able to see the stars from earth (and not just because of air pollution!) *Natura de-naturata.* In time, Gaia will be ashes. What then would divine creativity be other than a local phenomenon, an isolated system, occurring here and there in scattered places in the cosmos, and a completely temporary one, which ultimately succumbs to entropy?

Of course, I know there is an opposite hypothesis found in someone like Paul Steinhardt and his theory of an endless universe. On this hypothesis, the divine creativity would be endless, and its telos would be worlds without end. Now my point is this: there is nothing, really nothing, that the theologians and philosophers, process or classical, have to add to this debate that would determine the truth or falsity of either hypothesis. That determination depends entirely and in principle upon the experimental evidence and the mathematics. If the weight of the evidence shifts to the counter-hypothesis of Paul Steinhardt, he will win the Nobel Prize in physics. He will win, not the process theologians, who are speculative bystanders, cheering for one side, of course, but waiting on the sidelines like the rest of us for the outcome of this game. But we must let the chips of physics fall where they may and then incorporate these results into our thinking about our place in the cosmos—but it is physics that is going to tell us about the cosmos in which we are placed. If that is the case, then what Catherine and I are saying will prove to have been a cosmo-poetics, not a speculative cosmology. Why? Because what business do we have calling this cosmology when it lacks the wherewithal to settle or intervene upon this most fundamental of cosmological debates? Surely cosmologists should be able to settle a cosmological debate, at least *in principle.* I myself am not cheering for either side. I can live with either outcome. I love the idea of an endless universe of universes. But I see nothing nihilistic in entropic dissipation. It does not gainsay, in fact, it intensifies, our affirmation of our little blue ball of life, the divine Gaia, marking it as a precious but passing moment in, let's say, an expanding story. So I would prefer to say that physics is all the metaphysics we are going to get, and this weak metaphysics is a cosmo-poetics.

CC: So then what specifically is the insistence of God?

JDC: Here I sound a little more like Levinas and Derrida than Tillich and Whitehead. I have a concern to maintain a distinction between God and *khora*, between God and the *tohu-wa-bohu* and the *tehom*. Here, I believe, I am reading Genesis pretty much *ad literam*, by which I do not mean the way it is read in Alabama! In the opening scene of Genesis, the elements are co-original companions of God in what had been up to then, in the scene before the opening of Genesis, one of silence and inactivity. When the curtain opens, God is there, and the elements are there—*il y a, es gibt*—always already there, along with God, lifeless, like sleeping giants. Then God breaks the silence, decides to breathe life into their limbs, stirs them up by punctuating air and land and the deep with living things. So God and the elements are not the same, but God gives them life. I preserve a similar distance between the cosmos and God. So for me, God does not transcend being as the supreme being of theism, but neither is God immanent in the ground of being, the God in all and all in God of panentheism. God calls, as if from without, as a "may-being" soliciting being, not from above (theism) or within (panentheism) but from the future as the event. It is not so much that God eludes confinement in being but that God pleads for us to make God be.

Think of it this way. The actual world, actual events in Whitehead's sense, the world at any given moment, what is happening, is a cluster of relatively stable constructions or unities—from kitchen tables to the stars—otherwise there is pure chaos. But if relatively stable then also relatively unstable. But destabilized by what? Let us say by two tropics of instability, one from below and the other from above, one below being, the other beyond being. From below, on the underside (*khora*, *tehom*, et cetera), a differential matrix, a quasi-transcendental spacing-timing, *différance* in Derrida's sense, or a quasi-system of events in the Deleuzean sense, so that these constructions are constructed of unstable stuff. On the other side, let us say, from above, the undeconstructible, the not-yet, the absolute future, the promise/threat of the coming of what we cannot see coming, the pressure of the event in the Derridean sense, which destabilizes what is present and makes it restless for and with the future. That is condensed in the most economical way for me in the expression "the possibility of the impossible," which, is my favorite nickname for God. The insistence of God makes the world restless with promise. But the world exists; God insists. The distance I observe between God and the world is the distance between insistence and existence. They are not the same, and so I avoid any suggestion that they are. They differ not as creative ground and grounded creature but as call differs from response, as insistence differs from existence.

That is the transition from the second part to the third part of *Insistence*. Up to that point, I was still engaged in theopoetics, where there was still a danger of a kind of tête-à-tête, *apud deo*, between God and us. I think that a residual anthropocentrism or humanism threatens the name of God. So much God, so much self, Kierkegaard said. But what finally addresses us, what finally calls upon us, is the cosmos—whence the recurrent trope of the "stars" in *Hoping against Hope*. So I do not identify theopoetics and cosmopoetics, but I situate theopoetics within a larger cosmo-theo-poetics, in which theopoetics is itself inscribed, as in a certain *khora*, just the way that in the myth Elohim finds himself having to deal with *tehom* and the elements that coexist with him at the beginning of Genesis. When I write "the name (of) 'God'" the diacritical marks are signaling that this name, too, is inscribed in *khora*, as the name of something calling and calling to be recalled *in* the world, calling in the midst of a cosmic play of which God is not the author or the poet—if anything, the play of the world, what Heidegger called a *Weltspiel*, is the poet of God. God is not the ground of being, but neither is God *khora* or *tehom*—or *différance*, which is why I keep saying deconstruction is not mystical theology. The innovation of *The Insistence of God* is found in the third part of that book, in the cosmo-theo-poetics. That is new ground for me, ground I was forced to explore by my encounter not only with the Speculative Realists but also with Catherine Keller, with the process theologians generally.

CC: If that's the case, then what is left for philosophy and theology to do?

JDC: Everything! It is an infinite task—to follow the trace of a cosmic call, to understand our being-in-the-world as coming-to-be-in-response-to the call of cosmic forces. The task, to produce a radical hermeneutic rendering of the sense and non-sense of our place in the cosmos, of living *in* such a marvelous and mysterious cosmos, of life and death, of good and evil, of the beautiful and the ugly, of the true and the false. Philosophers and theologians raise all the "big questions," ever ancient and ever new. They confront the issues that cannot be mathematicized, that cannot be formalized, that cannot be programmed. They address events. Physics may be all the metaphysics we are going to get, but physics is not enough. It is not enough to subdue the mystery of the physical world or the mystery of our lives. Even if the physicists come up with a "theory of everything," that will not be every theory that we need. Such a theory would cover everything but not from every angle. Philosophy and theology have their own angle, their own hermeneutic "as," and this "as" can be multiplied without limit.

Philosophy and theology raise all the old questions, but this time around they must do so free from what Tillich called the mythological and half-blasphemous concept of the Supreme Being, and free from all the ethics and politics of divine sovereignty that attends the mythology of supernaturalism. This time around they must conduct their business in dialogue with physics and the natural sciences, as we see in Malabou, in Michel Serres and Bruno Latour, and in the process thinkers. They must avoid comforting themselves with the illusion that physics does not address the ultimate nature of reality. They must not elevate themselves by saying, as Gabriel Marcel said many years ago, that the sciences deal with "problems," but we philosophers acknowledge the "mystery," or like Heidegger, that science does not think. Trust me, physics thinks, and it is up to its experimental-mathematical ears in mystery and is fully cognizant of that. Philosophy and theology have their work cut out for them, and they have their own angle of access. But they must avoid congratulating themselves with the illusion that they are autonomous discourses that somehow have some privileged access—provided either by Divine Revelation or Speculative Reason—that hotwires them to a knowledge about the cosmos to which the natural sciences are not privy. In my *Truth* book, I said that this is the postmodern version to the ancient search (*philia*) for wisdom (*sophia*), which cannot be confined to the "philosophy" department.

CC: Earlier you mentioned the cosmic idea of entropy, but what about the more immediate crisis of ecology in terms of resource scarcity and global warming? How can philosophy and theology be responsive to the horizon of human existence in what some scientists are now calling the Anthropocene?

JDC: Without denying that having a good idea of the ultimate destiny of the universe is extremely important—speculative cosmology is not idle speculation—of course, you are right, we have more pressing problems. The climate change deniers are science deniers, and it is unbelievable, an embarrassment, a scandal, a catastrophe, that James Inhofe (Republican, Oklahoma), a militant denier of scientific evidence, is chairman of the Senate Environment Committee. That is a damning commentary on the American Right. Like every intellectual, especially if they are professors, we philosophers and theologians have a duty to blow the whistle on the ignorance of people like Inhofe or, when they are not ignorant, on their malice in wanting to earn a profitable living off the lives and well-being of future generations. Of course, radical hermeneutics means that interpretation goes all the way down, so it is always possible to strike a contrarian view. We cannot, for example, absolutely refute the idea of alien abductions or even of the young earthers. But in saying this, we are not saying that one interpretation is as good as another. We do not have Cartesian certitude about climate change, but we do have moral certitude, meaning evidence that compels us to act in good conscience. The evidence here is empirical and scientific, and we can show our students what "evidence" means. We can raise the question of the moral culpability of denying an overwhelming scientific consensus—97 percent of scientists—when public health and well-being is at stake. We can explain what culpable ignorance means. Of course, it is politically difficult to tell the families of coal miners that their livelihood, the way they have provided for their children for generations, is putting the globe at risk, putting all the children at risk, theirs included, and it is difficult to stir an indolent population, to get them to sacrifice now for a future evil. Very few politicians have the courage to take this on, and those who do can lose their own jobs. If we have no sense of the common good, we have nothing to which we can appeal. How do we persuade people to sacrifice now for something that has not happened yet, at least not on the scale that science predicts?

So it is a matter of the "spectrality" of justice in Derrida's sense, the duty we have to the dead to see that they will not have died in vain, and the duty we have to the future, not in the abstract, but a real future, our children and grandchildren and great-grandchildren. There is more to the real than what is present. The present exists, but the future insists. It is difficult to call for the justice due to those who are coming, who are not yet. From what I read, neither my generation nor yours will suffer much from this personally, "not yet"—that is the watchword of the "they" in Kierkegaard and Heidegger when confronting death. When the worst begins to happen, the droughts and floods, the food shortages, the poorest people will be more vulnerable, and the poorer nations, while the wealthier ones will be able to protect themselves, at least for a while. Even now, when the power grid fails, the comfortable suburbs buzz not just with Hispanic immigrants mowing their lawns but with back-up generators. So nothing is easier than to make the present more comfortable at the expense of the future—that is the one rule elected officials follow today. But as philosophers who can theorize the notion of justice, and as theologians who have inherited a prophetic sense of justice, we in particular have a special responsibility. We, better than others, can make plain that this is a matter of justice, and what a matter of justice means. We can articulate the notion of the justice due to an invisible, inexistent, insistent future. We are bound by something that does not yet exist, that calls for our response from the future. We can talk like that. Our thinking is conducted in a discourse like that. We can show that the living are stewards of the earth and that we have a duty to leave behind us a habitable world, and we can give "testimony" to this duty personally.

What else can we do, precisely as philosophers and theologians? We can supply, beyond the pressure of practical considerations, a "deep" ecology, a deeper discourse on the earth. One thing that has been tried by N. T. Wright is to back up environmentalism with Scripture.

In *Surprised by Hope*, he argues that, read carefully, the New Testament is saying that the Second Coming of Jesus will take place not in heaven, but here on earth, and so we must tend to the earth and make it habitable for the second coming of Jesus. We *do* have here a lasting city, he thinks. But even if you took the Scriptures as literally as Wright does, which I don't, and you are not a science-denier, as he is not, you would still have to admit that, *sub specie aeternitatis*, this is a temporary solution. The earth will eventually be reduced to ashes by an expanding sun, so Jesus and all those risen bodies will have to relocated. I take this to be a completely mythological scene. They will need a second, interstellar Noah, for when humankind (will the animals be risen too?) will have to pack up and move on before that happens! Presumably risen bodies can travel light. The panentheists try to back it up with metaphysical theology, arguing that the earth, the material world, is the body of God. Just as they see a radical democracy in the immanence of God in the world, so they see a radical environmentalism in taking the earth as sacred stuff, as God's body. I don't dismiss this, but I redescribe it. I think that what lies behind such theologies is a cosmotheopoetics, a way of giving words to our dwelling in the world, one that is very close to poetry. That does not mean it is not serious. Poetry is serious business and this is serious poetry about our dwelling in the world, about our habitat, about the habitat of all the species.

CC: This sounds like Heidegger. Do you see a role for Heidegger here?

JDC: Yes, despite his odious politics, we cannot dismiss Heidegger. His idea of a poetic, meditative "thinking," one that dwells on the earth, in the old fourfold mythology of gods and mortals, sky and earth—a paradigm you have invoked in your recent book—is very powerful. It is a great resource for a deep ecology and an example of cosmo-poetics. Heidegger reminds us that protecting the earth, conserving the land, used to be a conservative idea. The conservatives opposed the modernizers who wanted to blacktop the earth, the Marxists who put the interest of labor before the love of the land. But for today's Right, which believes only in money, the earth is a source of profits, "raw material" (Heidegger's *Bestand*) for making more money, and so these "conservatives" would conserve only their own stock portfolios. Talk about odious politics: right-wing campaigns for "saving the jobs" of the coal miners gets votes in the Appalachian states. But that means the coal barons want to keep the coal mines running for their own profit, while paying the miners as little as possible and while doing as little as possible to protect the health and safety of the miners—and the environment be damned. Of course, Heidegger did not know the word "Anthropocene," but already, in 1947, he launched a prescient critique of "humanism," of human exceptionalism. He warned us that it was becoming more and more difficult to find a place that has not been made over by humans, that is untouched by humans. Nowadays the wild, if you can find it, and the "wild animals," must be kept safe from us, not the other way around. Everywhere we encounter, not Being itself, but *human* being and its doings. I think Heidegger's "time of need" is the Anthropocene.

Heidegger was a classical conservative, but on this point, he made two stupid blunders. First, he thought the Nazis were on the side of conservation and that the *Wehrmacht* would be opposed to machine technology, which was a cruel joke. Second, he said, "Science does not think," which is another joke, a foolish one. Today, it is science, first and foremost, not the poetry of Hölderlin, which warns us of the coming catastrophe and also, and this is important, keeps us "open to the mystery" of the cosmos. This went hand in hand with his antediluvian attitude to technology. So we philosophers and theologians do have a voice of our own, a "deep ecological" voice, which says that our "dwelling" in the world is threatened, not only in a very basic way affecting our very survival, but also in a subtler way, in that it seduces us with a false paradigm of "sovereignty," of the sovereignty of the human and of its unchecked technological power. So, first, unlike Heidegger, we must understand that "science," which was the devil for him, is our partner, that "technology" can take many forms, especially "green" technologies. Second, unlike traditional divine omnipotence theology, we must understand the idolatry involved in thinking of a strong God who will come riding over the hill to save us. On the contrary, as Žižek quips, the therapy is over when you realize there is no Big Other! We must assume responsibility ourselves for what we are doing to this planet.

CC: I know that you care very much about progressive politics, but at times you have been reticent to engage in theorizing the political. In his introduction, Keith concludes that you have a "nascent political theology." Are you sympathetic to this claim, and how do you assess the contemporary work that is going on in terms of political theology?

JDC: The expression "political theology" goes back to Carl Schmitt's general theory, which I like, that in modernity theological concepts are secularized, that they show up in the so-called secular order, and—this part I don't like—therefore the political "sovereign" has the power to act like God, to decide over and above the rule of law, like Kierkegaard's transcendent God suspending the universal prohibition against murder. That sends us all scattering for an antidote to Schmitt, the most obvious being to dissociate politics from theology altogether, which is the secular solution. And in so far as that means keeping the official functions of church and state separate, I agree. But on a deeper level, and this is the postsecular option, Schmitt forces theology to rethink what it means by "God," which in a sense is my lifelong project. Vis-à-vis Schmitt, instead of a theology of sovereignty, I embrace a sacred anarchy. I pursue the "weakness of God," that is, the name of God as the name of the weak force of the call, not of a divine agent with sovereign power, who authors laws and so can suspend them, who punishes and rewards, who upsets us when "he" doesn't intervene on our behalf, all of which I consider "semi-blasphemous and mythological" [Tillich] So Keith is right to speak of a nascent political theology, because my concrete political views can be felt on a theoretical level in my critique of the theological paradigm of sovereignty, of divine omnipotence, of a strong theology, and of the politics of top-down political power that accompanies it—from God the Father all the way down to power politics of neoliberal capitalism, colonialism, sexism, and racism. The politics that accompanies weak theology is the politics of *ta me onta* (the non-beings or nobodies), of radical democracy, which means, to protect the weak against the strong. This requires a radical reversal of sovereignty politics, to give priority to the people at the bottom. That is a biblical order of rank, an anarchical one, the madness of the kingdom of God, of the year of the Jubilee, which is political theology that Schmitt opposes. In that sense, since everything I have written about for the last twenty-five years has to do with weak theology and the weakness of God, everything I write is political—in a "nascent" way.

Personally, I should add, I am a political "junkie"! I find political contests, not just elections but the day-to-day battles among the parties, among the three branches of government, more fascinating than sports. It is the first thing I read about in the morning—I subscribe to two daily newspapers—especially since it is rare for a Philadelphia sports team to be in the headlines! If the papers are not delivered in the morning, I panic and rush to my iPhone! Yes, I am like most academics, leftish and progressive. But you are also right that I tend to keep a certain distance from writing political *theory*. I have published a few things about the politics of sovereignty. But if I tried to do much more, to build a more specific political theory, I think I would end up taking the convictions that I have forged in concrete experience, observing how lives are destroyed by poverty and discrimination, and building a second-order theory to justify the views I already hold down on the first floor, and this would mostly be read by other academics who already agree with all this. I would simply take what I already think, jack it up a couple of degrees of abstraction, and declare it "grounded." *Voilà*, a political theory! If circumstances on the ground changed, I would simply adjust the "theory" accordingly. In Bush v. Gore, all of us who usually advocate the "principle" of the primacy of the federal government over state government, suddenly supported the state supreme court of Florida against the US Supreme Court, which has been in the pocket of the right wing for a while now. Is this justified? Of course it is, because that is where justice lies—in the singularity of the situation—not in the "principle," which is not justice but an after-the-fact justification. I think exactly the same thing about ethics. If I ever wrote a book about politics, I would call it *Against Politics*, just the way when I wrote a book about ethics, it was entitled *Against Ethics*, that is, against the hypocrisy that pretends to be deriving judgments from "principles," which I think gets it all backwards. That is part of the anarchy, the distrust of the "principle," of the universal *arche*, in sacred anarchy. So maybe it is better that I don't write a book on politics!

CC: Would you describe this anarchy as a version of liberalism?

JDC: No. I would not say liberal but social, not I but we, not even the nominative "we" but "us," in the accusative, as Levinas said, galvanized by the other, not the autonomous subject but the heteronomous decision of the other in me, not the individual self but "entangled" selves, not Kant but Hegel. You can see the drift. So, were I to jack up my concrete "politics" into a "political theory" I would describe it as a social—as opposed to a liberal—democracy. Again, I can only speak in the concrete: by that I mean, economically, the democracy that was beginning to take shape in the USA during the New Deal in the wake of the Great Depression, even as it was still steeped in racism and sexism. This was ultimately undermined by Ronald Reagan and his phony campaign against "welfare queens," which was just a cynical and transparent front for advancing the greed and racism of the Right. It wasn't even thinly disguised; it was blatant. So I advocate strongly progressive marginal tax rates, powerful social safety nets, robust support of public education and the healthcare system, strong regulation of the banks and the markets, breaking up monopolies, strong labor unions, controlling toxic emissions, all real possibilities before "deregulation" ruined everything. This sort of thing is most alive today in the Scandinavian democracies, although they, too, are under increasing pressure from nativist movements and right-wing reactionaries. I was sad to see how badly they dealt with the refugees from the Middle East. Sweden did well, but Denmark behaved badly. We used to call this a concern for the "common good," but that word has disappeared from our vocabulary.

So I am not sure what political theory accomplishes. Worse than that, theory can make people crazy, like saying that it makes no difference who wins these elections. Ralph Nader said, "Gore or Bush, what difference does it make?" Well, the difference gave us the war in Iraq, the single most destructive political decision since the war in Vietnam. How about Jim Inhofe? How's that "elections don't matter" thing working? I think the best political writing is found on the op-ed pages of good newspapers and highbrow journals, analyzing specific issues, not in philosophy books. Good political writing, like good sports writing, sizzles with brilliant, fiery, biting metaphors. It is found in insightful commentary on the politics of the day, not in writing the esoteric and unreadable papers we read at one at one another at the American Academy of Religion and then congratulate ourselves that we have thereby served the interests of the wretched of the earth. It is at its best when it takes a critical-polemical form, criticizing the inconsistencies of the Right and the failure of the Left to be true to itself. Here is the place for the public intellectuals like Cornel West. West is the best! Political writing should be strategic, the Socratic stingray, the gadfly.

For example, as I have just said, the Right today has little concern for the common good, but it is greatly concerned with the accumulation of personal wealth. The bottom line comes first; it precedes justice and truth. But money corrupts everything—journalism, religion, education, science, art, sports, entertainment, everything. So, as a matter of strategy, you have to show the Right that it actually costs more money in the long run if you destroy the environment, or ruin the public schools, if you put so many people in jail, or have working people living from day to day. It is more expensive to have so many people sick from lack of preventive care, so many people on drugs, to pollute the air and drinking water, etc. Don't appeal to the cruelty and injustice of the system. That won't work, because the Right thinks "those people" are doing very well "on the dole," sitting around collecting checks from the government. See Ronald Reagan, whom they all adore, who unleashed the worst instincts of Americans and made resentment against the poor politically respectable. That is what they actually think, especially when, as with the famous Romney clip—I think this cost him the 2012 election—we catch them behind closed doors. So we have to show them that the bottom line is that the current system ultimately costs too much money! Flint, Michigan is now spending millions of dollars because the government tried to save money by poisoning the water of people that they thought would not notice or have the power to protest. Why do you think the Koch brothers support prison reform? Because they have experienced *metanoia*—or because they think that, while they would like to keep as many of "those people" locked up, we just can't afford to? Then, only then, when you talk about money, do you have their attention.

I know that what I have just said is cynical, but I think it is true, at least it is true with the secular Right. They are the worst. They don't believe in anything except greed and white supremacy. Make America Great Again—that means: "Make America White Again!" When it comes to the religious Right—and here is where the question about political theology grows some teeth—there is a whole new element in play. We both start in the same place by asking, "What would Jesus do?" I completely embrace this question, in fact, I love it. I wrote a book about it, *What Would Jesus Deconstruct?* There I reminded everyone, Right and Left, that the question was coined by Charles Sheldon, who was a forerunner of the Social Gospel movement! That's a high irony, isn't it? So we say, look, let's do this together. Let's sit down at the same table, pen in hand, open up the New Testament, and together let's make a list of how many times Jesus brings up the poor and how many times he brings up sex. Now, having done that, let's ask this question again: what would Jesus do? After that, we could do the same thing with the Jewish prophets. Then the argument would shift to the next level: whether such matters should be left to private charity or to the "government"—this is a word they demonize, "statism" they call it, when of course the word means the "people," a usage still found in courts of law. As a practical matter, in a modern mass society, especially in this climate of gilded-age greed, it is a fairy tale to think it can be left to private charity. Furthermore, we don't want the richest people in the country deciding who gets to survive. But at least we can have that argument. There are signs that many younger evangelicals see all this.

By the same token, I think a lot, not all, but a lot of the criticism of the secular Left is on the mark. It's snotty, elitist, acidic, condescending and disdainful—and so the old joke, intellectuals love humankind, it is only individual people that they dislike! It is a rationalist Left, not a prophetic Left, a distinction Tillich made in *The Socialist Decision*. But the passion of the religious Left is compassionate, merciful, marked by the madness of the Kingdom of God. My oldest friends, people I deeply admire, belong to the Catholic left. So my political theology stems from the prophetic streak that runs from the Jewish prophets to the New Testament and shows up in people like Martin Luther King, Dorothy Day, the Catholic Worker Movement, the Berrigan brothers, the liberation theologians, and Bishop Oscar Romero. In *What Would Jesus Deconstruct?*, I singled out Fr. John McNamee, a Catholic priest who, against all the odds, managed to sustain a parish and parish school in a very bad neighborhood in north Philadelphia. So we on the religious Left can engage in concrete polemics with the aid of the powerful *Vorstellungen* (Hegel) of Jesus and the Jewish prophets at our side. The power of the *Vorstellung* is, as Hegel said, that it reaches the people, touches their heart. It gets them in the gut—maybe "gut" would be an interesting translation of *Geist*. Religion is where most people get their philosophy, Hegel said. That is where my political theology would start, by announcing the year of the Jubilee. So what Keith says is true. My political theology is that a genuinely just order would be the fruit, not of pure reason or the laws of dialectical materialism, but of a passion for the impossible, which is a deeply religious or theological passion, as it is embodied in concrete experience.

CC: But does this mean you think the distinction between the religious and secular remains valid? Hasn't it been deconstructed?

JDC: That is an important point. In postmodern theory, we have complicated the "religious" versus "secular" distinction, but we must not be too quick about this. As of today, right now, as a political reality, this is a tested distinction, and it is deadly serious. It still represents real voting blocks and voter patterns, which we would ignore at our own peril. So it must be taken into consideration strategically, in planning political campaigns and in making decisions about policy. On the other hand, in the academy, it is a contested distinction with a troubled history, about which we postmodern theorists have our theoretical doubts, not just on a strictly theoretical level but in concrete experience. When "secular" physicians abandon a lucrative practice and put themselves in harm's way to join "Doctors Without Borders" to fight Ebola in west Africa, that is on our accounting a "religious" act. It is an affirmation of something unconditional, of being seized by a matter of "ultimate concern," as Tillich would say. That is real theology, *in actu exercitu*, in the real culture; hence, we speak of a cultural or secular theology. A genuine political order would be driven by a genuinely religious passion for the impossible, with or without confessional religious bodies. Here I would recall what we said earlier, that many of my books these days are written for the growing number of "nones," for people, mostly younger people, for whom this distinction actually has collapsed and who cannot say whether they are religious or not, who are moved by a desire beyond desire for something, but they just cannot say what. My diagnosis is that this means they have discovered in their own experience that confessional theology is a *Vorstellung* of an event, and it is semi-blasphemous and mythological to take it too literally.

So we have good reasons to think this modernist distinction is waning as another postsecular sensibility waxes. Maybe we will be wrong, but that is our wager. Lacan would not agree. He thinks that, in the end, the old religion will always triumph. Maybe, maybe not. We know the mainstream congregations, both Protestant and Catholic, are losing their voice—and their congregations. But we must not congratulate ourselves that this is a fait accompli, and we certainly must not think this distinction has disappeared in real political work. But in fact, I think our deconstruction of the distinction can also be converted into real currency and can be put to strategic use in politics. It is a useful point to press against the secular Left—to help it get over its nose-holding contempt for religious people, to stop it from giving religion away to the Right. And also to press against the self-righteous religious

Right—it might remind them of the Parable of the Good Samaritan, that real religion is often found outside the so-called true religion, which is itself the seat of mythology and semi-blasphemy. That would be like what Derrida called the coming of a "new Enlightenment," one that is enlightened about the illusions of the old one, and critical of its pretentious "Critiques" and rigorous divides. But as always, he adds, "perhaps."

CLAYTON CROCKETT is Professor and Director of Religious Studies program at the University of Central Arkansas. He is author of *Deleuze Beyond Badiou: Ontology, Multiplicity, and Event* and editor (with B. Keith Putt and Jeffrey W. Robbins) of *The Future of Continental Philosophy of Religion* (IUP).

3
The Becoming Possible of the Impossible: An Interview with Jacques Derrida[1]

MARK DOOLEY

MARK DOOLEY (HEREAFTER MD): You once remarked that Jack Caputo reads you the way you love to be read. Why is that so?

JACQUES DERRIDA (HEREAFTER JD): I have many reasons for saying this. Firstly, he reads me the way I not only enjoy being read, but also in the way I strive to read others—that is, in a way which is generous to the extent that it tries to credit the text and the other as much as possible, not in order to incorporate, replace, or to identify with the other, but to "countersign" the text, so to speak. This involves approving and affirming the text, not complacently or dogmatically, but in and through the gesture of saying "yes" to the text.

What I love in Jack Caputo is this willingness to say "yes," as well as his willingness to countersign and to try and understand what he reads. He does this without giving up his own demanding rigor, his own culture and memory, as well as his singular relation to other texts that I don't know. So even when he is apparently reading me, I learn from him because he illuminates my text with his own culture and insight. To take an example, because he knows the work of many theologians, such as Meister Eckhart, Luther, and Kierkegaard, better than I do, he is able to write his own text according to his own trajectory and his own desire without, at the same time, betraying me. So that is why I don't really consider him simply as a commentator or interpreter. It is another kind of gesture.

MD: He's doing something new. . . .

JD: He is doing something new that, in turn, enriches my own text and gives it a wider scope. From a narcissistic point of view, I like being read in this way. Caputo sends me back an image of me and my texts that, of course, I enjoy. I would not, however, be so pleased if *his* text was not original in a certain way, if it was not very different from mine. For example, his book *The Prayers and Tears of Jacques Derrida*, helps me to understand how deconstruction is indebted, on the one hand, to Heidegger and, on the other hand, to the Lutheran tradition. In so doing, it helps me understand what is Christian and what is not Christian in my own text. This I could do only through Caputo, which is why he is for me a teacher in a certain way. It is very precious to be read by someone that I benefit from reading in my own turn, which is to say, that in reading him I am not simply looking at the reflection of my text in his. We write very different texts. No one will be surprised when I say that we have very different histories, very different backgrounds. It is not only a question of language and religion, but also our training is very different. Consequently, this encounter between Jack and myself is all the more surprising and, for me, a stroke of luck.

Another reason why I am so grateful for his writings is because when he reads my texts, which is especially the case throughout *Prayers and Tears*, he is the first one, and so far the *only* one, to bring the most philosophical and theoretical of my writings together with those which are most autobiographical. As some recent texts show, the two are for me sometimes indistinguishable. Jack has both the generosity and the competence to read these texts together, to pay attention to the *philosophemes*, so to speak, which are sometimes buried, sometimes embodied in an argument, as well as to the most idiomatic and singular references. He pays attention to tiny details, which are very significant for me, and he is the only one who really pays attention to significant motifs, details, metonymies, or subtle tropes and connections, which, as far as I can say, go unnoticed even by my most generous readers, my most friendly readers. These are the reasons why I am so grateful.

MD: From *Radical Hermeneutics*, his first major book to deal with issues raised in your work, to *The Prayers and Tears of Jacques Derrida*, Jack Caputo has tried to highlight an ethico-religious impulse which he sees at the heart of your ideas. How do you react to people like Jack, Richard Kearney, and others, who interpret you in this way?

JD: Don't forget that Jack Caputo speaks of religion without religion!

MD: I'll come to that!

JD: I am very grateful to Jack in that regard also, because he doesn't try to transform me in to a pious person. He respects the fact that I may be an atheist, and of course he takes into account all the complications which this suggests. I think he is right to mention this because my relation to religion is a very complicated one, and he respects how complicated it is. Without trying to attract me back to religion, he attempts to understand what I am struggling with myself. He is capable of appreciating this because of his background and probably because of his proximity to his religious tradition. That is, he appreciates the intimate relationship there is between faith and atheism, between radical doubt and faith. And not only does he know this in terms of discursive arguments and traditional discursive programs, but also in terms of the pathos and the effects it tends to engender. I must say that I am always so surprised by this because we are so different personally. But despite these differences, Jack has never shared certain prejudices about me or my work. For there are those who say that what I am doing is really a hidden or cryptic religious faith, or that it is just skepticism, nihilism, or atheism. He has never shared these prejudices.

MD: In fact, he has publicly defended you against such charges. He has never failed to come up with a paragraph every so often to trounce your detractors. . . .

JD: For which I am also very grateful. From the point of view of the cultural and academic wars that are going on, he is a very precious ally because he is not simply someone who takes sides with me because he is my friend but is someone who courageously and lucidly, in situations which I imagine are not always that easy for him, engages in the problems themselves. As you know, it is not easy, for me either, because there are battles all the time, there are enemies, and a lot of hatred. So I can imagine how difficult it is for him in his own social and academic milieu. It requires great courage of him, and that's the reason why I am so happy not only to be with him and to discuss with him, but also to attend the conferences he organizes at Villanova, a place where they are open and not reactive in the way other universities and other philosophy departments sometimes are. It is thanks to Jack that this milieu is open to these things. In the course of these conferences he does a wonderful job in terms of putting people together, people who come from different traditions and religious backgrounds, as well as from nonreligious backgrounds, and he organizes an ongoing discussion which goes far beyond myself and my own small contribution. His conferences should, I hope change the situation in philosophy and theology in the States and beyond.

MD: Is it a surprise that an American theologian, such as Mark C. Taylor, and an American philosopher of religion, such as Jack Caputo, have probably done more in recent years to promote your work than any other figures in the States? Are you surprised that you command such popularity amongst American theologians and professors and students of religion at this stage of your career?

JD: My answer would be a "yes" and "no" answer. I have been happily surprised in certain ways, but not so surprised in other ways. I should try to explain why I say "yes" and "no." Yes, because for someone like me who is French, a Jew, and so on, to be read and received that way by a Protestant theologian and a Catholic philosopher in the United States is, of course, something which might seem unpredictable. In a certain way, I am still surprised by this, happily surprised. On the other hand, I think there was from the very beginning good reasons to foresee this series of events. For long before the works by Mark Taylor and Jack Caputo, which were of course very impressive developments, there were signs of interest on the part of theology. It was discreet and it had to be interpreted, but I was nevertheless attentive to it. Indeed, long before I met Mark and Jack, I had asked myself why is this so? What is there in my own texts and my own gestures which draws the attention of American theologians? I knew from the very beginning that deconstruction, in the manner in which I was trying to elaborate it as deconstruction of theology or onto-theology, could be considered as a help to, or a model for, theology and theologians. I knew, for instance, that there had been in Germany, and in other places too, a similar gesture to deconstruct a certain type of theology, a certain philosophical theology, in order to uncover or unveil, so to speak, an evangelical Christian message. I also knew that around Heidegger there had been something similar. I felt that deconstruction, from the very beginning, could be considered as a good strategic lever for theologians. On the other hand, I was aware that the deconstruction of metaphysics or ontotheology didn't simply mean attacking God, the Divine, or the Sacred.

I was aware also that in the United States, much more than in France or Europe, there was a strong and vibrant life in theology and, consequently, that they might be interested in something which could appear both threatening and appealing at once. Due to the strong role which religion plays in the life of the United States, deconstruction could appear as an enemy and as a fascinating ally. During the very first years I was writing and publishing in the States, however, I was aware that for my detractors this was just one more "sin" of deconstruction. They would say that deconstruction's allies are theologians, and that it is a hidden form of theology and religion. Deconstruction is, on the one hand, nihilistic, relativistic, skeptical, and, on the other hand, a left wing anarchic radical movement, or, it is a hidden or cryptic religious sect. . . .

MD: You just can't win!

JD: Or one wins on all sides!

JD: This situation prevails not only in the States, but also in Europe. However, while the matrix is somewhat the same in Europe, the symptoms are nevertheless different. In the States it is more spectacular and visible.

MD: Even as early as *Glas* you seemed to be preoccupied with various "religious" themes, motifs, and problems, themes which Jack Caputo and Mark Taylor would later take up, such as the gift, speculative economies, the nature of the host and the Holy Family. Have you always had an interest in the phenomenon of religion and the religious?

JD: My interest in religion, as developed in *Glas* and elsewhere, is simply an interest in something that is in our culture, in our philosophy. From the very beginning I was interested in religion without, I must insist, having any *serious* religious context. My own family, even though we were more or less observant, had no religious culture. I knew very little of such things. Even when I was growing up as a student and a young professor, I knew, in principle that I should read the Bible seriously, something which I had not done up to that point. You see, on the one hand there is this orientation toward these religious problems, but on the other hand I am really ignorant of such matters. Each time, on the occasion of seminars, I learn just like a young student. This year, because I am giving a seminar on the "Death Penalty," I had to read and reread texts in the Bible, the Old Testament, and the gospels, and, in so doing, I just happen[ed] to discover things. That is what differentiates me from Mark Taylor, Jack Caputo, you, and others. While you were trained and grew up in a religious environment and context, I did not. My situation in this regard is strange; it's a mixture of, on the one hand, incompetence and, on the other, a terrible hunger to learn. This is just the way I work.

MD: Are you comfortable, therefore, with Jack Caputo's description of you as a Jewish Augustine from El Biar, one which he formulates on the basis of your own remarks in *Circumfession*?

JD: In a certain way, yes. *Circumfession* is both a tragic and an ironic text. I am constantly laughing in a way that is tragic throughout this text. At the same time, this mixture of tragedy, laughter, and irony is something which Jack manages to capture in a very lucid way. I always play with my religion, Judaism, in a serious way. When, for example, I say that I am the "last Jew"—meaning both the worst one and the last one—it is a play or a game, but a serious game nevertheless. Jack understood that he had to do the same with me. He understood that he had to make serious jokes. It is true that I was a young Augustinian Jew from El Biar. I could not deny this. I was born Jewish, I was circumcised, and I tried to understand what was going on with circumcision. This happened in a very specific and singular situation historically, that is, in a Jewish community in the colony of French Algeria in the thirties and forties. This is irreplaceable. Not only am I a Jew, but a Jew of this generation, of the suburb of Algiers, one who was ten years of age when the war broke out, one who was expelled from school, and one who read Saint Augustine one day and felt that he *had* to write this text, *Circumfession*. I knew, of course, for many years that I wanted to write a huge book on circumcision, and I accumulated a lot of material with that purpose in mind. Then this book was commissioned with Geoffrey Bennington, and I had to write one hundred pages approximately. But I don't remember how I decided to write the text with that particular structure, that is, with the references to Saint Augustine, the various layers, et cetera. At the time, as far as I can remember, I was reading Saint Augustine for other purposes. I was, for many years before I wrote *Circumfession*, fascinated by Augustine without reading him very seriously. But I cannot explain the precise chemistry which gave birth to this text. I cannot account for what happened there. The same is true of *Glas* and *The Post Card*, which, along with *Circumfession*, are the texts which are closest to me. These are the most fictional and autobiographical of my works. The three of them were written very spontaneously and artificially, in a very brief period, as if I was compelled to write them urgently. If you were to ask me what texts I would keep, I would say this kind of text.

MD: Jack Caputo has tried in his recent work to underscore the "prophetic" and "messianic" nature of deconstruction. I am interested to know if you were aware of this "prophetic" strain in your work before you thematized the idea of the undeconstructable notion of a "justice to come" in the early nineties, or was this something of a "turning" in the spirit of Heidegger?

JD: I don't think this is a turning. If I may oversimplify a little again, I would say that from the very beginning, from *The Introduction to the Origin of Geometry*, with its emphasis on the "end of history," "the telos," and so on, the project had what sounded like a prophetic tone. So the prophetic, the eschatological, or the apocalyptic tone, could be heard in my work from the very beginning. This could be shown very rigorously. At the same time, however, I was so vigilant and so anxious not to give in to or accept this tone that I multiplied the signs of irony.

Let us look at an example. In the text, "Of an Apocalyptic Tone Recently Adopted in Philosophy," I speak apocalyptically, while, at the same time, denouncing the strategy, the mystification, and all the abuses of this tone. I write as an *Aufklärer* in a certain way. There is both an apocalyptic tone and the tone of someone who denounces this, and both voices are intertwined. The theme of a multiplicity of voices within one voice is thematized in this text. So, from the very beginning, there was both this very prophetic, messianic, mystical tone, and its opposite. This is why I think that if there is an idiomatic tone in my texts, it is a mixture of the two—that is, the one who plays at being prophetic while laughing at himself. I know that my tone is prophetic, but I am not a prophet.

If I may make a confession here: I have always had the feeling, even more so of late, that my destiny as a writer and as a thinker has something prophetic about it, even though I know that I have no particular prophecy to make, nothing to foresee, nothing except catastrophe. Sometimes prophets foresee catastrophe. In fact, almost all of them foresee catastrophe! So this is a permanent *Stimmung*: I am a prophet without prophecy, a prophet without being a prophet.

Against the background of this permanent *Stimmung*, it is true to say that during the last ten years or so, something in the content of the texts—especially in the theme of the "to come," the reference to messianicity, and the reference to justice as different from the law—is more explicitly recognizable as being intrinsically or structurally prophetic, that is, pointing to what is "to come," which is not the future, in a certain way.

Is this original? There is something like that in Levinas, in Heidegger, in Nietzsche. Heidegger says somewhere that thinking is eschatological; when you think, you think the extreme, that is, the eschatological, the apocalyptical. The truth is apocalypse or, what he calls, "unveiling."

So if I wanted to address these questions in a non-improvised way, I should, of course, begin by analyzing the relationship between philosophy, thinking, poetry, and prophecy. Even if you don't say this in Heideggerian terms, you have to admit that there is no thought without the inscription of "the new." You have to think poetically in order to think something new. The difference between poetry and prophecy is difficult to determine because there is something prophetic in every poetic gesture. There is a strong relationship between poetry and prophecy. Of course, in a very dry and cold way, when, like the speech-act theoretician, you pay attention to "the promise," you will see that the promise has something prophetic in it, that the theory about the promise is a promise itself. The promise in language is in itself prophetic. Language is prophetic. You don't have to be a Messiah or to believe in one to say that the structure of language is messianic. I am simply saying, in a theoretical way, that the experience of language is messianic, and it is part of the experience of the messianic that the Messiah may come at any time. I am working on this limit between describing a prophecy and performing a prophecy without prophecy.

MD: Caputo suggests, in both the introduction and conclusion of *The Prayers and Tears of Jacques Derrida*, that there is an endless translatability, or an undecidable fluctuation between the passion for "*the* impossible" and the passion for God. He says that we will never be able to decide which is an example of which. How do you respond to this?

JD: If I had to react quickly, I would say that the difference between the passion for *the* impossible, on the one hand, and the passion for "God," on the other, is the *name*. "*The* impossible" is not a name, it is not a proper name, it is not some*one*. "God"—I do not say divinity—is someone with a name, even if it is a nameless name like the Jewish god. It is a nameable nameless name, whereas *the* impossible is a non-name, a common name, a non-proper name. "God" is a proper nameable nameless name. "*The* impossible" is a common non-proper name, or nameless common name. Now, you cannot and you should not translate one into the other. If there is a transparent translatability "the faith" is safe, that is, it becomes a non-faith. At that point, it becomes possible to name. It becomes possible because there is some*one* whom you can name and call because you know who it is that you are calling. Not only can I not say this, but I would not and should not say this. If I were sure that it was possible for me to replace "*the* impossible" by "God," then everything would become possible. Faith would become possible, and when faith becomes simply possible it is not faith anymore. So I see a danger for faith and for something which is the abyss of faith. This danger consists in stating, or in believing in, the mere translatability between these two things. I keep oscillating between the two.

MD: So would you concur with Caputo's contention that for you there is an endless or undecidable fluctuation between the two?

JD: Yes, absolutely. Once again, to be in undecidability does not mean simply that I don't *know.* It means, firstly, that it does not belong to the order of knowledge and, secondly, that I don't *want* to know. I know that I should not know. If I could rely on this translatability there would be no God anymore.

Now, when the God comes, when the Messiah comes, we will see! But I cannot foresee and program this. That is why I am an atheist *in a certain way*—a faithful one! I am faithful to this sort of atheism. So I agree with Jack Caputo when he says there is this undecidability, but to say that there is such undecidability doesn't mean that the two terms are replaceable one for the other. That is the problem of God.

MD: So when you appropriate the name of God in your text, are you *using* this name or are you just *mentioning* it?

JD: Do you think I can answer such a question?!This is an interesting question about the "use-mention" distinction. If I knew if I were using or simply mentioning the name of God, the answer would be given. Most often, I am sure that I am just mentioning it. God is a name which is in use everywhere, so I am always mentioning it. When I write I am not addressing people in a church. I am just reading texts, writing fictions and philosophical treatises. So I am constantly in the situation of *mentioning*, of using by mentioning; I am always referring to what others say, what the Bible says, what Hegel says, what Heidegger says, what Jack Caputo says, what my mother says about God. So it is difficult for me to use the word God.

Now, when and if I pray—Jack Caputo's book has to do with prayer, and I refer to my own *secret* experience of praying—I am not sure that even in that situation I would simply *name* God; you do not have to *name*, you can address someone, not knowing who this other one is, or how to name him or her. This is very interesting, but, in a certain way, it is impossible to answer such questions improvising before a tape recorder. On the other hand, you are compelled to say things that you might not say if you had more time. So what I should not say, but what I will say, is that beyond all the situations in which I probably just *mention* the name of God, as when I borrow it, read it, or analyze it in different situations, if I *use* it, or if I use something which looks or sounds like the name "God," it refers to the becoming possible of "*the* impossible"—that is, and here I come back to something which in my text I usually question or critique, a savior, a redeeming someone, someone who would save, not only myself, but save everything I am attached to exactly when I think nothing can be saved. So when I refer to some power, some saving power in which I don't believe in a certain way, God would mean this. The one who could finally make possible what I am sure is impossible. For me, God is precisely the one who would share my desire for the impossible, even if he doesn't respond to, or satisfy that desire. This is a dream.

I am not very happy with what I am saying here because I have a number of relations with God or divinity. I have the one I just tried to describe, but I also often think, not in a pantheistic fashion, that God is what puts in motion the question, is the fabric of existence. God is everywhere. To take the example of demythologization, once you have pushed this gesture as far as possible by psychoanalyzing or deconstructing everything in religion, you can still say God is not some*thing* else or some*one* else, that is, the product of a phantasm or a desire. God is precisely what produces this neurosis or this pathology. That is what God is.

MD: Neurosis?

JD: Once you account for religion through neurosis, then you have to account for neurosis. "God" is the name of what produces this neurosis, of what produces religion. Religion is fabulation, it is mythology. I remember once, when he was a young boy, my elder son was asked by my father: "Do you know what the Bible is?" Pierre, who was then five years old, replied "Yes, it is the mythology of the Hebrews!" So the force by which this mythology was produced is what I call "God."

Let us take the existence of "the secret," or the possibility to hide something, to spiritualize, or to interiorize. You can, of course, scientifically follow the evolution of animals and biological organisms, and you will see that a cat can hide something behind the door. He has a way of hiding. When, however, you climb up the scale you find that there are more subtle ways of hiding. Finally, we are brought to what we call consciousness—or that by virtue of which you can hide something in your head by lying. So hiding or keeping a secret is a long story of life. Nietzsche would say that "the ruse" or "the lie" is a part of life. You can also see the secret at work in Christianity, as in the case of Abraham on Mount Moriah. Christianity teaches that God can see into your soul.

Once you have reduced all this to a movement in life, to an evolution in a very flat positivistic way, you realize that this does not serve to deny the existence of God. It is God. This lie, this hiding, this transformation of life, from the most elementary forms of life to the more sophisticated forms of secrecy in religion and in the unconscious—this is God, we could call this "God"...

MD: Why?

JD: Because how else could you account for this progressive spiritualization which produces ultimately the idea of sharing a secret with God? Who could prevent me from calling this *unique* adventure "God," the power of God. This does not contradict the most scientific positivistic approach. Let us call life, and the ruses in life, "God." On the one hand, you can go as far as possible in the direction of this reduction, this scientific reduction. To do so is necessary. I am, from that point of view, an *Aufklärer*, in that I think we have to reexamine and question the limits between animality and humanity. We have to be as scientific and as reductive as possible. Such a reduction is not, however, incompatible with faith, divinity, and the sacred.

MD: Could you not call it, as you have in the past, *khora*, or *différance*, or anonymity? What you are describing sounds a lot less like God, and more like *khora* or *différance*. . . .

JD: Yes, but *khora* has something which *resists* historicization or revelation. *Khora* has something which is irreducible to any anthropo-theological revelation; it is something which is absolutely cold and which doesn't give anything. *Khora* would be, nevertheless, not part of the process but that out of which—not as an origin, but on the impossible background of which—something like God, man, and animal, take shape. *Khora* is not God. Non-God is part of this experience of the sacred and divinity.

You see, I have the feeling that no name, as such, is indispensable, and especially not in my texts. That would be true for the name of God also. I could have written almost everything I wrote without the name of God, and even without the name *différance*. Yes, I could do without it. This would not change the stakes and the content of what I am saying essentially. Of course, it would change both the strategy and the economy. *Différance*, for instance, is a way of describing, more economically, the economy itself, the principle of economy. So it is a better economy. Perhaps the word "God"—with all the precautions we have taken a moment ago—is also a metonym, or a more economic way to express something else. In using it, we are naming in the quickest and briefest way a lot of things: God is *the* impossible, the singular, what makes *the* impossible possible, the gift, forgiveness, pure hospitality. These are different names, and, at some point, I encounter the name of God at these limits. "God" is the name of the limit, the *absolute* limit, *absolute* transcendence, *absolute* immanence. Each time I write "the absolute" I think of "absolution," the moment when the debt is remitted absolutely. Each time I write "absolute," I could, of course, replace this common attribute with "God." So, I can imagine a transformation of my texts in which the words *God* and *différance* would simply disappear without causing any damage. This may mean either that the name "God" is useless, or because it is so powerful it can be replaced by any other. It is everywhere. It is a useless, indispensable name.

Now, given this very general axiom, why do I use the name "God" here and not there, more in this text than in that one, later rather than earlier, or earlier rather than later? I have no general answer for this; I have no criteria. It would be too simple to say that, for instance, I refer more frequently to God in the most recent texts. I don't know if I do. It is probable, but that is a matter of socio-historical analysis. During the last decade or so, mainly because both the scene and the way people now read me has changed, I have felt a greater freedom to use the word *God* than I did at the beginning. To good readers, my texts attest to the fact that I am not simply a dogmatic, religious person and that when I say "God," it is said with tongue in cheek. Levinas once said to me that when you say "God" you have to add "so to speak," or, as we say in France, "allow me, if you will, to speak that way." He was complaining, with a smile of course, that the name of

God is so obsolete that when you use it you have to apologize. So I know that today when I use the word *God* I don't have to apologize, because I assume that people know that when I use it I do so with tongue in cheek.

MD: Why do you say in *Circumfession*, that you "rightly pass for an atheist," instead of simply stating that you are an atheist?

JD: Once again, I am being ironic. Firstly, I prefer to refer to what *they* say, even if they are right in saying so, and even if they have good reasons for saying this, it is still what *they* say. So I feel free because I am not saying this. Even when I say that *they* have good reasons for saying this, I am not saying this of myself. *I* am just referring to them, to what *they* say. It is, however, not that simple. For I am more than one: I am the atheist they think I am, which is why I say that I "rightly" pass for an atheist, but I would also approve of those people who say exactly the opposite. Who is right? I don't know. I don't know whether I am or not. Sometimes it depends on the moment or the hour. It is not a matter of knowledge. I would prefer not to say who I am myself.

MD: But you are comfortable saying that you have a "religion without religion"?

JD: Yes.

MD: Caputo would say that it's a religion of justice, an openness to the other. . . .

JD: That is true. I try in more "scholarly" texts to explain what religion is or is not, and to explain the difference between faith and knowledge. So in a certain sense of "religion" I am religious. I am a very religious person, not because I pray or because I go to church or the synagogue, but in my relation to others, in my behavior as a citizen, as a father, and so on. I am obsessed with the problem of "perjury" and someone who is obsessed with the problem of perjury is someone who hates perjury, who wants to respect the other and the sacred. I have a religious temper without piety and practice.

MD: Would you say that if there is a word you privilege above others in your work it is *justice*?

JD: No. It is true that it has prevailed throughout the last eight or ten years. I felt that it was my duty, my responsibility as a professor, a writer, and a philosopher, to give *some* privilege to this word in this context for some time. I would not, however, privilege it absolutely, because even when I say that justice is not reducible to the law and that justice is always to come, there is still something totally enigmatic for me in justice. Someday I would like to do a very patient work on the history of this concept, of this name, *dike*. So while I have a strong feeling of some necessity in this distinction between justice to come and the law, its meaning remains very obscure. I would not transform such an obscure meaning into a master name.

Furthermore, I would be very slow to suggest that mine is a novel sense of justice. It is much more complicated than that. As Nietzsche taught, you may be on the side of the weak because the weak will prevail. In other words, I may be interested in the margin, the minority, the minor text, because I suffered myself and I want to exact revenge. If so, you are not doing this simply and purely out of a sense of justice. I think I have to do what I am doing with the word *justice* in this context, and this "I have to" is something which I would not, and cannot, deny, is something that is absolutely universal. You can, of course, translate this "I have to" into a call for justice or for duty. But, as you know, I interpret duty as something which should go beyond duty, beyond debt. These are the aporias.

MD: Can you say a final word on Jack Caputo's legacy?

JD: I think that people will consider Jack Caputo's work as a major contribution because of the way he has provided a powerful interpretation, not just of my own work, but also of the texts of Meister Eckhart and Heidegger. His legacy will be the legacy of someone who has transformed the picture in the United States, in the English-speaking world, transformed the relation between religion and philosophy through a confluence of the most radical attempts of the twentieth century—Heidegger and deconstruction. He has left behind a field in which thinking, writing, and religion have a new relationship, where religion would not be enclosed in a dogmatic field of revelation, but [would] open up to radical deconstructive questioning, open, without being threatened, to the naked minimal experience of faith. So that will provide a field in which new ways of reading and teaching will become available. While these new ways of reading and teaching will happen first with in the American academy, my hope is that they will extend far beyond. My hope and prediction is that Jack Caputo's work will someday be translated into many idioms, many other idioms.

NOTE

1. This interview was recorded in Paris on January 15, 2000, trans. J. P. Leavey, *Oxford Literary Review* 6, no. 2 (1984): 3–37.

Part Two

Radical Hermeneutics: Selections

§ 1
Pious Hermeneutics: From Aquinas to Heidegger

4
Meister Eckhart and the Later Heidegger: The Mystical Element in Heidegger's Thought, Part One

HEIDEGGER AND MEDIEVAL MYSTICISM

In the introduction to his habilitation dissertation at Freiburg, *The Doctrine of Categories and of Meaning in Duns Scotus* (1916), the young Martin Heidegger praised the "objective" orientation of medieval philosophy: "Scholastic psychology, precisely inasmuch as it is not focused upon the dynamic and flowing reality of the psychical remains in its fundamental problems oriented toward the objective and noematic, a circumstance which greatly favors setting one's sight on the phenomenon of intentionality" (*DS*, 15).[1] While modern philosophy is characterized by a keen sense of subjective experience, the Scholastic thinker is concerned primarily with the object of knowledge, with "being." The Scholastic, he says, is typified by an "absolute surrender" to the "content" of knowledge (*DS*, 7). In a sentence that is prophetic in the light of what he would later call the "subject matter of thinking" (*die Sache des Denkens*) Heidegger observes: "The value of the subject matter [Sache] (object) dominates over the value of the self (subject)" (*DS*, 7). Because thinking "tends into" (in-tendere) being, the medievals spoke of the "intentional" character of knowledge. Thus the Scholastics' neglect of subjective experience at least kept them free of the "unphilosophy of psychologism" (*DS*, 14). Heidegger found in the medievals an anticipation of the work of Husserl, who would come to Freiburg this same year (1916) and whose Logical Investigations he had been studying for some time (*SD*, 82). Both Husserl and the author of De modis significandi[2] reject the reduction of the laws of logic to the empirical constitution of the human mind; both seek a "pure" grammar which delineates unchanging relationships between the parts of speech and which holds true a priori of every possible empirical language (*DS*, 149–50). The simple but challenging task for thinking in the medieval world was to subordinate the "individuality of the individual" (*DS*, 7) to the demands of the subject matter, to its unchanging structures and "objective meanings." That is why one can read through the great *Summae* of the thirteenth century without once catching a glimpse of the personalities of their authors.

But it would be a mistake, Heidegger contends, to think that behind the objectivity and formalism of the Scholastic there is nothing "living." On the contrary, "the theoretical posture of the spirit is only one" of its possible attitudes and perhaps not even the most important

(*DS*, 236). Hence the text we cited above continues: "In order to reach a decisive insight into this fundamental character of scholastic psychology, I consider a philosophical, or more exactly, a phenomenological examination of the mystical, moral theological and ascetical literature of medieval scholasticism to be especially urgent. In such a way alone will one push forward to what is living in the life of medieval scholasticism" (*DS*, 15).

Behind the impersonal disputations of the scholastics there is the life of the soul which seeks God in the practice of morality and asceticism. The speculative theology and philosophy of the Middle Ages is not opposed to its mystical tradition but rather expresses in a conceptual way what the mystic has experienced:

> If one reflects on the deeper essence of philosophy in its character as a philosophy of world-views, then the conception of the Christian philosophy of the Middle Ages as a scholasticism which stands in opposition to the contemporaneous mysticism must be exposed as fundamentally wrong. In the medieval world-view, scholasticism and mysticism belong essentially together. The two pairs of "opposites" rationalism-irrationalism and scholasticism-mysticism do not coincide. And where their equivalence is sought, it rests on an extreme rationalization of philosophy. Philosophy as a rationalist creation, detached from life, is powerless; mysticism as an irrationalist experience is purposeless. (*DS*, 241)

Philosophy is the conceptualization of what the living historical man experiences. And for the young Heidegger, the experience of the mystic is the experience of medieval man intensified and "writ large."

The Heidegger who offers this sensitive interpretation of medieval thought is not only conversant with Husserl's "transcendental phenomenology," but is equally concerned with the problem of history, and especially with the work of Wilhelm Dilthey, whose *Collected Writings* were a significant source of his reflections in "the exciting years between 1911 and 1914,"[3] and of Heinrich Rickert, his mentor at Freiburg to whom the *Habilltationsschrift* is dedicated. With Dilthey and Rickert, the young Heidegger speaks of the necessity of understanding a historical epoch in terms of its "goals": "But where it is a matter of reaching a living understanding of an 'age' and of the accomplishments of the spirit that were productive in it, then an interpretation of its meaning which is guided by an ultimate conception of its goals becomes necessary" (*DS*, 231). And this is what he says he hopes to find in a study of medieval mysticism. For philosophy cannot be content with the abstract, thinking subject: "The epistemological subject does not signify the most important meaning of the spirit, let alone its whole content" (*DS*, 237–38). Philosophy must penetrate to the living, historical spirit. Thus philosophy must go beyond logic and the theory of knowledge to metaphysics itself. One can already see the author of Kant and the *Problem of Metaphysics* (*KPM*, 25–26): "One cannot see logic and its problems in a true light unless the context in which they are interpreted is translogical. Philosophy cannot for long dispense with its true optics, metaphysics" (*DS*, 235). There is need for a "metaphysical-teleological interpretation of consciousness" (*DS*, 235): metaphysical, because it goes beyond the logico-epistemological view of consciousness to the living historical spirit; teleological, because the living spirit is end-directed and meaning-seeking.[4]

No inquiry into medieval thought can prescind from "the world of experience of medieval man" (*DS*, 235). "The fundamental structure," Heidegger says, of the "whole attitude of life of medieval man" is to be found in what he calls "the transcendent and primordial relationship of the soul to God" (in *dem transzendenten Urverhältnis der Seele zu Gott* [*DS*, 1]). In this relationship, neither the absoluteness of God nor the integrity of the soul is destroyed, but the soul—"stretching out into the transcendent"—is given to share in God's absolute value. This contrasts sharply, he says, with our "modem experience," whose richness and variety is measured by its absorption in the "breadth of content" (*inhaltliche Breite* [*DS*, 240]) of sensible reality. The medieval man subordinated the variety and multiplicity of the sensible world to a "transcendent goal."

The importance of these texts for the historian of Heidegger's development should not be underestimated. For the notion of the soul "stretching out into the transcendent," of the primordial and transcendent relationship of the soul to God, foreshadows the relationship of *Dasein*[5] to Being. As the soul transcends beyond the multiplicity of sensible things in the world to God himself, so *Dasein* transcends beings to Being itself.

Of all the medieval mystics, Heidegger draws special attention to Meister Eckhart,[6] a thinker in whom the unity of "mysticism" and "philosophy" (*DS*, 241) is clearly exemplified. For not only was Eckhart one of the outstanding figures in the history of medieval mysticism, he was also one of the great Dominican "masters" at Paris. Some forty years later, Heidegger would say: "The most extreme sharpness and depth of thought belongs to genuine and great mysticism .... Meister Eckhart testifies to it" (*SG*, 71). The evidence of Heidegger's interest in Meister Eckhart at this time is indisputable. The 1915 inaugural lecture, "The Concept of Time in the Science of History," begins with a citation taken from Eckhart on the distinction between time and eternity.[7] In 1919 Heidegger held a lecture course on "The Philosophical Foundations of Medieval Mysticism" in which the role that Eckhart played is testified to by the fact that a student in this course wrote a book on Eckhart, approaching him from a very Heideggerian point of view.[8] And in the habilitation dissertation itself Heidegger promises us a work of his own on Meister Eckhart. "I hope on another occasion," he says, "to be able to show how Eckhartian mysticism first receives its philosophical interpretation and evaluation" in connection with "the metaphysics of the problem of truth" (*DS*, 232n1).

What does Heidegger mean by an interpretation of Eckhart in terms of the "metaphysics of truth"? A metaphysical investigation, we have seen, means a historical-teleological analysis of the living spirit, which in the case of medieval philosophy centers on the notion of the transcendent relation of the soul to God. "Truth" for the medieval philosopher means the "true" (*verum*), which is the "transcendental" relationship between thinking and being (*DS*, 80). The "true" is convertible with "being" (*ens*) itself, and so "transcends" the categories (of Aristotle); every being as such is true. In a text that Heidegger would later cite in *Being and Time* (*SZ*, sec. 4, p. 14), Aquinas calls the true a "relational transcendental," that is, one that arises from being considered in relationship to something, in this case to the intellect.[9] According to the scholastic notion of the true, every being is accessible to thought and all thinking is directed to being. Thus if the significance of Eckhart is to be found in connection with the metaphysics of truth, then this must mean that the living relationship between the soul and God represented in Eckhart's mysticism constitutes a "model" (*SD*, 54) in terms of which one can conceive the relationship between thinking and being. The relational transcendental (truth) is to be thought of in terms of the transcendent relation (of the soul to God).

Whether this is what Heidegger meant in 1916 we cannot be sure because the work on Meister Eckhart never appeared, nor have the lectures of 1919 been published. It is in any case a suggestion that Heidegger himself pursued in his own later works. For there is no stronger analogy to the relation between *Dasein* and the coming to pass of the Truth of Being in Heidegger's later thought than that between the soul and God in Eckhart. The extensive parallels between Eckhart and the later Heidegger are not accidental. Moreover, if Heidegger's references to the writings of Eckhart are any indication, his interest in the meister never subsided. In the works that have appeared since 1947 Heidegger cites Eckhart seven times to our knowledge. Twice (*K*, 39; *VA*, 175) he cites directly from the Middle High German text. On two other occasions (*WD*, 95–96; *G*, 36) he refers to pivotal elements in Eckhart's teachings. Twice (*SG*, 71; *FW*, 4) he comments on the depth of this man whom he has called both a "master of thinking" (*VA*, 175) and a "master of life" (*FW*, 4). On a seventh occasion (*FND*, 76) he refuses to call Eckhart a "modern" and therefore—for Heidegger—a "subjectivistic" thinker. Moreover, Heidegger's description of thinking as *Gelassenheit* (*gelâzenheit*) employs Eckhart's very vocabulary, as Heidegger himself points out (*G*, 36).

Heidegger has said that his beginnings in theology have determined his path of thought (*US*, 96). Hitherto it has been thought that Heidegger's theological interests culminated in his concern with Kierkegaard in *Being and Time* and in his discussions of "hermeneutics" in the later work. But it seems to us that a decisive source of Heidegger's thought in Western theology has up to now been overlooked, namely, Meister Eckhart.[10] The main burden of the present study, then, is first, to show the extensive parallels that exist between Eckhart and Heidegger and, second, to assess their philosophical significance. For after having shown that a relationship exists, one must still determine what to make of it. Are we to suppose, for example, that "thinking" (*Seinsdenken*), as Heidegger conceives it, and mysticism are the same?

One last remark before proceeding with this analogy. The relationship between Heidegger and Eckhart is a suggestive theme for the historian of German philosophy, for it brings together the earliest and the latest stages of German speculation. It suggests a fundamental continuity in German thought whose middle term is surely the great idealist system of the nineteenth century. In Eckhart, the Idealists, and Heidegger, one finds a similar structure: a transcendent reality (God, the Absolute, Being) comes to pass in man; and man is conceived not "anthropologically" but ontologically as the locus of the realization of the transcendent (as the "ground of the soul," "spirit," "*Dasein*"). This is a topic of such proportions that we cannot hope to do it justice in these pages. We must be content to offer suggestions about it where space permits. Moreover, we do not hold that the relation of Heidegger to Eckhart is mediated by the Idealists, but that it grows directly out of Heidegger's acquaintance with Eckhart from his earliest studies in Scholasticism, and out of the aborted effort he made to discover "what was living in the life of medieval scholasticism" (*DS*, 15).

The analogy between Heidegger and Eckhart can be conceived in terms which Heidegger has himself suggested. Speaking in 1960 to theologians at Marburg interested in his work, Heidegger recommended the following analogy: Being : thinking :: God : the thinking conducted within faith.[11] This structure, derived from the medieval doctrine of analogy (*DS*, 70is called the "analogy of proportionality." It signifies a similarity of relationships, a proportion of proportions. And it is an apt formula as well for relating Eckhart and Heidegger: as God is to the soul in Eckhart, so Being is to *Dasein* in Heidegger. This does not imply that Being is "really" God, or that Heidegger has "substituted" Being for God, for the relationship of the terms of this analogy is not direct but structural: each plays a similar role within similar structures.

Having established Heidegger's interest in Eckhart, our procedure now will be as follows: to work out the relation of the soul to God in Meister Eckhart (II); to compare the relation of Being and *Dasein* with Eckhart's mysticism (III); and, finally, to examine the import of this comparison for our understanding of Heidegger (IV).

ECKHART'S SPECULATIVE MYSTICISM

Our analysis of Eckhart will begin with a discussion of the metaphysical account of God in his Latin writings. We will then examine the major themes of his mystical doctrine, the "ground of the soul," the "birth of the Son" and "detachment," in his vernacular works. The metaphysics will provide a speculative foundation for the mysticism; the mysticism will offer the "living" correlate to the metaphysics.

The Metaphysics of God

In the prologues to the Opus Tripartitum, Eckhart sets out the "first proposition" from which, if one is careful, nearly all that can be known of God can be deduced (*LW*, I, 165). The proposition is: being is God (*esse est deus*). He does not say, as did Aquinas, that God is being (*deus est suum esse*), but he adopts instead the more extreme expression that being is God. Aquinas, realist and Aristotelian, emphasized that creatures possessed their own proper and proportionate share in being, while God possessed the unlimited fullness of being itself. But the mystic Eckhart stresses instead the radical dependency of creatures upon God.[12] Of itself, he says, the creature is "absolutely nothing" (*nihil penitus*), a "pure nothing" (*ein reines Nichts* [Q, 170]), not even a modicum. The creature does not have being "in itself" at all, but only "in God." Created things have being, Eckhart holds, the way air has light (*LW*, II, 274–75). The air does not "possess" the light; it simply receives it for as long as the sun illumines it. The light is not "rooted" in the air, but in its source, the sun. In the same way, the creature does not "possess" being, has no "hold" on it, but instead continuously receives being from its source, being itself. Being is God, that is to say, being belongs properly only to God, in whom alone it is originally "rooted" (*LW*, II, 282).

If being is God then it follows that nothing of the perfection of being is lacking to him. God is the purity and plenitude of being (*plenitudo esse, purum esse* [*LW*, III, 77]). He precontains and includes (*praehabeat et includat* [*LW*, I, 169]) in a preeminent way the limited and multiple perfections which have been "lent" (Q, 119–20) to creatures. Moreover, if being is God, then God is "one." He possesses His being in a timeless simplicity that entirely excludes the successiveness and multiplicity, that is, the "negativity" of creatures. God is the "negation of negation" (*negatio negationis* [*LW*, I, 175]).[13]

The neoplatonic emphasis that Eckhart places on the "unity" of the divine being is developed in the German works in terms of the distinction between the "Godhead" (*Gottheit, divinitas*) and "God" (*Gott, deus*). "God" refers to the divine being insofar as it is related to creatures and consequently insofar as it is named on the basis of these relationships. Hence "God" is called good as the cause of the goodness of creatures, wise because of the order he has established in the universe, et cetera. But the "Godhead" is the divine being insofar as it remains concealed behind all the names which are attributed to Him. The Godhead is the "One," which is purer than goodness and truth, which is even prior to the Son and the Holy Spirit. The "One" refers to God: "There where He is in Himself, before He flows out into the Son and the Holy Spirit. . . . A master has said: the one is a negation of negation" (Q, 252). The Godhead is the absolute unity of the divine being, the negation of all multiplicity, not only of the multiplicity of creatures but even of the multiplicity of Persons in the divine Trinity. The Godhead is the deeper "ground" (*Grund* [Q, 264]) from out of which even the Persons of the Trinity flow. But because this ground is "hidden," it is just as much an "abyss" (*Abgrund* [Q, 213]).[14]

While Eckhart frequently vests his thought in the language of Aquinas, the direction his thought is taking is quite different. Indeed, he goes on to deny the central tenet of Thomas's metaphysics, the primacy of *esse*. After accepting Aquinas's arguments for the identity of being (*esse*) and understanding (*intelligere*) in God, he states in his Parisian Questions that he has reached a very unthomistic conclusion: "I am no longer of the opinion that He understands because He is, but that He is because He understands, so that God is intellect and the act of understanding, and the act of understanding is the ground of being itself" (*LW*, V, 40). There is something higher—or deeper—in God than "being" and that is "understanding." God is not being, formally speaking: "In God there is neither being (*ens*) nor the act-of-being (*esse*), because nothing is formally present in both the cause and that of which it is the cause, if the cause is a true cause. But God is the cause of all being. Therefore being is not formally present in God" (*LW*, V, 45).

Eckhart attempts to reconcile this position with the one he adopted in the prologues—that *esse est deus* arguing that being does not belong to God "formally" but rather in a "higher" sense. This is because God is "a true cause," that is, one which is of an essentially higher kind than its effect, in this case, creatures. Now creatures have "being" properly speaking, for to be "created" is to receive being. But God is the cause of the being of creatures. And since he is a "true" or transcendent cause, he does not share "being" with creatures in a "univocal" sense (*LW*, V, 51). Thus God does not have being, properly speaking, but the "purity of being" (*puritas essendi* [*LW*, V, 45]).

But the purity of being is identified by Eckhart as understanding. For the understanding is not being, but that by which being is known. Ideas are not things but the means by which things are known. In order to know something, the soul, Eckhart says (following Aristotle), must be "pure" of, "unmixed" with, "separate" from that which it knows. If the eye were colored, then it would see all things under that color. The understanding is separate from being and contains the form of every being in a pure way. God is the highest "separate substance," the most removed of all from time and multiplicity, the absolute "purity of being." Hence God knows all beings and is not any particular being. His proper name is not being, therefore, but the purity of being, namely, understanding.

The "naked essence" of God, the pure, simple, inner life of God, is the life of understanding, or, as Eckhart translates intellectus in his vernacular sermons, the life of "Reason" (*Vernunft*):

> If we take God in His being, then we take Him in His vestibule, for being is the vestibule in which He dwells. But where is He then in His temple, in which He shines forth as holy? Reason is the temple of God. God dwells nowhere more authentically than in His temple, in Reason. As that other master said, God is His Reason, which there lives in knowledge of Himself alone, abiding there only in Himself, where nothing ever troubles Him. For He is there alone in His stillness. In His knowledge of Himself, God knows Himself in Himself. (*Q*, 197; cf. *Q*, *"Einleitung,"* 23)

By assigning such primacy to the understanding, Eckhart is defending the traditions of his order against the Franciscans, who emphasized the divine will. Eckhart takes over the "self-thinking thought" of Aristotle and contours it to the needs of his Christian metaphysics. As such, Eckhart's *Vernunft*, the life of God knowing himself, provides a neglected link in the familiar connection between Aristotle and Hegel. When Hegel identifies the Absolute as the absolute "Idea," he agrees with the Dominican-Aristotelian intellectualism of the Middle Ages, and with the German Eckhart in particular.

The activity of thought thinking itself is entirely self-contained, beginning and ending in the divine mind itself. Hence it is for Eckhart the supreme form of "life." With Aristotle, Eckhart held that a living thing is "that which is moved from itself as from an inner principle and in itself. But that which is not moved except by some external thing neither is nor is said to be living. From this it is evident that everything which has an efficient cause prior to and above itself, or a final cause outside of or other than itself, does not live in the proper sense. But such is the case with every creature. Only God as the ultimate end and first mover lives and is life" (*LW*, III, 51). God requires no efficient cause to set him into activity, nor does he act for the sake of any end outside of himself. He is the cause and principle of all things, but he requires no cause or principle for himself. Hence Eckhart cites with approval proposition VII of the *Liber XXIV Philosophorum*: "God is the principle without principle, the process without variation, the end without end" (*LW*, III, 16n1). The life of the self-thinking thought is self-sufficient, self-complete. The life of God, Eckhart says, is "without why." While it is the explanation (or "why") of all other things, it itself stands in need of no explanation of its own being (*LW*, III, 41). Thus God created the world, not out of any lack in himself that He hoped to fill up (a "why"), but out of the welling up within himself (*ebullitio*) of his own life that spills over into creatures. In an unusually rhapsodic passage for the Latin writings, Eckhart says: "Life means a certain overflow by which a thing, welling up within itself, first pours itself fully within itself, each part of itself in every other, before it pours itself out and wells over into something external" (*LW*, II, 22).[15] While it would be an exaggeration to see in Eckhart the first process theory of God, it is true that he emphasized the living and active quality of the divine nature.[16] He saw God as the process of life giving birth to life, a process which flows into the Trinity itself and then flows over into creatures.

The Ground of the Soul

The transition to Eckhart's mystical doctrine may be made by returning to the pivotal text, cited above, in which Eckhart spoke of the divine Reason. It continues: "Now let us take it [knowledge] as it is in the soul, which possesses a trickle of Reason, a little spark, a twig" (*Q*, 197). Eckhart sets up a correlation between God and the soul. As God possesses a hidden ground that is Reason itself, so the soul possesses its own hidden ground, which is but a "little spark" (*Fünklein*), a drop, a small share, of the divine Reason.[17] In virtue of this divine spark, the soul alone among all creatures is able to penetrate to the hidden ground of the divine being. Because of its small share in the divine intellectuality, the soul is akin to God and able to unite with God: "Intellect properly speaking belongs to God and 'God is one.' To the extent, therefore, that each thing possesses intellect or intellectual powers, to that extent it is one with God" (*LW*, IV, 269–70; e.t., 212). Because of their mutual intellectuality, there is an intimate and profound correspondence between the soul and God. As God's Reason is the hidden sanctuary of his Being, so the soul's spark of Reason is its inner temple (*Q*, 153). Here God and the soul unite: "Here God's ground is my ground, and my ground is God's ground" (*Q*, 180).

When Eckhart speaks of the "little spark" of Reason, it is important to realize that he is not referring to the faculty of discursive reasoning, the power that uses concepts and representations. In the vernacular sermon "*Impletum est*" he distinguishes three kinds of knowledge: "The one is sensible: the eye sees things, even at a distance, which are outside of itself. The second is rational and much higher. But with the third is meant a noble power of the soul, which is so high and noble that it grasps God in His own naked being. This power has nothing at all in common with anything else" (*Q*, 210).

The first two powers are directed outward to creatures, the first in terms of their sensible properties, the second in terms of their essential or intelligible properties. The second power, which Eckhart here calls "rational," proceeds by means of concepts and representations (*Vorstellungen* [*Q*, 138]; *Begriffe* [*Q*, 318]; in Latin, *species*), which in the classical Aristotelian theory are signs of external things and are themselves symbolized by words. But of the third power, "the ground of the soul," he says that it "has nothing in common with anything."[18] It is not concerned with creatures, nor is it in any way like creatures; it is related solely to God, and to his "naked Being" (the Godhead).

By means of its "faculties"—sensation, will, and (discursive) reason—the soul is directed outward to creatures. By the use of these faculties it performs "outer works," not only of laboring and eating, say, but also of praying and fasting (*Q*, 76). The ground of the soul, the very "being" (*Wesen*)[19] of the soul, on the other hand, is prior to the emergence of the faculties and is the "root" (*Wurzel* [*Q*, 318]) of all outer works. Hence Eckhart says that one should be holy in one's being, not merely in one's work; if a man "is" holy, his "works" will be holy. We are not sanctified by our works; our works are sanctified by us. There is no "activity," no commerce with creatures, in the ground of the soul because the ground of the soul is prior to the faculties by which one "acts." It was not in Aquinas but in the German Dominican tradition—in Albert the Great (d. 1280) and Dietrich of Vrieberg (d. 1310)—that Eckhart found the idea that the essence of the soul was a "hidden recess of the mind" (*abditum mentis*).[20] In this innermost ground, the soul is still and silent (Q, 237–38) and ready for a union with God that is denied to the "faculties," inasmuch as they are immersed in the daily business of life.

Stripped of all relationship to creatures, Eckhart invests the ground of the soul with all of those properties which be otherwise reserved for God. Like God, it is timeless, living in an eternal now, never "growing old" (Q, 162). Similarly, it is "one and simple" (Q, 164) because in it there is no distinction of faculties, no multiplicity of activities. Moreover, he says: "It is neither this nor that; despite this, it is something which is raised up above this and that like the heavens above the earth. Consequently, I name it now in a more noble way than I have ever named it. . . . It is free of all names and emptied of all forms, wholly simple and free as God in Himself is simple and free" (Q, 163). It has so little to do with anything created that it has no identifiable creaturely property. Like the Godhead itself, it is nameless.

There is thus a special correspondence, an exclusive reciprocity, between God and the soul. Only the ground of the soul is pure enough and simple enough to receive God, and only God is pure and simple enough to enter the ground of the soul (Q, 164, 252). "God is nearer to the soul," he says with St. Augustine, "than it is to itself." And again: "Where God is, there is the soul; where the soul is, there is God" (Q, 207). The soul is the place of God, as God is the place of the soul (Q, 213). The ground of the soul is a "place" among creatures into which God may come, a place for God's advent into the world.

The Birth of the Son

The advent of God into the soul, the event that takes place in the soul, is described by Eckhart as the "birth of the Son." The place that the soul makes for God, he says, is God's "birthplace" (Q, 415). Eckhart takes his point of departure for this doctrine from St. John, and from this point on, whatever affinities Eckhart may have to Eastern mysticism,[21] his position is distinctively Christian. He frequently cites the First Letter of St. John: "Think of the love that the Father has lavished on us, by letting us be called God's children; and that is what we are" (I John 3: 1).[22] For Eckhart John is to be taken at his word, and John says that we are not only "called" God's children, but "that is what we are." This can only mean one thing: "As little as a man can be wise without wisdom," he says, "so little can he be a son without the filial being of the Son of God" (Q, 317). And even more strongly:

> The Father bears His Son in eternity like to Himself. "The Word was in God and the Word was God." He was the same as God and of the same nature. Yet beyond this I say: He has begotten Him in my soul. . . . The Father bears His Son in the soul in the same way that He bears Him in eternity, not in any other way. He must do it, whether he wishes to or not. The Father bears His Son incessantly, and I say still more: He bears me as His Son, and as the same Son. (Q, 185)

The process by which the Father bears his Son in eternity is extended to the ground of the soul so that the Father bears his Son in the soul. Moreover, he bears the soul itself as that very Son. The Son is born in the place that the soul makes for him and the soul is assimilated to that Son. The generation of the Son in eternity and the Incarnation of that Son as man is a universal event for Eckhart that is extended to the soul itself: "It would mean little to me that the 'Word was made flesh' for man in Christ, granting that the latter is distinct from me, unless He also [was made flesh] in me personally, so that I too would become the Son of God" (*LW*, III, 101–102; cf. *Q*, 415).[23]

Although Eckhart's formulations are in the strongest possible language, his position is essentially orthodox (Théry 199; 242–44; 266–68). For not only is there a doctrine of mystical union expressed in terms of divine sonship in the Johannine gospel,[24] but the notion that the Son is born in the soul has a long history in orthodox Christian theology before Eckhart.[25] In keeping with this tradition, Eckhart distinguishes between the Son by nature and the Son "by grace" (*Q*, 119–20; 208). The Son by nature is the eternal Word himself; the Son by grace is the ground of the soul which has been "formed over" (*überbildet* [*Q*, 103]) in the image of the Son by reason of the residence which the Son takes up in the soul. Grace is the "co-dwelling" of the soul and God together (*Q*, 398).

Eckhart elaborates the doctrine of the birth of the Son in two important ways: first, in terms of an "image," and second, in terms of a "word." A father is one who generates his "image" (*Bild*) or likeness. For an image, there are two requisites (*Q*, 224–26). First, there must be a likeness between the original model and the image. But while this is a necessary condition, it is not a sufficient one: "There can be no image without likeness, but there can indeed be a likeness without an image. Two eggs are equally white, yet one is not the image of the other" (*Q*, 224). The second requirement is stronger, namely, that the image be sustained in its very being as an image by the model: "An image takes its being immediately and solely from that of which it is an image" (*Q*, 226). The image of a face in the mirror, for example, is not only like the face of which it is the image, but it also derives its being from the face, in the sense that the image persists only so long as the face is present; if the face were removed, the image would vanish. Now the relation of a son to his father fulfills both these requirements. Yet even here a distinction is to be made. A human father brings about the being of his likeness, his son, but because of the disunity between a human father and son—they are distinct and separate substances—the human son may continue to live after the father has died, thus impairing the perfection of the second requirement. The divine Father on the other hand is essentially a process of giving birth, the divine Son essentially a process of being born. The being of each is their relationship to one another. And since it is the same eternal birth process that is extended to the ground of the soul, the soul too is made in the authentic and true image of the Father. The soul is formed in the image of the Father (*überildet*) by the Father himself.

For the Father to bear his Son is also, according to Eckhart, for him to speak the eternal Word. According to medieval theology, the essence of the Second Person is to be the "thought" in which the Father knows himself. The "Son" is the "concept" or that which is "conceived" by the Father. The Second Person is thus the "Word" in the sense of a "*verbum cordis*," a silent inner word (or "concept") of which the vocal word (*verbum vocis*) is the outer sign.[26] If the Father bears his Son in the soul precisely as he does in eternity, then he also "speaks" his Word in the soul just as in eternity (*Q*, 236–38; 287). The Word has nothing to do with a spoken sound. Indeed it is even opposed to such. The Word that God speaks in the soul is "hidden" and easily ignored. To hear what is spoken in silence, one must be silent oneself: "All voices and sounds must be put away and a pure stillness must be there, a still silence" (*Q*, 237). And: "In stillness and peace . . . there God speaks in the soul and expresses Himself fully in the soul" (*Q*, 238). The truest word, the most perfect language, is silent. In the best tradition of negative theology, Eckhart denies the ability of human language to express the divine nature: "What one says about God is not true; but what one does not express is true" (*Q*, 242–43). But not only "voices and sounds" disrupt the silence that Eckhart has in mind, but all concepts, images and representations: "The best and most noble thing of all which one can attain in this life is to remain silent and let God work and speak. Where all the powers have removed all their works and images, there is this Word spoken" (*Q*, 419–20). Nothing created is able to express the divine being. Not only spoken or written words, but even inner concepts are incapable of comprehending the simplicity and plenitude of God (*Q*, 242–43). The only "concept" that adequately expresses the likeness of the Father is the uncreated "Word" itself, which the Father speaks. All human language, interior and exterior, must be silenced in order to let the Father speak.

Detachment

While the birth of the Son in the soul is the work of God, it cannot be accomplished without the soul's assistance. So necessary is the soul's participation in this process, so intimately does it share in the Father's work, that Eckhart does not hesitate to say that the soul "co-bears" (*mitgebiert* [*Q*, 161]) the Son, that it "collaborates" (*mitwirkt* [*Q*, 94–95]) with God. There is only one work, which the Father initiates and with which the soul cooperates.

The soul cooperates with God's action by the practice of "detachment" (*Abgeschiedenheit*). Eckhart uses the word *Abgeschieden* to translate the Latin *separatus* (*DW*, V, 438–39n1). The *substantiae separatae* (*die abgeschiedene Geiste*) are the substances that are "separate" from matter and its conditions (angelic natures). Eckhart also uses *Abgeschieden* as a translation of *abstractus*, that which is "removed from" or "drawn away from" matter and its conditions. The "separate substances" are pure of matter and so purely intellectual beings. For insofar as a substance is removed from (*separatus, abstractus*) material qualities, it is able to acquire knowledge of these qualities. But God is removed not only from matter but from every form of particularity, and so God comprehends all being. God is not being, formally speaking, but intellect. God is the absolutely abstract or separate substance.

Because this is so with God, Eckhart puts the same demand on the soul which would unite with God: "This immutable detachment brings man into the greatest likeness with God. For God is God because of His immutable detachment, and from detachment He has His purity and simplicity and unchangeability. Consequently, if a man should become like to God, insofar as a creature can have likeness with God, then this must come about through detachment. . . . And you should know this: to be empty of all creatures is to be full of God; and to be full of all creatures is to be empty of God" (*DW*, V, 541–42). The soul must detach itself from all creatures, and so purify and simplify its being, just as God is pure and simple. But what does it mean fur the soul to become "detached"? Eckhart means neither that one should become physically separated from things by entering a monastery (*Q*, 59), nor that one should long for death and "separation from the body," as the Phaedo counsels. Detachment is a matter of the "heart" (*DW*, V, 539). The detached heart considers creatures to be "nothing" (of themselves). It does not seek created goods, but desires only God himself. Detachment means "to be receptive of nothing other than God" (*DW*, V, 540), to desire nothing other than God, to serve no one but God. The detached heart has "nothing to do with anything," with "this or that," that is, with any creature. Having thus purified its heart of any affection for created things, the soul takes on the "separateness," the "nothing-ness," of God himself and so becomes a receptacle fit for God alone: "Only He [God] is so simple and subtle that He can be contained by the detached heart. Hence detachment is receptive of nothing other than God" (*DW*, V, 540). The unity of Eckhart's metaphysical and mystical thought of which the youthful Heidegger spoke (*DS*, 241) is nowhere more apparent. The *substantia separata* of the Scholastic metaphysician becomes the "detached heart" (*abgeschiedene Herz*) of the German mystic. The "living" or "existential" correlate of the metaphysics of *intelligere* is the mystical life of detachment.

Eckhart also discusses the way in which the soul readies itself for the birth of the Son in terms of what he calls *Gelassenheit*, a notion that we take to be identical with "detachment." The root of the word, *lassen*, means to let go, to relinquish, to abandon. The soul in *Gelassenheit* abandons or relinquishes whatever would impede God's advent into the soul. But *lassen* also means to "permit" or "let." Thus the soul that has abandoned the obstacles to the birth of the Son simultaneously lets or permits God to bear his Son in the ground of the soul. The first moment is negative (to be empty of creatures); the second is positive—(to be full of God).

The principle of perversity in the soul and the greatest obstacle to its union with God is "self-love" (*Eigenliebe*) or "self-will" (*Eigenwille*): "People say: Ah, Lord, I would very much prefer that I stood as well with God and that I had as much devotion and peace in God as other people have. And I would also prefer that things would go along for me in the same way [as with others] or that I too might be as poor" (Q, 55). Eckhart's diagnosis of such complaints is this: "In truth, it is your 'I' which is protruding. It is self-will and nothing else" (Q, 55); and his remedy: "Consequently, begin first with yourself and abandon yourself (*lass dich*)!" (Q, 55). It is not so much what a man does that matters, but what he is. He should do nothing because it is his own will, even if as an outer work it is praiseworthy (giving alms, say), but only because it is God's will, even if it is less praiseworthy (earning money, for example).[27] If a man abandons everything but not himself, then he has abandoned nothing. But if he abandons himself, then he has abandoned all (Q, 36, 185). The "resigned" (*gelassen*)[28] soul does not pray that God's will conform to its own—that it be given something it desires—for that is still self-will. Nor does the resigned soul even will that it itself should conform to the will of God. Rather it has no will at all of its own; it is entirely divested of willing (Q, 304).

Such a soul is completely at God's disposal; it is empty of creatures in order to be full of God: "Where the creature ends, there God begins to be. Now God desires nothing more of you than that you go out of yourself according to your creaturely mode of being and let God be God in you" (Q, 180). The fully resigned soul is a pure and empty vessel into which God can be received. Like a good vessel, it is closed on the bottom to creatures and open on the top to God (Q, 228). Like the power of seeing in Aristotle's *De anima*, which is pure of all color, the soul is pure of everything created, and so it can receive God purely, precisely as he is in his "unconcealed" (*unverhüllt*: Q, 147) Being, and not inasmuch as he is the "object" of human desire.

If the soul is fully divested of its own will and given over to God's, then Eckhart says it lives "without why." We have seen previously that Eckhart uses this same expression—"without why"—to describe God's being. A living thing is that which moves from within. This is preeminently true of God, who is the beginning of all things without himself having a beginning (*principium sine principio*). God lives without why. The soul too in *Gelassenheit* takes on this same quality of life without why. Some men love God, Eckhart says rather pointedly, the way they love a cow—for its milk (Q, 227). But the soul in *Gelassenheit* is disinterested in itself. If a man loves God for the good that God can give him, then he does not love God but himself. "Love has no why" (Q, 299). If a soul works for the sake of its own self-aggrandizement, of procuring external goods, then its works are not living but dead (Q, 268), for they are moved from without (Théry, 236–37). The soul must love God for no other reason (why) than God himself. Then it will be like life itself: "If one asks life for a thousand years, 'why do you live?' if it were able to answer it would say nothing other than 'I live in order to live'" (Q, 180). God—like life—needs nothing external to himself in order to be justified. The soul that lives with such perfect abandonment, such uncalculating love, enjoys a freedom and spontaneity like to God's own. It works for the sake of working. One must drive the money changers from the temple of the soul, Eckhart says (Q, 154); the money changers are those who love God only for profit. They are spiritual mercenaries who serve God for wages. They have not learned that they are now sons, not servants (John 15: 14; Q, 186), God's friends, not his hirelings (Q, 154–55), free men, not slaves.

Eckhart often says that God "needs" the truly detached soul in order to bear his Son there: "It is God's nature that He give, and His being depends on the fact that He give to us, if we are submissive to Him. If we are not and we receive nothing, then we do Him violence and kill Him" (Q, 172). God appears to be under the same necessity of nature to bear his Son in the soul as he is in eternity: "The Father bears His Son in the eternal knowledge, and He bears Him as fully in the soul as He does in His own nature. And He bears Him in the soul as His own, and His being depends on the fact that He bear His Son in the soul, whether He wishes to or not" (Q, 172). The soul apparently provides a necessary complement, an indispensable medium, in which the divine life is completed and fulfilled.

But this is not really Eckhart's view. It is quite clear that the divine life is a self-contained and self-sufficient process. Even the process by which God creates is a "welling over" and an overflow (*antequam effundat et ebulliat extra* [*LW*, II, 172]), not an attempt to fill up a lack. Moreover the birth of God is the result of grace (*gratia*), which is a free giving, and not of the necessity of nature. Finally, even in the vernacular sermons, where Eckhart states his position in the most extreme manner, he eventually qualifies his assertions. Hence the passage in which he spoke of "killing God" continues: "If we are not able to do this in Him Himself, still we may do it in ourselves and as far as it concerns us" (Q, 172). The death of God in question turns out to be a death in and for the soul, not in God's own being. We are able to stop the flow of God's life into our souls. No Dominican master at Paris, and certainly not the author of the prologues, would hold that anything of the perfection of *esse* could ever be lacking to God.

But what the German preacher did mean by this bold language is to be found in his defense (Théry, 241–42) of such texts as we have cited (Q, 172, 185). In the first place, he says, this is an "emphatic expression, commending God's goodness and love." This is the assertion of a preacher who means to inspire the soul to the "highest virtue" of detachment. Because Eckhart demanded a perfect abandonment—without why—to God, he found it necessary to assure his listeners of the goodness of God and of the fact that it belongs to the necessity of the divine nature to return love with love. Second, he wished to insist that it is the same Son which the Father bears in eternity and which the detached soul receives by grace. It is the same necessary process of filiation that occurs in eternity which is extended—by grace—to the soul that has prepared itself for it. The soul comes to be by grace the self-same thing that God is by the necessity of his nature.

Whatever Eckhart's own intentions may have been, his expressions have fathered a long tradition of the divine "need" of man in the German tradition. Among the mystics, God's need of man is found in Jacob Boehme and in the mystical poet "Angelus Silesius" (Johann Scheffler: 1631–1677), in whose *The Cherubinic Wanderer* it receives its classic expression:

> *God Does Not Live Without Me*
> I know that God cannot live an instant
> without me;
> Were I to become nothing, He must give
> up the ghost.
> One Sustains the Other
> God is as much set in me as I am in Him;
> I assist His essence and He preserves
> mine.[29]

In the philosophical tradition, God's need of man certainly recalls the nineteenth-century Idealists. Where Eckhart says that the "highest striving of God" (*Gottes höchstes Streben* [Q, 208]) is to bear the Son in the soul, Fichte's absolute Ego will also be a process of striving (*Streben*), not for the birth of the Son in man, but for the achievement of moral order in and through him.[30] And perhaps the most important representative of all is Hegel himself, for whom the Absolute is estranged from itself until it attains self-knowledge in and through speculative thought.[31]

NOTES

1. We refer to the works of Heidegger with the following abbreviations: *DS*: *Die Kategorien und*

Bedeutungslehre des Duns Scotus (Tübingen: J. C. B. Mohr, 1916); *EM*: *Einführung in die Metaphysik*, 2nd ed. (Tübingen: Max Niemeyer, 1958); *FND*: *Die Frage nach dem Ding* (Tübingen: Max Niemeyer, 1962); *FW*: *Der Feldweg*, 3rd ed. (Frankfurt: V. Klostermann, 1962); *G*: *Gelassenheit*, 2nd ed. (Pfullingen: G. Neske, 1960); *HB*: *"Brief über den 'Humanismus,'"* in *Platons Lehre von der Wahrheit Mit einen Brief über den "Humanismus,"* 2nd ed. (Bern: A. Francke, 1954); *HW*: *Holzwege*, 4th ed. (Frankfurt: V. Klostermann, 1963); *ID*: *ldentität und Differenz*, 3rd ed. (Pfullingen: G. Neske, 1957); *K*: *Die Technik und die Kehre* (Pfullingen: G. Neske, 1962); *KPM*: *Kant und das Problem der Metaphysik*, 3rd ed.(Frankfurt: V. Klostermann, 1956); *N* I, *N* II: *Nietzsche*, 2 vols. (Pfullingen: G. Neske, 1962); *PT*: *Phänomenologie und Theologia* (Frankfurt: V. Klostermann, 1970); *SD*: *Zur Sache des Denkens* (Tübingen: Max Niemeyer, 1969); *SG*: *Der Satz vom Grund*, 3rd ed. (Pfullingen: G. Neske, 1965); *SZ*: *Sein und Zeit*, 10th ed. (Tübingen: Max Niemeyer, 1963); *US*: *Unterwegs zur Sprache*, 3rd ed. (Pfullingen: G. Neske, 1965); *VA*: *Vorträge und Aufsätze*, 2nd ed. (Pfullingen: G. Neske, 1959); *WD*: *Was Heisst Denken?*, 2nd ed. (Tübingen: Max Niemeyer, 1961); *WG*: *Vom Wesen des Grundes*, 5th ed. (Frankfurt: V. Klostermann, 1965); *WM*: *Was ist M etaphysik?*, 9th ed. (Frankfurt: V. Klostermann, 1965); *WW*: *Vom Wesen der Wahrheit*, 4th ed. (Frankfurt: V. Klostermann, 1961). All translations are our own. When we consult the following translations, we refer to them by "e.t." after citing the original text: *G*: *Discourse on Thinking*, trans. John Anderson and E. Hans Freund (New York: Harper, 1966); *WD*: *What Is Called Thinking?*, trans. F. D. Wieck and J. Glenn Gray (New York: Harper, 1968).

2. Martin Grabmann would later show the author to be one Thomas of Erfurt, not Duns Scotus.

3. Hans Siegfried, "Martin Heidegger: A Recollection," *Man and World* 3, no. 1 (February 1970): 4.

4. Cf. Karsten Harries, "Martin Heidegger: The Search for Meaning," in *Existential Philosophers: Kierkegaard to Merleau-Ponty*, ed. G. A. Schrader (New York: McGraw Hill, 1967), 162–68, and Richard Schmitt, *Martin Heidegger on Being Human* (New York: Random House, 1969), 55–102.

5. We leave *Dasein* untranslated and always refer to it in the neuter.

6. Meister Eckhart of Hochheim (1260–1327/29) was the most celebrated preacher of his day and the foremost representative of fourteenth-century German mysticism. A bull in 1329 condemned twenty-eight propositions extracted from his writings. Consequently the Latin writings were largely ignored until H. S. Denifle revived interest in them in 1885. It was through his German treatises and sermons that Eckhart exerted his influence on the German tradition. Our references to Eckhart's works will be as follows: *LW*: *M eister Eckhart: Die deutschen und lateinischen Werke*, edited on behalf of the German Research Association, *Die Lateinische Werke*, ed. Ernst Benz (Stuttgart: Kohlhammer, 1936–); *OW*: *Die Deutsche Werke*, ed. Josef Quint (Stuttgart: Kohlhammer, 1936–); *Q*: *Meister Eckhart: Deutsche Predigte und Traktate*, ed. and trans. Josef Quint (Munich: Carl Hanser, 1963); Théry: Gabriel Théry, "Édition critique des pieces relatives au proces d'Eckhart," *Archives d'histoire doctrinale et littéraire du moyen age* 1 (1926): 129–268. There is no better antidote to the extravagant misinterpretation to which Eckhart is exposed than this document, which is the record of his defense against the charge of heresy. We have consulted the following in preparing our own translations: *Meister Eckhart: Selected Treatises and Sermons*, ed. and trans. James Clark and John Skinner (London: Faber and Faber, 1958).

7. Martin Heidegger, "Der Zeitbegriff in der Gescbichtswisscnschaft," *Zeitschrift für Philosophie und philosophische Kritik* 161 (1916): 173.

8. Kate Oltmanns, *Meister Eckhart*, 2nd ed. (Frankfurt: V. Klostermann, 1957); cf. especially p. 10.

9. Thomas Aquinas, *Questiones Disputatae de veritate*, Q. I, a. 1, c.

10. In a work that appeared after our study was completed, Reiner Schürmann-Maztre (*Eckhart ou la joie errante: Sermons allemands traduits et commentés* [Paris: Éditions Planète, 1972]) offers an excellent interpretation of Eckhart that relies heavily on Heidegger's views. As he notes (339n91) this has already been attempted by Oltmanns but with questionable results. His own efforts are more successful, I think, because he depends upon the later Heidegger and not, as did Oltmanns, upon *Sein und Zeit*. Schürmann's thesis is that the confusion that has surrounded Eckhart for six centuries is due to interpreting his thought as a "metaphysics" concerned with substances considered statically. In fact, Eckhart is concerned not with substance but event (66n46), and with the "path" of the soul en route to God ("peregrinal ontology"), which is the path of detachment (170).

A concluding section (380) confronts Heidegger and Meister Eckhart on *Gelassenheit* (and in particular, *G*, 23–28). See also Schürmann, *Eckhart ou la joie errante*, 11, 98, 164, 201n94, 210n112, 219, 283–84n28. There are at least two basic differences between Schürmann's work and ours: (1) His work is not a comparison of Heidegger and Eckhart, but an interpretation of Eckhart that has recourse to the thought of Heidegger; our concern is with an assessment of Heidegger on the basis of a comparison with Eckhart. (2) While Schürmann does discuss the differences between Eckhart and Heidegger (358–61, 365–67), he does not seem to hold that their consequences are as grave as we will point out below. Heidegger's "way" (*Denkweg*) is hardly one of joy (*la joie errante*), though this aptly describes Eckhart's experience (14, 367, last paragraph). Eckhart's importance for Heidegger is also briefly noted by Laszlo Versenyi, *Heidegger, Being and Truth* (New Haven: Yale University Press, 1965), 152, and Reuben Guilead, *Être et liberté: Une étude sur le dernier Heidegger* (Louvain: Éditions Nauwelaerts, 1965), 172–73.

11. *The Later Heidegger and Theology*, eds. James M. Robinson and John B. Cobb Jr. (New York: Harper & Row, 1963), 42–43.

12. Vladimir Lossky, *Theologie negative et connaissence de Dieu chez Maître Eckhart* (Paris: J. Vrin, 1960), 335–36.

13. If this phrase resembles anything in the Idealists, it is the "one" of Schelling's *Identitätsphilosophie*, although Eckhart's "one" does not stand in need of mediation or diversification because it is already the fullness of being (*plenitudo esse*).

14. The "abyss" *(Abgrund)* of the Godhead is another of those seminal ideas of Eckhart. It reappears again most notably in Jacob Boehme's *Un-grund* and so in Schelling (see n. 16). Some have—with good reason—placed Heidegger's *Nichts* in this tradition. Cf. William Kluback and Jean Wilde, preface of Martin Heidegger, *The Question of Being* (London: Vision, 1956), 9, and E. B. Koenker, "Potentiality in God: Jacob Boehme," *Philosophy Today* 15 (Spring, 1971): 44.

15. Compare this passage with the depiction of "life" in Hegel, *The Phenomenology of Mind*, trans. J. Baillie (London: Allen & Unwin, 1966), 220–24.

16. Cf. John Loeschen, "The God Who Becomes: Eckhart on the Divine Relativity," *The Thomist* 25 (July 1971), 405–22.

17. Heidegger refers to this "little spark of the soul" (*Seelenfünklein*) in *WD*, 96. He regards it as an unsuccessful attempt to transcend the notion of man as the "rational animal." Only the notion of *Dasein* and of its "memory" (*Gedächtnis*) seizes man in his relationship to Being. And of course, Eckhart's notion cannot "succeed" in Heidegger's terms, for Eckhart is not interested in conceiving of the soul as a relationship to Being, but as a relationship to God. In Eckhart's terms, Heidegger does not succeed in gaining a view of man in his essential relationship to God. Once again, the similarity between Eckhart and Heidegger is structural.

18. This indicates how free of any vestige of an anthropological conception Eckhart wished to keep the Fünklein. Heidegger's criticism of Eckhart in *WD*, 95 does not at all take this into account.

19. Eckhart uses *Wesen* as a translation of *esse* and hence in its original sense as "Being," the verbal sense that Heidegger of course wishes to revive. Cf. Anmerkungen, Q, S37–S38.

20. Martin Grabmann, *Der Einfluss Alberts der Grossen auf das mittelalterliche Geistesleben: Das deutsche Element in der mittelalterlichen Scholastik und Mystik* (München, 1926–1936), 2:324–72. Cf. Éttienne Gilson, *A History of Christian Philosophy in the Middle Ages* (New York: Random House, 1955), 431–36. The idea is ultimately of Augustinian origin.

21. D. T. Suzuki, *Mysticism: Christian and Buddhist* (New York: Macmillan, 1969); Rudolf Otto, *Mysticism East and West,* trans. B. Bracey and R. Payne (New York: Macmillan, 1962); Shizuteru Ueda, "Maître Eckhart et la buddismc zen," *La vie spirituelle* 53 (January 1971): 34–35, 40–41.

22. All scriptural citations are from *The Jerusalem Bible* (Garden City, NY: Doubleday, 1966).

23. The Idealists too insisted that the Incarnation was not restricted to the empirical individual Jesus of Nazareth.

24. *The Jerusalem Bible*, "The New Testament," 411, n. a.

25. Hugo Rabner, "Die Gottesgeburt," *Zeitschrift für Katholische Theologie* 59 (1933): 333–418. Rahner concludes: "The idea flowed to him from a thousand sources; it is age-old; it is one of the essential pieces of Christian mysticism of all centuries" (411).

26. Thomas Aquinas, *Summa Theologica*, Ia, Q. 27, a. l, c.

27. Eckhart's mystical doctrine seems remarkably at times to resemble Kant's "moral formalism." For both thinkers no merely "material" principle should ever determine the will; for both, material principles are principles of "self-love."

What Kant calls "heteronomous" activity, Eckhart calls "dead works."

28. Because *Gelassenheit* means surrendering one's own will and accepting God's, we have translated it sometimes as "resignation" and sometimes as "abandonment." In ordinary German it means "composure." Cf. n. 36

29. Angelus Silesius, *Cherubinischer Wandersmann*, introduced and reviewed by Will-Erich Peuckert (Bremen: Carl Schünemann, 1956), I, No. 8; No. 100.

30. Cf. Ernst von Bracken, *Meister Eckhart und Fichte* (Würzburg: Konrad Triltsch Verlag , 1943).

31. That is in part why Hegel cites the following text from Eckhart in his *Lectures on the Philosophy of Religion*: "Das Auge, mit dem mich Gott sieht, ist das Auge, mit dem ich ihn sehe, mein Auge und sein Auge ist eins. In der Gerechtigkeit werde ich in Gott gewogen und er in mir. Wenn Gott nicht wäre, wäre ich nicht, wenn ich nicht wäre, so wäre er nicht. Dies ist jedoch nicht Noth zu wissen, denn es sind Dinge, die leicht misverstanden werden und die nur im Begriff erfasst werden können" *(Sämtliche Werke: Vorlesungen über die Philosophie der Religion*, vol. 1 [Stuttgart: Frommanns, 1959], 228). For Hegel, Eckhart seems to say that the Absolute came to know itself in the same act in which man rose to a knowledge of the Absolute. Whereas in fact Eckhart is alluding to the Aristotelian doctrine that the knower-in-act and the knowable-in-act are one, and to *De trinitate*, Bk. IX, c. 12, in which Augustine says that the knower and the known, when thus united, conceive a common offspring—for Eckhart, the Word which is born in the soul (Théry, 224–25, 238). Moreover, Hegel's text is corrupt. The first sentence should read: "Das Auge, in dem ich Gott sehe, das ist dasselbe Auge, darin mich Gott sieht; mein Auge und Gottes Auge, das ist *ein* Auge und *ein* Sehen und *ein* Erkennen und *ein* Lieben" (Q, 216). The second sentence I find nowhere in Quint, although it is doctrinally akin to Q, 267–69. The third and fourth sentences, which would be easily misinterpreted if one were not familiar with the distinction between *Gott* and *Gottheit*, are found in another sermon altogether and should read: "Wäre aber ich nicht, so ware auch 'Gott' nicht: dass 'Gott' ist, dafiir bin ich die Ursache; wäre ich nicht, so wäre Gott nicht 'Gott.' Dies zu wissen ist nicht not" (Q, 308). *Gott* is a name assigned to the divine being in virtue of its relationship to creatures. Hence if I were not—that is, if I were not created—God would not be called "God," that is, the cause of being. Eckhart also refers to the ideal preexistence of the self as an Idea in the Divine Mind. The last half of the fourth sentence, which represents Hegel's but not Eckhart's views, I find nowhere in Quint.

5

Meister Eckhart and the Later Heidegger: The Mystical Element in Heidegger's Thought, Part Two

HEIDEGGER AND ECKHART

Space does not permit us to pursue Eckhart's thought in any greater detail. We must instead turn to Martin Heidegger and develop the striking parallel of the latter's thought to that of the mystic of Hochheim.

Dasein and the Ground of the Soul

Both Eckhart and Heidegger reject any merely "anthropological" account of the essence of man. Neither is content to say that man is one being among others, differentiated by his "rational faculty." Man must be understood instead in relationship to something which transcends beings altogether. The essential "greatness" of man is nothing human or anthropological, but rests in his being the privileged "place" (*Stätte* [*Q*, 213]; *Ortschaft* [*HB*, 77])[1] in which the "transcendent" comes to pass.[2] Hence neither Eckhart nor Heidegger speak of "man," but of the "ground of the soul" or the *Dasein* in man. And as the ground of the soul is the sanctuary or temple of God, so for Heidegger *Dasein* is the place which is needed by and used for the Truth of Being. Heidegger as much as draws this analogy of his thought to Eckhart for us himself. Referring to a text from the *Talks of Instruction* (*Q*, 57) in which Eckhart distinguishes those who are great in their "being" from those whose "outer works" alone are great, Heidegger comments: "Let us consider that the great being [*Wesen*] of man is that it belongs to the essence [*Wesen*] of Being and is used by the latter to preserve [*wahren*] the essence of Being in its Truth [*Wahrheit*]" (*K*, 39).

Let us take a closer look at this comparison. *Dasein* is not a term for anything psychological; it is not a "faculty" of the "mind," nor is it "consciousness." It is the process by which a "world," and the things that are in the world, become manifest. *Dasein* is the ecstatic relationship of openness to Being in which and through which Being reveals itself. *Dasein* comes to pass "in" man, but it is not equitable with man. For man is a being, and *Dasein* is the process by which beings come to be manifest.

But Eckhart makes a comparable claim about the ground of the soul. For the highest power of the soul is so noble, he says, as to be nameless. "This power has nothing in common with anything else" (*Q*, 210). It is neither "this nor that." It is not a faculty of the soul, but prior to all faculties. It is not identifiable with anything at all, anthropological or otherwise. It is not a being, just the way *Dasein* is not an existent entity (*ein Seiendes*), but a place within entities wherein God reveals himself in his "naked Being." The ground of the soul is not man's "specific difference." That is why we have underlined the importance of Heidegger's characterization of the enlivening attitude of medieval mysticism as "the transcendent and primordial relationship of the soul to God" (*DS*, 1). For Heidegger has taken over this same *structure* in his own mature philosophical writings: the structure of a relationship to the transcendent that comes about in man, but is not identifiable with anything "human."

By its "faculties," Eckhart held, the soul performed outer works and concerned itself with created things, thus running the risk of entirely forgetting the "hidden ground" that is deeper than all faculties. Heidegger too warns of the danger of becoming so preoccupied with the business of everydayness as to forget the question of the meaning of Being. In the later Heidegger, "fallen" *Dasein* is so devoted to the challenge of mastering and manipulating things that it is unmindful of the deeper Truth of Being that technology conceals. Both Eckhart and Heidegger describe a comparable "fallenness" into everyday existence, and both interpret it as a forgetfulness of a silent, hidden ground in which the everyday is transcended.

Moreover, neither Eckhart nor Heidegger claim that there is anything contemptible about the "outer" man, but only that it is something "derivative," resting on deeper grounds. For Eckhart, the ground of the soul is not the opposite of its faculties, but the root out of which they flow. Eckhart does not repudiate the Aristotelian definition of man as the rational animal; he simply denies that the entire essence of man is thereby circumscribed. By the same token Heidegger bolds that it is in virtue of its relationship to Being that all of *Dasein*'s relationships with beings are made possible (*WG*, 13; *WW*, 20). The way in which *Dasein* comprehends Being filters down into the way in which beings are understood (*SZ*, § 3). Like Eckhart, Heidegger is prepared to admit that the definition of man as the "rational animal" is not "false" (*HB*, 74–75) as far as representational thinking is concerned. His complaint is only that there is a realm beyond representational thinking, which alone can provide the most adequate interpretation of the Being of man (*HB*, 67–68).

Finally, *Dasein* and the ground of the soul are each related to the transcendent in terms of "identity." Both God and the soul, Being and *Dasein*, "belong together" and find in each other their "proper element." Eckhart repeatedly says that the soul and God are "one" in the sense that each alone is simple and pure enough as to be able to unite with the other. There is in Heidegger a comparable insistence on the togetherness of Being and *Dasein*. Being and *Dasein* are not two beings that are related to one another, but two poles of a pure relationship. All one may really speak of is the process by which Truth comes to pass: Being emerging out of concealment into unconcealment in its "there" (*HB*, 69) and *Dasein* letting Being be in its Truth. This is, according to Heidegger, the hidden truth of the *Satz der Identität*, of the "leap" (*Satz*) out of representational thinking into the "belonging together" (*Identität*) of Being and man (*ID*, 20–25). This reciprocity of Being and *Dasein* is clearly reminiscent of the intimate relationship of the soul and God in Meister Eckhart.

Birth and Event

According to Meister Eckhart, the ground of the soul provides the place in which the event of the "birth of the Son" occurs. According to Heidegger, *Dasein* provides a "clearing" in which the "Event of Appropriation" (*Ereignis*),[3] the Event of Truth, comes to pass.

In order to explain what he means by this event, Heidegger employs a structure very much like that used by Eckhart in his account of the birth of the Son, namely, a "relation." For Eckhart, the being of the Father is to bear and that of the Son is to be born, and this unique situation, found only in the Trinity, in which a relation is not an accidental feature superadded to a substance but the very substance of the beings themselves, is called by the medievals a "subsistent relationship." And since the birth of the Son is an extension of the inner life of the Trinity to the soul, Eckhart adopted this same vocabulary in speaking of the relation of the soul and God. The relation of Being and *Dasein* is of the same sort, because for Heidegger Being "is" (*west*) the very process of coming to pass in *Dasein*, and *Dasein* "is" the very process of letting Being reveal itself. The "Being" (*Wesen*) of each is their relationship to one another. Hence Heidegger might well have spoken of something like a "subsistent relationship" between Being and *Dasein*. In fact one does find a comparable expression in his works. In his lecture on "The Thing" he speaks of "mortals" (*Dasein*) as "*das wesende Verhältnis zum Sein als Sein*" (*VA*, 177). *Wesen* of course is taken verbally and so the phrase means, "The relation to Being [*Sein*] whose being [*Wesen*] is to be [*wesen* taken as an infinitive] a relation." Or using Adamczewski's translation of *Wesen* as "way to be,"[4] the phrase means, "The relationship to Being whose way to be is to be related." However it is translated, Heidegger means that the very Being of *Dasein* is its relationship to Being. Now the Event of Appropriation is the event of the "mutual relation" of Being and *Dasein*, in which both Being and *Dasein* come into their "own," that is, in which Being is provided with a place of disclosure and by which *Dasein* is opened to the truth of Being.

Moreover, the "relation" of *Dasein* to Being even fulfills Eckhart's requirements for the relation of an "image" to its original exemplar. We recall that it was not sufficient for the Son to be "like" the Father in order to be his "image" but it was also necessary that he be sustained in his very being as an image by the Father. Now Heidegger's account of the relationship of Being and *Dasein* conforms remarkably to what Eckhart demands of a "true image" and relation: "But how is Being related to ek-sistence, provided that we may so rashly ask this question at all? Being itself is the relationship [*Verhältnis*] insofar as it [= Being] holds [*halt*] ek-sistence [*Ek-sistenz*] in its existential, i.e., ex-static essence [*Wesen*] in itself and gathers it [= *Eksistenz*] to itself as the dwelling place of the truth of Being in the midst of beings" (*HB*, 77).

Heidegger here (and elsewhere: *WD*, 1–2) plays on the root *halten* in the word *Verhältnis*. *Dasein* is "held" in its relationship to Being by Being itself. And in a sentence which could very well have been written by Meister Eckhart, Heidegger says, "A relationship to something would be a true relationship if it [=x] is held in its [x's] own essence by that [=y] to which it is related" (*G*, 50). This meets Eckhart's requirement for a "true image" exactly. The relationship of *Dasein* to Being is not the "doing" of *Dasein* but of Being. Being itself brings *Dasein* into relationship with itself, and sustains that relation. What Heidegger means by this may be seen by contrasting this position, found in the later works, with the one that he holds in Being and Time. The author of *Being and Time* spoke of the necessity for *Dasein* to raise the question of Being anew, radically to interrogate Being. Even as late as 1935 Heidegger spoke of questioning Being as a matter of "resolving," of "willing to know" (*EM*, 16). But it seems to have been one of the decisive realizations of the later Heidegger that Being does not submit to human interrogation, that Being is not the "answer" to a "question" (*SD*, 20–21), but that it is rather a "gift," a "favor" (*Gunst* [*WM*, 49]) which is bestowed upon man. If Being is grasped at all, it is because Being reveals itself on its own initiative to *Dasein*, although of course man must be open to this revelation. But man himself cannot bring about this revelation of Being. This is exactly as with Eckhart. It is the Father who bears his Son in the soul, although the soul's cooperation is indispensable.

Eckhart also formulated the doctrine of the divine birth in terms of the "eternal Word": for the Father to bear the Son in the soul is to speak his Word (*conceptum*, *verbum*) in the soul. For Heidegger, too, the Event of Truth can be expressed in terms of a primordial language. In the Event of Language, Being comes to pass in the word and man is brought into his proper essence by means of this authentic discourse (*US*, 30, 258–59). Like Eckhart, Heidegger holds that this language is something over and beyond human talk, that it is a more original language which is nothing human at all. It is instead, according to Heidegger, the primal address of Being itself. It is not man who speaks, he says, but Language itself (*die Sprache spricht* [*US*, 12]). This seems to mean that the impulse to speak can on certain occasions originate in Being itself, so that, in this sense, Being speaks "through" man. Like Eckhart, too, Heidegger characterizes this primal language in terms of silence. Because the original speaking of Language itself is quiet (*US*, 30, 262–63), it is only heard in silence and listening (*US*, 252–54). The most authentic talk is reticence and reluctance to speak. Moreover, this "silence" to which both Eckhart and Heidegger refer is not only external but also involves the cessation of all images and concepts. In sum, as for Eckhart the most authentic speaking consists in letting the Father speak his Word in the soul, so for Heidegger the most authentic discourse consists in letting Being come to words in language.

One cannot overlook, however, the criticism which Heidegger voices of the "theological" interpretation of language (*US*, 14–15), in which Eckhart's views seem to be included. For even though theology attributes a divine origin to language, Heidegger says, basing this view upon the opening sentence of St. John's Prologue (exactly as Eckhart does), it nonetheless remains within the traditional metaphysical understanding of language. Theology still adheres to the traditional distinction between the "inner concept" and the "outer word," taking the latter to be the externalization of the former. With the tradition, theology holds that the inner concept is the "truer" language, but it insists that the truest concept of all is nothing created, but the uncreated Word itself. For Heidegger, on the other hand, this whole framework is faulty, for words are not to be understood as signs of concepts, and concepts as signs of things (*US*, 243). Rather the "thing" comes to be, that is, to "appear," in the first place, only through language (*US*, 232–33, 193–94). Language lets things be; it is the "condition" (*Be-ding-ung*) of things. What Heidegger calls for is a language tempered by silence, free of "conceptual" or "representational" thinking, and which overcomes the distortions of all metaphysical language. Hence while Eckhart praises mystical silence, Heidegger calls for a renewal of language, a renewal which he thinks is to be found in the poets. While in Eckhart we meet a classic representative of the *theologia negativa*, in Heidegger we find a thinking which is to be conducted in proximity to the poets, but which nevertheless retains in a "secular" way something of the flavor of negative theology.[5]

Gelassenheit

While the birth of the Son in the soul is the work of God, there is a sense in which it is the soul's work also, inasmuch as it cannot be accomplished without the soul's cooperation, without its "detachment" and "resignation." The self-disclosure of Being in *Dasein* is the "work" of Being, but it cannot be accomplished without *Dasein*'s cooperation. Speaking of the "thing" in which the fourfold intersects, Heidegger says, "When and how do things come about as things? They do not come about *through* the machinations of men. But they also do not come about *without* the watchfulness of the mortals" (*VA*, 180). Just as for Eckhart the soul must utter its *fiat*, so Heidegger's *Dasein* must open itself to the workings of the event. The proximity of Heidegger to Eckhart in this matter is so great that Heidegger can find no better word to describe the posture of *Dasein* than Eckhart's own: *Gelassenheit* ("releasement").[6]

To be sure, Heidegger immediately points out the difference between his use of the word and Eckhart's: "But what we call releasement obviously does not mean casting off sinful self-seeking and getting rid of self-will in favor of the divine will" (*G*, 36). For Eckhart the soul that had not attained resignation was full of "self-love" (*Eigenliebe*) and "self-will" (*Eigenwille*). Heidegger is not interested in the problem of "self-love," but of what he calls "subject-ness" (*Subjectität* [*HW*, 236]). Heidegger singles out a perversion that, while distinct from that described by Eckhart, is clearly analogous to it. The perversion is not "sinful self-seeking" but setting up the thinking subject as the highest principle of Being and subordinating everything to the dictates and demands of the thinking subject. On this point at least, Heidegger has no quarrel with the common understanding of the history of modem philosophy: it begins with the discovery of the *ego cogito* by Descartes, and it is consummated by the absolutizing of the ego in Hegel.[7] This is a perversion which entirely inverts the essence of man (*N* 2:366), for it refuses to acknowledge the priority of Being and sets up the priority of a being, man, in its stead (a failing quite analogous to the spiritual error of "pride," in which man—the creature—sets himself before God—the Creator).

With Descartes the being is reduced to an "object" presented to a subject. Leibniz leads this to its ultimate consequence by formulating the "principle of rendering a sufficient reason." With this principle human reason lays down the rules by which Being must abide: no being can be unless a sufficient reason is rendered to the thinking subject (*SG*, 31–75). There is no question of "sin" here, but there is the same ring of perverted self-importance. Rational thinking is "attached" to its own concepts (*Vorstellungen*) and rules (*Grundsätze*) to which it expects Being to conform. The history of metaphysics is the history of reason's prescriptions about what Being must be—idea, substance, spirit, matter, will, etc. (*ID*, 64). But for Heidegger, Being is "the Overwhelming" (*das Überwältigende* [*EM*, 115]), and man is but a "mortal" cast forth by the "throw" of Being (*HB*, 71, 75, 84).

If the *Dasein* of *Being and Time* was characterized by self-sufficiency and self- possession (*Eigentlichkeit*), the *Dasein* of the later works is described in almost opposite categories.[8] Man is not the "lord" of the earth, of "beings," but the "shepherd" of Being. The virtues of the shepherd are his watchfulness, his patient waiting, and of course his poverty and humility (*WM*, 49; *HB*, 90). The "poverty" of *Dasein* is that it has no power of disposal over Being, that it depends upon Being's "favor," if truth is ever to come to pass. It has "divested" itself of its rational presuppositions about what Being must be. But like Eckhart, indeed like the Sermon on the Mount itself, Heidegger ascribes the greatest "worth" (*Würde* [*HB*, 90]) to the "poor" in spirit, because it is through *Dasein*'s poverty that the truth of Being itself is preserved. The fault of the metaphysics of "subjectness" is, therefore, not that it assigns too much to man, but that it assigns him too little. For it does not see man as the place of the preservation of the Truth of Being (*HB*, 66). The true worth of *Dasein* is that, by releasing itself from its rational presuppositions, it "admits" (*einlasst*) itself into the Open in which Being reveals itself (*WW*, 14–15).

Like Eckhart, Heidegger distinguishes two "moments" of releasement, a negative and a positive. Where Eckhart said that the soul must be "empty of creatures," Heidegger speaks of the necessity of "being loosened" (*Losgelassensein* [*G*, 51]) from beings and the thinking concerned with beings ("representational," "calculative," or "transcendental-horizontal" thinking). Indeed, in *What Is Metaphysics?* Heidegger very nearly adopts the word *Abgeschiedenheit* to describe this moment of releasement, speaking of the need for a "separation from beings" (*der Abschied vom Seienden* [*WM*, 49]) in order to attain the "favor" of Being itself. In Eckhart this negative phase of detachment implied a discipline of freeing the soul from the love of creatures. In Heidegger, too, there are the same overtones of asceticism and self-discipline. The "separation from beings," he says, is the "sacrifice," that is, the surrender of the powers of calculation for the sake of a higher truth. It is this ascesis which enables Heidegger to insist that his thought is not "arbitrary" but "strict" (in keeping with Husserl's determination of the nature of phenomenology). Although it does not have the "exactness" of mathematics, the thinking concerned with Being (*Seinsdenken*) is strict and "disciplined," because it must strenuously resist the inclination to "rationalize" Being, to "explain" it in terms of cause and effect, to reduce it to the highest being and first cause. Strict thinking must stay purely in the element of Being itself (*HB*, 56).

But there is a second, positive moment of releasement. Just as for Eckhart detachment meant not only to be "empty of creatures" but also to be "full of God," so releasement means not only to be "loosened from beings" but also to be "open to Being" (*G*, 25–26, 51). The first moment is negative, a willing not to will, not to "represent." It is active and ascetic. The second moment attains the perfection of releasement. Here there is no question of willing of any kind, but a simple openness to Being which "lets" Being be, just as Eckhart spoke of letting "God be God" (*Q*, 180). And as to the resigned soul the unconcealed and truly divine God is revealed, so in Heidegger Being discloses itself in its truth, free of all metaphysical disguises, to the thinking which is released.

We are now in a position to clarify a criticism which Heidegger makes of Eckhart's view of *Gelassenheit*: "Releasement can still be thought within the realm of willing, as happens in the old masters of thinking, e.g., in Meister Eckhart" (*G*, 35–36). Now if Heidegger means by remaining "within the realm of willing" that Eckhart holds that *Gelassenheit* is a will to not will, then he is clearly mistaken. For both thinkers maintain that this is but a preliminary phase of *Gelassenheit*, and that the perfection of *Gelassenheit* is the suspension of willing altogether. This is a point on which Heidegger and Eckhart are in complete agreement. It is more likely that Heidegger means that Eckhart remains within the realm of willing insofar as Eckhart recommends that we be released into another, higher will. Heidegger's criticism amounts to the accusation that Eckhart remains within the history of metaphysics because he has replaced Being itself with a being, the will of the highest being. This is a point of great importance and we will have occasion to return to it in our concluding remarks below.

The proximity of Heidegger to Eckhart on the question of releasement is manifested in another way. We recall that Eckhart said the fully resigned soul should live "without why," that is, with a disinterested love of God. This same phrase—*ohne Warum*—reappears in Heidegger's *Der Satz vom Grund*. The reason for this is that Heidegger is commenting upon a couplet from Silesius's *Cherubinic Wanderer* that bears that same inscription:

> Without Why
> The rose is without why; it blossoms
> because it blossoms;
> It cares not for itself, nor does it ask if it is
> seen. (*CW*, I, No. 289)

Angelus Silesius's poem draws upon an anthology of mystical writings composed by the Jesuit Sandaeus, in which Eckhart and his disciples Suso and Tauler are amply represented.[9] Silesius, the contemporary of Leibniz, offers an apparent exception to the "Principle of Sufficient Reason," according to Heidegger: something—the rose—is without a "reason," a "why." But the poet has no interest in denying the Principle. He says that the rose is without "why"—not without "because" (*weil*). "Because" supplies the "ground," whereas "why" only seeks after it. The rose is not without a ground. Leibniz's principle is true *of* the rose, but not *for* the rose, says Heidegger (*SG*, 73). The rose does not *seek* the ground of its blossoming. It does not interrogate the origin and outcome of its blossoming, but is content with the simple activity of blossoming. The rose illustrates the same point which Eckhart makes when he says that the soul that lives "without why" is like life itself. Life does not need an explanation and a rationale for itself. Life is not desired *for* something other than itself but because it is life: life is without why; it lives because it lives (*Q*, 180).

In the way that Eckhart said the life "without why" befitted both God and the soul, so Heidegger sees in the rose a twofold model. In the first place, the rose is like Being itself (*SG*, 188). Like the rose, Being is the simple process of emerging out of itself: "The blossoming is grounded in itself, has its ground by and in itself. The blossoming is a pure rising forth from out of itself" (*SG*, 101–2; cf. 73). Hence the rose represents Being as physis (*SG*, 102): the emergent-enduring-power (*aufgehend-verweilend-Walten* [*EM*, 3]). The language of Heidegger in this matter is very close to Eckhart's talk of the "life" of God as the process of "welling up" within himself and then overflowing first into the other persons of the Trinity and finally into creation itself. Heidegger's *physis* and Eckhart's "life" are akin: each is a process of rising up out of an inner recess into manifestness (self-emergence); and each is a "self-sufficient" process in the sense that it rises up *because* it rises up, needing no outward impulse or motivation. The blossoming of the rose is equally a model for each.

But the rose has a further role to play for Heidegger: "What is unsaid in the verse, and everything depends on this, is rather that man, in the most concealed ground of his being [*Wesen*], never truly is until he is in his way like the rose—without why" (*SG*, 72–73). Thus the rose is also a model for *Dasein* (just as it was a model for the soul in Silesius's poem). *Dasein* must be "without why" inasmuch as it must suspend all rational interrogation of Being.[10] The thinking concerned with Being does not demand that a "reason" be "rendered" for Being. Being "is" (*west*) *because* it is. Being is the ground of beings, but there is no ground for Being itself. Hence it is just as much an "abyss" (*Abgrund*). Being is the final "because" for every question. With Being itself *Dasein* must surrender its search for further explanation: "The because is swallowed up in a play. The play is without why. It plays as long as it plays. There remains only play: the highest and the deepest" (*SG*, 188). Being is an inexorable "because," and all that *Dasein* can do is "let" Being be, free of reason's categories and "first principles." But that is the essence of releasement.

There is one last point to be made in connection with the notion of *Gelassenheit* in Heidegger and Eckhart. Eckhart, we noted above, unwittingly fathered a long tradition of God's "need" of man in German thought. Now the relation of *Dasein* to Being which Heidegger expresses in the word *brauchen* seems to stand in the shadows of that tradition. Ordinarily, *brauchen* means "to need" or "to use." But for Heidegger it does not precisely signify either of these. Being does not "use" *Dasein* insofar as this implies "utilizing" (*Benutzen* [*WD*, 114]). To "utilize" something is to subordinate it to the user, to make of it a mere instrument, like the hammer. *Dasein* is no "tool" for the "cunning" of Being. Nor should we think *brauchen* in terms of "needing." For it is not appropriate to imagine that Being—Truth itself—is dependent upon man (*G*, 665). This is to fall back into the error of Cartesian subjectivism. Nor is Being's relationship to *Dasein* one of "necessitating" (*Benötigen* [*WD*, 115]) it, for the "sacrifice" of *Dasein* to Being must be free (*WM*, 49), just as Mary's *fiat* was free.

If Being does not utilize or need or necessitate *Dasein*, just what does *brauchen* mean? Heidegger answers that "only proper use [*Brauchen*] brings what is used into its essence [*Wesen*] and holds it there. . . . To use something is to let it enter into its essence, to preserve it in its essence" (*WD*, 114; e.t., 189). *Brauchen* must be understood in the light of the fact that Being and *Dasein* belong together, that each complements and provides the proper element for the other. Each "helps" (*hilft* [*WM*, 50]) the other into the fullness of its being (*Wesen*). Without Dasein there is no clearing in which the Event of Truth may occur. Yet *Dasein* does not determine how the event will come out, which is the sense in which Truth is independent of *Dasein*. *Brauchen* means something like "assisting" or "helping," rather the way God and the soul "help" and preserve one another in the *Cherubinic Wanderer* (*CW*, I, No. 100). That is why Heidegger says that *Es brauchet* is to be thought in conjunction with *Es gibt*.[11] The "It" that "gives" is the same as the "It" that "uses," and the It that gives is the event itself (*SD*, 20). But the Event comes to pass as an appropriation process: it "bestows" upon *Dasein* its proper essence and, in so doing, the Event, too, comes about in a manner that is "appropriate" to itself. This mutual self-appropriating is the giving of the "It gives" and the using of "It uses." And while this position is not Eckhart's, it belongs to a philosophical and mystical tradition of which Eckhart is, willingly or not, the forefather.

Being and Beings

The last major theme in the writings of Meister Eckhart to which the work of Heidegger invites comparison is the relationship between God and creatures. The analogue in Heidegger's thought is the relationship between Being and beings. Thus our original proportionality may be expanded: God : soul : creatures :: Being : *Dasein* : beings.

Eckhart insisted, as we saw above, on the radical dependency of the creature upon God. Creatures have being the way the air has light. This position is not pantheistic, as the best modem scholarship points out;[12] but it does stress the intimacy and proximity of God and creatures. Creatures are "immediately touched" and "penetrated" by God, the way the air is totally filled by the light of the sun (*LW*, I, 173). The upshot of this is not that one should take flight from this world in order to find God but, on the contrary, since creatures are filled with God, that one should learn to find God in creatures. If God is concealed to a man by created things, the trouble is not with things but with the man (*Q*, 55). One must learn to seize God in creatures: "A man does not learn this [finding God] through flight while running from things and turning oneself into a solitude of an outward kind. He must rather learn an inner solitude, wherever and with whomever he may be. He must learn to break through things and to seize God in them and to hold his image steadfastly in himself in an essential way" (*Q*, 61). Creatures are nothing in themselves. Consequently, one must not take them "in themselves" but "in God" (*Q*, 379). One must not avoid creatures but must be related to them in the right way. To take creatures in themselves is self-love and attachment; but to regard them with a detached heart is to see them in God and to see God in them.

In Heidegger there is a comparable proximity between Being and beings. Being is always the Being of beings (*WG*, 15). Being "never is" (*nie west*) without beings (*WM*, 46).[13] And as there was with Eckhart, so there is in Heidegger an error that consists in taking beings apart from Being, in occupying oneself with beings and forgetting Being. The error is not worldliness" (cf. *WG*, 24–26) but "metaphysics": "Insofar as it always represents beings as beings (*das Seiende als das Seiende*), metaphysics never thinks upon Being itself" (*WM*, 8). Metaphysics falls short of Being itself because it invariably "represents" Being in terms of a being—the highest being (*God*), the thinking being (the subject), and so on. And as Eckhart warned that the desire for creatures was a desire for nothing (*Q*, 171), so Heidegger regards the present age, in which metaphysics has run its course to completion (*SD*, 61), the age of technology (*Technik*), as one of "nihilism." Nihilism, according to Heidegger, is the age in which Being has become a vapor, a vacuous abstraction (*EM*, 27–29), "nothing at all" (*NI*, 338). The phenomenon of "fallenness" described by the author of *Being and Time* now consists in thinking what is "given" while forgetting the "It" that "gives" (*SD*, 8), just as for Eckhart the worldly heart is concerned with creatures to the neglect of the Creator.

But just as Eckhart does not recommend that the soul leave the world to find God, so Heidegger thinks it only "foolishness" to suggest that we do away with technology. We are not interested in "some kind of renaissance of pre-Socratic philosophy," he says. This would be "idle and foolish" (*WM*, 11). Nor does he wish to relinquish the use of technological tools: "The equipment, apparatus and machines of the technological world are for all of us today indispensable, for some to a greater extent, for others to a less extent. It would be foolish blindly to assail the technological world. It would be shortsighted to wish to condemn the technological world as the work of the devil" (*G*, 24; cf. *ID*, 33; *K*, 24–25).

But neither does Heidegger make the by now familiar suggestion that it is not technology which is evil but the use to which it is put, that technology is "neutral" and that we must learn to master it, instead of letting it master us (*K*, 5). Technology is not neutral because it is a "mission of Being" (*Seinsgeschick*) in which Being remains concealed. Technology is a name for the epoch of Being in which the illusion is perpetrated that Being is nothing more than a "store of energy" that awaits man's use (*K*, 26), and that logico-mathematical thinking is the uniquely valid kind of thought (*G*, 26). This is nothing neutral, but a concealment of Being. The real problem that technology presents, according to Heidegger, is the distortion it makes in the essence of Truth and therefore in the essence of man (*VA*, 164). The problem is not with "machines and equipment." This is very much like Eckhart's diagnosis of the disconsolate soul: the trouble is not with peoples or places but with "you yourself" (*Q*, 55).

Eckhart advised the soul not to leave the world but to change its attitude toward it. Correspondingly, Heidegger tells us not to do away with technology, but to learn how to gain a new ground and foundation in it (*G*, 26). Man cannot change the course that Being takes in history—the way the soul cannot change the will of God. Hence man must learn to think the present historical situation in terms of the "mission of Being"—the way the soul must learn to view everything in terms of the will of God. Heidegger describes the new attitude that *Dasein* must have in the technological world as follows: "We are able to use technological objects and yet with suitable use keep ourselves so free of them that we are able to let go of them at any time. We are able to make use of technological objects as they ought to be used. But we are also able simultaneously to let them alone as something which does not concern what is innermost in us and proper to us" (*G*, 24).

The new attitude—which of course is "releasement"—says "yes" to the utilization of technological equipment, but "no" to the distortion it makes of the essence of truth. Viewing technology as a mission of Being itself, this attitude is alert to a truth that technology conceals: "The meaning of the technological world is concealed" (*G*, 26). And releasement stays open to this hidden meaning: "I call the posture in virtue of which we hold ourselves open for the concealed meaning of the technological world: openness towards the Mystery" (*G*, 26). One must not think upon technology technologically but in terms of the mission of Being. And in this light technology appears as a derivative and "untrue" form of a more primordial *technē* (*K*, 34) which is to be found among the early Greeks (*VA*, 160). As the soul finds God in all places and people and things, so meditative thinking finds even in modern technology the traces of a pristine disclosure of the Event of Truth. For the "thinking which thinks in terms of Being as mission" (*Seinsgeschickliche Denken* [*N* II, 335]), technology is a withdrawal of a primordial truth.

Original *technē* is a making which does not exploit "nature" but which is accomplished in harmony with it. Hence it does not conceal the truth of nature but it reveals it. Original *technē*, says Heidegger, brings about the "truth" in "things." The "things" of original *technē* are the subject of some of the later Heidegger's most interesting accounts, accounts that are at once "phenomenological" in the sense of *Being and Time* (hence in the sense of a phenomenology of the *Lebenswelt*), and yet profoundly in accord with the later *Seinsdenken*. We recall the bridge in "Building, Dwelling and Thinking" (*VA*, 145), the "jug" in "The Thing" (*VA*, 153). The jug, for example, unites the earth out of which it is made, the heavens whose rains it collects and contains, the gods to whom it can present a wine offering, and mortals whose thirst it satisfies. In the jug the "fourfold" of earth and heavens, mortals and gods, which represent to Heidegger an original and truer state of things, one which has all but been forgotten, is collected together and brought to appearance (*VA*, 170–172). With such making there can be a proper dwelling (*Wohnen*) in the world (*VA*, 159). The world becomes again a place in which man is born and ages and dies, in which he works and rests and prays, in which he discovers the sense of "being human."

Hence, as the soul for Eckhart is at peace with the world and no longer disturbed by its dangers, so Dasein is reconciled with technology (*G*, 25), while it nourishes the hope of another day (*K*, 31) in which technology is assigned its proper place and is no longer taken to be "something absolute" (*G*, 25).

THE IMPORT OF THE ANALOGY

The analogy that Heidegger's thought presents to Meister Eckhart is unmistakable. We must now tum to the implications that this analogy holds for our understanding of Heidegger. The proximity of Heidegger to Eckhart might very well represent to some a basis for writing Heidegger's work off as "true philosophy." To others it might show that he belongs to a long tradition of "deep thinkers." We shall steer a middle course between these predispositions by raising three simple and straightforward questions. In the first place, the parallel of Heidegger to Eckhart raises anew the entire problem of "humanism" in the later Heidegger, for it is characteristic of mysticism to allow man to be swallowed up in a "mystical self-effacement." What does this analogy suggest, then, about the loss or the preservation of the humanity of man in the later Heidegger? Secondly, to what extent are Eckhart and Heidegger saying anything different from one another? Heidegger might very well have "overcome metaphysics," but not in such a way as to have said anything that has not been said many times before by those who are not metaphysicians. Finally, is Heidegger himself a "mystic" and his thought a "mysticism"? What interest can "philosophy" have in a thinker such as Heidegger?

(1) The most serious question raised by the controversial "shift" in Heidegger's thought concerns the place of man in his philosophy. This is a troublesome issue, in which the deep transformation which Heidegger's thought has undergone comes plainly into view. *Dasein* is no longer conceived in terms of its freedom and self-possession, as the being that "has its Being to be" (*SZ*, § 4, p. 12), which must actively take over and choose its Being. Rather the Being of *Dasein* is to stay open to the address of Being. Its characteristic mood is not "anxiety" but "composure" (*Gelassenheit*). It does not raise the question of Being but lives "without why," waiting for Being's self-disclosure. And, as if intentionally to complicate the issue, Heidegger's later works frequently denounce the notion of "humanism."

As we have already shown, this position has all the earmarks of the mystic's—and in particular of Meister Eckhart's—notion of the surrender of the soul to God. However, Heidegger's views are not for that reason inconsonant with any form of "humanism," if "humanism" means the attempt to establish the dignity of man and to preserve his essence. For Eckhart himself considered the union of the soul with God to be something that brings the soul into the fullness of its being. It certainly is not effected at the cost of the loss of the identity of the soul. This was something that the youthful Heidegger sensed about medieval mysticism when he said that the "transcendent relation" of the soul to God is one in which both the absoluteness of God is affirmed and the integrity of the soul is preserved (*DS*, 239). The reason for this is that God and the soul are not "two things"; on the contrary God and the soul belong together: "Many simple people think that they should look upon God as if He stood there and they stood here. But that is not so. God and I are *one*" (*Q*, 186). Were they not "one" their union could be brought about only at the expense of one or the other. But the soul and God are of a kind: they are both so pure and detached, so removed from creatures, that they belong exclusively to each other.

Because the union of the soul and God is something that "befits" each, is "appropriate" to each, Eckhart is able to emphasize that nothing of what is "proper" (*eigen*) to the soul is lost when it unites with God. As living things, he says, we act "on our own," "out of our own grounds" (*wir aus unserm eigenen wirken*). If we are united with God, then God must take over our being, but not in such a way that we are then moved by God as "from the outside." Rather, God must become "our own" so that in being moved by God we will be moved "from within on our own": "If we should then live in Him or through Him, then He must be our own and we must work on our own" (*Q*, 176). So much "our own" does God become for the detached heart that Meister Eckhart will not only say that that it is God who bears his Son in the soul, but also that it is the soul itself which bears the Son in itself (*Q*, 160; Théry, 264–65).[14] Living "in Him and through Him," according to Eckhart, is not a form of self-diremption, as it is portrayed in Hegel's discussion of "unhappy consciousness," but a higher form of self-possession.

Eckhart's detached heart constitutes a model of "religious humanism," that is, the attempt to realize the fullness of being human by rooting human existence in the love of God. Whether or not such a program constitutes a "true humanism" is a problem that can be finally decided only "from within," by those who actually have undertaken such a life. But it is at least clear that there are no a priori arguments against the position that Eckhart adopts. Moreover, if we consult the history of Christian spirituality, we discover a number of interesting examples of individuals who testify in favor of what Eckhart says. One thinks for example of Francis of Assisi, a man whose love of God and spirit of poverty led him not to a "contempt of the world" but, quite the contrary, to a rather remarkable sense of joy. It is simply nonsense to find in Francis a joyless self-effacement, an "un-happy" and "divided" consciousness.[15] What seems to be the case instead is that in Francis, who practiced the detachment of which Eckhart spoke, some ideal form of "being human" was attained—to be sure, not one that all men must follow, but a unique and genuine one nonetheless.

The problem of "humanism" in Heidegger is quite comparable to that in Eckhart. One main thrust of the word *Ereignis* is to emphasize that Being and *Dasein* find in each other their "proper" (*eigen*) complement. Just as he had said of the medieval *unio mystica*, Heidegger can say of the Event of Truth that in it neither the "transcendence" of Being (*SZ*, § 7, p. 38) nor the integrity of man is destroyed. On the contrary, the Event of Truth provides the basis for a "higher" humanism: "Humanism now means, in the event we determine to hold on to this word: the essence of man is essential to the Truth of Being" (*HB*, 94). Humanism means to bring man into his essence and so to provide for the real "worth" of man (*HB*, 75), a worth that every metaphysical humanism is unable to grasp:

> One must be clear about the fact that, by this means, man remains enclosed in the essential realm of *animalitas*, even when one does not equate him with animals but rather attributes to him a specific difference. One is always thinking in principle of the *homo animalis* even if the *anima* is put as *animus* or *mens* and later as subject or person or spirit. Such a way of putting man is the manner of metaphysics. But man's essence is thereby taken in too lowly a way. . . . Metaphysics is closed off to the simple and essential certitude that man "is" [*west*] only in his essence [*Wesen*], in which he is addressed by Being. Only in this address has he found that wherein his essence dwells. (*HB*, 66)

The humanism which Heidegger repudiates is the metaphysical view which cannot rise above the conception of man as the rational animal. This rejection of humanism has nothing to do with recommending the inhumane (*HB*, 95), but with opening man up to the Truth of Being.

The "Event" (*Er-eignis*) of Truth takes over in the later Heidegger the role that was once assigned in *Being and Time* to "authenticity" (*Eigentlichkeit*), by which *Dasein* was brought back to its deepest and most individual possibilities and in which the hold that the "they" exerts was broken. But the "ownmost possibility" of *Dasein* in the later works is identified with its role in providing a place of disclosure for the Truth of Being. Nonetheless, one wonders whether this is anything more than a merely verbal maneuver. What possibilities for man lie in the "Event"? The whole notion in the later Heidegger of a "higher" humanism has a tendency to slip into a rather vacuous play on words.

However, it is possible to determine the renewal of human existence which Heidegger has in mind. Heidegger's thought originates, in part at least, in the phenomenological movement and so in Husserl's refutation of "scientism," the theory that the only objective account of the world and of man is that supplied by the physical sciences. Heidegger's work has always in one way or another been a continuation of this protest against scientism. Just as with the earlier phenomenological analyses, meditative thinking attempts to gain access to a world to which calculative thought is closed off, a world that the later works call the "fourfold." The technological world must be subordinated to the world in which man "dwells." To the extent that this is not done, man's "dwelling" in the world is disrupted and even destroyed. The world of the "fourfold," on the other hand, is eminently "humane"—because it is more attentive to man's "mortality" and to his belonging to the "earth" (*humus*), because it affirms the truly "divine" God and sees in the heavens the measure of lived time. It is interesting to note in this connection that the essay on the fourfold "Building, Dwelling and Thinking" (1951) was addressed by Heidegger to a postwar Germany that was in the midst of a great housing shortage. "Building," he holds, is more than a problem for civil and mechanical engineering; architecture is not merely a mathematical art. The real problem of housing, he concludes, is our ignorance of how to "dwell" (*VA*, 162). Like Husserl and Merleau-Ponty, Heidegger struggles to establish the primacy of the "life-world." But Heidegger's effort is considerably more enigmatic—some might say "profound"—because he thinks the world in which man dwells may be attained only by an attitude of "openness to the Mystery" concealed in technology (*G*, 26).

One might further object, however, that according to Heidegger it is impossible for man to remake the world, to render it humane. And that is true enough in the sense that the movements of history (*Geschichte*) originate in the mission (*Geschick*) of Being (*HB*, 81); they are not subject to human control. While that is so, it remains true that the world cannot be remade without man's cooperation (*K*, 34, 38–39; *VA*, 180). Unless man is "released" from the illusion that technology is something absolute and is open to the original *technē* concealed within technology, then the "turn" (*Kehre*) in Being will never come to pass. Man cannot remake the world himself (a Marxian revolution for Heidegger is "subjectivism" [*HB*, 88–89]), but he can "let" it be remade. Like the man of God who bolds that the world will never be reconstituted so long as men do not have recourse to God, Heidegger holds that the precondition for a renewal of the world is a thinking directed to Being. If man is open to Being, then—perhaps—Being will disclose itself to man. But in this "perhaps" lies one of the largest difficulties with Heidegger's thought, and one which we shall examine in greater detail in the second question.

(2) If the movements of Heidegger's and Eckhart's thought are in so many ways parallel, if they even stand together in offering a view of a "higher" humanism, then just where does Heidegger really differ from Eckhart? To answer this question, let us first turn to the concluding paragraphs of "The Talks of Instruction" in which, it seems to us, Eckhart expresses the "spirit" of his thought:

> To the extent that you are in God, to that extent will you have peace, and to the extent that you are outside God, you will be outside of peace. If only something is in God it will have peace. As much in God, so much in peace. By this test you will know how much you are in God: by whether you have peace or lack peace. For where you lack peace, you must necessarily lack peace, for the lack of peace comes from the creature, and not from God. Everything that is in God is only to be loved; there is nothing in God which should be feared. (*Q*, 100; e.t., 108)

Eckhart's God is a God of love. Of all the sacred authors, it is from John that be draws the greatest inspiration. It is John, the "beloved disciple," who writes: "Think of the love that the Father has lavished on us, by letting us be called God's children; and that is what we are" (I John 3:1). And around this text Eckhart is able to build his entire mystical speculation. God is first and foremost a loving Father for Eckhart, not a just judge or a supreme being or a first cause. The relationship between God and the soul is not one of fear—of offending God, of violating his Law—but of loving trust. Everything that is in God is to be loved, nothing is to be feared. "Love cannot mistrust," he says, "it can only trustfully await something good" (*Q*, 75). In the hands of a loving father one knows only trust and peace. And we are in the strongest sense God's sons, for we are not only "called" children, but "that is what we are."

The situation is radically different, however, in Heidegger's case. For Heidegger must never speak of Being as loving or benevolent or fatherly. This is to treat Being as if it were the good will of the highest being. And that, as we have seen, is precisely the point upon which he criticizes Meister Eckhart's conception of *Gelassenheit*: it remains confined within the realm of willing (*G*, 35–36).

Dasein must be released not to the good will of the Father but to Being itself. But what is Being? In *Der Satz vom Grund* Heidegger answers: "Being and ground [*Grund*]: the same. Being as grounding has no ground but rather as the abyss [*Abgrund*] plays that game which as mission [*Geschick*] plays up to us Being and ground." Being for Heidegger is not the "reason" (*Grund, ratio*) of Western metaphysics, but the ground which is equiprimordially an abyss. It is not a principle of thoroughgoing intelligibility, but it is just as much unintelligible. If the Heidegger of *Being and Time* protests what has become of "human existence" in Hegel (*KPM*, 127n196), the later Heidegger protests what has become of "Being." For in Hegel, whose claim to have consummated Western metaphysics Heidegger accepts, Being is identified with Absolute Reason and so is dissolved into a principle of lawfulness and regular development. The sequence of historical epochs is regulated by the principle of unfolding rationality. There is, as Leibniz demanded, a "why" for every historical event and every historical epoch. The distance that Heidegger has put between himself and Hegel's notion of Being is made plain in the minutes of the seminar on "Time and Being":

> By what is the succession of epochs determined? Whence is this free sequence determined? One naturally recalls Hegel's history of the "thought." For Hegel history is dominated by necessity, which is simultaneously freedom. Both are for him one in and through the dialectical course, which is the way the essence of the spirit is. With Heidegger, on the other hand, one cannot speak of a "why." Only the "that"—that the history of Being is such as it is can be said. Consequently, in *Der Satz vom Grund*, Goethe's verse is cited:
>
> How? When? and Where? The gods
> remain silent.
> You keep yourself in the *because* and do
> not ask *why*?
> (*SD*, 55–56; cf. *SG*, 206)

Heidegger's Being is a ground without ground, as Eckhart's God is "principle without principle" (*principium sine principio*) in the words of the *Liber XXIV Philosophorum* (*LW*, III, 16n1). For Eckhart this means that God is the fullness of being (*plenitudo esse*), a principle of consummate goodness and perfect intelligibility, the final explanation, the ultimate rationale which needs no reason beyond itself. But for Heidegger, Being is a ground which does not itself admit of explanation. Being comes to pass as it does. That is all one may say. At the end of "Time and Being," Heidegger writes: "What does there remain to say? Only this: the Event of Appropriation comes to pass [*Das Ereignis ereignet*]" (*SD*, 24). No further determination of the event can be made. One must be satisfied with "because" and not ask "why?" *Dasein* must be "without why." And whereas for Eckhart this meant that the soul should act not because God commands it to act, but rather in loving unity with, and on the basis of, God's indwelling presence (Théry, 236–37), for Heidegger it means that *Dasein* must openly acknowledge the inscrutability of Being.

Because the Event is both ground and abyss, Heidegger calls it, in one of his most striking characterizations, a "play" (*Spiel*).[16] The history of Being is the history of the play of Being, of its fluctuating retreat and advance, revelation and concealment. The process bas no more rationale than that, and to the extent that one gives it a rationale one forces the categories of metaphysics upon it. Thus Leibniz's remark "When God calculates the world is made" is emended by Heidegger to read, "While God plays the world comes to be" (*SG*, 186). And Heidegger cites with approval the following fragment from Heraclitus:[17] "Time is a child playing a game of draughts; the kingdom is in the bands of a child" (cf. *SG*, 187–88). Not only might one say "It gives" (*Es gibt*) and "It uses" (*Es brauchet*), but now we may add "It plays" (*Es spielet*): "Because is swallowed up in the play. It plays because It plays. There remains only play: the highest and the deepest" (*SG*, 188).

That is why, where the author of *The Book of Divine Consolation* can speak of peace, Heidegger speaks of a "venture," a "wager" on the outcome of a portentous game: "We must venture out into the play of language upon which our being is staked" (*WD*, 87). Again, man must confront "the high and dangerous play upon which the being of language has staked us" (*WD*, 84). Technology (*Technik*) is the "danger" (*Gefahr*) for Heidegger. It is a concealment of the Truth of Being. It distorts the meaning of nature, of dwelling in the world, of thinking and of man himself. It is a danger which man did not bring on himself but which Being itself has perpetrated. Being itself has withdrawn in its truth and has advanced in the form of an untruth. The illusions of the age of technology are mistakes for which no man is responsible.

Accordingly *Dasein* does not "trust," it can only "hope" (*VA*, 41–42). Indeed, Heidegger has undermined all possible "grounds" for trust (and even for hope). For, in the first place, having broken with the metaphysical tradition of the ultimate intelligibility of Being, he has divorced Being from all rationale, from all lawful becoming, from all rational governance. Moreover, he has also divorced Being from any possible personalistic conception. It is no accident that there is *no* talk of "father," "son," or "giving birth" in Heidegger's account of the relationship between Being and *Dasein*, whereas these are the dominant expressions in Eckhart's Christian, indeed Johannine mysticism. And in my view this must be counted as the most decisive difference of all between Eckhart and Heidegger. Heidegger uses many metaphors to explain the relationship of Being and *Dasein*—giving, using, thanking, playing, saying, etc.—but never "giving birth" as a "father" generates his "son."[18] The reason for this is not that the relationship of father and son is an "ontic" relation between things, because that is also true of giving and playing and all the rest. The point is that some ontic relations are capable of being reworked and transformed so as to become possible ways of speaking—in a "non-objective" way (*PT*, 37)—about Being and *Dasein*, and some are not. The relation of father and son is not susceptible of such a reworking because it is a radically personal relationship, and as such involves such dispositions as love and trust. And it is as plainly nonsensical to describe Being in these categories as it would be to describe it in terms of the categories of Hegel's *Logic*.

And so Heidegger asks: Will the illusions of the age of technology pass (*ID*, 71)? Will the "West" (which Heidegger takes to be a true "evening-land" (*Abendland*]) become the eve of a new day? Will man ever get beyond the conception of himself as the "rational animal" (*SG*, 210–11)? These are only questions: no one knows the answers. The answers depend upon the possibilities that inhere in the Event possibilities that Heidegger himself calls "dark" and "uncertain" (*SD*, 66). One does not "trust" in the outcome of the event. The best one can do is wait (*G*, 37); the only "serenity" (*Gelassenheit*) one has is to know there is nothing more one can do. *Dasein* may prepare for the possibility of a "new beginning": it may open itself to it. But *Dasein* can neither effect it nor trust in its coming to pass. Eckhart so trusted that God would return love with love that he said we could "force" God to come to us (Théry, 218–19). Eckhart said that although there are unknown depths in God, and the Godhead is an "abyss" of which nothing can be spoken, still there is nothing to fear in God; everything in God should only be loved (*Q*, 100). But there is nothing in Heidegger's *Ereignis* to love and almost everything to fear and mistrust. This seems to me to constitute a serious problem with Heidegger's thought, and one to which insufficient attention is paid.[19] It is hard to see how the "releasement" for which Heidegger asks can continue to make any sense once it is detached from its religious context, that is, from its relationship to a loving God, and is related to the idea of Being which he puts forward.

It is true that Heidegger does speak of the Event as "giving" and of *Dasein* as "thanking," which does endow the Event with something of a benevolent aspect (*WM*, 49; *WD*, 94). Such personalistic language is close to Eckhart's, for the Father gives the "gift" (*gratia*) of the Son and the soul is indeed grateful. However, while one may accept Eckhart's expressions quite literally, all Heidegger has done is to adopt another "model" for thinking out the relationship of Being and *Dasein*. The Event does not literally give, because literally to give is to give a "gift," and a "gift" is an expression of good will, whereas the relationship of Being and *Dasein* must be gotten beyond the realm of willing. Giving implies a benefactor and it implies gratitude, neither of which Heidegger seriously means to suggest. What Heidegger does mean by the model of "thanking" seems to be this. The revelation of Being is nothing that *Dasein* can bring about—for example, through its "questioning" as *Being and Time* supposed. Only Being itself can effect it. Consequently, if Being is revealed to *Dasein* it comes "gratuitously," as it were, and as a "gift" (or "favor"). *Dasein* however cannot and will not receive the gift if it is not disposed toward the giver as a recipient should be, that is, with "gratitude." The correct disposition of *Dasein* toward the self-revelation of Being is "openness" toward it or simply "thinking" (*Seinsdenken*). Hence *Dasein*'s "gratitude" is "thinking"; its "thinking" (*Denken*) is "thanking" (*Danken*). The whole notion of "thanking" therefore rests not on any personalistic overtones of the event but on the kinship—etymological or otherwise—of *Denken* and *Danken*. Indeed, the whole notion of "giving" arises out of a sentence in Being and Time which Heidegger would like to reinterpret and which uses the phrase *es gibt* (*SZ*, § 43, p. 212)."

There is nothing benevolent about the giving of the Event; there is no gratitude in the thanking of *Dasein*. Heidegger is not talking about any sort of personal presence, but about "manifestness." He does not conceive of the coming to be of manifestness in terms of the loving care of a father but, on the contrary, in terms of a "world play" (*Weltspiel*). While the "concern" (*Sache*) of Eckhart's thinking is with a loving Father, the "concern" of Heidegger's thought is history and the secular.

(3) Does it not emerge from this discussion that Heidegger is a mystic, although of a rather different cut than Eckhart? There are varieties of mystical experience, and not all mystics subscribe to the notion of a personal and loving Father, as Eastern mysticism testifies. One can amass an impressive argument in favor of "Heidegger's mysticism." To begin with, Heidegger himself has repeatedly said that what he is doing is *not* philosophy (SD, 61). The sum and substance of philosophy is metaphysics, he says, and his thinking goes beyond metaphysics. It is something of a strange phenomenon, after all, to see so many books and articles and lectures by professors of philosophy devoted to a thinker who vigorously protests against being considered a philosopher. How seriously have these authors considered Heidegger's protests?

If "mysticism" is a nondiscursive, directly intuitive experience of a "truth" that neither common sense nor rational argumentation can attain, then Heidegger seems to bear the essential trademark of the mystic. "Sound common sense" is for him the thoughtlessness of the "they." "Reason" is the illusion that Being submits to the prescriptions of the thinking subject. The "Truth of Being," to which reason and metaphysics have no access, can be attained only in a "leap" (*Satz, Sprung* [WD, 4–5; SG, 95–96]) which reminds us strongly of the *intuitus mysticus*. Heidegger does not offer arguments for his position. To "argue" is to fall victim to the illusion that "reason" is the final arbiter of what is true. In the later Heidegger, argumentation is replaced by a cryptic, even oracular tone. Compared to the later works, *Being and Time* is a carefully developed work.

To illustrate this point, a lecture is given in 1962 which bears the same title as the third, unpublished Division of *Being and Time*, "Time and Being." Some twenty-five pages long in its printed form, it concludes that all there is to say is *Das Ereignis ereignet*. And the last sentence of the lecture is an apology for the fact that the lecture itself is an obstacle to the saying of the *Ereignis*. The lecture makes affirmations, whereas the sentences in which the event is to be expressed are not assertions (*Aussagen*). They are not "true" or "false" nor do they demand a "justification" ("sufficient reason").

It is a long way from the Socrates of the Platonic dialogues, who does not relent until a sound argument is brought forth, to "Time and Being." The later Heidegger has intentionally left the Platonic dialogues behind, and with them the whole notion of argumentative thinking. If philosophy must give arguments, then Heidegger has indeed left philosophy, just as he says.

Nonetheless, it does not follow that he has left philosophy for mysticism. The book on Eckhart was never written, after all, but there are numerous essays on the poetry of Hölderlin and Trakl. If Heidegger's "thinking" (*Denken*) has gone beyond philosophy, it has moved more in the direction of poetry than of mysticism. We recall the divergence of Heidegger and Eckhart on the nature of language. Heidegger does not wish to cut off propositional language for the sake of silence—which would be a typically mystical move, and which Eckhart advocated—but for the sake of a nonpropositional language, a language akin to that of the poet. Heidegger insists upon reticence and carefulness about language, not upon mystical silence, and he finds this care only in poetry (*WM*, 50–51). Hence even if the mode or style of the later Heidegger is inconsonant with what most Western thinkers have traditionally called philosophy, it does not follow that it is mysticism.

However, there is an even stronger reason for distrusting the suggestion that Heidegger is a mystic, a reason which, it seems to us, justifies the great interest that "philosophers" have shown in his work. It concerns not so much the "style" of his thought but its "content." We remarked above, in contrasting Heidegger with Eckhart, upon the "secular" character of Heidegger's work. We wish to understand this word in its deepest sense: "secular" is that which characterizes the *saeculum*, the age; but an age or epoch is always, for Heidegger, a "mission of Being." Hence the secular character of Heidegger's work consists in his commitment to comprehending the history of the West and to comprehending the present age in terms of Western history, a commitment quite foreign to Eckhart who wished to see God in things so that we might one day—in eternity—see things in God (*Q*, 61). Heidegger's thinking is for a "time of need," the age of technology, in which he holds the "truth" of being human and of Being itself is covered up. The age of technology is for him a metaphysical event, and he wishes not to condemn it but to think it through. The technological age summons man, according to Heidegger, to a meditation upon the history of Western metaphysics.

Hence the question that Heidegger asked in 1929 remains the essential one: What is metaphysics? Metaphysics is to be overcome, but it is not to be laid aside (*WM*, 9). On the contrary, metaphysics contains the truth of Being in a concealed way (*WM*, 44). Heidegger's thought consists in a dialogue with the history of metaphysics in the hope of uncovering what it has concealed. From Aristotle's question about the being as such Heidegger "retrieves" the question about the Truth of Being. From Descartes's reduction of the world to *res extensa* he retrieves the primordial spatiality of *Dasein* (*SZ*, § 21, p. 101). In Leibniz's formulation of the principle "no being *is* without a *ground*," Heidegger hears the "ringing together" of Being and ground, the ringing of Being as the groundless ground. From the idea of truth is correspondence (*adequatio*) Heidegger is able to think truth as unconcealment. In Nietzsche's "history of nihilism" Heidegger finds the history of metaphysics itself (*N* 2:343).

Metaphysics has always been the medium in which Heidegger learned what he says.

His thinking has largely consisted in finding another way of saying what he has learned. He says what metaphysics would say were it able—the Truth of Being (*N* 2:353—54, 397). The history of metaphysics is the hiding place of Being, and Heidegger's thought has been a radical attempt to uncover the wealth hidden *in* and *by* that tradition (*HB*, 77). Heidegger does not renounce metaphysics but lays bare its essence. And who but "philosophers" would be interested in such a task? It is very doubtful that his thinking will interest any who are not interested in metaphysics, and even more doubtful that it can be comprehended by any who do not comprehend metaphysics. Heidegger has invigorated contemporary philosophical thinking and, despite what he himself says, deals with issues that are only of interest to those who think in that tradition which begins with the pre-Socratics and which all have called "philosophy."

What, then, does this question of Heidegger's mysticism amount to? Just this, I think: that one way of understanding Heidegger is to see his thought in an analogy with a mystic like Meister Eckhart; that certain analogies can be drawn between Heidegger and the mystics, analogies which are instructive and illuminating and indeed even based on the historical evidence of Heidegger's early interest in medieval mysticism. But to argue that Heidegger is a mystic is to distort much more of Heidegger's thought than it illuminates. The analogy is but an analogy.

One must be careful not to be fooled by Heidegger. He appropriates the talk of the mystic, and much of the structure of the "mystical union" of the soul with God, but he makes these things over for his own purposes and to his own liking. Heidegger has been interested in theological issues from the very beginning of his studies, and he has long been transforming the ideas and the language of the Western religious tradition. He did this in *Being and Time* (fallenness, guilt, conscience), and he has done it again in his later work. For Heidegger, Being is a "play" and the task of thinking is to "play along" (*mitspielen* [*SG*, 188]) with Being. To bring Being to language is a "game" (*WD*, 83), for Being as primordial language bolds itself back and resists saying. Hence Heidegger must resort to all available resources to bring Being to words; all are "fair game."

The mystic for Heidegger is a kin and an ally, who says a great deal of what Heidegger himself wants to say: there is more to thinking than reasoning; true language depends upon silence; in *Gelassenheit* a deeper truth reveals itself. And so Heidegger freely takes over and uses what he finds of service in the mystic, and particularly in Meister Eckhart. But Heidegger remains throughout his own man. The mystic is concerned with the eternal, the "thinker" with time. Even the poet is to be distinguished from the thinker (*WM*, 51), for the poet does not think Being as Being but as the "holy."[20] While Heidegger's thinking is conducted in proximity to the poet and to the mystic, Heidegger's abiding interest lies in the age old "issue" (*Sache*) of philosophy, the question of Being. It is this question that first stimulated his thinking, and it is to this question that he has subsequently subordinated all other alliances.[21]

NOTES

1. We refer to the works of Heidegger with the following abbreviations: *DS*: *Die Kategorien und Bedeutungslehre des Duns Scotus* (Tübingen: J. C. B. Mohr, 1916); *EM*: *Einführung in die Metaphysik*, 2nd ed. (Tübingen: Max Niemeyer, 1958); *G*: *Gelassenheit*, 2nd ed. (Pfullingen: G. Neske, 1960); *HB*: *"Brief über den 'Humanismus,'"* in *Platons Lehre von der Wahrheit Mit einen Brief über den "Humanismus,"* 2nd ed. (Bern: A. Francke, 1954); *HW*: *Holzwege*, 4th ed. (Frankfurt: V. Klostermann, 1963); *ID*: *ldentität und Differenz*, 3rd ed. (Pfullingen: G. Neske, 1957); *K*: *Die Technik und die Kehre* (Pfullingen: G. Neske, 1962); *KPM*: *Kant und das Problem der Metaphysik*, 3rd ed.(Frankfurt: V. Klostermann, 1956); *N* I, *N* II: *Nietzsche*, 2 vols. (Pfullingen: G. Neske, 1962); *PT*: *Phänomenologie und Theologia* (Frankfurt: V. Klostermann, 1970); *SD*: *Zur Sache des Denkens* (Tübingen: Max Niemeyer, 1969); *SG*: *Der Satz vom Grund*, 3rd ed. (Pfullingen: G. Neske, 1965);

SZ: *Sein und Zeit*, 10th ed. (Tübingen: Max Niemeyer, 1963); *US*: *Unterwegs zur Sprache*, 3rd ed. (Pfullingen: G. Neske, 1965); *VA*: *Vorträge und Aufsätze*, 2nd ed. (Pfullingen: G. Neske, 1959); *WD*: *Was Heisst Denken?*, 2nd ed. (Tübingen: Max Niemeyer, 1961); *WG*: *Vom Wesen des Grundes*, 5th ed. (Frankfurt: V. Klostermann, 1965); *WM*: *Was ist M etaphysik?*, 9th ed. (Frankfurt: V. Klostermann, 1965); *WW*: *Vom Wesen der Wahrheit*, 4th ed. (Frankfurt: V. Klostermann, 1961). All translations are our own.

Further abbreviations include *CW*: Angelus Silesius, *Cherubinischer Wandersmann*, introduced and reviewed by Will-Erich Peuckert (Bremen: Carl Schünemann, 1956), I, No. 8; No. 100; *LW*: *M eister Eckhart: Die deutschen und lateinischen Werke*, edited on behalf of the German Research Association, *Die Lateinische Werke*, ed. Ernst Benz (Stuttgart: Kohlhammer, 1936); *Q*: *Meister Eckhart: Deutsche Predigte und Traktate*, ed. and trans. Josef Quint (Munich: Carl Hanser, 1963).

2. We have chosen "transcendent" as a neutral term to refer indifferently to Heidegger's "*Sein*" and Eckhart's "God."

3. Joan Stambaugh's translation of *Ereignis*, "Event of Appropriation," takes into account both senses of the word which Heidegger intends, that is, "coming to pass" and "appropriation" (cf. Martin Heidegger, *Identity and Difference*, trans. Joan Stambaugh [New York: Harper, 1969], 14n1). Reiner Schürmann quite rightly stresses that Heidegger and Eckhart articulate the *Gottesgeburt* and the *Ereignis* in the language of "event" and "happening," and not of substance (see Reiner Schürmann-Maztre, *Eckhart ou la joie errante: Sermons allemands traduits et commentés* [Paris: Éditions Planète, 1972], 66n46, 201n94).

4. Zygmunt Adamczewski, "On the Way to Being," in *Heidegger and the Path of Thinking*, ed. John Sallis (Pittsburgh: Duquesne University Press, 1970), 13–18.

5. In assigning such importance to the poet Heidegger is anticipated by Shelling, not by Eckhart.

6. Since Heidegger uses *Gelassenheit* to emphasize the necessity of "letting" Being be, his English translators have rendered it as "releasement," a convention we shall adopt as well (cf. William Richardson, *Heidegger: Through Phenomenology to Thought* [The Hague: Martinus Nijhoff, 1963], 504. See *supra*, n. 28).

7. Cf. *FND*, 76, where Heidegger discounts the possibility of beginning "modern" philosophy with Eckhart instead of Descartes. This is because Eckhart repudiates the "ego" as the highest principle of philosophy, placing the value of the subject matter before that of the self (*DS*, 7).

8. In this context *Eigentlichkeit* sounds more like *Eigenwille* than its opposite, which raises the question of the compatibility of the later notion of *Gelassenheit* with *Being and Time*'s view of *Eigentlichkeit*.

9. Jeffrey L. Sammons, *Angelus Silesius* (New York: Twayne, 1967), 44–45. On Eckhart and this saying of Silesius, see Shizuteru Ueda, "Maître Eckhart et la buddismc zen," *La vie spirituelle* 53 (January 1971): 38.

10. How is the later Heidegger to be reconciled with the author of *Being and Time*, for whom the essence of *Dasein* consisted in raising the question of Being? See my "The Rose Is without Why: An Interpretation of the Later Heidegger," *Philosophy Today* 15 (Spring 1971): 3–15.

11. In ordinary German, of course, *es gibt* means "there is" (French: *il y a*). But Heidegger takes it literally as "it gives" (cf. *SZ*, § 43, p. 212; *HB*, 78; *SD*, 1–25).

12. Vladimir Lossky, *Theologie negative et connaissence de Dieu chez Maître Eckhart* (Paris: J. Vrin, 1960), 307–20.

13. See the controversy surrounding this text in Richardson, 562–65.

14. Gabriel Théry, "Édition critique des pieces relatives au proces d'Eckhart," *Archives d'histoire doctrinale et littéraire du moyen age* 1 (1926): 129–268.

15. Cf. Johan Huizinga, *Homo Ludens: A Study of the Play Element in Culture* (Boston: Beacon Press, 1955), 139-40; Evelyn Underhill, *Mysticism* (New York: Putton & Dutton, 1961), 439–40.

16. I have explained the "play of Being" more carefully in my "Being, Ground and Play in Heidegger," *Man and World* 3 (February 1970): 26–48. Using Heidegger's "play" of the foursome and Angelus Silesius (*CW*, II, no. 198) as a basis, Schürmann, *Eckhart ou la joie errante*, 204, construes a "play"—the word is not Eckhart's—between God and the soul in Eckhart. Even so, there is nothing of the ominous wager which belongs to Heidegger's play of Being in Schürmann's hypothesis.

17. Heraclitus, Fragment 52, in Kathleen Freeman, *Ancilla to the Pre-Socratic Philosophers* (Oxford: Basil Blackwell, 1962), 28.

18. Adamczewski's translation of *Ereignis* as "bearing" would therefore be misleading (cf. Zygmunt Adamczewski, "Martin Heidegger and Man's Way to Be," *Man and World* 1 (1968): 369.

19. Laszlo Versenyi has pointed out such difficulties (cf. *Heidegger, Being and Truth* (New Haven: Yale University Press, 1965), 152–58.

20. This seems to mean that the poet experiences Being but he does not express it in the language of the thought of Being (*Seinsdenken*). Hence it is up to the thinker to "translate" the poet.

21. One can hardly close the question of Heidegger and mysticism with an examination of Heidegger's relation to Eckhart. The whole area of his affinities to Eastern mysticism needs to be discussed. Cf. "Heidegger and Eastern Thought," *Philosophy East and West* 20, no. 3 (July 1970). See also Peter Kreeft, "Zen in Heidegger's *Gelassenheit*," *International Philosophical Quarterly* 11, no. 4 (December 1971), 521–45.

6
Heidegger's "Dif-ference" and the Distinction between *Esse* and *Ens* in St. Thomas

The history of Western metaphysics, according to Martin Heidegger, is a centuries-old "oblivion of Being" (*Seinsvergessenheit*), the shadow of which reaches all the way from Anaximander to Nietzsche (*WM*, 1 1/210).[1] If Heidegger himself claims to have recalled Being itself, Being in its truth, Western metaphysics has contented itself with various counterfeits for Being, either with generic categorizations of beings in general, or with a causal first-being, a being which causes other beings. No matter how loudly it protests to the contrary, in metaphysics Being is forsaken in favor of beings. Yet the followers of Thomas Aquinas have argued with equal fervor and a comparable vigor that it is in Thomas Aquinas, and Thomas Aquinas alone, that one finds a genuine philosophy of Being. St. Thomas alone has recognized Being in all its purity *as Being*, has captured Being as the very act-of-existing itself. Outside of his metaphysics there are only various counterfeits of Being: Being as unity (Plato), as *ousia* (Aristotle), as essence (Duns Scotus, Francisco Suarez, modern Rationalism and Idealism). Thus Étienne Gilson has elaborated a remarkable interpretation of the history of metaphysics as a history of *Seinsvergessenheit* from the standpoint of St. Thomas, an account that in many striking ways parallels Heidegger's own interpretations of Western philosophy.[2] Both Gilson and Heidegger are accused of writing the history of philosophy from a bias, but that is because both authors are thinkers, and they are not writing history but philosophy. And the striking thing is that both lay claim to the same land; both insist that they have found the sole access to the region of Being as Being. Outside of their way lies only the "oblivion of Being," lies "essentialism."

I have addressed the problem of these conflicting claims on a previous occasion and with results that the reader can survey for himself. I will not repeat them here.[3] Instead I want to take up the question again, and pursue the matter further, this time from a different standpoint. My argument will unfold in four stages. (1) I will begin with a sketch of how Western metaphysics, by neglecting the distinction between Being and beings, has fallen, in Heidegger's view, into an oblivion of Being; (2) I will then offer a defense of St. Thomas on this point and argue that the distinction between *esse* (Being) and *ens* (beings) is not only found in Aquinas, but his whole metaphysics turns on it; (3) I will then return to Heidegger to test this defense of St. Thomas against Heidegger's notion of the *Aus-trag* or "dif-ference," from which the truly radical character of Heidegger's critique of St. Thomas, and of all metaphysics, will be made plain; (4) finally, I will conclude by offering an interpretation of the relationship between these rivals for the throne of Being as such, an interpretation which does not settle the question but attempts to open it up in the proper way.

THE OBLIVION OF BEING

Let us begin by briefly rehearsing the main themes of Heidegger's interpretation of metaphysics as an oblivion of Being. Metaphysics, he says in his well-known commentary on Descartes's letter to Abbot Picot, is the root of the tree of Philosophy: what then, Heidegger asks, is the nourishing ground of these roots? "What is metaphysics, seen from its ground?" (*WM*, 7/207). He responds: "Metaphysics thinks beings as beings (*das Seiende als Seiende*). Wherever the question is asked what beings are, beings as such stand in view. Metaphysical representation owes this view to the light of Being. The light itself, i.e., that which such thinking experiences as light, does not come within the range of metaphysical thinking; for metaphysics always represents beings only as beings" (*WM*, 7/207).

Whatever metaphysics apprehends, it apprehends through the light of Being, but Being itself remains hidden from it. In its place metaphysics proffers various counterfeits:

> In whatever manner beings are interpreted—whether as spirit, after the fashion of spiritualism; or as matter and force, after the fashion of materialism; or as becoming and life, or idea, will, substance, subject or energeia; or as the eternal recurrence of the same events—every time beings as beings appear in the light of Being . . . when metaphysics gives answers to its questions concerning beings as such, metaphysics speaks out of the unnoticed revealedness of Being. The truth of Being may thus be called the ground in which metaphysics, as the root of the tree of philosophy, is kept and from which it is nourished. (*WM*, 7–8/207–8)

The history of metaphysics is the history of the various historical configurations which Being brings about within beings, while all the time the primordial event (*Ereignis*) by means of which this configuration occurs, the primordial light (*Licht*) by means of which this kind of a clearing (*Lichtung*) is made, remains out of sight. Metaphysics therefore occurs in and as an oblivion of Being; it does not "recall" or "think on" (*andenken*) Being: "Metaphysics, insofar as it always represents only beings as beings, does not recall Being itself" (*WM*, 8/208). And so Heidegger's thought, which comes to pass as the attempt to retrieve these forgotten origins, takes leave of metaphysics: "Insofar as a thinker sets out to experience the ground of metaphysics, insofar as he attempts to recall the truth of Being itself instead of merely representing beings as beings, his thinking has in a sense left metaphysics. From the point of view of metaphysics, such thinking goes back into the ground of metaphysics" (*WM*, 9/208). Now the surprising thing about metaphysics is that all the while that it is speaking only about beings, it gives every impression that it is thinking Being as such: "Metaphysics gives, and seems to confirm, the appearance that it asks and answers the question concerning Being. In fact, metaphysics never answers the question concerning the truth of Being, for it never asks this question. Metaphysics does not ask this question because it thinks of Being only by representing beings as beings. It means all beings as a whole, although it speaks of Being. It refers to Being and means beings as beings. From its beginning to its completion, the propositions of metaphysics have been strangely involved in a persistent confusion of beings and Being" (*WM*, 11/211).

Failing to attain Being itself, and persisting in confusion, metaphysics settles its accounts with beings, and this in either of two ways. First it may replace Being itself with beings in general—generic characterizations of Being drawn from particular groups of beings (life, matter, will, idea, and so on), which Heidegger calls the "beingness" of beings (*Seiendheit*). This is called "ontology." Or else it settles for an account of other beings in terms of a first being—cause of beings, an *ens realissimum*, and this is called "theology." Hence metaphysics is ontotheology (*WM*, 19–20/217–18; *ID*, 120/54).

THE *ESSE/ENS* DISTINCTION IN ST. THOMAS

Does St. Thomas in fact make the distinction which Heidegger claims is left out of all metaphysics? Does he recognize the "ontological difference" between Being and beings? Or does his thought persist in what Heidegger calls a "confusion" of these two orders, so that while Thomists are constantly saying "Being" they mean the being (*das Seiende*), not Being itself (*Sein*)?

The traditional rendering of St. Thomas's metaphysics serves only to confirm Heidegger's worst suspicions. According to this view, the fundamental principles of St. Thomas's thought are the principles of act and potency, which of course he has inherited from Aristotle. Aristotle, it is said, applied these principles to the level of the substantial makeup of a thing (prime matter and substantial form), of accidental change (substance and accidents), and of operation (faculty and operation). The distinctive contribution of St. Thomas is to have seen that there is indeed another level on which these principles apply, that of being (in the sense of *ens*), in which case potency and act mean essence and existence (*esse*). There are two important consequences of taking this kind of approach to St. Thomas. In the first place, it very closely assimilates St. Thomas to Aristotle and reduces the originality of Aquinas to a certain inventiveness in feeling around for a new order in which to "apply" the fundamentally univocal categories of act and potency. And that, as Gilson has shown so clearly, would destroy the unique contribution of Aquinas, who has transcended the categories of Greek metaphysics by reason of his confrontation with the doctrine of creation. The traditional rendering cuts off all access to the revolutionary quality of St. Thomas's notion of *esse*, which, Gilson claims, answers any and all of Heidegger's charges.[4]

Secondly, on this reading of St. Thomas, the notion of *esse* is clearly subordinated to that of *ens*. Let us reflect on this second point a bit further. If we ask the question as to whether St. Thomas subscribed to the difference between Being and beings, we are at a loss to respond. For this amounts to asking whether Thomas distinguishes *esse* (= *Being, Sein, einai*) and ens (= the being, *das Seiende, to on*). Yet when one turns to the texts of St. Thomas one finds that *esse* is distinguished, not from *ens*, but from *essentia*. On this reading both *essentia* and *esse* are taken to be component principles, *principia quo*, in virtue of which the concrete being, the *ens*, is constituted in its being. Metaphysics is defined as the science of *ens qua ens*; the whole focus of the doctrine is on *ens*. It is *ens* that is to be explained; it is *ens* that is thematized by metaphysics. *Esse* becomes the "actual principle" within a coordinate set of intrinsic principles that go to explain *ens*. This account of St. Thomas plays right into Heidegger's hands. What Thomistic metaphysics thematizes is *ens*, the thing which is (*id quod est*), and it offers an "ontological" account (*logos, ratio*) of the "being-ness" (*Seiendheit*) of *ens*, by delineating the intrinsic constitutive principles in virtue of which the *ens* comes to be. *Esse* is a subordinate, component principle in the science of *ens qua ens*.

On this reading, Thomistic metaphysics takes place entirely on the level of *ens*—of the component principles of *ens*, and of the *primum ens* in whom these component principles are identical with one another. There is nothing here to suggest that St. Thomas makes any use at all of a distinction between Being and beings. But this traditional rendering of St. Thomas is very suspect. To begin with, it is inconceivable, as anyone knows who is sensitive to the difference that history makes (as are both Gilson and Heidegger) that a set of categories employed by a Greek philosopher who antedates Thomas Aquinas by fully 1,600 years (over twice the distance that separates us from St. Thomas) could be taken up univocally by the thirteenth-century Dominican friar. And indeed the untenableness of this unhistorical way of thinking about Aquinas is confirmed by the texts themselves. First of all, in the Greek philosopher, the principle of *energeia* was a principle of form (*morphé*), whereas the potential principle signified something indefinite and indeterminate. Form and definiteness belong to the principle of perfection. But for the Christian philosopher, who has his eye on infinity, form belongs to the potential order and it serves only to constrict and restrain the infinity of being itself. For St. Thomas, form—which gives actuality and determination in Aristotle—restricts and contains the act-of-existing (*esse*).[5] Thus the meaning of the terms "actual" and "potential" has been inverted. "Infinity" now signifies actuality and form has become potentiality.

And there is a second difference in St. Thomas's use of the words act and potency. For the Greek philosopher, the potential principle precedes the actual principle in time. Potency—the bronze—preexists the form which it will receive at the hands of the artist. But essence can in no way preexist *esse*. Essence "is nothing before having *esse*."[6] It is absurd to suggest that for St. Thomas essence can somehow or another float about awaiting *esse*. Essence is not at all a potential principle in this sense, but only in the restricted sense of being the receptive principle, the principle which is susceptive of or able "to be." When one reflects upon both of these points, one begins to realize that the Aristotelian vocabulary is here an obstacle to understanding the uniquely metaphysical element in St. Thomas's authentic teaching. In my view, St. Thomas would have done better to have dropped all talk of potency and act here and simply spoken in terms of *esse* and that which receives *esse*. In other words, St. Thomas is not simply extending the application of a univocal set of categories inherited from Aristotle. His thought has shifted to an entirely different plane, the plane of *esse*, of the act-of-being, and he would have done better to drop the conceptual framework which was designed to account for *ousia* not *einai*, substance not being. Had he done so, it would be considerably plainer to the students of Heidegger that the focus of Thomistic metaphysics is on being itself (*ipsum esse*).

The true concern of St. Thomas's metaphysics becomes even plainer when one takes into account his repeated declarations that *ens* takes its meaning from *esse*. *Ens* is a participle which derives from the infinitive *esse*, an infinitive that becomes for him a verbal noun signifying the highest and most perfect actuality of all.[7] Hence he writes that if an entity is called "thing" (*res*), we primarily mean to signify its essence, which is Avicenna's position: "Whereas the name 'being' (*ens*) or what is, is imposed from the very act-of-existence itself (*ipsum esse*)."[8] To say *ens* is to signify a thing primarily in terms of its act of existing. *Ens* always means *ens-in-esse*, the being in its act-of-existing, the being in its being, the Being of beings. Hence the traditional definition of metaphysics as a science of *ens qua ens* (*to on he on*), which St. Thomas takes over verbally from Aristotle, becomes under his hand the science of *ens* in terms of *esse*. For St. Thomas, a philosophy of *ens*, if it is true to its purpose, must become a science of *esse*. Even if he pays lip service to the Aristotelian formula, which Heidegger takes to be a mark of its oblivion inasmuch as it commits metaphysics to the being (*to on*, *ens*) and not Being itself, it is dear that for Thomas Aquinas metaphysics has to do primarily with *esse* and not *ens*, and that it takes *ens* to mean that which has *esse*. It is for this reason that the proper name of God, the *ens* whose *essentia* is *esse*, is *esse* itself.[9] In the case of God, *ens* gives way entirely to *esse*, and it says more about God to say *esse* than to say *ens*. In every creature there is a distinction between its *esse* and its *ens*, for the *ens* is a way of having *esse*. We call a creature a being (*ens*) on the basis of its *esse* (*ens imponitur ab esse*). But with God we no longer make the distinction between ens and *esse*, and so we call him *esse*, indeed *ipsum esse per se subsistens*.

Nor is this merely a linguistic consideration. For the grammatical and verbal priority of *esse* over *ens* leads us to the heart of the Thomistic doctrine, and to the central teaching of St. Thomas as it has been brought to light by the last forty years of Thomistic research.[10] I refer of course to the doctrine of the participation of Being. Stated in its most general terms, this doctrine teaches that every being is a being (*ens*) in virtue of its participation in being itself (*ipsum esse*), whereas God is Being itself in an essential and unparticipated manner (*ipsum esse subsistens*). Thus the central teaching of St. Thomas is the distinction between subsistent Being and finite beings.

It is now clear how St. Thomas is to be extricated from Heidegger's charge of *Seinsvergessenheit*. For if, on the traditional rendering, St. Thomas's thought appeared to be a philosophy of *ens* in which *esse* is subordinate to *ens* as one of its intrinsic co-principles, the more thoughtful re-interpretation of recent years shows that it is clearly a philosophy of *esse*, in which *ens* is subordinated to *esse* as the participated is to the essential, and the imperfect is to the unlimitedly perfect. In other words, the enlivening and central move which St. Thomas makes is to open up the distinction between Being and beings. His thought moves within the element of the ontological difference. One begins to suspect that Heidegger's views of St. Thomas were formed on the basis of the old manual versions of Thomistic metaphysics in which the primacy of *esse* was entirely missed. Had he read this more probing interpretation of Aquinas he would undoubtedly have been led to revise his views and to make an exception of St. Thomas from his sweeping charges about metaphysics.

To reach a better understanding of how St. Thomas makes use of the distinction between Being and beings, let us take a somewhat closer look at his teachings on participation. He writes in the *Summa Theologica*: "Third, just as that which has fire but is not itself fire, is on fire by participation, so that which has existence, but is not existence, is a being-by-participation. But God is His own essence, as was shown above. If, then, He is not His own act-of-being, He will be a being by participation and not by-essence. In that case He will not be the *first* being, which is absurd to say. Therefore God is His own act-of-being, and not only His own essence."[11]

In this passage St. Thomas has shifted his paradigm from the Aristotelian doctrine of intrinsic constitutive principles to the Platonic paradigm of participation. Now God is said to be related to creatures as a pure perfection is related to its imperfect similitudes. God is related to creatures as the sun is related to the things which borrow its light and heat, as fire is related to the things it ignites. But God is not heat or light or any other form, but Being itself. There is only *esse*, for St. Thomas: the subsistent *esse* of God himself and the created entities to which *esse* is communicated. Every such thing as has *esse* points to that which is its own *esse*, beyond which there can be nothing further. The panorama of Being for St. Thomas is the community of *esse* constituted by subsistent *esse* and created *entia*. Because it is a science of *ens* it must become the science of *esse*. It is therefore not ontology, in Heidegger's sense, but rather, if we may be permitted to say "einailogy," the science of the very act of being. And because it is not ontology neither is it theology, in the sense of the highest being which causes other beings. For properly speaking, God is *esse* not *ens*, subsistent *esse* not an *individuum*, an *ens individuale*. To be sure, God is "individual" in the sense that His Being is uncommunicable to others, but not in the sense of being particularized.[12] God is assuredly not "*ein Seiendes*" (a being) as Heidegger means this. Thomas's metaphysics, therefore, is not the disjointed onto-theo-logic of which Heidegger speaks, but a single unified einailogy, a seamless garment which studies *esse* in its subsistent form and *esse* in its received, participated forms.

It could be objected that the doctrine of participation does not really depart from the traditional rendering of St. Thomas and that it is really reducible to the familiar Aristotelian account in terms of act and potency, in which terms Thomas himself often enough expresses it: "Everything which participates in something is composed of something participating and something participated, and the one participating is in potency to the thing participated."[13] And again: "It must be said that everything participated is compared to the thing participating as its act. . . . But participated *esse* is limited to the capacity of the thing participating. Whence God alone is His own *esse*, is pure infinite act. Now in intellectual substances there is a composition of act and potency, not indeed of matter and form, but of form and participated *esse*."[14]

In my view such texts as these show only how Thomas is able to move alternately between the language of Plato and that of Aristotle. And, of course, he is able to reconcile these diverse vocabularies of Being only because he himself stands on higher ground, metaphysically, than either Plato or Aristotle. He is able to effect an *Aufhebung* of the two Greek thinkers only because his thought moves wholly on the plane of Being—*esse*—a sphere which neither Plato nor Aristotle ever properly entered.

His transformation of Aristotle's thought is so thoroughgoing that it is actually misleading, as we have seen above, to articulate his doctrine of Being in terms of act and potency. These concepts belong originally to the Aristotelian interpretation of making and change in the order of sensible being, and they need to be thoroughly overhauled in order to enter the universe of St. Thomas's doctrine of Being. The essential thing in St. Thomas is found in his talk of *esse subsistens* (Being itself) and *esse participatum* (the created being). His genuine doctrine of Being has no need, in my view, even of the word *essentia*, which has a certain tendency in the traditional formulations to assume an equal place along with *esse* in the account of *ens*.[15] One does better to speak of *participans*, that which partakes of *esse*, than of *essentia*. The word *essentia* brings along with it the Suarezian misinterpretation and tends to make of existence something of an afterthought, as Gilson has shown so convincingly. Emerich Coreth has an interesting passage in his *Metaphysics* which brings this out very well:

> For the Suarezian, existence is nothing but the factual state of existing, of being posited, of being real, as contrasted with mere possibility. Such existence has no content, no positive determination, no grade of perfection in being. All of this is contributed only by essence or quiddity. . . . Hence even before it exists, while it is in the state of mere possibility, the existent is already fully determined, it has only to be transferred from the state of possibility into the state of actuality. The essence is not merely, as for the Thomists, an empty structural principle of that which this existent is, but the concrete positive determination of all that which it is. Whereas the Thomists claim that the whole positive content, the degree of perfection in being, derives from being as the principle of positivity, the Suarezians attribute it to the essence, to which existence only adds the state of actuality or reality.[16]

For Thomas, the role of essence is to limit the positive upsurge of being, contain it within certain borders, contract it. A thing is perfect for Thomas insofar as it is (*esse*), not insofar as it is not (*essentia*). But *essentia* is a positive word for a negative structure, an active word for a receptive structure, a perfective term for a principle of imperfection. It is far better replaced by *participans*.

Thomas Aquinas requires a deeper vocabulary of Being than is supplied him by Aristotle (act and potency) and Avicenna (*essentia*). In fact, he requires the Heideggerian vocabulary of Being and beings, *esse* and *ens*. As Gilson writes at the end of *L'Etre et l'essence*:

> Heidegger distinguishes in effect between *être* (*Sein*) and *étant* (*Seiende*). This is the Thomistic distinction

> between *esse* and *ens* (in Italian *essere* and *ente*) which has been erased by French usage, since the word *être* has assumed the two functions of verb and substantive. It is absolutely necessary to return, in metaphysics at least, to the old usage proposed by certain French translators of the Seventeenth century, who render *ens* by *étant*. There is no need for modifying the common usage, since the common language does not assume any metaphysical responsibility. But even if we may be enemies of useless neologisms, we ought to accept this necessary neologism. The present book would have been much clearer if we would have regularly used the word "*étant*" as a translation of *ens* and reserved "*être*" as a translation of *esse*.[17]

The long-standing habit of saying that the fundamental teaching of St. Thomas's metaphysics is that being (*ens*) is composed of essence and existence (*esse*) must be seen to be inadequate in terms of bringing out the full force of what Thomas teaches. For this formulation does not thematize the truly animating insight of Thomas Aquinas into the distinction between Being and beings, *esse* and *ens*, between subsistent Being and created beings.

In recommending this more extreme and streamlined vocabulary of Being, we are of course conscious that Thomas Aquinas expressed himself in the more conventional way, that he himself speaks of *essentia*, *actus*, *potentia* on nearly every page of his published writings. But we are invoking the right of the interpreter to understand a thinker in the light of the ages, in the light of the clarity that the intervening years afford, a light in which the merely external and time-bound elements of a text grow crusty and faded, in which the truly vital elements remain fresh and alive. The interpreter can indeed understand the thinker more perfectly than he understood himself, not because the interpreter is a better thinker than the thinker himself, but because he has the advantage afforded by the intervening years to see the text in its enduring significance and to separate this from what belongs to the idiosyncrasies of the age and the contingent setting of the thinker.

How then can there be any question of *Seinsvergessenheit* in the metaphysics of *esse*? Is it not abundantly clear in Thomas's doctrine of the primacy of *esse*, of the participation of every *ens in ipsum esse*, that we find a philosophy of Being *par excellence*? Thomas proved himself to be acutely aware of the difference between *esse* and *ens*. He has thematized the very act in virtue of which a thing is rather than is not. Does he not offer to us, with his notion of *esse*, a convincing analogue to what Heidegger calls *physis*, that is, the emergent thrust of Being as it rises up in beings, the thrust of a being into Being? How is *physis* different from *esse* properly understood? What sense can there be in Heidegger's talk of the withdrawal of Being from this metaphysics? What else can this charge be than an ignorance of the new understanding of Thomas Aquinas which has emerged in the last forty years, or a dogmatic prejudice against medieval thought?

These questions send us back to the text of Heidegger, against which we must test our renewed appreciation for the thought of St. Thomas.

HEIDEGGER'S DIF-FERENCE *(AUSTRAG)*

Up to now we have formulated Heidegger's position in terms of the distinction between Being and beings, a distinction which in the early works was known as the "ontological difference." In fact, as Heidegger's thought matured, this difference becomes considerably more complex and subtly nuanced. Indeed to adequately express Heidegger's view it is necessary, in my mind, to distinguish two different differences, if you will, or at least two levels of the same difference. Now it has not been difficult to rally to St. Thomas's defense so long as we have had the more straightforward difference between Being and beings in mind. But the terms of this problem are dramatically altered once we turn to Heidegger's more refined formulation of the difference.

Heidegger provides us with an excellent development of his later understanding of the difference in his interpretation of metaphysics in "The Onto-theological Nature of Metaphysics" (*ID*, 107/42), an essay that takes the metaphysics of Hegel as its point of departure. The aim in that essay is to carry out what Heidegger calls the "step back" out of metaphysics into the region of "thought," this in contrast to Hegel who aimed at a sublation (*Aufhebung*) of all previous positions into his own dialectical system. Instead of raising these systems *up* (*auf*), Heidegger is intent on moving *back* (*zurück*) to their unspoken origin. If we are able to carry out the step back, he says, we will enter into a confrontation (*Gegenüber*) with the very source from which a thinker's thought arises (*ID*, 116/50). We will enter the source from which Hegel's metaphysics—and presumably, for our purposes, St. Thomas's, too—arises. The step back is a movement from what the thinker explicitly thought to what is unthought in his thinking (*das Ungedachte*). What is unthought is precisely what is to-be-thought (*das Zudenkende*), for it is that which has fallen into oblivion. Hence, if we can gain access to this unthought source—of St. Thomas's thinking, Thomas's metaphysics—we will know precisely what the element of oblivion is which, Heidegger maintains, envelops St. Thomas's thinking.

Now Heidegger develops the step back by means of two different differences, or two levels of difference. To begin with, there is the straightforward difference, the ontological difference, between Being and beings. Of this Heidegger says: "The difference (*Differenz*) of beings and Being is the area within which metaphysics, Western thinking in the totality of its essence, can be what it is" (*ID*, 117/51). This difference *is* metaphysics. It sets forth the conceptual framework within which metaphysical reflection occurs. To do metaphysics, whether it be Hegelian or Thomistic, is to establish an ontological difference between Being and beings, to understand beings within a certain horizon of Being. All metaphysics is possible only as a distinction between Being and beings. But the task of thought is to step back "out of metaphysics into the essence of metaphysics" (*ID*, 117/51). That means that the step back is a step back out of the difference (*Differenz*) between Being and beings into that which makes the difference possible, to what is differing in the difference, to the difference *as such*. The step back moves from the naive acceptance of the difference into thinking the origin of the difference.

Now metaphysics, we have seen above, is onto-theo-logic. By the step back, then, we can understand how metaphysics arises as onto-theo-logic: "To accept the question as it has been put means however to carry out the step back. In this step we consider the essential origin of the onto-theo-logical structure of metaphysics" (*ID*, 123/56). Hegelian metaphysics, the paradigm which Heidegger uses in this essay, is a "logic." The word logic transliterates the Greek *logos*, which was translated by the Romans as *ratio* and into modern German as *Grund*. As such, Hegel's *Logic* seeks a ground of beings, the most general ground (ontology) and the highest ground (theology). All metaphysics, not just Hegel's, moves within an understanding of Being as ground and of beings as grounded. It thinks the difference between Being and beings in terms of ground and grounded. The onto-theo-logical nature of metaphysics, therefore, rests on a particular conception of the difference between Being and beings.

Heidegger articulates the difference within which metaphysics operates as a twofold process. In the first place, Being, as the Being of beings, gives itself up to beings, comes to pass in and as beings, discloses and reveals itself, un-conceals itself in beings: "Being comes to presence (*west*) here in the mode of a going-over to beings" (*ID*, 132/64). Being "goes over" (*geht über*) or "comes over" (*kommt über*) into beings. Being is the very process of "coming over" (*Überkommnis*). Beings on the other hand do not merely wait there, on the other side as it were, for the coming of Being, as if beings somehow preexist the coming of Being (rather as in St. Thomas *essentia* does not preexist *esse*, and wait for *esse*). Rather beings themselves appear only in and through this coming-over: "Being goes over into, comes unconcealingly over, that which arrives as something unconcealed, only through such a coming-over" (*ID*, 132/64). Thus the coming over of Being into beings is at the same time the coming in (*an-kommen*), the coming-on-the-scene of beings. Beings come on the scene, arrive in appearance, only in the coming-over of Being. The two processes are not only correlate, they are at bottom one; the coming-over of Being into beings is the coming-on (arrival) of beings in Being. Moreover, just as the coming-over of Being is revelatory (*ent-bergend*), so the arrival (coming-on-the-scene) of beings is concealing. For by the coming over Being reveals itself in and through beings, and by the coming on of beings Being itself remains concealed.

This twofold process is called by Heidegger the *Unter-schied*, literally (as the hyphen indicates) the "scission between" Being and beings, or in the Stambaugh translation, the "differentiating." Now in this *Unter-schied* the coming over (*Über-kommnis*) and the arrival (*An-kunft*) "are borne away from and toward one another" (*auseinander-zueinandertragen*), that is, kept apart while bearing in on one another. This process of *auseinander-zuneinander-tragen* Heidegger calls the *Aus-trag*, an expression that appears in this text almost as a shorthand version of the longer phrase. Now *aus-tragen* is the literal German translation of the Latin *de-ferre*, *dif-ferrens*, to carry or bear outside of or away from. Thus we will call the *Aus-trag* the "dif-ferring" in the difference between Being and beings, that which makes the difference between them, that which opens up the difference, holding them apart while sending them to one another in the appropriate manner, so that Being revealingly conceals itself in beings.[18] The differentiating (*Unter-schied*) is thus "the revealing concealing dif-ferring" (*der enterbergend-bergende Austrag*).

Let us try to make Heidegger's meaning somewhat plainer by means of the following diagram:

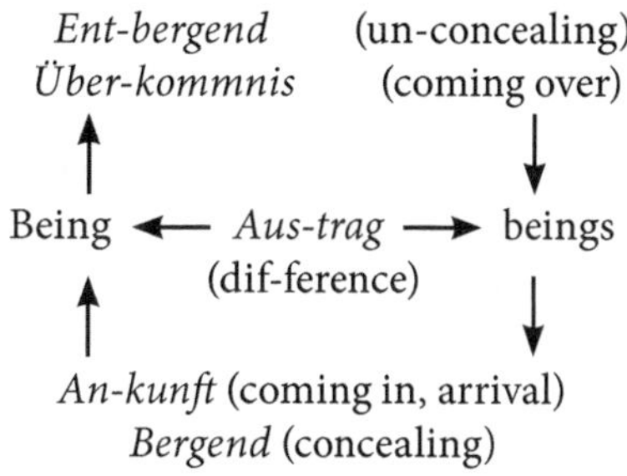

The step back is thus constituted out of two steps. First, there is the step back from beings to Being, the step that establishes the difference (*Differenz*) within which metaphysics occurs. Then there is the radical step back from the *Differenz* that belongs to metaphysics to the *Austrag*, the dif-ferring in the difference. Metaphysics thinks beings in their Being, it thinks the difference between Being and beings, it understands beings in terms of some idea of Being. But it never thinks the origin of this difference, that which makes the difference, that which opens it up as the particular kind of difference which it is.

In terms of Hegel's metaphysics, this means that his thought is possible because "being gives itself only in the light cleared for Hegel's thinking" (*ID*, 135/67). Being gives itself to Hegel, clears itself for him in a special way, a way that is unique to the epoch that makes a clearing for itself in and through Hegel. To understand a particular metaphysical system is to understand how the difference between Being and beings has been cleared and opened up in that thinker and in that epoch. It is to understand "the respective stamp of that difference of Being and beings to which corresponds a respective interpretation of beings as such" (*ID*, 135/67). The character of metaphysics is determined by the character of its understanding of the difference (*Differenz*), something which is in turn determined by the way in which the dif-ferring (*Austrag*) opens up the difference. The dif-ferring (*Austrag*) then is the hidden source, which has long been forgotten, from which the epochs of metaphysics take their origin: "The only thing that now matters for our task is an insight into a possibility of thinking of the difference (Differenz) as the dif-ferring (*Austrag*) so as to clarify to what extent the onto-theo-logical constitution of metaphysics has its essential origin in the dif-ferring (*Austrag*) which begins the history of metaphysics, governs all of its epochs, and yet remains everywhere concealed as the dif-ferring (*Austrag*), and thus forgotten in an oblivion which even escapes itself" (ID, 136/68). What remains in oblivion is then not precisely Being, for the distinction between Being and beings belongs to metaphysics, but the dif-ferring (*Austrag*) which makes this metaphysical difference possible. It is not so much an oblivion of Being as an oblivion of the dif-ference.

In the case of Hegel, then, the difference between Being and beings, which is for him the difference between ground and grounded, is now seen to be the issue of the dif-ferring (*Austrag*). The differing (*Austrag*) holds Being and beings apart, but it also holds them together, so that while Being grounds beings, beings in turn ground Being. Thus original *logos*, which was sent to the early Greeks as the "gathering of what unifies" (*ID*, 137/69), gives itself to onto-theo-logic as the unity of the most general and as the unity deriving from the highest being. The coming over and the arrival, coming on, mutually determine one another and constitute a circle, the circling of Being and beings around one another (*ID*, 138/69), as the above diagram illustrates. The onto-theo-logical nature of metaphysics originates out of an understanding of Being as the ground of beings, and of being—that is, the highest being, God—grounding other beings.

Now it is clear that metaphysics cannot itself comprehend what has been said here about metaphysics, for we have entered the region from which metaphysics has itself originated. And the words of metaphysics are no longer able to express what this thinking has accomplished: "That which bears such a name (*Austrag*) refers our thinking into the region for which the guiding words of metaphysics—Being and beings, ground and grounded—no longer suffice. For what these words name, what the manner of thinking that is guided by them represents, originates as that which differs by virtue of the difference (*Differenz*), the origin of which can no longer be thought within the scope of metaphysics" (*ID*, 136–40/71).

DIF-FERRING (*AUSTRAG*) AND THE DIFFERENCE (*DIFFERENZ*) BETWEEN *ESSE* AND *ENS*

With this account of Heidegger's *Austrag*, or dif-ferring, we find ourselves face to face with the full force of Heidegger's critique of metaphysics, and so with the true point of divergence between Aquinas and Heidegger. For while we have been able to show that St. Thomas does indeed establish a distinction between *esse* and *ens*, and so cannot on that account be charged with *Seinsvergessenheit*, we see now that there is a deeper level to this question which must needs be taken into account.

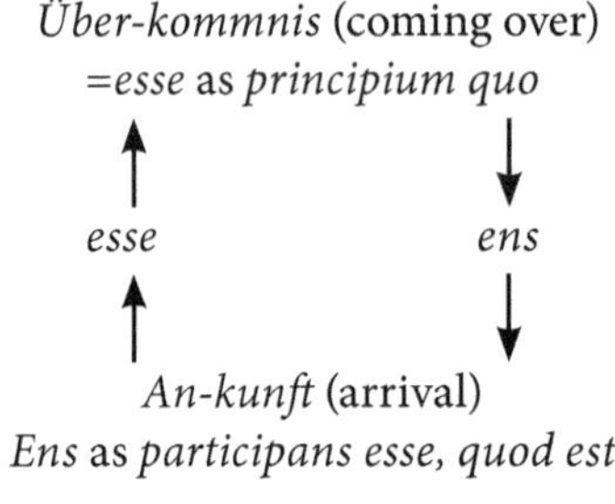

Thomas's thought does indeed move within the distinction between Being and beings, in the sense of *esse* and *ens*. Indeed, in the expression "being is taken from *esse*" (*ens sumitur ab esse*), we can see how the "coming over" and the "arrival" takes place within the framework of the metaphysics of participation. *Esse* comes over into the *ens* and lets it be, that is, renders it present, real, actual, so that the being (*ens*) exists, as St. Thomas often says, "*in rerum natura.*" The being (*ens*) on its part arrives in being (*habens esse*), comes to be in Being, comes to be as something having *esse*. This "participational" structure of Being in St. Thomas proves to be nothing else than this "circling around one another" of *esse* in *ens* and *ens* in *esse*.

Let us apply the above diagram to the metaphysics of *esse*:

The being (*ens*) comes into being (*esse*) in the coming over of *esse* to the *ens*. The *ens* arrives in *esse* by participating in *esse*, by sharing in *esse* itself. *Esse* on the other hand comes over to the being by giving itself to the *ens*. The textual basis for this way of construing St. Thomas is found in his *Commentary on the De Hebdomadibus of Boethius*. There, in one of the more important participation texts, St. Thomas writes: "For running and be-ing (*esse*) are signified in the abstract, as also is whiteness; but that which is (*id quod est*), that is a being (*ens*) and one who runs (*currens*) signify in the concrete, as also does white."[19] He continues: "Thus we are able to say that being (*ens*), or that which is, is, inasmuch as it participates in the act of being (*actus essendi*). Here Thomas is speaking of the concrete *ens* participating in the common perfection of *esse* (*esse in commumi*). But this level of participation is itself made possible only by a more radical participation of created *esse* in subsistent *esse*. Now the circle has become a *similitudo*- process, a circular process in which there occurs a kind of *exitus* and *reditus*:

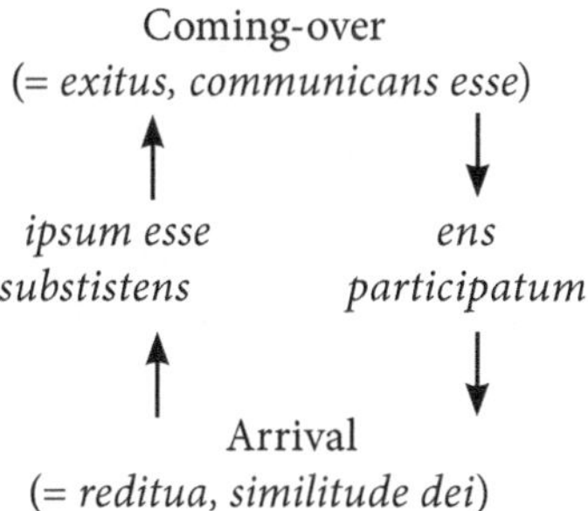

In the first movement God communicates, not his own *esse*, but the likeness of his *esse*, so that there is, as St. Thomas says, a kind of diffusion of the divine being, not in the sense that it is broken up and spread around, but in the sense that its likeness is everywhere reproduced. This is the *exitus* of the divine *esse* into the sphere of beings, the *exitus* of creatures from God, of *ens* from *esse*. In the second movement, creatures arrive in the likeness of God, they come to be by being like Being itself. Indeed their being (*esse*) is their being like to God (*similitudo esse*).

But if there is a difference (*Differenz*) in Thomistic metaphysics, a differentiation of Being and beings, this is no more than is to be expected of a metaphysics, for this is indeed what constitutes the nature of metaphysics. But what is lacking for Thomas Aquinas is any recognition of the *Austrag*, the dif-ferring, that origin from out of which the difference between *esse* and *ens* arises. Thomas's thought moves within the horizon of the difference between *esse* and *ens*, and there is nothing more ultimate in his thought. There is no act, no perfection, more perfect than *esse*. There is nothing more fundamental in the Thomistic universe than the community of *esse*, that is, of *ipsum esse subsistens* and *esse participatum*. St. Thomas's thought moves within the horizon of this difference, but without questioning how this difference opens up, without questioning the dif-ferring in the difference. While he thinks the difference between *esse* and *ens*, he does not think the "between" itself (*ID*, 132/65) which makes the difference.

It can be rejoined from the Thomistic side that such a demand is in principle meaningless. For if in thinking *ipsum esse*, either as the very *esse* of every *ens* or as subsistent *esse* itself, Thomas has succeeded in thinking Being itself, *das Sein selbst*, then the call to think that which is in some way beyond Being is in principle to be rejected. But this rejoinder brings us to the heart of the matter. For we must insist that Heidegger's *Austrag*, or dif-ferring, is a historical- aletheological structure, that is, that it is at once a process of clearing (*Lichtung*) and of historical dispensation (*Geschick*), and thereby a process which makes the Western historical tradition possible. Let us listen to his words: "In the dif-ferring (*Austrag*) there prevails a clearing (*Lichtung*) of what veils and closes itself off" (*ID*, 133/65). Thus the differring is a lighting- process, a clearing process, a process of opening up what in *Being and Time* and in phenomenology generally would be called the "horizon" within which metaphysics takes place. Heidegger continues: "The way in which it, Being, gives itself, is itself determined by the way in which it clears itself. But this way is dispensational (*geschicklich*), an ever epochal stamping (*eine je epochale Prägung*), which is for us only if we release it into the having-been which is proper to it" (*ID*, 135/67).

The *Austrag*, or dif-ferring, is thus the source from which the whole understanding of Being that prevails in any given age has been opened up. It assigns the shape of appearances, the horizon of manifestness, in a given epoch. Thus if we say that the basic structure of appearance, of the way things show themselves for St. Thomas, is the participation of Being, the distinction between subsistent Being and participated being, then this insight, this conceptualization, this articulation of a difference between subsistent and participated, is itself a bestowal of the *Austrag*, a way that the *Austrag* has opened up the difference for him. It is a gift of the historical giving of the *Austrag*, but not the "It" which itself "gives."[20] Heidegger is saying that Thomas has not thought the very process of manifestness, of rising into presence. If Thomas takes the first step from beings to Being, he has not taken the second and truly radical step back, which is required in order to achieve the face to face confrontation (*Gegenüber*) with the very splitting open of Being and beings that is at work in any epoch. In other words, Thomas had not thought *Geschick* and *aletheia*.

But how does Thomas Aquinas think Being? As *esse reale, esse extra animam*, as what in *Being and Time* would be called *Vorhandensein*, which is best translated as "objective presence" (no German hears the word "hand" in *Vorhandensein*).[21] *Esse* is what renders a thing actual, real, *in actu*. It is not that in virtue of which things are manifest, but that in virtue of which they are real. Thomas does not take *esse* as a principle of "presencing" (*Anwesen*) in the Heideggerian sense, that is, as a process of rising up into manifestness out of concealment which, lingering for a while in presence, drops back into concealment. If *esse* is an active upsurge for Thomas, it is not an aletheological upsurge, but an objectivistic analogate to it, a process of coming to be real. The objectivistic structure of this notion of Being is easily discerned by the perfect willingness of St. Thomas to speak of the relationship of Being and beings, God as subsisting Being and participated beings, in causal terms.[22] For Thomas wants to explain, to causally delineate the community of *esse*. If we have objected to calling Thomas's thought an onto-theo-logic, and have insisted that it has instead an einailogical character, it remains true that this thought is "a-logic," that logos for him means objectivistic, causal thinking.

But for Heidegger Being is the very light within which things are manifest, within which the real and ideal, the mental and extramental, both cause and effect, are themselves manifest. It is in what Heidegger calls the clearing that the Greek experience of *einai* and *on*, and the medieval experience of *esse* and *ens*, and the modern experience of ground and grounded, takes place. Unconcealment (*aletheia*) is the primal origin, the originary source of light, from out of which whatever is in any way illuminated is lit up. The *Austrag*, the "*ES gibt*," the "*Ereignis*," "*das Seyn*," or however it is named, is the very process by which every historical clearing is cleared. The aletheological character of Heidegger's *Austrag* (dif-ferring) is at the same time its historical-dispensational (*geschicklich*) character as well. From the point of view of Heidegger's attempt to expose the oblivion into which Western metaphysics has fallen, St. Thomas remains a captive of his times, one who has been victimized by the very ahistorical character which Being has taken on in his own times. He thinks Being as Being gives itself to be thought within the thirteenth century; he thinks within the clearing which has been cleared for him. He does not extricate himself from the historical dispensation granted to his thought in order to see that and how that age was imparted to him. He thinks on the gift of Being and beings in the thirteenth century. He thinks on subsistent Being itself, *ipsum esse subsistens*, but he does not think that primordial source of light which discloses God to him as subsistent Being. He thinks the God of Exodus 3:13 as "He Who IS," but not the historical dispensation which made that particular reading of that text possible only within the horizon of medieval metaphysics.

For Heidegger there are many historical shapes that the clearing can take, many ways that the difference between Being and beings can be opened up. And Thomas has brought one of them to words in the fateful language of medieval scholastic Latin. In so doing St. Thomas responds to the way Being is opened up for him, and that is his greatness. But the oblivion in which his thought is trapped is not lessened by this greatness; in fact, his greatness and his oblivion are one and the same, for this oblivion is no personal defect (*WM*, 11–12/211). He thinks Being as it is given in the medieval epoch, but not the epochal character of Being. He speaks Being as it has been apportioned to him to say, but he does not grasp the apportionment (*moira*) under which he stands. He stands under the dispensation of Being without understanding Being as dispensation (*Seinsgeschick*). The participation of Being is the final word for Thomas and for medieval metaphysics, but it is not the final word for Being itself. For Being itself, or better for the Event (*Ereignis*), for the dif-ference (*Austrag*), it is but an epochal coinage, a particular shape and structure of manifestness. For Being will move on beyond this particular constellation of meanings and transform itself into another coming. The medieval sending already harbors within itself the possibility of modern thought, as Gilson himself has shown better than anyone. It is not the medieval configuration of Being and beings, or the modern configuration, or some synthesis of the two in the manner of an *Aufhebung*, which contains the truth of "Being." It is the step back into the dif-ference (*Austrag*) itself, into the giving of the "it gives," from which the various shapes and manifestations of Being arise, which will alone provide us with an access to what Heidegger means by Being. And it is in the unmindfulness of the dif-ferring (*Austrag*) on the part of Thomas Aquinas and of all metaphysical thinkers, in the failure to carry out the final step back, that the oblivion of which Heidegger speaks consists.

It is perhaps now possible to understand the abyss that divides Heidegger and Aquinas. And it is possible to see why Heidegger's followers are so singularly unmoved by the vigorous protest that is made on behalf of the metaphysics of *esse* against the charge of the oblivion of Being. For no matter how forcefully one asserts that *esse* is an active upsurge into being—and I do think that is an enduring insight of St. Thomas's—one has not gotten to square one in dealing with what Heidegger means by the oblivion of Being. For the oblivion of Being of which Heidegger speaks means that the Being of metaphysics, even of the metaphysics of *esse*, is a gift of a historical sending, an issue of original dif-ferring, and as such the outcome of a more primordial origin which remains essentially unknown to, and in oblivion in, metaphysics.

CONCLUSION

What then are we to conclude about the relationship between Heidegger and Aquinas? Is Aquinas exempt from Heidegger's sweeping interpretation of the history of metaphysics as an oblivion of Being? Not if one understands the full force of Heidegger's critique, as I have tried to show. Aquinas is indeed the philosopher of Being par excellence, as his followers have repeatedly insisted. But Aquinas has left unthought that which gives Being. Indeed as Heidegger says in a note to the *Gesamtausgabe* edition of *Holzwege*, it is not enough to be a "philosopher" of "Being": "The differentiating (*Unter-schied*) is infinitely different (*verschieden*) from all Being (*Sein*) which remains the Being of beings. Consequently it remains inappropriate to still name the difference with 'Being'—be it with or without a 'y' (*Sein* or *Seyn*)."[23]

Beyond the philosophy of Being lies the step back into the forgotten origins of the dif-ference of which philosophy makes use. The oblivion of Being, as we said above, is in the end a misnomer. It is not an oblivion of Being but an oblivion of that which gives Being, of the dif-ference which opens up the way in which Being and beings are given in a particular epoch. And unless one is prepared to do violence to the text of St. Thomas, or to the text of Heidegger, it is not possible to say that St. Thomas recalls what Heidegger says has fallen into oblivion, that *esse* meets what Heidegger requires of the matter to be thought. Thomas Aquinas is separated by a gulf from Heidegger's historical-aletheological method. And it is only by choosing to ignore Heidegger's understanding of Being as a historical event of closure and disclosure that one will be able to reconcile these two thinkers.

Speaking for myself, I believe with Heidegger that Being must always be understood in terms of *phainomenon* and *aletheia*. I am not, however, as I hasten to add, an uncritical admirer of Heidegger's work.[24] And although this is not the place to take up the question of Heidegger's shortcomings, I will say here that, though I am in agreement with much of what Heidegger says about Being as *aletheia* and about the epoch of Being, I have serious difficulties with Heidegger's "dispensation" of Being (*Seinsgeschick*) and with the ominous "it" which gives. While I cannot, as does St. Thomas, subscribe to a deductive and objectivistic science of metaphysics, neither can I think, as does Heidegger, that the disclosure of Being is the doing of the "it gives," of an anonymous "event." I would myself like to see emerge a meditative aletheology which is unencumbered by the mythology of the *Ereignis* and of the *Aus-trag* and which reinstates man as the author of language and of the epochs of Western thought. But this is matter for a later study.

For the present, I want only to end on a promissory note, but not I trust, an empty one. It seems to me that if the confrontation of Heidegger and Aquinas is to be carried out in a meaningful way, this can only be accomplished by means of what Heidegger calls a "retrieval" (*Wiederholung*) of St. Thomas, a retrieval that uncovers the latent aletheological meaning of his work. I mean in part what Josef Pieper meant when he spoke of the "silence" of St.

Thomas. Pieper wrote: "It could be positively maintained that the doctrine of a thinker is precisely '*das im Sagen Ungesagte*,' the unexpressed in what is expressed. That is how Heidegger begins his own interpretation of a Platonic text. The phrase is no doubt deliberately strained, but it is clear that an interpretation which does not reach the unspoken assumptions underlying the actual text must remain, in essence, a misinterpretation, even if in other respects the letter of the text be commented upon with considerable learning; this latter fact may indeed make things worse."[25]

Pieper goes on to say that these assumptions are unexpressed in the text precisely because they are so self-evident to the author that he does not feel compelled to make them explicit. But I should have thought that the most important assumptions of all are those that are hidden from the author himself, which explains somewhat more effectively why they remain unexpressed. Thus, while Pieper's suggestion that the hidden key to Thomas's works is the doctrine of creation is true as far as it goes, it does not, from the point of view of the present study, go far enough. For what we require is a more radically Heideggerian hermeneutic of *esse*, a rethinking of it which disentangles it from the objectivistic treatment it receives in St. Thomas's scholasticism, one that looks for the concealed way in which St. Thomas speaks of Being as *aletheia*, as a rising up into presence, and so one which follows Heidegger's own suggestion: "*Aletheia* could be the word which gives us a hint, one which we still have not experienced, about the unthought of Being of *esse*" (*WM*, 11/210). And while such an understanding was indeed concealed from Aquinas the metaphysician, I believe that Aquinas the man, the saint, has opened the door for such an interpretation. It is St. Thomas himself who puts the causally minded objectivism of his metaphysics of *esse* into question. If we listen carefully to what he says at the end of his life, if we take him at his word, we will be compelled to rethink the whole of what he has said in favor of what he has left unsaid. It is recorded that on the morning of December 6, 1273, shortly after he had finished saying Mass, St. Thomas underwent what we can only regard as a transforming mystical "experience" (*Erfahrung*). After this experience he fell silent. And on one of the rare moments on which he broke this silence St. Thomas said to his friend and secretary Reginald: "All that I have written seems to me nothing but straw compared to what I have seen and what has been revealed to me."[26] These are among the last words that we know St. Thomas to have spoken. And they suggest that the discourse of his scholastic treatises must give way to a different interpretation, one in which *ratio* is transmuted into *intellectus*, *disputatio* into *pietas*, and in which Being as presencing (*Anwesen*) and the upsurge into unconcealedness has replaced the cool objectivism of *esse reale*. They suggest what Heidegger himself has said, that *aletheia* gives the clue to the unthought meaning of *esse*. For these words suggest that Thomas has passed from a speculative knowledge about *ipsum esse subsistens* to an intimate experience of the Godhead, from an objectivistic and detached disclosure about pure Being to the grace of being touched by Being itself. The text contrasts what has been written (in the language of scholasticism) with "seeing" and "being revealed," which is the language of *aletheia*. The Saint compares objectivism with aletheology as straw is compared with something precious. His words suggest that beneath the cool prose of the magister there is embedded a latent mystical content, that the metaphysics of *esse* is a concealed way of speaking of a mystical experience of Being (*Seinserfahrung*).

In some ways, Meister Eckhart, Thomas's Dominican brother and his successor in the Dominican chair at Paris by some twenty-five years, has already shown us how to begin the retrieval of which I speak here, that is, of finding the ultimately mystical meaning of the metaphysics of *esse*.[27] For Meister Eckhart turns the sober texts of St. Thomas into a fiery mysticism. He finds in Thomas's statement that God is his own Being (*deus est suum esse*), the mystical saying that Being is God (*esse est deus*). He finds in St. Thomas's notion that the soul is the root from which its faculties and powers flow, his own notion of the "ground of the soul" (*Seelengrund*), and so on. So we have a guide for this retrieval. And if his retrieval can be carried out, one will find a hitherto unnoticed harmony between *esse* and *aletheia*, a harmony mediated by Meister Eckhart himself who is, to my mind, a vital link between Heidegger and St. Thomas.

NOTES

1. I will use the following abbreviations to refer to Heidegger's works. *WM: Was ist Metaphysik?* 9th ed. (Frankfurt: Klosterman, 1965), translated in English as "The Way Back into the Ground of Metaphysics," trans. W. Kaufmann in *Existentialism from Dostoevsky to Sartre*, ed. W. Kaufmann (Cleveland: Meridian Books, 1956); *ID*: *Identity and Difference*, trans. Joan Stambaugh (New York: Harper & Row, 1975). The German text appears in the appendix. I will give the German pagination first and then the English, separated by a slash.

2. Etienne Gilson, *Being and Some Philosophers*, 2nd ed., corrected and enlarged (Toronto: Pontifical Institute of Medieval Studies, 1952); *L'être et L'essence*, 2nd ed. (Paris: J. Vrin, 1962).

3. See my "The Problem of Being in Heidegger and Aquinas," *The Thomist* 41 (1977): 62–91; and "Fundamental Ontology and the Ontological Difference in Coreth's *Metaphysics*," *Proceedings of the American Catholic Philosophical Association* 51 (Washington, DC: Catholic University, 1977), 28–35.

4. Gilson, *L'être*, 365–77.

5. *De Creaturis Spiritualibus*, art. 1, c. The distinction between St. Thomas's and Aristotle's doctrine of act and potency is given a penetrating formulation by Norris Clarke in "The Limitation of Act of Potency: Aristotelianism or Neoplatonism?" *The New Scholasticism* 26 (1952): 167–94.

6. *De Potentia dei*, III, 3, ad 2m, translated in *An Aquinas Reader*, ed. Mary T. Clark (Garden City: Doubleday Image Books, 1972), 74–75.

7. *Summa Theologica*, I, 3, 4, c., translated by James Anderson, *Treatise on God* (Englewood Cliffs: Prentice Hall, 1963)

8. *Scriptum super Sententiis*, I, d. 8, q. l, a. I (Clark tr., p. 44).

9. *Summa Contra Gentiles*, I, c. 22, n. 236c.

10. For a survey of these developments see Helen James John, *The Thomist Spectrum* (New York: Fordham University Press, 1966).

11. *Summa Theologica*, I, 3, 4, c., p. 10.

12. *Summa Theologica*, I, 29, 3, ad 4m.

13. *Commentarium in libros Physicorum Aristotelis*, XIII, lect. 21, no. 1153.

14. *Summa Theologica*, I, 75, 5, ad 4m.

15. See William Carlo, "The Role of Essence in Existential Metaphysics: A Reappraisal," *International Philosophical Quarterly* 2 (1962): 557–90

16. Emerich Coreth, *Metaphysics*, English edition by Joseph Donceel (New York: Seabury Press, 1972), 81–82.

17. Gilson, *L'être*, 367.

18. I do not find the translation of *Austrag* as "perdurance" very helpful. Fr. Richardson translates it as "issue." See E. Richardson, *Heidegger: Through Phenomenology to Thought* (The Hague: Martinus Nijhoff, 1962), 579n6.

19. In *Librum Boeui de Hebdomadibus exposito*, lect. II, n. 23 (cf. Clark, p. 51).

20. The relationship between the difference between Being and beings and the *Austrag* that is developed in "The Onto-theological Nature of Metaphysics" is also worked out in "Time and Being," in which it is thematized in terms of the "it gives" and the gift of Being. See Martin Heidegger, *On Time and Being*, trans. Joan Stambaugh (New York: Harper & Row, 1972), 1–24.

21. See Joan Stambaugh's translation of the introduction to *Being and Time in Heidegger: Basic Writings*, ed. D. Krell (New York: Harper & Row, 1977), 47.

22. See the texts which Clark has collected on 48.

23. Martin Heidegger, *Gesamtausgabe*, vol. 5, *Hofzwege* (Frankfurt am Main: Klosterman, 1977), 364, note (d).

24. See the last chapter of my book, *The Mystical Element in Heidegger's Thought* (Athens: Ohio University Press, 1978), 218, especially 271.

25. Josef Pieper, *The Silence of St. Thomas*, trans. Daniel O'Connor (London: Faber & Faber, 1957), 52.

26. See ibid., 45–47.

27. This suggestion is made by Bernard Welte, "Thomas von Aquin und Heideggers Gedanke von der Seinsgeschichte," in *Zeit und Geheimnis* (Freiburg: Herder, 1975), 203–19. On the connection between Heidegger and Eckhart, see my book (*The Mystical Element in Heidegger's Thought*, n. 24). On the connection between Aquinas and Eckhart, see my "The Fundamental Themes in Meister Eckhart's Mysticism," *The Thomist* 42 (1978), 197–225.

7
Demythologizing Heidegger: *Alētheia* and the History of Being

Martin Heidegger could never resist a good story. He could never resist giving what he had discovered about *aletheia* and the oblivion of Being a narrative form. In *Being and Time*, we were promised a story—which was to be written backwards—of the "destruction of the history of ontology." Beginning at the end, with Kant, it was to feel its way back through the tradition in a deconstructive gesture, looking for what had all along been blocking the discovery of the temporal meaning of Being which had at last begun to emerge in Kant. In the later works this story is considerably recast. Again, the vantage point is the end, but now the end is the age of the *Gestell*, the enframing, the "end of philosophy," which holds us all in its grip. The end is not conceived as a modern breakthrough but as an *eschaton*, a dead end into which the West has run. The task of thought is to make its way back into the primordial "Beginning" (*Anfang*) in order to recapture that fleeting moment which will make it possible for us today to begin anew, to make the present into an "authentic" end, which means a transition to another beginning.[1]

I want to argue in the present pages that Heidegger's best insights are obscured by his penchant for heroic tales and if privileged epochs, for first dawns and new beginnings. What Heidegger has to say about the history of Being must be understood in critical, not heroic terms. It is necessary to delimit the *mythos*—the story—in the history of Being, in order to get at what *aletheia* means. I am not arguing against the historical side of Heidegger, but rather insisting that historical thinking should serve primarily a critical and strategic, not a hierarchizing and memorializing, purpose. For *aletheia* is not a story but a structure, not a moment in time but a structure constitutive of time, which has to do with the essential oblivion or withdrawal of Being. *Aletheia* can never appear on the stage of history, not in the beginning, the middle, or the end, because it is the very staging, the mise-en-scène, of history.[2]

"Awakening" from the "oblivion" of Being (*Seinsvergessenheit*), accordingly, is not a matter of returning to a primordial beginning in order to find there the secret to a New Dawn.[3] It is rather a raised awareness of the oblivion and its inextinguishability that keeps its distance from historical hierarchies of any sort. The awakening, Heidegger says, consists in a turn *toward* the oblivion, in awakening *from* the oblivion by awakening *to* the oblivion.[4] It is thus a profoundly emancipatory thought that puts us all on the alert for the powers that be, or presume to be, which give themselves airs of ahistorical necessity and immutable presence. It practices a Socratic vigilance about whatever purports to be "present." It is a critical alertness that holds the epochs of Being and presence in question.

This, I argue, makes for rather a more liberated view of Heidegger, one no longer caught in the double bind between two beginnings, too late for the gods and too early for Being,[5] waiting for a god to save us. For this demythologized Heidegger, *a-lētheia* is not a Greek word. The hyphen breaks up its nominal unity, prevents it from belonging to any historical age or language. *A-lētheia* is not the Greek or any other historical master-name of Being but rather the inconspicuous open space within which the history of the names of Being unfolds. *Aletheia* can never appear *in* that space—not at the beginning or the end—for it is the very opening up *of* that space, granting the epochs of presence their space of play.

Consequently, everything I want to say about demythologizing Heidegger turns on his analysis of the history of truth and *aletheia,* which forms the main body of the present study. Then, at the conclusion of this paper, I will reexamine the question of Heidegger's stories to see if they cannot, after all, be reinscribed within the space of a critical history.

I

In the later writings, the privilege that was accorded modernity in *Being and Time* is surrendered and the transcendental determination of time defended there is rejected. The very thing for which Kant was praised—"he was bringing the phenomenon of time back into the subject again"[6]—becomes the reason he is criticized. The whole of modernity is looked upon, not as a period of breakthrough and discovery of the contribution of the subject (and hence of *Dasein*), but as a subjectivizing of Being. Modernity is the age of the *Weltbild*, of the world as picture and representation, as an object for the thinking subject which sets itself up as the measure of all that is and is not.[7] Heidegger's understanding of the history of ontology thus undergoes a profound upheaval. The end of the history of ontology is now the most extreme and radical oblivion of all, the *eschaton*,[8] where the Western tradition has run into a deadly end, an end-state which threatens to destroy man, nature, and the gods, even if the bomb never goes off. Now the history of ontology, or of metaphysics, is read as a steady deterioration or falling away (*Abfall*) from the primordial beginning (*Anfang*).[9]

Accordingly, the "destruction" of the history of ontology, which in *Being and Time* meant an exercise in trouble-shooting, looking for what went wrong somewhere back in the tradition in order to repeat and redo it (*wieder-holen*), is reconceived as a work of recollective thought (*an-denken*) which tries to recover something that has dropped out of sight. Plato and Aristotle are still the source of the trouble, but that is because there is in them a primordial experience of Being which was covered over. Hence Plato and Aristotle are not to be read backwards, from the standpoint of modernity, but forwards, as a falling away from the early Greeks, who now assume the place of historical privilege. Plato and Aristotle block off, not what was to be discovered *later*, but what had been experienced in the primordial beginning which had *preceded* them.

Thus the word *Wiederholung*, which belongs originally to *Being and Time* (actually it belongs to Kierkegaard), where it meant trouble-shooting, rooting out a critical error made at the beginning (Plato and Aristotle), is now transformed into *Andenken*, memorial thinking, that is, thinking back into the originary event of the Western tradition (prior to Plato and Aristotle) and repeating the first beginning. *Andenken* makes it possible to begin anew, with the same originality which characterized the first beginning, and hence to effect "another beginning."

With the recent publication of Heidegger's 1937–38 lectures on the early Greek experience of Being and *aletheia*,[10] we can now get a better picture of what Heidegger meant by the two beginnings, what sort of privilege the early Greeks enjoyed, and what limitations, if any, they experienced. Heidegger is here telling the story of the history of truth. Truth means the truth of assertions when the assertion conforms to the state of affairs about which it speaks; truth is correctness (*Richtigkeit, adequatio, homoiosis*). This conception, which goes all the way back to the beginning of philosophy in Plato and Aristotle, is treated today as self-evident and self-grounding. No attempt is or can be made to verify it—we could hardly check every true assertion against it—but it is taken as "a kind of eidetic insight into what truth must be."[11] Yet, Heidegger argues, *before* an assertion can be made about an entity, the entity itself must be manifest, out in the open. Hence the correctness of assertions presupposes the openness of entities. The self-grounding definition of truth has a concealed ground in the openness of beings. How did this concealed ground get concealed? How did it drop out of view?

The trouble, as we have said, started with Plato and Aristotle. For when they formulated this "definition" of truth, they set off its limits, cut truth down to size for philosophy's purposes, and introduced a formula that could be handed down in a decontextualized form across the centuries. Their recourse to conceptualizing thinking cut this formulation off from its living context, from the Greek experience of Being as the open and manifest realm in which things appear and are manifest. If we look "back" at Plato and Aristotle they appear to be the first ones to have introduced a clear definition of truth as correctness, and everything before them looks fuzzy. But looked at in terms of their own predecessors, they can be seen as producing a "formulation" which presupposes a shared experience of the openness of beings. Hence when Plato and Aristotle said *aletheia* is correctness, we today only hear the half of it. We hear the constriction of *aletheia* to correctness. We do not hear what the Greeks heard in a fully Greek way: that the correctness of assertions arises from and presupposes the manifestness and openness of entities themselves. The Greek view all along presupposes that truth is *homoiosis because* it is first and foremost openness. But only the shorthand, stenographic version was handed down, not the full experience.[12]

Thus the "precision" which Plato and Aristotle lent was in fact a dangerous incision into the essence of truth, incising it precisely at its point of origin—in the Greek experience of *aletheia* as unconcealedness, in accordance with its etymology. Plato and Aristotle are transitional thinkers, effecting a transition from the rich, poetic, experiential thought of their predecessors to the leaner conceptualizations of philosophy. Hence we must read them in the light of their antecedents, in light of the early Greeks. The history of truth in the Greeks must be seen to stretch from Anaximander to Aristotle.

This is not to say, however, that the early Greeks themselves had formulated a notion of truth as un-concealment. That was not their task, their appointed destiny, their need (*Not*). Their greatness lay in raising the question of the being (*das Seiende*) itself. Their vocation was to stay with the thought of the being itself, to persist with that thought, until they found the means to differentiate what is from what is not, as the present and enduring, the well-formed and delimited, which shows itself from itself (*physis*). The being for them is what rises up into well-formed and enduring appearance.[13] Their thinking arises from the sheer wonder (*thaumazein*) that the being emerges into appearance and perdures there.[14]

Now all of this takes place within the horizon (*Umkreis, Gesichtskreis*)[15] of the open space of unconcealment. But it is the being itself, not its unconcealment, which is thematized. *Aletheia* as the realm of unconcealment is the concealed clue, the implicit horizon, the unconceived realm, *within which* the Greek experience of Being unfolds. It was not for them to raise the question of *aletheia* as such, but rather of *to on* "in" its *aletheia* (*on/aletheia*). To have done otherwise would have skewed their destiny, subverted their task. Their vocation was to be the place where thinking, Being, and history itself are set into motion because there erupts in them the question of the being in all its wonder. In the first beginning (*Anfang*), Being is the most question-worthy of all (*Fragwürdigste*), even as today it has been flattened out into a self-evidence and taken without question (*Fraglosig*). And while *aletheia* was the invisible element within which the early Greeks thought, palpably present on every page of their writings, it could never be spoken as such.[16]

It belongs instead to us "late-comers" who live in the wake of the first beginning, at the ending and unraveling of this great beginning, to make the end-state a transition to a new beginning. And the only way to do this is to do again what they did, to think again what they thought. We must recapture the wonder of the beginning by experiencing again the wonder that the being is in its unconcealment. For *us*—though not for them—that means to go back and see what was at work in their experience, to see the implicit clue which functioned in and enlivened the beginning, which is the unspoken element of *aletheia*. We can think *aletheia* as such in a way that *they* could not.

Now the pieces of Heidegger's story are beginning to fall in place. It has a beginning, a middle, and an end—which, if it can become a genuine end, will effect a transition to another beginning. The early Greeks thought the being in its beingness as presence (*Anwesenheit*) within the element of *aletheia* (*on/aletheia*). Plato and Aristotle tried to "sharpen" this up with a "definition" of the link between thinking and the being which left the element of *aletheia* as unconcealment in the background. After that, the oblivion set in with a fury and *aletheia* got Romanized and christened as *veritas*, and then modernized as *certitudo* and *Richtigkeit*. *We* today stand at the end of this long devolution, and *accordingly* we must go back prior to Plato and Aristotle and find out just what was happening in the early Greek experience which gave it its richness and fire, made it the "hearth fire"[17] of the early Greek experience. That, we discover, is the implicit element of *aletheia* within which they were thinking. For the early Greeks had the persistence to stay with the being as it rises into unconcealment and to resist the explanatory mode of thinking (*Erklaren*) introduced by Plato and Aristotle which tries to dominate the being.[18] Instead, they let the being be in its presence as it stands forth unconcealed. That is what we today must learn to do again, at the end of this tradition, at this dangerous moment of decision. So, this is not a Romantic story with a happy ending but a modern one that leaves us hanging in suspense.

But how is it possible for us to begin again if we are so driven by the technological will to manipulate and dominate beings, if the experience of beings in their simple unconcealment is so far removed from us, at an extreme remove (*eschaton*)? We can begin again just by realizing that *our* removal from Being is in fact Being's removal, that is, its withdrawal, from us. This extreme falling out from the early experience, this lack of a *need* to think about Being—because of all the success and prestige that come from dominating beings—arises not from us but from Being. It is Being's own withdrawal that bears the best witness to Being today, in the age when Being has become nothing at all. It is a turning away (*Wendung*) on Being's part that constitutes the neediness (*Not-wendigkeit, Dürftigkeit*) by which we are beset today. If we today feel no need (*Not*) to ask the question of Being, that feeling is just the way we are tuned to Being. If the early Greeks were tuned to Being in wonder, the wonder is for us that we do not wonder. This experience that Being seems to have vacated the premises (*Seinsverlassenheit*), that it is nowhere to be found, is Being's own doing and *our way to Being*. In the first beginning, the task was to raise the question of Being; at the end, the task is to make questionable what at the end of this long tradition has been flattened out into a triviality, a self-evidence, a tautology. Thinking in the technical age means to see in the technical epoch the epochal withdrawal of Being, the *Gestell*.[19]

Were the early Greeks to have raised the question of *aletheia* itself they would have been deflected from their own historical destiny. Their work was to think the being *in* its unconcealment (*on/aletheia*) not *aletheia* as such (*aletheia* as *aletheia*). Inasmuch as *aletheia* provides the space of play within which early Greek thinking unfolds, to put that question itself would be to shatter that space and to disrupt that historical form of life.[20] *Aletheia* functions like a hidden clue, not a manifest theme. *Aletheia* is what it is when it is not to be found, when it constitutes the silence of the opening itself whose sole function is letting-be. But that means that, as the horizon, "*aletheia must* in a certain way be overlooked."[21] *Aletheia* itself cannot appear; it can only be pointed out subsequently as the element within which a given historical form of life unfolds.

II

Now that explains why, in his later publications, Heidegger spoke of the need to think "over and beyond" the early Greeks, to think *aletheia* in a way that is "no longer" Greek.[22] That means to think *aletheia* as such, and not merely the being in its *aletheia*. It is thus of the utmost importance to see the distinction Heidegger is making between the being *in* its *aletheia* (*on/aletheia*) and *aletheia* as such.

The virtue of the early Greeks is that they did not "objectify" the being, which means to turn it into an object for a subject, but rather they let it be what it is, as a self-showing rising into unconcealment (*on/aletheia*): "The Greeks were the first to experience and think of *phainomena* as phenomena. But in that experience it is thoroughly alien to the Greeks to press present being into an opposing objectness; *phainesthai* means to them that a being assumes its radiance, and in that radiance it appears. Thus appearance is still the basic trait of the presence of all present beings, as they rise into unconcealment."[23]

The Greeks experienced the phenomenality of the being, its radiant self-showing. But they left something out. For the experience of the phenomenality of the being presupposes the openness of the open, the open realm of the clearing of Being itself (which is what is meant by *aletheia* as such). Heidegger thus distinguishes two different steps in this regression: (1) from the correctness of assertions to the manifestness of the being (phenomenality; *on/aletheia*); (2) from the manifestness of the being to the openness of Being, to Being as the open, as *Seyn*, as *Lichtung*, *Ereignis* (*aletheia* as such).

Now the story runs like this: For Plato and Aristotle, the definition of truth as the correctness of assertions is made with the openness of beings in the background (and fast dropping out of sight). In the early Greeks, that defining gesture is resisted and the openness of beings (their phenomenality) is savored for what it is. But all of this remains within the *first* step, within the experience of the phenomenality of the being, of the being in its phenomenal unconcealment (*on/aletheia*). Thus nowhere in Greece, in the history of truth from Anaximander to Aristotle, is the second step taken, to *aletheia* as such, as the open clearing. The open remains an implicit, unconceived, unformulated horizon. The Greeks got to phenomenality but they never named the clearing itself: "This unconcealedness comes about in the unconcealment as a clearing; but this clearing itself, as *Ereignis*, remains unthought in every respect. To enter into thinking this unthought [*Ereignis*] means: to pursue more originally what the Greeks have thought, to see it in the source of its reality. To see it so is in its own way Greek, and yet in respect of what it sees is no longer, is never again, Greek."[24] The experience of *aletheia* is thus both Greek and not Greek, and this two-sidedness is of decisive importance. For it prevents Heidegger, at a critical juncture of his thought, from enclosing the *aletheia within* a historical period. The opening of the open is both Greek and not Greek, that is, is "somehow" displayed within the historical limits of a definite era and yet unable either to be found or to be confined there.

There are accordingly two distinguishable senses of the word *aletheia* at work in Heidegger's story. In the first, let us call it the phenomenal sense, *aletheia* means the phenomenality of the being, its self-showing (what is present in its unconcealment, *on/aletheia*), prior to its reduction to an object of an assertion, or later on, to an object for a thinking subject. That is a historical, Greek experience. In the second sense, let us call it here its more radical sense, *aletheia* means the opening up of the realm of the unconcealed, the very granting of the presence of the present. It is useful here to introduce the hyphenated form, *a-lētheia*, for one wants to stress the emergence of the field of presence itself from a radical, intractable concealment.

In the first sense, *aletheia* means the unconcealment that adheres to the presence of what is present, the self-showing being, *phainesthai*. In the second sense, which is withheld from the Greeks, it means that granting which bestows presence in its phenomenality, that opening which, always out of sight, is that *within which* every epoch of presence takes place; it means that a-lethic process which grants the epochs of presence. This is the sense of *aletheia* as such, the unthought element within which early Greek thought took place. In the first sense, *aletheia* means the epoch of presence as phenomenality. In the second sense, it means the granting of the epochs of presence, including the Greek epoch, even the early Greek epoch. More simply still, in the first case it means presence; in the second, that which grants presence.

To put it somewhat pointedly: We might say that in the first sense *aletheia* is a Greek word that describes the Greek epoch of presence as unconcealment (phenomenality). But in the second sense, the hyphenated sense, it is no longer a Greek word and cannot be enclosed within Greek experience, for it is no longer a quality of their experience, no longer a feature *of* the Greek experience of presence, but rather that which grants (gives, bestows, lets be, opens up) the Greek experience of presence as unconcealment (phenomenality). In short, *a-lētheia* is no longer a Greek word. The hyphen breaks up its nominal unity, prevents it from belonging to a particular, epochal, historical language (just as does the crossing out of *Sein* or the attempt to respell *Sein* as *Seyn*).

Now this puts us in a position to understand the controversy about the etymology of *aletheia* and Heidegger's supposed retraction of his interpretation of Plato.[25] Heidegger had written in 1943 that prior to Plato *aletheia* meant unconcealedness, whereas in Plato's own writings a transition begins in which *aletheia* as unconcealment comes to mean *orthotes* or correctness. But in 1969 he concedes that the use of *aletheia* in the sense of the correctness of statements can be found as far back as Homer: "In the scope of this question, we must acknowledge the fact that *aletheia*, unconcealment in the sense of the opening of presence, was originally only experienced as *orthotes*, as the correctness of representations and statements. But then the assertion [in *Plato's Doctrine of Truth*] about the essential transformation of truth, that is from unconcealment to correctness, is also untenable."[26]

To get this straight we have to distinguish three different issues. First, there is the etymological issue, as to whether *aletheia* contains an alpha-privative. That is a purely philological (*historisch*) issue, and on this point Heidegger is probably right, and he has nothing to retract here, although that debate is still going on. In any case, what Heidegger is after would not be affected one way or the other by the outcome of the etymological issue. Secondly, there is the question of linguistic usage (another issue for the science of philology), that is, the question of how, regardless of its etymology, the word was actually used. This is the level on which Heidegger's retraction is offered. He no longer thinks that one should single out Plato as bearing the responsibility for using the word *aletheia* in the sense of correctness. But this is so, not because Plato did indeed take truth as un-concealment, but because Heidegger now thinks that no one uses *aletheia* as un-concealment, whether in poetic, philosophical or everyday usage. That is, truth always is used in the sense of correctness, before and after Plato.

Finally, there is the level of the matter for thought itself, which has nothing to do with scientific philology. On this level, which is the only one Heidegger is concerned with, Heidegger does not retract anything. He does not budge an inch: as a matter for thought, truth as *orthotes*, *homoiosis*, derives from *aletheia*, unconcealment. And so what he said in the thirties remains in place—but with one major exception. He no longer thinks it possible to translate *aletheia* with "truth" ("*Wahrheit*"), for truth *always* means some form of correctness:

> Insofar as truth is understood in the traditional "natural" sense . . . *aletheia*, unconcealment in the sense of the opening, may not be equated with truth. Rather *aletheia*, unconcealment thought as the opening, first grants the possibility of truth. For truth itself, just as Being and thinking, can only be what it is in the element of the opening.
>
> The natural concept of truth does not mean unconcealment, not in the philosophy of the Greeks either.[27]

As a "natural concept," as a word spoken in an historical language, *a-lētheia* (the open) is not to be found. The most we can come up with is *aletheia* as phenomenality. But even this is to be found only as background sense, which starts dropping out with Plato and Aristotle and which means correctness both in ordinary usage and whenever it is thematized. If you *ask* the Greeks what *aletheia* means they will always say correctness, but they will have unconcealment and phenomenality in the background. What neither the Greeks nor anyone else will say, what is nowhere to be found in any natural language, among any historical people, is *a-lētheia*, the opening of presence: "Instead we must say: *Aletheia*, as the opening of presence and presencing in thinking and saying, originally comes under the perspective of *homoiosis* and *adequatio*."[28]

"Truth" always means the relation of presence and thought that constitutes and defines a particular historical age, an epoch of presence, but *aletheia* names the a-lethic process which grants presence (Being) and truth. It is the opening itself, in which all Being (as presence) and all truth (as phenomenality, *veritas*, *certitudo*, *Richtigkeit*) are given and granted. *A-lētheia* means the *es gibt*, the very granting of the historical epochs. The history of the West is the story of the manifold determination s of Being and of truth, of so many accounts of the presence of what is present and of its presence to thought. That historical happening, which is the matter for thought, cannot be contained in, or show up in, some historical epoch because it itself is what contains an historical epoch. It gives the space (*Raum*) within which the plurality of entities belonging to that epoch play themselves out (*Spielraum*).

The disruptive hyphen names the opening of the open. The hyphen breaks up the nominal and natural unity of the word and prevents it from taking up residence within any natural, historical language. Like Derrida's *différance*, *a-lētheia* is neither name nor concept and possesses no nominal unity.[29] "The natural conception of truth does not mean unconcealment, not in the philosophy of the Greeks either."[30] "Natural" (*natürlich*) means historical—as when we speak in English of natural languages, by which we mean languages that exist in historical fact. It also means "natural" in the sense of Husserl's natural attitude, the level we inhabit prior to reflective thematization. Thus Heidegger is saying that no historical language thinks and says *a-letheia* as such. What any given historical language calls truth is something less than *a-letheia*—which grants presence and truth.

Thus it is necessary, structurally necessary, that even the Greeks failed to hear their own word *aletheia*. That follows from the very makeup of *a-letheia* itself. This failure does not arise from carelessness on their part but from the withdrawal of what grants from whatever is granted, even if what is granted is unconcealment as *phainesthai*. The failure arises because *lethe* belongs to the heart of *a-letheia*.[31] *Lethe* means not only concealment but selfsheltering. The opening that grants the shining presence of what is present is itself concealed and sheltered. The matter for thought is not the shining presence of the present but the opening that grants the history of Being and truth, from the early Greek experience of Being, to the experience of Plato and Aristotle, and so on all the way up to the current epoch of the end-state, the deadly and decisive end, the *eschaton*.

The ambiguous privilege of the early Greeks is then nicely encapsulated by Heidegger when he says that we cannot get to the matter for thought unless: "We experience *aletheia* in a Greek manner as unconcealment and then, *above and beyond the Greek*, think it as the opening of self-concealing."[32] Notice the two separate steps: (1) first, the Greek experience of *aletheia*, the return to the ancient beginnings and the Greek experience of *aletheia* as *phainesthai*, the shining gleam of appearances; (2) then, the movement beyond that historical, epochal determination of Being, that historical experience of Being and truth, that historical language called Greek, to *a-lētheia*, the opening of the open, within which every historical epoch occurs and by which it is granted.

Now we can identify the historical "privilege" of the early Greeks: they are the privileged historical portal through which thinking passes in order to get to what is ante-historical, the very *Wesen* or coming to presence of history, which cannot be itself historical. How so? Because *a-letheia* as the open leaves its traces behind in the Greek experience of *aletheia* as *phainesthai*. The Greek *aletheia* is a trace of the originary, more-than-Greek *a-letheia*. But how is that possible? How can that *Wesen* of history, the process of letting history be, which can never be itself something historical, leave its tracks behind in some particular historical epoch? How can Heidegger make this claim stick, given the gulf between the historical experience of the phenomenality of Being in the Greeks (*aletheia* in the first sense) and the ante-historicality of *a-letheia* as the opening? How can any epoch of presence be more marked by the opening, bear more traces of the opening, than any other? How can anything made possible *by* the opening serve as a privileged due *to* the opening?

Heidegger's answer comes in terms of a kind of phenomenology of horizonality. The history of the West is the history of successive epochs of Being and presence, and *a-lētheia* is the element within which that history unfolds, the open space in which a clearing is made for the various epochs of presence—from Anaximander to the present. But *a-letheia*, in virtue of its very structure as *a-letheia*, remains out of sight, and is in a certain way always overlooked—even as it is implicitly at work, functioning. But the advantage the early Greeks had, according to Heidegger, is that this implicit clue was still functioning for them, that it was still a palpable, felt horizon, that everyone felt the power of its granting rather than just taking it for granted. That means that it must show up somehow, somehow leave a trace of itself, that *aletheia does* appear somewhere *inside* the very history which it is otherwise supposed to *grant*, namely, as something implicitly, prethematically experienced, but not thought as such. After all, it is one of the fundamental achievements of phenomenology to have shown how the unthematic, horizontal, functional clues at work in experience are, not "given" or perceived, but co-given or apperceived along with what is thematic. There is no paradox in principle in saying that the early Greeks had a prethematic experience of *a-letheia* and that this implicit border became progressively obscured by the subsequent history of metaphysics that was more taken by what the Greeks made thematic, the Being of beings, than with its implicit horizontal clues.

Now the story that Heidegger tells in his "history of Being" is beginning to look a lot like Husserl's story in "The Origin of Geometry," which both were telling just about the same time (the 1930s). Both stories turn on the notion of an originary experience which became impoverished as a proposition, cut off from its enlivening historical world, and then passed on in its dehydrated form to the subsequent generations who lost its nourishing sense, and that produced the present crisis. Both stories invoke a notion of reactivation, or of "beginning again," doing again for ourselves and in our own way what was done in its own way at the time of the creative beginning (*Anfang*) or primal institution (*Urstiftung*).

But the most telling comparison of all is that both stories have recourse to a kind of a priori history. Suppose we ask ourselves how Heidegger *knows* all this about the early Greeks. He denies that this is a factual, historical matter, a matter of ordinary historical research or "historical inspection" (*historische Betrachtung*). As we have already seen, Heidegger is prepared to believe that, as a factual matter, *aletheia* may turn out not to contain an alpha-privative (which, philologically speaking, would reduce his rendering of the word to a pun). Furthermore, he is prepared to admit that no Greek ever in fact *used* the word *aletheia* in the sense of *a-letheia*. So then how does he know *what* is implicit and prethematic here? He could only have come upon this rendering of the early Greeks, which situates them at the beginning of what is quite a story, by way of *geschichtliche Besinnung*, a meditative-historical thinking in tune with the matter of thought, which thinks in terms of the history of Being.[33]

But such an issue-oriented (*sach-lich*) reading of the early Greeks amounts to a declaration about what the early Greeks *must have meant*, because the "very notion" of truth as correctness issues from a deeper notion of un-concealment. In other words, Heidegger here engages in what Husserl called an a priori sense-history, an a priori history of the genesis of sense, so that Heidegger's early Greeks are beginning to look a lot like Husserl's proto-geometers. But this a priori history is but the flip side of the genetic fallacy. In the genetic fallacy one tries to reduce the validity or meaning of something to the historical circumstances under which it arises; its *historisch* origin is taken to be the basis of its *sachlich* validity. Heidegger follows the opposite tack: because the very meaning of truth as correctness derives ontologically from truth as *aletheia*, there "must" be a historical correlate that instantiates this genesis. Because correctness arises from unconcealment as a matter for thought, that is how it "must have been" historically. Because truth as correctness depends for its condition of possibility upon unconcealment, that is what *aletheia* must have meant before it was historically formulated as correctness. Now if this history is not to be found by means of ordinary historical research (*historisch*), it does yield itself up under a deeper historical meditation (*geschichlliche Besinnung*). And that is the very essence of a transcendental history.

Heidegger cannot resist assigning a historical correlate to this deep structure (the open). He cannot resist rooting around old words for the barely discernible traces of this onto-genesis which "must" be there somewhere. He cannot resist giving the onto-genesis of *orthotes* from *aletheia* the form of a story—whatever the *historisch* case may be. If we can detect this onto-genesis in the word *aletheia* when we meditate upon it in a *sachlich* way (as *a-lētheia*), then we *must* be able to hear it in the old, founding words, the words of elemental power at the beginning and the first dawn.

Now that is the essence of the mythological gesture which I find in Heidegger. It is a myth of origins, of a great beginning, of a great founding act back at the beginning of the tradition, which gives flesh and blood—mythic form—to a philosophical insight. In the beginning was the *logos*, a great flash of early Greek fire and lightning, which vanished quick as a flash, but left an afterglow which steadily diminished over the centuries, until it finally devolved into the present crisis.

It is not very difficult to find places where Heidegger sings a mythic anthem to the early Greek firestorm:

> There was a time when it was not technology alone that bore the name *technē*. Once that revealing that brings forth truth into the splendor of radiant appearing was also called technē.
>
> Once there was a time when the bringing forth of the true into the beautiful was called technē. And the *poiesis* of the fine arts was also called technē.
>
> In Greece, at the outset of the destining of the West, the arts soared to the supreme heights of the revealing granted them. They brought the presence of the gods, brought the dialogue of divine and human destinings, to radiance.
>
> When then was art—perhaps only for that brief but magnificent time?[34]

The whole thing sounds a little like Camelot: "one brief shining moment," and all. (Camelot itself is a grand and enduring story, a point to which I will return at the end at the end of the essay.) But it is rather a tall story too, and easy to debunk—if that is really required. One would not be inclined to sing such anthems to the Greeks if one were writing a history of power—of women, say, or of slaves. The Greek world was built around a set of exclusionary and hierarchical power relations which placed male over female, free man over slave, Greek over non-Greek, of which the divided line provides the metaphysics, and the Pythagorean table of opposites the "early Greek experience." Do women and slaves also share in the clearing? Do the slaves who hauled the stones for the temple also participate in "setting the truth into the work"? How are the excluded present in the open? Heidegger would have had very different results if his perspective were the history of power instead of the poetics of truth. Or indeed if he had chosen to heed other poets than Friedrich Hölderlin, if, for instance, he had actually listened to Georg Trakl instead of making him say what he must have meant, or if he had listened to James Joyce, e e cummings, or Mallarmé.

In fact, Heidegger weaves a marvelous yarn about the early Greeks that is guided by a litany of eminent Germans: in addition to Hölderlin (whence the "Fourfold" and the "two beginnings"), the early Rhineland mystics like Meister Eckhart, mystical poets like Angelus Silesius (*Gelassenheit*), and, let us not forget, Husserl's phenomenological access to the *phainomenon*, the self-showing of what appears. Heidegger chose to listen to Husserl with Greek and poetic ears, and to listen to the Greeks with ears tuned by Hölderlin and Husserl. (This is not a criticism—it is a description of his genius.) Heidegger is exceptionally good at making the early Greek texts dance. He can bring them alive, and he has a feel for them which few can match. But it is possible to listen to others, to nourish and savor and meditatively muse over many texts—from the scriptures, to the writings of the Eastern thinkers, to medieval mystics—and to hear in them a deeper voice, find in them a deeper structure.

I am arguing that Heidegger's view is strengthened, not weakened, if it is disentangled from this story, if it is understood that this story is just a good story, if it is understood that his essential thought is not dependent upon really swallowing such a tall tale.

III

Now let there be no mistake: here is always room for a good story. We do our best teaching and learning in stores. That is why we must come back to Heidegger's stories and the place they in fact have within critical history. Before we do that we must be clear about this breach between critical and memorial history, clear about how austere a picture we are drawing of Heidegger. Hence we must ask ourselves what is left of Heidegger once he has been divested of the splendor of the early Greeks and the tale of the two beginnings. How are we to understand this more austere, more radicalized, demythologized Heidegger?

A-lētheia is not truth and cannot be translated as "truth" because it is that which grants the epochs of truth. It is not Being because it is that which grants Being and presence. Demythologizing Heidegger drives us back to the extremity of the *es gibt* which grants the epochs of presence, so that all "there is" is the springing up of the epochs, the epochal movements, the relentless un-folding of *a-lētheia*.[35] There is no epoch of (*des*) the *Ereignis*, he says, for the epochs spring from (*aus*) the *Ereignis*.[36]

On this reading, Heidegger's thought comes back full circle to its original point of departure. In *Vier Seminare*, the seminar notes mark off three stages along the path of thought.[37] The first is the attempt to think the *meaning* of the Being of beings, to put its finger on the "upon which" that organizes any projection of Being of beings. That was given up because "meaning" is too closely tied to the structure of transcendental subjectivity. Then the effort shifted to locate the "truth" of Being. It is that middle period which we have been trying to demystify, as if the truth of Being implied that somehow, somewhere, some historical people actually thought and experienced Being "in its truth," as if Being actually *has* a singular "truth."

Finally, the seminar says, there is the attempt to think the "place" of Being, its *Ortschaft*, the open space within which Being and time play themselves out, and here the guideword is neither meaning nor truth but *Ereignis*. In the final stage, the task of thought is to think the happening of the place of the epochs, that which grants the space and time of the epochs their play (*Zeit-Spiel-Raum*). Here there is no privileged meaning or truth of Being but only the unfolding of the many meanings and truths of Being across the epochs—none of which can be privileged, from Anaximander to the present.

I say that Heidegger has come full circle here, that there is but one Heidegger, not three, not because I want to deny the developmental, shifting character of the "path of thought," but because I think this path traces out a circle that comes back to a kind of *Ur*-Heidegger, the Heidegger whose path of thought was set in motion by Franz Brentano's book about the manifold sense of beings (*die mannigfache Bedeutung des Seienden*). Heidegger began by asking about the multiple senses of Being and ended up conceding its multiplicity, acknowledging that all there is, is the multiple senses, the manifold unfolding of the senses, meanings, or truths of Being. The truth of Being is the delimitation of truth and the proliferation of truths across the epochs. He began by trying to make a reduction *of* that multiplicity and ended by making a reduction *to* it. He began and ended with the "there is/it gives," the multiple sendings of Being and truth.

Thus, the thinking that is turned toward the *Ereignis* has so radicalized the idea of history, has become itself so radical a thought, that it can no longer be cast as a history of Being in the narratival sense, of telling a story about great beginnings and dangerous turning points. It is precisely by succumbing to this narratival impulse that Heidegger's "history of Being" becomes implicated in *Historie* and chronology and falls into privileging some historical epoch. But what this demythologized Heidegger has in fact accomplished is a description of every epoch in terms of a structurally necessary withdrawal, a moment of *lēthē*, in which the open space itself, the opening up of the open within which a given epoch happens, withdraws from view precisely in order that what is granted in that epoch may come to presence. That means that every epoch is equally epochal, inhabited by the structure of withdrawal, and no epoch can be privileged. On this accounting, "history'" is "leveled," not in the sense that it is decimated, but in the sense that the hierarchizing of the epochs is undone and privileged historical spheres are robbed of their advantages. We get rid of dominating historical mountain peaks, not for a flat plain, but for a populous range of competing peaks. The "danger" on this reading—if we may be granted an eschatological moment—arises precisely from absolutizing *one* of the historical epochs, one of the periods of presence, in particular, to fill up the clearing with a particular and undisplaceable form of presence.

On this reading, *Wiederholung* as a theory of the historical "retrieval" of primordial beginnings is replaced by a more radical "repetition" conceived as the springing up of the different, the emergence of diversity, without hierarchical privilege. Heidegger has isolated the structural withdrawal of the open—*Ereignis, das "Es" das gibt, Austrag*—which precisely makes possible the presence of the present which constitutes a given epoch al sending. What he has isolated is "ontologically" primary—it is what is first in the order of the *Sache selbst*—but it is precisely the most elusive of all in the order of "thinking" because of its very withdrawal.

Now the effect of this discovery is not to rush headlong into hierarchizing the epochs of presence from the radiant splendor of the early Greeks to the filthy smokestacks of the

Gestell, but precisely to see how the prestige of any *particular* epoch of presence has been compromised. Its effect is therefore to drive us from a memorializing to a critical conception of history. As something granted and given, as a partial sending of presence, no epoch has more than transient authority, no epoch sets the rule for another. The only rule the epochs recognize is the rule of justice, of *dikē*, according to Heidegger's fabulous reading of Anaximander, where *dikē* means precisely to let the moments of presence while away. Injustice, *adikia*, results from the stiff-necked persistence of presence which refuses to go under, to give way to another, to give its place to another. *A-dikia* is the refusal to make space for another. And that is what happens when the authority of an epoch asserts itself.[38]

It is not from sheer perversity that I want to bring Heidegger's reading of the early Greek epoch down a notch or two, but from a concern with the matter of thought. The matter for thought is not the early Greek experience of presence—for that is to remain on the level of what is granted—but the granting itself, the open space of the clearing. And the thought of the clearing delimits the prestige of *any* epoch, something which from time to time shows up in Heidegger himself. In the 1930s, some three decades before Kuhn, Heidegger defended Aristotle's theory of falling bodies against Galileo, not because he thought that Aristotle is right and Galileo is wrong, but because he thinks it makes no sense to pass such a judgment which conflates two different epochs of presence.[39] To do so is to put "correct assertions" from different (read: "incommensurable") "worlds" of unconcealment into meaningless combat with each other. To compare Aristotle and Galileo directly on this point is as nonsensical as it would be to rank Aeschylus and Shakespeare. The competition among the various names of Being, the nominal unities of the various epochs of presence, is a lovers' quarrel. We have neither the right nor the means to evaluate the epochs.[40]

It is important to see that, more critically understood, Heidegger is not engaged in a search for the master name of Being. He is instead engaged in underlining the historical contingency and dissolubility of all the master names for Being that have been forthcoming in the history of the West—*eidos*, *ousia*, *esse*, *res*, *Geist*, *Wille zur Macht*. To appreciate the contingency of the epochs of presence is to delimit the authority of all the names of Being and to preserve and shelter the mystery of what withdraws, of the clearing which, while itself never named, is that which grants the names of presence. And that is what it means to keep the question of Being *open*, to let Being waver in questionability, tremble in irresolvability, according to the memorable demand of the first pages of *Being and Time*. It is to make that which has congealed into an easy self-evidence into an uneasy questionability, to transform that which has become a matter of unquestioning assent (*Fraglosigkeit*) into a matter of the deepest questionability (*Fragwürdigkeit*). We keep the question of Being open by letting the epochs of Being and presence rise and fall in the open space of the clearing.

In a "critical" theory of history, the names of Being have only a contingent authority (rather like the contingent necessity of which the scholastics spoke). An epoch of presence is nothing more than a temporary configuration or grid which has been thrown over beings, whose pretense to immutable validity must be kept in check. If history is possible only in virtue of the withdrawal, then the whole of history is the errancy in which the epochs are set adrift. "Error is the space in which history unfolds."[41] The history of Being is the "forgetting" (*lēthē*) of something that never was known. The epochs of presence are but temporary ways of filling the clearing with the brushstrokes of presence, subject to the *dikē* which finally commits it back to the flux.

And that is why the best use of the history of presence is critical, not memorializing. It should be used to play the epochs off each other, to let each be the corrective of the other, to put down the pretensions of one with the successes of the other, to use one to tell stories on the other, critical stories, in an effort, not so much to fuse the horizons as to keep each in check, to humble the pretensions of any one in particular. Historical thinking is necessary but it is necessarily critical.

IV

Only now is it possible to make room for Heidegger's stories—having first delimited them and situated them within a critical history. Demythologizing permits a certain *re*mythologizing.

The narratival impulse is not without a purpose. Heidegger could not have done without his stories. The promise of the "destruction of the history of ontology" gave *Being and Time* a punch that no mere "existentialist" treatise could have mustered up. His fabulous account of the early Greeks and of the lightning flash that lit up the early Greek countryside was a large part of the power of the later Heidegger, and I have my doubts as to whether the later Heidegger would have made half the impact he did had he not spun such a magnificent yarn. After all, not all stories are of equal merit and power. Great stories have power and impact. They have a "moral," make a point, impress upon us an otherwise lost lesson, and vividly embody a purely *sachlich* point.

We do our best teaching and learning in stories, and nobody has ever said that Heidegger was not a great teacher. Heidegger often tried to write poems and with uneven success, perhaps because his real talents lay elsewhere, perhaps because his real skills are narratival, epical (epochal?). He was extremely good at fiction, and I say this without a whit of sarcasm, because I do not situate this remark within a metaphysical opposition of truth and fiction, historical objectivity and fanciful artifacts, unprejudiced factual accounts and wishful thinking. I take it that such historical positivism has long been discredited. We have to do instead with (hi)stories which compete with one another for insight, depth, and persuasive power. Everything is an interpretation.

Heidegger has told a very powerful tale on contemporary technology, one with teeth in it. He very adroitly plays his poetic, Hölderlin-ish world of the early Greeks against the turbines and computers of modern "cybernetics" and the awful, grinding wheels of the *Gestell*. Of course, he very conveniently forgets a long list of the very forgettable things about the early Greek world—from its infant mortality rate to the place it accorded (or better, denied) to women and slaves—but that is part of the rules of the game in good storytelling. We ought to have the good manners not to interrupt a master storyteller with such considerations.

His critique of technology is the most powerful part of his work, the part where everything he has to say comes to a head, where everything is, as he would put it, "gathered together" in the sense of *logos*. It is the tip of Heidegger's pen. Indeed, the confrontation with technology stands at the heart of the "reversal." This critique, almost entirely missing from *Being and Time*—as a matter of fact, *Being and Time* offered a quite positive phenomenological account of science[42]—appears for the first time only in the '30s. Once again, Heidegger starts at the *end*, with what was coming from modernity, but this time with a radically *critical* point of view. Heidegger's reading of history begins with his own time, from his own time, about the needs of his time. Every great thinker regards his time as needy, as a turning point, a point of decision, an *eschaton* wavering between destruction and a new beginning, and wonders whether this darkest night of all is to be the dawn of a new day. Everybody looks back upon the past and sees it leading up to them and then tells a story about how they got there and where the way out is to be found. Thinking is essentially historical (and one can write the history of those who think otherwise). Thinking is essentially *geschichtlich*, that is beginning with the present and worried about the future,[43] an issue of "care," and not merely *historisch, dispassionately* rummaging through the archives of bygone days.

But the point of such storytelling is essentially *critical*. It is a way of delimiting the pretensions of the present, of the powers that be, which take themselves to be present instead of having come to be, which lay claim to the master name, which set themselves up as master. Such historical thinking means to cut them down who give themselves airs of ahistorical importance and permanent presence, showing the earthly genealogy of everyone and everything which purports to have dropped from the sky. Heidegger is writing what Foucault calls a history of the present, a history anchored in a present crisis, telling a certain story about how we have come here and how we can get out, telling a story on the powers that be.

The essence of that story is to be found in the claim that technology issues from the withdrawal, that what comes to presence (*an-wesen*, verbally) in technology is withdrawal.[44] The *Gestell* is the way that presence currently has of filling up the clearing, a way it is granted in, and by the withdrawal of the clearing. Technology is what issues from the invisibility of the clearing; it is not what Being is, but the way it pretends to be, one more way of presencing, but not the granting of presence itself. Technology is not the clearing, not the *Ereignis*, not the *Es gibt*, but rather something given, the presence which has descended upon us in our day. It is but one more master-name with illusions of mastery.

And against this pretentiousness and arrogance, which is indeed dangerous, *the* danger for us in our dangerous times, he tells the tale of another time when things were better, more gentle, when thinking let beings be in their radiance and phenomenality. And that, it seems to me, is to say with all due flourish that there is indeed another possibility for thought, a possibility scattered here and there, among Greek and German mystics and poets, and even, *pace* Heidegger, outside Greece and Germany, perhaps even in North America. There is another relationship to the world in which we do not reduce ourselves to such a ravaging assault upon things. There is the possibility of letting things be, of being captured by the mystery by which the being emerges into Being, by the splendor of the simple.[45] In short, there is the possibility of all the things that Heidegger has been writing about.

The thing (*die Sache*!) is not to be encumbered by the additional and unnecessary burden of taking all this to be the singular privilege of a particular epoch, back at the great beginning, in the first dawn, where once there was a spot which is known as Camelot. The phenomenality of the phenomena, by way of example, is as alive and well in the painting of the French Impressionists as in anything produced by the early Greeks. There is as much radiant splendor of the being in its Being, as much rising up into unconcealment, in Paul Cézanne as there is in Anaximander, and it makes no sense, on Heidegger's own terms, to rank-order them. As a matter of fact, *pace* Meyer Schapiro, Heidegger has already made this point.[46]

The "other possibility" does not come first, before philosophy. It is not something aboriginal, primordial, at the dawn of the *Abend-land*. It is and always has been marginal, excluded, on the fringes, and it always took someone with an exorbitant turn of mind to take it up. Meister Eckhart, who gave Heidegger the word *Gelassenheit* (for which he gets a grudging acknowledgment in Heidegger's book of the same name), was a fringe figure in his day, suspect and eventually excluded by the Roman Curia that twisted his arm into retracting some of his best lines. Thales has become famous for being out of step, extra-ordinary, and *he* lived in the golden dawn. We may assume that the early Greeks exhibited their fair share of pushing and shoving and everydayness and that Thales would have been just delighted if someone had taught him how to convert water into hydroelectrical energy, which is something he believed possible in principle anyway (without having the details at hand). It was ever thus.

Therefore, let us treat this account of the early Greeks as a good story, not a sheer fabrication, because it exploits certain things about the pre-technical world, but which at the same time is not tied to some historical, epochal correlate. Let us remember that all good storytelling requires a conveniently short memory.

Memorial thinking is uncannily good at active forgetting, which is a big part of the way it works. Let us take it for what it is, a philosophical myth, and inch Heidegger a little closer to Plato the mythmaker—which he may not have liked. That, I think, will liberate the considerable power of Heidegger's thought from an enervating nostalgia and new-dawn-ism which makes him the butt of too many good jokes and trivializes his thought. Nothing is accomplished if Heidegger's history of Being is taken to be anything more than a good story with a good punch line. Otherwise we are stranded in a nostalgic longing for a lost world and longing hope for a new dawn, trapped between the two beginnings, too late for the gods and too early for Being, feeling bad that we no longer speak Greek and afraid of being in bad faith if we buy a computer .

Now that is an undeservedly ignoble end for a thinking as powerful as Heidegger's to suffer. In its place, we put a critical history that sets about the work of epochal delimitation, which robustly marks off the epochality and transiency of the diverse names of Being, which shows how every epoch is marked by withdrawal and granting, violence and letting-be, by possibilities for either, *mutatis mutandis*. Every epoch is possessed of its own grace and its own malice. Critical history takes aim at the hierarchy of epochs, levels the peaks and valleys in Being's own history, and claims, in accord with Difference itself (*Unter-Schied*), that the epochs, that wander about in errancy, are not better or worse but only different, that there are only the manifold senses of Being, the manifold ways in which the twofold unfolds, many Beings and many truths, playing themselves out in endless self-differentiation.

In critical history, the history of Being is the history of errancy. The matter for the thought, the springing up of the epochs in virtue of the withdrawal, is thereby released, let be. The history of the effects of the withdrawal is emancipated from the rule of nostalgia and hope, from every *telos* and *eschaton*. Critical history releases the *Geschehen* in *Geschichte*, the *schicken* in *Geschick*. Thinking is released from the hermeneutic demand to decipher the one true message, meaning, truth, and is admitted (*eingelassen*) into the place of the unfolding of the play, of the rising up and passing away of the epochs. There remain only the coming-to-be and passing away of the epochal formations, the unfolding of the twofold, the issue of the *Aus-trag*, describable only and best as a *Spiel*. Here the only *archē* a child-king who rules without why. It plays because it plays, Heidegger says, without ground and without why.[47]

Heidegger wants to think the *a-lētheia* process itself, the unfolding of the manifold epochs of presence, the manifold senses of Being and truth. And he makes it a lovers' quarrel, or a storyteller's prerogative, to take sides with one or the other of these historical configurations, even with *aletheia* itself in the age of the Greeks. What matters for him is the matter for thought that is the mystery of what withdraws and shelters itself behind the epochs that it makes possible. All there is (*es gibt*) is the multiple truths and changing faces of presence, so that the matter for thought is to be "located" in the a-lethic process itself, the dwelling place (*Ortschaft*) of presence.

Demythologizing Heidegger is, like all demythologizing, an attempt to avoid idolatry. It separates out the contingent and mutable structures that metaphysics stretches across the abyss, and it does so precisely in order to shelter what withdraws and to preserve it in the mystery of its play. It sets the play of withdrawal deeper than the contingent configurations in which it issues. It puts the play of the *archē* before the violence of hierarchy and the mystery of the clearing before the idols of presence.[48]

NOTES

1. Martin Heidegger, *Gesamtausgabe*, vol. 45, *Gundfragen der Philosophie: Ausgewahlte "Probleme" der "Logik,"* (Frankfurt: Klostermann, 1984), 145.

2. Martin Heidegger, *Vier Seminare*, translated from the French by C. Ochwadt (Frankfurt: Klostermann, 1977), 104–5.

3. Martin Heidegger, *Gesamtausgabe*, vol. 5, *Holzwege* (Frankfurt: Klostermann, 1971), 327; Martin Heidegger, *Early Greek Thinking*, trans. D. Krell (New York: Harper & Row, 1975), 18.

4. Martin Heidegger, *Zur Sache des Denkens* (Tübingen: Niemeyer, 1969), 31–32; Martin Heidegger, *On Time and Being*, trans. Joan Stambaugh (New York: Harper& Row, 1972), 29–30.

5. Martin Heidegger, *Poetry, Language, Thought*, trans. A. Hofstadter (New York: Harper & Row, 1971), 29–30.

6. Martin Heidegger, *Sein und Zeit*, 10th ed. (Tübingen: Niemeyer, 1971), 24; the translation used is that of E. Robinson and J. MacQuarrie (New York: Harper & Row, 1962), 45.

7. Martin Heidegger, *The Question Concerning Technology and Other Essays*, trans. W. Lovitt (New York: Harper & Row, 1977), 115.

8. Heidegger, Holzwege, 327; Heidegger, *Early Greek Thinking*, 17; cf. Heidegger, *Zur Sache des Denkens*, 63; and Heidegger, *On Time and Being*, 57.

9. Heidegger, *Grundfragen der Philosophie*, 145.

10. Ibid.

11. Ibid., §§ 20–24.

12. Ibid., § 26.

13. Ibid., §§ 30–33.

14. Ibid., §§ 36–39.

15. Ibid., 147.

16. Ibid., 147.

17. Ibid., 146.

18. Ibid., § 38.

19. Ibid., 40.

20. Ibid., 137–38.

21. Ibid., 147.

22. Cf. Heidegger, *Vier Seminare*, 104.

23. Martin Heidegger, *Unterwegs zur Sprache* (Pfullingen: Neske, 1965), 132; Martin Heidegger, *On the Way to Language*, trans. P. Hertz (New York: Harper & Row, 1971), 38.

24. Heidegger, *Unterwegs zur Sprache*, 134–35; Heidegger, *On the Way to Language*, 39.

25. For a careful accounting of this debate, see Robert Bernasconi, *The Question of Language in Heidegger's History of Being* (New York: Humanities Press, 1985), chap. 2. For more on the etymological issue, see Alexander Mourelatos, *The Route of Parmenides* (New Haven: Yale University Press, 1970), 63–67.

26. Heidegger, *Zur Sache des Denkens*, 78; Heidegger, *On Time and Being*, 70.

27. Heidegger, *Zur Sache des Denkens*, 76--77; Heidegger, *On Time and Being*, 69--70.

28. Heidegger, *Zur Sache des Denkens*, 78; Heidegger, *On Time and Being*, 71.

29. See Jacques Derrida's famous essay "Différance" in *Margins of Philosophy*, trans. Alan Bass (Chicago: University of Chicago Press, 1982), 3, 7.

30. Heidegger, *Zur Sache des Denkens*, 77; Heidegger, *On Time and Being*, 70.

31. Heidegger, *Zur Sache des Denkens*, 78; Heidegger, *On Time and Being*, 71.

32. Heidegger, *Zur Sache des Denkens*, 79; Heidegger, *On Time and Being*, 71. Emphasis is mine.

33. Heidegger, *Grundfragen der Philosophie*, § 13.

34. Martin Heidegger, *Die Technik und die Kehre* (Pfullingen: Neske, 1962), 34; Heidegger, *Question Concerning Technology*, 34.

35. Heidegger, *Zur Sache des Denkens*, 20; Heidegger, *On Time and Being*, 19–20.

36. Heidegger, *Vier Seminare*, 105.

37. Ibid., 73, 82–87.

38. Heidegger, Holzwege, 357, 368; Heidegger, *Early Greek Thinking*, 45–46, 54.

39. Heidegger, *Grundfrage der Philosophie*, 51-53; Heidegger, *Question Concerning Technology*, 117–18.

40. Heidegger, *Zur Sache des Denkens*, 62; Heidegger, *On Time and Being*, 56.

41. Heidegger, Holzwege, 337; Heidegger, *Early Greek Thinking*, 26.

42. Heidegger, *Sein und Zeit*, § 69c.

43. Heidegger, *Grundfrage der Philosophie*, § 13.

44. Heidegger, *Question Concerning Technology*, 23–35.

45. Heidegger, *Poetry, Language, Thought*, 7.

46. I am thinking not only of the famous case of Heidegger's admiration for Vincent van Gogh but of his great admiration for Paul Cézanne. See Heinrich Wiegand Petzet, *Auf Einen Stern Zugehen: Begegnungen und Gespräche mit Martin Heidegger (1929–76)* (Frankfurt: Societäts-Verlag, 1983), 143.

47. Martin Heidegger, *Der Satz vom Grund* (Pfullingen: Neske, 1956), 186–88.

48. That is why I think there is an ethics of nonviolence implicit in his critique of metaphysics.

§2

Cold Hermeneutics: From Phenomenology to Deconstruction

8
Hermeneutics as the Recovery of Man

When Constantine Constantius—the Kierkegaardian pseudonym—undertook a return trip to Berlin, he made an experiment in "repetition" which was, I want to argue, of some consequence for hermeneutics. I believe that what we nowadays call "hermeneutics"—Heideggerian and post-Heideggerian hermeneutics—defends the view that repetition is possible and indeed that everything in hermeneutics turns on its possibility. On this account, hermeneutics is always a work of retrieval (*Wiederholung*), a laying out (*auslegen*) which fetches back (*wiederholen*), an explicating which retrieves what is latent and puts it into words for the first time, as Heidegger says (*SZ*, § 63, 314–15/62).[1] Hermeneutics is set on restoring something has remained withdrawn, on bringing out into the open something which has been closed off. And that is what I mean by speaking of hermeneutics as a philosophy of "recovery," from the Latin *recuperare,* which means to recoup, to retrieve or restore, and also to recuperate. It means at once to get back something lost or latent, and also to get "better," to get over an illness (in our case, of the spirit).[2]

Now I will devote my time in the present essay—which is part of a larger project—to the word "recovery" although I appreciate the fact that the word "man" in my title is not uncontroversial, especially today when we not only want to overcome humanism but even to be pitiless about the death of man. I will say here only this much about the word "man" in my title. I stand with Heidegger's *Letter on Humanism*, and I believe that Derrida is right to say that Heidegger's treatise remains in a sense still a species of humanism, albeit of a higher sort. Derrida is right, I think, but I do not take that to be a criticism of Heidegger. I am worried more by the "end of man" than by remaining within a humanism of a higher sort.[3]

The point of the present essay then will be to thematize the project of recovery, to probe and unfold it, and to defend its role in an adequately conceived hermeneutics. I will argue as follows. There are two philosophies of recovery or retrieval which feed into the hermeneutic strategy of *Being and Time*—the Kierkegaardian notion of existential "repetition" and the phenomenological return to beginnings in Husserl. In *Being and Time,* Heidegger demonstrates that these two versions of retrieval are of a piece, that they represent as it were twin circles. I will show that the one circle—existential repetition—belongs to what Kierkegaard calls the "foundering of metaphysics," while Husserlian phenomenology, as Derrida shows so well, remains under the spell of the metaphysics of presence. I will argue that Kierkegaardian repetition controls and decisively modifies the phenomenological element in *Being and Time*,[4] and hence that the hermeneutics which is at work in this book has broken with metaphysics. After Heidegger, hermeneutics means a recovery of origins, a return to the more primordial, which has nothing to do with the "nostalgia for presence" but on the contrary everything to do with what Kierkegaard calls the "courage" for repetition. Finally, without pretending to know what Derrida in the long run wants to say, and fully cognizant that I may be deconstructed on the spot, I want to conclude that Derrida's critique of Heideggerian hermeneutics is misled by the Husserlian element in *Being and Time*. It is a mistake, I will contend, to make the critique of presence into a critique of the whole project of retrieval, and hence a mistake to think that hermeneutics is a matter of the free play of signs—even as it is a mistake for Richard Rorty to think that hermeneutics has to do merely with keeping the lines of communication open between the diverse "language games."[5]

KIERKEGAARD'S EXISTENTIAL REPETITION

The hermeneutic circle is the oldest official—if the office of philosophy was instituted with the Platonic Socrates—philosophical theory about man and knowledge. The Being of the soul is to return whence it came, to recover its origins in the sphere of primordial Being, to recover its lost home in the sphere of pure presence. The Being of the soul is circular, belonging primordially to the super-sensible world, falling into the sensible things, and destined for return.[6] And if the Being of the soul is circular, then knowledge too has a circular structure; knowledge is recollection, the reactivation of a former cognition that has somehow lost its life. Philosophy opened its doors with the doctrine of the circle.

But in Platonism the circle is through and through metaphysical; indeed, Platonism inaugurated metaphysics and it is more or less what metaphysics has meant for over two thousand years. Aristotle made his reputation, in part, by showing what had gone wrong with the Platonic undertaking, but the price of the Aristotelian critique is high—the replacement of the circle with the hypothesis of the *tabula rasa*. What was needed was a thinker with Aristotelian instincts who understood the dynamics of the circle. That, I contend, is what we find in Kierkegaard, and if it is true that it is found in Heidegger, as I think it is, that is in no small measure due to Kierkegaard.[7]

Kierkegaard made a penetrating critique of the metaphysical version of the circle—"recollection"—and opposed it to the authentically Christian version, which was for him the opposite of metaphysics, and this he called "repetition." In the book that bears that title, Constantine Constantius writes: "*Repetition* is a decisive expression for what 'recollection' was for the Greeks. Just as they taught that all knowledge is a recollection, so will modern philosophy teach that the whole of life is a repetition. . . . Repetition and recollection are the same movement, only in opposite directions; for what is recollected has been, is repeated backwards, whereas repetition properly so called is recollected forwards. Therefore repetition, if it is possible, makes a man happy, whereas recollection makes him unhappy" (*Rep.*, 33).[8]

The common problem to which both recollection and repetition are addressed is the transition from time to eternity, and that is why Constantine says that they are the same movement. How does the existing, temporal individual make his way from time to eternity? The Greek solution, Constantine says, is to move *backward*, from time to an eternal preexistence. Now there are two things to be emphasized about this characterization. In the first place, it holds that eternity is, or has been already, present and that its presence has been lost. Eternity is in the past; it is a lost actuality. Secondly, the backward movement signifies for Constantine the attempt to extricate oneself from time, to back oneself *out* of it. That is why in the *Postscript* Johannes Climacus says that Platonic recollection is the "temptation" to recollect oneself out of existence, and that it belongs to the greatness of (the historical) Socrates to have resisted this temptation.[9] Recollection then is a nostalgia for a lost eternity which sees the temporal as copy, imperfection, transiency, and it wants to extricate itself from time by means of speculative thought. Recollection is metaphysics, and metaphysics wants to be disengaged speculation.

Repetition, on the other hand, is the way from time to eternity that is taken by existence itself. Eternity in this sense is not a metaphysical object but a religious goal, the whole point of Christian life. Now for the existing individual eternity is the *vita ventura*, the life which is to come—in this *ventura* we already hear Heidegger's *Zukommen*—the life which is promised to those who fight the good fight, who set their hands to the plow without looking back. That is why Constantine calls repetition a movement forward, not backward. For it does not have to do with a past actuality, with a presence lost, but with a presence which is yet to be realized, with the *possible*. It is not a matter of reawakening a recollection of a previous existence, but of bringing about a new life. In repetition what is to be repeated has not previously existed, has never enjoyed a prior presence, but remains something to be brought about. Consequently, if the backward movement of recollection signifies evasion, escape, disinterest, retreat, then repetition moves forward, presses forth, engages the battle, pushes ahead, resolves upon the one thing necessary and clings to that resolve even unto death. In the Christian conception, time (temporality) is a trial and test that sorts out the wheat from the chaff. If metaphysics wants to think its way out of time, Christian life in time is a test in which every moment is urgent, every moment an occasion for a decisive action, for a decision upon which everything—that is to say, all eternity—hangs in the balance. Whence the Christian sees time in terms of futurity and decisiveness. Christian time is futural; the Christian labors each day for the *vita ventura*, the life that is to come. But in metaphysics time is an imperfection, an imitation, not something to be worked through; it lacks urgency, decisiveness. Nothing is decided in time; the point is rather to transcend time for the sake of eternity, to put it out of action.

Platonic recollection therefore belongs to—indeed inaugurates—the metaphysics of presence. Platonism remains for Kierkegaard under the spell of the Eleatics, whereas Kierkegaard bids us think in terms of *kinesis*, movement.[10] In an astonishing commentary on Aristotelian *kinesis*, Kierkegaard writes in his private papers: "When even Aristotle said that the transition from possibility to actuality is kinesis he was not talking about logical possibility and actuality but about the possibility and actuality of freedom, and therefore he quite rightly posits motion." (*Rep.*, 21) Kierkegaard wants us to think not in terms of permanent presence but in terms of movement where movement means principally existence and freedom.

That is why Kierkegaard sees no essential difference between Platonic and Hegelian recollection, even though Hegel wants to think Being in terms of time and motion. The doctrine of *Aufhebung* does not constitute an essential improvement over *anamnesis*. For Hegelian time is not authentic, radical, Christian temporality, in which everything hinges on the moment, the decision; it is not a time in which we are exposed to the flux and contingency. Hegel's is a time made safe by eternity, underwritten by reason, regulated by necessity. It lacks what is uniquely proper to time: contingency, freedom, exposure to the future. It makes only a show of embracing *kinesis* while in fact subordinating it to a rational teleology of history. Hegel's time is a time reworked by metaphysics, made over into its image and likeness, and in which the groundlessness of radical freedom is covered up (*Rep.*, 20 and 52).

The proper element of repetition is time. Repetition moves through time, grapples with it, exposes itself to the flux. But if it cannot, like recollection, simply negate time and nullify the flux, neither can repetition merely submit to time and turn itself over to the flux. Its unique task is to persevere in time and to maintain its constancy, identity, and continuity. What was a theoretical question for Hume and Kant concerning the "identity" of the epistemological subject became for Kierkegaard the concrete problem of how the existing individual achieves identity as an ethicoreligious agent. Hence, if Kierkegaard wanted a philosophy of *kinesis* and not pure presence, this was to be a kinesis this was to be a *kinesis* with constancy, with identity, with "repetition."[11] The lack of repetition for Kierkegaard means momentariness, opportunism, the inconstancy that busies itself from moment to moment. Just as in Nietzsche's conception of eternal return, in repetition we fuse Being and becoming, not in the fraudulent manner of the Hegelian *Aufhebung* , but existentially, by maintaining constancy within the flux of time.[12]

That also is why the love of repetition is happy, for it presses forward robustly to victory; the happiness of repetition is the exhilaration which comes of an earnest struggle. But the love of recollection is unhappy, for it is a melancholy longing for a lost paradise, dreamy will-lessness. The unhappiness of recollection lies in its nostalgia for a presence lost. Recollection is flaccid and voluptuous, while repetition is courage, reality, the seriousness of life (*Rep.*, 33–35).

Repetition we said, has the courage to impose constancy on the flux, the constancy of the circle in which in the midst of change, we return to the same. It fuses Being and becoming, constancy and novelty. But what precisely is the constancy of the circle of repetition? Does it mean the return of the same, repetition in the *literal* sense? Not at all, for literal repetition remains within the metaphysics of presence; literal repetition is re-presentation, making present again a presence lost. Indeed the point of Constantine's treatise is to show that the attempt to repeat the same, to reenact a moment which is over, is doomed to failure. That is why repetition is impossible on the aesthetic level. One can never repeat a pleasure that has flown by: there are too many contingencies, too many fortuitous contributions for us to be able to bring them all together again; whence aesthetics must practice the rotation method, and it dreads repetition (*Rep.*, 23). Constantine Constantius's return visit to Berlin ends in failure; this whole whimsical tale, Kierkegaard writes, is a parody of true repetition (*Rep.*, 14).

Kierkegaard wants to show that repetition is possible only in the religious sphere, in the sphere of inner man, and that means that it belongs to the category of existence and freedom. It has an existential sense, and it has nothing to do with the recurrence of something present (*vorhanden*). The circle of repetition therefore is the circle in which freedom works itself out. It is the process by which freedom becomes what it already is, by which it becomes itself. Repetition does not mean that we get something external (*vorhanden*) back—that we are able to make present again a presence flown—but that "consciousness (is) raised to the second power" (*Rep.*, 135). It does not signify the repossession of lost goods or even, as Kierkegaard learned to his regret, that one gets one's fiancée back, but rather that one gets one's freedom back.[13] But not precisely "back," for repetition does not move backward; rather one acquires freedom for the first time. But then what is repeated? An innermost potentiality, the latent possibility to be or become oneself, which we have neglected, overlooked, "forgotten." In repetition the existing individual learns that, to regain his soul, he must suffer the loss of the whole world. Repetition is a growth in freedom, a shattering of worldly ambitions and selfish goals in order to be brought back to the one thing necessary, to one's innermost and utmost potentiality.

This is made clear in the young man's use of the story of Job in the second part of the book. Kierkegaard thinks that Job and Abraham—he uses Abraham of course in *Fear and Trembling*—as great as they are, are only fighting out border skirmishes on the outskirts of faith, and are not full-fledged "heroes" of faith (*Rep.*, 115). Their sufferings are only a temporary "trial," and hence a merely probationary period, after which their goods will be restored, made present again. Abraham and Job recuperate their losses—Abraham gets Isaac back, and Job's goods and reputation are also restored. But the condition of true repetition is the permanent loss of presence. Freedom must suffer shipwreck; it must undergo the agony of absence. The genuinely religious individual must be prepared to lose all. In this way he will learn that God, who is the true teacher of repetition, is leading him back to himself, wondrously directing him on a wholly unsuspected course, by means of which he discovers what he did not realize he even sought—himself. He seeks the world but, in losing it, finds himself; he seeks to restore something external and, in the process, recovers his own inner freedom. In Kierkegaardian repetition there is neither a prior presence nor literal recurrence, but rather the emergence of the new from the possible. Repetition is not the re-presentation of a presence lost, as in Platonic *anamnesis*, nor the making explicit of what was necessarily and logically implicit, as in Hegelian *Aufhebung*. It is rather freedom's discovery of itself, a self which was latent, unknown, although it was known all along to God, who has mysteriously led us back to ourselves. We should neither have known it by ourselves, nor found it by ourselves. But it "is" there—where "is" does not mean "present"—all along, calling us, beckoning to us. God alone elicits it from us, prompts us, moves us, casting us down only to lift us up anew, reborn, remade in the new man who has all along stirred within us. Repetition is the self's recovery of itself.

It is clear then, and let us conclude our sketch of Kierkegaard on this point, that the movement of repetition eludes the metaphysics of presence, that it is an overcoming of metaphysics. This is pointed out by Constantine Constantius himself. He writes, "Repetition is the *interest* of metaphysics"—that is, that point in modern thought at which metaphysics realizes that it can no longer remain disinterested speculation—"and at the same time the interest upon which metaphysics founders"—that is, the point at which metaphysics, which is necessarily speculative and necessarily a philosophy of presence, breaks down and gives way to the philosophy of concrete existence (*Rep.*, 53).[14] Metaphysics looks on, with the detachment of the disinterested spectator, at the spectacle of presence. But repetition is not a speculative problem, and it cannot be resolved by speculative means. It does not have to with restoring the fullness of presence but with the abyss of freedom. It has nothing to do with Greek ousiology but with saving oneself only by first losing oneself.[15]

When *Repetition* was translated into German in 1909 in the Diedrichs edition, the Danish title *Gentagelse* was rendered *Wiederholung*, and it was that early German edition, which Heidegger knew, that stands in a decisive way behind the hermeneutic phenomenology of *Being and Time*.[16] Now one cannot proceed directly from Kierkegaard to Heidegger without first passing through Husserl, to whom we turn now. But I have offered this reading of this Kierkegaardian text in order to underline something essential about Heidegger's hermeneutic strategy in *Being and Time*, something that is threatened today by those who, like Rorty and Derrida, often speak as though they were continuing what Heidegger has set in motion.

HUSSERL'S RETURN TO BEGINNINGS

The work of retrieval in *Being and Time* is multilayered. It has to do not only with existential retrieval (it is not only an existential hermeneutic) but also with phenomenological retrieval (it is also a hermeneutic phenomenology). As an existential hermeneutic it wants to recall us to ourselves, to restore our authentic selfhood and being-with others (*Selbstsein, Mit-sein*). As a hermeneutic phenomenology it invokes a new methodological consciousness which says that to philosophize is to recover an understanding in which we already stand. Now if the inspiration of Heidegger's existential hermeneutic is Kierkegaard's notion of repetition, the inspiration of his hermeneutic phenoenology is Husserl's phenomenology, on which account it is proper to regard Husserl's work as a proto-hermeneutics. We have said that the genius of *Being and Time* was to find a way of bringing these two levels of retrieval together and to make of them a single garment. For of themselves they are at odds with one another on the issue of the "metaphysics of presence." Hence we want to see, not only how Heidegger draws upon Husserlian phenomenology in constituting his new hermeneutics, but how the Husserlian element is controlled by the "foundering" or destruction of metaphysics.

Husserl had given an account of perceptual consciousness that maintained that everything in perception turns on the decisive role played by the "horizon" or field to which the perceptual object belongs. We are conscious of the orchestra playing, not of the silence in the rest of the hall; of the film we are viewing, not of the darkness in the theater. The phone ringing in the stillness of the night is alarming even though it is commonplace for the same phone, with the same decibel level, to ring in the middle of a busy day. A word or a sentence taken out of context takes on a wholly new sense. A severed human hand is ghastly, even though it is well preserved and "looks no different" than a living member of a whole body. The facade of a building that is being leveled is no longer the same but stands as a mute testimony to the ravages of urban progress. We pay explicit attention to the object which appears within the bounds of the horizon while the horizon itself remains implicit, playing a decisive but mute role: "The focal is girt about with a 'zone' of the marginal; *the stream of experience can never consist wholly of focal actualities*."[17] The stream of experience is thus a complex of an actual (focal), thematic and an inactual, non-thematic halo that surrounds but decisively affects the structure of the thematic object.

Now it is always possible to shift the arrow of intentional attention away from the focal to the non-focal, and to make the inactual actual. That is the task of reflection. Rays of attention, Husserl says, can be sent by the ego to penetrate the "dimly apprehended depth or fringe of interminate reality," piercing its vagueness and "fetching out" from it the hitherto inactual.[18] And here, in this fetching out (*herausholen*) carried out by transcendental reflection, Heidegger encountered another form of that fetching back (*wiederholen*) that makes the implicit explicit, that turns the phenomenological look from the thematic entity to its implicit horizon. Here, in this Husserlian distinction between actual object and inactual horizon,[19] Heidegger found the housing for the ontological distinction between the entity and its Being that he had learned from his years of study of Scholasticism and Aristotle.

Now it is clear that transcendental horizonal consciousness moves in a circle. It is only in virtue of the prethematic and implicitly grasped horizon that it is possible to grasp an object; yet it is only by scrutinizing our consciousness of the object that we find in it the lines that reach out to the horizon. The work of phenomenology is carried out by moving back and forth between horizon and object, between thematic and prethematic. Nor is there anything vicious in this circle, for the implicit horizon is the *causa essendi* of the thematic object, while our consciousness of the object is the *causa cognoscendi* of our discovery of the horizon. The viciousness of the circle is removed as soon as one takes into account the distinction between implicit and explicit.

Husserl himself considered the work of fetching objects back off the horizon as an infinite task, an idea in the Kantian sense. It is in principle possible, even if it is not so factually, to make the absent horizon present. Whence if the experienced object is a complex of actuality and inactuality, presence and absence, this is not to be conceived in opposition to the principle of all principles, the principle of self-givingness, but as a task imposed upon reflection to bring every component in our experience to explicit consciousness. Derrida would insist, and rightly in our opinion, that Husserl's argument actually worked against his own purposes, and that he had in fact established the opposite: that there is no pure presence, no purely self-giving object, and that presence is only possible on the horizon of absence.[20] It is precisely the absence of the horizon, its implicit, prethematic status, which makes the presence of the object possible. What if, Heidegger would ask, our capacity for reflection, our capacity to convert absence into presence, is finite? What if the infinite task is not merely a dream but a misunderstanding of the facticity of *Dasein*?[21]

Somewhere shortly after 1920, Husserl began to pay more attention to the "world" as the horizon or horizons and, at the same time, to consider the genetic and historical dimensions of his theory of intentionality. This joint emphasis on world and history gave rise to the famous *Lebenswelt* phenomenology that has so decisively influenced Continental philosophers of this century. I want here to pull but one thread in the rich texture of Husserl's later philosophy that is of special importance to the story we are presently telling, which seems to have decisively affected Heidegger's hermeneutics of retrieval, and that is Husserl's theory of predication.

Husserl had always held to the perceptual base of all knowledge, and defended a stratified theory in which higher order objects are founded (*fundiert*) upon the lower order and ultimately perceptual objects. In *Formal and Transcendental Logic*, and especially in *Experience and Judgment*, Husserl traced with meticulous care the lineage of higher order judgments in perceptual experience. Perhaps because of a renewed appreciation for Wilhelm Dilthey, Husserl came to realize that this perceptual base, after it is a perception of material objects, is also a cultural-perceptual world, and hence is historically qualified; the perceptual ground upon which higher-order judgments are founded has a historical coefficient. Not only are the higher-order predications of mathematical physics founded on perception—that had always been his position—but furthermore science has a history and the work of reduction cannot be separated from the history of the formation of scientific judgments. And so when he argued in the *Krisis* that the Galilean science had simply taken over naively and without transcendental reflection on higher-order mathematical cognitions, this constituted a failure in historical retrieval. What is missing in modern physicalist objectivism is a capacity to fetch back the historico-epistemic (a new alliance!) beginnings of its own cognitions. The failure to carry out the reduction now means a failure in historical sense, an incapacity for the historical reduction—which means retrieval, repetition, or, as Husserl puts it, reactivation. Reactivation is Husserlian repetition. Our incapacity for this reduction allows the abstract constructions of modern physics to lead a life of their own, to acquire an autonomous voice, and to speak imperiously to modern man. We have forgotten their origins, forgotten to repeat to their beginnings, and that failure in repetition has precipitated the contemporary crisis.

And so everything in phenomenology turns on retrieval. From the very start, phenomenology meant for Husserl a search for beginnings, for forgotten origins, and the method it used, reduction, *re-ducere*, meant a leading back to beginnings. Reduction, reactivation—these are the Husserlian versions of recovery and repetition. What is reduction if not retrieval? And what is the naïveté of the natural attitude if not forgetfulness? The transcendental ego leads an anonymous life, forgotten in the midst of our preoccupation with the natural life that it makes possible. We live out our intentional life, inhabit our intentional acts, without heeding the transcendental activity that gives shape to our world. And transcendental phenomenology recalls us out of this oblivion, back to the hidden and forgotten origins of our world. If transcendental phenomenology always had a genetic sense, it was inevitable that it would finally take a historical turn; hence there could have been no more consistent outcome to Husserl's development.[22] Transcendental reduction was all along destined to become historical retrieval.

But what is the character of this retrieval? Does it amount to a making-present-again, a literal representation, or is it a repetition that endures the loss of absence? I think it is to Derrida's credit to have shown that this phenomenology remains a captive of the metaphysics of presence. We have already seen how this was the case with the phenomenology of horizons; and it is also the case with the task of historical retrieval. This I take to have been ably demonstrated in Derrida's commentary on "The Origin of Geometry."[23] In the historical reduction, everything turns on leading the higher-order structures back to their foundations in the living present, in the primordial perceptual experiences of the first geometers who first gave sense to our inherited mathematical idealizations. At the beginning of our scientific tradition there lie rich and pregnant experiences that have nourished the whole subsequent history. It is all a matter of returning to this limpid moment—one that we can determine a priori without recourse to factual information; this is the way it "must have been"—in which a light dawned upon the first geometer and he was motivated to pass from a practical concern to an idealized reconstruction of it. Here was a moment of transcendental truth, now long forgotten and buried over by a history of neglect and naïveté. The transcendental-historical reduction breaks the spell of this naïveté and we reenter the region of pristine light.

The reduction turns out to be recollection in the Kierkegaardian sense, recapturing a lost world, moving backward to a former presence, reinstating a past actuality. The circle moves from presence to absence, and from absence to presence restored. The work of phenomenology is to make present again what has lost its presence. Now on this point—which goes to the heart of the thesis of this paper—we must say that Kierkegaard was the more radical thinker who understood that repetition in the literal sense is impossible. One cannot restore a presence lost. That is the illusion of metaphysics. Kierkegaard understood the foundering of metaphysics; his "thunderstorm" had taught him the limitations of repetition. Constantine Constantius had undertaken repetition—if we may paraphrase Merleau Ponty's famous remark about the reduction—precisely in order to discover the impossibility of carrying it out literally. He learned that repetition must become a more oblique recovery, one which instead of retrieving pure presence learns to endure the harshest absence.

HEIDEGGER'S HERMENEUTICS OF RETRIEVAL

What Heidegger says in *Being and Time* was that the two philosophies of retrieval by which he had been affected so deeply—Kierkegaard's philosophy of repetition and Husserl's return to beginnings—belonged together. He saw that the circle of repetition, the self's recovery of itself, belonged together with the circle of understanding, the phenomenological recovery of the implicit and prethematic. He saw that the existential-ontological recovery, by which *Dasein* hands itself back to itself futurally, is of a piece with the hermeneutic-phenomenological recovery. The philosophy of retrieval provides a determination not only of the Being of man but also of the method of investigation[24] whence there are always two tiers of retrieval at work in the existential analytic, two distinguishable but related circles—the one ontological, the other methodological; the one existential and the other hermeneutic. And each mirrors the other. The ontological circle grounds the hermeneutic; and the hermeneutic circle befits a being with the Being of *Dasein*.

We have seen, however, that in their original and native settings—in Kierkegaard and in Husserl—these philosophies of retrieval are not of a kind. For the one, Kierkegaard's, has made a breach with the metaphysics of presence, and the other, Husserl's, wants to make present again the anonymous ego, the sedimented sense, the implicit horizon, to bring everything into the clarity of a philosophy of intuition and self-givenness. And so we want to interrogate *Being and Time* as to the sense of the retrieval that is at work there, as to the character of the hermeneutics that it practices and its relationship to metaphysics. Is this a retrieval in the traditional metaphysical sense, which wants to reinstate a lost presence and bring it into the light of the day—as the word "phenomenology" indicates—or has it made its break with metaphysics so that it understands the loss of presence?

Now it has been our contention all along that the relationship of Heidegger to Kierkegaard is much more intimate than either Heidegger himself or his commentators have been prepared to admit. In our view, the genius of Kierkegaard, the academic renegade and tormented "exception," is amplified by the genius of Heidegger, the German professor, a species about whom Kierkegaard had not a few things to say. We want to show that Heidegger's proximity to Kierkegaard is the controlling element on this question of retrieval and that his hermeneutics is not a philosophy of presence. In *Being and Time* there is, of course, no question of making one's way from time to eternity, but rather from fallenness and inauthentic time to authentic being-a-self. The *vita ventura* becomes authentic futurity. But structurally the positions are the same: the call of conscience is a call back to our thrown Being-in-the-world. The caller of the call of conscience is *Dasein* itself (in its authentic Being), and that which is called is also *Dasein* itself (in its inauthenticity), and what is said to *Dasein* in the call is to become itself, to be the being which it already is, to take up its authentic potentiality for Being. Here there is an existential circle: *Dasein* calls itself to become itself. Just as in Kierkegaard, *Dasein* is not Being but *kinesis*, and the structure of the movement is circular: from *Dasein* to *Dasein*, to become the being which we already are, to be (*wesen*, taken verbally) that which we have been all along (*gewesen*).

It is in virtue of this existential circularity of *Dasein*'s Being that Heidegger can claim both that authenticity is a modification of inauthenticity, and also that inauthenticity is a modification of authenticity (cf. *SZ*, § 27, 130/168, and § 64, 317/365). Ontologically, in the order of Being, inauthenticity is a falling out of, and hence derivative from, authenticity: in its average day-to-day-ness, *Dasein* fails to be true to its ontological makeup and falls in among things. But on the other hand, ontically and factually, authenticity is a modification of inauthenticity: finding itself factually dispersed among things, the transition to authenticity is a movement back to existential-ontological Being, a retrieval of its thrown-projection into the world.

Now the essential point here, for our purposes, is that this recovery is not to be construed as making-present-again of a lost presence; it is not the restoration of a past actuality. On the contrary, it does not recover presence but absence; it recovers *Dasein*'s own absence from which it has all along been in flight.[25] The call says "nothing," precisely so: no-thing. It recalls *Dasein* to the brute contingency of its Being, the thrownness about the origin of which *Dasein* has nothing to say. It recalls *Dasein* to the nothingness of its potentiality for Being: *Dasein* is all along a null project, a project into death, running forth (*vorlaufen*) into the end. This is a recovery that *Dasein* would just as soon forgo. This is no return ticket for a trip to Berlin but an invitation to take up the anxiety of Abraham and Job. It is more like the *memento mori* of Christianity, enjoining us to recall our finitude and death. This is a retrieval of absence, of the abyss. Inauthenticity on the other hand clings to the present, the actual, and it moves like the aesthete in volume 1 of *Either/Or* from one actuality to the next, practicing the rotation method, avoiding true repetition in favor of the curiosity of the ever-new. But authentic *Dasein*, which has the courage for anxiety, the courage of repetition, recovers the absence which underlies this presence; it breaks the grip of the actual upon its Being and, in so doing, recovers its freedom. The freedom of

Dasein is that it is no longer held fast by the actual; it is a transcendence beyond things that stretches out into the Nothing.[26]

This is not to say that *Dasein*'s freedom is an impotent brooding over finitude, that it is nihilism or Stoic freedom. On the contrary, freedom is a taking action that liberates the possible (*SZ*, § 59, 294/340–41). Hence, in the breach with everyday *Dasein*'s preoccupation with the actual (presence), in order to confront its own nothingness (absence), *Dasein* uncovers the true Being of the possible. The Being of *Dasein* is neither presence (*Vorhandensein*) nor absence, but possibility (*Seinkönnen*). *Dasein* projects itself into a potentiality for Being, not a free-floating and wholly untrammeled possibility, but a possibility into which it has been thrown. *Dasein*'s recovery of itself, its self-retrieval (*Wiederholung*), is then not a recollection of a previous state as in Platonism, nor a reactivation in Husserl's sense, which makes actual again. On the contrary the initiation of something new, a retrieval in which *Dasein* discovers (uncovers, recovers) what it is capable of, what it has all along been "sent" to do. We must hear the *schicken* in Heidegger's use of the words *Schicksal* and *Geschick* in *Being and Time*. These words have nothing to do with fate and determinism, but with sending, *mittere*, mission. The authenticity of *Dasein* lies in retrieving what it has been sent or commissioned to do in this historical situation, in taking up that for which it has all along been sent. Recovery is the repetition of the possible (*SZ*, § 74).

Just as in Kierkegaard, repetition does not consist in restoring a lost possession—it does not mean we get the girl back. Rather, we are led by it into a new sphere, one that is unexpected, unforeseen, previously unknown, but yet somehow always mysteriously familiar, obliquely and darkly pre-understood. And we are brought into this sphere not solely by our own resources. For, as in Kierkegaard, *Dasein* requires a teacher of repetition. If in Kierkegaard this teacher is God, in Heidegger it is the historical situation itself, the movement of history in which and by which we see the traces and hear the echoes of a forgotten possibility, a possibility that can indeed be felt only by those who have the eyes to see and the ears to hear, that is, by resolute *Dasein* bent on recovering itself.[27]

We are now in a position to situate Heidegger's hermeneutic method in *Being and Time*. I want now to show that Heidegger's hermeneutics is through and through a philosophy of retrieval, and hence that the methodology of *Being and Time* is a mirror image of its ontology. And I then want to argue that this means that the Kierkegaardian moment controls the Husserlian, that the ontology of finitude modifies the phenomenology of presence, reshapes it and gives it a new sense, which nowadays goes under the name of "hermeneutic phenomenology."

Ontologically, the call of conscience is a call *back* from inauthenticity and fallenness; methodologically, hermeneutic phenomenology reverses the movement of fallenness in order to make its way *back* to *Dasein*'s authentic constitution. *Dasein*'s Being is characterized by a certain drift or tendency to fall in among things, to degenerate in the literal sense of becoming more and more removed from its origins.[28] We tend to drift further and further from ourselves, ontologically, even though ontically we are this very being. But if fallenness is a certain *Zug*—drift, pull, tendency—then hermeneutics must be the *Gegenzug*, the counter-pull, the counter-tendency; any adequate interpretation of *Dasein* can come about only by countering this tendency, reversing this drift, wrenching *Dasein* in the opposite direction. That means that interpretation, *Aus-legung*, is a forceful setting free (*Freilegung*) of *Dasein* which checks its tendency to fall and makes its way back to its primordial or originary (*ursprünglich*) makeup: "The setting free of *Dasein*'s primordial Being (*ursprünglichen Seins*) must rather be *wrested* from *Dasein* by following the *counter-tendency* (*im Gegen-zug*) from that taken by the falling ontico-ontological tendency of interpretation" (SZ, § 63, 311/359).

On the existential level, authentically being oneself (*eigentliches Selbstein*) is the counter-tendency to inauthentically being like everyone else (*das "Man"*). On the hermeneutic level—that is, on the level of a thematic interpretation such as is undertaken by the author of *Being and Time*—an authentic interpretation of *Dasein* in terms of existence and temporality is the counter-tendency to a falling interpretation of *Dasein* in terms of presence. Our prethematic fallenness (as existing beings) is mirrored in a fallen ontology. If on the prethematic level fallen *Dasein* takes refuge in the *actual*, then on the level of an explicit hermeneutic thematization this results in a metaphysics of presence. Hence we need an interpretative moment which corresponds on the hermeneutic level to existential resoluteness, which cuts through the ontology of presence even as resoluteness breaks the grip of the actual. That is what Heidegger means by hermeneutics, and that is why hermeneutics is this counter-tendency (*Gegenzug*).

This mirroring of anticipatory resoluteness in hermeneutics also explains why hermeneutics proceeds by way of fore-structures.[29] The methodological forestructure, the preunderstanding, reflects the existential-ontological being-ahead-of-itself; *Vorstruktur* reflects *Vorwegsein*. Hermeneutic fore-structures cut through the disguises of fallness and make their way back to *Dasein*'s originary structure, even as resoluteness returns *Dasein* to itself. They are a movement *back* to *Dasein*'s structure precisely because they are a projective movement *forward*. Inasmuch as they projectively sketch ahead the horizon within which *Dasein* (or whatever being is under interpretation) can appear, they are at the same time a movement back to *Dasein*'s concealed Being. The forestructures carry out the regress. To mimic the later Heidegger: *Vorstruktur und Rückgang: dasselbe*. Here then is the dynamics of the circle: the fall into the dominant ontology of presence is a falling out, an *exitus*, an ontological de-generation, while the hermeneutic projection is a *reditus*, return, retrieval. Hermeneutics is the thematic recovery of *Dasein*, even as resoluteness is its prethematic recovery.[30] Hermeneutics is methodological repetition, even as resoluteness is existential repetition.[31]

But what guarantee is there that the projective forestructures effect the *reditus*, that they manage to recapture the being in its primordial Being, that they are drawn from the things themselves and are not arbitrary fancies? As Heidegger puts it: "But is not anything of this sort *guided* and *regulated* in a way of its own? Where are ontological projects to get the evidence that their 'findings' are phenomenally appropriate? Ontological interpretation projects the entity presented to it upon the Being which is that entity's own, so as to conceptualize it with regard to its structure. Where are the sign-posts to direct the projection, so that Being will be reached at all?" (SZ, § 63, 312/359)

The only positive response to this question is to be found in Heidegger's notion of the preunderstanding,[32] and it is here that Heidegger's Husserlian strategy comes into play. The legitimacy of the forestructures is secured only if the forestructures, which are to be structures which reach forth beyond the being to its Being, also reach *back* and *link up* with our preunderstanding. *This linking up is the only possible control in hermeneutic phenomenology*. We can ensure that the forestructural violence will be a wresting loose, a setting free, and not simply sheer caprice, only by insisting that such forestructures effect a movement of return to or retrieval of a prior understanding, a preunderstanding that Heidegger simply takes to be constitutive of *Dasein*. That is what *Dasein is*: a being that always and already is possessed of an understanding of Being—and hence of its own Being, of the Being of others, and the Being of things. If this preunderstanding is denied or undermined, the whole edifice of hermeneutic phenomenology collapses. This is not to say that this preunderstanding is not at times badly defaced or distorted, but even then it remains at work in everything which *Dasein* does: "No matter how far removed from an ontological concept the distinction between existence and reality may be, no matter even if *Dasein* proximally understands existence as reality, *Dasein* is not just present-at-hand but has already understood itself, however mythical or magical the interpretation which it gives may be" (SZ, § 63, 313/361). Here Heidegger invokes the dynamics of Husserl's phenomenology of horizons and the distinction between the implicit, prethematic horizon and the explicitly thematic object. We live and move about within a certain horizonal understanding, and these "forgotten" horizons make our explicit awareness possible. Heidegger takes over this Husserlian structure and gives it a more properly ontological cast. The horizon within which *Dasein* moves about is its understanding of its own Being (and of Being in general), an understanding (*Verstehen*) which does not get to be a concept (*Begriff*), which remains anonymous, even though its effects are felt in every corner of our experience. The hermeneutic forestructures then are "guided and regulated" by this preunderstanding. Their role is to explicate it, to bring it out into the open, to give it explicit, thematic shape where previously it remained anonymous and prethematic. The work of hermeneutics is *aus-legen, ex-ponere*, to lay out in the sense of drawing out into the open, to make explicit what we all already implicitly understand.

Notice then how Heidegger has redefined the traditional hermeneutic circle along Husserlian lines (and at the same time drawn Husserl into the hermeneutic circle). He has transformed the old circle of the whole and the parts into a phenomenological circle of implicit and explicit, of prethematic and thematic, of anonymous horizon and explicitly named object. And he saw that these phenomenological dynamics obey the laws of repetition and retrieval. That is why there is nothing vicious in hermeneutic circularity: it conforms to classical phenomenological science, and Derrida is certainly right to say that the hermeneutic circle in *Being and Time* is controlled by the logic of implicit and explicit.[33] Phenomenology is already a protohermeneutics, for its work of fetching out (*herausholen*) what is only horizonally given, or pregiven, is a work of laying-out (*auslegen*) an understanding in which we already stand.

A primordial interpretation, Heidegger says, "will let that which is to be interpreted *put itself into words for the very first* time" (SZ, § 63, 314– 15/ 362). Where understanding previously remained vague and inarticulate, in interpretation it becomes articulated and explicit. But that means that in hermeneutics everything comes down to recognition—*recognitio, Wiedererkennung, Anerkennung*—knowing that comes back to what we already know. A knowing again, renewing our primordial acquaintance with ourselves. Everything comes down to our capacity for retrieval and repetition; there is no proving and disproving in hermeneutics but only a self-examination, a self-discovery, in which we find ourselves in the account or fail to do so. Hermeneutics provides this prior understanding with the words with which to come into language. In so doing, it brings us to stand in the place which we already occupy. It returns us to ourselves, brings us home. It is appropriation and homecoming: coming in to our own again.

But we have said that the hermeneutic phenomenology is the mirror image of the existential ontology,[34] and hence that this Husserlian moment is controlled by the Kierkegaardian. Hence we must not make the mistake of thinking that in this hermeneutics we want to make everything present and explicit, to restore presence everywhere. For the ontology of existence culminates in resoluteness, which is a readiness for anxiety, openness to the absence. And so that too is mirrored in the hermeneutics.

To see how this is so, we must follow up the clue that is provided us by the ontology of existence. When resolute *Dasein* returns to itself from fallenness, it does not seize again a lost presence, or recapture a pure but hitherto concealed Being. On the contrary, it returns to the nothingness of its Being, and faces up to that from which it has all along been in flight, its own nullity (*Nichtigkeit*). By the same token, if hermeneutic phenomenology projects the Being of this being in terms of existence and temporality, and claims thereby that it has drawn this projection from primordial sources, that it has thereby entered the circle "wholly and primordially" (*ganz und ursprünglich*, SZ, § 63, 315/363), it has not claimed to have made

Dasein's being *transparent*. It does not claim to have restored a lost presence and brought it out into the light, but rather to have restored the mystery, the absence, the "lethic" element in *Dasein*. Hence the effect of this hermeneutic retrieval is to have recovered our "openness for the mystery" (*Offenheit zum Geheimnis*)[35] of existence. Retrieval for Heidegger does not mean the retrieval of presence, the recovery of a lost actuality, but precisely the opposite. For his grievance with metaphysics has all along been that it turns Being into presence. It treats *Dasein* as a fully definable thing, a circumscribable presence, which, however much we qualify it with uplifting predicates (person, spirit, and so on), remains something present. But the Being of *Dasein* is finitude, contingency, nothingness, lacking a secure grasp of its whence and its whither, thrown and mortal. Whence what is brought to words for the first time in this projection of *Dasein* is a self-understanding of ourselves as mortals. Heidegger wants to recover the mystery of mortality; the retrieval is a *memento mori*, the recovery of the abyss. The *terminus ad quem* of this retrieval, of this phenomenological *Rückgang*, is no transcendental ego, no *res cogitans* or absolute spirit, but the being whose Being is a nullity. Heidegger's hermeneutic is bent on restoring our finitude, mortality, and humanity—if *homo* means *humus*.

In Husserl the recovery of origins is intended as a transcendental movement, as a movement of pure freedom, in which the ego disengages itself from its situatedness within the horizon of the world. The movement from thematic to prethematic is made possible because of the ability of the reflecting ego (*das reflectierende ich*) to loosen the grip of any worldly horizon and to thereby to secure for the ego reflective clarity. But in Heidegger there can be no question of loosening ourselves *from* our horizonal situatedness but rather of awakening ourselves *to* our situatedness, awakening our sense of *being* situated. In *What Is Metaphysics?* he argues that we cannot thematize the world as such and as a whole by some pure effort of thought—for that would result in an unphenomenological and vacuous construction—but we can, through anxiety, become profoundly attuned to our situatedness *within* an encompassing (and hence non-bracketable) totality.[36] Husserl's phenomenology of horizons is meant to be part of a presuppositionless science which would reduce every prethematic horizon (in principle, if not in fact) to thematic awareness. But Heidegger means instead to unfold and penetrate our horizons, not to entertain the illusion that we can disengage them. The task is not to deny our presuppositions, he said, but to penetrate them more deeply (SZ, § 62, 310/358).

Heidegger stands with Kierkegaard on this point, not Husserl. And his critique of Husserl is an echo of Kierkegaard's critique of Plato. Platonic recollection, Hegelian remembering (*Erinnerung*) of the form through which the spirit has passed, Husserlian *epoché*—all of these are so many versions of what Kierkegaard called "disinterest," which he regarded as a fantastic creation. The project of repetition and of retrieval is radically interested, and the metaphysics of presence founders on this interest: "Repetition is the interest of metaphysics and at the same time the interest upon which metaphysics founders" (*Rep.*, 53). As long as one remains on the level of interest—*inter-esse*, being betwixt and between, being caught up in the world, Being-in-the-world, existence—there can be no illusion of transparency. Transparency and pure presence are illusions of distance, illusions induced by the impossible attempt to shut down the workings of existence, to disengage the existing self, to forget that one exists, as Johannes Climacus put it. And it is to this forgetting that retrieval and recovery are opposed, so that when one recalls existence, one has dismissed the illusion of presence and thereby restored the mystery of existence.

That is also why, I should add here, concrete and practicing hermeneutics—the hermeneutics of texts in the usual sense, as opposed to the exclusively ontological hermeneutics we have pursued here—must guard against the same illusion of objective presence. We have seen that existential retrieval means that *Dasein* recovers not a lost actuality but a possibility, and that hermeneutic retrieval recovers not a transparent presence but the enigma of a thrown project. But that implies that concrete, working hermeneutics must aim its interpretations, not principally at restoring lost monuments and documents, but at what is possible in a text. Its goal cannot be to reconstruct a past actuality, to restore it to its original condition, but, as Hans-Georg Gadamer argues, to find out its possible sense for us today, to find out what it says to us, here and now.[37] We shall do this in any case, as Gadamer argues—or else interpretations would not have a history. As Nietzsche says in *The Advantage and Disadvantage of History for Life*, the strong one knows how to assimilate the past and to bring it into the service of the present and future, and he does so at the expense of pure objectivity.[38] Indeed pure objectivity, were it ever possible—and not instead an ontological folly that flies in the face of the facticity of *Dasein*—would be of no use at all. We would then have to learn how to wean ourselves away from such things as from a form of escapism. The perfect reconstruction of past actuality would leave us speechless and mute insofar as we are existing beings, and would be of no use to life, as Nietzsche would say. This is not to say that the reading of a text is a capricious affair in which any reading is allowed. That is precisely what Heidegger rules out when he criticizes the notion of a free-floating construction (SZ, § 7, 28/50). We have seen that the one, decisive hermeneutic control is what we called the *linking* up of a projection with the preunderstanding. Unless the Being in terms of which a being is projected reaches back and articulates a preunderstanding, then it is groundless and uprooted. And that means that the labors of a concrete, working hermeneutics must be enlisted in the service of articulating our self-understanding. The interpretation of a past historical epoch, of a work of art, or of a scriptural text, must be governed by their ability to tell us who we are, to say something to us here and now about the beings which we ourselves are or, better, must become. All hermeneutics, on whatever level, is the recovery of man and is governed by the existential imperative to become oneself.

DERRIDA'S CRITIQUE OF RETRIEVAL

We have made everything in the hermeneutic strategy initiated by *Being and Time* turn on the dynamics of retrieval. We have followed the complex interweaving of two levels of retrieval, the one existential the other phenomenological. And we have said that everything depends upon our ability to make the transition from fallenness—whether into the naïveté of the natural attitude or the tranquility of everydayness—to *Dasein*'s primordial Being. But Derrida wants to deconstruct this very distinction between the primordial and the fallen on the grounds that it too belongs to the metaphysics of presence: "Yet is not the contrast between primordial and derivative properly metaphysical? Is not a demand for an *arche* in general—whatever precautions are taken with this concept—the essential operation of metaphysics? Is there not at least some Platonism in the notion of *Verfallen*?"[39] On Derrida's view, Heidegger's notions of authenticity and primordiality remain under the spell of the metaphysics of presence: "The primordial and the authentic are determined as the proper (*eigentlich*)—i.e., as the *near* (*prope*, *proprius*), the present in the proximity of presence to self. It could be shown how this value of proximity and presence to self enters, at the beginning of *Being and Time* and elsewhere, into the decision to pose the question of the meaning of Being starting from the existential analytic of *Dasein*. The force of metaphysics in such a decision and in the credit accorded here to the value of presence to self could also be demonstrated."[40] For Derrida, the very structure of retrieval is metaphysical, for it implies a movement from a temporary absence to a permanent presence. *Dasein* is at first dissipated and dispersed among things, estranged from itself, then it returns to itself, gathers itself up into a unity and self-identity, a unity which is of course at the expense of difference, of differance.

That is what leads Derrida, at the conclusion of "The Ends of Man," to distinguish two different sorts of deconstruction. The first, Heidegger's, attempts deconstruction "without changing ground, by repeating what is implicit in the founding concepts and original problematics, by using against the edifice the instruments or the stones available in the house." The second, Derrida's extension (and deconstruction) of Heidegger, goes further: "To decide to change ground, in a discontinuous and eruptive manner, by stepping abruptly outside and by affirming absolute rupture and difference."[41] Heideggerian deconstruction is at fault precisely because it is an attempt at retrieval, at repeating the primordial beginnings, because it wants to go back and find what is primordial. Derrida's undertaking is however a more pitiless breaking with every possible form of metaphysics and humanism and stands altogether outside it. There is no question of repeating or retrieving its innermost sense, but of breaking with the very illusion of an innermost sense. Heidegger's overcoming befits the higher man, but not the *Übermensch* himself: it is not pitiless enough.[42]

I should like to respond to this criticism by taking my point of departure from a text from *Vom Wesen des Grundes*, which, in conjunction with the argument we have developed in this paper, throws Derrida's reading of Heidegger into doubt. Here Heidegger says that insofar as *Dasein* is characterized by "existence," "transcendence," and "possibility"—words drawn from metaphysics but that acquire a new and unmetaphysical sense in Heidegger—then, far from being a being of nearness, as Derrida would have it, *Dasein* is precisely a being of distance (*ein Wesen der Ferne*): "And so man, as an existing transcendence which bounds forth towards possibilities, is *a being of distance*. Only through the primordial distances he establishes in his transcendence towards all beings does true nearness to things arise in him. And only being able to hear into the distance, effects in *Dasein* as a self an awakening to the answer of *Dasein*-with, in being-with which *Dasein* can surrender its egoism (*Ichheit*) in order to win itself as an authentic self."[43] This text flatly contradicts the attempt to define authentic *Dasein* in terms of self-presence, self-nearness, self-identity. For authentic *Dasein* is characterized by transcendence: it is stretched out beyond itself—beyond its factual presence or present factuality—into the possible, into its uttermost potentiality for Being. And it is precisely this self-absence, its being held out into Nothingness (*Gehaltensein in das Nichts*),[44] from which inauthentic *Dasein* is in flight. Inauthenticity is the flight from absence to presence. Inauthenticity is a refusal of transcendence, of that stretching forth into the possible which constitutes its genuine Being; it is a flight in to the actual. Authentic *Dasein*, on the other hand, has the courage for absence, for the uncanny; it is ready for anxiety, for the nullity of its ground and of its projects, for the possibility of its own nullity, which it cultivates precisely as a possibility. In the language of metaphysics this ec-static stretching out of *Dasein*'s Being is called transcendence, and that means, Heidegger says here in a language beyond metaphysics, self-distancing. *Dasein* is what it is only by staying open to the distance that constitutes its very Being. To be a self is to have the courage for self-distancing, to keep the wound of finitude open—whereas inauthenticity collapses upon itself, collapsing into the present and the actual. The controlling metaphor in all of Heidegger's diverse accounts of *Dasein* over the years is not nearness but openness, disclosedness, and that always means keeping itself open or stretched out into the distance.[45] Authenticity is a matter of distance, not of nearness. (And it is this same distance—*ec-statis*, *Ausstehen*—that constitutes the projectedness of *Dasein* upon which all Heideggerian hermeneutics turns.)

In my view, Derrida has been misled by his critique of Husserl. He rightly—quite brilliantly, I think—saw in Husserl's phenomenology a metaphysics of presence, and he showed in his introduction to *The Origin of Geometry* that Husserl wanted a metaphysical making-present-again, that he wanted to reactivate a lost meaning, to repeat it literally. Whence he says in the essay on Descartes and Foucault: "The attempt to write the history of the decision, division, difference runs the risk of construing the division as an event or a structure subsequent to the unity of an original presence, thereby confirming metaphysics in its fundamental operation."[46] But if this movement from presence to absence, and then from absence to presence restored, holds true of Husserl's teleology of reason, it cannot be said either of the retrieval of authenticity in *Being and Time*, or of the step back into the origin of metaphysics in the later writings. For the recovery of the primal and primordial of which Heidegger speaks—whether in his early writings or late—is never the recovery of a primal presence. It is the recovery or a primordial *experience* (*Erfahrung*), but this is always an experience of finitude and absence. In other words, and here one can put our counterpoint to Derrida succinctly, *in Derrida the critique of presence tends to pass over surreptitiously into a critique of retrieval itself.* And that is what I deny. For the one is not the other. Retrieval can indeed take the metaphysical form of a retrieval of presence—that is what Platonic recollection, Hegelian *Erinnerung*, and Husserlian *Reaktivierung* surely are. But a more radical doctrine of retrieval, such as we find in Heidegger, has given up this nostalgia for presence and has become instead a readiness for anxiety, an openness, a self-exposure to finitude, limit, and negativity. It wants precisely to return us to the finitude from which we have all along been in flight and for which metaphysics is constantly seeking the cure. In Heidegger the movement of *return* means having the courage to face up to the nothingness that inhabits Being and the thought of Being. It is not nostalgia but courage for the hard and inhospitable. It is the acknowledgment of our finitude, fallibility and mortality. It is a recovery of man; for man, *homo*, means *humus*. This recovery is the call to remember, man, what you are: *memento homo, cineris est et in cinerem reverteris*. It is the recovery of the *memento mori*. And that is a recovery that we would soon enough do without. If it is nostalgia, it is a pathological nostalgia.

The critique of presence cannot be passed off as a critique of all return and all retrieval, not if retrieval, instead of meaning the restoration of presence, means the restoration of the mystery, of the wholly other, of the nameless. Derrida thinks that repetition means you get the girl back.[47] But he has not taken adequately in to account the Kierkegaardian element in repetition. He gets no further in the understanding of repetition than Constantine Constantius, who has an aesthetic theory, and not as far as the anxiety of Job and Abraham. Indeed even Job and Abraham remain only on the outskirts of true repetition: for their deferral and difference were only temporary; they got their goods back. Genuinely religious, genuinely non-metaphysical repetition means the agony of real and permanent loss, means that the recovery of the self is carried out only in the agony of absence.

If retrieval means the recovery of the abyss, of the mystery, of the absence that inhabits human experience, that is also what I take hermeneutics to be. Hermeneutics thinks—contrary to Derrida (and Rorty)—that there is something deeper to be sought, something more primal. Hermeneutics turns on this commitment to the primordial. The movement of its circle is always circling back on something more essential. Hermeneutic violence is always practiced in the service of retrieval. If recovery is the life of hermeneutics, then deconstruction is but a moment through which it passes. And that is why I reject the disjunction which Derrida proposes:

> There are thus two interpretations of interpretation, of structure, of sign, of play. The one seeks to decipher, dreams of deciphering a truth or an origin which escapes play and the order of the sign, and which lives the necessity of interpretation as an exile. The other, which is no longer turned towards the origin, affirms play and tries to pass

> beyond man and humanism, the name of man being the name of that being who, through out the history of metaphysics or of ontotheology—in other words throughout his entire history—has dreamed of full presence, the reassuring foundation, the origin and end of play.[48]

For in this dichotomy Derrida has fused the search for the originary with the nostalgia for presence, and that is precisely what I deny. We have seen in Heidegger the search for something originary which is not the fullness of presence but which has the courage for the abyss. In Heidegger, both early and late, the return to the primordial has nothing to do with escaping from the play in which *Dasein* (or Being) is caught up. On the contrary, it is entering into that play and taking one's stand within it. As a readiness for anxiety, it is precisely the acknowledgment that *Dasein* is the being whose Being is at stake, whose Being is not secured by an *essentia* or *natura*, not underwritten by *eidos* or *ousia*, but is precisely an issue for *Dasein*.

And who can deny that this very confrontation with the abyss of *Dasein* is a return to origins, a recovery of that more primordial Being from which everyday *Dasein* is in constant flight? Here we have a breaking through to a concealed sense from which every day *Dasein* is in flight that is at the same time a denial of presence, a readiness for the void.

And so everything comes down to the question with which we began, about whether repetition is possible. Hermeneutics has all along maintained that it is, and the point of hermeneutic violence has always been to wrest loose what tends of itself to remain concealed. Deconstruction belongs in the service of retrieval; active forgetting—as Nietzsche himself says[49]—belongs together with recalling. Whether it is taken on the ontological level which we have pursued here, or on the concrete level of the interpretation of texts, hermeneutics always means that there is a deeper sense, a latent understanding, that needs to be brought to words. That means, for example, that the interpretation of a classical text, or of a work of art, of a moment in human history, is never finished, never exhausted. There is always a new and primordial way for these things to speak to us. And in each case they speak to us about ourselves; they tell us who we are and recall us to our finitude. The texts of the great metaphysicians always address the question of our finitude whether to embrace it or to find a way around it. The works of the great artists sing the song of our incarnation and mortality. The sacred texts recall to us our dependence upon an encompassing power. It is the task of hermeneutics as I see it, to give words to this self-understanding, to bring it into language and that means into appearance. These are words which we would sooner leave unsaid in favor of the public interpretation of our lives. Such words are neither a mere play of signs nor a monument to ageless presence and pure Being; they are words which hermeneutics enlists in the service of the *Sache selbst*, words of elemental power, words that have put themselves at the disposal of a primordial *hermeneuein*.

NOTES

1. *SZ*: Martin Heidegger, *Sein und Zeit*, 10th ed. (Tübingen: Niemeyer, 1063); the pagination after the slash refers to the English translation, *Being and Time*, trans. J. Macquarrie and E. Robinson (New York: Harper & Row, 1962).

2. Hence one can connect this sense of *recuperare* with the Husserlian "crisis," which is an illness of the spirit.

3. Jacques Derrida, "The Ends of Man," *Philosophy and Phenomenological Research* 30 (1969): 31–57.

4. With the notable exception of Calvin Schrag, Heidegger commentators tend to keep a safe distance from acknowledging the Kierkegaardian element in Heidegger's work, for fear, no doubt, of being declared "ontic." That is a serious mistake, not because Heidegger's work is indeed ontic, but because a good deal of Heidegger's

"onto-logical" revolution is prepared for by Kierkegaard. I might also recommend in this connection William Spanos, "Heidegger, Kierkegaard and the Hermeneutic Circle: Towards a Postmodern Theory of Interpretation as Disclosure," *Boundary* 2 (Winter 1976): 455–88, which is one of the few essays I know that has seen the connection between Kierkegaardian repetition and Heideggerian hermeneutics. The point of this essay, which is obscured by the highly opaque style in which it is written, is that "existential" hermeneutics means self-appropriation, a point I heartily endorse although it is not the point of the present chapter.

5. See my "The Thought of Being and the Conversation of Mankind: The Case of Heidegger and Rorty," *The Review of Metaphysics* 36 (March 1983): 661–85.

6. In the Middle Ages this became the basis of a mystical circle of *exitus* and *reditus*—for example, in Meister Eckhart. See my "Fundamental Themes in Meister Eckhart's Mysticism," *The Thomist* 42 (1978): 197–225.

7. This point has been pursued in a penetrating way in various essays by Thomas Sheehan; see his "Heidegger's Topic: Excess, Access, Recess," *Tijdschrift voor Philosophie* 41, no. 4 (December 1979): 615–35.

8. *Rep.*: Søren Kierkegaard, *Repetition: An Essay in Experimental Psychology*, trans. with introduction and notes by Walter Lowrie (New York: Harper & Row, 1964).

9. Søren Kierkegaard, *Concluding Unscientific Postscript*, trans. Walter Lowrie and David Swenson (Princeton, NJ: Princeton University Press, 1941), 184–85, including the "note."

10. See note 7above.

11. It is precisely this problematic that occupies Heidegger in *SZ*, § 64.

12. There is an important doctrine of repetition in Nietzsche, which goes under the name of eternal recurrence.

13. It is painfully obvious that Kierkegaard has in mind here his own loss of Regine Olsen. When he wrote *Repetition*, he still entertained the hope that he would be reunited with her, only to find, shortly after he had completed the book, that she had married Friedrich Schlegel. Whence Kierkegaard's unpleasant introduction to the shortcomings of the philosophy of presence. But there it seems to me is a classic case of having to kill the author and to forget Kierkegaard himself.

14. Interest for Kierkegaard means *inter-esse*, being in the midst of, and clearly anticipates Heidegger's *in-der-Welt-sein*. See Søren Kierkegaard, *Johannes Climacus or De omnibus dubitandum est and A Sermon*, trans. T.H. Croxall (Stanford: Stanford University Press, 1958), 151–52.

15. For more on Kierkegaard's notion of repetition, see the bibliography under the entry "Repetition," in *Søren Kierkegaard's Journals and Papers*, 5 vols., ed. and trans. Howard Hong and Edna Hong (Bloomington: Indiana University Press, 1975), 3:20–22.

16. See Jens Himmelstrup, ed., *Søren Kierkegaard: International Bibliografi* (Copenhagen: Nyt Nordisk Forlag-Arnold Busck, 1962), no. 808, p. 26; Hans-Georg Gadamer, *Philosophical Hermeneutics*, trans. David Linge (Berkeley: University of California Press, 1976), 214.

17. Edmund Husserl, *Ideas: General Introduction to Pure Phenomenology*, trans. W. Boyce Gibson (New York: Collier Books, 1962), 107.

18. Ibid., 92.

19. For more on Husserl's discussion of horizon, see *Ideas*, §§ 27–28, 44, 47, 63, 69, and 83; see also the distinction between attentional actuality and the wakeful ego, on the one hand, and implicit, non-attentional, potential consciousness of the horizon in §§ 35 and 37.

20. This kind of argument runs throughout Derrida's Husserl interpretations; but see, for example, Jacques Derrida, *Speech and Phenomena*, trans. David Allison (Evanston, IL: Northwestern University Press, 1973), 81–83.

21. See Heidegger's letter to Husserl of October 22, 1927, in Edmund Husserl, *Phänomenologische Psychologie*, Husserliana 9 (The Hague: Martinus Nijhoff, 1962), 600–603. One should beware of overstating the opposition between Husserl and Heidegger, which is in part the point of the present discussion.

22. Jacques Derrida, *Edmund Husserl's "Origin of Geometry": An Introduction*, trans. John Leavey, ed. David Allison (Stony Brook, NY: Nicolas Hays, 1978).

23. Derrida makes this point in his "'Genesis and Structure' and Phenomenology," in *Writing and Difference*, by Jacques Derrida, trans. and introduction by Alan Bass (Chicago: Chicago University Press, 1978), 154–68.

24. Heidegger does not censor the word "method," as Gadamer does. See Martin Heidegger, *Der Satz vom Grund* (Pfullingen: Neske, 1957), 111.

25. Thomas Sheehan, "On Movement and the Destruction of Ontology," *The Monist* 64 (October 1981): 539–40.

26. See Martin Heidegger, "What Is Metaphysics?" in *Martin Heidegger: Basic Writings*, ed. David Krell (New York: Harper & Row, 1977), 101.

27. Heidegger writes: "The resoluteness which comes back to itself and hands itself down, then becomes the *repetition* of a possibility of existence that has come down to us. *Repeating is handing down explicitly*—that is to say, going back into the possibilities of the Dasein that has-been-there" (SZ, § 74, 385/437).

28. "In the field of ontology, any 'springing-from' (*ent-springen*) is degeneration" (*SZ*, par. 67, 334/383).

29. That, of course, is why Gadamer claims that in *Being and Time* hermeneutics is given an ontological foundation.

30. Actually, interpretation (*Auslegung*) may be either thematic or prethematic, but the work of the author of *Being and Time* is clearly meant to be a thematization.

31. That is why the word *Wiederholung* can be used to apply either to *Dasein*'s own existential self-actualization (par. 74) or to the reading of the history of ontology—in Martin Heidegger, *Kant and the Problem of Metaphysics*, trans. James Churchill (Bloomington: Indiana University Press, 1962), 211–12.

32. Part of the answer to this question is negative: if a conception has become popular, common (*völkisch* [*SZ*, § 32, 153/195]), then we may be sure that it is degenerate, diluted, commonplace, fallen out of its elemental power. But such negative criterion will ensure only that our forestructures will be exotic, not necessarily recuperative, restorative of the things themselves. It is a necessary but not a sufficient condition.

33. Derrida, "Ends of Man," 47–48.

34. Whence either the ontology or the methodology may be called hermeneutic.

35. Martin Heidegger, *Discourse on Thinking* (New York: Harper & Row, 1966), 55.

36. Heidegger, "What Is Metaphysics?," 101.

37. Whence Gadamer's critique of historical objectivism is in the essential spirit of *Being and Time*.

38. See Friedrich Nietzsche, *The Advantage and Disadvantage of History for Life*, trans. Peter Preuss (Indianapolis: Hackett, 1980), pars. 2 and 6.

39. Jacques Derrida, "*Ousia* and *Gramme*: A Note to a Footnote in *Being and Time*," trans. Edward Casey, in *Phenomenology in Perspective*, ed. Joseph Smith (The Hague: Martinus Nijhoff, 1970), 89.

40. Ibid., 90n36.

41. Derrida, "Ends of Man," 56.

42. In the same spirit, Rorty speaks of Heidegger's "fatal attachment to the tradition," a "pathetic notion." See his "Overcoming the Tradition: Heidegger and Dewey," in *Heidegger and Modern Philosophy*, ed. Michael Murray (New Haven, CT: Yale University Press, 1978), 256.

43. Martin Heidegger, *The Essence of Reasons*, bilingual edition, incorporating the German text of *Vom Wesen des Grundes*, trans. T. Malick (Evanston, IL: Northwestern University Press, 1969), 130–31.

44. Heidegger, "What Is Metaphysics?," 105.

45. There is a threefold distancing at work here: (1) *Dasein* stretches out toward its own potentiality for Being, which makes its *Selbstsein* possible; (2) toward the Being of others, which makes its *Mit-sein* possible, and (3) toward *Vorhandensein* and *Zuhandensein*, which makes its every day *in-sein* possible. All three of these ecstasies are made possible by its primordial projection of Being itself.

46. Derrida, *Writing and Difference*, 40.

47. There is to be sure a thematic of "repetition" in Derrida, but it is always in the sense of the supplement, trace, or vestige, but not in the genuine sense of Kierkegaard and Heidegger. See the concluding pages of Jacques Derrida, *Of Grammatology*, trans. G. C. Spivak (Baltimore: Johns Hopkins University Press, 1974), esp. 312.

48. Jacques Derrida, "Structure, Sign and Play in the Discourse of the Human Sciences," in Derrida, *Writing and Difference*, 292.

49. Nietzsche, "Advantage and Disadvantage," par. 1, p. 10.

9
Heidegger and Derrida: Cold Hermeneutics

INTRODUCTION

I want to undertake here a double-reading of Martin Heidegger and Jacques Derrida. I do not intend a comparison, in any usual sense. Rather I want to let the texts of Heidegger and Derrida mingle with each other to the point of infiltrating and subverting each other. I want first to let Derrida insinuate his way into Heidegger and then, in a return movement, to let Heidegger insinuate his way into Derrida.

Heidegger and Derrida: by that I do not intend an *Aufhebung* but rather a double-cross in which each, taking the side of the other, is co-opted and corrupted by the other in a kind of friendly subversion. Heidegger and Derrida: double agents, each trying to infiltrate the other organization of the other, trying to steal each other's secrets, trying to compromise the other. Heidegger and Derrida together, each trying to keep the other honest, or at least on the alert, each protecting the other from himself. Heidegger and Derrida: a cross-insemination, a commingled product which, were one under any constraint to give it a name, instead of just letting it play itself out, one might temporarily describe as a kind of hermeneutics without illusion and without comfort, a cold hermeneutics.

I am interested in Derrida's critique of the "postal principle" which, since it regards message-bearing, is the principle of all hermeneutics, Hermes, the message-bearer from the gods, is the first and paradigmatic postman. If Heidegger dissociates himself from hermeneutics inasmuch as it belongs to transcendental-horizontal thinking, he does not reject hermeneutics in the larger, looser sense of waiting for the message of the gods. Hermeneutics means waiting for the dispatch—*Schickung, envoi*—which is on its way, courtesy of the "it gives." Only a god can save us now, that is to say, only a saving message from the *Ereignis,* a call that arrives just before the hour of execution, a message borne by a modern-day Hermes, perhaps one from Freiburg. *Hermes Friburgiensis.*

Derrida makes the postal principle questionable. He questions the assumption that an unambiguous message can be transmitted from an identifiable sender to a clearly designated addressee. Thus he puts into a central element—the "eschatological" element—in Heidegger's thought—even the so-called later Heidegger. But questioning is the piety of thought and, by thus questioning Heidegger, Derrida pushes us into another reading of Heidegger. He displaces the apocalyptic and eschatological element in Heidegger's thought, exposing thereby a more radical streak in his work, one that is prepared to live without such hermeneutic comfort, ready for the free play of dispatches, without postal expectations.

But this is a game that two can play; it is a game of double-agents. By letting Derrida insinuate himself into Heidegger, Derrida himself infiltrated. For Heidegger puts Derrida into question, and the question goes like this. Once we have come to grips with the *ébranler*, once we have recognized the tremor by which all things are shaken, the play which cannot be arrested, what then? It will of course be said that there is no such "once," no such place, that it is oneiric and utopic to dream of such a place, that the wavering means that we waver always in undecidability between coming-to-grips and not-coming-to-grips. Still, in the name of Martin, we press further: in what terms are we to describe those who take their stand in this very undecidability, in the breakdown of the postal principle, in the withdrawal and retreat of the *Sache selbst*? To what extent is this not indeed what is meant by overcoming the oblivion, which has nothing to do with eschatology? And if it is, then have we not infiltrated Derrida, caught him in a moment of deadly earnest, of a certain deep hermeneutics when he thought no one was looking? For everything deep loves the mask.

I will carry out this subversive plot in four steps. (1) I begin by marking off Derrida's critique of postal eschatology, and (2) I follow this immediately with the Heidegger who plays into Derrida's hands—let us call this the "eschatological Heidegger." This sets the stage for my double-reading in which I show first (3) how Derrida opens up another reading of Heidegger, "beyond eschatology," and then (4) how such a reconceived Heidegger opens up in turn another reading of Derrida, an eye-of-the-storm Derrida who practices a more elusive, less innocent hermeneutics.

DERRIDA'S CRITIQUE OF THE POSTAL PRINCIPLE

Derrida wants to tell the truth on apocalyptic utterances, to put an end to all talk about ends. Such utterances always lay claim to a privileged experience, to a revelation that they pretend to pass on to the rest of us. We have been unfounded recently by a profusion of competing eschatologies, each claiming to go one better in "eschatological eloquence":

> I tell you this in truth; this is not only the end of this here but also and first of that there, the end of history, the end of the class struggle, the end of philosophy, the death of God, the end of religions, the end of Christianity and morals (that, that was the most serious *naïveté*), the end of the subject, the end of man, the end of the West, the end of Oedipus, the end of the earth, *Apocalypse Now*, I tell you, in the cataclysm, the fire, the blood, the fundamental earthquake, the napalm descending from the sky by helicopters, like prostitutes, the nuclear thunder and the great whoring, and also the end of literature, the end of painting, art as a thing of the past, the end of psychoanalysis, the end of the university, the end of phallocentrism and phallogocentrism and I don't know what else. (*Fins*, 464/80)[1]

We recognize a familiar list of heroes in that eschatological catalog no less redoubtable masters of suspicion than Marx, Freud, Nietzsche, Heidegger, and Derrida. And Heidegger in particular: "And if Heidegger thinks the *Überwindung* of metaphysics or of onto-theology like that of eschatology which is inseparable from it, he does so in the name of another eschatology. Several times he says of thought, here distinct from philosophy, that it is essentially eschatological. That is his word" (*Fins*, 465/81). Apocalyptic utterances demand a privileged standpoint, an insight into the essence (*Wesen*) in the verbal sense, into what is happening and coming to pass in things—be it technology, religion, or metaphysics—along with the authority to declare a "coming dawn."

This is not to say that there is a clear and decidable difference between apocalyptic and non-apocalyptic utterances. For one thing, the critique of apocalypticism is usually waged, as it is by Kant, in the name of reason and the rational light. But that Enlightenment ideal is as vulnerable to deconstructive critique as is its adversary. It too thinks it has seen the light, which is here the light of reason (*Fins*, 466/82). Furthermore, even the critique of apocalypticism declares the *end* of apocalypticism, tells the *truth* on apocalypticism, and so has an eschatological streak of its own—with its own revelation and declamations. There is no standing clear on either side of the divide between the apocalyptic and non-apocalyptic. There is a mystagogue and an *Aufklärer* in each of us. As Derrida writes, "Each of us is the mystagogue and the *Aufklärer* of the other" (*Fins*, 462n8). The best one can do is to remain on the alert, mindful that one has no secrets to disclose. But even "vigilance" implies a light. Finally, the critique of apocalypticism should not underestimate the disruptive power of the apocalyptic, its capacity to defy political censorship and the ruling concordats. Apocalypticism is an effective way to disrupt the ruling postal system that monitors the messages that are permitted to be sent out over public lines. It can be an act of defiance of *la police postale* (*Fins*, 473/89). Indeed, everything that disrupts will be made out as apocalyptic by the powers that be; they will want to make it look that way.

The apocalyptic then is not a malady that infects only seers and German metaphysicians. It represents the very structure of writing itself. It is the "double bind" of writing, suggesting by its very structure that it has a message to deliver, even while it fails in principle to do so (*Fins*. 445/46/64). In postal terms, the postman has no message to deliver. But if we can get over the expectation that he does, then perhaps we can enjoy the free circulation and exchange of letters for their own sake. And "getting over" that expectation turns out to be a Derridean way of "overcoming" (*verwinden*) the "postal principle."

Apocalypticism follows the logic of the postal principle. It pretends to tell the truth, to deliver a message. It claims to have a destination, a destined hearer (*destinaire*); it turns on the unity of sender and addressee, of *destinateur* and *destinaire* (*Fins*. 467/84). The postal principle governs a teleo-system, a teleo-logical network of messages—*logoi*, dispatches, *envois*, *Schickungen*—sent out across the lines, from end to end, *telos* to *telos*, from computer terminal to computer terminal. Now given everything that Derrida has otherwise argued about the differential play, the postal system breaks down. It turns on a dream about identifiable origins, about the unity of meaning transmitted across the wires, and identifiable destination. He illustrates the dream that inheres in every apocalypse by taking the *Apocalypse* itself, the one by John, and finding there a fold, a seam, a *pli*, in which the text becomes uncontrollably complicated. The drift and slippage in the *Apocalypse* lies in its complicated angelic-courier system. Elohim gives the message to Jesus to show to his servant John. But Jesus sends the message through a messenger, an *angelus*, thus creating a confusion of voices: so many people on the line; such a complicated dispatch. Like the cover of *La Carte Postale*, there is always someone speaking behind the back of the one writing. And it finally gets to the point that we no longer know who is speaking to whom: "No longer do we know very well who lends his voice and his tone to the other in the Apocalypse; no longer do we know very well who addresses what to whom" (*Fins*, 470–71/87).

It is in virtue of this angelic complication that the *Apocalypse* becomes truly, and paradoxically, apocalyptic, that is, revelatory—namely, of the very structure of writing as the endless sending of confused signals without sure origin or definite destination, a postal system set free from postal regulations:

> But by a catastrophic overturning here more necessary than ever, we can as well think this: as soon as we no longer know very well who speaks or who writes, the text becomes apocalyptic. And if the dispatches always refer to other dispatches without decidable destination, the destination remaining to come, then isn't this completely angelic structure, that of the Johannine *Apocalypse*, isn't it also the structure of every science of writing in general? . . . Wouldn't the apocalyptic be a transcendental

> condition of all discourse, of all experience itself, of every mark or every trace? And the genre of writings called "apocalyptic" in the strict sense, then, would be only an example, an exemplary revelation of this transcendental structure. In that case, if the apocalypse reveals, it is first the revelation of the apocalypse, the self-presentation of the apocalyptic structure of language, of writing, of the experience of presence, either of the text or of the mark in general: that is, of the divisible dispatch for which there is no self-presentation, no assured destination. (*Fins*, 470–71/87)

The apocalyptic occurs when we are no longer able to identify who is saying what to whom. Dispatches refer to dispatches without decidable origin and destination. We do not know where the rumor started, or just what it means, or who is supposed to take it up. The postal principle is disrupted and we are admitted into a sphere of *destinerrance*, of messages running awry (*Fins*, 474/91).

And that spells the end of eschatology, including any eschatology based on the *Ereignis*. *Ereignis* calls us beyond Being—the call itself coming from beyond Being—towards that which sends Being. *Ereignis* wants to lead or conduct us—from oblivion into memorial thought, from *Gestell* into *Geviert*. But with the breakdown of the postal principle all such "conductive violence" is brought to a halt. And all that remains is the call itself, the sheer "Come . . ." of every apocalypse: come, lord Jesus; come, beyond Being. But with this difference: "'Come' does not address itself, does not appeal, to an identity determinable in advance. It is adrift (*une derive*) underivable from the identity of determination. 'Come' is *only* derivable, absolutely derivable, but only from the other, from something that may be an origin or a verifiable, decidable, presentable, appropriable identity, from nothing that may not already be derivable and arrivable without "*rive*" (without the source, spring, rivus)" (*Fins*, 477/94).

We are called beyond eschatology.

> Perhaps you will be tempted to call this the disaster, the catastrophe, the apocalypse. Now here, precisely, is announced—as promise or threat—an apocalypse without apocalypse, an apocalypse without vision, without truth, without revelation, of dispatches (*des envois*) (for the "come" is plural in itself, in oneself), of addresses without message and without destination, without sender or decidable addressee, without last judgment, without any other eschatology than the tone of the "Come" itself, its very difference, an apocalypse beyond good and evil. "Come" does not announce this or that apocalypse: already it resounds with a certain tone; it is in itself the apocalypse of the apocalypse; "Come" is apocalyptic. (*Fins*, 477/94)

The result is a releasing of the movements of *Ereignis* from eschatological violence, from fixed destination and stored up destinies, so that *legein* now means a sheer letting-be rather than a gathering up which means to deliver itself of the goods with a kind of momentous reversal and parturition:

> Our apocalypse now: that there is no longer any place for the apocalypse as the collection of evil and good in a *legein* of *aletheia*, nor in a *Geschick* of the dispatch. *L'envoi*, of the *Schicken* in a co-destination that would assure the "come" of the power to give rise [*lieu*) to an event in the certainty of a determination. But then that is what someone doing who tells you: I tell you this, I have come to tell you this, there is not, there never has been, there never will be an apocalypse, the apocalypse deceives, disappoints? There is the apocalypse without apocalypse. (*Fins*, 477–78/94–95)

It is true that Heidegger has put metaphysical tele-communications into question. But he has done so only in the name of another version of the postal principle. The meaning of

Being is not, as in Plato, Hegel and Husserl, an ideal and repeatable message, fully constituted in its ideality, sent across the epochs, borne by different translations, copied by different copyists, xeroxed, collated, and distributed, and then entrusted to professionally trained couriers. Rather it is something that has all along remained behind, sending out emissaries and dispatches while itself remaining in concealment. The history of metaphysics, which is organized around the transmission of ideal meanings—the Platonic-Husserlian postal principle[2]—is itself the concealment of the authentic letter of Being, which was spoken once, in the earliest dawn of the tradition. Thinking today is essentially preparatory thinking, *Vor-denken*, preparing for the day of repetition, retrieval, the new coming, the second coming, the new dawn. Come!

If we stand at the end of the false postal principle, which keeps delivering the dangerous message of presence—from *ousia* to *Gestell*—that in turn poses the task of thinking, to think the more mysterious postal principle, the dark play of the Janus-faced message, which is to be read backwards, in reversal, and hence turn into the saving message. But that is just a more mysterious hermeneutics, a darker decoding system, which says the way to understand the message is to read it backwards. The saving is the danger spelled backwards.

Because Heidegger's version of the postal principle is eschatological, not teleological, it is no less apocalyptic. It seeks to find a new beginning in the end, which is all around us: the end of philosophy, of metaphysics, of the old-Platonic-Hegelian postal principle. It looks for a new dawn in the growing darkness of the evening-land. It calls for the vigilance of thought, to keep watch, like a shepherd, through the world-night, waiting for the traces of a new day.

Derrida poses the objection to himself that this reading of Heidegger is already displaced by Heidegger, for whom the postal principle would be nothing more than a form of technology, a communication systems technique, which Heidegger has already delimited in advance. But what is Heidegger's delimitation of technology? The *Gestell is for him the last and most extreme* (*eschaton*) possibility, the final sending of the *Seins-geschick*, the last *Schickung*, in which we are taken in by what is sent, to the neglect of the "it sends." Whence Heidegger's critique of technology belongs entirely within the framework of "sending" (*Schicken*) and the postal principle. But is that not just a metaphor, an incongruous juxtaposing of *Ereignis* with a mailman? If so, Derrida thinks, it is the "catastrophic" metaphor that he describes in "The Retreat of Metaphor," in which vehicle and tenor, primary and secondary analogates, are reversed. If language is the house of Being, Heidegger says, that does not mean that we must think language in terms of housing, but housing in terms of language. Accordingly, if *Ereignis* is a postal system, that does not mean we are to think the *Seinsgeschick* in terms of letter-sending, but letter-ending in terms of the *Seinsgeschick*. That is to say, for Derrida, *Ereignis* is the place—which he himself would call writing, or *arché*-writing—where all transfers, metaphors, correspondences and communications take place. And his point is that this central processing unit has been scrambled, jammed, decentered, and thrown into confusion, its wires crossed, its lines downed: "If the postal (technology, position, 'metaphysics') is announced in the 'first' dispatch, then there is no longer 'metaphysics,' etc. (this I would attempt to say one time and differently), nor even the "dispatch," but only dispatches without destination. For to order the different epochs, stations, determinations, in brief the whole history of Being, to a destination of Being, this is perhaps the most unheard of postal snare. There is not even post or dispatch, there are only posts and dispatches" (*CP*, 73–74). (Still, one wonders how far removed this account really is from Heidegger, from *Spiel* of which he says: "*Es spielet, weil es spielet*": it plays because it plays.[3] And Derrida wonders too. In a parenthetical remark, he whispers to us, "And this movement [which seems to me at once very far and very close to Heidegger]" [*CP*, 74]. That is the point of the double-cross. Within those parentheses is enclosed another reading of Heidegger.)

In any case, on Derrida's reading the postal system is broken down into a free play of *différance*. "There is" (*il y a*) only *différance*, postal agency, delays, and the unavoidable possibility, and fatal necessity, of detour, of lost letters. One cannot even write a history of these dispatches, because history, tradition, transmission, are all constituted effects of the postal play. The desire for a history is eschatological, metaphysical, apocalyptic.

Were there such a history, then we would receive one day—today, it is what *is* today, all around us on the earth[4]—the dispatch of the *Gestell.* Perhaps it would come on the back of a card with a picture of a loathsome smokestack belching into the sky. But we who know how to think would know to read it backwards and also to see in it another possibility like those trick cards that show different scenes when held at different angles. In so doing we would make the way clear for the reversal, for the *Geviert*—"the most beautiful postcard which Martin has sent us from Freiburg," and the most simple (*CP*, 74). That would bring the epoch of postal technology to an end. That would represent the end of the post, the end of the course, the end of all couriers (*CP*, 37). Everything would be released into a new beginning. But for Derrida, that is the dream of presence: eschatology now.

HERMENEUTIC ESCHATOLOGY

We cannot deny the "eschatological" Heidegger. Indeed, as Derrida says, this is his own word. The eschatological Heidegger thinks the way, the beginning overtakes and outstrips the end. And such an eschatology is essentially hermeneutical for it demands the capacity to hear the saving message in old words. It requires the ears to hear how the oldest of the old tells us what is coming so that we can understand the end as a transition to new beginning.

To confront this Heidegger we can do no better than to follow closely Heidegger's efforts to hear what Anaximander has to say. Getting in touch with Anaximander is the long distance philosophical call par excellence. For what Anaximander says is the very earliest recorded message we have from the Greek thinkers. But are we drawn to this task merely as a challenge, to see if we can actually decipher a message that old? That would reduce the call to a kind of technological-historical feat, without substance or weight (*HW*, 325/6), without a bearing on the *Sache*, which is just what Derrida suspected Heidegger would say (*CP*, 73). It would diminish an effort at thought to an exercise in philosophical and psychological technique, to see if we could get inside the head of a man named Anaximander, who lived long ago at this address in Miletus (*HW*, 328/18).

The authority (HW, 325/16) of this message, in Heidegger's view, has nothing to do with its age and/or the idiosyncrasies of its author. The interest we have in stringing a line of communication between Anaximander and us should not center on its length, on mere chronological-historical distance (325/16). Rather it arises because the early (*die Frühe*) has a claim (*Anspruch*) on the later, especially the last. The saying (*Spruch*) of Anaximander is a claim (*Anspruch*) (325/16). This is not just any call; it is a priority call with the right to interrupt the work-a-day conversations we are accustomed to have. And so it is not that the call is long-distance that matters, but that there is a voice of authority on the other end. In fact, for one so far away, the voice is surprisingly near (*Nähe*, 325/16), speaking to us now, about something that is coming (*in das Kommende hinausspricht*), perhaps any day now. (We know neither the day nor the hour.

Which means it may not come at all. And that is why Anaximander is calling: to serve up a warning/reminder, to put us on watch for something which needs hearing and heeding. He wants to set us thinking, to recall to mind (*an-denken*), something that we tend to forget. We have preserved but one saying of Anaximander but it contains a double message. For it tells us about how it was in the beginning—it is a long-distance call—but also about what is coming, maybe any day. And the power of this saying, the authority of this voice, lies in the fact that these are the same thing. The same (*dasselbe*), but not identical. Anaximander's call stretches from one end to the other, so that it looks like a standard tele-communication. But the end in question is not a *telos*, but an *eschaton*. Not a linear *telos*, but a more ambiguous, playful *eschaton*.

The end of which we are speaking is not a tele-linear goal and consummation in which the accumulated potencies of the Western tradition reach their fulfilment, but quite the opposite. It is the emptying (not the filling), the spending, the exhausting of a great beginning. The *eschaton* means we have reached the point where the potency of the tradition has been spent, and it is a question as to whether we will persist indefinitely in this dead-end or whether the eschaton will turn itself inside out and become the point of departure for a new beginning, an opening on to what-is-coming. And that is the point of Anaximander's call, the force of his claim (*An-spruch*) on us: to remind (*an-denken*) of this decision, to mark the decisiveness of the point we have reached.

Eschato-logy is not teleo-logy. Teleology is metaphysics. It is a rule-governed process in which the seeds of success are sown from the very beginning; in which the *rationes seminales* are planted at the start. In teleology the beginning is small, progress is steady, and the end is a great fulfilment and *parousia*, an *Aufhebung*. Eschatology is a play. In eschatology, the beginning is a great dawn, a tremendous burst of lightning, a flash illuminating the whole countryside. But it vanishes as quickly as lightning, and then its memory is diminished and erased, until finally, through a series of transformations whose rule no one knows, there is only night, only *Abend-land*. And then, in that dark night, there lies the possibility of another beginning, another sudden turn in which the lightning flashes again:

> Do we stand on the eve (*Vorabend*) of the most monstrous transformation of the whole earth and that era in which it is suspended? Do we stand on the eve of a night which heralds another dawn (*Frühe*)? . . . Is the land of the evening (*Abend-land*) only now emerging? Will this land of evening overwhelm Occident Orient alike, transcending whatever is merely European to become the location of a new but primordially fate history? . . . *Are* we the latecomers (*Spätlingers*) we are? But are we also at the same time precursors of the dawn of an altogether different age, which has already left our historiological representation of history behind? (*NW*, 325–6/17)

It is not a question of reckoning what is coming (*rechnen das Kommende*) through scientific historical research, through a calculus of possibilities carefully drawn from the past. That historical calculus systematically destroys our true relation to the future (*Zukunft*), to what is arriving (*An-kunft*), maybe any day. It is systematically blind to the genuine message that is being sent across the epochs, systematically destructive of what is arriving in the mail, to the coming dispatch (*die Ankunft des Geschickes*) (*NW*, 326/17).

There is thus an essential difference between the tele-communications of teleology and hearing the call of the beginning in eschatology. The present epoch is an age of sophisticated historical research, of the most advanced historical consciousness, which is likewise the age of the most advanced and sophisticated system of nationwide and international communications. We have at our disposal the most advanced techniques for getting in touch with everything past and present. But it is in just such an age—which Heidegger calls an epoch of "historicism," for we are the least confined of any people before us to the present time and place—that we have become deaf and blind to the message which is sent across the epochs, to the genuine dispatch of Being: "Historicism has today not only not been overcome, but is only now entering the stage of its expansion and entrenchment. The technical organization of communications throughout the world by radio and by a press already limping after it is the genuine form of historicism's dominion" (*HW*, 326/17).

The press is slower to pass the word along than the radio. The radio limps after the television, which puts us on the spot, eyewitnesses. The eye of the video is slowly becoming all-seeing in fulfillment of the pan-opticon described by Foucault.[5] It is a question of how quickly and how efficiently end can be joined to end, *telos* to *telos*, and that is what has doomed the newspaper and appears now to doom the book. Teleology is the science of getting from end to end with maximal efficiency. In tele-communications, teleology reaches its peak but the lines of eschatology go dead. The age of advanced tele-communications is the age of deafness and blindness to the dispatch of Being. The clarity of the message that is sent in eschatology is in inverse proportion to the technical organization of tele-communications. The noise of technological communication systems drowns out the word that Being sends.

In eschatology the earliest is not a seed that slowly ripens into the last, but rather a flash that, having been all but extinguished by the last, is capable of flashing again and turning darkness into light, the evening-land into a new morning. In teleology the last always comes after the first, after a long period of maturation; but in eschatology the first can overtake (*überholen*) the last, and with a suddenness that could not be anticipated: "But what if that which is early overtakes everything late; if the very earliest thoroughly overtakes and outstrips the very latest?" (*HW*, 327/18). Then we would be in an eschatological position, which means openness to something new, a new beginning in the midst of the old. And that is the most decisive difference of all between eschatology and teleology. Teleology reaches fulfilment, satisfaction, peace, rest when it reaches the *telos*. *But in eschatology, the eschaton* is the transition point to a new beginning, a new flash of lightning and the commencement of a new postal service. Whence Heidegger answers his own question: "What once occurred in the dawn of our destiny would then come as what once occurred, at the last (*eschaton*), that is, at the departure of the long-hidden destiny of Being" (*HW*, 327/18). The beginning would come again at the end, would overtake the end. And that is what we mean by eschatology: when we are driven into the end in such a way that the beginning can overtake it, so that the end turns itself around, reverses itself and becomes a commencement. Then the whole accumulated wealth of the history of Being is collected together in one glimmering moment of reversal. The *eschaton* of itself is but an end, a spinning out of possibilities, the danger of a dead end. But an eschatology means that the beginning overtakes the end, that everything harbored and hidden in the interval between the beginning and the end is gathered together and pushes the end beyond itself, outdistances and outstrips it (*überholt*) and precipitates a new beginning. This gathering-together (*logos*, *legein*) of the whole history of Being in the end (*eschaton*) is the eschatology of Being: "The Being of beings is gathered together (*lethestai*, *Logos*) in the ultimacy of its destiny. The essence of Being hitherto disappears its truth still veiled. The history of Being is gathered in this departure. The gathering in this departure, as the gathering (*logos*) at the outermost point (*eschaton*) of its essence hitherto, is the eschatology of Being. As something fateful (*geschickliches*) Being is inherently eschatological" (*HW*, 327/18).

In teleology the beginning is separated from the end as seed from mature form. In eschatology the beginning overtakes the end and precipitates a reversal. Eschatological thinking then is precisely the capacity to see in what is coming the coming again of the early. When the early overtakes (*über-holen*) the late, the late retrieves (*wieder-holen*) the early: "If we think in terms of the eschatology of Being, then we must someday await what once belonged to the early in what is one day coming. Today we must learn to ponder the former dawn on its own terms" (*HW*, 327/18). In eschatology the beginning overtakes the end, puts an end to the end; in teleology, the end fulfills the beginning and puts an end to the beginning. In eschatology the beginning outstrips the end so that the end is driven beyond itself. The most extreme end is consequently the point of transition to a beginning. And if the most extreme end is the greatest danger, then it is likewise the place of salvation. And that indeed is the note on which the essay on Anaximander concludes. "Is there any rescue? Rescue comes when and only when danger *is*. Danger *is* when Being itself advances to its farthest extreme (*Letzte*), and when that oblivion that issues from Being itself reverses itself" (*HW*, 373/58). Eschatology is then a logic of reversal, a movement in which the beginning spins itself out into oblivion, and then turns itself around into a new beginning. It is a reverse hermeneutics which know how to read backwards. And this eschatological logic—which is a primordial *logos* and not a metaphysical method-logic, teleo-logic, theo-logic—is simultaneously a salvation history, a way the danger is reversed, and night is turned into day, a way we can be saved by the grace of an *eschaton* that reverses itself, that is to be distinguished from a way of serving ourselves.

And *that* explains the claim that Anaximander's call has upon us. It is a rescue call meant to save us from the *eschaton*, to avert the fate that the end would be a terminal illness. Anaximander has an urgent message to deliver, and he has placed an emergency call to us, though it comes in the form of a one-line telegram, the rest of the page ripped away. We do not have the whole message, but only a fragment. But we can tell from what we do have, if we decipher those words carefully, that the message is important, that there is an alternative to the current impasse, a "rescue" from the "danger." And those are Heidegger's words. We require only a hermeneutic eye to decipher this message of salvation.

BEYOND ESCHATOLOGY

But such a hermeneutic eschatology cannot escape the charge of metaphysics. Teleology and eschatology alike are caught in the grips of the same metaphysical circle, each finding a way for the end to repeat the beginning, each functioning within a metaphysics of recuperation, salvation, comfort and rescue. *Eschatology* suffers from a metaphysical-hermeneutic illusion that there is *a meaning* of Being, and that it was once granted to us, but has since dissipated, and that it is the task of thought to recover and restore it. The whole project flies in the face of what Heidegger means by *lethe* as primordially constitutive of *aletheia*. It flatly contradicts the very notion of the *Seinsgeschick* that any age would be privileged, that any epoch would be blessed with a particular revelation denied to others. How can any epoch, which is defined as a phase of withdrawal, be singled out as in any way less of a withdrawal?

Without denying that this hermeneutic eschatology is there I want to show now that Heidegger's task is not unambiguous, that Heidegger knew better, that there is another, more radically critical, deconstructive thought at work, and that it was there from the start. Here we see Derrida looking over the shoulder of Heidegger.

I have in mind the Heidegger who was not interested in Being but in moving *beyond* Being, for whom the question of the "meaning" of Being was a way of saying that the point is to get beyond Being to what lets Being be, to the horizontal operation which grants Being its play, its space. From *Being and Time* on there is a relentless effort to get beyond Being, to move thought into the region where we are loosened from the illusion that there is a privileged sense of Being which we should find and hold close to our breasts.

In other words, the whole postal metaphysics breaks down, the whole metaphysics of the "tradition" as message bearing is surpassed, and it is no longer a question of recovering an original message which gets sent across the ages. Teleology and eschatology differ only in the means they to deliver the mad. Teleology uses regular lines and has regular deliveries and we know when to expect the postman. Eschatology is more wanton, more playful, and we know neither the day nor the hour when the mail is being delivered. But in both cases there is a primordial message to be carried across the epochs, a tradition that bears a unique message. This second, more radical Heidegger knows that the message is that there is no message, no privileged sense-of-Being, no special instructions from Milesia.

Let us follow the tracks of this Heidegger. (If there has to be a Heidegger I/Heidegger II distinction, this is I think a better candidate than the early Heidegger/late Heidegger distinction.) When we follow this Heidegger, we find him slowly undermining and discarding the notion of the meaning of Being, the truth of Being, and Being itself, in order to bring himself before the matter to be thought. The point is to give up the postal expectation, to get beyond waiting for the mailman, to cease waiting for the letter which will reveal the secret word, the master-name for Being. We are brought before the matter for thought just at that point where we surrender the illusion that Being has a privileged meaning or truth.

But does that mean that the *saving* message will be that there is no saving message? Is this the eschatology that consists in putting an *end* to all eschatologies? Is this thus a new, higher, more critical eschatology, a new hermeneutics, the new secret, the new apocalypse? But before we are buried in a sea of paradoxes, let us briefly trace the steps of the post-eschatological, post-postal Heidegger.

There is an important distinction in *Being and Time* between Being and the *meaning* of Being, but it is a distinction that is easily overlooked, and this because of an easily missed distinction that Heidegger is making between a "primary" and a "secondary" projection. In the first place, Heidegger says, the being is projected upon its Being; this is a preliminary, primary projection. Then it is projected more decisively in terms of the "meaning" of that Being. He says: "What does 'meaning' signify? In our investigation, we have encountered this phenomenon in connection with the analysis of understanding and interpretation. According to that analysis, meaning is that wherein the understandability [*Verstehbarkeit*] of something maintains itself—even that of something which does not come into view explicitly and thematically" (*SZ*, 323–24/370–71). Meaning is not exactly the object of understanding, what is understood by the understanding, but that in which what is understood is suspended or held (*hält sich*). It sustains what is understood, giving it a pivot around which understandability can organize itself. He continues: "'Meaning' signifies the 'upon-which' (*das Woraufhin*) of a primary projection in terms of which something can be conceived in its possibility as that which it is" (*SZ*, 324/371). It is because the being is projected in its Being in the first place—the "primary" projection—that it is something understood. But it is because we point to a certain center of reference, a certain pivot or organizing point *in* this primary projection—which Heidegger calls the "upon-which" (*das Woraujhin*) of the primary projection—that we can lay claim to knowing the "meaning" of what is understood. The meaning makes the projection-of-Being possible, which in turn makes the appearance of the being possible. Meaning always has to do with making-possible: "Projecting discloses possibilities—that is to say, it discloses the sort of thing which makes possible" (*SZ*, 324/371).

This is not to say, however, that there are two projections, but rather two phases of one and the same understanding-projective undertaking: the first, in which the being is projected upon its Being, the second, in which we determine the lines of force in that projection that sustain and hold it together.

One can see that Heidegger is already set on breaking up the binary Being/being pair and replacing it with a ternary, tripartite articulation in terms of: (1) the being that is to be understood (projected), which is of course no "bare fact" but always something projected within its horizontal setting; (2) the *Being* of that being, which provides its horizontal frame; (3) the *meaning* of the Being of that being, the *upon-which* of the projection of the being-in-its-Being. This is to distinguish being/Being/meaning; or again the projected/its projection/the upon-which of the projection.

The problem with the history of metaphysics then is not that it has no theories of Being—indeed that is all one ever finds there—but that neglects to take the further step, that it fails to realize that the step-back is a two-step—from beings to Being, and from Being to the upon-which of its projection. Whence metaphysics functions naively, missing the hidden upon-which, even though the understanding of Being feeds off, nourishes itself on (*sich nährt*) it: "All ontical experience of entities . . . is based upon projections of the Being of the corresponding entities—projections which in every case are more or less transparent. But in these projections there lies hidden the '"upon which" of the projection; and on this, as it were, the understanding of Being nourishes itself" (*SZ*, 324/371).

It is therefore not Heidegger's point, although he sometimes suggests that it is (and when he does, that is *our* candidate for Heidegger I), to offer a competing Being/beings distinction. He does not propose a superior theory-of-Being that will surpass its competitors just because it reaches being while they invariably speak of beings and hence never succeed in crossing the line, the slash, between Being/beings. On the contrary, he is after the slash itself, the way the line is drawn in metaphysics between Being and beings, the rule that all metaphysics follows in distinguishing Being/beings. Heidegger does not want to get into the fray, to enter a names-of-Being contest with the latest and best name for "Being." He wants to move quietly and inconspicuously around the edges of this debate and to pick out the rule that organizes the various entries in the contest.

He is not interested in the message but the nature of the delivery-service. He does not seek the "meaning of Being" in the conventional sense—that is just what populates the history of metaphysics like the various "world-views" (*Weltanschauungen*) described in the introduction to *Grundprobleme*. Rather he seeks to make a transcendental-horizontal-hermeneutical gesture that puts its finger on what sustains (*hält*) and maintains in subsistence (*nährt*) all such projects. Heidegger has already dropped out of metaphysical competition in *Being and Time*. He is already asking *about* metaphysics, which is to ask *beyond* it. He is already on his way, not towards Being, but *beyond* it, as he says in the *Grundprobleme*.

Metaphysics is an architectural business of *sketching* Being/beings proposals, of drawing Being/beings grids, the point of which is to frame things out, to secure them, organize them around a solid center, ground them on rock-sure foundations, situate entities. It is not Heidegger's point to get into that business with a rival grid of his own, but to *question beyond* it and see what is going on *in* all such undertakings.

That became slowly clearer over the years, even though *our* Heidegger I, the hermeneutic-eschatological Heidegger, kept intervening, keeping the ambiguity of the text alive. Heidegger gave up speaking of the "meaning" of Being, because that word belonged too irrevocably to the transcendental-phenomenological tradition. But when he turned to the "truth" of Being—in a gesture meant to turn away from subjectivism—he complicated things in a different way. For the truth of Being suggested even more forcefully that there is (or was) one surefire, luminous disclosure of Being that descended on the early Greeks and has since dropped out of view. The truth of Being suggested that the other views—not exactly world-views but views of Being, *Seinsanschauungen*—were not true, that they were concealments, coverings-over and that Heidegger, heeding the early Greeks, knew the secret name.

But then there are the numerous marginalia in the *Gesamtausgabe*, which gloss "Being" as *Ereignis* and the "truth" of Being as *a-letheia*, stressing the *lethe*, the coming-to-pass of a sphere of manifestness from ineradicable concealment. Here the post-eschatological, the post-postal Heidegger glosses the hermeneutic Heidegger, giving us the meta-hermeneutics that interprets the hermeneutic Heidegger. And occasionally the post-postal Heidegger breaks out into the clear even in the text itself, making it clear that there is no privileged meaning or "truth" of Being, that no sending enjoys any rights over any other, there is no secret letter being sent special delivery to/from Freiburg. There can be, he says, no assessing of progress in the history of the Western epochs: "Not only do we lack any criterion which would permit us to evaluate the perfection of an epoch of metaphysics as compared with any other epoch, the *right* to this kind of evaluation does not exist. Plato's thinking is no more perfect than Parmenides'. Hegel's philosophy is no more perfect than Kant's. Each epoch of philosophy has its own necessity. We simply have to acknowledge that a philosophy is the way it is." And that is the real difference between an *epoch* of metaphysics, a dispatch or *Schickung* from Being, and a *Weltanschauung*; the latter are subjective preferences, value-judgments, whereas the history of Being proceeds with a rigor that surpasses subjective preference. Hence the text continues: "It is not for us to prefer one to the other, as can be the case with regard to various *Weltanschauungen*" (*SZ*, 62-63/375). And there are texts of this sort even as early as 1938:

> When we use the word "science" today, it means something essentially different from the *doctrina* and *scientia* of the Middle Ages, and also from the Greek *episteme*. Greek science was never exact, precisely because, in keeping with its essence, it could not be exact and did not need to be exact. Hence it makes no sense whatever to suppose that modern science is more exact than that of antiquity. Neither can we say that the Galilean doctrine of freely falling bodies is true and that Aristotle's teaching, that light bodies strive upwards, is false; for the Greek understanding of the essence of body and place and of the relation between the two rests upon different interpretations of beings and hence conditions a correspondingly different kind of seeing and questioning of natural events. No one would presume to maintain that Shakespeare's poetry is more advanced than that of Aeschylus. It is still more impossible to say that the modern understanding of whatever is, is more correct than that of the Greek. Therefore, we must first free ourselves from the habit of comparing the new science with the old solely in terms of degree, from the point of view of progress.[6]

The history of Being unfolds as it does. That is all one can say. *Eidos, ousia, actualitas, res cogitans et extensa, Geist, Wille-zur-Macht*: these are so many master-names that have been put forth, so many ways Being has been projected, that Being sends itself. There is no question of preferring one to the other, or of rank-ordering them, no question either of waiting for the delivery of the letter that holds the secret, the master-name. It is a question only of attentiveness to the giving and the sending that is at work throughout the postal epoch, the epochal-postal system.

Ereignis is not the master name of Being. And Heidegger explicitly warns us against misconstruing it that way: "'Being as Ereignis': Formerly, philosophy thought Being in terms of beings as *idea, energeia, actualitas*, will—and now, one might think, as *Ereignis*. Understood in this way, *Ereignis* means a transformed interpretation of Being, which, if it is correct, represents a continuation of metaphysics" (*SD*, 22/21). *Ereignis* would then be reduced to Heidegger's entry in the contest for the master-name. But his point is to take the step-back from this contest, from this sequence of epochal faces and guises which Being presents, so that we are no longer taken in by the disguise, so that we are on the alert to the game metaphysics plays with us. The *truth* of Being would then turn out to be the recognization that *there is no truth*, no one truth, no privileged sense or meaning of Being, and hence no privileged epoch either. There is simply the incessant giving and taking, bestowal and withdrawal of presence in one form or another over the ages. But if that is so then to overcome metaphysics, to get beyond the "oblivion of Being," would turn out to mean a certain awakening to this state of affairs, a certain Socratic realization that there is no truth, no master-name. The only release *from* the oblivion would be to awaken *to* the oblivion. And *that* is just what is said in the "Seminar" to "Time and Being": "Thinking that begins with *Being and Time* is thus, on the one hand, an awakening which must be understood as a recollection of something which has never been thought—but on the other hand, as this awakening, not an extinguishing of the oblivion of Being, but placing oneself in it and standing within it. Thus the awakening from oblivion of Being to the oblivion of Being is the awakening into *Ereignis*" (*SD*, 32/29–30). This "awakening" (*Erwachen, Entwachen*) is the demythologized version of the new dawn to which we would awaken in the eschatological, apocalyptic Heidegger. We awaken, not to a new day, to the brightness of the dawn, but rather our eyes are opened to the night itself. There is no question of replacing the night of the *Abend-land* with the dawn of a new day, but rather of awakening to the night itself. We awaken to concealment itself: "The withdrawal which characterized metaphysics in the form of the oblivion of Being now shows itself as the dimension of concealment itself. But now this concealment does not conceal itself. Rather the attention of thinking is concerned with it" (*SD*, 44/41).Now thinking is on the alert to metaphysics, and it recognizes metaphysics for what it is, which is concealment, oblivion, withdrawal. It is not withdrawal itself which is overcome—that is ineradicably constitutive of the history of Being—but the withdrawal *of* the withdrawal. The withdrawal itself is now recognized for what it is. The only "truth" of Being then is *a-letheia*, which means the acquiescence of thought to the ineradicable *lethe* of which the various epochal guises, the names of Being are the modification.

The truth of Being is demythologized. The history of metaphysics turns out to be a set of dispatches of Being, mailed and stamped, which turn out to be no more than promissory notes, letters of intent, which never deliver the promised message. The Seminar puts this in postal language: "Metaphysics is the history of the way Being is stamped (*der Seinsprägungen*), that is, seen from the *Ereignis*, the history of the withdrawing of the *sender* in favor of the dispatches (*Schickungen*) which were sent along, of the current letting-presence of the present." (*SD*, 44/41). Being is packaged and stamped in the form of presence, parcelled out (*moira*) as presence, in epochally differing ways, and we are lured away from the sending power, that is, the whole postal process, which remains in primordial concealment, in favor of the packages we receive.

But if the only truth is *a-letheia* itself, that is, the rule of *lethe* over the epochs, does that not still privilege the Greeks, who named and thought truth as *aletheia*? That too must be given up. The end of philosophy must entail the end of the Greeks as well, and all the special privileges that German philosophers have accorded them. And our Heidegger II, our post-postal Heidegger, seems ready for this:

> The natural concept of truth does not mean unconcealment, *not in the philosophy of the Greeks either.* It is often and justifiably pointed out that the word *alethes* is already used by Homer only in the *verba dicendi*, in statement and thus in the sense of correctness and reliability, not in the sense of unconcealment. . . .
>
> In the scope of this question we must acknowledge the fact that *aletheia*, unconcealment in the sense of the opening of presence, was originally only experienced as *orthotes* as the correctness of representation and statements. But then the assertion about the essential transformation of truth, that is, from unconcealment to correctness, is also untenable. (*SD*, 78/70)

The privileges of the Greeks are curtailed. Even *aletheia* was originally experienced as *homoioses* and *adequatio.* And what else can that mean than what grants presence and the present is always unheeded? "Only what *aletheia* as opening grants is experienced and thought, not what it is as such. This remains concealed. Does this happen by chance? Does it happen only as a consequence of the carelessness of human thinking? Or does it happen because self-concealing, concealment, *lethe* belongs to *a-letheia*, not just as an addition, not as a shadow to light, but rather as the heart of *aletheia*?" (*SD*, 78/71). *Lethe* belongs so primordially to *aletheia* that *aletheia* itself remained in concealment to the Greeks themselves. The Greeks too belong to the epochal withdrawal. Thus Heidegger makes the startling concession, not only that—contrary to *Plato's Doctrine of Truth*—the early Greeks do not have a privileged experience of *aletheia*, but also that it is necessary to experience *aletheia* in a way that moves "*over and beyond the Greek*" (*über das Griechische hinaus*). Not only do we have to get beyond Being, we also have to get beyond the Greeks. With that we reach the end of the eschatological Heidegger: "What does *ratio*, *nous*, *noein*, perceiving (*Vernunft-Vemehmen*) mean? What does ground and principle and especially principle of all principles mean? Can this ever be sufficiently determined unless we experience *aletheia* in a Greek manner as unconcealment and then, above and beyond the Greek, thinking is the opening of self-concealing?" (*SD*, 79/71).

There remains only one essential point to make regarding this post-eschatological Heidegger, and that has to do with the connections between *lethe* and sheltering. But this is the most important point of all. In the self-concealing (*sich verbergen*) of the Open, of that which sends, there lies an essential sheltering (*Bergen*) and preserval (*Verwahren*): "And does not even a sheltering (*Bergen*) and preserving (*Verwahren*) rule in this self-concealing of the opening of presence from which unconcealment can be granted to begin with, and thus what is present can appear in its presence?" (*SD*, 78/79). The *Verbergen*, the concealment, is a harboring, keeping safe, sheltering (*Bergen*), giving it a place of safekeeping. And it is this that seems to me to interest Heidegger above all. The task of thought is sheltering and keeping safe, to protect what Heidegger once called "Being" from the harsh lights of metaphysical conceptuality, to preserve the mystery of the withdrawal of its mystery. What Heidegger came more and more to realize over the years was that metaphysics represents a kind of assault upon things, a power-play on the part of human conceptuality, and his critique of "humanism" was meant essentially to counter the pretentiousness and the will-to-power that all metaphysical mapmaking involves. The history of metaphysics is the story of so many attempts to throw a Being/beings grid over things, to lay them out (*aus-legen*) in some kind of encompassing interpretation, to catch them up (con-cipere, be-greifen) in one of its webs, to see to it that things are subdued by its will-to-power as knowledge, its power-knowledge. And if the eschatological Heidegger set out to displace these metaphysical conceptions with an alternate, non-metaphysical experience of Being in its glimmering Ionian radiance, the post-eschatological Heidegger came to a more sober, but deeper, perhaps more Socratic realization that the truth is concealed that the truth is the concealment, that truth is *lethe* sending its dispatches with epochal regularity while all along remaining behind.

But the truth is not only that there is no truth, no revelatory explosion, but also and more importantly, and as a part of this realization, the sense of reverence, openness and respect for the mystery of what holds itself back—all of which is named in the word *Gelassenheit*. The final realization of Heidegger is that the highest truth available to thought lies in the acknowledgment of the withdrawal of things from our conceptual grasp, the refusal of truth in the sense that metaphysical and eschatological thinking expect and demand. Thinking is surrendering these ambitions and pretensions and acquiring a sense of reverence and letting-be in which we are admitted into an experience of ourselves as mortals and of the world as the fourfold.

But are we not then right back into the eschatological Heidegger with his privileged experience of Being? Is not the account of mortals dwelling poetically *precisely* what Derrida calls "the most beautiful card which Martin has sent from Freiburg"? That is, is it not a privileged dispatch, special delivery, the truth of Being for those that have the eyes to see? I think not, and for two reasons. (1) We have been disillusioned, once and for all, by

Derrida, and by Heidegger himself, that there is some post-metaphysical dawn, some genuine turn in the sequence of epochs in which there would be a non-epochal dispatch, a sending with nothing remaining behind. Hence we do not confuse this experience of the breakdown of metaphysics with a new dawn. It is nothing more than alertness to the darkness of the world-night. (2) The experience of "mortals" under the heavens, upon the earth, is not vision, revelation, eschatology, apocalypse, but precisely the poverty of thought, the humility of one who has less to say than metaphysics. It is the experience of one who has opened himself to the abyss, to the play in which all things are caught up, to the *ébranler*, the trembling. He is on the alert to the illusions of ground-laying and foundation-seeking; he is open to the play of the child-king. And in that openness, he reaches a kind of understanding, the understanding of one who understands the limits of conceptual handicrafts. In letting the world play be, in exposing himself to the abyss, he experiences the truth of truth's very withdrawal. Deconstruction cannot avoid circling around on itself and effecting a deeper, more radical retrieval. And when it does it hits upon what we will call the cold truth.

COLD HERMENEUTICS: DOUBLE-CROSSING DERRIDA

If we have allowed Derrida to infiltrate Heidegger, then, according to the logic of the double-cross, we must now allow Heidegger to weave his way into Derrida's network. Now it is Derrida's turn to be seated in the chair and to let Heidegger whisper in his ear.

Let us begin by conceding Derrida everything. Let us admit at once the *ébranler*, the trembling and the tremor, the lack of grounds. Let us concede the slippage, the uncontrollable drift, dissemination. Let us give Derrida to understand that we are on his side. Let us acknowledge the breakdown of the tele-communications system: that there is no hotline between Freiburg and the early Greeks, that there are no privileged insights into what is coming, or what has been. Let us concede the play in which all things are swept. In short, let us give Derrida his way, which is the best way to gain his confidence, to infiltrate his corporation.

In so doing Derrida's project becomes question-worthy. And the question is this: What then? What have we accomplished? The answer is and must be: Nothing—what did you want? Where have we gotten ourselves? Where have we ended up? And the answer is and must be: Nowhere—where did you want to go? But what are we to do? And the answer is: whatever you like; *dilege, et quod vis fac.* There can be no question here of assured destinations, neither for messages nor travelers. The whole undertaking is a-telic and u-topic. It has neither goal nor assured place of arrival. It is not, after all, as if Derrida is in search of an alternate metaphysics, an alternate program that would hold its own in the world-market of competing metaphysical systems. It is not as if Derrida has another *Weltanschauung* for us to settle into, to curl up in before the hearth fires of philosophical speculation. On the contrary the idea was to be put out into the cold, to be divested of the comforts of philosophy, to shake the whole, to make—to let—the ground tremble.

But let us concede *that* too. We relinquish any claim to find a competing metaphysics, or anti-metaphysics, in Derrida. We give up the need to land on our feet after a go-around with *différance*. But we still insist that there is something question-worthy in all this, although it is not easy to know how to put the question. Once we have given Derrida everything, once we have exposed ourselves to the abyss, to the mirror-play of signifiers, what effect does that produce? What has it done to us? What have we done, or let be done, to ourselves? What has become of us? But that is *undecidable*. It does not produce a decided and definite effect with circumscribable results. On the contrary, it throws us into undecidability. It is not a question of standing clear on one side or the other—of metaphysics, of the apocalyptic.

That too we give to Derrida. But that does not lay our question to rest—which would, after all, be a peculiar kind of undecidability—but rather it keeps it in motion. What is this undecidability doing? How are we, who are caught up in undecidability, doing? How do we find ourselves, we who are tossed about by the *ébranler*, wandering two-headed in the maze of differential interweavings, with no footing, on constantly slipping grounds? We who are not even sure about this "we," about "interpreting us"? How are we to describe this groundlessness? What's to become of us? What sort of situation is this to be in? *Wie befinden-Sie sich*? Martin would ask. How are you doing? How are we doing? We who have given Derrida everything'?

It is here, in pondering this question, that a hermeneutic element insinuates itself into Derrida's corporation. It is here that a moment of "truth" intervenes. And by "truth" I mean neither *adequatio* nor *aletheia*, but rather the "cold truth" about ourselves, the comfortlessness of it all. The cold truth is the effect that one imagines Socrates produced in those he cross-examined: outrage and indignation at first, and then, after an unguarded moment of reflection, a cold shiver of recognition: that one indeed does not know what piety is, or justice, or how to define a good state. Socrates kept telling the truth on the Athenians, kept embarrassing them, producing disconcerting thoughts. He kept disrupting the concerted efforts of a few to run the *polis* to their own advantage, and to avoid cross-examination and gadflies. What effects did Socrates produce? Discomfort, discomfiture, disconcertion, anxiety. *Wie befinden-Sie sich*? *Ängstlich.* If one conceded everything to Socrates, what did that do to you? It put you in the position of being unable to discriminate what comes by nature and what can be taught, between what piety is and what is impious, between what a good state is and what it is not. It threw you into undecidability and robbed you of your sleep. And that is what this modern-day Socrates, roaming the streets of Paris, does, or tries at least.

It is in this cold shiver of recognition—which is nothing like a Cartesian moment of translucence, nothing like an idealist theory of reflection—that I locate a certain hermeneutic element in Derrida, one that links him with other practitioners of cold hermeneutics, like Kierkegaard, Nietzsche and Heidegger. It is a cold and heartless hermeneutics; it does not recover hidden meanings and lost treasures from the tradition. On the contrary it brings us up short, startles us, exposing us to the play that plays without why. It catches us off-guard, in an unsuspecting moment. Derrida's effect is to keep us "ready for anxiety," as Martin said, even as metaphysics wants to reassure us; to expose us to the abyss, even as metaphysics wants to fill it up, so that being clings to being, presence to presence, in a well-rounded whole. The moment of hermeneutic truth in Derrida is a moment of heartless honesty. Derrida's hermeneutic truth is like the truth of which Nietzsche spoke when he said that too much of it would kill you, and when he said that the strength of a spirit could be measured by the degree to which it needed the truth "attenuated, veiled, sweetened, blunted and falsified." What Derrida "knows" is like the knowledge that Nietzsche attributes to the sufferers, whom he calls the "elect of knowledge," who are almost sacrificed by their knowledge, which carries them into "distant terrible worlds."[7]

The end of the apocalyptic tone, the end of all calling to an end, of calling to a halt to one thing or another, means that there is no apocalyptic delivery service, no saving message. The "good news" is bad news. But then, is that not just another way to carry around apocalyptic secrets? Is that not the apocalypse all over again, but with no salvation no salvific word? Bad news is just as much news as good news, and sometimes more. And just as much grounds for an apocalypse.

That is why Derrida can never *say* what we have said here, can never write what we have written here—about hermeneutic truth. That would be to assume the very apocalyptic-hermeneutic tone that he means to renounce. His *daimon* must always be prohibitive; his dialectic must always be negative. He must always stay on the move, remain a moving target. Writing is a praxis of disruption that must remain on the alert, roaming the street, suspicious even of every attempt such as ours to pause and take stock. For then he would have something to defend; he would speak with the authority in order to enforce views, to suppress dissent. We cannot stop the perpetual motion of the mail. Socrates must outdrink everyone; we cannot get him drunk and wring from him just what he thinks justice really is. *In vino veritas* remains within the metaphysics of truth.

It is in this cold hermeneutics, this hermeneutics of the shiver that issues from the *ébranler*, that we see Heidegger peering over the shoulder of Derrida, whispering in his ear. Heidegger infiltrates this Socratic conversationalist with the taciturnity of the thinker; he finds the calm, meditative eye in the Dionysian storm. Under Heidegger's subversive influence the *abîme*, the uncontrollable mirror play of reflections, becomes the *Abgrund*, the dark and silent abyss, the quiet moment when we are struck with awe. Derrida sets about the deconstruction of all mystagogues and rationalists, of all who have claimed to see the light. Heidegger whispers in his ear that putting all metaphysics under the sign of suspicion, questioning every claim to privileged access, is a way of sheltering what conceals itself, of protecting it from harsh lights—whether those of metaphysics or of *Schwärmerei*. At that point a certain hermeneutic element intervenes—an apophatic, not a cataphatic hermeneutics, to be sure—a moment of recognition of the depths of the play in which we are caught up, a moment of openness to the mystery that everywhere invades us. It is this dark and mysterious play that we systematically attempt to avoid, to arrest, to dominate, to explain away with an arsenal of explanatory-hermeneutics devices, the instruments of comfort devised by cataphatic hermeneutics. Thus, having granted Derrida everything, having exposed ourselves to the play, we are readied for anxiety, to go on without illusion. And what is that, if not a certain recognition of the mystery that infiltrates and surrounds us?

To put this subversion as pointedly as possible, what Heidegger whispers in Derrida's ear after the breakdown of the postal principle is "*die Sache selbst*." But is that not the transcendental signified, the packaged goods, the *ousia*, that the postal system claims to be able to deliver? Not at all. In the breakdown of the postal principle we witness the power of the *Sache* to elude all such manipulative devices, every technique designed to package and deliver it, every attempt to dominate it. In the free circulation of postcards we see the very coming to pass of the *Ereignis*. The *Sache* for Heidegger does not refer to a vision—whether rational or mystagogical—of something supremely present, nor to patient waiting for something absent of which we can now but dream. Rather it addresses the very movement of the sending that holds itself back, the very process by which one master-name after another is put forward in an endless contest. It is, above all, the power of that process to take us in (*Eingenommenheit*), to hold us in its grips, to draw us into the contest. Freedom and letting-be for Heidegger mean to awaken to *that*, to that process that keeps unfolding in Western language and metaphysics, and keeps drawing us in. It is to awaken to what is happening today.

In so doing, in such releasement, we discover that the gods are all around, even in front of the oven (Heraclitus) or hanging on the fireplace. All things are filled with gods, with souls. One does not have to go far off to strange lands or to church, Meister Eckhart said, in order to find God. God, and the gods, are already here, in your backyard. We do not need angels and courier systems, we do not have to wait for the mail. The mailman has nothing to deliver. The postal system is a diversionary strategy devised by *Errance*, *Destinerrance*. The *Geviert* is not a postcard from Freiburg. It is the glint on things once we have experienced the breakdown of the postal system, as soon as we cease to play the game of apophantic hermeneutics, which tries to decode secret messages. With the breakdown of the postal principle, Hermes is out of a job.

That is the truth (the truth that there is no truth, no master name) which will set men free (among whom, slightly more than half are women). Derrida carries this into the marketplace, gives it an ethico-political cutting edge, makes of it a *praxis* of protest. It is in the name of truth (in the postal sense) that the postal police—within the university and without—have hitherto done their work. Every good delivery service has a security force, has its armed guards, protecting their goods, their secrets, their valuable packages, their packaged values. But if one is on the alert to the delivery system, one knows how to disrupt its claims, to dispute its authority, to throw it into confusion, to put it in play. Heidegger never saw the ethico-political edge of his critique of metaphysics, and when the *Der Spiegel* interviewers pressed him, he faltered.[8] He did not see the role that deconstruction plays in the *agora*. He was never a good Socrates. So we must, on this point, put him back in the chair and let Derrida whisper in his ear. In so doing we can seduce Heidegger into ethico-political critique, repeating his critique of the will-to-power, which he rightly said is all around us today, in terms of its ethical and social dimension.

But in doing that we mean to subvert Derrida as well, or to let Heidegger subvert Derrida, by enticing him to consider what is in play in the play, the mystery that withdraws behind the barrage of mail, the *Sache* that is always and already in play. The breakdown of the postal principle shelters the *Sache* from the delivery service and it armed guards, opening us thereby to the mystery of what shelters itself in concealment, the mystery in which we live and move about. The breakdown draws us into the play, the *ébranler*, reminding us of the limits of our projects and the darkness of the play. This darkness is still and solemn and the stuff of which poetic dwelling is made. But it is just as likely to leave us with a cold shiver when we ponder its impenetrable blackness. The *ébranler* takes the shape of a cold shiver; it describes the dynamics of a cold hermeneutics.

NOTES

1. I will employ the following abbreviations in the body of the text. The pages following the slash in the text are to the indicated English translations. For the works of Derrida: *CP*: *La Carte Postale: De Socrate à Freud et au-dela* (Paris: Aubler-Flammarion, 1980); *Fins: Les fins de l'homme: A partir du travail de Jacques Derrida* (Paris: Editions galilee, 1981), translated in English as "Of an Apocalyptic Tone Recently Adopted in Philosophy," trans. John Leavey, *Semeia* 23 (1982): 63–97. For the works of Heidegger: *HW*: *Holzwege, Gesamtausgabe* vol. 5 (Frankfurt: Klostermann, 1971), translated in English as "The Anaximander Fragment," in *Early Greek Thinking*, trans. David Krell (New York: Harper & Row, 1975); *SD*: *Zur Sache des Denkens* (Tübingen: Niemeyer, 1969), translated in English as *On Time and Being*, trans. Joan Stambaugh (New York: Harper & Row, 1962); *SZ*: *Sein und Zeit*. 10 ed. (Tübingen: Niemeyer, 1963), translated in English as *Being and Time*, trans. J. MacQuanie and E. Robinson (New York: Harper & Row, 1962).

2. See Derrida's *Edmund Husserl's "Origin of Geometry": An Introduction*, trans. John Leavey (Stony Brook, NY: Nicholas Hays, 1978), 50. For a superb account of *La Carte Postale*, see Gregory Ulmer's review in *Diacritics*, 11 (1981): 39–56.

3. Martin Heidegger, *Der Satz vom Grund* (Pfullingen: Neske, 1957), 188.

4. Martin Heidegger, *Einfuhrung in die Metaphysik* (Tübingen: Niemeyer, 1958), 155; Martin Heidegger, *An Introduction to Metaphysics*, trans. Ralph Mannheim (Garden City, NY: Doubleday, 1961), p.170.

5. Michel Foucault discusses the "panopticon" in Michel Foucault, *Discipline and Punishment: The Birth of the Prison*, trans. Alan Sheridan (New York: Vintage 1975), 195–228.

6. Martin Heidegger, *The Question Concerning Technology and Other Essays*, trans. William Lovitt (New York, Harper & Row, 1977), 117–18.

7. Friedrich Nietzsche, *Beyond Good and Evil*, trans. R. J. Hollingdale (Baltimore: Penguin Books, 1972), Nos. 39, 270.

8. "'Only a God Can Save Us': Der Spiegel's Interview with Martin Heidegger," trans. J. Caputo and M. Alter, *Philosophy Today* 20 (1976): 267–84, see especially 277–80.

10
On Not Knowing Who We Are: Madness, Hermeneutics, and the Night of Truth in Foucault

In this essay, which I take as the point of departure for the present study, from which indeed the whole has drawn its name, I argue that Michel Foucault's thought is best construed as a hermeneutics of *not knowing* who we are. I construe Foucault's work to operate according to what Jacques Derrida calls the logic of the *sans*. That means that we get the best results by proceeding *sans voir, sans avoir, sans savoir*, without sight, without savvy, and without seizing hold of what we love. This is a bit of a perversity, turning as it does, not on uncovering the truth or illuminating us, which is the standard hope philosophers hold out to us, but on living with the untruth, with what early on Foucault calls the "night of truth." The night of truth is the truth that there is no capitalized Truth, no "truth of truth." In the spirit of a certain Saint Augustine, I read Foucault as if he were engaged in a confessional practice, making a confession in writing, *confiteri in letteris*, that from the start, as Derrida says, the secret is there is no Secret. For there is no way around the beliefs and practices in which we are steeped, by which we are shaped from time out of mind. I see Foucault's work as very circumfessional, confessing that we are all circumcised, cut off from the heart of unconcealed truth, but this without nostalgia, without concluding—as Richard Rorty attributes to him[1]—that we are thereby lost and have no grounds for hope at all.

So contrary to the received view of Hubert Dreyfus and Paul Rabinow,[2] according to whom Foucault's thought moves "beyond hermeneutics," I would rather say it moves beyond a certain "tragic" hermeneutics toward a more radical one, toward what I will call here a "hermeneutics of refusal." Foucault as I see him rejects a hermeneutics of "identity" in favor of a hermeneutics of "difference," negates an assured and positive hermeneutics in order to affirm joyously and positively a *hermeneutica negativa*. I will take my point of departure from Foucault's early writings on madness, although I am also clearly interested in confessions, and so in what he says later on about Christian "confessional techniques." At the end, I will attempt to push out beyond Foucault, to a Foucault without Foucault, in keeping with this logic of the *sans*, by addressing the question of what I will call the "healing gestures" that should accompany all confession. Those who, like us, confess the humility of our condition should not be left to shiver through the night of truth all alone. I push forward in a direction that, while Foucault did not take it, is perhaps suggested by him, is one of the potencies of his thought, belonging to the wake of his passing ship, in which we push past a hermeneutics of refusal to one of response and redress.[3]

TRAGIC HERMENEUTICS: MADNESS AND THE NIGHT OF TRUTH

In his earliest writings on "mental illness" (*maladie*), Foucault drew a fascinating portrait of *déraison*—"unreason," the failing or giving way of reason—"before" it was interned and reduced to silence. By the nineteenth century, unreason had been constituted as "mental illness," an object for the "psychology of madness" (*folie*), which overwhelmed madness simultaneously with the external force of internment and the internal force of moralizing. The effect of this psychology was to foreshorten "the experience of Unreason," an experience in which, Foucault says, "Western man encountered the night of his truth and its absolute challenge," which once was and still is "the mode of access to the natural truth of man."[4]

What Foucault had in mind at that time might be described as a "destruction of the history of psychology" that parallels Martin Heidegger's project of a "destruction of the history of ontology" in § 6 of *Being and Time*.[5] Were psychology to reflect on itself, it would effect a kind of *Destruktion* that would constitute at the same time a *retrieval* of a more essential truth. It would suffer a kind of auto-deconstruction, coming under the scrutiny of its own eye. That is because psychology is the alienated truth of madness, the truth in a "derisory" or alienated form that precisely on that account harbors within itself and maintains contacts with something "essential." While deriding madness under the hypocritical veil of moralizing internment, psychology "cannot fail to move toward the essential," toward that originary point from which it itself arises as a science, namely, "those regions in which man has a relation with himself." "If carried back to its roots, the psychology of madness would appear to be . . . the destruction of psychology itself and the discovery of that essential, non-psychological because non-moralizable relation that is the relation between Reason and Unreason" (*MIP*, 74).

Beneath its moralization by the humanist reformers—viewing madness as somehow a moral failing, an effect of ill will—lies its more essential truth. Psychology cannot master the truth of madness because the truth of madness is the soil from which psychology springs, the prior, anterior sphere of unconcealment of which it is itself the alienating, scientific derivative. Madness is the founding experience from which psychology derives, from the distortion of which it itself arises. Occasionally, Foucault points out, the founding, originary experiences of madness do find a voice—in such artists as Friedrich Hölderlin, Gerard de Nerval, Raymond Roussel, and Antonin Artaud—and "that holds out the promise to man that one day, perhaps, he will be able to be free of all psychology and be ready for the great tragic confrontation with madness" (*MIP*, 75). Lying prior to the scientific truth of psychology, the poetic experience of the truth of madness represents a more radical unconcealment of madness.

"Mental illness" is "alienated madness," madness in an alienated form. The aim of Foucault's work at this point is to bring us "face to face" with madness in its unalienated truth, to let it speak in its own voice, which is not the voice of reason or science, to regain "madness freed and disalienated, restored in some sense to its original language" (*MIP*, 76). But what can this original experience be? What would unreason say were its voice restored? What is the truth of madness, the truth that madness knows but we have silenced? Madness is "difference," extreme, disturbing difference, inhabiting a "void." The Renaissance took the "risk" of exposing itself to this void. It let itself be put into question by madness, without shutting madness away. It allowed itself to be invaded by the "Other," the "insane." It allowed the familiar, the *heimlich*, to be invaded by the strange and *unheimlich*. It allowed reason to be tested by unreason: "It thought itself wise and it was mad; it thought it knew and it knew nothing" (*MIP*, 77). But in the seventeenth century there began what Foucault describes as "the negative appraisal of what had been originally apprehended as the Different, the Insane, Unreason" (*MIP*, 78).

So we have in the last two hundred years constituted *homo psychologicus*, the object of psychological science. Psychological man is a substitute that puts in the place of man's "relation to the truth" (*MIP*, 87) the assumption that psychological man is himself "the truth of the truth." By this Foucault means that the "real"—let us say "cold"—truth of our divided condition is explained away and forgotten by the "truth" of psychological science and its purportedly scientific explanations of an inner mental pathology. But the truth of truth, the truth of psychology arrives too late, only after madness in its truth has been closed off. Indeed, psychology itself is constituted as a science only on the basis of having closed off madness and turned it into a phantom of itself. Psychological truth is a way of forgetting the truth and reducing it to silence. Foucault refers to this truth that psychology allows us to forget, and that can be recognized in the modern world only in "lightning flashes" with names like "Friedrich Nietzsche," as a "tragic split" and "freedom" (*MIP*, 88).

Foucault thus pursues in these early writings an original approach to madness. He is not interested in its "physiological" basis, which he does not deny, or in its "cure," which he does not "oppose" (*MIP*, 86), but in the "truth of madness," in what the mad—shall we say—"know" or "experience." He is not addressing its physiology or its therapeutics but its "hermeneutics" and the way in which psychological science conceals, represses, forgets, and silences the truth of madness (rather the way that Hans-Georg Gadamer thinks that "method" objectifies and alienates "truth"). In these early writings the mad "know" something that we want first to diagnose and then to treat (and in recent years simply to anaesthetize with powerful psychotherapeutic drugs), whereas Foucault wants to linger with it for a while, to listen and to learn from it, to hear what it has to say.

What do the mad know? What truth would they speak if we lend them an ear? A "tragic" truth, the truth of a "split," let us say, a tragic knowledge. This is the sort of truth that would kill you—or drive you mad—of which Nietzsche spoke. Was Nietzsche's madness a function of what he knew? Was his knowledge a function of his madness? Foucault suspends both alternatives because they are causal, etiological; he subjects both questions to a kind of *epoché* that puts physiological and therapeutic questions out of action. His interest is hermeneutic: he wants to hear what one says who has been driven *in extremis*. While Foucault does not cite it here, one is reminded of the passage in *Beyond Good and Evil* in which Nietzsche repudiates the need to have the truth "attenuated, veiled, sweetened, blunted, and falsified"—which is pretty much what Foucault thinks happens to madness in psychology. Foucault seems to have in mind what Nietzsche calls the "elect of knowledge," who are almost destroyed by their knowledge, which carries them off into "distant, terrible worlds."[6]

The mad, in these early writings, have experienced a terrible truth; they sail on dangerous seas, have been released from ordinary constraints; they are extreme points of sensitivity to the human condition. They are not truly "other" than "us." That is only the alienating gesture in which "we" constitute ourselves as sane and normal and constitute "them" as "other." The mad speak of a truth to us for which we have neither the nerve nor the ear, which is the truth of who we are. They instruct us about our hostility, meanness, aggressiveness, combativeness (*MIP*, 80–81). "Man has become for man the face of his own truth as well as the possibility of his death" (*MIP*, 82).

Foucault is not saying that the mad are the true philosophers but rather that they are precisely not philosophers at all, that they are the most forceful testimony to the breakdown of philosophy. They speak not with philosophical knowledge but with tragic knowledge. They have broken through the veil that philosophy lays over reality and that, in the form of psychology, philosophy tries to lay over them. The mad speak *de profundis*, from the depths of an experience in which both the reassuring structures of ordinary life and the comforting reassurances of scientific or philosophical knowledge have collapsed. They experience the radical groundlessness of the world, the contingency of its constructs, both social and epistemic; they speak of and from a kind of ineradicable terror. They speak to us from the abyss by which we are all inhabited; they are voices from an abyss.

This discussion, which Foucault inserted as the new Part 2 of the 1962 revised edition of *Maladie mentale et Psychologie*, is an incisive summary of *Madness and Civilization*[7] published a year before, whose preface and conclusion it closely parallels. *Madness and Civilization* opens with a reference to the madness of not being mad, the dangerous and unhealthy (*in-sanum*) condition of failing to recognize that "we" too are a little mad, invaded also by unreason, and that it is mad to want to make reason a wholly insulated and pure region, a seamless sphere of the same insulated from its other. He speaks of the madness of sovereign reason, the madness of a reason that thinks it has purified itself of the madness that inhabits us all, whose exclusion constitutes us as "us," the madness that speaks in a "merciless" language of madlessness. The goal of *Madness and Civilization* is to arrive at a zero point, a point *before* madness is divided off from reason, before the lines of communication between the two are cut, before reason looks sovereignly—that is, without risk or threat—upon madness as its pure Other. This is a region in which "truth" and "science" do not obtain, which is prior to and older than science, which is older than the merciless "difference" between reason and madness, a region of an originary undifferentiatedness in which reason mingles with and is disturbed from within by its other. Such a return to the original scene of madness will isolate "the action that divides madness," the "originative . . . caesura" by means of which reason and science are made to stand on the side, or better to look on from above, while unreason spreads out beneath its gaze as its object" (*MC*, ix). Then unreason is constituted as madness, crime, or mental disease. That deprives madness of its voice—reduces it, in Jean-François Lyotard's words, to a *differend* in which it is impossible for madness to state its case—and establishes the monologue of reason with itself that we call psychology and psychiatry.[8]

The Greeks, by way of contrast, thought of *sophrosyne* and *hybris* as alternate possibilities—of moderation and excess—within *logos*, but they did not constitute some sphere of exile, of *a-logos*, outside *logos* (*MC*, ix). The discourse on madness Europeans conducted beginning in the Middle Ages gives a "depth" to Western reason that irrupts in some of its greatest artists and poets (Hieronymous Bosch, Nietzsche, Artaud) (*MC*, xi). Reason without unreason is a smooth surface, a superficial transparency; reason with unreason speaks from the depths, *de profundis*. Unreason reduced to its scientific "truth," constituted as a scientific object, is a surface event, a thin, transparent, placid object. If that depth is still apparent in the "dispute" conducted between reason and madness in the Middle Ages and Renaissance, the depth is gone and the dispute is hushed in the silent corridors of the mental institution. The task of *Madness and Civilization* thus is one of archaeological restoration, a vertical plumbing of the dark sedimented depths from which *homo psychologicus* emerges, of which it still bears a faint trace, reminding us of these hidden depths even as it tries to make us forget them.

What is the "great motionless structure" (*MC*, xii) lying beneath the surface that is reducible neither to the drama of a dispute nor to an object of knowledge? Foucault's answer is again the tragic ("the tragic category"). By the tragic he means a radical breach or split within human being, a profound rupture that makes it impossible for reason to constitute itself as an identity, to close round about itself, to make itself reason and light through and through. Reason is always already unreason; the truth of man is this untruth.[9] The attempt to find the "truth of truth" is the attempt to expunge this untruth, to take leave of a more disturbing and disturbed region, to simplify and reduce human beings to pure reason by constituting the twin transparencies of reason on the one side and madness as the object of knowledge on the other.

In the conclusion to *Madness and Civilization*, after tracing the story from the great confinement to the birth of the asylum, Foucault returns again to the theme of the tragic. At the end of the story, by way of a summation to his discussion of the asylum, he mentions the advent of Sigmund Freud. Freud, he says, reproduces in the person of the psychiatrist the confining structure of the institution of the asylum. For that reason, "psychoanalysis has not been able, will not be able, to hear the voices of unreason, nor to decipher in themselves the signs of the madman." Psychoanalysis can unravel some of the forms of madness; it is even able to let it speak (*MIP*, 69); but it remains a stranger to "the sovereign enterprise of unreason" (*MC*, 278). Were they freed from the fetters of moralizing internment, the voices of unreason would speak of "human truth" and "dark freedom," Foucault says. That is the role of the artists who lend unreason an ear, who give it a voice, or lend it a canvass.

Of Francisco José Goya's *The Madhouse*, Foucault remarks: "Within this madman in a hat rises—by the inarticulate power of his muscular body, of his savage and marvelously unconstricted youth—a human presence already liberated and somehow free since the beginning of time, by his birthright" (*MC*, 279). In Goya's *Sleep of Reason*, "man communicates with what is deepest in himself" (*MC*, 280). In Goya we experience madness as "the birth of the first man and his first movement toward liberty" (*MC*, 281), the freedom to dissolve the world and even to dissolve man himself. The madman, Foucault suggests, lives *in extremis*, at the limits of the constitution of the world, where the world threatens to come undone, to deconstitute itself in a kind of pathological parallel to Edmund Husserl's famous hypothesis of the thought-experiment of the destruction of the world.[10] But whereas, in Husserl, such a deconstitution would leave sovereign consciousness still standing, Foucault suggests that, in Goya's work, the reduction of the world leads us back to naked unreason.

In Marquis de Sade we discover the truth of nature, the savage truth that nature cannot act contrary to nature, that every desire arises from nature. As an "ironic Rousseau," Sade teaches the ethic of a more savage "fidelity to nature," "natural liberty." But Sade pushes beyond the truth of natural freedom to the "total liberty" of pure subjectivity that dashes even nature itself by its violence. Sade traverses the terrible path from "man's violent nature" to the "infinity of nonnature" (*MC*, 284), thus to a point where nature itself breaks up and reveals its own nature, its dissension and abolition. Sade dwells at that limit point where the world comes undone, where it is unmade, at "the limits of the world that wounds" the mad heart (*MC*, 285).

In Goya and Sade unreason finds a way to transcend reason in the path of violence and thus finds a way of "recovering tragic experience beyond the promises of dialectic" (*MC*, 285). The tragic always means the split, the rupture of human being—without the dream of dialectical rejoining and reconciliation—and here it means the unmaking and destruction of the world that reason builds around itself.

The final pages of *Madness and Civilization* are devoted to Nietzsche, who represents the tragic voice par excellence, the dominant voice from the abyss. Foucault's early writings are very much keyed to *The Birth of Tragedy* (and not, like the later writings, to *A Genealogy of Morals*), to which, Foucault says, all of Nietzsche's texts belong (*MC*, 285). Nietzsche is the philosopher of the tragic category, that is, of unreason and the undoing of philosophy. In Nietzsche unreason acquires a voice of "total contestation" of the world, contestations that restore "primitive savagery"! What interests Foucault about Nietzsche, however, is that his writing fell silent under the blow of madness, that his final word to us after a lifetime of writing was the howl of madness followed by silence.

Foucault is not leading up to the conclusion that madness is, in Heidegger's language, the "origin of the work of art," but to an opposite conclusion, that it spells its death. "Pure" madness is not the origin of the work of art but its absence and abolition; there is no work where there is pure madness.[11] Madness is but the parting gesture of the artwork, its final word or non-word just as it subsides into chaos. The work of art springs not from pure madness but from the invasion of reason by madness, from the tension or confrontation between reason and unreason, Apollo and Dionysus. But it is rendered impossible if this tension is broken from the side either of pure reason or of pure unreason.

The work of art carries out a kind of *epoché* of the world, suspending its hold on us, which it does just to the extent that it is "interrupted" by madness, or exposed to it and held in communication with it. The work of art puts the rationality of the world in question, making the world, and not the madman, guilty, arraigning the world before the work of art. What is the world's fault? What has it done wrong? For what is it to be held responsible? For what does it owe reparation? The guilt of the world is that it has suppressed the world of unreason, and it is precisely the restoration of unreason that the work of art demands, or better, the "restoration of reason *from* that unreason and *to* that unreason" (*MC*, 288). So it is not exactly unreason that is restored to itself so much as it is reason that is restored to itself, to its originative belonging-together with unreason. Reason is itself only insofar as it is also unreason; otherwise—and this is how *Madness and Civilization* begins—it is quite mad. Foucault has turned the tables—or the couch—on the doctor. Now, instead of the madman as patient silently observed by the figure of science, the world itself is put into question by the madman as artist, by a Dionysian artist.

These early works of Foucault are not only or even primarily histories of psychology and madness. As archaeologies of the silence to which unreason is reduced in the asylum, they offer a positive view of being human, a view best expressed by the category of the "tragic." Human beings are inwardly divided, inhabited by an abyss, by both reason and unreason. We dwell in both the truth and the untruth. In such a view, neither "science" (the human sciences) nor "morals" can be what they are (or want to be) all the way through. They are at best limited, incomplete, or distortive, and hence in need of correction—the view that Foucault held in the 1954 edition of *Maladie mentale et personalité*. At worst, they are useless illusions and even hypocritical attempts to suppress the unreason by which they are inhabited and hence they are beyond correction—the view both of the 1962 revised edition of *Mental Illness and Psychology* and *Madness and Civilization*. The human sciences promote the illusion that unreason is a disturbance to be quelled, an abnormality to be normalized, a cry to be silenced. Ethics promotes the illusion that virtue is a unity, that the law is universalizable, that conscience is God's voice, suppressing the violence and confusion by which we are inhabited.

Against the illusions of science and morals, Foucault advocates a more originary tragic experience, an experience of reason's undoing and auto-deconstruction by unreason, which is the "truth" of the human condition. This truth is destroyed if it is allowed to evaporate into the "truth of truth." The truth is the night of truth, the midnight hour when reason allows itself to be interrupted and invaded by unreason. That happens in certain works of art that flash like lightning in the night of truth, illuminating for a moment a more originary and cragged human landscape.

BEYOND TRAGIC HERMENEUTICS

Foucault's early writings came under fire both by his critics and by Foucault himself. In the first place, these texts are marked by a kind of phenomenological naïveté. The goal of the early writings, which is to find an "undifferentiated" experience of unreason, before it is differentiated into reason and madness, before the lines of reason are drawn in its virginal sands, perfectly parallels the phenomenological goal of finding a realm of pure "prepredicative" experience, prior to its being carved up by the categories of logical grammar. To be sure, where Husserl thinks to find pure *Sinn* lying beneath the categories of logical *Bedeutung*, Foucault suggests that we will find a pure *Unsinn*, a kind of perfect, pure, free, natural, undistorted, prepredicative madness, beneath the categories of the prison or the asylum. It was with this in mind that Derrida says it is an impossible dream to think that one could write the history of madness from the standpoint of madness itself. Writing and history already represent the standpoint of reason and are already violent; they have already incised this virginal terrain with their cuts and divides.[12]

This point is well made and Foucault has clearly not avoided this objection. Still, we should recall that in the concluding pages of *Madness and Civilization*, Foucault makes it plain that pure madness gives rise only to silence, that it leads to the end of the work of art. Now that surely implies that no work of history or archaeology could ever enter the domain of pure madness. The voices of unreason issue in works of art, or works of any sort, only inasmuch as they interrupt, invade, intermingle with, and confront reason. So Foucault is aware that there is no access to a "pure" madness or unreason, to a pure, antehistorical essence of madness, but only to the confrontation of reason and unreason in this or that concrete historical context.

Second, in a not unrelated way, Foucault criticized *Madness and Civilization* (he never spoke of the first book, in either edition, on mental illness and opposed its re-publication) on the grounds that it labored under the "repressive" hypothesis, that is, the notion that power works by excluding and repressing.[13] "I think that I was positing [in *Madness and Civilization*] the existence of a sort of living, voluble and anxious madness which the mechanisms of power and psychiatry were supposed to have come to repress and reduce to silence. . . . In defining the effects of power as repression, one adopts a purely juridical conception of such power, one identifies power with a law which says no, power is taken above all as carrying the force of a prohibition."

It is certainly true that in *Madness and Civilization* Foucault thought that unreason is repressed, suppressed, excluded, silenced, denied, obstructed, and occulted by reason. On this point I think he was right and that virtually the whole power of his book rests precisely on his being right about this. Furthermore, I do not think he means to retract this point. In an interview he gave in 1977, he says that the repressive mechanisms of *Madness and Civilization* were "adequate" to his purposes in that book, that "madness is a special case—during the Classical age power over madness was, in its most important manifestations at least, exercised in the form of exclusion; thus one sees madness caught up in a great movement of rejection" (*P/K*, 183–84). Yet, Foucault was subsequently led by way of his investigations into the history of sexuality to see another mechanism of power, the productive one, which proceeds not by repressing and saying no but which "traverses and produces things . . . induces pleasure, forms knowledge, produces discourse" (*P/K*, 119). But this other form of power reflects not so much a change in Foucault's thinking as a discovery about a change that takes place in the later history of power and madness. "However, in the nineteenth century, an absolutely fundamental phenomenon made its appearance: the interweaving, the intrication, of two great technologies of power: one which fabricated sexuality and the other which segregated madness. The technology of madness changed from negative to positive, from being binary to being complex and multiform. There came into being a vast technology of the psyche, which became a characteristic feature of the nineteenth and twentieth centuries" (*P/K*, 185).

One important result of this interweaving is that "sexuality" assumed the place—as the truth of madness—that Foucault would have earlier said belonged to the "tragic category." This is an important point to which I shall return later in this selection. The essential thing to see at the moment, however, is that at a certain juncture, instead of being repressed, unreason is forced to talk. At a certain point, one that Foucault ascribes to the rise of confessional practices in the Catholic Church in the seventeenth and eighteenth centuries, instead of being doused with water, berated with moral criticism, and subjected to a rigorous regimen, the mad are encouraged to say what they have on their minds, to associate freely, to dredge up their dreams, to tell us all about themselves and their parents especially their parents) and childhoods, to reveal their innermost secrets, to bring them out in the public view of the world. In short, to talk, talk, talk, for in the talking is the cure.

Now it would be a mistake, I maintain, to think that the repressive hypothesis is somehow inconsistent with productive power. In fact, the two are quite compatible and, indeed, produce a similar effect. I would even say that the hypothesis of a productive power is a continuation of the repressive hypothesis by another means. The unreason by which reason is inhabited is again silenced, this time not by real, physical, institutionalized silence but, still more effectively, and rather more pleasurably, by talk. The notion that more and more talking is an effective way to silence what requires a voice was noticed early on in the nineteenth century by Søren Kierkegaard, who found that the idle chatter of the press addressed to the "millions," and the numerous compendia of Hegelianized Christian doctrine that were being turned out by the dozens were proving to be an exceptionally effective way to silence the quiet terror of authentic faith.[14] One of the most famous Kierkegaardian pseudonyms bore the name Johannes de Silentio because he was charged with the task of describing the indescribable "fear and trembling" of Abraham, who was unable to explain himself to others and whom everyone else took to be quite—well—mad. Kierkegaard played such silence against the foil of the sane and sensible stockbrokers of the finite" with whom he draws a consistent contrast throughout *Fear and Trembling*.[15] In an age of top-down monarchical power, outright repression will do just fine but in the democratic age of the "millions," productive power does an even better job of silencing.

The fact of the matter is that unless power has a univocal essence, unless power means just one thing, it is impossible to sustain the idea that power is only or essentially or primarily "productive" and not also repressive. Power is only a descriptive category for Foucault and it means many things, in keeping with the plurality of historical situations in which it is deployed. There is no power as such; we can only describe the "how" of "power relations" (*BSH*, 217, 219). Power is now repressive, now productive, and now something else that Foucault had not noticed, and later on something else that perhaps has not yet come about. So there is nothing about Foucault's later adoption of the hypothesis of productive power to invalidate his notion that the work of reason is to silence and reject the voices of unreason by which it is inhabited, and hence to invalidate the early notion of the "tragic category." On the contrary, the two exist in a continual "interweaving" and "intrication."

The strongest challenge to the continued viability of "tragic hermeneutics" in Foucault's work is voiced by Dreyfus and Rabinow, who claim that after *Madness and Civilization* Foucault disavows any form of "hermeneutics," and, specifically, using Paul Ricoeur's term, the "hermeneutics of suspicion." By "hermeneutics" Dreyfus and Rabinow mean the unmasking and ferreting out of a repressed truth that tells the truth of man. In his foreword to the California edition of *Mental Illness and Psychology* (1987), Dreyfus says that even the 1962 revised edition remains under the spell of a Heideggerian conception of "'anxiety' in the face of madness" that is silenced by morality and science. Foucault is convinced that there has been a "repression of a deep, nonobjectifiable truth" (*MIP*, xxxii). So there is still a "conspiracy theory" at work in this book, a notion that something is being suppressed that, if we could just face up to it, would result in liberation (in the way that Heidegger talks about being ready for anxiety). In the first edition of the book, Foucault thought it was a matter of facing up to the alienation produced by social contradiction; in the second edition, he has succeeded only in replacing a Marxist conception of social alienation with a Heideggerian and existential conception of "strangeness" (*Unheimlichkeit*) but the overall (hermeneutic) scheme of reducing madness to its unalienated, liberating truth remains intact.

In the following years, Dreyfus argues, Foucault came to reject any such "hermeneutics" and with it the claim that there is some deep truth begging to be deciphered, some latent content that awaits "commentary,"[16] some meaning at once more hidden and more fundamental that demands a "hermeneutics,"[17] some interrogation of "the being of madness itself, its secret content, its silent, self-enclosed truth"[18] that would traverse what is said about madness at any particular historical time. There is no message from the depths. Madness is simply constituted in different ways at different times and nothing is being left out. There is no inexhaustible residue, no cover-up story, no buried saving truth (*MIP*, xxxiii). There is no ahistorical essential structure of madness (analogous to the ahistorical structure of *Dasein* yielded by the existential analytic), but only the changing, historical constitution of human beings. For Dreyfus and Rabinow, the critique made in volume 1 of *The History of Sexuality* of the search for a secret self—sexuality—as a "construction of modern thought," and hence as an important kind of modern power, is to be applied to *Madness and Civilization*. The latter sought to locate that secret, not in sexuality to be sure, but in "the sovereign enterprise of unreason" that is delivered over to us in flashes of lightning with names like Nietzsche and Hölderlin (*MC*, 11). But Foucault is led to give up this hermeneutic ontology that locates the transcendental being of unreason behind the play of the historical appearances of madness and *homo psychologicus*. He turns his attention instead to the patient description of the multiple historical forms in which modern man is constituted.

But if that is so, then what difference do the different historical constitutions of madness make? If madness is just produced in various ways, if nothing is repressed, lost, or silenced, why worry about what historical form the historical constitution of madness takes? If nothing is repressed, then nothing is to be liberated. If nothing is repressed, then there is nothing to offer resistance and no historical formation is better or worse than another. As Dreyfus and Rabinow query at the end of their book, "What is wrong with carceral society? Genealogy undermines a stance which opposes it on the grounds of natural law or human dignity. . . . What are the resources which enable us to sustain a critical stance?" (*BSH*, 206).

A good deal of what Foucault wrote in the years that followed *Madness and Civilization* raises these objections. In the remaining sections of this essay, I shall argue that an adequate answer turns on understanding what becomes of the hermeneutic impulse that is so clearly evident in the early writings that it turns, in short, on seeing that Foucault has moved beyond a certain hermeneutics toward another hermeneutics more radically conceived.

THE HERMENEUTICS OF REFUSAL

In "The Subject and Power," the afterword to the Dreyfus and Rabinow book, Foucault speaks of the two "pathological forms" of power, two "diseases of power"—fascism and Stalinism—that the twentieth century has known (*BSH*, 209). Are we to think that these are "alienated power," power gone wrong, power that divests human beings of something un-alienated or even inalienable? Foucault says they are marked by an "internal madness," but that such madness is merely the extension of contemporary "political rationality," of a kind of unlimited rationalization. Are we to think, then, that this is something like a political equivalent of the "other form of madness" that consists in not being mad, a political analog of the "merciless language of nonmadness" (*MC*, ix)? Are we to think that something is lost, repressed, or occulted by fascism and Stalinism?

Foucault puts these expressions in scare quotes. They are normative expressions that seem to edge out beyond a felicitous positivism. He is perhaps concerned that he is drifting in the direction of the earlier writings that speak of a more originative sphere. He is worried that he is making himself look like the "doctor." In the next paragraph the metaphor switches to Immanuel Kant, to what Lyotard calls Kant's "critical watchman,"[19] and Foucault speaks of a need for a Kantian-like critique of the limits of political reason that keeps watch for "excesses" (*BSH*, 210). Still, although it is helpful—this is what the Frankfurt school has already done—it is not enough, Foucault says, to study the Enlightenment and the excesses to which it has led "if we want to understand how we have been trapped in our own history" (*BSH*, 210).

We are trapped in our history. But *who* is trapped? And how *trapped?* What is the opposite of being trapped? Does being trapped mean that something has been prohibited, occulted, blocked off, or repressed (*P/K*, 183), that is, trapped? What would it be like to be untrapped? Who would be untrapped? Who is the "we" who would be untrapped?

Instead of pursuing the strategy of the Frankfurt school, of analyzing the "internal rationality" of such excesses, Foucault says that he thinks it would be more instructive to approach such processes of subjection by way of a consideration of the "resistance" that is offered to them, of the "antagonisms" that they engender (*BSH*, 211). Insanity and illegality, for example, are (negative) indicators of what a society calls sanity and legality. Consider the "struggles" we witness nowadays against the power of men over women, of psychiatry over the mentally ill, of bureaucracy over people at large. Such struggles "assert the right to be different and they underline everything which makes individuals truly individual" and they fight against everything that "ties [the individual] to his own identity in a constraining way," which reduces the individual to the identity of "madman," "mentally retarded," "alcoholic," "handicapped," and so on.

These struggles, Foucault says, "are not for or against the 'individual,' but rather they are struggles against the 'government of individualization'" (*BSH*, 212). It is not as though Foucault has a positive, affirmative normative idea of what an individual should be in the name of which he thinks these struggles should be waged. What the individual should be in some *determinate* way is none of Foucault's business. More important, the business of coming up with normative ideas of what the individual should be, and of developing administrative practices and professional competencies to see to it that such individuals are in fact produced, is precisely the problem, not the solution: it is exactly what these struggles are struggling *against*.

In sum, Foucault suggests, all such struggles "revolve around the question: 'Who are we?'" (*BSH*, 212). But Foucault's idea is not only *not* to answer this question in a determinate way but to see to it that no one else is allowed to answer it, or rather to answer it on behalf of anyone else and above all to enforce their answer. It is a question that each of us, in our singularity, requires the privacy to raise and answer for ourselves, without sweeping up everyone else in what we come up with, so that, contra Jean-Paul Sartre, we are not creating an essence for all humankind. It is like Derrida's adaptation of Augustine's question, "What do I love when I love my God?"[20] Foucault wants to keep this question open, and above all to block administrators, professionals, and managers of all sorts from answering this question on our behalf, thereby closing us in on some constituted identity or another that represents a strictly historical, that is, contingent constraint. While the tonality of hope and expectation is stronger in Derrida's slightly atheistic messianic expectation, in Derrida's *viens, oui, oui*, I think that the positions of Foucault and Derrida, their common desire to keep the future open, are close at this point. That goes some way to explaining what

Foucault means by being "trapped by our history." There are too many theories out there of what Foucault earlier called "the truth of truth," of the scientific or therapeutic truth of who we are, too many ready responses to the question "who are we?" Foucault's program is to block off or delimit the truth of truth—and to leave us to what he named in the earlier writings our (simple) truth, to the truth that there is no truth of truth, which is not a statement of despair but a hope for the freedom to invent something new. Foucault wants to defend the impossibility of reducing us to truth, to shelter the irreducibility and uncontractability of being-human, its refusal of identity and identification, its refusal of an identifying truth, in order to open up the possibility of new modes of self-invention. Such refusal issues from a felicitous nominalism about the irrepressibility of being-human, from its irrepressible capacity for being-different, for mutation and transformation.

Like Derrida, Foucault thus has a negative, nominalistic, and nonessentialistic idea of the individual. He struggles against any "positive" theory of the individual that takes itself seriously, that thinks it has the truth of truth, that thinks it can positively identify who we are. He opposes all "cataphatic" discourse about the individual, all discourse that tries to prescribe what the individual is or should be, and he does so in the name of a kind of "apophatic" discourse, of preserving a purely apophatic freedom. The gesture is actually classical, reminding us, as James Bernauer argues powerfully, of negative theology.[21] What you say God is, is not true, Meister Eckhart wrote; but what you do not say God is, that is true.[22] Foucault wants to keep open the negative space of what the individual is not, of what we cannot say the individual is, to preserve the space of a certain negativity that refuses all positivity, all identification, for that is always in the end a historical trap. To paraphrase the meister, whenever the social sciences tell us who we are, that is not true; but what they do not say about who we are, that is true. Whatever lays claim to being the truth of truth, that is not true; but whatever concedes that we do not know the truth of truth, that is true. Whatever way the individual is historically constituted is not true; but whatever alternatives there are to the way we are constituted, that is true.

The modern exercise of power on Foucault's account represents a peculiar "double bind" (*BSH*, 216) that produces individuals (productive power) precisely in order to block off individuality (repressive power). Modern power combines the production of individuals ("individualization techniques") along with the repression of individuality and difference ("totalization procedures") (*BSH*, 213). Far from having abandoned the repressive hypothesis, the double bind depends upon the combined and simultaneous effect of both productive and repressive power, upon their "interweaving" and "intrication" (*P/K*, 185).

Productive power takes its rise from the spread of "pastoral power" over the social body (*BSH*, 215). In pastoral power the pastor gives himself over to the production of an individual soul (the "individual" is an invention of the Christian confessional). The pastor needs to know what is going on in individuals' hearts, to get inside their minds, to have them "confess" their innermost secrets, in order to give spiritual direction. Pastoral power depends upon producing the truth, the truth of truth, in order to produce good Christians. In the modern world, pastoral techniques are multiplied everywhere: among the police, state investigative functions, and criminal justice and social work professionals; medical and healthcare professionals; clinical and counseling psychologists and psychiatrists; and educationists, demographers, and so on. Wherever a "file" is kept, wherever an individual "case history" is to be written, the "individual" is the target of knowledge and power, of power/knowledge.

Against this totalizing, normalizing production of individuals, Foucault holds out for the "individual." This is the double bind. Not the individual in the sense of the individual case history, of the "subject" whose secret code we—psychiatrists, moralists, or educationists—know, but rather the individual who resists all secret codes, who has no identity, who is not reducible to one or another of the hermeneutic techniques of pastoral power, who is marked by the "right to be different" (*BSH*, 211). Against the positive production of individuals in keeping with some normative standard, Foucault holds out for the negative freedom of the individual to be different. Whatever the social engineers want the individual to be, that is what the individual wants not to be, what the individual refuses to be in this hermeneutics of refusal.

So what philosophers must do is ask not, like René Descartes, "What am I?"—as if there were a general answer—but, like Kant ("What is the Enlightenment?"), who are we *now*, at this particular moment of our historical constitution. Who are we high-tech, late capitalist, mobile, post-Enlightenment—shall we say—postmodernists? And how can we be otherwise? Or better still: "Maybe the target nowadays is not to discover what we are but to refuse what we are. We have to imagine and to build up what we could be to get rid of this kind of "double bind" which is the simultaneous individualization and totalization of modern power structures" (*BSH*, 216). The idea is to liberate us not only from the state but from the sort of individualization that the state produces. The idea is "to promote new forms of subjectivity through the refusal of this kind of individuality which has been imposed on us for several centuries." (Ibid.).

Foucault's position is comparable to Lyotard's call for continual experimentalism, not only in art but in the artwork that we ourselves are, for the formation of new forms of subjectivity, for finding what Lyotard calls new idioms that provide a space for the right to be different. It corresponds, too, to Derrida's call for *l'invention de l'autre*, the coming, the in-coming, of something other.

We are now in a position to address the question of what difference the different historical constitutions of madness make. If madness is just produced in various ways, if nothing is repressed, lost, or silenced, why worry about what historical form the historical constitution of madness takes? If nothing is repressed, then nothing is to be liberated, there is nothing to offer resistance, and no historical formation—including fascism and Stalinism—is better or worse than another. It is, I think, clear that Foucault does believe that something is repressed, and the cogency of speaking of a "double bind" depends upon it. The claim that every historical constitution is a contingency that threatens to become a historical "trap" means that something is being trapped. The idea that no particular historical constitution is exhaustive or totalizing means that there is always a residue, an irreducibility, a fragment that cannot be incorporated.[23] I do not mean a "transcendental residuum" like Husserl's pure consciousness, or a historical essence or nature of being human, but rather a purely negative, always historical capacity for being-otherwise, which is what Foucault means by freedom.

That is the answer to the objection that Foucault's writings provoke after *Madness and Civilization*, that he treats human beings as a kind of pure *hyle* capable of taking on indefinitely many forms, of being historically constituted in an indefinite multiplicity of forms, no one of which is any better or worse than another. Foucault clearly distinguishes the power that is exerted over material objects, for example, by means of instruments, from the power that individuals exert over other individuals, which is not power over things but power over freedom. Power is not a mere violence exerted on an object, like cutting wood or bending a piece of steel. Violence or force are effected on a "mere passivity" (*BSH*, 220). But the power in which Foucault is interested is exerted over "the other," over another person who acts and reacts. Power is a set of actions upon other actions. Nor is power *consensus*, a free renunciation of one's own freedom for the sake of a general arrangement. "Power relations" occur in the space between pure force and free consent, and they may or may not obtain in the presence of either. Power is a matter neither of pushing boulders about with great bulldozers nor of a pure dialogue between Platonic souls.

Power is a way of inducing, seducing, conducing (*conduire*, conduct [v.], conduct [n.]); power is conductive. It is stronger (more coercive) than what Husserl calls "motivation," which is pure intentional freedom, because it is a way we have of being led (*ducere*) around (con), but like motivation it belongs in a quasi-intentional sphere of human behavior and is not to be reduced to physical causality. Power is a way of "governing," shaping, forming—the seventeenth-century religious orders that Foucault discusses in *Discipline and Punish* called the time of apprenticeship in the order years of "formation." Power sets up (*stellen, auf-stellen*) or frames out (*Ge-stell*)[24] a preset range of possibilities within which action can take place, broad "ducts" through which actions are led; power "structures the field" of actions (*BSH*, 222). Thus "power is exercised only over free subjects, and only insofar as they are free" (*BSH*, 221). Slavery is not power but constraint because in slavery the range of possibilities has been "saturated," that is, determined to a specific outcome (*determinatio ad unum*). Power is exerted only over beings capable of being recalcitrant and intransigent. Power implies freedom since without freedom power is just constraint or force. Power and freedom belong together agonistically, in an ongoing "agonism," a struggle, in which there are winning and losing strategies, a victorious consolidation of power on the one hand or successful strategies against power on the other hand. If power is cunning and pervasive enough, it will coopt freedom; if freedom is resistant and persistent enough, it will cause power to tremble.

Power is not something that could be removed, the result being a perfectly free society. A society without power would not be a society but a physical aggregate; as soon as human beings come together (and when have they not?), in virtue of their coming together, power relations spring into being. A society is essentially a network of power relations that are more minute than its larger institutional structures. The idea for Foucault is not to abolish power relations—that would make no sense—but to alter them by means of winning strategies, to open up new possibilities, to restructure the field such that something else (being-otherwise) is possible (*BSH*, 223). Such an alteration is driven by the ongoing agonism between power and freedom that sees to it that any field of power is an unsteady state, an unstable and hence ultimately open, alterable system. The idea is to keep open "the free play of antagonistic" relations, to refuse to let the social system harden into place with stable mechanisms that are overeffective in regulating conduct (*BSH*, 225).

So far from excluding or reducing freedom, power over freedom implies resistance. Freedom for Foucault is a kind of irrepressibility, a refusal to contract into an identity, a continually twisting loose from the historical forms of life by which it is always already shaped. Freedom is not a nature or essence but a lack of nature or essence, a capacity for novelty and innovation. Bernauer calls it "transcendence,"[25] the capacity to move beyond a particular historical constitution. That is in keeping with Bernauer's guiding motif of Foucault's "negative theology" (God transcends whatever we say about God), which I would say is rather a "high" theology for Foucault. I think Foucault has in mind a more modest freedom from below, a refusal, a resistance, a certain stepping back, not so much a transcendence, let us say, as a *re*scendence, which seeks to twist free from the trap of the present in order to find a variation.

We are now in a position to evaluate the claim of Dreyfus and Rabinow that, by turning himself over to detailed genealogies of the various ways in which bodies and minds are historically constituted, Foucault moved beyond all hermeneutics. This claim is tied up with the assertion that he dropped the idea of the repression of something deep and replaced it with the notion of describing the surface of productive relations of power.

I think this position is partly right. In the early writings Foucault clearly believed in "The Secret" and in finding the hermeneutic key to The Secret. The hermeneutics of suspicion he practiced at that point (suspecting psychology of repressing the tragic truth) turned on a positive idea of who we are, a particular—indeed, I would say a Dionysian—idea of a "tragic unreason." The authoritative account of who we are was to be found in *The Birth of Tragedy*, an account the human sciences would like to dismiss or forget. It is clear that by the time of the last works Foucault had given up the idea that there is some *positive* idea of "who we are" to be recovered, some *particular* identity that is being repressed which needs to be shaken loose ("destruction") and retrieved.

But if he has dropped the idea that there is some particular identity that is being repressed, he has not given up the idea that *something* is being repressed, something much looser, more unspecifiable and indefinite, something negative and unidentifiable. It is no longer an *identity* we need to recover (a secret tragic identity) but a *difference*. It is no longer a positive ideal that needs to be restored but simply a certain capacity to resist the identities that are imposed upon us just to set free our capacity to invent such new identities for ourselves as circumstances allow.[26] In short, the movement has not been beyond hermeneutics and repression but beyond a hermeneutics of identity (a positive tragic hermeneutics) to a hermeneutics of difference (a negative hermeneutics of refusal).

The later writings turn on the idea that there is always something other than or different from the various historical constitutions of human beings, some "freedom" or resistance that is irreducible to the several enframing historical forms of life, some power-to-be-otherwise, some being-otherwise-than-the-present that radically, irreducibly, irrepressibly belongs to us, to what we are (not). We never are what we are; something different is always possible. As Derrida says in *The Other Heading*, what is proper to the "identity" of a self or a culture[27] "*is not to be identical to itself.* Not to not have an identity, but not to be able to identify itself, to be able to say 'I' or 'we'; to be able to take the form of a subject only in the non-identity to itself or, if you prefer, only in the difference with itself (*avec soi*)." The "I" or the "we" is marked by its capacity to be otherwise. That is why I think that Foucault has not dropped the hermeneutic project. He has not abandoned a *certain* hermeneutics, a negative hermeneutics, a hermeneutics of refusal, of what we are not, which I like to call "radical hermeneutics."[28] In such a hermeneutics, there is no question of deciphering a "master name," of reapprehending through the "manifest meaning . . . another meaning at once . . . more hidden but more fundamental."[29] On the contrary, such a hermeneutics turns on the loss of fixed or determinate meaning, and on an understanding of being human as an abyss that refuses identification, contraction, or reduction to a fixed meaning. If Foucault has abandoned the hermeneutics of suspicion, that is because, in my view, he has taken up a hermeneutics of refusal.

Foucault's more radical hermeneutics rejects the idea of the truth of truth, of some nameable, masterable truth of being human. It rejects a whole series of humanisms of truth—*homo psychologicus*, *homo economicus*, *homo religiosus*, including his own earlier contribution to this theme, *homo tragicus*. But he has done so, not in order to skim along the surface of positivistic descriptions, but in order to open a hermeneutic dimension of negativity: that we do not know who we are. He has abandoned the truth of truth, the mastery of knowledge, in favor of the "cold truth," of the truth that there is no truth of truth, of the truth that our being is always already disturbed by untruth, which means an irreducibility to truth. This I think is close to Derrida's notion of the *khôra*, that the things we come up with when we describe our condition are written in the sand, a desert sand that is vulnerable to the next storm. The essence of such Foucauldian freedom, were there such a thing, is its untruth, its irreducibility to the truth of truth. Beneath the layers of *homo psychologicus* and all the "idols" of the human sciences, of all the "graven images" of modernity that we might collectively call *homo cyberneticus*, Foucault hears the murmur of a capacity to be otherwise. His is a refusal of the idols of the present, the idolatrous worship we are prone to offer the images that present themselves to us today and threaten to hold us captive. That critique of idolatry, in my view, is linked to the critical power of the messianic idea in Derrida. The later writings respond to a plea that quietly calls for something different, what Derrida and Levinas call "the call of the other." Conductive, productive power is *de*ductive: by leading us along (con) certain paths, it leads us away from (de) others, cutting off, closing off, the capacity to differ. Productive power is interwoven with repressive power. It wants to produce human beings of a certain sort because it is at the same time "anxious" about the human capacity for being-otherwise; it is not a little anxious about difference. Far from giving up on the idea of hermeneutic anxiety, pace Dreyfus, I think the power of Foucault's analyses, early or late, depends upon that anxiety.

We do not know who we are, not if we are honest about it. That is a hermeneutic point, albeit a negative one. It is the issue of a specific kind of ruthless facing up to the facts that neither ethics nor the human sciences can tell us who we are or what to do. It is, I would say, the issue of a certain "responsiveness" to the abyss that we are, to our endless ability to be otherwise. Dreyfus is mistaken to think that Foucault gave up on the hermeneutic idea of "facing up to the truth" (*MIP*, xxviii–xxx) if by that one means the "cold truth," the truth that there is no truth of truth, the truth that is invaded and fragmented by untruth. Whatever is called "Truth" and adorned with capital letters masks its own contingency and untruth, even as it masks the capacity for being-otherwise. For our being-human spins off into an indefinite future about which we know little or nothing, which fills us with a little hope and not a little anxiety, a future to come for which there is no program, no preparation, no prognostication.

BEYOND FOUCAULT: HEALING GESTURES

I wish to close with a word about madmen and confessors, a word that Foucault does not utter but that belongs to the space he opens up, to the potentialities he awakens. Foucault's analysis of the normalization of the mad in psychology and psychiatry, and of the normalization of the faithful in the confessional, addresses the anxiety of modernity about difference and abnormality, and it does so in an incisive way. But it does not discuss another issue and concern, the issue of what *healing* means in such an analysis, since we can hardly think we are all okay. This would represent a final step, from hermeneutics to therapeutics.

Let us return to the question of madness. Madness is a "disturbance" but in a twofold sense both of what is "disturbing" and "disturbed." Foucault does a masterful job of showing what is "disturbing" about madness. To put it in the terms of Heidegger in *Being and Time*, Foucault treats madness as a particular way the world is "understood," not in a theoretical sense, of course, but in the sense of what Heidegger calls in *Being and Time* a certain *Weltverstehen*, a practical understanding that is heavily "mooded" or "tuned" (*bestimmt*). The disturbing thing about the mad is the nagging fear that they are "at-tuned" to something, to some deep-seated dissonance, from which the rest of "us" seek to be protected. We are apprehensive that, living at the margins of normal life, *in extremis*, the mad have been exposed to something the rest of us prefer to ignore. "We" are beset by an apprehensiveness that our sane, healed, whole lives mask a deeper rupture, that the settled tranquility of the sane is acquired only by repressing the "up-set" of the mad. We are disturbed that "the disturbed" are responding to a definite *turbatio* that is "there." "We" find the "disturbed" disturbing. Madness is a mirror of ourselves. It tells us who we are. If the mad exhibit "infantile regressions," it is only because childhood is infantilized to begin with, unrealistically insulated from real conflict. If madness takes on the form of "schizophrenia," it is because the mad reflect the contradictions of a world in which humans can no longer recognize themselves, because the social world itself is marked by struggle, hostility, and foreignness. It is the world that is mad, alienated, un-free, divided, and contradictory, and it is such madness that the mad take as their model and in which the world ref uses to see itself (*MIP*, 80–81). That is what gives Foucault's analyses their bite.

But madness is also a being-disturbed, *patheia*, a way of suffering that causes *pain*. The mad *suffer from* their attunement, from what they experience/feel/undergo. Their ruptured lives are the site of a wound. Itis not as though the lives of extreme manic depressives would be felicitous if we just left them alone or if the world would adjust to them. They live with terror; they wrestle with demons; their works are impaired, ruined, suicidal, brought to halt, reduced to inertia. Their lives are disrupted and destroyed, "disturbed." They have fallen prey to madness. They need healing. Their cry of pain is also a call for help. They lay claim to us, we who are whole (enough) to help, we who are perhaps not so much whole and sane as just a little less mad and better skilled at repressing our madness. There are, after all, only a few Nietzsches, Hölderlins, and Vincent Van Goghs among the mad. It was in the long run better to let Van Gogh and Nietzsche alone, to let mad genius run its course into the dark night of truth. But for the majority madness does not mean genius but pain, and they cry out for help, not for the immortality of the work of art.

I take it there is nothing in what Foucault says that opposes "a strategy of cure" (*MIP*, 76); it is simply not his subject. Indeed, I see in his work the makings of a certain therapeutic "direction," let us say, of a therapeutic of non-knowing. Such a therapeutic does not come from on high, does not proceed from the heights of science or episteme, and so does not suffer from the illusion that it knows what madness is (when madness is not clearly physiological). Such a therapy of non-knowing would take madness "seriously," that is, as another from which we have something to learn. Indeed, it undergoes a change of direction by letting the mad come to us from "on high," in their extreme otherness. It does not look on the mad as "patients" in the sense of "objects" of medical knowledge, but as *patiens*, as ones who suffer greatly, who suffer from their knowledge, as Nietzsche says, and its look is not objectifying but *com-patiens*, compassionate. Such a patient would not be an object of knowledge but an author or subject of knowledge, one from whom we have something to learn. Such patients are not stretched out before the medical gaze as objects but come to us from on high, but rather lifted up by their suffering, in the manner of Levinas. We are not panoptical observers of madness, but we are put into question by the mad, seen and interrogated by them, above all, solicited by them. We have something to learn from the mad, above all that they are not "they" but who we ourselves are. We are instructed by them; they have set foot where the sane fear to tread. They tell us, unhappily, who we are; they tell us of our own unhappiness. The mad are not the subject of a medical observation but the source of a call that calls upon us and demands our response.

The mad do not ask for analysis and objectification by us but friendship, support, companionship, solace, joy. The healing gesture, the gesture meant to heal their suffering, is not intended to explain anything away or fill in the abyss but simply to affirm that they are not alone, that our common madness is a matter of degree, that we are all siblings in the same "night of truth." The healing gesture is not to explain madness, if that means to explain it away, but to recognize it as a common fate, to affirm our community and solidarity, and to divide their pain in two by taking on half of it in attentive compassion and counsel.

A comparable point can be made about the "confessional practices" of the seventeenth and eighteenth centuries that Foucault has adroitly analyzed. The meticulous ruminations of an Alphonse Liguori into the secret recesses of the soul are lurid exercises in a kind of confessional voyeurism, which are useful only as candidates for an inverted, perverted *ars erotica*. But they are also, and more importantly, from what I like to call a more authentically religious point of view, profoundly insufficient and, I would say, quite irreligious. The institutionalization, regularization, and methodologization of "confession" are religious perversity. The confessor (in the sense of *confiteor*, I confess) is a "sinner." "Sin" is like "madness": it is a larger-than-life term for life *in extremis,* at the limits, for life that has strayed beyond the safe and reassuring boundaries of everyday life, beyond the wide swaths of normalcy cut by our everyday practices. Sin is not reducible to wrongdoing—no more than madness is reducible to error. It is an expression, perhaps a mythic expression—that is arguably the status of "madness," too—that provides an idiom for a deeper breach, a profound rupture in the human heart. We are divided against ourselves. Like the madness by which we are all beset and upset, and from which we have something to learn, sin bears testimony to a deep divide. But, unlike madness, sin is not a disturbance in the sphere of reason and "truth," but in the sphere of justice and "good." "Sin" seeks to give words to profound self-diremption, a rupture, a radical unhappiness in our condition.

I believe that sin requires a healing gesture analogous to madness, a gesture of compassion and commonality. The sinner tells us who we are, tells us of our own unhappiness. Sin is not the object of a Liguorian gaze, not a secret to be ferreted out by confessional techniques, not an object of interrogation. Sin is not an object at all, but the Being of the being we ourselves are.[30] The language of sin provides an idiom for what Levinas calls the "murderousness" of freedom, the murderousness of our power. We who are free and well fed, we who are whole and hearty, fit and on the move, we who move easily within the relations of power, are murderous and we cause others to suffer. "Sin" likewise provides an idiom for our weakness, our infidelities to those to whom we owe loyalty. Sin is not the Other but who we are. Sin is the Other within, the serpent and the apple within our hearts. Sin comes to us from on high and gives us something to understand by telling us about ourselves, by telling us of the abyss within.

The healing gesture handed down to us by the great religious traditions is not analytic objectification, not minute, ruminating subjectification. The great healing gesture that sweeps down over us in Buddhism is called the "great compassion" and in the New Testament is called "forgiveness"! Jesus was the discoverer of forgiveness, Hannah Arendt says.[31] Forgiveness loosens the knots of the social network, slackens the ties in the relations of power, even as revenge draws them tighter and makes them more intractable and oppressive. Forgiveness opens the space of the social network; it makes the future possible and denies to the past its role as fate. Forgiveness makes new forms of subjectivity possible, even as revenge condemns us to repeat the past in endless cycles. Forgiveness releases and opens; revenge traps, incarcerates, and closes. Forgiveness is not given to minute interior rehearsing of the past and intensive subjectification, but is rather dismissive and forgetting. Go and sin no more! Forget it! Forgiving is active forgetting. Forgiveness does not ask questions, but understands that it has itself been put in question by sin. Forgiveness lets itself be interrogated; it does not interrogate. Forgiveness readily makes itself guilty for the sake of the other. Forgiveness asks who among us can cast the first stone; it looks lovingly on sinners, with whom it consistently consorts to the scandal of the Good and the Just. Forgiveness heals not by analyzing but by holding out a hand of compassion, by offering a forgiving word that affirms and confesses for its own part that we are all sinners, all siblings of the same dark night.

That is the "truth" of confession, the truth that there is no "truth of truth," no confessional techniques, no methodological examinations of conscience, no objectification by way of subjectification. That is also why Julia Kristeva thinks that Christian confessional practices have a notable, albeit mystified, healing power. (But then what is more mystifying than the creatures that psychoanalysis invents?) That is particularly true, she thinks, when confession centers on words of forgiveness and not on the rites of "penance," which is the view of Duns Scotus, whom Kristeva regards as the great theologian of confession.[32] Scotus of course lived before the age of subjectification/objectification, the age of the world reduced to a picture for the subject's gaze (*Weltbild*), as Heidegger says, and offered an antidote to the Tridentine confessional practices that Foucault has ruthlessly exposed.

The secret is, there is no Secret. The truth is that we cannot gain the high ground of a capitalized Truth, insulated from violence and unreason, destruction and self-destruction, "madness" and "sin." The truth is what Foucault calls—in a wonderfully unguarded moment—the "night of truth." His analyses constitute a remarkable hermeneutics of that night of truth, a cold and more merciless scrutiny of the human condition that is, at the same time, bent subtly in a direction not at all at odds with mercy.

NOTES

1. See John D. Caputo, *More Radical Hermeneutics: On Not Knowing Who We Are* (Bloomington: Indiana University Press, 2000), chap. 4 for a discussion of Derrida, Rorty, and politics.

2. Hubert Dreyfus and Paul Rabinow, *Michel Foucault: Beyond Structuralism and Hermeneutics*, 2nd ed. (Chicago: University of Chicago Press, 1983). Hereafter cited as *BSH*.

3. See the discussion of "cold hermeneutics" in John D. Caputo, *Radical Hermeneutics: Repetition, Deconstruction, and the Hermeneutic Project* (Bloomington: Indiana University Press, 1987), chap. 7. Hereafter cited as *RH*.

4. Michel Foucault, *Mental Illness and Psychology*, trans. Alan Sheridan (Berkeley: University of California Press, 1987), 74. Hereafter cited as *MIP*. This is a translation of the 1962 French edition, *Maladie mentale et Psychologie*, which is an extensive revision of the 1954 edition, *Maladie mentale et personalité*. The important difference between these editions is examined carefully in James Bernauer, *Michel Foucault's Force of Flight: Toward an Ethics for Thought* (Atlantic Highlands, NJ: Humanities Press International, 1990), 24–36 and app. I.

5. Dreyfus discusses Foucault's interest in Heidegger in his instructive foreword to *MIP*, ix, xviii–xix, xxviiiff. Martin Heidegger, *Being and Time*, trans. E. Macquarrie and J. Robinson (New York: Harper & Row, 1962).

6. Friedrich Nietzsche, *Beyond Good and Evil*, trans. R. J. Hollingdale (Baltimore: Penguin, 1972), no. 39, p. 50, no. 270, pp. 189–90. See my discussion of these texts of Nietzsche in *RH*, 189.

7. Michel Foucault, *Madness and Civilization: A History of Insanity in the Age of Reason*, trans. Richard Howard (New York: Pantheon, 1965). Hereafter cited as *MC*. This is an abridgment of *Histoire de la folie à l'âge classique* (Paris: Gallimard, 1972).

8. Jean-François Lyotard, *The Differend: Phrases in Dispute*, trans. G. Van Den Abbeele (Minneapolis: University of Minnesota Press, 1988), xi.

9. "Untruth" is an expression used by the later Heidegger in such a way as to say that there is always a radical core of untruth within truth; truth is not truth "all the way through," concealment is the hidden ground of unconcealment, a wresting of unconcealment from a prior concealment. See Martin Heidegger, "On the Essence of Truth," trans. John Sallis, in *Martin Heidegger: Basic Writings*, ed. David Krell (New York: Harper & Row, 1977), 132–35. Foucault seems to think of unreason as a prior untruth and concealment embedded in the core of reason.

10. Edmund Husserl, *Ideas Pertaining to a Pure Phenomenology and to a Phenomenological Philosophy*, bk. 1, trans. Fred Kersten (The Hague: M. Nijhoff. 1983), §§ 47–49.

11. See Michel Foucault, "Madness, the Absence of Work," trans. Peter Stastny and Deniz Sengel, in *Foucault and His Interlocutors*, ed. Arnold Davidson (Chicago: University of Chicago Press, 1997), 97–104.

12. Husserl, *Ideas Pertaining to a Pure Phenomenology*, §§ 124–27. "The attempt to write the history of the decision, division, difference runs the risk of construing the division as an event or a structure subsequent to the unity of an original presence, thereby confirming metaphysics in its fundamental operation." Jacques Derrida, *Writing and Difference*, trans. Alan Bass (Chicago: University of Chicago Press, 1978), 140; see Foucault's hostile response in Michel Foucault, "My Body, This Fire," trans. Geoffrey Bennington, *Oxford Literary Review* 4, no. 1 (1979): 5–28. For a good account of the acrimonious character of this exchange between Foucault and Derrida and for a sensible appraisal of the convergence of their thought around the themes of power and ethics, which I am also suggesting here, see Roy Boyne, *Foucault and Derrida: The Other Side*

of Reason (London: Unwin Hyman, 1990). For Derrida's most recent statement on Foucault, see Jacques Derrida, "'To Do Justice to Freud': The History of Madness in the Age of Psychoanalysis," trans. Pascale-Anne Brault and Michael Naas, in *Foucault and His Interlocutors*, 57–96.

13. Michel Foucault, *Power/Knowledge: Selected Interviews and Other Writings, 1972–1977*, ed. Colin Gordon, trans. Colin Gordon, Leo Marshall, John Mepham, and Kate Soper (New York: Pantheon, 1980), 118–19. Hereafter cited as *P/K*.

14. See Søren Kierkegaard, *Two Ages: The Age of Revolution and the Present Age*, trans. Howard Hong and Edna H. Hong (Princeton: Princeton University Press, 1978), 68, especially 92–102.

15. Søren Kierkegaard, *Fear and Trembling and Repetition*, trans. Howard Hong and Edna H. Hong (Princeton: Princeton University Press, 1983), 36.

16. Michel Foucault, *The Birth of the Clinic: An Archaeology of Medical Perception*, trans. A. M. Sheridan Smith (New York: Pantheon, 1973), xvi–xvii.

17. Michel Foucault, *The Order of Things: An Archaeology of the Human Sciences*, trans. Alan Sheridan (New York: Pantheon, 1970), 373. Dreyfus and Rabinow use this text to set the terms of their own understanding of hermeneutics.

18. Michel Foucault, *The Archaeology of Knowledge and the Discourse on Language*, trans. A. M. Sheridan Smith (New York: Pantheon, 1972), 32.

19. Michel Foucault, "Judiciousness in Dispute, or Kant after Marx," in *The Lyotard Reader*, ed. Andrew Benjamin (Oxford: Basil Blackwell, 1990), 328.

20. Jacques Derrida, "Circumfession: Fifty-Nine Periods and Periphrases," in Geoffrey Bennington and Jacques Derrida, *Jacques Derrida* (Chicago: University of Chicago Press, 1993), 122.

21. I have found James Bernauer's work (see note 4) to be singularly insightful in its approach to Foucault and congenial to my notion of "radical hermeneutics," a notion I developed in connection with Derrida, not Foucault. For more on Bernauer's notion of Foucault's negative theology, see James Bernauer, "The Prisons of Man: An Introduction to Foucault's Negative Theology," *International Philosophical Quarterly* 27 (December 1987): 365–81, and his excellent conclusion in *Michel Foucault's Force of Flight*, 175–84, on "ecstatic thinking." For more on the long-range consonance between Foucault and Derrida, which focuses on the question of reason and unreason, see Boyne, *Foucault and Derrida*.

22. James M. Clark, ed., *Meister Eckhart: An Introduction to the Study of His Works with an Anthology of His Sermons* (London: Thomas Nelson and Sons, 1957), 159.

23. The motif of the irreducible residue, the unassimilable fragment, the remains, the leftover that cannot be *relevé*, is central likewise to Jacques Derrida, *Glas*, trans. John P. Leavey and Richard Rand (Lincoln: University of Nebraska Press, 1986), which like so much of recent French philosophy is on the lookout for something that cannot be consumed and incorporated into the Hegelian "dialectic." Cf. *MC*, 285.

24. There are late Heideggerian tones in late Foucault: where Heidegger has analyzed the *Gestell* that is the "essence of technology," in its application to nature, Foucault discusses the *Gestell* that is applied to us in the various "technologies of the self," or technologies of behavior. Michel Foucault, *Discipline and Punish: The Birth of the Prison*, trans. Alan Sheridan (New York: Vintage, 1977, 1979), 135–69.

25. "This . . . force of resistance, this Foucaultian spirituality, bears witness to the capacity for an ecstatic transcendence of any history that asserts its necessity." Bernauer, *Michel Foucault's Force of Flight*, 180–81.

26. Foucault does not have a theory of pure or radical freedom, of the sort he suggested in his early work on Ludwig Binswanger, but of a circumscribed, circumstantial (circumcisional!) freedom, a capacity for contextual alteration, for modification of the circumstances one finds oneself by way of refusal. It is also a theory of local revolt as opposed to total revolution. See John Rajchman, *Michel Foucault: The Freedom of Philosophy* (New York: Columbia University Press, 1985), chap. 1, "The Politics of Revolt."

27. Jacques Derrida, *The Other Heading: Reflections on Today's Europe*, trans. Pascale-Anne Brault and Michael Naas (Bloomington: Indiana University Press, 1992), 9.

28. I have expanded on the notion of a hermeneutics that gives up on the idea of a hermeneutic secret, of uncovering the master name, and that finds itself in an abyss in *RH*, chaps. 6–7.

29. Foucault, *Order of Things*, 373.

30. That is fundamentally the argument in Søren Kierkegaard, *The Concept of Anxiety*, trans. Reidar Thomte (Princeton: Princeton University Press, 1980), which is the reason that Heidegger had a fairly easy time of rewriting this concept in

a secularized or, as he said, "formalized" way in Heidegger, *Being and Time*.

31. Hannah Arendt, *The Human Condition* (Chicago: University of Chicago Press, 1958), 236–43. "Trespassing is an everyday occurrence which is in the very nature of action's constant establishment of new relationships within a web of relations, and it needs forgiving, dismissing, in order to make it possible for life to go on by constantly releasing men from what they have done unknowingly" (240). Forgiving is releasing, forgetting, and moving on.

32. Julia Kristeva, "*Qui tollis peccata mundi*," in *Powers of Horror: An Essay on Abjection*, trans. Leon S. Roudiez (New York: Columbia University Press, 1982), 131–32. Duns Scotus located the essence of the sacrament in the word of the confessor, not in doing penance. Hannah Arendt says that *metanoein* (Luke 17:3–4) is better understood as "change of heart," retrace your steps and sin no more than as "repent" (the usual translation), penance, which means, of course, to revisit yourself with pain. Cf. Arendt, *The Human Condition*, 240n78.

11
Beyond Aestheticism: Derrida's Responsible Anarchy

Deconstruction is sometimes accused of being a version of aestheticism. It appears to be frivolous and playful, to abdicate its duty to read literary and philosophical texts responsibly, and perversely to prefer arbitrary misreadings to serious interpretation. Viewed thus, Derrida sounds like the aesthete in Kierkegaard's *Either/Or* who advises us to situate ourselves at a point prior to the principle of contradiction, anterior to its field of force, so that, exempted from the harshness of having to choose between its terms, we will be free to frolic in a world without consequences. On this rendering, deconstruction practices its own version of the rotation method and aesthetic repetition. It engages in an endless free play of variant readings which are indulged in for the sheer pleasure they give but without regard for truth.

The result is calamitous, not only for the interpretation of texts, in which it is made to appear that anything goes, but also for ethics and politics, where the notion that anything goes is downright pernicious.[1] Hermeneutic nihilism is one thing, for that may be confined to the academy and the reading of old books. But ethical and political nihilism is dangerous, for that may spill over into the streets. So it looks like we should read Derrida the way we read the *Diary of the Seducer*, that is, with a growing realization of the amorality of it all that finally drives us beyond deconstruction.

That is what I want to contest. If you want to push the Kierkegaardian analogy, then I am arguing that there is an ethical side to Derrida, which is not just a "side," but goes to the heart of the deconstructionist project. There is an ethical analog to Derrida's defense of the underprivileged terms in binary systems (supplement, writing, margins, lost mail, and so on), for the systems that he critiques have concrete ethical and political instantiations. Furthermore, by siding with those who are marginalized by the system, deconstruction even has certain religious resonances which make their way into his text through Levinas. That means you can push the Kierkegaardian analogy all the way through, that there is an "ethico-religious" quality to the way deconstruction overcomes aestheticism. Thus construed, Derrida's knack for disturbing the academic peace locates him closer to Socrates than to the aesthete on the Kierkegaardian map, a notch or two higher on the "stages of existence."

Deconstruction takes aim at the "powers that be," an excellent English expression that shows very nicely the ethical spin that Derrida has put on his critique of the metaphysics of presence. The powers that be: that means the powers that have presence, that claim to "be" rather than to have "become," to have timeless validity rather than an historical genealogy. It wants to delimit the *arche* which metaphysics always sets at the head of every hierarchical system. Yet it does not do this irresponsibly, but with a sense of what might be called a "responsible anarchy." That at least is what I propose to show.

THE VOCATION OF DECONSTRUCTION

One of the things that the aestheticist reading likes to stick to Derrida is that he does not believe in anything, that deconstruction is not moved by the call of anything, that it has no responsibility, no vocation. Hermeneutics, on the other hand (Gadamer is one of these critics), is just as pleased as it can be with itself for being open to the other, and it constantly pats itself on the back for heeding the call of Being.[2] Hermeneutics looks a little like Judge Wilhelm who works over the aesthete for not having a self or continuity, for being incapable of ethical repetition: I hope to show that looking like Judge Wilhelm is not ultimately an enviable position, not if you read as far as the "Ultimatum" in *Either/Or.*

So, the first thing to settle is whether deconstruction is *bound* to anything, whether there is any room in it for the prized terms of hermeneutics and indeed of Western morals generally: call, answerability, responsibility. Does deconstruction experience any obligation, or have a sense of responsibility, or experience a call? In short, does deconstruction have a vocation?

I would say that the notion of responsibility, of responsiveness, goes right to the heart of the deconstructive project. Not only is it not missing from deconstruction, a sense of responsibility is pretty much what deconstruction is (and the way I would have defined it had the editors of *The New Random House Dictionary* asked me). Derrida gives us an idea of the responsibility of deconstruction in "The Principle of Reason: The University in the Eyes of Its Pupils."[3] He is discussing Heidegger's notion that the "principle of sufficient reason" (*der Satz vom Grund*), "every being has a reason," has us all in its grip, that it lays claim to us (*in Anspruch nehmen*) today with a particular force. The twist that Derrida gives to these Heideggerian formulations is to show that this principle is subverting the university—the vocation of the university—in a particularly disturbing way.

For the university is constantly being driven on and driven about by this powerful principle. That is so not only because it is in the business of rendering reasons and so provides reason with a home. But it is even more important to see that the university has very much submitted itself to the idea that it itself has a reason. The university is an entity—it is an institution—and as such is answerable to this powerful principle: it too has to give an account of its raison d'être. So the university is eager to serve a purpose, to perform a service. Its "function" is to train the leaders of tomorrow, as they always say at commencement, to fund the professions with trained minds, to supply the brain power for the will-to-power, the technological minds to keep the wheels of the *Gestell* turning. Its job is to cure cancer, to turn out the accountants and the computer people whom an advanced industrial world requires, and even to help build bombs. No one can fault the university on this point: it responds to the claim which that principle makes upon it; it answers the call.

The question is, is this the only way to answer the call, the only way hear what is calling in the call? Would anything else be unresponsive and irresponsible? Heidegger points out that because the principle of sufficient reason is itself something, an entity, a *Satz,* it is possible to let the principle recoil on itself and ask for the reason for the principle of sufficient reason. At that point, something very embarrassing happens: the principle of ground that every entity has a *Grund*, turns out to be itself groundless, an *Abgrund*. The *Satz* stops here; the *principium*/prince/emperor has no clothes. For it is not possible to ground the principle that claims that everything has a ground, and does so with such power that it brings the university and everything else under its claim.

But is this responsible, to question the highest principle of thought, to put the *arche* itself in question, to demand a reason for the *principium rationis*; does it not risk irrationalism, anarchy? Will not such questioning precipitate thinking into an abyss? Or is it not a "higher responsibility" for us to question even this most prestigious of all principles, to put the prince on the spot, since no one is above the law, including the law itself?

It is turning out that there are two ways to respond to the principle of reason: the first is, like a dutiful subject, to obey it, to be responsive to it, to submit to the *arche*, which is what metaphysics has always meant by responsibility. But Heidegger, and Derrida after him, is on the tracks of another kind of responding and responsibility, one which, by putting the principle itself, the *arche* into question, wants to be *responsible for* the university and the first principle of all thinking (PR, 8). It is possible to answer *for* the principle of sufficient reason, to question its prestige and to wonder whether it has not gone too far. To do that is to answer the call not by obeying it but by questioning it. We are being both responsible, because we assume responsibility for it, and reasonable, because we ask whether the principle of reason is out of control.

But such a question makes the university tremble. A questioning that puts grounds and grounding into question looks groundless, abyssal, anarchic, irrational. The university is threatened by such deconstructive gestures, which look like aestheticism or nihilism. Yet it is the Derridean-Heideggerian claim that nothing is more essential to the well-being of thinking and of the university, and nothing more responsible. For the university is bending under the weight of the principle of reason: everything it does is done for a reason, a purpose—a social purpose, a professional purpose, above all a national purpose, even as it leaves the question of the origin of the principle and the source of its authority unasked.

There is no easy way to twist free of this encumbering of the university by insisting upon the distinction between "oriented" (applied) and "basic" research, free from outside interference, or to insist on the "autonomy" of the philosophical faculty as Kant had done. Heidegger has shown the inextricability of science from technology, of the will to know from the will to power; there is no knowledge that can be shielded from power. There is nothing that cannot be put to work in the war effort—even hermeneutics itself (PR, 13). Everything can be used—and everything can be regulated: by the grants that are approved and rejected, by the style of speech that is admitted into the university. So long as they speak well, the university is able to assimilate even the most radical elements to its campus greens. Faculty row is, after all, safe housing for radicals of all sorts, a way of keeping them off the public streets. The university feels no discomfiture with Marxism, Derrida points out, for Marxism speaks the language of the university and has made itself at home there: "[Marxism] does not threaten the fundamental axiomatics and deontology of the institution, its rhetoric, its rites and procedures. The academic landscape easily accommodates such types of discourse more easily within its economy and its ecology" (PR, 16).

The idea is to hold in question "the essence of reason and the principle of reason, the values of the basic, of the principial, of radicality, of the *arche* in general." But that can only be done by "sounding a call for a certain practice" (PR, 16). That is why Derrida thinks that deconstruction exercises its responsibility by challenging the university in its very style of thinking, flaunting its language and its staid good manners: "It is a matter . . . of preparing oneself thereby to transform the modes of writing, approaches to pedagogy, the procedures of academic exchange, the relation to languages, to other disciplines, to the institution in general" (PR, 16–17). And that transformation includes transforming the way in which the university reproduces itself, certifying the professional competence of future professors by seeing to it that they likewise will respect the code.

Such subversiveness cannot be *simply* an-archical, however—it is always around a *simpliciter* that a metaphysical economy is organized—for that is decidably ir-rational, ir-responsible. Thinking responsibly does not mean anything irrational but rather asking what has been excluded by what calls itself reason and *arche*. Assuming responsibility for the university and for the principle by which it is ruled thus calls for a "double gesture," a style of operating both within the principle of reason and outside it. It is a question of proving oneself by all the standards that the university sets *and* of speaking and writing differently, of operating within the constraints of the university *and* of opening it up to what is essentially outside the university, opening it to its own other, to something that its infinite Hegelian appetite cannot digest. It is a question of proving that one can live by the discipline of the university even while doing something to scandalize it:

> Those who venture forth along this path, it seems to me, need not set themselves up in opposition to the principle of reason, nor need they give way to 'irrationalism.' They may continue to assume *within* the university, along with its memory and tradition, the imperative of professional rigor and competence. There is a double gesture here, a double postulation: to ensure professional competence and the most serious tradition of the university even while going as far as possible theoretically and practically, to think at one and the same time the entire thinking about the abyss beneath the university. (PR, 17)

Being responsible for the university situates us on the margins, both within and without, inside and outside the university. A flat-out plunge into an-archy will just reproduce the hierarchy. Anarchy is not insidious; it cannot get inside or insinuate itself; it is a clumsy frontal attack that invites repulsion. We need both the *arche* and the an-archy, both the law and the transgression; both to have ends and to beware of ends.

The result of the double gesture, Derrida concludes, would be to give ourselves a "chance," a little opening through which, in an unguarded moment, something different may slip—a chance and a moment which Derrida describes as Kierkegaardian: "It is the chance for an event about which one does not know whether or not, presenting itself *within* the university, it belongs to the university: It may also be brief and paradoxical, it may tear up time, like the instant invoked by Kierkegaard, one of those thinkers who are foreign, even hostile to the university, who gives us more to think about, with respect to the essence of the university, than academic reflections themselves" (PR, 20). Derrida concludes this lecture by setting chance—an irruptive moment, a tear in the fabric of time's continuity—along with memory, the continuity of tradition, of the memory of what the university is, as a double guard over the university. A guardian, we have learned from Heidegger, is one who preserves, *wahren*, as in *Wahrheit*, *veritas*. By inscribing *veritas* on its coat of arms, the university calls upon these guards to watch truthfully over itself and the way it responds to the principle of reason.

Whence the lameness of the aestheticist charge against Derrida: he thinks that Kierkegaard is on *his* side. The whole point of deconstruction is to assume responsibility, not simply, in the manner of metaphysics, by responding to—the readier and more rapid the response, the more dangerous it is—but by assuming responsibility for. The height of responsibility is to wonder about the origin of what calls for a response. The comparison to *Either/Or* is holding up, but it is beginning to work in the favor of deconstruction. The Judge works over the aesthete for his self-indulgent and wanton playfulness, for his avoidance of the principle of great power—the principle of contradiction, *der Satz der Identität*, the principle that gives one entry into the ethical universal. The Judge insists upon a decision and decidability, upon having a conscience and good will.

But you only have to read *Either/Or* through to the end to know that the Judge is hurling boomerangs at the aesthete, that the arrows he aims land on his own posterior. At the end, ultimately, the Judge is felled by a little ultimatum from a country parson that informs the Judge that before God no man is just. Everything the Judge threw up to the aesthete comes back at him: the truth is the particular not the universal, the exceptional one, not the law; the truth is undecidability—the things that I will, I do not, the things that I do, I will not—not the decisive victories of an ethical athlete; the truth is confessing the mess we are in, not the braggadocio of insufferable Judge Wilhelm. The parson outlines the possibility of a religious replay of aesthetic particularity that makes the Judge eat his universals.

We can see the Derridean counterpart, the Wilhelmsonian result of hurling aestheticist arrows at Derrida. The part of the Judge is played by the defenders of the principle of reason who call for solid and scientific thinking in the natural or social sciences, or for responsible interpretation in the humanities, and in general for honoring the serious ends of the university, or of any of our honorable institutions, which pass on truth and the tradition. But the question is whether this loud voice that calls for obedience to the universal does not silence the call of the different, cut off our chance for something different, for an irruptive moment, for the difference which appears in the blink of an eye. The responsibility of deconstruction is to issue a little ultimatum that confesses that we do not know what reason means and that reason itself has a hard time giving a reason for itself. It wants to open the university and what it calls reason to something other, particular, different, to the *claim* of the different which is being excluded.

Derrida thus occupies a space on the Kierkegaardian map that corresponds structurally to the religious rather than to the aesthetic. Derrida systematically defends the rights of the different not the same, of the particular not the universal, of the exception not the rule, of everything that is excluded and marginalized by the rule of the same, or the *arche/principium/*prince.

The aestheticist critics have been unable to hear all the resonances of the word "responsibility." They have missed the double gesture: not only of responding *to* the principle, but of assuming *responsibility for* it, of holding it in question, of delimiting the power of the *arche* and of seeing what it excludes. They have mistaken Derrida's refusal (merely) to respond to the *arche*, to serve all its ends, as an irresponsible anarchy, whereas the point of it all has been to assume the highest responsibility in a highly "responsible anarchy":

> [INTERVIEWER:] Could one describe the political equivalent of deconstruction as a disposition, as opposed to a position, of responsible anarchy?
>
> [DERRIDA:] If I had to describe my political disposition I would probably employ a formula of that kind while stressing, of course, the interminable obligation to work out and to deconstruct these two terms—"responsible" and "anarchy." If taken as assured certainties in themselves, such terms can also become reified and unthinking dogmas. But I also try to re-evaluate the indispensable notion of "responsibility."[4]

That is why Kierkegaard is a Derridean figure par excellence, a deconstructionist model. Kierkegaard is one of those thinkers who could not possibly have survived in the university, who could not *think* in the university, but who gave the university more to think than all its professors, core requirements, and final examinations. Excluded by the university, he was emancipated from its protocol, freed of its good manners, and able really to write. This was something that Professor Heidegger never saw when he himself wrote about Kierkegaard. (There is another well-known example of the same type: Nietzsche.) The critique of *homo metaphysicus* is inextricable from a critique of *homo academicus*.[5]

THE CLAIM OF THE OTHER

I am arguing that deconstruction is always responsible in just this way, that it responds to the claims that every reasonable and responsible person experiences, but with a double gesture: both by responding to them and by making itself responsible for them in order to see what they have *excluded*. It suspects that along with the resounding fame of prestigious principles there is a lot of sounding brass, a lot of drowning out and exclusion. And it is to this excluded one, this "other," that deconstruction tries to be especially responsive. The argument then is that deconstruction arises as a response to the claim of the other.

Openness to the other, then, is not a point on which hermeneutics alone can pat itself on the back. All that bragging in *Truth and Method* about responsiveness to the call of the other, putting our self-understanding at risk, getting experienced at expecting the unexpected, which is supposed to define hermeneutics, is not the private property of hermeneutics after all. For deconstruction, too, we can perfectly well say, "experiences" (properly deconstructed) the "claim" (properly deconstructed) of the other, of the different. Of course, in its straightforward, metaphysical sense, Derrida keeps a safe distance from the word "experience." That is because "experience" has tended to mean the experience of immediate presence, something shot from guns. I myself think it better to rewrite deconstruction as a philosophy of experience where experience is willing to confess to its limits, to its inextricable complicity with the textual system in which it operates. Having an experience is to a great extent a matter of knowing how to move around within a textual system that both enables that experience to happen and disables it from trying to detach itself from that system, as if it were some atomic bit of data.

So given the deconstructive delimitation, I would venture the formula that deconstruction arises from the experience of *différance*. That helps bring the ethical dimension into sharper focus. Deconstruction opens up an ethics which experiences the claim, not of presence but of absence, not of identity but of difference. Unlike the mainstream metaphysics of morals, of which there are in Western philosophy more than enough examples, deconstruction does not invoke universal, rational, or natural laws. It does not just respond to them, but it assumes responsibility for them and investigates their extraordinary power to abolish everything that they consider particular, irrational, or unnatural. Deconstruction is set in motion by the rights of the different. It does not heed the mainstream call of Being, presence, and the same, but keeps its ear peeled for the call of the other.

Lest anyone think that Derrida must be a friend of mine whom I feel called upon to defend, I can, with the best manners of the university, cite a text. In the same interview from which I draw the title of this paper, Derrida says: "I mean that deconstruction is, in itself, a positive response to an alterity which necessarily calls, summons or motivates it. Deconstruction is therefore a vocation—a response to a call. The other, as the other than self, the other that opposes self-identity, is not something that can be detected and disclosed within a philosophical space and with the aid of a philosophical lamp. The other precedes philosophy and necessarily invokes and provokes the subject before any genuine questioning can begin" (K 118).

Hermeneutics has picked the wrong fight when it criticizes deconstruction on this point of responsibility, and it comes off looking a lot like Judge Wilhelm. Difference is after all what deconstruction is famous for. If anything, hermeneutics—I mean Gadamer and Ricoeur, not what I would myself call "radical hermeneutics," which is a hermeneutics that has wised up—has curtailed the call of the other by means of a Hegelian metaphysics of identity, which is too quick to assimilate the other to the same. In hermeneutics, the idea is to effect a fusion of horizons between the same and the other. It is a philosophy of digestion that is always interested in assimilating the other, making it part of its substance. Gadamer, for example, objected to nineteenth-century hermeneutics in just these terms. He criticized its project of "reconstruction," of turning the past into a lifeless object that it can then inhabit, walking around it silently, presuppositionlessly, as one would tiptoe around an Egyptian tomb. In the place of that, Gadamer puts integration, mediation (*Vermittlung*), appropriation (*Aneignung*), a relation of life to life in which the life of the one is consumed by and assimilated into the life of the other and thereby acquires a new form.[6] Gadamerian hermeneutics, moved as it is by its Hegelian mainsprings, is preoccupied with digestion.

In hermeneutics, the breaching of my horizon, the rupture that the advent of the other brings, is always taken to be provisional, a negative moment in a larger movement. There is always a "projection of completeness" in which I commit myself to the idea, in principle and in advance, that what is alien can be assimilated, that the differences can be reconciled, that agreement can be reached, that the different can be made the same. But in deconstruction there is a more radical toleration of the plurality of voices that does not try to make them sing the same song, or dance to the tune of the same logos. Deconstruction practices a more radical *Gelassenheit*, which is bent not on assimilating the other but on letting the other be. Hermeneutics starts out with an experience of the otherness of the other and has its sights set for how the differences can be mediated. Deconstruction, on the other hand, wants to make room for a chance, a tear in the continuous garment of time, to savor the different, which keeps getting extinguished by the same. Hermeneutics wants to cross distances while deconstruction wants to make space for the other.

Diane Michelfelder has recently put this point in a particularly insightful way.[7] She says that in Gadamerian hermeneutics the other appears as question (*Frage*), but in Derrida the other appears as claim (*Anspruch*). In Gadamer the other is a dialogue partner who appears "across" the space of a conversation, on the same level, in a more or less homogeneous space. The idea of a Gadamerian conversation is to get the logos going back and forth in such a way that the particulars—the participants—tend to give way to the play of the universal, the *Sache selbst*. Gadamer has in mind the to and fro of a conversation on a single level in a bi-polar game (like a tennis game on a perfectly flat surface). But the space of a Derridean "exchange" is neither bi-polar nor level. Derrida does not think of two neatly divided partners exchanging views, keeping the logos in the air. Such a dia-logue is logocentric, a kind of dia-logo-centrism. Instead, he has in mind a tangled maze of messages, not a dialogue but a colloquy, so that even when there are just two of us, I am not sure how many voices speak through me or the other, how many voices we have, whether we are individuals or corporations.

Furthermore, Derrida thinks perfectly level surfaces are artificial and can be found only in an unreal transcendental space as flat as a sprawling shopping mall, where people can walk and walk until there is nothing left to consume. Real space is curved, unequal, unfair, where the voice of the different one is excluded, distorted, silenced. So deconstruction sets about effecting a strategic reversal in favor of the different one, curving that space in the other's favor. In deconstruction, the other comes to me not across a level and homogeneous space but with the power of a claim, with the force of a disruption whose otherness I am not out to assimilate. To let the other be—that is the point of deconstructive work—is to leave them their otherness, to tolerate the difference, not to sublate it in a fusion of horizons.

So I would give Michelfelder's insightful distinction between question and claim a Levinasian twist. The relationship between the same and the other is not level but curved. The other is both lower and higher: lower because excluded, higher because his/her exclusion cries out, calls for, claims my response. That is why Levinas says the other comes to me from "on high." We run up against the other as a source of initiatives that are not our own, which come toward us with an autonomy and unpredictability that puts us to the test, which in general arise from a recess to which we are denied access.

On Levinas's accounting, the language of others is the point of contact we make with them, and the one way they have of revealing themselves to us. Language arises from plurality, from the difference between us, so that to listen to someone else is always to be instructed, that is, to hear something that is not our own. The idea is not to bring all discourse under the rule of reason, of the universal that extinguishes particulars, which would eventually be to silence everyone, but to keep the lines of communication open, for there can be no end to the novelty and otherness that arise when people get together. Instead of looking for ways to bring us into agreement, Levinas prefers to let them be *kath auto*.[8]

In the biblically inspired metaphysics that Levinas defends, plurality is a positive feature, belonging to a positive plenitude that he describes as anti-Parmenidean. Parmenides set the stage for onto-theo-logic by so privileging unity, by so identifying being with unity, that multiplicity and diversity have been suspect ever since. Plurality is not a fall from unity, a decline, a loss, nor even sheer numerical multiplicity. Plurality is the excess of the being of the other over and above my own projections.[9] Plurality is a creationist view that sees multiplicity in terms of fertility, superabundance, the emergence of difference and the novel, and not in the Platonic and neoplatonic categories of participation, analogy and emanation (TI, 80).

In such a view, the notion of "community" has been radically solicited as a Parmenidean, onto-theo-logical notion. Communities are defined in terms of unity, the capacity of individuals to swallow their differences and to come to common convergence, to stand as "one." So defined, a community resists otherness, cannot tolerate the existence of "individuals," and it ends up adopting excommunicative practices. That is why we need another idea *of* community, and maybe even another idea *than* community, one which is conceived in terms of its capacity to tolerate difference, its openness to the other, that is, to just the sort of people for which communities have historically shown such low tolerance (cf. PR, 16).

JEWGREEK ETHICS

It cannot go unnoticed that the ethics of Levinas is not only philosophical but religious, not only Greek but Jewish. "JewGreek is Greekjew."[10] In putting the question of the other to philosophy, Levinas in fact raised the question of the other *of* philosophy. In Levinas's ethics, the religious experience of the other, the passionate intensity of a biblical ethics of mercy, irrupts in the center of phenomenology and disrupts its project of comprehension. That rupturing of phenomenology, Derrida says in the Kearney interview, is what interests him most about Levinas—functioning as a "model" for his own attempt to delimit and deconstruct the metaphysics of presence (K, 107–8).

That is why all of that talk in Levinas about the stranger, the widow and the orphan sounds so odd to our philosophical ears—it is picking up on something biblical, something "other" than philosophy. It follows that deconstruction's focus on what has been "excluded," its responsiveness to the claim of the other, is marked with detectable overtones of a biblical ethics of the outcast one, of the despised and lowly, needy and helpless. Responding to the claim of the other is an old biblical idea, although this is not anything which Derrida has tried to monitor: "Though I was born a Jew, I do not work or think within a living Jewish tradition. So that if there is a Judaic dimension to my thinking which may from time to time have spoken in or through me, this has never assumed the form of an explicit fidelity or debt to that culture" (K, 107). The religious backdrop of the ethics of the other, while no more than a backdrop for Derrida personally, is more than a little interesting to us, who have taken upon ourselves to answer the charge of aestheticism, which is thrown up against deconstruction. For it completes the Kierkegaardian analogy: the overcoming of aestheticism in deconstruction has not only an ethical, but even a religious "dimension" to it. Not only is deconstruction not an irresponsible playing with words, not only is it committed to thinking responsibly, but there are resonances in it which a "religious thinker" immediately recognizes.

So I wish to conclude these remarks in a way calculated to scandalize the faithful, with a few deconstructive remarks on the ethics of the outcast, one that is to be found in the New Testament. That will concretize the suggestion that there is a religious element on the back-burners of deconstruction. It is also interesting to see what light deconstruction throws on religious texts. I, for one, think that deconstruction puts Jesus in an interesting light—though this will be received with little joy in either the Vatican or Paris. On this point at least, on the ethics of the outcast, Jesus is as Jewish as can be. That is why the New Testament scholar Edward Schillebeeckx remarks, near the end of his masterful *Jesus: An Experiment in Christology*: "It says something that it was a Jewish thinker and philosopher, E. Levinas, who could speak of the irresistible power of the 'defenceless other one' who goes on trusting."[11]

JEWCHRISTIAN IS CHRISTIANJEW

Deconstruction attempts to disrupt and intervene upon the totalizing projects of philosophy and philosophical ethics rather the way that Jesus attempted to intervene on the Law. Jesus was not opposed to the Law but to its totalizing tendencies. He did not think it either likely or desirable that the Law would be done away with. He wanted to transgress it strategically, to disrupt it where it had become repressive, exclusionary. He was urging, to put it in the terms we have been using here, not only to respond *to* the Law—there was quite enough of that already—but to be responsible *for* the Law, that is, to see that the Law had been given to the Jews by the father but it was not to be confused with the father. You might say Jesus was working on some way for the Jew to be both inside and outside the Law. This, of course, fits the picture of the "responsible anarchy" which we sketched above. The idea is not to throw the Law to the wolves but to check its totalizing tendencies and to see what it has been excluding.

That sort of project is easily misunderstood, and so Jesus became notorious as a transgressor (a "deconstructor"), as one who wanted to destroy the Law and the temple, though that was not his point at all. It did not help his image any that his first appearance on the public scene was in association with a bizarre wilderness prophet who dressed in animal skins and lived off locusts. If there was a word for it in Aramaic, someone probably called Jesus an anarchist. The fact is, he held no punches with the religious *arche*, the authorities in Jerusalem. He leveled blistering attacks upon them that eventually cost him his life, calling them at one point a "brood of vipers"—an "uncommonly sharp expression," Schillebeekx remarks (S, 128). (That, interestingly, puts Kierkegaard's *Attack upon Christendom* in excellent company.)

The interesting thing about Jesus from our point of view—as philosophers we want to know what was Jesus's "idea," what was he after (we are always already Greek)—is that he does not seem to attach an ethical quality to sameness but to *difference*, which is the light deconstruction throws on him. (You would have a devil of a time, if I may say so, finding a natural law theory in Jesus, basing everything on a common nature—although the Church has been trying that for some time now). What seems to have been preeminently "ethical" to him was openness to the different. The whole idea behind what he called the "kingdom of God" was mixing with the different, not preserving the purity of the same.

He did not think it much of an ethical feat to tell the rich and the powerful, or those who are already quite fond of us, or who come from the same part of Galilee as we do, that they are loved by the father (although they are). His pitch was that the father loved the Samaritans, the lepers, the lame, the possessed, the prostitutes and the adulterers, the lost sheep and prodigal sons, even tax-collectors and outright enemies. Any reader of postmodern writings cannot help but be stuck by the Foucauldian quality of this cast of characters. The mad, the ill, and the law breakers are just the sort that Jesus singled out. He was more drawn to the marginalized people about whom postmodernists write than to the career diplomats that dominate official Christianity ("Christendom") and who, Kierkegaard said, have made a prosperous business out of the crucifixion.

He went around in search of the excluded, scandalizing the guardians of truth in the process. He practiced a kind of strategic reversal, systematically singling out everyone who was last and putting them first. Of course, the idea was not simply to reverse the hierarchies but to displace them altogether (S, 145). He shocked the pharisees by *mixing* with everybody (the Aramaic *perishayya* meant "separate"). He told parables about prodigal sons and about a dinner party at which the crippled and lame were given the place of honor. His association with Mary Magdalen left the pharisees speechless. He would eat and drink with tax collectors and sinners (an interesting association of ideas!). He transgressed the Sabbath laws, because he said the Sabbath was made to give people a break, not a pain. When called to account for himself before the Sanhedrin, his defiance was absolute. He refused even to speak. He would not grant in principle the right of this institutional power to pass judgment on his mission to those whom that power systematically excluded (S, 315).

He found the face of God in the face of the different. The richer and more powerful you are, the weaker the divine trace; the more outcast you are, the stronger the trace. His *abba* seemed to have particular fondness for the lepers and the lame, the poor, and sinners of all sorts. The mark of divinity for Jesus was otherness, difference—and it is that very Jewish idea that Levinas is picking up. It is upon the least of our fellow human beings, the most errant and aberrant, that the love of the *abba* is inscribed (Jesus). The only access we have to the face of God is the face of the other, who comes to me from "on high" who "resembles God" (TI, 293).

In sum: the ethical turn that is taken in deconstruction, the anarchic responsibility for what is excluded by every *arche*, seems to me to arise from the height of responsibility (properly deconstructed). Furthermore, its turn toward the other has a long history and is interwoven with an old religious gesture. So I am not troubled by the analogy of deconstruction with the aesthete in *Either/Or*—not if you promise to read the whole book.

NOTES

1. As a case in point, see Allan Bloom's reactionary indictment of American "relativism" in *The Closing of the American Mind* (New York: Simon & Shuster, 1987) and the superb refutation of it by Martha Nussbaum, "Undemocratic Vistas," *New York Review of Books* 34 (November 5, 1987): 20–26.

2. Gadamer criticizes aestheticism in *Truth and Method*, trans. G. Barrell and J. Cumming (New York: Seabury, 1975), 73–90; his endorsement of Kierkegaard's argument in *Either/Or*, 85–86, against what he calls "hermeneutic nihilism" (in reference to Paul Valêry) seems to me a lot like what he thinks is going on in Derrida. See Diane Michelfelder and Richard Palmer, eds., *Dialogue and Deconstruction: The Gadamer-Derrida Encounter* (New York: SUNY Press, 1989). Allan Megill thinks that all postmodernists are aestheticists, although he thinks there might be a way out for Derrida; see Allan Megill, *Prophets of Extremity: Nietzsche, Heidegger, Foucault,*

Derrida (Berkeley: University of California Press, 1985), 3–4, 332–36. Finally, I must include an earlier piece of my own in this ill-begotten critique: "Hermeneutics as the Recovery of Man" reprinted in *Hermeneutics and Modern Philosophy*, ed. Brice Wachterhauscr (Albany: SUNY Press, 1986). While I am still fond of 416–37, I would today have written 437–42 quite differently, something I did succeed in doing in *Radical Hermeneutics* (Bloomington: Indiana University Press, 1987), chaps. 6–7.

3. Jacques Derrida, "The Principle of Reason: The University in the Eyes of Its Pupils." Trans. C. Porter and E. P. Morris, *Diacritics* (1983), 3–20 (hereafter PR). Modesty forbids me from referring the reader to an extended account of Heidegger's *Der Satz vom Grund* in my *The Mystical Element in Heidegger's Thought* (New York: Fordham University Press, 1986), chapter 2, and of Derrida's "Principle of Reason" in my *Radical Hermeneutics*, chap. 8.

4. Richard Kearney, "Deconstruction and the Other: An Interview with Derrida," in Richard Kearney, *Dialogues with Contemporary Continental Thinkers: The Phenomenological Heritage* (Manchester: Manchester University Press, 1984), 120–21 (hereafter K).

5. See Pierre Bourdieu, *Homo academicus*, trans, P. Collier (London: Polity Press, 1987).

6. Gadamer, *Truth and Method*, 146–50.

7. Prof. Michelfelder's remarks were part of a symposium run by Richard Palmer on Gadamer and Derrida at the 1987 meeting of the Society for Phenomenology and Existential Philosophy held at the University of Notre Dame.

8. Emmanuel Levinas, *Totality and Infinity*, trans, A. Lingis (Pittsburgh: Duquesne University Press, 1970), 71–72 (hereafter TI).

9. I believe that there is a similar notion of plurality and of the unforeseeable initiative taken by the other (natality) in another Jewish thinker, Hannah Arendt. See Hannah Arendt, *The Human Condition* (Chicago: University of Chicago Press, 1958), part 5, "Action."

10. A citation from James Joyce's *Ulysses*, of course, used by Derrida at the end of "Violence and Metaphysics" in Jacques Derrida, *Writing and Difference*, trans. Alan Bass (Chicago: University of Chicago Press, 1978), 153.

11. Edward Schillebeeckx, *Jesus: An Experiment in Christology*, trans. Hubert Hoskins (New York: Crossroad, 1985). 638. (Hereafter S). The account of Jesus that follows here is drawn from Schillebeeckx.

12
On Not Circumventing the Quasi-Transcendental: The Case of Rorty and Derrida

RORTY: ON NOT SUSPENDING THE NATURAL ATTITUDE

Richard Rorty has given up the traditional idea of "philosophical knowledge," the idea that there is some sort or entity or principle or condition which philosophers can come up with, so long as they argue carefully, that "explains" or "grounds" what the rest of us are doing. Rorty has given up the Kantian idea that there is a "philosophical tribunal"[1] whose job it is to adjudicate conflicting claims about science or morals or art, in virtue of something that philosophers know and that nobody else knows, not unless they become philosophers, too. He rejects the idea that philosophers, in virtue of some method or capacity, can cut through appearances and get to what is "really" going on, can penetrate beneath the surface or rise above the lower world the rest of us live in. He rejects the idea that it is the office of some "nonempirical super science" (*CIS*, 4) called philosophy to establish entities like the Form of the Good, the *prima causa*, the monad, absolute *Geist*, the Will to Power, Being (as opposed to beings)—or generally anything we feel an irresistible urge to capitalize—whose role it would be to keep order either in the sciences or in the everyday world we live in.

Put in Husserlian terms, Rorty sees absolutely no reason whatever to suspend the natural attitude, which, as far as he is concerned, can take care of itself and does not stand in need of transcendental aid.[2] Some natural attitudes are better than others, but it is the business of the natural attitude itself to put its own house in order, without foreign intervention. There is no need to acquire, and no way to establish, the transcendental conditions of possibility which back up the empirical world, which ground and found it, which adjudicate its disputes and provide an overarching hook upon which the empirical ego can grasp whenever things get too stormy in the empirical world below.

Rorty rejects the idea that philosophers can come up with an idea of human nature that would pick out something quintessentially human which would not be a function of socialization, which would see to it that socialization does not go all the way down (*CIS*, 185). He rejects the idea that philosophers have found a way to come up with anything quintessential, with any essence at all, human or natural. He rejects the idea that the physical sciences can come to the rescue, now that religion and philosophy have faltered, and cut through the world of familiar objects, like Eddington's table, to the mathematical properties of Physical Reality itself.

The urge to capitalize in the physical sciences is just as unjustified as it is in metaphysics and religion.[3] He shows a steadfastly nominalist and historicist (*CIS*, xvi, 74) skepticism about essence, reality, overarching principles, ahistorical conditions of possibility, and whatever else is dreamed of in our philosophies.

Rorty has no knock-down arguments against these entities and principles; he does not think you can drive your opponents up an argumentative wall (*CIS*, 53). He does not want to be drawn into the fray, get caught arguing the inverse side of metaphysics (which is philosophy, Heidegger says), defending an inverted metaphysics, which is metaphysics all the same. Rorty is just incredulous toward such constructs: he greets them with a blink, a yawn, and particularly a smile. On this point, at least, he fits Lyotard's famous definition of postmodernism as "incredulity towards metanarratives," toward *grands récits*, big stories.[4] When it comes to big stories, Rorty is a big skeptic; he is very incredulous about the sorts of things that philosophers have allowed themselves to believe, and he has set about, very adroitly, finding a way of not letting himself be drawn into these beliefs. His idea is to back himself out of the vocabularies of the classical theories, to ease himself out of their language games, by simply "redescribing" the situations which the philosophers think are so troubled as to drive them to seek a uniquely philosophical solution.

The effect of a good redescription on Rorty's terms will be therapeutic, to make the problem go away by seeing that, on this alternate description, there is no problem, that things can get along just fine without the philosophical intervention, that the natural attitude can take care of itself, that nobody in the natural attitude is feeling the pain that the philosophers are trying to cure. All you really need to see on Rorty's terms is that the vocabulary with which we describe the world or one another can always be revised, that any person or object or event can always be recontextualized, that any description can be replaced by redescription which will not suffer from the disadvantages of the prior description. Of course, the new vocabulary will generate new disadvantages of its own. But as Nietzsche might have said, final vocabularies are something to be overcome. All this Nietzschean-Rortian insight requires is a certain ironic distance from our current "final" vocabulary which sees that it is not final at all but "contingent" (*CIS*, 73).

What lies behind all this is the philosophical cramp that language is a "medium," either of representation, as in the realist correspondence theory of truth, or of expression, as in the more romanticized idealist theories that language is the way Spirit, Thought, History, or Being comes into words and so comes to be as Spirit, Thought, History, or Being. Rorty's notion is to kick this habit of thinking that language is a medium, that it is anything at all, anything *philosophical*, that is, like a medium, and to realize that it is just a tool by means of which we make our way around the world.[5] Apart from the various natural languages which are the object of study in linguistics and in the various language departments, there just is no philosophical thing called language (*CIS*, 14–15).

The skill and the adroitness, the grace and the good humor, the originality, insightfulness, and wide-ranging literateness with which he has set about the delicate operation of articulating and defending this version of neo-pragmatism are pretty much what we mean nowadays by "Rorty." The name of the thinker, Heidegger says, stands for a matter to be thought. But what does "Rorty" stand for? How shall we *classify* it? (The problem of classification is a central question raised by Rorty.) What is its genre? Does "Rorty" stand for a "philosophy"? If you like. So long as you do not get in heat over that. So long as all you mean by "philosophy" is a kind of writing,[6] a frank and literate line of reflection which expresses itself about a wide range of human affairs, without pretense to expert knowledge (*episteme*), with an eye toward uncomplicating some of the muddles that philosophers, scientists, theologians, and artists have created for the rest of us, toward untying a few knots, and letting the natural attitude take care of itself. The whole idea is to give the natural attitude some room to breathe and to allow it to straighten out its own affairs. To refer to it as "philosophy" at this point is mostly aimed at offering relief to desperate catalog librarians, and it is based upon little more than checking the footnotes to see what books are being cited. But it does not have much more punch than that (*CIS*, 135–36).

One might object that the "very idea" of the "natural attitude" is a *philosophical* idea. Nobody who actually *lives in* the natural attitude ever thought of it. The "very idea" of a natural attitude arises only from a transcendental standpoint, only by distinguishing the natural attitude from the transcendental attitude, so that the very identification *of* the natural attitude already presupposes the *epoché*, that is, that you have stepped outside of the natural attitude.[7] So Rorty has, as I said, a delicate operation (cf. *CIS* 7–8) on his hands, which it seems to me must always involve two stages. First, he must defend the natural attitude against its metaphysical detractors and transcendental *conquistadores*, those who think the natural attitude cannot conduct its own affairs, that it requires transcendental monitoring and colonizing by a more "advanced," high-order consciousness. Secondly, he must eventually talk philosophers out of making this distinction at all, so that eventually even talk about the "natural attitude" would disappear, even as Nietzsche hoped that the apparent world too would disappear, and even as Heidegger said we should leave metaphysics to itself and cease all overcoming of metaphysics.[8]

The idea is to just knock off philosophizing in the traditional way, to kick the traditional philosophical habit, the way one would quit smoking. This of course drives "professional philosophers" mad, that is, people who get tenure and promotion, sabbatical leaves and cushy grants, people who in general make a profitable living from "philosophy." They do not want Rorty's line to get back to their academic deans or to the National Endowment for the Humanities. The delicious thing about Rorty's line is how nicely it cuts across the once well-entrenched divide between analytic and Continental philosophy, how he overruns both their camps, and leaves a lot of very unhappy philosophical campers shaking their fists in anger at him. Analytic philosophers: because he has, unforgivably, made philosophy interesting and significant to a larger public; because he has broken ranks with a narrow in-group in the prestige universities who have made a career of patting each other on the back and recommending one another for prestige appointments while no one else reads or cares about their precious little papers. Continental philosophers: because he has invaded their turf, laid hands on their favorite thinkers, explained them in a way that can be understood, and stolen some of their best lines—like "the end of philosophy" or "overcoming metaphysics."

Professional politics aside, it is truly interesting how Rorty's line converges with the more radical developments in Continental thought in the last twenty years. His work intersects in interesting ways with Nietzsche and the late Heidegger; with the work of "postmodernists" like Derrida, Lyotard, and Foucault; it bears on the exchanges between Gadamer, Lyotard, and Habermas. Rorty's ability to spot this convergence and to translate it into his own terms has made him, like it or not, the most widely read "philosopher" writing in English. Of course this convergence has been reached by tunneling toward the same center from entirely different directions: Rorty from a skeptical antimetaphysical tradition which has been shaving down metaphysical pretensions ever since Ockham unsheathed his razor; the postmodernists from the high-flying speculations of Hegelian dialectics, Husserl's transcendental phenomenology, and Heidegger's History of Being. But they have joined rails in a middle which Rorty was the first to spot.

RORTY'S "DERRIDA"

Rorty shows a particular appreciation for the work of Derrida. In Rorty's terms, Derrida is a master of "self-creation," a genius of "autonomy," that is, of creating idiosyncratic, virtually *unclassifiable* texts which hold our interest, which repay endless rereading, and which leave us wondering at how he does it. Derrida has succeeded in making himself different, has come to grips with the anxiety of influence with great aplomb by writing in a magnificently assimilative but creative manner, sounding now like Husserl, now like Rousseau, now like Heidegger—or Freud, or Lacan, or Blanchot, or Hegel, or Levinas (this could get to be a long list)—but always sounding different. Derrida has mastered the art of being idiosyncratic, of repeating the people he happens to have read but with a difference, a difference that is immensely creative, highly associative, ingeniously complicated (*CIS*, 126; cf. xiv). Derrida composes fantastic "texts," rich, lush, overfull texts that overlap with other texts, that allude to philosophers, psychoanalysts, poets, and novelists in a way that sends his readers scurrying to the library to track down the disseminative excess of allusion, citation, creative misrepresentation, miming, playing; texts full of multilingual puns and tremendously funny jokes. Derrida is not a master of thought, which is the highest compliment grave old Heidegger could pay anyone, but a master of writing, of texts, of invention, an impressario who stages breathtaking productions, a genius at being brilliant, a philosophical virtuoso the likes of which we have not seen since Nietzsche and Kierkegaard.

Derrida has made himself into a work of art, has created a text out of the uncontrollably dense complex of people he has met (like Proust [*CIS*, 100]), books he has read, cities and even campuses he has visited, talks he has given. Derrida is utterly scandalous in this regard. He incorporates the most extraordinarily "contingent" things into his "philosophical" texts: the landscape at Cornell University, which is woven into a discussion of the philosophical problem of the "abyss," that is, of non-foundationalism; or the spelling of his own name, which leads him to associate the "da" in Derrida with *Da-sein* (Heidegger) and Freud's *fort-da*. He writes a book, *The Post Card*, which is paradigmatic for Rorty of Derrida the writer, which consists of a series of love letters that are filled with private allusions, including an account of his visit to Oxford and a trip with Jonathan Culler to the Bodleian Library. The "book" itself includes a series of fantastic, entertaining, outrageous, obscene speculations on a postcard that he found in the library bookstore—and which could still be found there as late as a visit I made to Oxford in 1988—in which a diminutive Plato appears to be standing behind (whence the obscenity) a much larger, seated Socrates, who is writing. Derrida's delight in this seeming reversal of the most honored filial relation in Western philosophy knows no limit, and the "book" he writes on the "subject" is only to be compared with the "aesthetic writings" of Kierkegaard for wit and imaginativeness.[9]

Unless you consider *Glas*,[10] which I would say is his masterpiece and is even more complex, more unreadably readable and idiosyncratic than *The Post Card*, and which is more germane for considering Rorty's relationship to Derrida, although Rorty tries to duck *Glas* (*CIS*, 126). *Glas* requires a companion volume entitled (what else?) *Glassary* in order to track down the allusions to Hegel, in the left column, and Genet, in the right column. "Philosophically" (I can hear the good reader gasp), it turns on a series of interrelated philosophical problems.

The problem of the author: which Derrida addresses by means of a "theory" and practice of "auto-graphy," which means that a writer is always signing his or her own name. In the left column, Hegel is *aigle*, the soaring eagle of *sa*, *savoir absolute*, his/her, *s(ignifi)a(nt)*, *Ça* (the unconscious), and whatever else you can come up with. *Sa*, the soaring eagle of speculative knowledge that swoops down on every unsuspecting particular, lifts it up (*relever*) into the universal and carries it back in its grasping (*begreifen*) conceptual claws to its cold mountaintop of absolute knowledge. On the right side, in a parallel column, Genet who cannot stop signing *genêt*, the mountain flower, who keeps spreading flowers all over the place, Genet whose fags wear flowers in the most embarrassing places. On the left, a column made stiff and hard by the rigor of the absolute

Begriff; on the right, cut flowers, headcuts of criminals cut from newspapers hanging on the prison wall, guillotines, castrations, all of this cut and stitched together into the text of *Glas*, with the glue of *Glas*, which likes to slide these slippery (*glissant*) signifiers the one inside the other, maybe even *a tergo*, with the aid of a little vasoline.

The problem of the family: on the left, the life of Jesus in Hegel's *Early Theological Writings*, that is, his *"Jugend"-Schriften*, the child-writings which are the father of the mature man/Hegel, according to any good teleological genealogy (e.g., Bourgeois's). Hegel is always telling the story of the "speculative family" in which the Father generates his Son who must be broken up and spread out as Spirit. That involves a holy family composed of a man with only an actual mother but a father being in itself; and the bourgeois family, a good Prussian patriarchal family, whose son leaves the inwardness of hearth and home for the outwardness of commercial life, in order finally to be reconciled by the *Staat*; and a number of very improper fag families in the "other" column.

The problem of woman: Antigone, the sister who defies the public law of the father, of the state, of day, in name of the inwardness of the family, mourning, the night. While in the right hand column Genet is telling the story of transvestites, men/women, and of outlaw families, unfamilies of fags and homicidal rapists who make "unnatural" love and who bear the most delicately beautiful names, religious names like nuns who have left the world, names like Our Lady of the Flowers, First Communion, and so on.

The problem of the proper name: when they are arraigned before the judge, and called by their "proper," legal names, the names that have been attached to them by the law for the purpose of surveillance, their bourgeois names, then they know they are already dead men.

The problem of the system: a rich thematics of "fragments" and remnants which means to say, like Johannes Climacus, that the system can never close over, that there are always remainders and fragments, always outlaws, always the inassimilable, indigestible, ungraspable. *Individuum ineffabile est.* There is something always already incalculable in the infinite Hegelian calculus. And this "calculus" contains an almost perfectly private allusion, except that Derrida gave it away. In 1987, while lecturing on *Glas*, Derrida told his audience that the thematics of "calculus" in *Glas* was also making allusion to his mother (the woman, who is daughter/mother/sister, is important in *Glas*) who was suffering from gallstones (*calculs*) at the time. That was a little joke, for Mom, who would appreciate being immortalized, or at least mentioned, in what would get to be a very famous book. A little like having a book dedicated to her, but inside the margins, and more importantly privately, until Derrida let his joke out in public.

I could go on—which is of course the whole idea. One could always go on, enjoying more and more of this inexhaustibly complex text, more and more *jouissance*, so long as you get these jokes. But you "get the idea." Which is *not* the idea, just what Derrida does not want, that you sum it up and "grasp" its logocentric "point" with your eagle claws, consume it and then move on. The quasi-idea is to linger and languish in the gooey glue of *Glas*. Now that is the Derrida whom Rorty admires, Derrida on his best day, the Derrida who is making himself beautiful and different by one of the most fascinating exercises in "autonomy" of this century, by weaving a rich full text out of his most private life, even out of the contingencies of his own name.

Still, there is a side of Derrida that Rorty does not admire, and that is the side where Derrida gets serious, when he is no longer a comic writer but starts trotting out new metaphysical creatures of his own devising, "quasi-entities" whose hiddenness reminds us of the hidden God in negative theology.[11] As you might expect, you can only get to know these quasi-entities if you are a philosopher and have the credentials to make the right arguments. That is the side of Derrida that argues for philosophical ideas like *différance*, *archi-écriture*, supplement, un- decidability, and so on. For a while, in his early writings, Derrida even adopted an unmistakeably apocalyptic tone about these quasi-entities, announcing the end of the age of the book and the beginning of writing. While Derrida has shaken that particularly bad habit, he still talks like "metaphysics" is an inescapable, encompassing something or other that has a hold on us that is deeper than we can say. That makes Rorty squirm in his seat because Rorty thinks that deconstruction on its best day should help us circumvent metaphysics, not mystify it all the more.[12]

The central claim that is made on behalf of *différance* which Rorty goes after is that it is a transcendental "condition of possibility" for speech and writing in the empirical sense. That brings Derrida squarely back to a version of transcendental philosophy, a variation on Kant and Husserl, which has an explanation for everything that is going on in the natural attitude. That puts Derrida and deconstruction in the superior position of knowing, in virtue of a philosophical theory, what is going on in language and what sorts of traps those folks down there in the life world—for example, literary critics—keep walking into. The clearest instance of this adaptation of Derrida is that of Paul de Man, who thinks that Derrida gives him the wherewithal to straighten out the "naive" literary critics who still think that language refers to the world.[13] According to de Man, naive literary critics "resist theory," that is, "literary theory" just because "theory"—or, Derrida's theory of *différance*—problematizes this naive belief in the worldliness of literary language by discovering the purely literary quality of language whose virtue is that, unlike scientific language, it refers to nothing other than itself. That Diltheyan split (between natural and literary language) gives de Man his elegiac tone, always mourning the loss of the world, which picks up on the nostalgic, negative-theological, apocalyptic side of Derrida, which is the worst side of Derrida, the side that has forgotten that he is a comic writer. Derrida's job is to make fun of philosophy, to make it look bad by making it look funny. The worst thing he can do is to get drawn into the game of which he makes such stupendous fun.

But that is just not true, according to Christopher Norris and Rodolphe Gasché, whose readings of Derrida Rorty strongly opposes.[14] Norris says that it is a big mistake for Rorty and others to think that Derrida is just making fun of philosophy, that Derrida just throws philosophy into confusion by showing that every time it thinks it has come upon reference all it really finds is difference, that philosophical arguments always get washed out by their literariness, that philosophy is just writing and has no gifts or expertise of its own, that philosophy is always deluded to think that it has an argument over and beyond rhetorical force. Norris thinks that Derrida has rigor—he stands erect, like the left-hand column of *Glas*. Derrida gives rigorous and close readings of philosophers, and his deconstructive analysis of Husserl is an exemplary piece of close argumentation, which shows how Husserl needs what he has excluded. What Derrida does, Norris says "amount[s] to a form of Kantian transcendental deduction. . . . [It] pose[s] the question: what must be the necessary *presuppositions* about language if language is to make any kind of coherent or intelligible sense?"[15] Derrida has "earned" his eagle's wings as a philosopher; he can soar with the best of them. He does deconstruction in a philosophical way that reminds us, as Norris says in *Derrida*, of the Enlightenment tradition of making arguments and doing critiques.[16] Derrida is not against philosophy but against a false idea of philosophy that is fed by logocentric delusions, like thinking that it has God's point of view. The Western philosophical tradition is all we have, and you have to work within it; you can't go beyond philosophy, no more than Foucault could write a history of madness from the standpoint of the mad.[17] You can't have God's point of view, or the madman's; all you have is human reason. But Derrida's aim is to be relentlessly critical of what calls itself reason, particularly when the university starts building nuclear bombs in the name of reason, which would see to it there is nothing rather than something. You work from within, including from within professional philosophical expertise, and you try to make a difference.

But Rorty thinks it really would be odd for Derrida to end up like that, delivered over to the hands of Gasché and Norris. If *différance* picks out the transcendental conditions of possibility of speaking and writing in the empirical sense, then that "would require us to envisage all such inventions before their occurrence. The idea that we do have such a metavocabulary at our disposal, one which gives us a "logical space" in which to "place" anything which anybody will ever say, seems just one more version of the dream of 'presence' from which ironists since Hegel have been trying to wake us" (*CIS*, 125). Rorty is right, in my view, not to challenge the "accuracy" (*CIS*, 123) of Norris's and Gasché's treatment of Derrida. Their commentaries, in my view, play the strategically useful role of emphasizing (perhaps overemphasizing, and generating an accuracy problem of their own) Derrida's more serious transcendental side (since Derrida's wilder side is well known).[18] Rorty's portrait just waves off every serious moment in Derrida as a kind of philosophical hangover, and it reads works like *The Post Card* too one-sidedly. But Rorty thinks that, if it is accurate, the Norris-Gasché line accurately portrays Derrida at his worst. Setting accuracy aside, the question is whether it is not just incoherent of Derrida to make a transcendental move, whether that is not just one more unfortunate relapse into the metaphysical dream of presence, just as Rorty says. How can Derrida possibly think that with his notion of *différance* he has attained some logical space within which he can place anything that anybody is ever going to say?

DERRIDA: A KIND OF TRANSCENDENTAL PHILOSOPHER

In my view, Derrida is indeed committed to something like what Norris and Gasché attribute to him. Derrida does indeed have a certain "philosophical idea" about language. You might even say he has a (kind of) "theory"—that is a strong word that Derrida is not comfortable with: it implies mastery and a totalizing overview. He has a theory about what is going on in language and other sign-making or meaning-making or more generally effect-producing quasi-systems or "economies," as he might call them (like painting and architecture).

To put things in too simple a way, I would say there are two phases to this quasi-theory. The first phase is the part that Derrida has borrowed from Saussure. Derrida thinks these economies produce their effects by a kind of "spacing," by producing marks or traces which make nominal unities called "words" or concepts or meaning—or beauty, rhythm, symmetry or asymmetry, or whatever you *need*—not merely and not primarily in virtue of the intrinsic "substance" of the "signifier" but in terms of the "differential" relationship—the "space"—between the signifiers. It does not matter whether you speak or write, whether you use "give" or "*geben*," what does matter is that the "difference," the space between "give" and "live," *geben* and *leben*, be discernible. Derrida calls this spacing "*archi-écriture*" or "*différance*," which are not quasi-entities but, to put it the way Rorty would prefer, just an odd sort of vocabulary Derrida adopted as a contingent result of the books he was told to read, or that he got interested in, when he went to school in Paris. Specifically it was something he was getting from Saussure, mediated through the Copenhagen school of structural linguistics.

Derrida does have an idea of what language "must be" be if it is, as Norris says, to make "any kind of coherent or intelligible sense." So Derrida is a transcendental philosopher—*almost*. He is very close to the edge of transcendental philosophy; he hovers around its margins, is in between the columns of *Glas*, in their interplay, working the levers between the columns. But that transcendental side, played up by Gasché and Norris, is only the *half* of it, and this brings us to the second phase of his "theory." For Derrida is also supplying the presuppositions for thinking that whatever sense language does make will also be *unmade*, that the things we *do* with words will come *undone*. You might say, from Rorty's standpoint, he is asserting that, and explaining why, final vocabularies are *never* final, that and why final vocabularies are always contingent and revisable, and that you need different vocabularies for different things. That is why Gasché is circumspect enough to call this a *quasi-transcendental* philosophy, borrowing a (pretty funny) move in *Glas* (although the joke dies under Gasché's knife) in which Derrida, commenting on the analysis of *Antigone* in Hegel's *Phenomenology of Spirit*, addresses the question of something which a system cannot assimilate (a constant issue in *Glas*): "And what if what cannot be assimilated, the absolute indigestible, played a fundamental role in the system, an abyssal role, rather, playing. . . ." The left-hand column text breaks here, is followed by twelve pages of inserted text drawn from Hegel's letters to and about his sister, and then continues: "a quasi-transcendental role" (*Glas*, I 71–82a/151–62a).

The "quasi-transcendental" entity in this text is the sister, not just Antigone but the "figure" (*Gestalt*) of the sister in the *Phenomenology*, a little fragment of this vast book to which no attention has been paid but which for Derrida is both necessary and impossible in the system, which makes the system both possible and impossible, that is, plays a "quasi-transcendental role." So the second step in Derrida's "quasi-theory" is to see to it that it is a theory that says that you cannot have a theory in a strong sense, without the "quasi." Derrida is arguing that linguistic systems are differential; that they produce nominal and conceptual unities as effects of the differential play (or spacing) that is opened up between the marks or traces; that this differential spacing is, as Louis Hjelmslev showed, indifferent to the distinction between phonic and graphic marks; and finally that this notion of meaning as an effect of differential spacing displaces the primacy of intentional subjects expressing their thoughts by means of external signs.

But what Derrida added to all this, the twist he put on it—which is analogous to what Gödel does to mathematical systems—was to radicalize that argument, to push it further. He shows that Husserl's and Hjelmslev's attempt to enclose or regulate such a differential play by a purely formal system, to close the circle of its play, to formalize it, was misbegotten on the very grounds of a differential play. For it belongs to the very idea of differential play that the play is of itself self-differentiating, disseminating, and that any such formal rules as one could devise would be themselves "effects" of the play not the "basis" of it, subsets of the play of signifiers, not rules which govern it.[19] In Rorty's terms, any rules you would devise about what future final vocabularies would look like would themselves be contingent features of the final vocabulary you currently favor, without predictive power for what future vocabularies will look like. In Derrida's terms, it is always too late to assert our superiority over, our transcendental mastery of, language, for we are always already speaking and drawing on its resources. We have said yes to language before we say yes to anything else. Yes, yes.[20]

But of course it is also true that anything Derrida himself would say about the differential play would be in the same predicament, an effect of the play, not the play itself (rather the way that anything Rorty would say about the contingency of final vocabularies would still be contingent). It is always already too late for Derrida too. That is why he devised the strategy of inventing words like *différance*, with the purely graphic alteration, which is not a word or a concept—at least not the first three or four times he used it, as Rorty rightly points out,[21] after which it is too late again. But at least the first couple of times he uses you see what he is up to, what he is pointing to. Once it sediments and becomes part of the established vocabulary of "deconstruction," he has to move on and try it another way. In his earlier works Derrida tended to spell all this out; in his later works he takes it for granted. In *Glas*, which is his major work, he is just putting it to work.

So what does that do to Derrida? Does that make deconstruction a practice with a philosophical theory behind it to back it up (which is what the title of one of Norris's first books suggests),[22] which is just what philosophy has always been doing and about which Rorty has well-known complaints? Well, yes and no. Almost.

Yes, inasmuch as Derrida did not just drop out of a tree one day and start talking funny. He was led to what he had to say by Saussure, Husserl, Heidegger, Nietzsche, and Freud (among others), and he works it out case by case with painful detail. That is, Derrida has reasons for saying what he is saying and every once in a while he will lay them out—as in his argument with John Searle who it seems to me (pace Rorty, *CIS*, 132–43) to this day does not get what Derrida is up to. If you make Derrida abandon this side, then the whole thing is just crazy, and Derrida is just running off at the mouth, albeit in a most entertaining way. Now that is what Rorty seems to want, that is, that Derrida would write in this entertaining way but for no good reason, or for his own amusement and that of those with a similar sense of humor. He is just having fun. He is making himself beautiful and carving out a sphere of autonomy for himself in a particularly brilliant way. So where's the problem? Derrida: that's not philosophy, that's entertainment.[23] Now that may be Rorty, but it's not Derrida. (But can it even really even be Rorty? I will come back to this point at the end.)

So if Derrida is a philosopher who gives reasons if you disagree with him or make fun of him, it is true that Derrida is also not a philosopher, not a transcendental philosopher, and that is the side that Rorty likes. For what Derrida comes up with when he starts talking like a philosopher is that you cannot come up with anything like a philosophical theory, or with distinctions between theory and practice, or the *Geisteswissenschaften* and *Naturwissenschaften*, or analytic and synthetic, at least not for long. For sooner or later the differential play in what your theory is trying to stick together will make it come undone. Sooner or later, someone will give you a close reading; they will descend upon you and disclose that your *arche/principium*/emperor-prince has no clothes, that the distinctions you are making have sprung a leak, that you need and use what you are excluding, that your metaphorics contradicts your thematics, that you can't make the distinction between metaphorical and literal stick, and so on. And that goes for deconstruction too were deconstruction ever to be so foolish as to state itself baldly as a theory.

The upshot of this is that Derrida is both inside and outside philosophy, on the margins of philosophy, that he is a "certain kind" of philosopher. He has reasons for thinking that what philosophy calls reason does not hold water, that is, is without reason or has become unreasonable. The reasons (plural) for not believing in Reason (capitalized, singular) are better than the reasons for believing in it.

But his whole idea is to stay inside/outside philosophy and the university, to be adept at its games, to move with ease within its habits of thought and institutional corridors, and to disrupt its tendencies to start congratulating itself for being the home of Reason, the house of Being, the capital of everything that is Capitalized, including capital (money), or the place where the revolt against capital will be fomented, or the defender of bourgeois liberalism, or the guardian of truth, or any of the other unguarded things we say on behalf of academic learning or the university at commencement exercises. That is why Rorty is badly mistaken to think that "there is no moral to these fantasies, nor any public (pedagogic or political) use to be made of them" (*CIS*, 125; cf. 68, 83). Derrida stays close to philosophers and the university, moves with ease among their arguments, cultivates their language, reads them with a punishing closeness, gains their confidence, finds what is closest to their heart and then pulls the string, the loose thread in the text. After meeting all the standards of the philosophers, he breaks free and produces a scandalous writing which writes differently.

Now it is precisely this marginality, this non-positionality of being inside/outside, which constitutes the "transcendental" motif in Derrida, the moment of what is called in *Glas* the transcendental ex-position (out of place). Antigone's place is both necessary and impossible. It is necessary because it provides the transition from natural to spiritual desire. That is, the relation of brother and sister is both sexual—they form a couple, a single pair of members of the opposite sex—and not sexual; without desire, and so it is the mediating *réleve* between the two. Yet this is impossible, for it contradicts everything that Hegel says about the battle for recognition; this is a mediation and reconciliation of what has never done battle. The sister has transcendental status for Derrida because she is a possibility which the system must exclude even as she is needed as a stop or a station in the progress of absolute knowledge, an interruption to be assimilated, on the way to the reconciliation of divine and human law. You can't have absolute knowledge without the sister, but once you do, you do not have the system any longer. It makes the system possible and impossible. The sister is inside and outside the system. The very thing that is excluded is what makes the system possible and must be included (*Glas*, 170a–71a/150a–51a).

That is what Derrida is always doing with philosophical texts, showing how the very thing that makes them possible also makes them impossible, which is something he can predict will happen inasmuch as any assembly of signifiers is always already set adrift by *différance*. That is his almost transcendental, quasi-transcendental role. Almost. A broken, split transcendental. But notice that is not what he does in the other column with Genet, a text that he just lets play. Genet is already set adrift, already in play; Hegel has to be reminded of the play; but Derrida, who is neither Hegel nor Genet, is the inter-play, is the space and the spacing between them, as their columnizer.

Rorty is pushing Derrida into the Genet column, and Norris is pushing him into the Hegel (Kant) column, while Derrida himself is doing a double writing. Rorty's "Derrida at his best" transgresses philosophy, strays outside its borders into a scandalous, comic, different discourse, which has dropped the pretention of being transcendental. Rorty's "Derrida at his worst" remains inside philosophy, has reasons for his distrust of Reason and sounds for all the world like a philosopher. Norris on the other hand does not take enough precautions to keep Derrida out of the Hegel column. His transcendental Derrida is too strong, too erect, too stiff.

A CRITIQUE OF PURE AUTONOMY

But this is an odd sort of transcendental, even for a quasi-transcendental, because it is a transcendental without a subject. It is a kind of anonymous transcendental, an impersonal field, populated by neither an empirical nor a transcendental subject, by no subject at all, but only by the play of differences. The standard transcendental is a subjective condition that makes the unity of objects possible, but the field of *différance* is a different transcendental, which makes any kind of unity, subjective or objective, im/possible.

Rorty, on the other hand, despite his account of the "contingency of the self" (*CIS*, 23) and of its utter "socialization," operates within the most classical assumption of individual, subjective autonomy. His redescription of Derrida in terms of "autonomy" is the part that falls the widest of its mark. It is not a redescription but a contradiction of Derrida. The whole point of Derrida's analysis of discourse in terms of *différance*, that is, of differentially related signifiers, is to underline the notion that languages are not "invented" by "subjects" (and I would think that the same thing is true of any adequate conception of a "language game"). The very idea of thinking of language in terms of a language game or of a play of signifiers is to get over the idea of a game invented and played by the players, which is the familiar, common-sensical, classical, subjectivistic, and "metaphysical" model of language, one which in other respects Rorty seems intent on abandoning.[24] The idea is rather to think of language as a game which plays the players, which exceeds and overtakes, which precedes and antedates, the interiority of a private subjectivity. On both the Derridean and Wittgensteinian models, a language is not something a private, interior self devises in order to enter the world and communicate its inner thoughts. Rather it is a game into which one is entered from the start by being thrown into the world, a game which plays the "I," which brings the "I" about, and marks it forever with the contingencies of its birth and upbringing. Language is not a matter of an "I" which expresses its "inner thought" by outer marks. It is rather a behavior which is acquired by picking up the conventions of making marks in the ways adopted by those who "bring me up," by means of which "I" am slowly brought up or drawn into the higher order operations of thinking and imagining, and get to be a certain sort of "I." The "I" thus is not the interior, anterior inventor of the language, but one of the things produced by it, an "effect" of the game. So the extent to which I will be able to acquire these higher-order operations is very much a contingent function of the subtlety, complexity, and nuances of the "vocabulary" (and the grammar) with which I am presented by my birth and education, of the degree to which the differential play to which I am exposed is differentiated enough, of the subtlety of the strategies that have been devised in the game I am taught to play.

On such a model it would be quite perverse and wrongheaded to think in terms of the "autonomy" of the subject, of the "freedom" to engage in "self-creation." The point of this model is exactly the opposite, to stress the impersonal, structural, community-wide, historical, and unconscious forces which rule over—but not with formalizable rules—or hold sway in the language game to which I belong. Such quasi-structures prevent "self-creation" in any strong sense; indeed they make the "self" the "creation" (or effect) of the linguistic play. If anything enjoys "autonomy" here, it is not the self but the game which seems to carry the selves along by its own momentum, which is the "text" in the Derridean sense, For Derrida autonomy is a more likely predicate of a text, of writing, that orphan, which having lost its voice and its father to speak on its behalf, is "on its own," cut off from its father/author and its reference to the world.

That is why Derrida would never want to describe *Glas* or *The Post Card* in terms of a virtuoso performance of autonomy or self-creation, in terms of anything done by Jacques Derrida, the one who "signs" this text on the outside. He did not "invent" the linguistic chains that are strung together in *Glas*, the historical, etymological, graphic, and phonic associations out of which it is woven. He is not responsible for the connection between *glas* and *classicus*, for its connection with bells and tolling, for the emblematic character of *glas* for language itself as a system of "classifying," for the Hegelian impulse to let the classifying universal assimilate the classified particular. He found them—and he confounds them; he points to them and he exploits them; he lets them loose. He shows us how we are all a little lost in them, that no one can keep his head above water in the midst of them, that we are all always already swept up by them. That is why he says we sign our names, not only on the outside of the text, outside the margins or on the covers—which would signify mastery, superiority, domination of the text, as if we really were the authors and knew what we are doing—but also, always and inevitably, inside the text. We cannot help ourselves, we too are drawn into the text, sucked up by its tendencies and metaphorics, caught in its complexities and weblike traps. Autography flatly contradicts autonomy.

Derrida does not "deconstruct" something by means of his facile and inventive capacity for redescription or recontextualization. Rather, the language games are consistently undoing themselves and Derrida is like the first reporter on the scene of an earthquake, sending field reports back from the scene, reporting on the fissures and gaps that are breaking out all around him, even as he reports new formations that are gathering before his eyes.

Far from being a paradigmatic exercise in autonomy, the point of *Glas* is to confess the loss of autonomy, the loss of the self, of the author, of the subject, of self-creation. Rorty objects to *Glas* because it is not "readable" (*CIS*, 126). That is only partly true. Derrida would never want something purely unreadable, purely Joycean (nor would Joyce). But it is true up to a point, true that it is unreadable, which is its point, the stylus tip that Derrida wants us to be pricked by: to experience unreadability, undecipherability, the loss not only of authorial but also of readerly authority, just the way Johannes Climacus does. Derrida wants us to get a little lost, to lose our autonomy. In *Glas*, that is not so much a theory he has but a performance that is being staged.

This is also why Derrida is quite insistently and consistently concerned, not with autonomy, but with heteronomy. What strikes him about language is not the ability of the subject to keep its head in the midst of the play—autonomy—but the dispersal of the subject into the play, the loss of the autonomy of the subject, and the loss of the identity of the object, in an anonymous transcendental field. That is first of all an epistemological and metaphysical point which bears against Rorty's analysis. For, ironically enough, Rorty is still clinging to a seventeenth- and eighteenth-century metaphysics of the subject. His nominalism turns on a freely inventive name-making subject who invents "vocabularies," not an impersonal field whose quasi-structural laws produce certain temporary nominal unities calls "words" and "concepts." Rorty shows no interest in another nominalism, one which sees names as the effects of impersonal, structural forces, of an anonymous quasi-transcendental field, which is "other" than the subject, and hence heteronomous. *Ça*.

But this talk of heteronomy also has an ethico-political point which Rorty either misses or dismisses, that is, the turn to, the other, the openness to the other. The politics which goes along with Rortyian autonomy is bourgeois liberalism, while the politics which goes along with Derrida is suspicious of the bourgeoisie and is turned toward the marginalized and excluded, the oppressed and the victimized. Derrida is radically suspicious of ethnocentrism and Eurocentrism, while Rorty is unfortunately prone to think that the North Atlantic nations play the only politically worthy game in town (cf. *CIS*, 93), a role analogous to Hegel's Prussia, except that we happened on it by chance instead of aiming the labor of the Spirit at it teleologically. Derrida is radically suspicious of saying "we" and Rorty loves to say "we liberals," which is, it seems to me—on his terms—not only an empty but a dangerous pat on the back. Derrida is radically suspicious of the power plays that tend to shape the prevailing language games and the vested interests that keep them in place, while Rorty thinks they can be flipped with a flick of his Wittgensteinian bic.[25]

I frankly think that Rorty knows better than this and he has been trying to respond to this sort of criticism which, on a more radically postmodern version of liberalism, one ought to have no truck with. But Rorty is having a hard time shaking this criticism because his theory of the autonomous subject ("I") is too strong, and his suspicion of the "we" is too weak, for his postmodernism. He ought to give up this talk of autonomy as one more piece of seventeenth-century metaphysics and of the contingencies of Indo-European grammar, which he doesn't need and which causes more trouble that its worth. Rorty argues with clarity and persuasiveness that the self is contingent, that it is shaped all the way down by socialization—yet he still talks about liberal subjects and autonomous self-creators. He would do much better to drop the idea of autonomy, to celebrate more forthrightly the plurality of possible non-Western and non-European language games, to suspect more deeply the vested interests which have their way in the Great American Way, to analyze more carefully the sociopolitical factors which are deeply embedded within any socialization process and which make changing vocabularies harder than it looks. He needs to give more play to the notion of an other whom we cannot bring into our conversation,[26] who doesn't belong to NATO, and who cannot keep up with the fast clip of Rorty's highly sophisticated Euro-American conversation.

That is not Marxism, which I agree is now dead in the water—although not before leaving a lot of others dead, too—but it retains Marxism's distrust of vested power interests. Nor is it bourgeois liberalism, because it is much more self-suspicious and much less self-congratulatory than that, more concerned with the thousands of lives—American Indian lives, black American lives, Latin American lives, black South African lives: one could go on—that have likewise been sacrificed to the interests of maintaining "our" economy and the vested economic and political interests of the United States. But it retains liberalism's interest in giving people some space, in trying to reduce their suffering, in defending the weak against the strong. Call it a kind of radicalized, postmodern liberalism or call it a non-Marxist left. Either way it is what I think Rorty—"at his best"—is or should be after. That is why Derrida seems to me to have gotten further down the road on this point than Rorty. Derrida does not think you can "circumvent" metaphysics and change vocabularies at the drop of a hat. Derrida thinks you are always already stuck in the prevailing system and that the status quo must be the terminus a quo for any changes you have in mind. He advocates not circumvention but intervention, alterations here and there, wherever possible, wherever you happen to be, making some space, creating an opening, carefully inserting a little monkey wrench here or there just when the prevailing powers are about to have their way one more time and grind somebody up. Derrida does not think in terms of my autonomy to re-create and redescribe myself, of self-creating subjects, but of local action aimed at reducing the subjection of "others" to "us." He is inclined to problematize the "we," to see us as part of the problem, and to worry over the other, the heteronomous. He is less inclined to want to bring others into our conversation, to bring them up to North Atlantic speed, than to let others be and give them some space. Derrida is after a kind of praxis of the other, answering the call of the other, and he thinks of this as a matter of intervening strategically within well-entrenched systems of power on behalf of those whom "we" are oppressing. This is neither a Marxist Apocalypse nor liberal subjects coming up with a new description of themselves with the ease with which American advertisers can redescribe carcinogens as "better things for better living."

Put in a way to appeal to a pragmatist, Derrida gets a lot more done with the language of heteronomy than Rorty does with the language of autonomy. In particular, he gets a lot more done of what Rorty himself wants to do. On this point of autonomy, Rorty's redescription of Derrida is a regrettable regression.

THE UNCIRCUMVENTABILITY OF THE QUASI-TRANSCENDENTAL

What I am arguing then comes down to this. Rorty needs a quasi-transcendental theory of the sort one finds in Derrida, even though he does not feel that need himself. It comes to down to classifying: "Rorty" too is a kind of transcendental philosopher. I say this for two reasons.

First, Rorty needs a quasi-transcendental theory in order to avoid the illusions, both epistemological and political, of a free autonomous subject. He needs to bracket the naive empiricist idea of a free subject and see that it is the "effect" of an anonymous, quasi-transcendental field. He needs to put that particular residue of the old metaphysics of the subject, which Heidegger calls "subjectism" (*Subjektität*), to the knife of a quasi-transcendental critique, one which avoids, however, the Kantian and Husserlian mistake of reproducing the empirical subject on a higher, transcendental notch. That is what *différance* does and what a "language-game" theory, adequately conceived, seems to do. That is what I argued in the previous section.

Second, Rorty needs a quasi-transcendental theory to account for what he himself does quite successfully, in particular in those areas of genuine convergence between himself and Derrida. For if, as I have argued, Rorty is not right in redescribing Derrida in terms of the "autonomy" of a subject freely inventing his own vocabulary, then his account of Derrida in terms of the "contingency" (Derrida's "chance") of our vocabularies, in terms of Derrida's deployment of private allusion, of the search for an arbitrary, idiosyncratic, unclassifiable text is right on the money, if I may be so capitalistic.

So what I want to ask now, by way of a conclusion, is this: what is the status of "Rorty," of his "theory" of the "contingency" of any "final vocabulary"? "Rorty," I claim, is extremely close to "Derrida"; "Rorty" is trying to occupy pretty much the same marginal space that Derrida is trying to straddle—without falling off. Rorty too is, or should become, a quasi-transcendental philosopher who cannot go cold turkey on philosophy, who illustrates just what Derrida means about being inside/outside philosophy, even when the whole idea is to just leave metaphysics to itself and forget about it. Rorty too has a "theory" about final vocabularies that is *almost* a philosophical one, a quasi-philosophical one. He rejects the idea that language is some sort of I-know-not-what medium which mediates between us and the world, either by representing the world accurately or bringing the world to expression. We should cut out that sort of unnecessary quasi-entity-building, which simply reproduces all the old problems—Is the medium good or bad? faithful or distortive? transparent or opaque? and so on—and just content ourselves with the fact that vocabularies, as Donald Davidson and Wittgenstein show, are tools we use which vary with the purpose and are either efficient or inefficient (*CIS*, 11–12), which is why anybody's final vocabulary is always revisable.

Now that is to entertain a philosophical theory about language, one which uses Wittgenstein and Davidson pretty much the way Derrida uses Saussure and Hjelmslev—a pragmatic, language-game theory, albeit one which flies along at a much lower altitude than those metaphysical theories about language which soar with the eagles. But it remains a philosophical theory, not in the weak sense of a pacifier for overwrought librarians, but in a stronger sense, one which requires a little bit of expertise of a distinctly philosophical sort. For after all, nobody "down there" in the natural attitude thinks that language is a "tool."[27] The folks in the natural attitude think that hammers and pens are tools, but not language. They think that some people are good with words and others not, some things can be expressed and others—the usual example is "love"—not. But above all people in the natural attitude have what Rorty calls "common sense" (*CIS*, 74). It is in this critique of common sense that Rorty gets—understandably—a little bit transcendentally uppity. That is not a criticism; it is just part of the philosopher's trade, something I am arguing that Rorty needs because he is still implicated in a certain kind of philosophizing in a stronger sense than he is willing to let on. The folks in the natural attitude "know" that their language tells it like it is, that other people may use "different words" but these others must mean the same thing as "us," because our words pick out "chunks" (*CIS*, 5) of the world which are really there, whether you dress them up in English or French, classical Greek or Sanskrit. The world is sitting out there in itself begging to be named and there really is only one way to do that, even though some people are better at it than others.

In other words, people in the natural attitude do *not* appreciate the "contingency" of their vocabularies. They *identify* with their vocabulary and do not preserve the *ironic distance* which is required by Rorty (and Derrida), the distance between ourselves and the vocabulary of which we are currently enamored, between our current vocabulary and any possible alternative. They lack a higher-order reflectiveness about language that disengages a speaker and user of a vocabulary *from* the vocabulary he or she uses. They are unable to make that much of an *epoché*, unable to effect that much of a quasi-transcendental distancing or disengaging from the contingent vocabulary they employ. After all, to recognize a contingent vocabulary *as contingent* is already to have risen "above" it or gotten "beneath" it just this far, that one no longer *lives naively* in it. So Rorty is reproducing many key features of the transcendental reduction: disengagement, reflective distancing, the breach of naïveté, thematizing of the natural attitude as such.

By putting any final vocabulary into relief, Rorty has raised himself up a notch (*relever*) and worked himself into a transcendental position. Almost. Not quite. For it is only a certain kind of transcendental, a quasi-transcendental, a broken or split transcendental, a transcendental ex-position. He certainly does not want, and has not embraced, "a metavocabulary" which "gives us a 'logical space' in which to 'place anything which anybody will every say'" (*CIS*, 125). On the contrary he has given us reasons to give up the search for such a space. His notion of the "contingency" of any "final vocabulary," which turns on the notion that language is a "tool," plays a distinctly quasi-transcendental role. It explains, in Wittgensteinian and Davidsonian terms, how we do things with words, even as it predicts that we will never have any final terms or unrevisable final vocabularies at our disposal. That is very much what Derrida thinks and what Derrida means when he speaks of "conditions or possibility and impossibility," that is, quasi-transcendental conditions. That is, Rorty and Derrida have reasons to believe that we will *never* (that's pretty transcendental talk) attain a metavocabulary within which we can place everything anybody will ever say, which will enable us to envisage what people are going to say before they say it (which is very untranscendental).

Let me illustrate this point with an example. In his early writings on Husserl, Derrida tried to defend the linguistic string "Green is or" against Husserl, who rejected it on the grounds that it was not only material nonsense but formal nonsense as well. On Husserl's theory, the sentence "The English language is dead" is false but meaningful. "The English language is green" is "countersensical" (*Widersinn*) but in good form, for its logical form is such that it could, with the proper substitutions, be rendered both meaningful and true. But "Green is or" for Husserl is just a plain *Unsinn*, not only semantically but logico-grammatically incoherent; it makes no sense at all, true or false, sensical nor countersensical. Derrida responded to Husserl's analysis by showing that you could *always* recontextualize "Green is or" and make it both meaningful and true—for example, by making it the response to a request for a string of English words, or by color-coding disjunctives, or by changing its inflection, or by a homophonic play, or by a literally indefinite number of other available means.[28]

"You can always recontextualize"—that is the transcendental move: it breaks the naivete of common sense and the natural attitude by calling upon the resources of a language-game theory, or a *différance*. But the notion that what you can always do is *recontextualize* a word or a sentence is the *anti*transcendental move, the one which shows the slipperiness of language, the unavailability of a final vocabulary, the sheer contingency and literally endless reconfigurability of the vocabularies we use and of the beliefs we entertain. That's the move with the historicist and nominalist drift, the one which preserves an ironic, quasi-transcendental distance.

So I would say, do not go gently into that dark night which Rorty describes, the one in which something like transcendental philosophy will have passed from the scene. If you do, do not expect to find either Rorty or Derrida there. They will be both back at the university—although it is not clear what department they are in—writing more books that the catalogue librarians, driven to the edge of despair, will finally, *faut de mieux*, classify (*classicus*, *glas*) as philosophy.

Would it not be wonderful to write a book that no one could *classify*, for which no librarian, philosopher, encyclopedist, hermeneut, speech-act theorist, communications rationalist, curriculum specialist, realist, or idealist could find the *glas*? Would that not be a magnificent idea? Would it be a transcendental ideal?

Well, almost.

NOTES

1. Richard Rorty, *Contingency, Irony, and Solidarity* (New York: Cambridge University Press, 1989), 197. Hereafter cited in text as *CIS*.

2. Rorty came to the defense of the "natural attitude" in the discussion that followed a presentation of "Two Meanings of 'Logocentrism': A Reply to Norris" at a conference sponsored by the Greater Philadelphia Philosophy Consortium in October 1988. I found this defense singularly enlightening about Rorty's views. My comment

on Rorty's and Norris's papers that day was the first draft of the present study. "Two Meanings of 'Logocentrism'" was subsequently published in *Redrawing the Lines: Analytic Philosophy, Deconstruction, and Literary Theory*, ed. Reed Way Dasenbrock (Minneapolis: University of Minnesota Press, 1989), 204–16.

3. Still, there are curious tendencies in his work toward a naturalistic reductionism that turns everything over to charged particles migrating through empty space. See *CIS*, 17.

4. Jean-François Lyotard, *The Postmodern Condition: A Report on Knowledge*, trans. G. Bennington and B. Maussumi (Minneapolis: University of Minnesota Press, 1984), xxiii–xxiv.

5. That is also how Rorty reads Davidson. Davidson's critique of the very idea of a conceptual scheme, on Rorty's view, is not primarily that it would cut off communication between the users of different schemes. That would make Davidson look too much like Karl-Otto Apel and Habermas, that is, like a defender of transcendental conditions of communication. Rorty takes Davidson to be objecting that the "very idea" is a *philosophical* one and makes language into some kind of magical mystical something, some sort of unknown somewhat, another Transcendental Object = X. And who needs that? All a pragmatist needs are the physical causes of particular beliefs; everything else is a redundant backup. See Richard Rorty, "The World Well Lost," in Richard Rorty, *Consequences of Pragmatism* (Minneapolis: University of Minnesota Press, 1982), 3–18. This talk of physical causes is what I mean by physicalistic reductionism.

6. Rorty's first piece on Derrida was entitled "Philosophy as a Kind of Writing," in Rorty, *Consequences of Pragmatism*, 90–109.

7. Edmund Husserl, *Ideas Pertaining to a Pure Phenomenology and to a Phenomenological Philosophy*, first book, trans. Fred Kersten (The Hague: M. Nijhoff, 1983), sec. 30, pp. 55–56: Husserl would never have been able to formulate the principle *of* the natural attitude in this section without having already implicitly *made* the *epoché*, which is not announced until sec. 31.

8. Friedrich Nietzsche, *Twilight of the Idols*, trans. R. J. Hollingdale (Baltimore: Penguin Books, 1968), 40–41; Martin Heidegger, *On Time and Being*, trans. Joan Stambaugh (New York: Harper & Row, 1972), 24.

9. "Apart from his incredible, almost Nabokovian, polylingual linguistic facility, he is a great comic writer—perhaps the funniest writer on philosophical topics since Kierkegaard." Rorty, "Two Meanings of 'Logocentrism,'" 209.

10. Jacques Derrida, *Glas* (Paris: Galilee, 1974), translated in English as *Glas*, John Leavey and Richard Rand (Lincoln: University of Nebraska Press, 1986); Gregory Ulmer and John Leavey, eds., *Glassary* (Lincoln: University of Nebraska Press, 1986).

11. Rorty, "Two Meanings of 'Logocentrism,'" 208.

12. Richard Rorty, "Deconstruction and Circumvention," *Critical Inquiry* 11 (1984): 1–23.

13. Rorty, "Two Meanings of 'Logocentrism,'" 209. See Paul de Man, *The Resistance to Theory* (Minneapolis: University of Minnesota Press, 1986).

14. Norris criticizes Rorty in "Philosophy as a Kind of Narrative: Rorty on Postmodern Liberal Culture," in Christopher Norris, *The Contest of Faculties* (London: Methuen, 1985), 139–66, and Christopher Norris, "Philosophy as Not Just a 'Kind of Writing': Derrida and the Claim of Reason," in Dasenbrock, *Redrawing the Lines*, 189–203. See also Richard Rorty's review of Rodolph Gasché, *The Tain of the Mirror* (Cambridge: Harvard University Press, 1986), in "Is Derrida a Transcendental Philosopher?" *Yale Journal of Criticism* 2 (1988): 207–17.

15. Norris, "Philosophy as Not Just a 'Kind of Writing,'" 193; cf. 195.

16. Christopher Norris, *Derrida* (Cambridge: Harvard University Press, 1987), 142; cf. 150–55.

17. Norris, "Philosophy as Not Just a 'Kind of Writing,'" 198.

18. See my review of Gasché: "Derrida: A Kind of Philosopher," *Research in Phenomenology* 17 (1987): 245–89.

19. See Jacques Derrida, *Of Grammatology*, trans. Gayatri Spivak (Baltimore: Johns Hopkins University Press, 1974), 57–63.

20. See Jacques Derrida, "A Number of Yes" (*Nombre de Oui*), trans. Brian Holmes, *Qui Parle* 2, no. 2 (1988): 118–33.

21. Rorty, "Deconstruction and Circumvention," 18.

22. Christopher Norris, *Deconstruction: Theory and Practice* (London: Methuen, 1982).

23. Rorty, "Two Meanings of 'Logocentrism,'" 212.

24. I have complained about this before, in an earlier piece on Heidegger and Rorty. Cf. "The Thought of Being and the Conversation of Mankind: The Case of Heidegger and Rorty," *Review of Metaphysics* 36 (1983): 661–85; cf. 672–74, where I

argue that the notion of language as freely invented by human subjects for their own use belongs to the most classical metaphysical idea of language. It is not a neutral nonphilosophical idea (*CIS*, 14–15), but philosophy's most classical gesture, as Heidegger shows (for example, in "Language," in Martin Heidegger, *Poetry, Language, Thought*, trans. A. Hofstadter [New York: Harper & Row, 1971], 1871–72). Like Rorty himself, I think the main value of this earlier piece of mine is the way it differentiates Rorty from Heidegger. And I have to confess that I am now more in sympathy with Rorty's more Derridean skepticism about how Being itself comes to words in human talk, about which Rorty, as I now think, rightly complains in response to my earlier treatment (*CIS*, 122–23n4). I am much more sympathetic now, via Derrida, with a lot more of what Rorty—via Derrida—is up to. Nonetheless, I still think he is steadfastly stuck in metaphysics when he treats language as a man-made tool, as I hope to show here.

25. Which is the point of Rick Roderick in "Reading Derrida Politically (Contra Rorty)," *Praxis International* 6 (1987): 442–49. For Derrida's politics, see Norris, *Derrida*, 155; and my "Beyond Aestheticism: Derrida's Responsible Anarchy," *Research in Phenomenology* 18 (1988): 59–73.

26. This is a point on which Mark Taylor takes Rorty to task. See "Paralectics," in Mark Taylor, *Tears* (Albany: SUNY Press, 1990), 123.

27. The notion that language is a tool is, in my view, separable from the theory of autonomy. I think—contra Heidegger—that language is like a tool, but a tool (this is a little more Heideggerian) forged not by autonomous subjects but by communities, slow historical tendencies, erratic and contingent circumstances, collective-impersonal impulses, structural and unconscious forces. Language is filled with inertia, is a culture-wide phenomenon, is not subject to individual volitions or subjective fiats. When Derrida speaks of "prag-grammatology," he is also I think trying to appreciate the pragmatic point, which is that language is a way of coping with the world, of getting through the day. But I must say the notion of "tool" leaves a lot out for me.

28. Jacques Derrida, *Margins of Philosophy*, trans. Alan Bass (Chicago: University of Chicago Press, 1982), 319–20; cf. *Speech and Phenomena*, trans. David Allison (Evanston: Northwestern University Press, 1972), 97–99. For a further account of this example, see my "The Economy of Signs in Husserl and Derrida," in *Deconstruction and Philosophy*, ed. John Sallis (Chicago: University of Chicago Press, 1987), 99–113, and *Radical Hermeneutics* (Bloomington: Indiana University Press, 1987), 138–45. Husserl discusses "Green is or" in sec. 15 of the *Logical Investigations*, vol. 1.

§ 3
Devilish Hermeneutics: From Augustine to Derrida

13
Shedding Tears beyond Being: Derrida's Confession of Prayer

I simply place my fingers or lips on it, almost every
evening . . .
I touch it without knowing what I am doing or
asking in so doing,
especially not knowing into whose hands I am
entrusting myself,
to whom I'm rendering thanks. But to know at
least two things
—which I invoke here for those who are foreign
(get this paradox: even more ignorant, more
foreign than I)
to the culture of the tallith, this culture of shawl
and not of veil:
blessing and death. (*V*, 46/44–45)[1]

BEYOND BEING

The resources and strategies of negative theology, its "detours, locutions and syntax" (*Marg.*, 6/6),[2] have always fascinated Jacques Derrida, and that is because for Derrida, as for negative theology, our desire beyond desire is for what lies "beyond being," to use a venerable expression from Christian Neoplatonism. But what lies "beyond being" for Derrida is tears, prayers and tears, tears shed beyond being (*V*, 42/40), prayers sent like sighs beyond being, truth, and knowledge. That produces, on the one hand, a remarkable proximity of his work to negative theology, even as, on the other hand, it opens up an abyss between him and negative theology. I will develop this contrast by drawing the unlikely and disconcerting portrait of Derrida as a man of prayer.

In "How to Avoid Speaking: Denials" (1985), Derrida remarks that, faithful to a fault to the title of his essay, he has indeed avoided speaking of something essential. In this essay on negative theology that takes its point of departure from Plato, Dionysius the Areopagite, and Heidegger, that is, from a massively Greco-Christian tradition, he has avoided speaking of what is neither Christian nor Greek: the Jewish and Islamic traditions of negative theology. Here as elsewhere, he finds himself speaking of foreigners in a language that is not his own. Of course, French is his "own" language and it is not "foreign," but it is not his language: "I have only one language; it is not mine."[3] This is the language that he does not have although he does not have another, as Hélène Cixous says.[4] He speaks what he calls "Christian Latin French," by which he means the language of French colonial Algeria, which is a linguistic condensation of an ancient Greco-Romano-Christian history. Hence, the one thing he has not spoken about in this essay on "not-speaking" (*ne pas parler*), the one thing about which he has been completely silent in this essay on mystical silence, is the very thing that is closest to him: "For lack of capacity, competence, or self-authorization, I have never yet been able to speak of what my birth, as one says, should have made closest to me: the Jew, the Arab."[5]

In a beautiful, if enigmatic autobiographical journal entitled "Circumfession" (1991), Derrida breaks this silence and professes, confesses, exposes the secret of his Algerian birth, which makes of him a "little black and Arab Jew" (Circ., 57/58).[6] Or rather, it makes him the last, the least of the Jews (Circ., 146/154; 178/190) inasmuch as his relation with the Jew is both continuous and ruptured, so that he is not *simply* Jewish (or Arab or North African or French). But of all the secrets he springs on Geoffrey Bennington in "Circumfession," all of which turn around the privacy of his Jewish "circumcision" (a Latin word) in an Arab country colonized by the French, the secret that interests me here is his confession that he is privately a man of prayer, that he has been praying all his life. He wonders aloud (or in writing): "If I ought to tell them that I pray, and describe how that could happen, according to what idiom and what rite, on one's knees or standing up, in front of whom or what books, for if you knew, G., my experience of prayers, you would know everything" (Circ., 175–76/188). The private matter made public by the author of "Circumfession" is that he has been praying all along and that his experience of prayer is the secret source of "everything."

In another passage he wonders "if those reading me from up there see my tears, today . . . if they guess that my life was but a long history of prayers," for these readers have understood everything "except that I have lived in prayer, tears" (Circ., 40–41/38–40). That is why he loves his prayer shawl: "A prayer shawl I like to touch more than to see, to caress every day, to kiss without even opening my eyes" (*V,* 44/43), a prayer shawl he has kept safe at home all his life. "Up to the end, never, whatever may happen: in no case, whatever the verdict at the end of so formidable a journey, never can one get rid of a tallith. One must never, ever, at any moment, throw it away or reject it" (*V,* 69/71).

But how can he, who says that "I quite rightly pass for an atheist" (*je passe à just titre pour une athée*) (Circ., 146/155), be praying? Where (*ubi*) and to whom is he to address his prayers? That is precisely what he desires to know, what he is praying to know. As he says to "G.": "You who know everything, you would tell me whom to address them to" (Circ., 175–76/188). This passage from "Circumfession" is then interrupted with a graph/graft from the *Confessions* in which Augustine asks where, had he died in sin, the prayers of Monica for his salvation would be (*ubi essent*), to which Augustine himself answers, *nusquam nisi ad te*, nowhere but with you, or, even more precisely, nowhere but toward you (*ad te*). But Derrida is at a loss to say where his prayers rise, if they rise at all, or where they drift, if they are adrift, like letters lost in the mail.

The destination of his prayers is kept secret from his readers because it is first kept from him. Where do his prayers arrive? *Nusquam nisi ad te*, he can say with Augustine, but with this difference, that Derrida does not know who this "you" (*te, toi*) is. To or with God, whom he loves, he can also say with Augustine. But then he must also ask with Augustine, "What do I love when I love you?" or when I love "my God" (*Confessions*, X, 6–7). What else can he do but make that question his own, he asks (*Circ.*, 117/122–23). You know that I love you, he can say, but what do I love when I love you? The difficulty posed to us by Derrida's "Circumfession" is described nicely in the opening lines of Augustine's *Confessions* (I, 1). Bearing about in his body his mortality (*circumferens suam mortalitatem*), Augustine says, being but this tiniest bit of creation, still, he "desires to praise you." But must the soul first call upon you to praise you, and must it first "know you before it can invoke" you? he asks (*utrum scire te prius sit an invocare te*). "For it would seem clear that no one can call upon you without knowing you, for if he did he might invoke another than you, knowing you not. Yet may it be that a man must invoke you before he can know you?" That marks the point where their paths part, for Derrida pursues the way of *non-knowing*, of invoking without knowing, of praying without truth—for the prayer shawl has nothing to do with the veil, with the veiling and unveiling of truth. This path, which Derrida elsewhere calls the "passion of non-knowing,"[7] is precisely the path staked out by Derrida in "Circumfession" and other recent autobiographical writings. Augustine, on the other hand, casts his lot with St. Paul, who says, "But how are they to call on one in whom they have not believed?" (Rom 9:14), the same Paul who, upon finding the altar with the inscription "To an unknown god" (*agnosto theo*), told the Athenians, "What therefore you worship as unknown, this I proclaim to you" (Acts 17:23). If Paul will remove the veil that covers the Athenians eyes and reveal to them the name of the Unknown God, Derrida, on the other hand, will write an "epistle against Paul" (*V*, 73/77), opposing Paul on unveiling the un-known God, on unveiling men and veiling women, on resurrection, and, finally, on circumcision.

Still, has not Augustine himself gone a long way toward showing us that one needs to love something in order to know it? If so, then Derrida's path is at least quasi-Augustinian; for Derrida, loving and calling upon precede knowing, so that the prayer of "Circumfession" is a prayer "without truth" (*sans vérité*), "shedding tears beyond being" (*V*, 42/40). By this he means that he is invoking a God who does not belong to the order of being, truth, and knowledge, directing a prayer to a God who has nothing to do with knowing or unknowing. What lies "beyond being" for Derrida, is tears. What constitutes, if anything does, the God beyond being, or God without being, is not the *Gottheit* beyond *Gott*, not the *hyperousios* of Pseudo-Dionysius, but tears. For God is called upon in prayers and tears, which are otherwise than being, otherwise than the order of concealment and unconcealment, hiddenness and manifestation, knowing and unknowing. To invoke the name of God is to enter an entirely different order than the history of truth, to belong to a history, not of *vérité* but of *verser les larmes*, shedding tears, the way one's blood is shed.

The meaning of the name of God in deconstruction never comes down to a decision made in the order of being or knowledge, to deciding whether or not God exists; its meaning is shifted out of the circle of knowing and non-knowing, concealment and non-concealment, being and non-being, and located in a "logic or a topic" (*V*, 71/75) that is otherwise than knowing, in a sphere of tears *au-delà de l'être*. That is the order of the tallith, not of the veil; of the call for justice, not an inquiry into truth; the order of the heart, of blood, of faith, of circumcision, not of creedal propositions; the order, not of knowing but of doing the truth (*facere veritatem*); the order, not of things but of the event. Its meaning is not nominative, to pick out and name something somewhere, but invocative and provocative, to make something happen.

The text that most closely approaches the rhetoric and syntax of "Circumfession" is *The Post Card*, which is another text addressed to "you," where we are also unsure of who is being addressed. So it is no surprise that the text of "Circumfession" contains italicized grafts from a notebook that Derrida was keeping in the 1970s and 1980s, at the time of the composition of *The Post Card*. In the final entry in "Circumfession," Derrida writes: "Resurrection will be for you, '*more than ever the address, the stabilized relation of a destination, a game of a-destination finally sorted out, for beyond what happens in the P.C., it is now the work to dispatch it that must win out, toward the secret that demanded, like a breath, the "perversity" of the P.C., not to be finished with a destinerrancy which was never my doing, nor to my taste, but a still complacent and therefore defensive account of the Moira*'" (7-6-81) (Circ., 290/313–14). He lacks the "salvation" and "resurrection," the stable destination taught by the "grand masters of the discourse about the resurrection, Saint Paul or Saint Augustine," and he seeks a "quasi-resurrection," that is, a "return to life" that would consist in an event to come that would "open up a new era" (*V*, 35/32) otherwise than Pauline resurrection (*V*, 26/22). Life will have been so short—and late will this quasi-resurrection come; *sero te amavi* (*V*, 35–36/33). Being a little lost, his "Circumfession" is like a postcard gone astray, beset by *destinerrance*, sent off only to arrive heaven knows where, addressed to the "secret," which is not to be identified with the *deus absconditus*, which is in fact a more assured destination and the stuff of a *docta ignorantia*. For the secret kept from him is that there is no Secret Truth, that we are circum-severed from the Truth (Circ., 291/314), deprived of *vérité* and *savoir absolue*; and so he does not know to whom to pray, his condition of non-knowing being more adrift, more radical, than the prayer of a negative theologian to the *deus absconditus*.

In the spirit of his epistle against Paul, one might imagine Derrida defending the prayers the Athenians offer to the unknown God where this altar is meant to keep the name of God safe from knowledge. The God to whom he prays in "Circumfession" is unknown (*ignotus*) but not ignored. Neither an epistemic puzzle we cannot solve nor the divine abyss of negative theology, the name of God draws us beyond knowing and unknowing, leads us outside the circle of hidden and revealed, to the order of the tallith, beyond being and without truth. The Messiah of whom he dreams, for whom he prays and weeps as he caresses his tallith, the one whom he calls to come, "comes to strike dumb the order of knowledge: neither known nor unknown, too well known but a stranger from head to foot, yet to be born" (*V*, 34/31). "My white tallith belongs to the night, the absolute night" (*V*, 80/85; cf. Circ. 83/84). The coming of his Messiah is not a matter of truth (*vérité*) and manifestation, but it represents instead a verdict (*vere dictum*) without verity or truth, for the Messiah belongs to the order of the order, the order of the command, of the Law, which is a demand for justice. His Messiah belongs to the "culture of the tallith," of the prayer shawl whose fringes remind us of the Law, and not to the culture of the veil (*V*, 44/42–43, 73/77), to the long history of veiling and unveiling, of appearing and not-appearing, that stretches from Plato to Heidegger, which is the Greco-Christian history of truth (*V*, 34/31). He is "fed up" with this trope of the veil, infinitely weary of that "tiresome, tireless, tired out" history of concealment and unconcealment, driven to "tears beyond being," to dreaming of justice beyond being's truth and unconcealment (*V*, 42/39–40). His call to "come" is a call for justice, a prediction of the verdict of justice, foretelling in the sense of calling for a justice to come. Residing "beyond any truth as ontological revelation" (*V*, 79/83), it has nothing to do with foreseeing the future.

But is it possible to pray to God in an absolute night? Can one kiss one's tallith and pray to God, or, like a certain Augustine, to "you," if I do not know who you are, who this "you" is? Would that still be a prayer, really a prayer?[8]

THE WOUNDED WORD

In "The Wounded Word," Jean-Louis Chrétien describes the structure of praying to an unknown God that is of some help in this matter. He cites a verse from the French poet Jules Supervielle:[9]

> How surprised I am to be addressing you,
> My God, I who know not if you exist . . .

Chrétien describes this as a prayer to a virtual God, a "watered-down" God, as Supervielle himself says, but not a virtual prayer; it is a real and actual prayer, belonging properly to the religious order, "with the virtual character of the God to whom it says 'you' constituting a moment in its religiosity."[10] An "actual prayer" directed toward a "virtual God," a "virtual you": but what, or who, pray tell, is that? A real and earnest prayer, heartfelt, unfeigned, and full of tears, directed to God, *s'il y en a*. Is this perhaps something of an "anonymous prayer" on the model of Rahner's anonymous Christian, the prayer of someone who is praying to God even though he does not know that it is God to whom he prays? And what if there is no God, *s'il n'y en a pas*? Then it is a prayer directed somewhere, who knows where (God knows where!), but a prayer nonetheless.

This is a thin and diluted prayer, Chrétien observes, a more robust form of which is to be found in the prayer of the father of the child possessed by a demon in the Gospel of Mark, "I believe, help my unbelief" (9:24), which is both a prayer for prayer and an act of faith in faith. This remarkable formula from the New Testament recognizes that all faith proceeds from faithlessness, and all prayer proceeds from an inability to pray, so that to pray that one be able to pray constitutes indeed a most authentic prayer. A prayer is a performative act—the very act of directing one's words to God *is* the prayer—with a unique reflexivity, so that to pray for the prayer itself, to pray that one be able to pray is already to pray. Indeed, this would be so even if one is not so sure that one believes in God, *especially* if one is not sure one believes in God, which also means that one is not sure one does *not* believe in God. When Derrida is asked why he says "I quite rightly pass for an atheist" instead of simply saying that he *is* an atheist, he responds by saying that he is not, in fact, sure that he is an atheist. This is what others say about him, and perhaps they are "right"—in the order of cognitive assertions and creedal assent—but he is not so sure himself that he is one. That is, that he is *one*. For there is a certain *sic et non* that goes on within him, within all of us, such that we are each inhabited by advocates of opposing sides, and the one will not give the other any rest. Accordingly, while he kisses his tallith and prays *viens, oui, oui*, he cannot be sure of the destination of his prayer, for his prayer is "*destinerrant*," sent on a journey that may very well go astray like a lost love letter.

For Chrétien, prayer arises from a destituted, de-constituted subject, a subject dispossessed of subjective authority, suppliant and in need of help. But what subject has less authority than the one who, lost in prayer, does not know to whom he or she is praying, who prays, "Oh God, if there is a God," or even "*Dieu qui n'est pas, pose ta main sur notre épaule*" (Oh God, who is not, put your hand on our shoulder).[11] When would the destitution of the praying subject, the "nudity" of the voice in prayer, as Chrétien puts it, be greater? When would the voice in prayer be more in need of prayer? When would the prayer for prayer, and hence prayer itself, be more intense?

Prayer, as Chrétien argues, is the very element or stuff of religion: where there is prayer, there is religion; and where there is religion, there is prayer. But can there be a religion and a prayer without God? If that is so, as Chrétien argues, would it not follow that it is the prayer of a religion without religion, a prayer *sans Dieu* in a *religion sans religion* of the sort that Derrida describes in *The Gift of Death* (*Donner la mort*)?[12]

The bareness and the barrenness of the prayer to the unknown God lays bare the intentional structure of prayer in a way that no other prayer can, for it exposes the structure of prayer as an act directed at someone, at "you," even and especially if one has no assurance that there is such a "you." This prayer enacts a kind of phenomenological reduction of the real existence of an *ens reale*, or an *ens realissimum*, which has been bracketed in order to lay bare the structure of the intentional act. The directedness of prayer to "you" holds so radically that it holds even if one has no assurance that someone is listening, reducing the one who prays to praying that someone be there to hear the prayer, so that one is praying for the prayer itself. The intentionality of the act does not require that someone indeed be there, or be known to be there, but that the prayer be directed to someone, if they are there. Indeed, and this in virtue of its performativity, there would be prayer as long as one is praying that there be someone to whom to pray, as long as one send one's prayers to someone, whoever and wherever they are, to someone of uncertain destination. Prayer, even in its most classical and orthodox forms, arises from the groundless ground of praying that there be someone who hears our prayer. *Domine, exaudi orationem meam*: O Lord, hear my prayer; *et clamor meus ad te veniat*: and let my cry come unto you. Whenever we say *oremus*, let us pray, we are saying, let us preface our prayer with a prayer; before we even begin praying let us begin praying for our prayer; let us begin with a prayer that there be someone who hears. The uncertainty does not dissipate the prayer but constitutes it in the first place and intensifies it, for that is the very reason to pray in the first place and all the more reason to keep on praying, to pray like mad, to pray that our prayers "to heaven go" (*Hamlet*, III, 3). The very uncertainty that seems to make it impossible to pray is what makes it necessary, what reduces us to prayers and tears.

Like the law of inverse proportions that governs the structure of faith according to Johannes Climacus, the objective (or destinational) uncertainty of the prayer raises to a fever pitch its subjective intensity, its prayerfulness. While the prayer to the virtual God may be a "thin" prayer when measured by the doctrinal standards of the actual and concrete historical faiths, it is for that very reason a profoundly passionate movement of the heart (*inquietum est cor nostrum*). The thinness has to do with the determinacy of the doctrinal content of the prayer and the identifiable determinacy of its destination. But a more robust prayer by this standard would not be a more prayerful prayer, more of a prayer; it would be a *more determinate* prayer, a prayer marked by more constants and fewer variables, by more proper names and fewer pronouns. A more robust prayer would be safer, having a more secure place within a rich and determinate historical tradition of texts and prayers and names for God. For a Christian, for example, it would join itself with Jesus's prayer to the Father in the Spirit and insert itself in the long history that ensues from Jesus's prayer. It would be, in short, less lost.

The prayers that emanate from the author of "Circumfession," on the other hand, are the adrift, *destinerrant*, a-destinal prayers of someone deprived of salvation and resurrection; his prayer is more aporetic, more uncertain of its outcome, more exposed to encountering the very opposite of what he is praying for. His prayer lacks a determinate and identifiable destination, is deprived of the inherited vocabularies of age-old prayers, and is radically exposed to failure, even to something fearful. The Messiah for whom he prays is both desired and feared, awaited and not awaited. Waiting for the Messiah for him is like a defendant awaiting a "verdict" (which is a good "nickname" for the Messiah) of a jury in a trial. The verdict lies in an unforeseeable future which befalls us like death, for the future does include death, which means that it is a future that we are waiting for and postponing.[13] He is waiting for justice, waiting to hear the verdict, but then again, if it is going to go against him, he does not want to hear, so that he does not want what he wants (*V*, 27/25). I do not know what is to come when I call for the coming of the *tout autre*. When I pray, "Come," when I ask, "When will you come?" I am worried that someone is really going to show up, and worried about who, worried about what will be demanded of me, worried that the Messiah will not be at all what I expected (which is, of course, just what is to be expected of the *tout autre*). One should always be careful about what one prays for, lest one's prayers be answered. So when I say or pray, "When will you come?" that longing ("How long, O Lord, how long?") always comes admixed with fear and a desire for deferral, for the Messiah is both a promise and a threat. The call "*viens*" is a *contretemps*, a single gesture in which "the other is made to come, allowed to come, but his coming is *simultaneously* deferred."[14] Still, does being more "lost" and exposed, more lacking in salvation, diminish the need for prayer? And should not every prayer be admixed with a fear of what we are getting ourselves into? Must we not always divest ourselves of our own preconceived ideas about who God is and what God has in mind for us when we pray? Must not our intention always be to renounce our own intention? Must not our desire be to renounce our own desire? "Not what I want but what you want" (Mark 14:36). Does not all this intensify and provide the very conditions of prayer?

Let us look at things from Derrida's point of view. The movement by which one determines the destination of prayer as the "God" of the inherited biblical faiths is an attempt to still or arrest this indeterminacy and destinerrancy; but such a determination must always be inscribed within the more radical translatability and determinability that affects all language in virtue of *différance*. For it would always be possible to determine otherwise what is called "God" in the concrete biblical faiths, always possible to ask what I love when I love my God. That is why Derrida says of his mother that she must have known that the "constancy of God in my life is called by other names" (Circ., 146/155). What gives constancy in Derrida's life is subject to irreducible plurality and translatability, whereas in the inherited religious traditions this constancy goes under the constant name of "God." From Derrida's point of view, the determinacy of the direction of the prayer is a way of trying to appropriate the secret, to make it one's own, to utter its secret name, revealed only to the believers or insiders, instead of confessing more radically its unknowability. On Derrida's point of view, we would never be authorized to determine the secret, to arrest the play, to still the endless translatability of the various names to which we pledge our troth. Where would we be situated when we attempted such a thing? How would we have gained access to such a standpoint? In that regard, Derrida's "Circumfession" is more radically confessional than Augustine's *Confessions*, his word more wounded. For when Augustine confesses his wounded and mortal nature, he is also confessing/professing a faith in which these wounds would be bound up. But Derrida confesses the secret, the non-knowing, the destabilized and destitute state of his confession, his confession without a confessional bond. His is a confession without confession, a confession of the "without," of the *sans*, by which his heart and flesh are marked, *sans voir, sans avoir, sans savoir, sans s'avoir*.

I would argue that the unknowing in this prayer to the unknown God is a structural element of prayer itself, of *any* prayer, the most classical prayers of the faithful included; it is not restricted to certain poets or philosophers who may as a contingent fact rightly or wrongly pass for atheists. For inasmuch as prayer is inscribed within the movement of faith—Lord, I believe, help my unbelief—there is a moment in every prayer where it finds itself thrown back on itself, finds itself praying for the prayer itself, praying that there is some point to prayer, praying that there is someone to hear our prayers, praying that our prayers find someone who hears them. There is, furthermore, always and essentially something unknown about the one to whom we pray, an uncertainty about their response, an irreducible uncertainty about the future, which is why we are praying rather than confidently forecasting a successful outcome. That ring of unknowing is a condition of prayer that is not only found in those who rightly pass for atheists but is also a mark of prayer itself, even and especially the most saintly prayer, the passionate prayer that issues from that passion of non-knowing called the dark night of the soul. At that point in mystical prayer, the soul comes to question whether she believes in God, or believes in prayer, having reached a point where she has to pray to be able to pray, pray to be able to believe in prayer, pray to be able to believe at all.

The point of prayer, its intentional aim, is God, if there is a God; in prayer, one stands *coram deo*, before God, like Augustine in the *Confessions*. In *Being and Time*, Heidegger distilled the structure of the *coram deo* in Augustine into what we might call analogously a *coram morte*, a being before death (*Sein zum Tod*), a running forward into death (*Vorlaufen in den Tod*), which he treated as a "formal indication" of the one-to-one relationship of the soul with God in the *Confessions*, a text that was mediated to him by Luther and Kierkegaard. Augustine's *coram deo* is for Heidegger an ontic specification, a de-formalized instantiation, of this formal indication. But in my view, Heidegger's formal indication leaves out something crucial. Far from formalizing the *coram deo*, Heidegger has transformed it into something of an entirely different form and truncated its intentional type. For his formalization has omitted the very intentionality of the *coram deo*, that is, of the prayer. The discourse (*Rede*) of *Dasein* standing before death, being brought back before its own death, is a soliloquy, a dialogue of *Dasein* with itself, an examination of its conscience in which *Dasein* makes itself ready to hear the call of conscience, in which *Dasein* calls out to *Dasein* to return to itself. The wound of mortality, the wounded word that *Dasein* speaks to itself standing before death, is the wound of a being that has to pull itself together from its dispersion, its scattering abroad (*Zerstreuung*), which is the *distensio animae* that Augustine describes in Book X of the *Confessions*. That wound is healed in authentic resolve, which corresponds to Augustinian *continentia*, the gathering or self-collecting of the soul, its ability to abide within itself. But when in *Being and Time Dasein* collects and recollects itself, when it gathers itself together into an authentic resolve, that self-centering constitutes a certain self-possession or autonomy that Marion rightly describes as a kind of "autarchy" or self-rule. The wounded word of prayer, which is the very structure of the *coram deo*, on the other hand, is the wound of a being torn outside itself and directed to another, to "you," whose help it seeks, whoever this you is, even if I do not know if this you exists, especially if I do not. The wounded voice is a voice of supplication, an- archic, not autarchic, deprived of being an origin, *sans voir, sans avoir, sans savoir, sans s'avoir.* Prayer is a dialogue, not a soliloquy, in which abyss calls to abyss.

In "Circumfession," Derrida has preserved the intentionality of the prayer, the intentional structure of the address, of the *confiteor*, the confessional mode that is turned to "you." The fifty-nine periphrases of "Circumfession" are so many words cut by the wound of circumcision, "that wound I have never seen" (Circ. 66/66), a "virtual," "unmemorable," and "indecipherable" wound (Circ. 271/293), which strikes down the proud heart, which circumcises the heart and the word, the ear and the tongue. His tallith, he says, does not protect him and make him invulnerable but "recalls me to the mortal wound" (*V*, 62/64), that he is under the law, laid claim to by the call of the other, that he is circumcised. The tallith is like the cloth wrapped around the wounded infant penis; "the tallith hangs on the body in memory of circumcision" like a detached prepuce (*V*, 68/70). The words he speaks in "Circumfession" are not the self-possessed words of radical and erect resoluteness, not the words of a being which has become transparent to itself (*Erschlossen*) and resolute (*Entschlossen*) about its ownmost course of action. They are rather the words of one who is lost and adrift, cut, cut loose, and cut down to size; words deprived of erection and resurrection, not so much incisive as incised words, not self-possessed but confessional, circumcised, circum-fessional. Circumcision is what makes him write (Circ., 188–89/202), the writing that is incised on his body and inscribed on his soul, the inscriptions of his stylus reproducing and reinscribing the incisions of the mohel's blade.

The difference between "Circumfession" and a negative theology is not that negative or mystical theology is inscribed in prayer whereas "Circumfession" is a memoir of an atheist to himself. Rather, they are both constituted by movements of prayer—that is the surprising thing that unites them—but the prayer of the negative theologian has a determinate and identifiable destination, *à Dieu*, where the name of God is a constant historical and biblical name, the name that has been handed down to us by the Scriptures and tradition. That is a name that is both unnameable and omni-nameable, as Meister Eckhart says, a name that contains the perfection of every name within itself and by that very fact both excites and exceeds every name we send God's way. The name of God is the name we must save because God is everything save the name, *sauf le nom*, by which God is addressed. The God of negative theology is not simply unknown, for the negative theologian, who takes her bearings from an historical faith, knows to whom she directs her prayers, *nusquam nisi ad te*. If the God of negative theology is called unknown, this is meant as a compliment, as praise, and it is to be taken strictly in the sense of the cloud of unknowing and the learned ignorance. We know that it is to the God of Abraham and Isaac to whom we pray, and we know that we can never know this God. But we know this God whom we do not comprehend is more intimate to us than we are to ourselves, and we know that if something is comprehended, then it cannot be God whom we comprehend. There is nothing higher, nothing greater we can know about this unknown God than that.

But the name of God in Derrida is more desert-like and radically adrift than the God of negative or mystical theology; the absolute night of his white tallith is not the dark night of the soul in John of the Cross. His prayer is, for all that, not less actual, not less real, not less earnest and heartfelt, not less full of tears. It is fully actual within an order that is otherwise than knowing and being, an order of shedding tears beyond or without being, where the whole order of knowledge, of the very distinction between knowing and unknowing, has been struck dumb (*V*, 34/31). He does not love his tallith less than an orthodox believer, but his prayer is less determinate, less clear about its destination, not able to be identified with any of the historical names of God that are handed down to us by the Abrahamic religions. But that indeterminacy does not undermine the prayer; it intensifies it, leaving his word wounded, suppliant, and errant in a radical and disturbing way; his is the prayer of a desert wanderer, a white tallith in an "absolute night" (*V*, 80/85), a circumcised word, where circumcision means to be "severed from the truth," *sevrée de la vérité*, cut off, circum-severed from the truth, awaiting a *verdict sans vérité*. Of the two men who went up to the temple to pray, his prayer would be rather more like the one who does not feel fit to pray (Luke 10:18), which is more and not less of a prayer. The more unfit one feels for prayer, the more un-able, the more prayer is prayer. He lacks the "truth" about God in the sense of lacking any theology or dogma, and in the sense of being unable to identify himself with a determinate historical community of faith, with a fixed textual and institutional faith tradition. But over and beyond that cognitive indeterminacy, *au-delà de l'être*, the very idea of God, the meaning of the name of God, resides in an order that is otherwise than truth and being. Derrida's prayer will always maintain a certain ironic quality inasmuch as he will always maintain a certain *ironic distance* from the name of God, because the name of God for him is endlessly translatable, "the constancy of the name of God" for him going under many names. But at the same time, and for the same reason, it will always be in earnest, bathed in the blood and tears of existence.

DIFFÉRANCE AND THE NAME OF GOD

We can shed some light on the question of the meaning of the name of God for Derrida if we briefly mark an interesting evolution that this name has undergone in his work. The name of God first appears in Derrida's early writings under the theme of the "reduction" or the "effacement" of the trace, the "lifting" of the trace in favor of "full presence." What begins in Platonism, he says, culminates in "infinitist metaphysics": "Only infinite being can reduce the difference in presence. In that sense, the name of God, at least as it is pronounced within classical rationalism, is the name of indifference. . . . We must not therefore speak of a 'theological prejudice,' functioning sporadically when it is a question of the plenitude of the logos; the logos as the sublimation of the trace is *theological*" (*OG*, 104/71).[15] The name of God, which is the "theological" name par excellence, at least the "rationalist" pronunciation of it, is taken to be something that must be effaced in the name of God's utter transcendence of every name or concept. The name "God" arises from "speech dreaming of plenitude," from a dream of "life without *différance*" (*OG*, 104/71), from a dream of presence without *différance*, of which classical negative theology is a case in point. To seek such pure and perfect transcendence is, as with Levinas's "dream of a purely heterological thought," to pursue a thought unconditioned by a subject and unencumbered by any horizon, which is a dream that "must vanish *at daybreak*, as soon as language awakens" (*ED*, 224/151).[16] The name of God should be a self-effacing trace, like a comet that burns itself out and disappears as it streaks across the sky of language. Negative theology knows that the straightest way to the Godhead beyond God, to the God beyond the trace, is to take the detour of the apophatic (*ED*, 398 n. 1/337 n. 37), for God is infinite, ineffable, and inconceivable (*Marg.*, 6/6).

To be sure, Derrida's point in all this is critical and delimitative. It is not to consign the name of God to the rubbish heap of illusions, although that is a conclusion drawn by both his (secularizing) admirers and (religious) critics alike, but to bring this name down to earth. He does not deny that this name has reference but seeks to reinscribe it in *différance*. It is not as though there is some sort of negative ontological argument lodged deep in deconstruction, in virtue of which the very idea of *différance* would disprove the existence of God and discredit negative theology. But Derrida insists that whatever reference this name has is a function of difference, of the system or chain of differences within which it is inscribed. That means that it cannot be insulated from an irreducible translatability into other names that could do service for it. The name of God, like every name, is a nominal "effect," which means, of course, an effect of lettering but not a literal effect, because *différance* is a quasi-transcendental condition of nominal unities of meaning, not a real, entitative or transcendent cause of equally real or transcendent entities. The name "God," like every name, acquires significance by the differential relations within which it is always and already inscribed—God/human, God/world, God/gods, infinite/finite, eternal/temporal, and so on. It is inescapably inscribed within the multiple systems—syntactical, semantic and pragmatic, phonic and graphic, social, historical, institutional, and gendered—by means of which it is forged as a certain linguistic, historical, and nominal unity. Whatever the nominative power of this name, whatever the real or entitative status of its referent—and Derrida is not saying, and he is not authorized to say, one way or the other, what that is—the name "infinite" is a finite name, the concept "inconceivable" is quite conceivable, and the name "ineffable" is very speakable. Rather than bringing discourse to a halt, these are among our very best words, supplying the stuff of the most beautiful, poignant, and soaring discourses, giving rise to the most stunning and audacious sermons and treatises. I never tire of pointing out that "Meister" Eckhart, that master of mystical silence and ineffability, whose prayer to God was to rid him of God, was the greatest preacher of his day in the Order of Preachers, and one of the veritable creators of the modern German language, a master *of Lesen und Leben*.

But we would be missing something important in Derrida's early writings if we did not see that, beyond critique and delimitation, he has been stirred in an affirmative way by this discourse on God in negative theology. He has, of course, and this is what has drawn most of the attention in the literature, very considerable regard for the strategic resources of negative theology. He has always admired its "detours, locutions and syntax," the extraordinary economy with which it enacts the self-effacing trace and the "rarefaction of signs" (*Sauf*, 41/48).[17] For this is a language that would exceed language, a "sweet rage against language" that operates "at the edge of language," (*Sauf*, 63–64/59–60), upon which he does not hesitate to borrow (*Marg.*, 6/6). For Derrida, the language of negative theology is a wounded word, driven by passion to go where we cannot go, to name the unnameable God:

> —It is this passion that leaves the mark of a scar in that place where the impossible takes place, isn't it?
>
> —Yes, the wound is there, over there (*Sauf*, 63–64/59–60)

The scar left behind on the language of negative theology is the wound inflicted by the impossible.

I would emphasize, however, that the early Derrida's interest in this name has another side, less mystical than prophetic, less Neoplatonic than biblical, more Jewish than Christian, more religious than theological, which also makes its first appearance in the early writings. I refer to his fascination with the evocative discourse of Levinas on the *tout autre* in "Violence and Metaphysics," an essay that it would be a mistake to reduce to a simple critique of Levinas. Let us entertain the "hypothesis," he says at the end of this essay, that "this experience of the infinitely other" is to be called "Judaism," which represents a kind of "non-philosophy" or "absolute empiricism" that comes to "solicit" the "autistic syntax" of Greek philosophy: "Therefore nothing can so profoundly *solicit* the Greek logos—philosophy—than this irruption of the totally other (*tout autre*)" (*ED*, 26/152). The issue of this solicitation is for Derrida a fruitful aporia, a productive impossibility. We find ourselves faced *both* with the necessity to speak and articulate, to conceive and philosophize, to have recourse to the categorial system handed down to us by the Greeks—how could we avoid that and why would we want to?—*and* at the same time with the necessity to disturb that conceptuality, to open it up from within to the outside, to awaken it from its autistic dream. Both of these at the same time, both Greek and Jew, living in the difference between the Greek and Jew, being "attached to both the philosophers and the prophets," as Levinas says. This is achieved, not in a reconciling *Aufhebung*, but in the mutual solicitation and incessant disturbance of the Greek by the Jew and of the Jew by the Greek, of the one by the other. "Jewgreek is greekjew. Extremes meet." "Are we Jews? Are we Greeks? We live in the difference between the Jew and the Greek, which is perhaps the unity of what is called history" (*ED*, 227/153).

So the affirmative point that emerges from a deconstructive analysis of the name of God, even in Derrida's early writings, is to welcome the shock that "Judaism" delivers to "philosophy," to open Greek logos to its other, to "circumcise" the logos of the philosophers and so open philosophy to its outside, like the circumcised ear and the circumcised heart in Jeremiah:

> See, their ears are closed [uncircumcised], they cannot listen. (Jer, 6:10)
>
> For all those nations are uncircumcised, and all the house of Israel is uncircumcised in heart. (Jer, 9:25)

In Derrida, circumcision cuts both ways—it is both the literal defining inscription that marks the Jew off from the peoples (*goyim*), and it is the figure of welcoming the other that cuts open the circle of the same. Like his tallith, his circumcision is literal, not merely a figure indifferent to its literality, which is what divides him from St. Paul (*V*, 72/7–76). Unlike Heidegger, who thinks that the name of God closes down questioning and stops the question of Being in its tracks, for Derrida the name of God is the open-ended name of the *tout autre*, a name that disturbs and solicits the Greek logos and keeps it turned to the other for which it cannot be prepared.

THE PROMISE

That is why a careful and theologically sensitive reading of Derrida's early writings, of which there is not an oversupply, would not have been surprised by the force and saliency with which the name of God would resurface in his later writings, in particular in "Circumfession." What I wish to emphasize here is that in "Circumfession" the name of God is not a theological name: "Well, I'm remembering God this morning, the name, a quotation, something my mother said . . . to quote the name of God as I heard it perhaps the first time, no doubt in my mother's mouth when she was praying, each time she saw me ill, . . . I heard her say, *gràce a Dieu, merci Dieu,* when the temperature goes down, weeping in pronouncing your name, . . . I'm mingling the name of God here with the origin of tears" (Circ., 112/117). The name of God is mingled with prayers and tears, mingled like water and wine. It is not a theological word but a religious one, especially if, as Chrétien argues, the defining feature of religion is prayer. It does not function nominatively, to pick out an entity, but invocatively, to call upon and provoke an event. The name of God does not belong to "the logic or the topic of the veil," to the order being, presence, and truth, as he says in "A Silkworm of One's Own," but to the order of the tallith, of prayers and tears (*V*, 71/75). The name of God in "Circumfession" does not pick out an object of metaphysical theology, nor the subject matter of rationalist metaphysics; it does not have to do either with ontic truth of entities or the ontological truth of Being. It is the name of "you," *te, toi,* "my God," not of a dream of full plenitude and presence. It does not name this "you" as an entity, but calls upon it. "God" is not an *ens realissimum*, but an addressee to whom I direct my prayers and tears, by whom I am always already addressed and solicited, "my God."

Now if this name does not signify the dream of presence without *différance*, it is no less a name forged by dreaming. But far from being a dream from which we "awaken" at the dawn of language, it is the dream of language, language's own dream of the coming or the incoming of the other, which is the very promise by which language is provoked, the promise of which language dreams, which is accordingly the dream that fires deconstruction, which constitutes deconstruction. For what else is deconstruction but a dream of the coming of the other, indeed, a prayer for the coming of the Messiah? In the final passage of the text of "Circumfession," which also contains an allusion to the *sero te amavi*, which is the epigraph of "Silkworm," Derrida writes: "You have spent your whole life inviting calling promising, hoping sighing dreaming, convoking invoking provoking" (Circ., 290–91/314).

Deconstruction is the dream and desire for the coming of the other: *Viens, oui, oui.* He is always saying, praying, Amen, yes, yes, to the coming of the *tout autre*. Yes, I said yes. Amen. Yes, to the justice to come, to the democracy to come, to the gift to come, to the forgiveness to come, to the hospitality to come, to the friendship to come. As such, deconstruction is structured around a prayer which in its most economical form reminds us of the final words of the last book of the New Testament. Like every prayer, Derrida's prayer is what Chrétien calls a wounded word, a notion explicitly articulated by the cut of circumcision, whose decisive, or incisive, character is summed up in this final passage of "Circumfession." He has been "hoping sighing dreaming": "What, the witness, you my counterpart, only so that he will attest this secret truth, i.e., severed from truth, i.e., that you will never have had any witness, *ergo es*, in this very place, you alone whose life will have been so short" (Circ 290–91/314–15). *Sevrée de la vérité*: the cut in Derrida's circumcised word is this severed truth, this severing of him from the truth, the sign by which he carries about his mortality, as Augustine said, *circumferens suam mortalitatem*. His prayers arise *de profundis*, from the depths of the cut, which opens a desire for the coming of the other, for prayer "opens the religious dimension, and never ceases to sustain, to support, and to suffer it," as Chrétien says,[18] even as his prayers are directed toward the secret from which he is cut off, "convoking invoking provoking" the unknown God. *Abyssus abyssum invocat*.

Cut off from the truth, praying for the coming of the *tout autre*, for the fulfillment of the promise, he prays to remain faithful to the promise. But what is this promise, and who is promising what to whom? In what can he have faith? For what and on what basis does he hope? What does he love when he loves his God? We are awash in questions.

The promise, as I construe it, is the promise that is inscribed in language itself, the promise language makes to which we are always already responding. This promise is not a particular speech act, as when one person promises something definite to another person, but the very promise of language itself. In this sense:

> "A language is promised," which at once precedes all language, summons all speech and already belongs to each language as it does to all speech.
>
> The promise of which I speak . . . and of which I am now proposing that it promises the impossible but also the possibility of all speech; this strange promise neither yields nor delivers any messianic or eschatological *content* here. There is no salvation here that saves or promises salvation.
>
> But the fact that there is no necessarily determinable *content* in this promise of the other, and in the language of the other, does not make any less indisputable its opening up of speech by something that *resembles* messianism, soteriology, or eschatology. It is the structural opening, the messi-an*icity*, without which *messianism* itself . . . would not be possible.[19]

Language is opened by the promise of a language to come, and our speech comes always and already in response to such a promise; our language comes to us as the in-coming of the other. But we are not in a position to determine in advance any specific content, to hold up a determinate ideal or program. The "given language," the language given us, is astir with many gifts, made restless (*inquietum*) with words of an elemental "donatative" force, words like *gift* and *forgiveness*, *hospitality* and *friendship*, *come* and *welcome*, *yes* and *amen*, *justice* and *democracy*. These given words, our least bad words for something to come, come in response to a promise inscribed in language itself. Our hearts are restless, and we will not rest until we can recall a call that never was present, until we welcome a future that will never come, which is an impossible future, the future of *the* impossible. But that restless heart is not consigned to hopelessness; on the contrary, that indeterminacy belongs to the very structure of the promise. This restlessness describes the groaning of history and language to bring forth the "event," the *événement*, the *évenir* of the in-coming (*l'invention*) of the wholly other, that is, of the unforeseeable future (*l'avenir*). For history and language move about in the ambience of the promise, of the space opened up between the absolute past and the absolute future.

The author of "Circumfession" does not and cannot determinately identify what he desires, but his desire is aroused (*tu excitas, ut laudare te delectet*, I, 1) by something that stirs in those words in particular, which are not chosen arbitrarily—he does not dream of a monarchy to come, or an enmity to come. Something is promised to us by them; something calls to us from afar. They come to us from of old, from an ancient memory, from a time out of mind, and they summon us to a future to come. To be sure, these are our words, but we do not have them; they have us, and we speak in answer to their call. Our words are at bottom the words of the other in us, the other who addresses us. Such words call to us, and we answer, "*Viens, oui, oui*," come, yes, come; but our "come" comes second, as an answer, a second yes, *oui, oui*, to the call addressed to us in these words, which is the first yes, the yes that language calls to us, *tu excitas*, the yes that language is, the promise that language is. That means that for Derrida the prophetic and messianic texts of the three great religions of the Book, all of which turn on a messianic coming, as well as the philosophical eschatologies of Hegel, Marx, and Heidegger, are more definitely and determinately destined sendings, directed at a more assured, that is, a more fixed and identifiable destination.

But the author of "Circumfession" is a little more lost, a little less assured, a little more adrift, a little more confessional, a little more deprived of salvation, kissing and caressing his tallith, shedding tears beyond being. Periphrasis 59 continues, and these are the last words of the book: "The voyage sent, scarcely organized, by you with no lighthouse and no book, you the floating toy at high tide and under the moon, you the cross between these two phantoms of witnesses who will never come down to the same" (Circ., 290–91/314–15). He does not know to whom he is praying, which means he does not know by whom the promise of the future has been made, if it has been made by anyone at all, or whether the promise does not arise in some middle-voice operation that gets itself made in the given language, in what is handed down to us by language and tradition, coming from a past that was never present, promising us an unforeseeable future. He does not know whom to thank for "a gift for which thanks should be given to goodness knows what archaic power. . . . The day I would know to whom gratitude must be rendered for it, I would know everything, and I would be able to die in peace. Everything I do . . . resembles a game of blindman's bluff . . . [he] holds out his hand like a blind man seeking to touch the one whom he could thank for the gift of a language, for the very words in which he declares himself ready to give thanks."[20]

His prayer lacks the security of an assured destination, the fixity of a definite point of arrival, but that lack is an opening that intensifies its passion, impassioning it with the passion of the impossible, with the passion of non-knowing. To be sure, there is a considerable passion when passion has a determinate destination, when we set our hands to the plow with a fixed goal and do not look back (Luke 9:62). But there is no less passion, and perhaps there is more, at least there is a different passion, in this passion of his that is not quite sure of how to proceed or where it is heading, a passion that is thrown back upon itself and gropes like a blind man in the dark, which risks getting lost, which is a little lost. Getting lost is what he risks, but his risk is no more risky than the opposite risk, which is the danger to which they are exposed who, thinking themselves to know the way, risk getting complacent, self-assured, dogmatic, or routinized. But when we do not know where we are going, or how things will turn out, then the tensions are tightened, the stakes raised, and the passion pushed to its highest pitch, in accord with the law of the raising of subjective intensity first formulated by Johannes Climacus.

SERO TE AMAVI

It is not so much a question of his faith in his tallith, Derrida says, but of his tallith's faith in him. Happily, his tallith is very understanding and forgiving of his inconstancies:

> I love the peaceful passion, the distracted love my tallith inspires in me, I get the impression it allows me that distraction because it is sure, so sure of me, so little worried by my infidelities. It does not believe in my inconstancies, they do not affect it. I love it and bless it with a strange indifference, my tallith, in a familiarity without name or age. As if faith and knowledge, another faith and another knowledge, a knowledge without truth and without revelation, were woven together in the memory of an event to come, the absolute delay of the verdict, of a verdict to be rendered and which is, was, or will make itself arrive without the glory of a luminous vision. My white tallith belongs to the night, the absolute night. (*V*, 79–80/84–85)

He is a man of prayer, a man of the tallith, who has a tallith of his own, not because it belongs to him but because he belongs to it. His tallith does not keep him safe or make him invulnerable, but it reminds him of the wound of his mortality, the open-endedness of his aspirations and the uncertainty of what is to come. That is why one should never, never get rid of one's tallith, even as one must never be late for prayer (*V*, 69/71, 65/67). That is why, every night before going to bed, he places his hand on his tallith and presses it to his lips.

Our tears are sent beyond being, drawn beyond being; we weep and pray for what, beyond being, beyond truth, calls up our tears. Our hearts are restless, *inquietum est cor nostrum*, with an incessant aspiration for the impossible, *viens, oui, oui*, astir with hope in the promise of an unforeseeable event. To invoke the name of God, which he associates with tears (Circ., 112/117), is not to name a being or a non-being, something known or not known. The name of God does not have a nominative power for him but an invocative one; it does not name something but calls for an event (*événement*), something to come (*à venir*), something to be done (*facere veritatem*). The name of God draws us outside the closed circle of being and truth into an open space without borders, where tears are shed beyond being, into a desert place where the distinction between knowledge and non-knowledge is struck dumb, luring us like a love that we will have always loved so late, *sero te amavi*, life having always been too short (*V*, 35–36/33). The prayers of circumfession are prayers of "peaceful passion" and its love is a "distracted love." Its prayers and tears are sent beyond being, like sighs lovers send God knows where for their future, for something futural, for the coming of something wholly other, even as they steel themselves for the threatening promise of what is to come, for the open-ended possibility of the absolute surprise.

NOTES

This essay previously appeared as "Tears beyond Being: Derrida's Experience of Prayer," in *Théologie négative*, ed. Marco M. Olivetti (Padua: CEDAM, 2002), 861–80, and is here reproduced with permission of CEDAM.

1. Hélène Cixous and Jacques Derrida, *Voiles* (Paris: Galilée, 1998), translated in English as *Veils*, trans. Geoffrey Bennington (Stanford: Stanford University Press, 2001). Hereafter referred to as *V*. This book contains a short piece entitled "Savoir" by Cixous on the severe myopia from which she suffered from birth, which was cured by laser surgery, and her subsequent and unexpected mourning for the loss of her myopia, her lifelong companion, and a second longer piece by Derrida entitled "A Silkworm of One's Own (Points of View Stitched on the Other Veil)" ("*Un Ver à soie: Points de vue piqués sur l'autre voile*"), which deals with his lifelong companion, another veil, which is not a veil at all, but a white tallith, a prayer shawl.

2. Derrida, *Marges de philosophie* (Paris: Éditions de Minuit, 1967), translated in English as *Margins of Philosophy*, trans. Alan Bass (Chicago: University of Chicago Press, 1982). Hereafter referred to as *Marg*.

3. Jacques Derrida, *Monolingualism of the Other; or, The Prosthesis of Origin*, trans. Patrick Mensah (Stanford: Stanford University Press, 1998), p. 1. This essay is an extended meditation on this phrase.

4. Hélène Cixous, *Portrait de Jacques Derrida en Jeune Saint Juif* (Paris: Galilée, 2001), 9.

5. Jacques Derrida, "*Comment ne pas parler: Dénegations*," in *Psyche: L'inventions de l'autre*, by Jacques Derrida (Paris: Galilée, 1987), 562, 562n13; Jacques Derrida, "How to Avoid Speaking: Denials," in *Derrida and Negative Theology*, ed. Howard Coward and Toby Foshay (Albany: SUNY Press, 1992), 100, 135–36n13.

6. "*Circonfession: cinquante-neuf périodes et périphrases*," in *Jacques Derrida*, ed. Geoffrey Bennington and Jacques Derrida (Paris: Éditions du Seuil, 1991) (hereafter referred to as Circ.); the number following the slash is the page number of the English translation by Geoffrey Bennington: "Circumfession: Fifty-Nine Periods and Periphrases," in *Jacques Derrida*, ed. Geoffrey Bennington and Jacques Derrida (Chicago: University of Chicago Press, 1993). For commentaries, see John D. Caputo, *The Prayers and Tears of Jacques Derrida* (Bloomington: Indiana University Press, 1997), § 18; Cixous, *Portrait*; Gideon Ofrant, *The Jewish Derrida*, trans. Peretz Kidron (Syracuse, NY: Syracuse University Press, 2001); Jill Robbins, "Circumcising Confession: Derrida, Autobiography, Judaism," *Diacritics* 25 (1995): 20–38; Elisabeth Weber, *Questions au Judaïsme* (Paris: Desclée de Brouwer, 1996). Citations of the Latin text of the *Confessions* are from Loeb Classical Library (Cambridge: Harvard University Press, 1916), vol. 26. I am using the translation of the *Confessions* by F. J. Sheed (Indianapolis: Hackett, 1970).

7. Jacques Derrida, *Cinders* (*Feu le cendre*), a bilingual edition, trans. Ned Lukacher (Lincoln: University of Nebraska Press, 1991), 75.

8. In Derrida's account of prayer, as distinguished from his practice of prayer in "Circumfession," prayer is composed of two elements: (1) a pure invocation of the other as other, any other, God, for example; (2) an element of praise, which inevitably involves a predicative content. One never finds invocation in its purity but always mixed with a predicative element, which makes

it Christian, Jewish, and so on; see Derrida, "*Comment ne pas parler: Dénegations*," 572; Derrida, "How to Avoid Speaking: Denials," 110; for commentaries, see Caputo, *Prayers and Tears of Jacques Derrida*, 38–39, and Hent de Vries, *Philosophy and the Turn to Religion* (Baltimore: Johns Hopkins University Press, 1999), 135–41.

9. Jean-Luis Chrétien, "*La parole blessée: Phénoménologie de la prière*," in *Phénoménologie et théologie* (Paris: Criterion, 1992), 41, translated in English as "The Wounded Word: The Phenomenology of Prayer," trans. Jeff Kosky, in *Phenomenology and the "Theological Turn": The French Debate*, ed. Dominique Janicaud, Jean-François Courtine, Jean-Louis Chrétien, Jean-Luc Marion, Michel Henry, and Paul Ricoeur (New York: Fordham University Press, 2001), 147; Jules Supervielle, "*Voilà que je me surprends à t'adresser la parole/ Mon Dieu, moi qui ne sais encore si tu existes*," in *La fable du monde* (Paris: Gallimard, 1950), 39.

10. Chrétien, "*Blessée*," 42/Chrétien, "Wounded," 147.

11. Yves Bonnefoy, "*La Lumière, Changée*," *Poèmes* (Paris: Mercure de France, 1978), 211.

12. Jacques Derrida, "*Donner la mort*" in *L'Éthique du don: Jacques Derrida et la pensée du don* (Paris: Métailié-Transition, 1992), 53, translated in English as *The Gift of Death*, trans. David Wills (Chicago: University of Chicago Press, 1995), 49.

13. See Jacques Derrida, *Sur Parole: Instantanés philosophiques* (Paris: l'Aube, 1999), 54.

14. See Jacques Derrida, *Politiques de l'amitié* (Paris: Galilée, 1995), 197–98, translated in English as *Politics of Friendship*, trans. George Collins (London and New York: Verso, 1997), 173–74, and Jacques Derrida, *Deconstruction in a Nutshell: A Conversation with Jacques Derrida*, edited with a commentary by John D. Caputo (New York: Fordham University Press, 1997), 24–25.

15. Jacques Derrida, *De la grammatologie* (Paris: Éditions de Minuit, 1967), translated in English as *Of Grammatology*, corrected edition, trans. Gayatri Spivak (Baltimore: Johns Hopkins University Press, 1997). Hereafter referred to as *OG*.

16. Jacques Derrida, *Écriture et la différence* (Paris: Éditions de Seuil, 1967), translated in English as *Writing and Difference*, trans. Alan Bass (Chicago: University of Chicago Press, 1978). Hereafter referred to as *ED*.

17. Jacques Derrida, *Sauf le nom* (Paris: Galilée, 1993), 41–46, translated in English as *On the Name*, ed. Thomas Dutoit (Stanford: Stanford University Press, 1995), 48–60.

18. Chrétien, "*Blessée*," 41/ Chrétien, "Wounded," 147.

19. Derrida, *Monolingualism of the Other*, 67–68.

20. Ibid., 64.

14
The Good News about Alterity: Derrida and Theology

Derrida's work is often mistakenly criticized as a kind of linguistic subjective idealism which traps us inside a chain of linguistic signifiers, unable to do anything but play vainly with linguistic strings. In fact, Derrida's thought is through and through a philosophy of "alterity," of openness to the other, which provides a rich and vigorous catalyst for religious thought. After demonstrating the wrongheadedness of the subjectivist reading of Derrida, I go on to show the richness of this philosophy of alterity for theology: first, in terms of the negative theology, where alterity refers to God as the absolutely Other; and then in terms of ethics of alterity, in which it is shown that, like Levinasian ethics, deconstruction is a philosophy of responsibility for the singularity of the other. I conclude with a note on Jesus as a master of alterity.

MISUNDERSTANDING DERRIDA

"Postmodern" thinking, if it means anything at all, means a philosophy of alterity," a relentless attentiveness and sensitivity to the "other."[1] Postmodernism stands for a kind of hyper-sensitivity to many "others": the other person, other species, "man's" other, the other of the West, of Europe, of Being, of the "classic," of philosophy, of reason—the list goes on. This approach has produced numerous, sometimes brilliant and sometimes merely eccentric results, a vast body of unorthodox and provocative approaches to madness; illness; criminality psychoanalysis; architecture; the university; literary, historical, and legal interpretation; the history of philosophy; and philosophy itself.

But the philosophy of alterity provides an equally fertile and suggestive opening for religious reflection, which is something that I hope to show here is especially true of the work of Jacques Derrida. Unfortunately, the significance of Derrida's work has been obscured by a particularly perverse misunderstanding of deconstruction, one which, to anyone who has taken the considerable trouble required to gain familiarity with his texts, seems quite ironic (if not amusing). For the notion has gained currency that deconstruction traps us inside the "chain of signifiers," in a kind of linguistic-subjective idealism, unable to do anything but play vainly with linguistic strings. That, were it true, would be an odd result for a philosophy of alterity, a very unkind fate to visit upon a philosophy whose every effort is bent upon turning toward the other. Were that true, Derrida's work would surely be of no use for understanding Christian faith and tradition, since it would make nonsense out of the interpretation of classical texts and the articulation of shared beliefs. I hope to show that the unique strength of deconstruction lies in exactly the opposite tendency of this misunderstanding, in the special skills it has cultivated in awakening us to the demands made by the other, and that this has interesting and provocative implications for theological reflection. Deconstruction is a rich and vigorous catalyst for religious thought, but that point is largely lost in the midst of the ill-conceived and panicky reactions it provokes.

This misunderstanding of deconstruction, which even supposes that the very idea of "misunderstanding deconstruction" is undermined by deconstruction, is often the result of too hastily construing the texts of a difficult, elusive, and playful author whose project is far more affirmative—deconstruction is affirmation[2]—than it sometimes sounds to more traditional ears. But this distortion of Derrida is not without political significance, for it is frequently attached to a reactionary political agenda that vigorously opposes the efforts of women, homosexuals, and ethnic minorities to have their voices heard.[3] Yet these are the very voices of alterity—the "call of the other"—in which deconstructive analyses take an interest.

After briefly indicating how this misunderstanding is to be set aside, I turn to the profit that deconstruction holds for theological reflection, which is, I hope to show, to lend a hand in announcing the good news of alterity. While there are numerous issues in terms of which this point could be developed I have chosen to address but two here: the questions of God and of religious ethics.

THE OTHER OF LANGUAGE

Derrida's justly famous, but unjustly notorious, declaration, "There is nothing outside the text" (*il n'y a pas de hors-texte*),[4] has been widely interpreted as a denial of reference, as if Derrida thinks there is nothing other than words and texts. That, were it construed as a metaphysical claim, would constitute a sort of linguistic Berkeleyianism, incoherent on its face (texts are after all material objects), with which Derrida has nothing in common. Alternatively, and somewhat less madly, Derrida is taken to advocate a vague subjectivistic skepticism, according to which signifiers are seen as leading only to other signifiers, leaving in doubt the character of anything outside of signifiers, anything real or really other, and leaving us in a cloud of confusion, undecidability, and inaction. One way to see the error here—and I apologize for the dogmatic tone—is to see that it conflates the *hors* of *hors-texte* with the "other of language," the referent (*ens significatum*). For while there is nothing for Derrida which escapes the constraints of textuality, it is no less true that everything that Derrida has written has had in mind the other of language, the alterity by which language is claimed:

> There have been several misinterpretations of what I and other deconstructionists are trying to do. It is totally false to suggest that deconstruction is a suspension of reference. Deconstruction is always deeply concerned with the "other" of language. I never cease to be surprised by critics who see my work as a declaration that there is nothing beyond language, that we are imprisoned in language; it is, in fact, saying the exact opposite. The critique of logocentrism is above all else the search for the "other" and the "other of language." Every week I receive critical commentaries and studies on deconstruction which operate on the assumption that what they call "post-structuralism" amounts to saying that there is nothing beyond language, that we are submerged in words—and *other stupidities* [my emphasis] of that sort. Certainly, deconstruction tries to show that the question of reference is

> much more complex and problematic than traditional theories supposed. It even asks whether our term "reference" is entirely adequate for designating the "other." The other, which is beyond language and which summons language, is perhaps not a "referent" in the normal sense which linguists have attached to this term. But to distance oneself thus from the habitual structure, to challenge or complicate our common assumptions about it, does not amount to saying that there is *nothing* beyond language.[5]

And again: "This misinterpretation is not just a simplification; it is symptomatic of certain political and institutional interests—interests which must also be deconstructed in their turn. I totally refuse the label of nihilism which has been ascribed to me and my American colleagues. Deconstruction is not an enclosure in nothingness, but an openness towards the other."[6] Deconstruction means to complicate reference, not to deny it; it insists that there is no reference without difference, no reference (*il n'y a pas*) outside of a textual chain (*hors-texte*). It argues that the range of reference of a term is set by its place within a systemic code, that its reference is both made possible and limited by the space that it occupies within a linguistic system (difference). Deconstruction wants to trouble the expression "reference" as an excessively subjectivistic term which overestimates the *ego cogito* of the speaking subject while underestimating the power of the linguistic system within which the speaker operates.[7] This delimitation of reference is motivated not by subjectivism or skepticism but by a kind of hypersensitivity to otherness, by a profound vigilance about the other of language. Derrida is constantly alerting us to the constructedness of what we call the "reality" of the extra-linguistic," and he is relentlessly, systematically, let us say, Socratically suspicious of the prestige of the ruling discourse, of the system of exclusions that is put in place when a language claims to be the language of reality itself, when a language is taken to be what being itself would say were it given a tongue.

This can be seen from the special attention Derrida has paid to the problem of the proper name.[8] For the reference of a proper name is the singularity of an unrepeatable individual, that being whose being is incommunicable, and this by means of the coded, repeatable, commonly shared signifiers of a spoken or written discourse. A truly or absolutely proper name would be a unique, unrepeatable, idiosyncratic mark or sound that would be unrecognizable by the members of any linguistic community. If a name were truly proper, it would not be a true name; if it were a recognizable name, it would not be truly proper. Derrida's work here, as elsewhere, is to explore the limits of our most common notions and to keep a Socratic watch over the elusiveness both of the singularity which slips through the grids of discourse and of discourse itself. He puts us on warning about the claims of language to lay hold to the things themselves. Every claim to the "things themselves" is a claim made within and by means of the resources of a certain language which has its own limits and within the framework of a complex set of contextual presuppositions which can never be saturated. There are no things themselves outside these textual and contextual limits, no naked contact with being which somehow shakes loose of the coded system which makes notions like the "things themselves" possible to begin with and which enables speakers to refer to them. But all this is said not in order to throw the speaker into confusion or to lock the speaker up in a linguistic prison, but out of a hypersensitivity to the other of language. This "other" is neither reducible to language and strings of linguistic signifiers nor is it something which can shake loose from language as if it fell full blown and wholly constituted from the sky.

Deconstruction is a work of delimitation, of understanding the limits under which we labor, a "new Enlightenment"[9] which raises our level of vigilance about what calls itself reference or subjectivity or objectivity. Similar analyses could be undertaken about the deconstruction of "truth," "tradition," "ethics," and so on. The impetus and the point of all such work is never destructive, never aimed at simply leveling or razng these structures. The point of deconstruction is to loosen and unlock structures, to let the shock of alterity set them in motion, to allow them to function more freely and inventively, to produce new forms. Deconstruction gives old texts new readings, old traditions new twists; it urges that regularizing structures and normalizing institutions—everything from literature to democracy—function more freely, more open-endedly, by exposing them to the trauma of something unexpected, something to come, to the *alter* which remains ever on the margins of texts and traditions, which eludes and elicits our discourse, which shakes and solicits our institutions. Deconstruction warns against letting a discourse or a discursive tradition close over or shut down, for that can only have the effect of silencing and excluding. I do not mean to suggest that deconstruction is the doing of a cunning and powerful subjective deconstructive agent. Rather, in a deconstructive analysis, one lets it be seen that the system in question lacks the cohesiveness and closure to which it lays claim, that it is not what it says it is. But by letting this out, one points to something there, in these systems, which struggles to twist free of the system. The watchword of deconstruction, one of them at least, is the open-ended call *viens!*, come, let something new come.[10]

Seen thus, deconstruction is not the sworn enemy of faith or religious institutions, although it can cause a lot of well-deserved trouble to a faith or an institution that has frozen over into immobilty. Deconstruction is, as I hope to show, a way to approach faith, one which lets faith say *viens!*, lets it function more ad-ventfully, with an enhanced sense of advent and event, gladdened by the good news of alterity by which we are always and already summoned.

THE OTHERNESS OF GOD

The other is never simply inside or outside language. The other is never conceivable or referable except by means of the resources of linguistic difference, yet it is never reducible to a string of signifiers. The other is a being of marginality, on the margins of language, occupying the point of contact where language opens up to things and where things break in upon and break open language. Derrida has put this argument about "marginality" to work on many levels: on that of the "things themselves" of Husserl's and Heidegger's phenomenologies, and also on that of the "absolutely other" (*autrui*) of Emmanuel Levinas which is or wants to be beyond being and phenomenality, to be more radically transcendent than the Being or the phenomena of phenomenology. Derrida has also made the argument from marginality, the argument of the inside/outside, in his recurrent discussions of negative theology. He shows a persistent interest in "apophatic discourse," a discourse that, by denying and negating, affirms the God beyond being and language. The God of negative theology who in habits the desert of silence beyond thought and word is an unavoidable matter of concern for Derrida.

Derrida was first drawn into a discussion of negative theology because deconstruction has been at times "accused of—rather than being congratulated for"[11]—being itself a negative theology. According to Derrida, *différance*, which is the organizing motif of his work, is neither a word (it is at best a word mutilated by a misspelling) nor a concept (the content signified by a word), nor an entity, nor any kind of a phenomenon which makes an appearance. That makes *différance* sound and look a little like YHWH or the *deus absconditus*, like an occulted and hidden deep ground of being and knowing and appearance. Now while it is true that *différance* tends to provoke a certain apophatic discourse, and true too that it tends to borrow certain rhetorical devices from negative theology, such an objection (or confusion) can be more or less directly dispatched.

However negative negative theology is or intends to be, however much it wants to negate and say that God is not this and not that, even to the point of saying that God is not Being, however much it prays God to rid us of God, negative theology is still making a positive point. The negation, says Derrida, is a *dénegation*, a denial which de-negates or un-negates itself, a denial that by denying names of God affirms the unnameable God; a denial that by denial effects the rerurn of the denied.[12] This is illustrated in a classic way by Meister Eckhart, the great Dominican preacher and Rhineland mystic who inherited the tradition of neoplatonic negative theology: "When I said that God was not being and was above being, I did not thereby contest his being, but on the contrary attributed to him a *more elevated being*."[13] Thus, to deny that God is Being is by denying to affirm that God is a superessential being, a *hyperousios*,[14] a hyperbeing beyond being, being-otherwise because otherwise-than-being. The negation of God's being is at the same time a denegation. Moreover, this radically negative discourse is a promise of deferred presence and intuition, for by suspending words and concepts, by purifying itself of creatures, the soul clears away the obstacles that impede the unity of soul with God.

But *différance* is something different. For if *différance* is not a word or a concept, if *différance* is something quite unnameable, that is because it is the grammatical, semantic, and grammatological space in which names and concepts are generated, a generative matrix whose effects are words or concepts. Neither active nor passive, *différance* is not itself some sort of superessential being, but the space between or the discernible difference that separates "run" and "gun," or "*laufen*" and "*kaufen*," as opposed to their positive content. *Différance* thus enables these signifiers to function significantly; it constitutes their signifying operation. *Différance* is not (only) one of its own effects, rather "[t]his unnameable is the play which makes possible nominal effects, the relatively unitary and atomic structures that are called names,"[15] including even the textual practice which constitutes negative theology. *Différance* is not a name but the condition of possibility of names, the generating matrix of names. Of course, that is only true the first few times Derrida used it; after that, *différance* settles into Derrida's vocabulary and becomes (by use) one of his most famous names, which is why it was necessary for Derrida to move on. Neither name nor concept, neither entity nor super-entity, *différance* is rather a certain transcendental or quasi-transcendental condition of possibility (and impossibility) of speaking of entities.

But over and above this purely negative difference between deconstruction and negative theology, that one is not to be confused with the other, Derrida has taken a positive interest in negative theology as a "textual practice,"[16] in the protocol of apophatic discourse, which has its own rules and rhetoric. Derrida comes back again and again to negative theology; he does not know how to avoid speaking of it. That is because, in my view, the discourse of negative theology is paradigmatic of discourse itself as it is conceived in deconstruction. Language for Derrida is always promising but never quite making good on its promises. It is not that *die Sprache spricht*, language speaks, but rather *die Sprache verspricht*, language promises, to follow Paul de Man's paraphrase of Heidegger. Language promises to deliver the things themselves, being in itself, undistorted *Ansichsein*, pure reference without difference, perfect and unimpeded intentionality. But that is a promise it cannot keep. The thing itself, *die Sache selbst*, *la même chose*, always slips away, is always already deferred as well as referred, differred as well as referred, always delivered under the constraints of a system of differences by which it is framed and figured. Whatever we say of God is not true, the apophatic theologian teaches us, and something like that is true of everything for Derrida: whatever we say is not true, i.e., not true in some encompassing way that escapes the constraints of *différance*. That is the situation of language itself for Derrida, whether the referent is God or a perceptible object.

Or else, language promises not to say a thing, to keep quiet about the thing itself, not to say a thing, to observe perfect silence about what is absolutely unnameable—God, for example. But it is too late; negative theology has already been speaking and making promises. It has in fact cultivated an abundant, rich and complex discourse, among the most memorable and beautiful discourses the West has known. The notion of the naked Godhead, and of the desert union of the naked soul with the naked Godhead, is caught up in the chain of memorable metaphors and soaring images which flow from the pens of the great mystical poets and mystic-preachers. Such notions as these, of the silent union of the soul with God, of the wordless desert, of living "without why," of the still point of *Seelengrund* and *Gottesgrund*, of abyss united with abyss in a timeless, spaceless, motionless now: those beautiful images belong to the most soaring discourses the West has known, to the great classics of Western spiritual literature. Quite literally. These great spiritual masters, these masters of desert silence and wordlessness, do not know how to keep quiet. They do not know how to avoid speaking of the great secret about which they say—again and again—that we must all keep quiet.

That is because, for Derrida, over and above any promise that I make or even that language makes, there is the promise by which the I is promised over to language, the promise that is "older than I am," the promise that "has seized the I," which delivers me over to language, a *zoon* promised to *logos*.[17]

That promise, that archi-promise, puts Derrida at odds with those who think that ontology, the *logos* about being, is an "idolatry," a kind of paganism that turns the absolute transcendence of God, God's absolute alterity, into a graven image. That is the view of Levinas. Such a view is also shared by the great negative theologians who, like Levinas, seek a "God without Being," to use the wonderful expression of Jean-Luc Marion, a God beyond and above Being.[18] Levinas demands an absolutely altruistic approach to the absolutely other. He thinks that the Heideggerian concept of Being or of the preunderstanding of Being blocks the otherness of the other, anticipatorily diminishing the absolute alterity with which the other shocks us. Taken in its radical alterity, the other is not being or a mode of being, something immanent in the world of understanding, but an excess beyond being, a radical transcendence, a movement beyond (*au déla*), something coming from on high, over and beyond (*meta*) being (*physis*). What Levinas says of the other person (*l'autrui*), and by extension of God, Marion holds quite explicitly of God. God is without Being (*Dieu sans l'être*) because God is beyond Being, because God is love, not Being. If God is without being, and if being belongs together with thought and language, then God inhabits the desert place staked out by negative theology, the place of the *alogos*, untainted and uncompromised by word or thought. The "ontological difference" of Heidegger and the *différance* of Derrida are antecedent horizons that compromise the absolute transcendence of God and constitute for Marion a higher or "second" idolatry, higher than worshiping graven images, to be sure, or the constructs of metaphysical theology, but no less able to insinuate the idolatrous presence of traces and images into the absolute emptiness of the Godhead beyond God.

Given what he has to say about marginality, Derrida does not think that it is possible to inhabit an absolutely desert place in which neither words nor concepts grow. The argument that Derrida mounted against Levinas in "Violence and Metaphysics,"[19] that the archi-violence of language, the incisions of discourse, are unavoidable, that an absolutely inviolate alterity is a dream, applies *a fortiori* to Marion and negative theology. By taking a stand with "being," with the unavoidability of the discourse of being, Derrida lines himself up not only with Heidegger but also with Thomas Aquinas,[20] who is sharply criticized by Marion for his interpretation of the Pseudo-Dionysius.[21] For Derrida does not think we can elude the horizon of Being and language. Like Aquinas, Derrida takes the God beyond being of the Christian mystical tradition as the superessential being of the *via eminentioriae*. Commenting on the *Book of Causes*, Thomas says, "The first cause is beyond being (*supra ens*) inasmuch as he is infinite *esse* itself."[22] The first cause is not a finite *ens* but the plenitude and perfection of *esse subsistens*, which is what Eckhart called the *puritas essendi*. The horizonality of being is inescapable for Heidegger, Aquinas—and Derrida.

Derrida thinks that the secret that negative theology wants to keep, the absolutely secret namelessness of God, is de-negated, that is, unnegated and divulged, as a secret by negative theology, as the secret that negative theology harbors, indeed as the secret that defines and constitutes negative theology. Keeping a secret is an operation of *différance*. The *deus absconditus* is the secret that negative theology promises to keep, and the promise of negative theology to avoid saying a thing is what *constitutes* negative theology; it is what makes negative theology be what it is, allowing its distinctive discourse, its protocols and tropes, to take shape. Of God, negative theology promises not to say a thing. That is what negative theology *is*. But by then it is already too late. It has already taken place[23] because promising is a mode of *différance*, a discursive function, a performative speech act. For negative theology is a discourse whose object is the secret, a discourse that constitutes its object as the secret, as the nameless, dark, unutterable, unthinkable desert of the Godhead beyond God. Were negative theology to grow silent, were it to be struck dumb, were it to be silenced by the Vatican (as it sometimes is), then the secret would be lost; the secret that there is a secret would go unnoticed. It is necessary to say again and again that there is a secret. It is necessary to spread the word, to let the word go forth, that of God we cannot say a thing. This was the mission of Meister Eckhart, for example, who preached this word widely. Meister Eckhart, O.P.: Order of Preachers and of praisers and predicators, the author of the boldest and most beautiful sermons Christianity has known, and a veritable founder of the German vernacular. Do not say a thing, for whatever you say about God is not true: That is what Meister Eckhart says. But it is always too late. "Language has started without us, in us and before us. . . . Indeed, it must have been possible to speak in order to allow the question 'how to avoid speaking?' to arise."[24]

As the space in which things get said, *différance* is the space of negative theology, the space in which the fine things that Meister Eckhart says take shape. *Différance* is indeed beyond being, not because it is like the Platonic and neoplatonic *agathon* but rather because it is like Plato's *chora*, like a kind of archi-matrix or primal place in which words and things are figured and reconfigured, in which speaking and writing take place.[25]

But if Derrida emphasizes that negative theology is further testimony to the unavoidability of language, to the encompassing character of *différance*, he also emphasizes the *responsiveness* of this discourse to alterity, for this discourse is always traced by the other by which it is summoned and to whom it directs itself in a prayer. The *Confessions* of St. Augustine, the *Divine Names* of Dionysius, the sermons of Meister Eckhart, all are begun, ended, and punctuated with prayers to God who is the beginning and the end of these discourses, their cause and their content. Even though it tries to "deprive itself of meaning or of an object," apophatic discourse "takes place," and in just such a way that this very lack of an object, this very being-beyond-being is exactly what beckons it. This beckoning call is the "call of the other," which always precedes, elicits, and solicits speech. Even the most utterly negative discourse "preserves a trace of the other. A trace of an event older than it."[26] When Meister Eckhart says that God is neither this nor that, when he tries to eradicate God from speech, that eradicating, apophatic speech is a trace of what it is trying to deny. For Meister Eckhart or Dionysius, the power to speak well of God, "even if, in order to speak *rightly* or *truly*, it is necessary to avoid speaking entirely," is "a gift and an effect of God." God is both the origin and the reference of apophatic discourse, which is the trace of its absent origin: "This is what God's name always names, before or beyond other names: the trace of the singular event that will have rendered speech possible even before it turns itself back toward—in order to respond to—this first or last reference. That is why apophatic discourse must also open with a prayer that recognizes, assigns or assures its destination: the Other as Referent of a *legein* which is none other than its cause."[27] This "singular event" is always presupposed and has always already taken place. This event is "at least, the 'already there' of a phrase, the trace of a phrase,"[28] a trace that wants to be absolutely singular, which is impossible, for its singularity is effaced just in virtue of its being repeatable, coded speech. So it is a trace that effaces itself, that reduces itself to ashes, to the ashes of negative theology.

We stand always already under the call of the other, always already in the trace of the other, which in the case of negative theology is the God of whom we cannot speak. So it is only because language is always already going on in us that we are led to ask how not to speak. It is necessary for us to speak, we who stand under a "language before language," for we are always already addressed by the other, always already provoked and solicited (which means both asked and shaken), always already asked to be responsive, responding, responsible before this address. We are the beings promised and delivered over to *legein*, the ones who ask, too late, how not to speak, for whom, sometimes, not speaking is the best way, the only way, to speak well.

Negative theology de-negates: in being as utterly negative as possible it bears constant witness (*martyr*), like a good martyr, to what it negates; negative theology is an unmistakable trace of what it negates. It keeps divulging (denegating) the secret of the secret, the secret that it has a secret of which it cannot speak, a secret situated on the very margins of language and silence. But that secret marks apophatic discourse, leaving its trace, and is traced out in its discourse. Were it not for negative theology, the secret would be lost; it would disappear without a trace; there would be no witness or martyrs.

Différance is a certain archi-trace, a trace neither in the sense of a secondary effect of a transcendent cause, like tracks left in the snow, nor in the sense of the active cause of its object, like the tracings of the brush that produce the portrait. Neither active nor passive, between active and passive, in the middle voice, on the margins or threshold, *différance* is the condition in which and under which the call of the other is inscribed and encoded, recalled and recorded, formed and figured, thought and articulated, written and spoken. In virtue of *différance* language is always going on, before us and without us, enabling us both to hear and to respond, to be addressed and to address, to call and recall and be recalled. Apophatic discourse is one of the things going on in *différance*, in the de-negating mode, in the mode of bearing witness to what it denies, for it cannot say a thing. Apophatic discourse is the most important way we have found not to speak of God.

When Derrida says that this is what theology calls God, that in negative theology alterity goes under the name of God, he is saying that there is of course nothing about deconstruction that allows us to determine, affirmatively or negatively, just what it is that solicits the response of the apophatic discourse, whether it is something infinite or finite, divine or mundane. It makes no difference whether the trace is the trace of something infinite or finite, whether the other is God, as in theology, or something in the world. For what is said here applies to the trace "in general," the distinction between the finite and the infinite, the "space" or the difference between them, being itself a matter of *différance*. It is the role of deconstruction to insist that discourse is always already the discourse of the other, solicited, awakened, drawn out of itself, by the other of language; that language is the mark or the trace of the other, in the double sense, the active/passive sense, of both marking off and being marked, of tracing and being traced, by the other of language. Without the trace of the other the other disappears without a trace; without the trace of the other, alterity itself would slip out of view. But there is nothing about deconstruction that settles the debate about the referent of apophatic discourse, nothing that affirms or falsifies the claims of faith; nothing that confirms or denies the claims of physiological reductionists who see there only the marvelous promptings not of the Spirit but of certain neurotransmitters. That is the age old dispute between belief and unbelief.

Deconstruction comes equipped with a kind of armed neutrality:[29] as a certain quasi-transcendental condition of possibility and impossibility, *différance* neither includes nor excludes the positive existence of any particular entity. It simply sets forth the conditions—the archi-condition—under which existential claims are made, while raising our level of vigilance about these claims, arming us with a heightened sense of suspicion about the constructedness of our discourse, including the constructedness of the discourse that claims to transcend discourse. The result is to leave faith in fear and trembling; but then that is a very religious result, and one of the oldest conditions of faith.

THE ETHICS OF THE OTHER

Fear and trembling not only beset the faith of postmodernism but also its ethics, where the philosophy of alterity has no less interesting implications for philosophy and theology. Indeed, I would say the very point of this philosophical movement is made clear only when one looks to its ethical—and ethico-political—upshot.[30] Instead of seeking basic principles, universalizable laws, or general criteria for judgment, Derrida's attention is turned toward "singularity" and difference. The singular is not the particular that is subsumed under the universal by the operations of judgment, but the idiosyncratic, the idiomatic, the unique and unrepeatable individual or individual situation in which ethical action must be taken. The most familiar antecedent for the direction taken by Derrida is Kierkegaard, whose famous treatment of the story of Abraham in *Fear and Trembling* was focused on the unique and nonuniversalizable situation in which Abraham was caught up by the incomprehensible command he received from God. If the singularity of this situation was of the essence of the category of the "religious" for Kierkegaard, then Derrida has in fact taken up a characteristically religious (as opposed to an aestheticizing) direction. Derrida points to the time of the Kierkegaardian "moment"—a philosophical category Kierkegaard derived from the *New Testament* notion of the *kairos*—as the time of ethics, the time of undecidability in which the ethical decision must be made. Like Kierkegaard, Derrida also thematizes the fragment, the idiosyncratic singularities that cannot be assimilated without remainder into and by the "System."[31]

The difference that separates Derrida from Kierkegaard is that Derrida's interests do not turn quite so much on the existential subject that must decide in fear and trembling as on the "other," on the singularity of the other one whose claims are visited upon the subject. Thus if Derrida does not seek the universal principles that secure the "legitimacy" of "moral claims," that is because he thinks rather of the subject that is always already "laid claim to" by the "other" who, to put it in the language of Levinas, come to us from "on high."[32] He is focused not on the "autonomy" of the ethical "agent" but rather on a profound and thoroughgoing "heteronomy," which means the rule of the other, in virtue of which the other comes to the subject and makes it freedom and autonomy questionable. The rule of the other gives the rule to the philosophy of alterity; it sets its standards, gives it its bearings, but in just such a way as to lead this philosophical—or quasi-philosophical—thinking up to its limits, to the limits or margins of singularity, alterity, and heteronomy. These are the "margins of philosophy," the limit situations that philosophy has always resisted, evaded, or struggled to master. Rather than resisting them, deconstruction lets itself be defined by them, settling in to these unsettling, dark interstices where traditional philosophical reflection has felt least at home, inhabiting the margins between the universality of language and the silence of singularity.

In a recent paper, first delivered at a conference on deconstruction and law, Derrida gave his most striking and provocative formulation of the ethical—and legal and political—implication of deconstruction, by arguing that, far from being reduced to silence by the question of justice, deconstruction "is justice," that it is defined and constituted by its attachment to justice. The "law," he says, is deconstructible. That is because laws are a function of *différance*, that is, they are written, historical, contingent, positive, constructs, effects of *écriture* in the Derridian sense. Laws are sometimes just, but they are also sometimes unjust. Conforming to law sometimes means only mere legality whereas the demands of justice are often served only by opposing the law and even spending time in jail. Laws mean to be just, and justice needs good laws in order to be rendered, but there is always a gap, a structural difference, between justice and the law. For while the law is always deconstructible—and if it were not, then the law would be not only an ass but a monster and a tyrant—"[j]ustice in itself, if such a thing exists, outside or beyond law, is not deconstructible."[33]

The undeconstructibility of justice does not refer to a Kantian Idea, to a Platonic *eidos* or *agathon*, to the eternity of God or some noumenal being in itself, but to the radical singularity of the other to whom justice is owed. The singularity of the other is a structural limit toward which deconstruction is always straining, and this is almost perfectly exemplified in the ethical situation. A good law is a law without proper names, without rigged definite descriptions.[34] But justice is owed to the singularities that bear proper names. A perfect set of laws would be like a perfect map; it would end up being the same size as the region of which it is supposed to be the map. That would undo it as a map or a set of laws. A perfect set of laws is impossible,[35] not only practically but theoretically. The point of deconstruction is to inhabit the structural gap between justice and the law—or between language and the other of language—and to sensitize the law to the singularities to which the law is structurally blind, which the law excludes, omits, dismisses, disregards, forgets, silences, injures. Such singularities and alterities, which can never assume the force of the law, are what gives deconstruction its force. They drive, solicit, and appeal to deconstructive analyses to keep the law open, pliable, revisable, flexible, self-correcting, that is, to keep it oriented toward justice, which has to do with singularities.

The particular predilection that deconstruction shows for singularity, and the resistance it has to a thematics of autonomy and universality and to cultivating universalizable rationalization procedures, are, I believe, to be attributed to the fact that at a crucial point deconstruction has recourse to a Jewish rather than a Greek paradigm. In my view, deconstruction does not have a Greek but a Jewish law in mind. It does not seek a philosophical conception of justice but a more biblical justice. This is to be explained not because there is anything devout about Derrida—the point of view of his work as an author is not religious—but because the strains of biblical religion have made their way into his work by way of his considerable interest in the work of Levinas. In Levinas, we witness the strange occurrence of an almost prophetic voice raised up among the postmoderns, of a modern-day Amos crying out for justice in the muted terms of a certain phenomenology of ethical obligation, a phenomenology which is neither Husserlian nor Heideggerian, which is even in a sense not quite phenomenological. From the very start—from his earliest criticism of Husserl for treating the "other" as the transcendental analog of the ego—Levinas has been convinced that philosophy cannot absorb the shock of genuine alterity. The sights of philosophy are incorrigibly set—to use Levinas's idiom—on being and phenomenality, while the other person comes to us from beyond being and beyond appearance, as a kind of moral infinity that bursts asunder the finite horizons of philosophical categories. As the most important of the European thinkers of this century to philosophize explicitly out of an experience of the Holocaust, Levinas insists on the irreducible alterity and unencompassable infinity of the other person, from whose face issues the categorical command "thou shalt not kill." Levinas's is a philosophy of the impossibility of murder, of the other whose claim on us is unavoidable. The other, Levinas says, is emblematically "the widow, the orphan and the stranger" of *Exodus* 22:21, the one who is laid low, the helpless one who calls out for help, the outcast who abridges and lays claim to our freedom and agency, who elicits and solicits our responsibility.

Levinas's unmistakably biblical, even Yahwistic, philosophy of alterity has been a central motif and an important impulse for Derrida's deconstruction, one whose centrality we are just really beginning to appreciate. Levinas does not constitute an ad hoc addition to Derrida's repertoire, a source to which Derrida beats a hasty retreat when pressed about the ethics of deconstruction. Levinas is an essential and an original impulse of deconstruction, one of the primary sources of the experience of alterity from which the philosophy of *différance* first took its bearings.[36] Although Derrida is not a religious writer and does not, as far as I know, hold any religious views, his thought seems to me in no small part driven by a kind of biblical sensitivity, let us say a hyperbolic sensitivity or hypersensitivity, to the demands of the other, to the claims laid upon us by the different one, by the one who is left out or cast out, who lacks a voice or a hearing, a standing or stature.

This is, I think, a rather more biblical than Greek and philosophical way to think about ethics. If we try to think philosophically about the sort of "ethics" contained in the *New Testament* we find a systematic valorization of the "different," not the same; of the other, not the self; of the singular, not the universal. The interest of the *New Testament* is in the leper and the lame, the Samaritan and the prodigal son, the prostitute and the sinner. The kingdom of God is vested in what St. Paul called the *me onta* of the world (I Cor. 1:28), those who are not so much "beyond being" as beneath being, less than being, the things which are not, which lack what the world, and what philosophy which belongs to the world, calls being. The scandal of Jesus lies in the preferential option he shows for these *me onta*, for the humble, the impure, the outcast, and in his willingness to set aside the rule of law and a law of rules in order to heal on the sabbath or to sit down to dinner with the ritually impure. One can hardly imagine a more characteristic story in the *New Testament* than that of the man with the withered hand who is brought before Jesus by the Pharisees to see if Jesus would break the laws of the sabbath by healing the man's hand (Mark 3:1–6). From a deconstructive point of view, the law of the sabbath is deconstructible, but justice, which is not deconstructible, demands that the man's hand be healed. The man with the withered hand calls to us from beyond the law, from beneath the law, and calls for justice. For the law was made for the singularity, not the singularity for the law.

CONCLUSION: TOWARD A CHRISTIAN DECONSTRUCTION

If deconstruction is a philosophy of alterity, if it has nothing to do with the caricature of philosophical tricksters playing with words, then it has important bearings upon the self-understanding of Christian faith. It helps, as I have only indicated here, to cultivate a nuanced sense both of the alterity of God and of the impossibility of treating God as absolutely other; and it refocuses Christian ethics on the ethics of the other, the lame and the leper, the widow, the orphan, and the stranger. However, many other implications remain to be explored. Deconstruction can also play an important role in delimiting the institutional power that Christianity has accumulated and in sensitizing Christianity to the victims of that power, to women and the Jews, for example, to its almost structural antisemitism, antifeminism, and Eurocentrism. Deconstruction can awaken Christianity to the deeply historical and textual character of the sacred scriptures themselves and to the contingency of dogmatic formulations that have evolved in the tradition. It can give a renewed appreciation of the multiplicity of the Christian tradition, of the voices that are silenced in and by the tradition, producing thereby the illusion of "the" tradition. Christian tradition is many traditions, many forgotten and suppressed voices which need to be heard. Deconstruction can sensitize Christianity to the other of Christianity, not only to the other Christianities within Christianity which it silences, but also to the equiprimordiality of religious experiences outside of the Christian confessions.

The deconstruction of Christianity eventuates in a Christian deconstruction. That is not a destruction of Christianity but a radical pluralizing and opening up of the many Christianities that are possible. Christian deconstruction would represent not a destructive diluting of Christianity but rather the most rigorous loyalty to the oldest Christian example of all, to the One who did not hesitate to deconstruct the law of the sabbath in the name of divine justice, or to sit down to dinner with sinners and the outcast. A Christian deconstruction would not amount to a negative destruction of Christian faith and tradition but to the most radical allegiance to a certain *rabboni* who was, to the scandal of all, a teacher of alterity, who to everyone's consternation kept spreading the good news about alterity. *Usque ad mortem.*

NOTES

1. Jean-François Lyotard's more familiar characterization of it as an "incredulity toward metanarratives" is also very useful; see Jean-François Lyotard, *The Postmodern Condition*, trans. Geoffrey Bennington and Brian Massumi (Minneapolis: Minnesota University Press, 1984), xxiv, 37.

2. Jacques Derrida, "A Number of Yes," trans. Brian Holmes, *Qui Parle* 2 (1988): 120–33.

3. See Derrida's response to the uninformed attack on him by William Bennett, then chairman of the National Endowment for the Humanities, in "The Principle of Reason: The University in the Eyes of its Pupils," trans. Catherine Porter and Edward Morris, *Diacritics* 13 (1983): 3–20.

4. Jacques Derrida, *Of Grammatology*, trans. Gayatri Spivak (Baltimore: Johns Hopkins University Press, 1974), 158.

5. Richard Kearney, *Dialogue with Contemporary Continental Thinkers* (Manchester: Manchester University Press, 1984), 123–24. For a good account of reference in Derrida, see Rodolphe Gasché, *The Tain of the Mirror* (Cambridge: Harvard University Press, 1986), especially 280–82.

6. Ibid., 124.

7. By the same token, deconstruction does not claim that the speaking "subject" is an unreal fiction. As Derrida says, "To deconstruct the subject does not mean to deny its existence. There are subjects, 'operations' or 'effects' (*effets*) of subjectivity. This is an incontrovertible fact. To acknowledge this does not mean, however, that the subject is what it *says* it is. The subject is not some metalinguistic substance or identity, some pure *cogito* of self-presence; it is always inscribed in language. My work does not, therefore, destroy the subject; it simply tries to resituate it" (Kearney, 125). The "deconstruction" of the subject shows that the subject lacks the sovereignty, the autonomy, the pure spontaneity and authorial authority by which it wants to be defined. The subject is always already caught in the grips of wider systems that antedate and surround it. The time of the subject is a past that has never been present. The subject is all along antedated by and lives under the constant influence of systems that are older and deeper than it: by unconscious and preconscious forces, by systems of social and political power, by bodily forces, by the linguistic system in which we are always and already immersed. These forces at once limit the subject, delimiting the scope of its beliefs and practices, while also making it possible. Derrida's efforts are always bent toward minimizing the effects of regularizing subjectivity and maximizing the possibilities of alterity, of inventing new forms of subjectivity.

8. The proper name is a central concern of *Glas*, trans. Richard Rand and John Leavey (Lincoln: University of Nebraska, 1986).

9. Derrida, "The Principle of Reason," 19.

10. The thematics of *viens* is present throughout Derrida's writings, but see Jacques Derrida, "Of an Apocalyptic Tone Newly Adopted in Philosophy," trans. John Leavey, in *Derrida and Negative Theology*, ed. Harold Coward and Toby Foshay (Albany: State University of New York Press, 1992), 61–67.

11. Jacques Derrida, "How to Avoid Speaking: Denials," trans. Ken Frieden, in Coward and Foshay, *Derrida and Negative Theology*, 74.

12. Derrida, "How to Avoid Speaking: Denials," 95. I have developed Derrida's argument against this confusion in John D. Caputo, "Mysticism and Transgression: Derrida and Meister Eckhart," *Continental Philosophy* 2 (1989): 24–39.

13. Josef Quint, ed., *Meister Eckhart: Deutsche Predigte und Traktate* (Munich: Carl Hanser, 1965), 196; Derrida, "How to Avoid Speaking: Denials," 78. For a commentary and a fuller development of Meister Eckhart's views, see John D. Caputo, *The Mystical Element in Heidegger's Thought* (New York: Fordham University Press, 1987), chap. 3.

14. Derrida, "How to Avoid Speaking: Denials," 77.

15. Jacques Derrida, *Margins of Philosophy*, trans. Alan Bass (Chicago: University of Chicago Press, 1982), 26–27.

16. Derrida, "How to Avoid Speaking: Denials," 74.

17. Ibid., 84.

18. Ibid., 90; Jean-Luc Marion, *God without Being: Hors-texte*, trans. Thomas Carlson (Chicago: University of Chicago Press, 1991); for a commentary on Marion's book from the point of view of Derrida, see John D. Caputo, "How to Avoid Speaking of God: The Violence of Natural Theology," in *The Prospects for Natural Theology*, ed. Eugene Long (Washington, DC: Catholic University of America Press, 1992), 128–50.

19. Jacques Derrida, *Writing and Difference*, trans. Alan Bass (Chicago: University of Chicago Press, 1978), 79–153.

20. Derrida, "How to Avoid Speaking: Denials," 102.

21. Marion, *God without Being*, 73–83.

22. Thomas Aquinas, *In de causis*. I. 6, n. 175. For a commentary, see John D. Caputo, *Heidegger and Aquinas* (New York: Fordham University Press, 1982), 131.

23. Derrida, "How to Avoid Speaking: Denials," 97.

24. Ibid., 99.

25. Ibid., 103.

26. Ibid., 97. Derrida is here invoking a very Levinasian theme: that the subject is constituted by a primordial responsiveness to and responsibility for the other, who is older, higher, more excellent, and prior to the subject and the subject's freedom. By insisting that negative theology is a prayer, not just a predication, Derrida is also, like Levinas, displacing the primacy of the *what?* and taking up the privilege of the *who speaks?* See Levinas, *Otherwise Than Being or Beyond Essence*, trans. Alphonso Lingis (The Hague: Martin Nijhoff, 1984), 3–20, for a general sketch of the argument.

27. Derrida, "How to Avoid Speaking: Denials," 98.

28. Ibid.

29. See Caputo, "Mysticism and Transgression," 25–29.

30. I have explored the ethical implications of deconstruction in detail in my *Against Ethics: Contributions to a Poetics of Obligation with Constant Reference to Deconstruction* (Bloomington: Indiana University Press, 1993).

31. These are the thematics of *Glas*.

32. A great deal of what I am saying here about ethics and Derrida also applies, *mutatis mutandis*, to Lyotard.

33. Jacques Derrida, "Force of Law: The 'Mystical Foundation of Authority,'" trans. Mary Quaintance, in *Deconstruction and the Possibility of Justice*, ed. Drucilla Cornell, Michael Rosenfeld, and David Carlson (New York: Routledge, 1992), 3–67; see 14–15. For a commentary on this article, see my "Hyperbolic Justice: Deconstruction, Myth and Politics," *Research in Phenomenology* 21 (1991): 3–20.

34. John Rawls, *A Theory of Justice* (Cambridge, MA: Harvard University Press, 1971), 131.

35. Notice the pattern: a perfect law is not a law; a perfect proper name is not a name. Derrida systematically explores such limit situations.

36. In his 1968 article, "*Différance*," when discussing the historical sources of his notion of *différance*, Derrida singles out Ferdinand de Saussure, Heidegger, Nietzsche, Freud, and Levinas, who together form a network that "traverses our 'era' as the delimitation of the ontology of presence" (Derrida, *Writing and Difference*, 21).

15
The Time of Giving and Forgiving/Edifying Divertissement No. 3

The gift, one might say, is *how* things "come," how *the* impossible happens.

The gift is an event, *é-venir*, something that really happens, something we deeply desire, just because it escapes the closed circle of checks and balances, the calculus that accounts for everything, in which every equation is balanced. The circle prevents the event, blocks the incoming of the new, tethers the *tout autre* to the horizon of the same. The tighter the circle is drawn, the less there is of gift. For when a gift produces a debt of gratitude—and when does it not?—it puts the beneficiary in the debt of the benefactor, who thus, by giving, takes and so gains credit. Hence, there is no gift and what gifts there are, if there are any, turn to poison (*Gift*).

Of the pure gift we may say what we say of justice and the absolute secret: it is nowhere to be found. The gift is of a kind, of an unkind, with the secret. The gift pure and simple does not make an appearance, never presents itself in the order of presence, like a Messiah who is never going to show up. The gift, if there is any, does not give itself to be seen, even as the absolute secret is that there is no secret to be learned.

But that is why the gift impassions, like justice and the secret and the absolute future, igniting a passionate desire for the impossible. The secret and the gift are equally unphenomenalizable, equally desirable, coequally the impossible. That is why they arouse so much passion.

The aporia of the gift goes to the heart of Derrida's "religion without religion," as well as to his "hyper-ethics" (DM, 70/GD, 71) or "ultra-ethics."[1] For there can be no question of simply voiding or avoiding the circle, no question of occupying a site that is simply exterior to the circle, but only of learning, pace Heidegger, how to *leave* the circle in the right way. There is no question of wiping away narcissism without a trace, but only of degrees or economies of narcissism, so that "[w]hat is called non-narcissism is in general but the economy of a much more welcoming, hospitable narcissism, one that is open to the experience of the other as other" (PdS, 212–13/Points, 199).[2] Even the relation to the other, which affirms and welcomes and loves the *tout autre*, preserves a trace of reappropriation. To welcome the other, to be as hospitable as possible, still involves remaining master of one's house.[3] When I love the good of the other, I am doing what I love—and I will not brook interference. It is never a question of simply stepping outside the circle, but of keeping the circle as loose as possible so as to let the impossible come. Giving means giving the other some slack, with more and more hospitality. Uninterrupted narcissism, on the other hand, draws the circle of the self ever tighter, turning the gift to poison.

THE TIME OF THE GIFT

"*Commençons par l'impossible*": Let us begin by the impossible, not with the impossible, as *with* some initial object of inquiry or interrogation judged to be impossible, but *by* the impossible, jolted or shocked by it into action. Let us allow ourselves to be engaged, impassioned by the impossible, set in motion by something that shatters the assured horizons of possibility and jars us off dead center.

To that end, we must ask: What is the time of giving, the time that befits the gift? How does it relate to what we called "messianic time"? Certain times are gift times; on birthdays and Christmas, for example, "presents" are "exchanged," mutually presented, among circles of friends, on the spot, right away. If you exchange presents on birthdays with someone, with people in certain circles, and it is the other's birthday, then you are willing to wait for your birthday to roll around, for the year is a circle or a cycle and your time will come, and so will your present. Whether immediately or with a little deferral, presents move in a circle of time, forming a circulation, a circular economy of exchange, like the *kula* described by Marcel Mauss in which gifts make their way around a circle of islands. Indeed, the subtitle of Mauss's *The Gift*, which gets this whole discussion going in French letters, into which Derrida too is now putting his two cents, is *The Form and Reason for Exchange in Archaic Societies*.[4] Presents always come home, right away or after some time, like Ulysses, circling back economically to the *oikos*, as opposed to father Abraham who left the land of his fathers, never to return again.

But would not the gift, if there is any (*le don, s'il y en a*), be something that breaks this circle of time and interrupts this schedule of departing and arriving presents? Would it not defy the symmetry of reciprocity or return so that it would be in the end an-economic (*DT*, 18/*GT*, 7)?[5] "It is perhaps in this sense that the gift is the impossible. Not impossible but *the* impossible. The very figure of the impossible" (*DT*, 19/*GT*, 7). But how can we escape this circle? Why would we even want to? Who wants to give up Christmas or birthday presents? (Is Derrida the Grinch?) Does not Heidegger say that the issue is not to escape the circle but to learn how to enter it in the right way? But who are we to believe, in whom are we to put our trust, Abraham or Heidegger? Is it a question of choosing between these two patriarchs?

If time is a circle, if it always has been a circle from time immemorial, from Aristotle to. Hegel, Husserl, and Heidegger, then the gift, if there is any, must belong to an eccentric time, an exorbitant, aneconomic moment in which the circle is torn up. It would take place in a moment of madness, like a paradoxical *Augenblick* in which Abraham, for example, visited by the law of the *tout autre*, tore time up. When Abraham raised the dagger and resolved to plunge ahead, to give (death) without return, without knowing where this mad leap would land him in the next moment, then, in that very moment when the angel stayed his dagger from Isaac's breast, Abraham severed the circle of time and left it gaping open: "There would be a gift only at the instant when the *paradoxical* instant (in the sense in which Kierkegaard says of the paradoxical instant of decision that it is madness) tears time apart. In this sense one would never have the time of a gift. In any case, time, the 'present' (*présent*) of the gift, is no longer thinkable as a now, that is, as a present bound up in the temporal synthesis" (*DT*, 2/*GT*, 9). A gift does not belong to the circle of presents (*présents*) or among the presents exchanged within certain circles of friends. You can never get a *gift* (*don*) on your birthday or Christmas. Presents (*cadeaux, présents*) are exchanged within certain circles of friends (and of time), within the horizon of now-time, the time of the present, the rounded circle of the give and take of time. The *cadeau* is a little link, from *catena*, which enchains you. But the gift (*don*), if there is one, eventuates in the excess of the moment, the *Augenblick* and, breaking loose from the closed circle of friends, heads out for the *tout autre*.

Over and beyond the circulation of presents, of the time of the present, the horizon of the presentable and representable, Derrida dreams and desires, prays and weeps over the unrepresentable gift, if there is any. To "think"—in a sense a little like Kant and a little like Heidegger—the gift is, accordingly, to direct oneself at something disproportionate, at the disproportion of the impossible, while leaving the possible—the proportionate, properly graspable objects—to other determinate operations, like perception, science, or intuition. That is a distinction that parallels, up to a point, Heidegger's distinction between thinking and philosophy (grasping), and Kant's distinction between thinking and conceiving (determining).

What then is the gift, the thought of the gift, of "this impossible thing, this impossible itself" (*DT*, 22/*GT*, 10)? An avowed antiessentialist to the end, Derrida maintains that the "essence" of the gift is that it not answer to its own essence, that it must not be what it ought to be (*DT*, 94nl/*GT*, 69n23). For a gift, "according to our common language and logic," means that someone "intends-to-give" (*vouloir donner*, as in *vouloir dire*) (*DT*, 43/*GT*, 27) something to someone, that A intends to give B to C (*DT*, 23/*GT*, 11), an idea that trades in the coin of intentional consciousness and self-identical elements. As soon as there is an identifiable donor and an identifiable donee, as soon as there are intentional, conscious subjects who know what they are doing, and an identifiable object/gift, as soon as there is an identifiable transaction between subjects about an object, then the "gift-event" (*événement, il y a*) which has just taken place is annulled and presents have been exchanged instead.

The conditions that make the gift possible simultaneously make it impossible. For in the act in which A gives B to C, C comes to be indebted to A, if only by gratitude, which means that C has not been given something but has been put in debt. A, on the other hand, has not given anything away, but has been taking under the guise of giving, having acquired credit, whether material or symbolic, even if only silently in A's own mind, just in case A chose to remain an anonymous donor. "For there to be a gift, there must be no reciprocity, return, exchange, countergift, or debt" (*DT*, 24/*GT*, 12), no chain of creditors and debtors. Otherwise the gift is undone in the very giving, which can be seen most easily in the extreme case that C would immediately return B to A, on the spot, just give it back. The more tactful thing is to defer the return until a later time and even then to return not the same thing but something different of a comparable price or value.

The impossible gift then is one in which no one acquires credit and no one contracts a debt. That in turn requires that neither the donor nor the donee would be able to perceive or recognize the gift as a gift, that the gift not appear as a gift. The gift must "happen" below the plane of phenomenality, too low for the radar of conscious intentionality (*DT*, 25–26/*GT*, 13). The mere consciousness of giving sends the gift hurtling back to the donor, "sends itself back to the gratifying image of goodness or generosity, of the giving-being who, knowing itself to be such, recognized itself in a circular, specular fashion, in a sort of auto-recognition, self-approval, and narcissistic gratitude" (*DT*, 38/*GT*, 23).

Nothing is gained by having recourse to the unconscious, since a subject can certainly contract a debt unconsciously, unconsciously feel and be indebted. As a deep stratum within consciousness, a layer thicker and darker than the flow of conscious time, the unconscious is still a structure of the subject. Indeed, in the unconscious the roots of subjective debt and credit are sunk even deeper. Because what is repressed is still kept in memory, if only in a more secret place, "unconscious repression" is by no means the "absolute forgetting" required by a "pure" gift, by no means the absolving, forgetting, forgiving that does not leave a trace behind, or which leaves only a trace, an ash, a cinder, which is the "destruction of memory" (*DT*, 28–30/*GT*, 15–17; PdS, 221–23/*Points*,

208–209), which burns the trace of gift-giving behind it and makes a holocaust of its holocaust (*Glas*, 270–71/243).[6]

ES GIBT

That is why Derrida's search for an absolutely presubjective stratum of giving leads him to Heidegger, to the *es gibt* of the 1962 lecture "Time and Being" (*TB*), the "gift" (*Gabe*) of time and Being by the It, which gives. There he finds a *Vergessenheit* that is structurally deeper than any conscious or unconscious forgetting.[7] What is given in the *es gibt* is no thing, but Being, which is not an entity but a mark of entities, and time, which is nothing temporal but a mark of temporal things. Here, too, what gives is "forgotten" not by slipping the mind of someone's *psyche*, but by a structural withdrawal from the phenomenal field, withdrawing in and through the giving, and this withdrawal is the very condition of the appearance of beings in their Being. What Heidegger's remarkable, formidably difficult lecture addresses is the givenness of things, the sheer happening of things, in virtue of which things happen as they happen, and that is all, "without why." "Only the 'that'—that the history of Being is in such a way—can be said" (*SD*, 56/*TB*, 52). Only the "because" (*weil*) endures. Things happen because and for the while (*dieweil*) that they happen and then sink away into the concealment from which they emerge, fleeting, fragile triumphs over all-consuming *lethe*. Of entities, we may say that they "are" and of Being, that "there is/it gives" (*es gibt*) Being. But of the giving or the granting of Being, of the "event" (*Ereignis*) which gives, "[w]hat remains to be said? Only this: the event events (*das Ereignis ereignet*)" (*SD*, 24/*TB*, 24). The event happens, and it happens because it happens.

But then what about this "It"? The mistake would be, Heidegger warns, following the admonition of Nietzsche about the seductiveness of grammar, to hypostasize or reify the *Es* (the avoidance of which is not promoted by Heidegger's decision to capitalize "It" and to speak of "*das Es*"). For *das Es* is not some entity, nor the Being of entities, no more than there is a separable subject doing something when we say, in Latin, *pluit* ("it's raining"). By "*das Es*" we mean nothing more than the very event or happening of entities, the epochal process of the granting and withdrawal of presence, the corning to presence and passing out of presence of entities, which is the "sending" (*schicken*) of the epochs and the "reaching over" (*reichen*) of the dimensionalities of time. We can bring the "It" in "It gives" into view only by thinking "It" in terms of the "giving" (SD, 19–20/TB, 19), the extending of time and the sending of the epochs, allowing the "It" to sink back into giving, to collapse into giving, the way the "it" that "rains" sinks into the rain that falls.

So then we are faced with something faceless, an "anonymous" process, a "sheer" eventiveness, hollow and heartless, without depth or "distance," in which there is no doer separable from the deed, no "one"—but "It"—"doing" anything. Instead, things are happening because they are happening and for the while that they are happening; it plays because it plays, without why. But that is not without a danger of its own and Heidegger is not about to leave things happening so starkly: "There is a growing danger that when we speak of 'It,' we arbitrarily posit an indeterminate power which is supposed to bring about all giving of Being and time. However, we shall escape indeterminacy and avoid arbitrariness as long as we hold fast to the determinations of giving which we attempted to show" (*SD*, 17/*TB*, 16–17). We escape the danger of a faceless, indeterminate anonymity as long as we think in harmony with the tune of giving, of a certain beneficence, which gives Being and time (rather like a eulogy that says that so and so was "given" to us, without saying by whom). It is at this point that Heidegger strikes up the tune of propriety, of the "*eigen*" in *Er-eignis*, which keeps a kindly eye over what is given.

The "It" sends Being into its "own" (*eigen*), and extends time into its own, and, owning Being and time to each other, owns both to "humans," to whom both are given, and so brings humans into their own, in a multiply appropriate act of appropriation. The arbitrary, indeterminate anonymity of *es gibt* is expunged by the generosity of a process that gives things their *Wesen*, truth, and ownness.

That is what Derrida flags (*DT*, 36/*GT*, 21–22), for the thematics of propriety, the "desire of the proper"—as opposed to desiring, dreaming, of the *tout autre*—is a thematics of identity, which draws the withdrawal of the "It" away from the ominous indeterminacy that Heidegger sought to avoid, but in so doing draws it back into the circle of a proper or identifiable Giver which gives us a proper or identifiable Gift. That is why Derrida says: "It is in this direction that we would have a few reservations to indicate regarding the most essential Heideggerian motifs, whether it is a matter there of determining what is originarily proper to Being, time, the gift, or of acceding to the most 'originary' gift" (*DT* 205/*GT*, 162). These Heideggerian motifs serve to reactivate the circle of credit and debt, and puts "us"—first "us Germans," and then, after the war, "us Westerners" (which is only slightly better, but we should be thankful even for little things, little gifts)—all back in the debt of father Parmenides and other Greek fathers and creditors, of the entire line of a distinctly Heideggerian *patrologia graeca* upon whom Abbé Migne never made a profit. For back there in *Greichenland*, which is the true spiritual *Heimat* and *Vaterland* of the *Abendland*, Being was spoken in its proper tongue (Greek), nestled and nurtured in the native land of Being and thinking, given a good and proper name, a holy and a hale name, *aletheia*, at the sound of which every Greco-German knee is obliged to bend, at the mention of which Greco-Germans everywhere should fall on one another's breasts, sighing and heaving for the first beginning, back in the homeland of Being and thought. The effect of Heidegger's "history of Being," which traces everything back to the Greek opening, is massively to indebt us all, to put us all back in the debt of the Great Fathers who spoke Greek, sending us back on a pilgrimage to the old country of Being, seated at the feet of Greek temples with the pages of "The Origin of the Work of Art" spread out like Sacred Scripture before us. Then, in that blessed time, the Proper Event gives Proper Gifts and so appropriates us to what is Proper to us, drawing us back into a Proper Debt to the Proper Father of us all, to Proper Greeks and their Proper sons and heirs, which is rather a "calculating" way to deal with what is *grundlos* and *sine ratione.* Against all that Derrida invokes the motif of the "superabundant" "from Nietzsche to Bataille" (*DT*, 205 I *GT*, 162).

Thinking now means thankfully-thinking-back on (Greek) Being, bound over in memorializing thinking-thanking (*denkendes Danken*, or *dankendes Denken*), which thinks on (*an-denken*) and never forgets that to which thinking is bound in endless debt. On Being, which is a Greek Gift, on Greece, which is Being's Gift. Watch out for Greeks bearing gifts! *Das Ereignis ereignet. Die Gift vergiftet.*[8]

All of which would be "wildly funny," as Derrida says, were it not so "horribly dangerous" (DLE, 109/OS, 68).[9] For such gratitude is exceedingly ungrateful to and unthoughtful about whatever is not Greek or Greco-German, whatever is Hebrew or Christian, Latin or Romance, which are disdainfully brushed off as "derivatives" or "fallings," not to mention whatever is African or Third World.[10] So if there is a danger in the indeterminate, ominous, anonymous "it" in the *es gibt*, the danger of all this propriety, all these proper tongues and proper homelands, is greater still.

By taking the turn toward propriety, by identifying the it (*Es*) as propriety's own happening (*Ereignis*), Heidegger turns out to be a part of "the great transcendentalist tradition" (*DT*, 74/*GT*, 53), which would station a hermeneutic guard around the disseminative excess of *es gibt*. For otherwise, without the monitoring properties of propriety, *es gibt* would just give because it gives, in a certain "dissemination without return" (*DT*, 130/*GT*, 100). Of itself, *es gibt* is a little wild, a little excessive and overflowing, a bit out of order, out of control, out of joint, an excessive *Un-fug* for which

Heidegger is not prepared and which seems dangerous to him, threatening to let everything go up in smoke (or turn to ash), its fumes dissipating into the air, leaving traces here, there, and everywhere (cf. *DT*, 129–32/*GT*, 99–101).

To guard against *this* "danger," in which Heidegger finds nothing saving, Heidegger inscribes the gift of Being in something Originary, which puts him in the transcendental tradition of inscribing things in "the originary given of a gift which comes down to and comes back to Nature, Being, God, the Father—or the Mother—as well as in the phallus in general (transcendental signifier sealing a symbolic order that guards the gift against its dissemination, which is perhaps to say, against itself)" (*DT*, 74–75/*GT*, 53). *Ereignis* too then operates as a kind of seal that holds dissemination in check, sealing the leaks in *es gibt*, not unlike Levinas's seal, which seals the cracks in ethics. *Ereignis* is likewise made to function in a way analogous to the Good in the Republic, which is a Father that engenders children from a place beyond Being, the proper father of legitimate children.

If Heidegger's *es gibt* serves Derrida's purposes as a subjectless process, a wholly nonpsychological event, prior even to the unconscious, it does not escape deep *identitarian* tendencies that want to own the giving process, to hold it in check, under the sway of the rule of the proper and the proprietary, of the originary granting of the Origin of all of us, all of "us" (Germans, Europeans, Euro-Americans, Westerners, NATO types). However grateful Derrida may be to Heidegger for the *es gibt*, he is driven to look in a different direction for the "gift," if there is one.

NO THANKS TO *DIFFÉRANCE*

That is why Derrida said in *Khôra* that it is risky business to see in *il y a là khôra* "the equivalent of an *es gibt*, of the *es gibt* which remains without a doubt implicated in every negative theology, unless it is the *es gibt* which always summons negative theology in its Christian history" (*Khôra*, 30/ON, 96).[11] The way around this risk is to stick with *il y a*, or *khôra*, or *différance*, since *khôra* is the interval or spacing of *différance*, and *différance* demands no thanks.

Différance is a subjectless process, an anonymous field in which "effects" are produced below the level of conscious subjects, and below the unconscious as well, in which events happen below the level on which conscious subjects intend to do anything. Hence *différance* resists the lure of propriety, the dream of the Proper and the Originary, the prestige of the Father of us all, of Greek fathers and creditors, the lure of the Good. For the Good too is a father, of life and knowledge, beyond *ousia* because it is the progenitor of all *ousia*, whereas *différance*, in an almost perfect anti-Platonism, is something like a *khôra*, a more maternal simulacrum, a non-originary origin (cf. *DT*, 204–5/*GT*, 161).

Différance is an anonymous, quasi-transcendental, pre-subjective field in which effects are produced without control. Events happen in *différance* not *from* (*par*) a spirit of generosity, but *with* generosity (*DT*, 205/*GT*, 162), that is to say, with a profusion and abundance that is the issue not of a subject's generosity but of a certain disseminative excess. Events happen with a kind of aleatory gratuitousness and anarchic abandon that lets something different come, with a grace or graciousness that unbinds events, which lets them loose, lets them eventuate. Events happen in *différance*, no thanks to *différance*. We should not think, Derrida writes, that *écriture* is a generous fellow, a giving subject, because it is not a subject at all. Indeed, "[w]e will venture to say that this is the very definition of the *subject as such*." The "very idea" of a subject is, as something conscious, that which *never* does anything, never gives anything "without calculating, consciously or unconsciously, its reappropriation, its exchange, or its circular return—and by definition this means reappropriation with surplus-value, a certain capitalization" (*DT*, 131–32/*GT*, 101). A subject is a capital fellow, a capitalist and an old boy, bent on making a profit.

One could say of this quasi-transcendental, *pre*-subjective something-I-know-not-what, something like what the medieval masters said of the transcendental bonum, that it is disseminativum sui, that it disseminates itself, not diffusing itself, however, like the God of Christian Platonism with boundless generosity, but in the middle voice, profusely, without the police of propriety to keep it in check. When the Neoplatonists said that the bonum is diffusivum sui they had in mind a more orderly, circular process, of exitus and reditus, of going out and coming back, a veritable hyperousiological kula, a good exchange of credit and debit (a reditus is also income, "revenue"), a very perfect circle in which everything is returned to its proper place, without loss. Dissemination, on the other hand, is almost the perfect opposite of that kind of giving, profuse and non-returning, although nothing is perfect.

Indeed, when one looks for a classical correlate to this sort of non-generous dissemination, Derrida points us in the direction, as we have insisted, not of the *agathon* which is *epekeina tes ousias*, but of *khôra*. If the *khôra* gives place this "does not come to the same thing as to make a present of a place." *Il y a khôra*, but she/it does not generously "give" anything and this "does not refer to the gesture of a donor subject" (*Khôra*, 37–38/ON, 100). Rather she/it is the spacing within which an unlimited number of events take place, in her/its place.

In dissemination, events come, and there is a powerful "donative eventiveness" (*événementialité donatrice*), but without the benefit or the encumbrances of anybody's good intentions, no thanks to anybody. A gift is an event (*DT*, 152–53/*GT*, 119–20), not an intentional act but something that happens, and always as a bit of a surprise, a fortuitousness, a fortunate break, something aleatory, beyond the horizon of anticipation, something irruptive, tearing up time, an instant (*Augenblick*), the effect of nothing foreseen (*DT*, 156–57/*GT*, 122–23), an unforeseeable sequence, neither the deep longing of the *Seinsgeschick* heaving and sighing toward its long-concealed eschatological issue (*Austrag*), nor the tidy circle of Neoplatonic *exitus* and *reditus*.

But *différance* could care less. *Différance* gives, no thanks to *différance*. *Différance* gives without being generous, the way *khôra* gives, which is the "interval or the spacing" of *différance*, a strange mother who gives without engendering (*Khôra*, 92/ON, 124–25). So do not start falling all over *différance* with gratitude. *Différance* does not love you or even know you are there. *Différance* gives, but *différance* could not care less.

(When you pray, do not say thanks.)

BY THE IMPOSSIBLE

But what about the subject, since there are subjects, indeed subjects are given all over the globe, the very idea of the subject being that the subject never gives without expecting a return? *Différance* opens the space—and keeps it open—within which the self-seeking subject moves about. But how can the subject make a move? That brings us back to the beginning that Derrida deferred (*DT*, 19/*GT*, 7), to beginning *par l'impossible*: "For finally, if the gift is another name of the impossible, we still think it, we name it, we desire it. We intend it. And this *even if* or *because* or *to the extent that* we *never* encounter it, we never know it, we never verify it, we never experience it in its present existence or its phenomenon" (*DT*, 45/*GT*, 29). As something we never come upon, the gift pure and simple—*le don lui-même, le don en soi*, which never presents itself in the order of presence—drives us on, drives us mad, like the secret, which engenders endless interpretations. The gift belongs to a thought beyond knowledge, a desire beyond mere wishes, a naming beyond ordinary nomination. Indeed, there are names and thoughts and desires *only* to the extent that we name and think and desire the gift, *the* impossible. There is passion only to the extent that we are impassioned by the impossible. Anything else, anything less, would be too parochial and presentable, too pedestrian and too possible, to be worthy of "thinking" or "desire" or "passion." Anything less would remain within the horizon of the same, as inventions of the same, as merely new moves within old games. So, "[o]ne can desire, name, think, in the proper sense of these words, if there is one, *only*" to the extent that we seek, we desire, we name the gift, which is the measure without measure, *modum sine modo*, which is *the* impossible, which is not and cannot be present (*DT*, 45–46/*GT*, 29).

Deconstruction inhabits the distance between *le présent* and *le don*: between the empirical objects of determinate concepts and wishes, the empirical passions and particular *présents*, which remain within the subject's circle of the same, and the gift, *le don*, which never presents itself. But does that mean, when one desires the gift, that one is grasping at a specter or a ghost? Does one succumb to a "transcendental illusion," in which a concept (which determines something *présent*) loses its empirical traction and is allowed to spin freely on its own in the empty air of ideality (*l'aire de temps de don*)? Would not everything in deconstruction then go up in smoke or turn to ash? The secret, the gift, justice, the democracy to come, *à-venir*—would they not all become a transcendental illusion? Almost, sort of (*sorte de*). There would indeed be a certain "analogy" to a transcendental illusion, and the analogy might help us out, since there is in deconstruction something analogous to Kant's transcendental desire and thought. There would be a certain *quasi*-transcendental illusion, which would not simply reproduce a Kantian illusion (DT, 46/GT, 29–30). For after all, we do not make the mistake of thinking *the* impossible is real, nor do we make the Kantian move of treating it as a foreseeable regulative ideal. The gift of which deconstruction dreams and by which it is impassioned will not be the object of a simple Kantian faith in a nonempirical ideal which exceeds the limits of experience and science, no future-present which establishes an ideal horizon of expectation that we simply seek after.

Accordingly, the gift implies a double risk, of illusion and of hypocrisy: on the one end, the risk of entertaining a transcendental illusion; on the other end, the risk of "entering the destructive circle," of getting ground up in the wheels of giving-in-order-to-get-back, the hypocrisy of taking under the guise of giving. The way to negotiate this double risk is with the delicacy of a double gesture. Everything comes down to seeing that the gift is a *quasi*-transcendental, slightly messianic engagement (*gage*) that both plays the economic game and outplays it: "On the contrary, it is a matter—desire beyond desire—of responding faithfully but also as rigorously as possible both to the injunction or the order of the gift ("give" [*donne*]) as well as to the injunction or order of meaning (presence, science, knowledge): *Know* still what giving *wants to say, know how to give*, know what you want and want to say when you give, know what you intend to give, know how the gift annuls itself, commit yourself [*engage-toi*] even if commitment is the destruction of the gift by the gift, give economy its chance" (*DT*, 46–47/*GT*, 30). Derrida enjoins a double injunctive, both to move within the grooves of the existing circles of knowledge and economy and also to outmaneuver them, both to give beyond economy and to give economy its chance. There are always circles of exchange, contractual ties and duties, marriage contracts and financial contracts; the law we will always have with us. The idea is not utterly to demolish them—we are all for the law and knowledge—but to interrupt them, to loosen them long enough to let something new happen, to let the gift be given. *Le désir au-delà du désir*, the desire for the *don* beyond the commerce and transactions of daily life, both is and is not outside every economy and circle of exchange. It is impossible, in the straightforward sense of the simple modal opposite of the possible, to do without subjects of knowledge and action who retain a certain measure of self-interest, who know what they are doing and do what they know. Where would we be, you and I and Jacques, if that were not true? Still, give, *donne* (*la donna bella*), give beautiful gifts, give without reserve. The way Abraham gives. Now, as we shall see, we do not know what is going on in secret, in Abraham's heart. (Nor does he.) How would we ever be able to get back past Genesis to find that out? Even if, *per impossibile*, we were able to invite Abraham himself to give a seminar at the College International—perhaps with an eye to giving him tenure and a reduced teaching load, as Johannes Climacus quipped about the god[12]—how would Abraham himself know why he gave his *me voici* to this unknowable voice? God says "*donne*" and that is what he meant to do.

In order to give, we need to know everything that undermines giving and draws it back into the circle of exchange, but still be engaged in and by giving. We need to appreciate what is going on with gifts, but still give. We plunge ahead, knowing full well that knowing and wanting work constantly to undermine and annul the gift, the idea being that, if we know the trap that giving sets, at least we will not walk into it straightaway: "For finally, the overrunning of the circle by the gift, if there is any, does not lead to a simple exteriority that would be transcendent and without relation. It is this exteriority that sets the circle going, it is this exteriority that puts the economy in motion. It is this exteriority that *engages* in the circle and makes it turn" (*DT*, 47/*GT*, 30). The dream and the desire for the gift, the passion that the gift impassions, are the passion and the desire to exceed the circle *even while not remaining entirely outside the circle.* That is what Derrida means by the *mover* of the circle, by the impossible impulse that engages the circle and sets it in motion, so that it will not be a perfect circle but just a little skewed and will not stay on dead center. That is why he speaks of beginning, getting underway, by the impossible, being impassioned by the impossible. We know in the instant in which the gift tears up the circle, in the instant of madness that ruptures the circle of time, at the same time, in that same instant, alas, the gift is inevitably drawn back into the circle. That is because the very idea of the conscious subject is to be a *vouloir* and not a pure *désir* or a pure *passion*; the subject is a wanting to give, to say, to have for oneself, a *Sorge* and a *conatus essendi*, an economic being. *There is no simply stepping outside that.*

But it is no less true that the aneconomic gift keeps the circle turning, so that *the circle depends upon the very thing it excludes, the gift.* The circle needs the gift no less than the gift cannot avoid the circle. For Derrida's point is not to find a spot of simple exteriority to the circle, but to loosen the circle and to create an opening for the *tout autre.* The point is not to escape the circle nor even to enter it in the right way but, to turn Heidegger on his head, to know how to breach it in the right way. That is why Derrida says that there are many narcissisms, various degrees of narcissism, the best of which are hospitable and welcome the other. There is always a movement of narcissism in any gift and, indeed, "without a movement of narcissistic reappropriation, the relation to the other would be absolutely destroyed." Even love, the affirmation of the other, would be impossible without the trace of narcissism (PdS, 212–13/*Points*, 199).[13] When I love the good of the other, that is the good I love. In the most hospitable, open-ended narcissism, the good I seek for my self is the good of the other. If you don't believe that, try getting in the way of someone who is intent on doing good for the other. They will chew you up if you try to stop them from getting what they want—which is to give to the other. That is what they want, and don't try to take it away from them.

"Beginning by (*par*) the impossible" means that the circle turns on a gift even as the gift is turned into a circle. When workers decide that they are just going to "work the contract," that means they are angry and they will do only what they are obliged to do. That means that not a lot is going to get done and the circle is not going to move very much at all. A pure contract will stop dead in its tracks. To do the work well requires "more" of us than is spelled out in the contract; the contract requires a little supplement by the gift. Doing the work well requires a gift, but without contractually obliging it. The work must be done with passion and love, beyond duty. The circle turns on a gift. The gift works, not like a regulative ideal, but like a kind of efficient cause that sets a circle in motion, gets it going and keeps it open, makes something happen, a little like a Kantian noumenal freedom.

The circle cannot turn without the gift, and the gift has nothing to exceed without the circle. The gift will be inevitably drawn back into the circle, but the circle will not spin without gifts. Pure gifts without circles are empty; pure circles without gifts are blind. It is not a question of one or the other, of the gift pure and simple, if there were one, or of pure economy, if there were one, but of inhabiting the distance between the two with as much grace and ambiance and hospitality as possible.

LITERARY GIFTS

Up to now we have ignored the inscription of *Given Time* within the texts of Marcel Mauss, Claude Levi-Strauss, and Charles Baudelaire. To Mauss's *The Gift*, the text first published in 1950 that has provided the context for a steady stream of French discourses on the gift ever since,[14] Derrida pays the gratitude of ingratitude. He upbraids Mauss for speaking always of the circle (*kula*) of exchange in archaic societies, that is, for speaking of everything *except* the gift, and, then, forgives him. For Mauss never really meant to say (*vouloir dire*) anything else to begin with, and there is no fault in that (*DT*, 145–46n1/*GT*,113n4). In the end, Mauss wanted to put us all in the debt of this archaic, eternal, natural, bedrock morality, that kinder, gentler Rousseauistic world of reciprocal giving (*DT*, 88–89/*GT*, 65), as opposed to the crassness and artifactuality of modern commercial transactions, even to one of the spirits of a certain Marx (*DT*, 61–66/*GT*, 42–45).[15]

So Mauss's title *The Gift* is a counterfeit, which provides Derrida with the transition to Baudelaire's story "Counterfeit Money" (*La fausse monaie*), within whose context Derrida inserts his most important commentary. In this story, the narrator's friend gives a two-franc silver piece to a beggar, eliciting first surprise from the narrator and then, upon hearing the friend's confession that it was a counterfeit, a series of speculations on the narrator's part as to the friend's intentions and the consequences of the deed, culminating finally in a condemnation of the stupidity of a man who could think to win heaven economically. Derrida, who is exploring the link between "money" and "literature," proceeds by way of nibbling at the margins of the text, first at its title and then at its dedication.

Because "Counterfeit Money" is fiction about a fiction; its title is an autonym that proclaims, "I am a counterfeit." Of course, it does not say this outright, partly because it does not want to discredit itself from the start, and partly because it has no "I," no *cogito*, with which to tell the truth or to lie (*DT*, 127–28/*GT*, 98). The story is a fiction about a counterfeit coin, about a fictive thing, a sign, a simulacrum, but a false sign, or rather a true sign with a false value (*DT*, 121/*GT*, 93). It is thus a story about story-telling, about all stories. A "real" author invents a "fictional" narrator who tells a "true" story about "false" money. Literature is (like) a counterfeit, a fiction we "credit" with being true, that we "believe" in the sense of suspending disbelief. The difference is that the reader's trust is not being abused; the reader is not being duped or deceived by literature, whereas a "true" counterfeit's success depends upon deception.

But suppose the friend were being deceptive about his deception and in fact gave the beggar a real coin while passing it off to the narrator, for whatever reason, as a counterfeit, so that he was only making a simulacrum of a confession to the narrator? What, then, Derrida asks? (*DT*, 125/*GT*, 96). In a sense, Derrida will devote the rest of the text of *Donner le temps* to this question.

We must be wary of a trap at this point. For a text is not a solid piece of *ousia*, like a piece of personal property, a *datum* lying before our eyes, around which an awake and conscientious Husserlian could, with steady pace, take in its perspectival perceptual variations, slowly accumulating more and more presumptive force for the intuition of this given. A text is but a misty, ephemeral, spectral thing, an event (*événement*) with a kind of merely mystical force that seems to sustain it above an abyss. That is to say, a text is a matter of faith, of credit, and of the credence we give to traces and to the conventions that surround, sustain, and constitute them, that keep their play in play, which thereby links economics, religion, and literature, all of which are kept from dissipating into thin air by some sort of religio-mystical force, like Marx's magical, mystical table (*DT*, 126/*GT*, 97). If you believe in economics or literature—and who does not?—you believe in ghosts. If with your right hand you denounce religious superstition, you had better find a way not to let it know that with your left hand you participate in literary and economic practices.

That leads Derrida into the question of the dedication, of the one(s) to whom the text is given. A text is given, not like a datum for a *gebende Anschauung*, but given to be read by a reader. For while Baudelaire dedicated "Counterfeit Coin" to Arsène Housaye, it is also true that "from the moment he let it constitute itself in a system of traces, he destined it, gave it . . . above and beyond any determined addressee, donee, or legatee" (*DT*, 130/*GT*, 100), he let it be handed over to a long and endless line of readers over whom he could exercise no control or maintain no authorial authority. He delivered it up to a "dissemination without return" and he cannot have it back. The structure of the trace overflows the phantasm of return which goes to the heart of a "gift." "That is why there is a problematic of the gift only on the basis of a consistent problematic of the trace and the text." The text or trace is just the sort of thing, or non-thing, the sort of ghostly apparatus, in which things are happening, events are given, beneath or beyond the control of intentional consciousness. Texts give, but no thanks to *différance*. Texts give, but not like generous, giving subjects with whose narcissism we all have to cope, who are always calculating a return, if only unconsciously: "[T] here where there is trace and dissemination, if only there is any, a gift can take place, along with the excessive forgetting or the forgetful excess that, as we insisted earlier, is radically implicated in the gift" (*DT*, 132/*GT*, 101–2). Texts forget their authors much more deeply than subjects forget those whom they should remember, more deeply than the neurotic has forgotten his desire for his mommy.

So the gift depends upon the death of the donor, who leaves us something in her will, over and beyond and even against her will. For no matter how rigorously an author writes her will, we can always break it, her fatal mistake being that she left it in writing (instead of living on forever), and writing can always be read otherwise. Whatever the *vouloir dire* or *vouloir donner* of their authors, texts are a little legacy, a perpetual gift that keeps on giving and (quasi-)living, long after the death of their authors, even if the latter are, biologically speaking, alive and well, in the next room autographing copies of their books. This is not to say that only the dead can give but rather that giving is a matter of life and death, life I death, *survivance*, neither pure death nor immortal life. Literary gifts require a living author who by committing herself to words and texts agrees to death, agrees to deal herself death, *donner la mort*, to give a gift without return and let her text go up in smoke, or turn to ash, that is to say, to disseminate without return, however fit she may feel when she signs her contract and checks the royalty clause.

BEGGARS AND THE DUTY TO GIVE

The mute subject in Baudelaire's story who never gets to say a thing is the beggar. Beggars are of course the most jewgreek, biblical, Levinasian figures of all, figures of paradigmatic disfigurement, figures of flesh laid low that come to us from on high,[16] the most literal marginalia, scandals to Fukuyama and the new world order, the last stand of Marxists and post-Marxists everywhere, if there are any.

Derrida is talking about chance, about how the narrator and his friend, having turned down a particular street, chance upon the beggar, but not entirely by chance, since nothing ever is "absolutely aleatory." When one turns one's step down a certain street, one well knows just how likely it is that we will chance upon a beggar. We always know where to head if we do not want a visitor to our city to see our beggars. You can almost calculate it, like the narrator's friend, who seemed, paradoxically, to be calculating a *kairos* in which he could pull off his ruse, having also very carefully distributed the coins in different pockets so that he could seem spontaneously to reach into his pocket and give the beggar whatever his hand chanced to find. The nomadic paths of beggars are predistributed within a regulated space: in the shadows of tall city buildings, over steam grates, under bridges, living in the subterranean "pockets" of the city, outsiders tucked inside, along lines of distribution that have been brilliantly traced by Michel Foucault (*DT*, 171–72n1/*GT*, 134–35n18).

In another story, "Beat Up the Poor," Baudelaire describes "those unforgettable looks" of beggars, the accusatory eyes of the poor who represent "the absolute demand of the other" (*DT*, 173–74/*GT*, 136–37), an absolute demand for the gift. But, can a gift be demanded? As soon as giving alms is bound and obligated, it is calculative or distributive justice and duty discharged (*DT*, 174–75/*GT*, 137–38). But it is no longer the gift. "A beggar always looks threatening, incriminating, accusatory, vindictive in the absolute of his very demand" (*DT*, 176/*GT*, 139). He is saying to us, "You must give—or else." When those who have more than enough share with those who have not, that is just an equitable redistribution.

The beggar poses an aporia. On the one hand: If I am obliged to give to the poor, then giving is simple distributive justice, not giving but simply sharing with others what is rightfully theirs to begin with, the result being that I have merely fulfilled an obligation, avoided guilt, and so done myself a favor. On the other hand: If I am not obliged, then the gift is merely self-will, giving only when I will to give, when I give because it gives me joy. When I see the beggar on the steam grate, is that a shallow pool that sends back to me an image (*psyche*) of my own generosity and not *l'invention de l'autre*? In short, if it is an obligation, it is not a gift; if it is not an obligation, it is a personal fancy that gives me pleasure. Either way, the gift does not happen. In short again, how can I keep the "I," which is always a principle of calculation and self-interest, out of the picture?

This is an old and delicate problem and we must proceed cautiously to see what Derrida has in mind. To this end I solicit the help of the Book. According to one of the jewgreek stories in the Book, a gift happens when I give not what I have but what I do not have. For example, if I do not have enough to eat for myself, or enough money to get by, but give of my very substance to the other, that is the gift. The widow who gives two copper coins—Are they counterfeit? Just what is this cunning old widow up to, anyway?—not from her superabundance (*ek tou periseuontos*), but from her lack and deprivation (*ek tes hystereseos*) (another hysterical, hysterematic woman), giving what she herself needs to live and of which she herself does not have enough (Mark 12:41–44).

The widow's gift is an absolute surprise, shattering the horizon of expectation, unplannable and unforeseeable, immoderate and immeasurable (even though we can count to two), a tear in the circle of time and in temple giving practices, an *événement* in which something other breaks through, breaks out, and shatters the regular flow of now-time, in which something inconceivable, hardly possible, *the* impossible, happens. So, the story of the widow that we take from the Book is also a thoroughly Derridean story, a paradigmatic example of Derrida's gift. (Or, is Derrida's gift a good example of the story of the widow? How am I supposed to know that?) No one would say it was the widow's duty to redistribute her possessions with the have-nots, or that she was just doing her duty, because she herself, having nothing, already is one of the have-nots. By the same token, no one should say that the widow was unconsciously, or even with conscious craft, just seeking to give herself pleasure, since that would carry us beyond the text into a psychoanalysis of the *hors*-textual widow to which we have no access. We have to stick to the story, in which, according to the oldest and most venerable teaching of Derrida, we are always stuck. We cannot silently slip out the back door of the text and steal away to some transcendental signified and then triumphantly march back in the front door with the Secret Key to the story.

The story underlines the madness of the giving that does not calculate the interests of the subject, and it is that madness that belongs to the essence (or non-essence) of what Derrida calls the gift. The giving happens *not* because the widow is trying to discharge her duty and to give herself a good name and a good conscience; and *not* because it gives her great pleasure to discharge of her overflow, to give herself a good time. She gives without why (*ohne warum*), as Meister Eckhart said, and this is what he meant by love; she gives because she gives, which means, because she has let go of her I, which is the principle of self-love, of calculating a return. (Some people love God, Meister Eckhart said, the way they love their cow: for its milk.) She is no longer in the calculation, even though she can count to two, and everything is given over to the *tout autre*, to whom she has given her all (*son tout*).

The story of the widow also explains what Derrida means by the "duty without debt" described in *Passions*, an uncalculating giving that acts not in order to discharge a duty or satisfy a principle, but in order to give to the other, in which is lodged, as he says, the "ethicity or morality of ethics" (*Pass.*, 75n3/ON, 133n3), although for clarity's sake he might do better to speak of a "responsibility" without debt or duty.[17] The madness of the gift is outside the economic equilibrium of duty, beyond duty (*DT*, 198/*GT*, 156). A gift happens not as a duty, not as a principle of redistribution that binds me and coerces me to give up what I have, but as an affirmation of the other, a *oui, oui* to the coming of the other. A gift happens when the singularity of the *tout autre* calls upon and solicits me, and I answer with a gift, I give the answer of a gift.

That, I think, reminds us of nothing so much as Augustine's *dilige, et quod vis fac*, which is a little axiom whose market value I have been trying to raise for some time now.[18]

THE TIME OF FORGIVING

The question of the gift or giving is inseparable from that of forgiving, that is, of giving "away" or "forth" (as in the German *fort*), giving away what is due to come back to us, whether that be a debt or an obligation, real or symbolic. The gift is a giveaway. *Le don* is inseparable from *le par-don*. As the gift must not be a secret calculation of a way to get a return for oneself, so it must not encumber the other with a debt. Whatever debts, whatever guilt, the other incurs must be forgiven.

Derrida addresses this question in the last chapter of *Given Time* by way of the narrator's reflections on the friend's explanation of, or his excuse for, his surprising gesture, when the friend confesses to the narrator, "it was a counterfeit." What does he mean to say (*vouloir dire*)? What does he want (*vouloir*)? Is he boasting? Or trying to be excused from appearing too prodigal? Does he think this confession will permit him to get away with the ruse? How is the narrator to judge his friend? (*DT*, 189–90/*GT*, 149–50).

Indeed, is the friend even telling the truth? Might he not be masking a true generosity under the cover of a falsehood? But what sense can there be to such speculation? Is the reader not structurally so situated as to have to take the man's word for it? Are we not obliged to take him on credit? Whether the friend is lying or not is a secret we can never access, *not* because it is so difficult to decipher that no one can hope to succeed, but because the secret is a structural secret, an unreadable, inaccessible secret, in principle: "[T]he readability of the text is structured by the unreadability of the secret, that is, by the inaccessibility of a certain intentional meaning or of a wanting-to-say in the consciousness of the character and *a fortiori* in that of the author who remains, in this regard, in a situation analogous to that of the reader" (*DT*, 192–93/*GT*, 152).Baudelaire does not know, anymore than we do, what is going on in the mind of the friend, which belongs to the secret of literature, whose essence is to have no essence, to the truth of the secret, which is that it has no truth, not even a little something secreted away somewhere. This is the "essential superficiality" of literature, which has "no consistency, no depth," no truth. What is true of literature is also true of money. It does not matter what it is made out of or what it is printed on: it is a pure surface that does not need a vast gold reserve secreted away somewhere to back it up; it is a simulacrum that runs on faith, which is mightier than mountains or Fort Knox.

So we believe the narrator's friend, assume he is telling the truth, that it was in truth a counterfeit coin. The narrator could approve of his friend if he thought the friend were trying to open up an aleatory sequence, to let events happen in. the poor fellow's otherwise miserable life (*DT*, 158/GT, 124). But however much the narrator tries to credit the friend's action, the latter proves himself unworthy: "And does one have to deserve forgiveness? One may deserve an excuse, but ought not a forgiveness be accorded without regard to worthiness? Ought not a true forgiveness (a forgiveness in authentic money) absolve the fault or the crime even as the fault and the crime remain what they are?" (*DT*, 206/*GT*, 163). The crucial *Augen-blick* in the story, Derrida thinks, lies in the moment the narrator looks deep into his friend's eyes, *dans le blanc des yeux*, and sees clearly that the man actually thought he could cut a good deal for himself while seeming to do a good deed, that he could "win paradise economically." That appalling ruse is condemned by the narrator, who occupies the place of moral judgment, and his judgment is without appeal (*DT*, 207/*GT*, 163–64). The judgment is based on what the narrator thought he saw in the friend's eyes. But in looking into those eyes he could not see the friend's secret *vouloir dire*. Is not the Other constituted by his secret, by the hiddenness of his motives, both in the story and outside? The narrator does not know what is going on with the friend, any more than does the beggar, neither of whom is given a chance to tell his own story in this story. Everything is seen through the eyes of the narrator, from the perspective of the narrator's judgment seat. But what the narrator finds unforgivable is not a diabolical ill-will in the friend, which is the seat of radical evil in Kant's *Religion within the Limits of Reason Alone*, but his stupidity: did he really think he could win heaven for a steal? He should have known better, should have known how stupid he was being; he should have made a better use of the natural gifts, the gift of intelligence with which nature has endowed him. He has dishonored the debt he had contracted with nature. That cannot be forgiven.

The narrator sits in the judgment seat, which is the seat of nature itself, and passes judgment on whatever is ungrateful to nature's beneficence. But that is a very hot seat indeed to occupy, Derrida thinks, because the narrator is trying to bi-locate, to be in two places at once, to occupy at once the place of nature (of *Sein* and *physis*), while speaking from the place of literature (*nomos*). Baudelaire undertakes a "naturalization of literature," crossing the wires of nature and art, as if his story were speaking the truth of nature, as if, when he opens his mouth, it is nature that speaks. By trying to pass off a simulacrum, art, as nature itself, the narrator proves himself a counterfeiter, just like Marcel Mauss, whose *The Gift* is about everything but the gift, and who also thought to bring everything under the sway of a natural communitarian society. What is called nature by Mauss and Baudelaire is, of course, what they take nature to be, the way they see and read and interpret nature, from which squinting perspective they pass judgment on what is against nature, that is, against their judgment.

Peut-être. Who knows? Who knows what is going on inside the head of the friend or the narrator, or even of Mauss or Baudelaire? God knows that it's a secret! It is a secret. God knows. If there is one. Without interiority, thickness, or depth, the secret is "spread on the surface of the page, as obvious as a purloined letter, a postcard, a banknote, a check, a 'letter of credit'—or 'a silver two-franc piece'" (*DT*, 215-16/*GT*, 170). Literature will have already begun. We will always be caught by a text, convinced we are wrestling with *die Sache selbst, la chose même*, only to awaken to find the bed-linens of a text in our hands, that it is a pillow to which we were about to deal a deadly blow. We are never escorted to the chair of nature from which to pass decisive judgments: "There is no nature, only effects of nature: denaturation or naturalization. Nature, the meaning of nature, is reconstituted after the fact on the basis of a simulacrum (for example, literature) that it is thought to cause" (*DT*, 215/*GT*, 170). We lack the wherewithal to judge what goes on in secret and we can always read the action of the other otherwise. For the other is wholly other, every other is wholly other, *tout autre est tout autre*, and we can hardly know what is happening with something wholly other; it's a secret. No one has appointed us to pass judgment on the other, to determine what is going on in secret. No one has shown us the back door out of textuality by means of which we may sneak away to a rendezvous with *la chose meme. La chose même toujours se dérobe*. Even if, by some ruse or stealth, we got to read the other's secret diary, we would still be reading texts.

Derrida would thus "exceed" the malignant operations of the secret, slip beyond its rueful exercise of power, which is the work of hypocrites and counterfeiters, a way of securing an advantage over the other, in order to move on to the benignity of the absolute secret: "One can stop and examine a secret, make it say things, give others to believe that [*donner à croire*] there is something there when there is not. One can lie, cheat, seduce by making use of it. One can play with the secret as with a simulacrum, with a lure or yet another strategy. One can cite it as an impregnable source. One can try in this way to secure oneself a phantasmatic power over others. That happens every day" (*Pass.*, 69/ON, 30). To which Derrida adds, "But this very simulacrum still bears witness to a possibility that exceeds it" (*Pass.*, 69/ON, 30). Instead of being on the take under the name of giving, instead of giving precisely to earn an even greater reward, say a hundredfold, the secret can also be the way to let the other be, to respect alterity, and not presume to pass judgment on what goes on in the other's heart. Who knows what is going on in the other? God knows, I do not! We are neither God nor Dupin nor a Persian detective. We are not master hermeneuts of the secret interiority of the other which we can penetrate with our institutionalized confessional machines, whether they are deployed by the police, psychoanalysts, fathers confessor, or literary critics.

Judge not.

Not only must we not be on the take when we give, we must also give away whatever we take, whatever we have on the other. We must give away what we think the other owes us, even if we get something on the other seven times a day, or seven times seven. We must; it's a responsibility, a responsibility without duty, a duty without debt, a debt that does not cut off possibilities. If we would give ourselves to the gift, we would also give ourselves to forgiving.

Donne. Pardonne. Oui, oui.

TRADITIONS AND THE WORLD-PLAY

Derrida's discourse on the time of the gift is deeply evocative in many directions. Here, while giving ourselves time to prepare for a reading of the fearsome story of Abraham, let me indicate, in a passing divertissement, two directions the analysis of the gift-so far-gives: (1) traditions; (2) the "world-play."

Our Debt to Tradition: A Bizarre Mixture of Responsibility and Disrespect

"Traditions" give—they hand things over, *trans-dare*—and we owe a "debt" to them. So traditions trace out the circle of a debt. We owe our predecessors who have given us everything. Derrida is not against traditions or having a debt to a tradition. It would never be a question of occupying a site of simple exteriority to the circle of tradition. He is only against debts and traditions that tie our hands, that lay down encircling horizons of possibility so forcefully as to wall us in and cut off *the* impossible. He is against being poisoned by the tradition's gifts. For example, if you happen to be a woman in an all-boys tradition, or gay in a straight clergy, and if you would like to be ordained but the ever-so-straight sacerdotal boys' club objects, then you are being poisoned by this gift. Derrida himself certainly wants to acknowledge a debt to Marx, which he would like the new world order also to acknowledge, or a debt to Shakespeare and Mallarmé, Husserl, Plato and Aristotle, and so on. But the debts he affirms are debts that liberate and open up the impossible. The tradition of which he dreams is a polyvalent, elusive, profusive structure among whose several spirits we must learn selectively to choose.

The tradition is a gift that passes through the trace and the dissemination that follows upon the trace, which means it is something that needs to be interpreted. Understood in terms of the trace, a "tradition" is a certain profusion, even a generous one, *with* generosity but not springing *out of* generous motives (*DT*, 205/*GT*, 162), one that occurs on a radically pre-subjective (textual) plane, on a level prior to the effects of subjectivity, like an anonymous, autonomous, quasi-transcendental field.[19] A tradition, for him, provides the occasion of an event (*événement*), of something happening and always as a bit of a surprise, a fortuitousness, a fortunate break, something aleatory breaking through the horizon of anticipation, an irruption, tearing up time, occasioning an unforeseeable sequence.[20] A tradition for him is neither the teleological development of the Spirit nor the deep eschatological sighing of the *Seinsgeschick* heaving and groaning toward its long-concealed issue. The gift of tradition is the effect of a "donative eventiveness" (*événementialité donatrice*), which is the interplay between the intentional and the unintended, the play of *différance* and subjects struggling to keep their head above the waves of *écriture* (*DT*, 156–58/*GT*, 122–23).

Traditions happen when quasi-systems of traces—not just books, of course, but institutions, laws, works of art, beliefs, practices, whatever you need, whatever is around—are fluid, open-ended, supple, flexible, reconfigurable, and reinterpretable, like a language that is rich in associative possibilities and the possibilities of a pun. It happens when quasi-systems shower effects upon those who stand in them like falling stars or meteors raining down from the heavens, when quasi-systems produce surprising, innovative, amazing, and unexpected results, when they produce something new and unforeseeable, when they repeat with a difference. It happens when these quasi-systems do all this in virtue of their own differentiality—shall I say, do I dare, when *différance* is good to us, no thanks to Derrida? But he resists thinking of the gifts of tradition in terms of generous, kind, beneficent, though slightly self-serving subjects who end up becoming canonized and memorialized creditors, to whose generosity and beneficence we are all indebted, at the sound of whose names we all have to bend a knee or bow a head or erect a statue on Monument Boulevard. The highest gratitude would always involve ingratitude about such monumental debts, which opens up the possibility of letting a new gift loose.

Tradition's gifts eventuate in the interface, the interaction between subjects and quasi-systems, for there are subjects and they are always dreaming of impossible gifts. Derrida does not imagine or dream of a world without subjects, which would be the nightmare of pure death; he is not dreaming of a world in which subjects are actually dead, dead in any more than just a structural sense. Quite the opposite, it is in the name of life that he insists upon life/death, since pure life would be stifling, even lethal, like pure light. It is never a question of choosing be- tween a world of pure dissemination or *différance* or *écriture* without subjects (which would make no sense) and a world of pure Husserlian intentional agents who mean what they say and say what they mean (which would make too much sense and keep everything under univocalizing, absolute, angelic control), but of something in between Husserl and James Joyce, to recall that memorable observation (HOdG, 104–6/HOG, 102–4).[21] Derrida keeps an eye out for an instant, a moment of chance, an *Augenblick*, which occurs in the *inter-esse*, in the being-in-between life and death, Joyce and Husserl, which is for him the time of giving and the giving of time, no thanks to *différance*.

One is always working inside a tradition or the institutions founded upon them; it is not possible to work elsewhere, to collect a check without a bursar or a controller. Traditions require agents who act and agents who understand the limits of action and the undesirability of their getting into every act, of making everything into their act, their action, the outcome of what they say and do and plan and want, who understand that they act within and from out of chains of *différance*. It is a question of actors who act in such a way as to open up possibilities for others to act on their own, which is not a bad way to run a democracy to come, of *vorausspringende Fürsorge* (*Being and Time*, § 26), even if (especially because!) Heidegger had no faith in democracy, present or coming. Acting within a tradition becomes a matter of releasing aleatory chains, of initiatives which initiate unforeseeable possibilities and unexpected initiatives from others, over which the initiators neither can nor want to maintain control. It is a question of acting by reacting, by inhabiting certain regular concatenations and altering them, by interrupting well-established patterns into which one has first settled, acting just enough to set them off in new directions, of learning first to operate within the most traditional institutional codes and then to push them to their limits, to mime and mimic them into something different. Aleatory action sets off effects beyond its intentional control, effects that exceed their origin and cause, rather the way a long and mighty train can be sent barreling down another track by a little alteration in a switch.

Having a tradition is a question of inheritors of a tradition who find themselves in a fix, responsible for selecting among an unfathomable complexity and perplexity of voices, a perfectly confusing plethora of polyvalent, polymorphic possibilities, among which both scholars and the faithful have to find their way. To have a tradition—*sans avoir*—as to have resolved neither to go it on one's own nor simply to repeat the tradition, one problem with which is we would not know which among the many traditions and *counter*-traditions competing for a voice in "the" tradition, if there is one, to repeat. To appeal to the authority of a tradition is to fall back upon a confusion and profusion of voices so that one is not sure who is saying what to whom, not to mention who got silenced.

Having a tradition for Derrida is a matter of being an heir, of being "faithful as far as possible, loving, avid to reread and to experience the philosophical joys that are not just the games of the aesthete," a "bizarre mixture of responsibility and disrespect": "We have gotten more than we think we know from 'tradition,' but the scene of the gift also obligates us to a kind of filial lack of piety, at once serious and not so serious, as regards the thinking to which we have the greatest debt" (PdS, 139/*Points*, 130). To have a tradition is to practice, at one and the same time, the greatest fidelity and a filial lack of piety, to feel the paralysis of owing a debt and owing it to ourselves to forget the debt, for only then will the tradition really move ahead. Pure fidelity is death, but so is pure infidelity. The art of the heir is to maintain the greatest possible tension between fidelity and infidelity (PdS, 160–61/*Points*, 150–51), between the circle and the gift, to be paralyzed by this aporia and then to make a move (when it is impossible).

That is for Derrida, pace Gadamer and Habermas, both tradition and Enlightenment (because it is not quite either). It is *traditio*, giving, giving-over, *trans-dare*, the very process of giving or transmitting the gifts of the tradition, which departs from the traditional idea of tradition (*DT*, 26/*GT*, 13), for the latter involves erecting tall monuments that tax our budgets, monumental erections honoring momentous founders. Tradition ought not to flatten us into submission by its massive dead weight, by the boulders that are rolled down its hill with all the weight of the great blockbusters of the past, the great texts and practices of the fathers, which we are all supposed immediately and unquestioningly to shoulder like good children who know the debt they owe their venerable ancestors. Tradition is not univocal but polyvocal, among whose multiple voices we must learn to make our way, selectively and judiciously. Tradition alters as it repeats, repeats as it alters, producing what it repeats (which is a good Kierkegaardian repetition, with a difference), which is the only way to be grateful to a tradition. For literal gratitude to a tradition paralyzes everybody and makes the tradition look like a monster, which is what Drucilla Cornell says of the law if it is not tempered by a Derridean coefficient.[22]

But it is also Enlightenment, a *new* Enlightenment, not the wide-eyed sclerotic Enlightenment of *Aufklärers* who want to monitor everything, to foresee and plan and program everything, to monitor and regulate every judgment with critical criteria that shut everything down in advance, that close off every possibility except the one that is inevitably predicted and pre-dictated and prevalidated by the criteria (DDP, 466/PR, 5).[23] The gift belongs to another Enlightenment, to the Enlightenment of the *Augenblick*, to the Kierkegaardian moment that cuts us a break, which breaks open a possibility, an impossibility, which deals us not death but a break, delivering the shock of something different, tearing up the circle of time.[24]

The gift gives us all a break (but give no thanks to *écriture*, which is not trying to be generous). The gift, which is both tradition and Enlightenment, *gives* us all a chance, an aleatory opening, a tear in the circle of necessity and duty. The injunctive *donne* calls upon us to give others a break, to open up the impossible for the other, not to close the other down within the horizon of possibility and normalization, not to remake others in the image of the Same (us), to let the invention of the other happen, to let events happen.

The Play of the World: Zarathustra, Nagarjuna—and Abraham

I also can envisage a certain theology of the world as gift that would not belong to the creationist tradition of the great monotheisms. Derrida has quite successfully fended off the suggestion that God is *différance*, that all this apophatic discourse about *différance* arises from the fact that deep down, after all, *différance* is Elohim, the unknowable Lord of Hosts, *epekeina tes ousias*, the *Gottheit* beyond *Gott*, the *mysterium tremendum*, the God of the Book. Who could believe that? But that is not the end of the matter. For one could, were one so minded, turn this equation around and speak of *différance* as all the God one wants, or needs, or knows, or can imagine. One could think of *différance* as a kind of fortuitousness and open-endedness inscribed in things, or in which things are inscribed, to which one attributes a divine trait, a mark of a certain divinity. Then, without being implicated in saying that the biblical God is *différance*, one could say the divine—and we would be better off saying "the divine" (*theios*), not God (*theos*)—would mean the opening in things, a certain resistance to closure, a divine "creativity" inscribed in things that keeps the quasi-system open to novelty, innovation, renovation. *Renovabitis faciem terrae*, thou shalt renew the face of the earth, but without the "thou," and in the middle voice: the possibility of the face of the earth being renewed.

Such a divine *différance* would be something like Nietzsche's notion of *Götterung*, a divinizing mark of the quasi-system, a trait of the state of the forces as a whole, which would from time to time be "blessed" by particularly fortuitous configurations and constellations, issues and outcomes. For even old Nietzsche, who became as grumpy as possible whenever theological tones were sounded, whenever church-dark, incense-infested organs began to grind out solemn hymns, had to admit that one idea of God that made sense is the thought of having something on which to hang one's gratitude. When life surges up all around us in a joyous dance of the elements, like the moon glistening on ten thousand waves in a midnight surf, then we look, if not "up" in pre-Copernican wonder, at least "around," for someone or something to thank, upon which we may expend our gratitude without reserve. When the system of forces reaches a peak of perfection, when the forces hum with beauty and harmony, that, says Nietzsche, is a state of divinization (*Vergötterung*), for which we should all be grateful. In this Nietzschean theology, or theodosia, it would not be a question of thanking someone with good intentions, someone with a heart, for the doer is not separable from the deed, but of being grateful for how things happen, for the dance the forces dance. One would expel the dense stupidity in things, what Levinas called the *il y a*, with a certain *Gottheit, divinitas*, which would be the mark or trait of innovation and experimentation, the gift-giving spirit in things.[25]

The opposite of this state for Nietzsche is that of *Entgötterung*, of de-divinization, when the quasi-system would grow dull and flat, monotonous and monochromatic, and the possibility of something new is cut off, when all invention subsides into the invention of the same. When those lulls set in, when everything levels off, when the divine spark is driven into measured-out mediocrity, which very much offended his delicate, aristocratic nose, then Zarathustra is filled not with gratitude but with nausea and dread. Whatever is has been: that is Zarathustra's "*Eli, Eli, lema sabachthani*." (Well, almost.)

One might also think of a theodosia a little like Nagarjuna and the play of dependent co-arising. For Nagarjuna there is what there is, *es gibt*, and that is all; it plays because it plays, and that is all, but what there is, is taken to be a gentle play of harmony and benignity, like the play of moonbeams on the ten thousand waves, with everything perfect just as it is, and everything mirroring everything else all quite perfectly.[26]

Zarathustra and Nagarjuna have invented different ways of saying, according to the quiet quasi-rule of *différance*, that momentary openings emerge here and there, wherever possible. *Und nichts außerdem*! The "divinizing" operation here is a hyperbolic gesture that is reaching for a predicate to express one's pleasure at how things are going when they are going well and things are opening up, a hyperbole that language puts at our disposal. Events happen, open up and close off, arise and fall back, come to be and pass away. Gifts, like falling stars, flicker for an instant against this greater night. And then you die.

But that is not the biblical gift, or the prophetic drift of the religions of the Book, nor does it quite capture the tone that Derrida has recently adopted, which is distinctively more messianic, more biblical, more prophetic, a little more Jewish than Buddhist, tilted more toward the *tout autre*. That messianic tone puts Derrida's gift more in touch with hospitality toward the stranger. For Derrida's gift has less to do with a cosmic play than with the *Augenblick*, with the chance of justice for the *tout autre*. Derrida's gift—and Derrida is thinking these days in more Jewish and prophetic terms—is concerned with the possibilities that open up for the outsiders, the political, social, national, sexual outsiders, the victims of "racism, nationalism, and xenophobia" (AC, 77/OH, 78).[27] That is a *genos* (or *agenos*) that corresponds very congenially with the biblical category of the least among us, a kingdom of little ones, the little breaks and openings that open up fortuitously in the kingdom. In the moment, the *Augenblick*, something impossible happens, time is opened up, and something new breaks through. In the aleatory opening religious faith feels the movements of God's gracious, gift-giving power. A loving hand, a finger of God, lines the interstices of the event, outlines the conditions of the momentary occurrence. The moment, the chance of an opening, breaches time's continuous flow and harmonious synthesizing, and in that breach, within it and from out of it, one catches a glimpse of God passing by, the back of someone hurrying from the scene.

That gives us a read, and a bead, on the miracle stories, a way to hear them as a "poetics" rather than as eyewitness accounts of well corroborated divine interventions on natural processes, which is the graceless, unliterary, literalist way they are treated by apologists and fundamentalists. For these stories of the interruption and suspension of the natural course of events, of the ordinary flow of continuous time, which breach the flow of causality and temporality, are so many modes of inventing the other and the time of the other, the time of the gift. Dividing the sea in half in order to let the Israelites go (although this is a Jewish story and one ought not to conclude that God is out to drown Egyptians); suspending the natural order of life and death in order to let Lazarus step out of the tomb, stepping out of a breach in time—if only Jesus had arrived a little sooner our brother would not have died; shattering the proportionality of cause and effect, the steady drip of moments in empirical time, or the economy of supply and demand, by feeding five thousand with five loaves of bread. God always passes by in the breach, in the *Augenblick*, in the chance of an occurrence, in the event of a gift, in the gift of an event, giving a new time. Being and time, nature and economics, good measure and steady presence must be breached, in order to let the hand of God, or her back or finger, be caught sight of, in an *Augenblick*. The miracle stories are stories of chance, of the moment, of the aleatory gift, writ large, in stunning tales and gilded letters.

That is why, for a teacher of the gift-giving virtue, Derrida looks next, not to Zarathustra or to Nagarjuna, but to Abraham.

NOTES

1. Jacques Derrida and Pierre-Jean Labarriere, *Alterités* (Paris: Éditions Osiris, 1986), 74. Jacques Derrida, *"Donner la mort,"* in *L'Éthique du don: Jacques Derrida et la pensée du don* (Paris: Métailié-Transition, 1992). Cited as DM. English translation Jacques Derrida, *The Gift of Death*. Trans. David Wills (Chicago: University of Chicago Press, 1995). Cited as GD.

2. Jacques Derrida, *Points de suspension: Entretiens*. Ed. Elisabeth Weber (Paris: Galilée, 1992). Cited as PdS. English translation Jacques Derrida, *Points . . . Interviews, 1974-94*. Ed. Elisabeth Weber. Trans. Peggy Kamuf (Stanford: Stanford University Press, 1995). Cited as *Points*.

3. In a recent series of lectures on hospitality that follows the etymology of the word "hospitality," *hostis*, the stranger, + *potis*, mastery, Derrida says that hospitality begins just when we are paralyzed by this aporetic, to be as welcoming as possible to the other while not surrendering the mastery of one's house.

4. Marcel Mauss, *The Gift: The Form and Reason for Exchange in Archaic Societies*, trans. W. D. Halls (New York: Norton, 1990). On "*kula*," see 21–31.

5. Jacques Derrida, *Donner le temps, I. La fausse monnaie* (Paris: Galilée, 1991). Cited as DT. English translation Jacques Derrida, *Given Time, I. Counterfeit Money*. Trans. Peggy Kamuf (Chicago: University of Chicago Press, 1991). Cited as GT.

6. Jacques Derrida, *Glas* (Paris: Galilée, 1974). English translation Jacques Derrida, *Glas*. Trans. Richard Rand and John Leavey, Jr. (Lincoln: University of Nebraska Press, 1986). Both texts cited as *Glas*.

7. Martin Heidegger, *Zur Sache des Denkens*, 2nd ed. (Tubingen: Max Niemeyer, 1976) (hereafter *SD*), translated in English as *On Time and Being*, trans. Joan Stambaugh (New York: Harper & Row, 1972) (hereafter *TB*).

8. For a more detailed account of Heidegger's worst, most mythologizing side, as opposed to a more austere demythologized Heidegger, see my *Demythologizing Heidegger* (Bloomington: Indiana University Press, 1993), chap. 1.

9. Jacques Derrida, *De l'esprit: Heidegger et la question* (Paris: Galilée, 1987). Cited as DLE. English translation Jacques Derrida, *Of Spirit: Heidegger and the Question*. Trans. Geoffrey Bennington and Rachel Bowlby (Chicago: University of Chicago Press, 1989). Cited as OS.

10. See Robert Bernasconi, "On Heidegger's Other Sins of Omission: Asian Thought and Christian Philosophy," *American Catholic Philosophical Quarterly*, 69 (1995): 333–50.

11. Jacques Derrida, *Khôra* (Paris: Galilée, 1993). Cited as *Khôra*. English translation Jacques Derrida, *On the Name*. Ed. Thomas Dutoit (Stanford: Stanford University Press, 1995). Cited as ON.

12. Søren Kierkegaard, *Philosophical Fragments*, trans. Howard Hong and Edna Hong (Princeton, NJ: Princeton University Press, 1985), 57.

13. For a comparable argument, see Julia Kristeva, *Tales of Love*, trans. Leon S. Roudiez (New York: Columbia University Press, 1987), 170–87, a remarkable essay on the *ratio diligendi* in Thomas Aquinas.

14. For an American contribution to this tradition, one which nourishes no desire to see the gift escape the circle of exchange, see Lewis Hyde, *The Gift: Imagination and the Erotic Life of Property* (New York: Random House, Vintage Books, 1983). Hyde himself confesses a debt to Marshall Sahlins, *Stone Age Economics* (Chicago: Aldane, 1972). Cf. Derrida, *Donner le temps, I. La fausse monnaie* (Paris: Galilée, 1991), 40n1/*Given Time, I: Counterfeit Money*, trans. Peggy Kamuf (Chicago: University of Chicago Press, 1991), 25n15. (Hereafter *DT/GT*)

15. Derrida is no less forgiving with Levi-Strauss for paying Mauss a poisoned tribute, for sharply criticizing Mauss for "going native," for being taken in by the charm of native logic, for accepting the natives' claim that the spirit (*hau*) that inhabits the gift/thing is what drives the giving and taking, that is, the circle of exchange. Mauss, Levi-Strauss complains, should have seen past these material charms to the formal logic of relations, to the relational system rooted in the unconscious and instantiated in language, of which "gifts" are but contingent embodiments. Against Levi-Strauss's rationalism, his "exchangist, linguisticist, and structuralist" systematizing of Mauss, Derrida opposes the "gift" as the instant that tears up the relational totality (that is, the gift as post- or extra-structural, exceeding structure), and even as "giving reason" itself (*DT*, 102–3/*GT*, 77). Derrida's criticism of Levi-Strauss's structuralism should not obscure the fact that Derrida, like Levi-Strauss, wants to distance himself from the moralizing humanism of Mauss and to find a "gift" that has nothing to do with intentionalist structures and everything to do with an anonymous play of differences. Derrida is seeking a dissemination that will be equally, even more, unconscious than that of Levi-Strauss.

16. See my *Against Ethics: Contributions to a Poetics of Obligation with Constant Reference to Deconstruction* (Bloomington: Indiana University Press, 1993), chap. 8, for a beggarly notion of flesh or a fleshly notion of the beggar.

17. Jacques Derrida, *Passions* (Paris: Galilée, 1993). Cited as *Pass*. English translation cited as ON.

18. See my *Radical Hermeneutics: Repetition, Deconstruction and the Hermeneutic Project, Studies in Phenomenology and Existential Philosophy* (Bloomington: Indiana University Press, 1987), 212–13, and *Against Ethics*, 41, 92, 121–22.

19. Very early on, in commenting on Husserl, Derrida said that *écriture* "creates an autonomous transcendental field from which every present subject can be absent," or what Jean Hippolyte calls "a transcendental field without a subject," notions that, in a sense, Derrida has been reworking ever since. See Jacques Derrida, *Husserl: L'origine de la géométrie*. 2nd ed. (Paris: PUF, 1974), 84–85/*Edmund Husserl's* Origin of Geometry, trans. John Leavey Jr. (Boulder: John Hays, 1978), 87–88 (*HOdG/HOG*).

20. I think that Hannah Arendt's notion of the "frailty of action" captures a good deal of this idea; see *The Human Condition* (Chicago: University of Chicago Press, 1956), 192–97, 220–30.

21. Jacques Derrida, *Husserl: L'origine de la géométrie*. 2nd ed. (Paris: PUF, 1974). Cited as HOdG. English translation Jacques Derrida, *Edmund Husserl's Origin of Geometry*. Trans. John Leavey, Jr. (Boulder: John Hays Co., 1978). Cited as HOG.

22. Drucilla Cornell, *The Philosophy of the Limit* (New York: Routledge, 1992), 158.

23. Jacques Derrida, *Du Droit à la Philosophie* (Paris: Galilée, 1990). Cited as DDP. English translation Jacques Derrida, "The Principle of Reason: The University in the Eyes of its Pupils." Trans. Catherine Porter and Edward Morris. *Diacritics* 13 (1983): 3-20. Cited as PR.

24. When Derrida expresses his admiration for a certain *Aufklärung*, a new one, and Habermas presses for a pragmatic and hermeneutically sensitive idea of critical reason, the two poles of modernism and postmodernism, if there are such things, begin to touch.

25. Friedrich Nietzsche, *The Will to Power*, trans. Walter Kaufmann and R. J. Hollingdale (New York: Vintage Books, 1968), No. 639, pp. 340–41; No. 712, pp. 379–80.

26. David J. Kalupahana, ed. and trans., *Nagarjuna: The Philosophy of the Middle Way*

(Albany: SUNY Press, 1986). For some interesting work on Derrida and Nagarjuna, see David Loy, ed., *Healing Deconstruction: Postmodern Thought in Buddhism and Christianity* (Atlanta, GA: Scholars Press, 1966), and Robert R. Magliola, *Derrida on the Mend* (West Lafayette, IN: Purdue University Press, 1984).

27. Jacques Derrida, *L'autre cap* (Paris: Éditions de Minuit, 1991). Cited as AC. English translation Jacques Derrida, *The Other Heading: Reflections on Today's Europe*. Trans. Pascale-Anne Brault and Michael Naa. (Bloomington: Indiana University Press, 1992). Cited as OH.

16
Toward a Postmodern Theology of the Cross: Augustine, Heidegger, Derrida

In this age of the death of God, it is of no little interest and significance that two of the major European philosophers of this century, two of the masters of postmodernity, if this is a word we still can use, have chosen (at different points in their work: one very early on, the other only later) to comment on the ageless power and beauty of Augustine's *Confessions*. In the summer semester of 1921, at the very beginning of his work, when he was still thinking within a Christian context, the young Heidegger (then thirty-two years old) devoted a lecture course to the tenth book of the *Confessions*; the course is a remarkable anticipation of the main lines of *Being and Time*, arguably the major work by any Continental European philosopher written in this century. In 1989–90, at the age of fifty-nine, an age when he says he was learning the meaning of the word "dying," Derrida, supposedly a very secular and antitraditional philosopher, wrote a beautiful autobiographical piece entitled *Circonfession*, which, like the famous narrative of his North African "compatriot" Saint Augustine, tells the story of his life, including the story of his dying mother, by grafting it upon numerous and sometimes lengthy citations of Augustine's Latin text.

Heidegger and Derrida produce very different texts and find strikingly different Augustines. Heidegger's Augustine is mediated to him by Luther and Kierkegaard—this lecture course was held two years after his formal break with Catholicism—while Derrida's Augustine seems indebted to Levinas and is hence a much more Jewish Augustine. Heidegger's *Confessiones* recounts a battle with concupiscence, while Derrida's tell the story of his circumcision, of the cut in his flesh that also signals a deep cut or severance from which all his thinking originates. Heidegger's Augustine is a very Pauline Christian soldier, fighting the good fight of faith, outfitted in the breastplate of hope and the helmet of faith, one for whom the Christian faith spells battle and trouble, so that his "confessions" read like a war journal. Derrida's Augustine is a man of prayers and tears, a much more womanly man, weaving together womanly tears and a manly circumcision, a man for whom confession is a matter of asking pardon, of confessing one's faults, of concern for the other.

Interestingly enough, and at the risk of shocking devout and orthodox readers of Heidegger, Derrida, Augustine, and the Scriptures (both Jewish and Christian), I would say that Heidegger and Derrida offer different renderings of the cross—two different, let us say postmodern, versions of what Luther called the *theologia crucis*—and it is around this thematic of a postmodern theology of the cross that I will organize my remarks here.

Heidegger's reading of the *Confessions*, while it is quite brilliant in its own right and though it provides a fascinating glimpse of the genesis of *Being and Time*, is extremely one-sided and very much held captive by the spiritual militancy of Paul, Luther, and Kierkegaard. Inspired by Luther's *theologia crucis*, Heidegger singles out the trials and tribulations by which factical life is buffeted in fighting the good fight of faith. But the phenomenon of the cross admits of another and significantly different emphasis, for the cross stands for suffering flesh and for the solidarity of Jesus with everyone who suffers. Seen thus, the cross points in the direction of an ethics of compassion rather than to an existential analytic of authentic self-possession. As I have argued elsewhere, that is a direction which Heidegger never took and, indeed, to which he seems endemically, systematically blind. When he read the New Testament, he found there only a *Kampfsreligion*, a Pauline battlefield with a self that wills what it does not and does what it wills not.[1] Heidegger seems never to have noticed the widows and the poor, the lame and the lepers, the young man raised from the dead, the blind and the crippled, and the systematic work of *therapeuein*, of healing, of *cura* as healing, around which the ministry of Jesus was organized. That, in turn, explains why Heidegger was so defenseless against the *Kampfsphilosophie* of the Nazis and against the bizarre extremes to which *Kampfsphilosophie* was taken by Ernst Jünger and Jünger's strange version of Nietzsche, which cleared the way for Heidegger's embrace of National Socialism. Had Heidegger a little more care for *cura* as healing, had he cared more for the cross as a symbol of solidarity with the suffering other, and had he cared less for a heroic freedom that stares into the abyss—out there all alone in the dark night of *Eigentlichkeit*, *coram morti*—he might have been less inclined to lend his good name and considerable genius to the Nazi nightmare. *Qui amat periculum, incidet in illum.*

What interests me in the present study is the entirely different reading of Augustine's *Confessions* to be found in Derrida's *Circonfession*. Without trying to undermine or simply jettison Heidegger's provocative gloss upon the *Confessions*, I maintain that Derrida provides the more sensitive rendering of Augustine, indeed, one that is quite sensitive to the *theologia crucis* and, let us say, more generally, to the biblical theology of suffering, Christian or Jewish. The spirit of Derrida's rendering of the *Confessions* is nicely captured in Daniele da Volterra's *Woman at the Foot of the Cross*, a stunning drawing of a weeping woman that Derrida includes in *Memoirs of the Blind* (the text accompanying his Louvre exhibit). This magnificent figure of a woman bent by grief, of a woman of sorrow, is not narrowly Christian but more broadly biblical, and not narrowly biblical but a broader figure of the human condition generally. That is why Derrida can say—this is the hope, the risk, the wager—both that *Circonfession* is a story of something that happens only once, with him, "It only happens to me" (*Circ.*, 282/*Circum.*, 305), and that this is "Everybody's Autobiography" (*Circ.*, 288/ *Circum.*, 311).

AUGUSTINE, HEIDEGGER, AND THE HERMENEUTICS OF FACTICITY: QUI AMAT PERICULUM, INCIDET IN ILLUM

(He who loves danger, perishes by it.)

—Eccles. 3:27; Augustine, *Confessions*; Derrida, *Circonfession*

In a remarkable footnote in *Being and Time*, Heidegger says that the analysis of "care" (*Sorge*) "is one which has grown upon the author in connection with his attempts to interpret the Augustinian (i.e., Helleno-Christian) anthropology with regard to the foundational principles reached in the ontology of Aristotle" (*SZ*, 199n1; *BT*, 492nvii).[2]

With the recent appearance of Heidegger's 1921 lecture course on Augustine's *Confessions*, it is at last possible to make sense of this fascinating remark.

Heidegger's reading of the *Confessions* is important for two reasons. In the first place, Heidegger undertakes there an existential phenomenological *Destruktion* of Augustine's work,[3] that is, he attempts to break through, or read back past, the heavy overlay of Neoplatonic metaphysics in Augustine in order to find the concrete, historical experience of life, what he calls in the early Freiburg period the "factical life" that pulsates beneath it. For the *Confessions* are not a metaphysical tract but a *confiteri*, a distinctive way of interpreting things that is rooted in Augustine's experience of Christian life (*GA* 60, 212). The distinction between the "metaphysical" and the "factical" thus amounts to a distinction between the Greek and Christian, a distinction which is also an indistinction inasmuch as Heidegger thinks that by the time of Augustine, it is not possible perfectly to distinguish Greek and Christian, the two having become already inextricably intertwined in the Patristic period. In order to find the authentically Christian, one would need to return to the early Christian, to primitive Christianity (*Urchristentum*), of which the only record is the New Testament, an effort undertaken by Heidegger during the preceding semester, in which he offered a commentary on Paul's letters to the Thessalonians, the earliest documents in the New Testament.[4] In the second place, Heidegger seeks to formalize Augustine's account of factical life—that is, to raise it to the level of an existential-phenomenological formality, a structural generality, or what in the 1920s he calls a "formal indication," so that what results from the analysis is broader than its specifically Christian contents and could stand as an indicator of factical life in general, rather like the distinction in *Being and Time* between the existential and the existentiell.

Heidegger's lecture course, entitled "Augustine and Neoplatonism," focuses on Book 10 of the *Confessions*. The heart of the *Destruktion*—that is, of the hermeneutic retrieval of Christian facticity from the *Confessions*—is the analysis of the soul as a *terra difficultatis* (*SZ*, 43–44; *BT*, 69), a land of difficulty (*Confessions*, bk. 10, chap. 16) and struggle (*Kampf*), a being that has become a question to itself (*GA* 60, 247), beset by *molestias et difficultates* (*Confessions*, bk. 10, chap. 28). The analysis focuses on the phenomenon of *tentatio*, the life of the soul as trial and temptation. In its mode of *confiteri*, the soul is not a stable self-identity, a substance at rest and at one with itself, but rather a being that has become a question unto itself, at odds with itself and pulled in opposing directions. *Ecce ubi sum*, Augustine says. See in what a state I am, in what turmoil and unrest. *Flete mecum et pro me flete.* Weep with me and weep for me, all you who feel within yourselves that goodness from which good actions come. *Tu autem, domine deus meus, exaudi et respice et vide et miserere et sana me.* But do thou O Lord my God hear me and look upon me and see me and heal me, *in cujus oculis mihi quaestio factus sum*, in whose eyes I have become a question to myself (*Confessions*, bk. 10, chap. 33). Life is through-and-through insecure, and "no man ought to be oversure that though he is capable of becoming better instead of worse, he is not actually becoming worse instead of better" (*Confessions*, bk. 10, chap. 32). This phenomenon of the questionability of the self to itself, of the insecurity of the self, is what organizes Heidegger's reading of the *Confessions*.

To be sure, the question of the self for Augustine is inseparable from the question of God. As Kierkegaard, whom Heidegger cites at this point, says: "The greater the conception of God, the more self there is; the more self, the greater the conception of God" (*SUD*, e.t., 80). What constitutes the self *as* a self, Kierkegaard says, is that in the face of which the self takes its measure, that before which it stands face to face, and what "an infinite accent falls on the self by having God as the criterion" (*SUD*, 79; *GA* 60, 248). The more immediately the soul stands before God, *coram deo*, taking God as its measure, the more deeply it enters within itself. Heidegger emphasizes that struggle is thus the measure of life *coram deo*. "God is there," Heidegger comments, "in troubling over the life of the self" (*GA* 60, 289). The life of the soul before God, the very facticity of factical life, is struggle (*Kampf*), difficulty (*Schwierigkeit*), burden (*onus*), trouble (*molestia*) (*Confessions*, bk. 10, chap. 28). *Vita . . . tota tentatio [est]* (*Confessions*, bk. 10, chap. 32).[5] Life is all trial and temptation, an "inner *Kampf*" (*GA* 60, 275) of the self with itself. To take the easy way out (*leichtnehmen*), to give in to the drift into the "world," to "fall" into the world—that is to decline the invitation to Christian life. The dynamics, or better, the "kinetics," of *tentatio* are described in terms of a pull (*Zug*) and a counter-pull (*Gegenzug*) having to do with the force of "concupiscence," the pull or lure that worldly things exert over our heart's affections, dragging us into the world and turning us away from God. A *moles* is not to be understood as it ordinarily is, as a natural thing, like a stone, Heidegger comments, but rather as a suction or a pull that draws me away from myself (*GA* 60, p. 267). *[C]adunt in id quod valent* (*Confessions*, bk. 10, chap. 23): some men fall in among what they prize while others resist, fighting the good fight against the "concupiscence of the eyes, the concupiscence of the flesh, and the pride of life" (1 John 2:16), the famous tripartite division of the spiritual battleground around which Augustine has organized Book 10.

In short, for Heidegger, the life of the soul before God is *cura*, a condensation of Augustine's text in transparent anticipation of the central claim of the existential analytic, that the Being of *Dasein* is care. But Heidegger translates *cura* in 1921 as *Bekümmerung*, being troubled, anxious, or disturbed, and not yet as *Sorge*, as in *Being and Time*. "The end of care is delight (*delectatio*)" (*Ennarationes in Psalmos*, bk. 7, chap. 9); the goal and telos of care is the delight it takes in that for the sake of which it has troubled itself. Augustine says that we "are scattered abroad in multiplicity" and dispersion (*in multa defleximus*), dissipated by many worldly cares, but by "continence we are collected and bound up into unity within yourself" (*Confessions*, bk. 10, chap. 29), turned back to the one thing necessary. Just so, in *Being and Time*, "everyday" *Dasein* is scattered and disseminated (*zerstreut*) in the world of the "they," and by resolutely projecting upon death, it is brought back to itself. *Tentatio*, Heidegger adds (*GA* 60, 248–49), is not a property of something objectively present, not something that may or may not accompany experience, but rather it is the very stuff of experience, the fabric of which factical life is woven. For factical life is not a thing with properties but a possibility—with the freedom either to fall into the world or to gather itself together before God. To exist is to live radically in possibility (*GA* 60, 249). The possibility and the counter-possibility, the movement toward God/self and the counter movement, are not isolable psychic events but co-given tendencies, each constituted by its strife and contention with the other. So, Augustine says, I am made a burden to myself because I weep over sorrows in which I should rejoice and rejoice in pleasures over which I should sorrow. Again, when I am in adversity, I desire prosperity; but when I am in prosperity, I fear adversity. Each is what it is over and against the horizon of the other, in an interplay of desire and fear, rejoicing and sorrowing. The pull and the counter-pull, the tendency to scatter and regather, belong together in a unity of opposing tensions.

Tentatio has what Heidegger calls a "*Vollzugsinn*," translated by Theodore Kisiel as "actualization-sense" and by John van Buren as "fulfillment sense," meaning, as van Buren says, "the sense of enacting, performing, actualizing, or fulfilling the horizonal prefiguration of the whole intentional relation."[6] The notion is perhaps best seen as an existential adaptation of Husserl's distinction between an intention and its fulfillment, the difference being that a *Vollzugsinn* is sense that demands not intuitive but actional or actualizing fulfillment. A *Vollzugsinn* is grasped *in actu exercitu*, in the very doing of it, actionally and existentially. *Tentatio*, accordingly, is not to be understood as signifying a constative or theoretical content but as a formal indication of a disturbance in life that is understood only if is undergone. "Weep with me and weep for me," Augustine says, "all you who feel within yourselves that goodness from which good actions come. Those of you who have no such feeling will not be moved by what I am saying" (*Confessions*, bk. 10, chap. 33). My life will be alive (*viva erit vita mea*), Augustine says, when I will adhere to you with all of myself (*Confessions*, bk. 10, chap. 28). My life is authentic (*eigentliches*), Heidegger comments, I truly exist, when I let the whole of my facticity be permeated and transfixed by You, when my life is "so actualized (*vollzug*) that every action is carried out before You" (*so vollzogen, daß aller Vollzug vor Dir vollzieht*) (*GA* 60, 249).

The three directions of concupiscence, of the *defluere*, the three directions in which the soul's life may run off, are three "dangers" (*Gefahr*) (*GA* 60, 211) to the soul not "objectively" (bringing about its metaphysical destruction) but "factically" (confessionally, concretely, existentially, having to do with a corruption of its *cura*, the ruination of that which the heart treasures). They are not to be taken as objective items on a list, but "in their full factical 'how,' in which I have and am the world and my life" (*GA* 60, 214). They cannot be analyzed in terms of metaphysical distinctions like body and soul, reason and senses, but rather in terms of the *quotidianum bellum* (*Confessions*, bk. 10, chap. 31), of the daily war the soul wages against the tendencies that pull it apart and scatter it abroad, *malitia diei et nocti*, the evils of the day and night, the little skirmishes of everydayness, whether waking or sleeping. Thus, as I am pulled off course by the flesh (*caro*), so that I eat not in order to nourish myself but in the disorder of taking delight in food instead of God, so I must counter this tendency with fasting (*Confessions*, bk. 10, chap. 31). Again, the eyes (the cognitive sphere, generally) are disordered by *curiositas*, by the desire for something novel (*Neugier*), by a throng of endless vanities, and this under the pretense of seeking knowledge, an excess carried to the point of "morbid" curiosity, which takes a perverse delight in seeing a mangled corpse (*Confessions*, bk. 10, chap. 35). Augustine's analysis of the three tendencies of concupiscence makes an explicit appearance in *Being and Time* in the analysis of the way that everyday *Dasein* "falls" into the world (§ 35–38): a generous citation of the text of *Confessions*, Book 10, chapter 35, on the *curiositas occulorum*, appears in § 36.

The first two forms of concupiscence, Heidegger comments, are "*umweltlich*," having to do with our worldly commerce with things (*weltliches Umgehen*)—with people and things in which we seek sensual gratification. But the third struggle—with worldly pride and ambition (*ambitio saeculi*)—has more directly and explicitly to do with the self, with being a self (*Selbstsein*), with how the self "is there" (*GA* 60, p. 228), because in it we take delight in the validity and importance of the self in the world. Here the energies of *cura* are spent in winning ourselves standing in the with-world (*Mitwelt*), in winning "with-worldly validity" (*GA* 60, 229). This war is conducted on the battlefield of language: *quotidiana fornax nostra est human lingua*; "*we are tried daily in the furnace of the human tongue*" (*Confessions*, bk. 10, chap. 37). Here, language is conceived as a battlefield—not as a medium of expression or communication but as the medium in which the soul strives with itself, with its vanity, with the regard in which it is held in the *Mitwelt*. I make my way around the world *emendicato*, like a beggar, in search of words of praise and approval from other people (*Confessions*, bk. 10, chap. 37). More insidious still (*intus etiam*), I am inclined by pride to make myself important in my own eyes, to be secretly pleased with myself in the interior of my own heart. After all, I am doing things for which I should indeed be praised; am I supposed to do evil in order to avoid praise? The fault is to regard my good deeds as my own doing, not God's in me.

When Augustine writes "[i]n all these and other similar perils and toils, You see the trembling of my heart," Heidegger comments, "Augustine clearly sees the difficulty and the ultimately anxiety-producing character (*beängstigende*) of *Dasein* in such having-of-the-self (in full facticity)" (*GA* 60, 241). Still, captured as he is by Neoplatonic metaphysics, Augustine lacks the full methodological resources, lacks the conceptuality adequate to the demands of factical life that could articulate fully the land of difficulty he has discovered, the hidden regions of the self he would explore (*GA* 60, 230). The most one can do at this point is to stake out the direction that a factical interpretation would take, a direction that tends finally toward *Being and Time* itself.

For Augustine, the whole of life is trial and temptation, and it is only in temptation that a human being knows of what sort (*qualis*) it is. Life is hard and beset by difficulty, tending by an inner momentum to fall away from itself, transfixed by the *possibility* of being drawn away from its own inner course. This possibility grows more intense, Heidegger says, "the more life is lived," that is, the more intensely our *cura* is directed into the world of our concerns (*umweltlich*), into the with-world (*mitweltlich*), and toward oneself (*selbstweltlich*). Again, this possibility of falling grows more intense "the more life comes to itself," that is, the more the very being of life as a concern about itself is intensified, which means the more life takes itself as its own measure. Life grows as *molestia* grows; conversely, as molestia increases, we become increasingly aware of the full determination and genuine sense of life. *Molestia* was misunderstood by Greek asceticism and by Christian asceticism, too, insofar as it had come under the spell of the Greek, as if it were some sort of objective thing that could be simply cut off or detached by *apathia*. The Greeks failed to see that life is trial and trouble all the way down. Life would not be life, would not be living, were it not shot through with the possibility of falling, were not the task of winning oneself back from the pull of *Abfall* dangerous all the way down (*GA* 60, 244–45). To work all this out, Heidegger says, a radically new categorical determination of "life" is required (*GA* 60, 243–44). To be sure, this project of thinking through factical "life" was ultimately superseded for Heidegger—life (*vita*, *Leben*) would be regionalized as a "biological" category in *Being and Time* (§ 10)—by the problematic of "*Dasein*," whose "essence" is "*Existenz*."

THEOLOGIA CRUCIS

The distinction Heidegger makes between the Neoplatonic metaphysics of Augustine and the experience of factical life draws heavily upon Luther's distinction between the *theologia crucis* and the *theologia gloriae*, something which is made clear in the Oscar Becker manuscript that appears as appendix 2 in *Phänomenologie des religiösen Lebens*. Augustine's neo-Platonism turns on what Heidegger calls Augustine's "axiology," a schema for rank ordering higher and lower values, from the lowest objects of use (*uti*) to the highest objects of enjoyment (*frui*). As the fundamental characteristic of life, *cura* is itself distributed into *uti*, a care for the temporal things we need to use, and *frui*, the ultimate and irreducible enjoyment of unchangeable things (*GA* 60, 273). The *vita beata*—the highest, happiest, most blessed life of all—is to enjoy the highest value, God, the *summum bonum*, while the worst and lowest life—one in which care is set adrift by the pull of concupiscence—is to use the invisible and unchanging things of God in order to enjoy the changeable things of this earth. When Augustine says that God is "*decus meum*," "my pride and glory," Heidegger comments that "this is a Neoplatonic thought" (*GA* 60, 286). The good life is a well-ordered life: you obey God, and the flesh obeys you! A good man is a good valuator ("*integer aestimator*," *De doct. Christiana*, bk. 1, chaps. 27–28; *GA* 60, 279). Heidegger emphasizes that this axiology has a fundamentally "aesthetic" sense—"the beautiful belongs to the essence of Being" (*GA* 60, 271)—for *frui* means to take delight in beauty and in the good, too, insofar as it is also beautiful. Heidegger claims that the *fruitio dei* is a "specifically Greek" conception—going back not to Paul but to Plato (*GA* 60, 277), to Greek conceptions of *nous* and *theoria*—which is decisive for the subsequent history of medieval theology and mysticism. Nonetheless, *frui* is redirected by Augustine away from its Greek orientation to "intuitive" enjoyment and is "rooted in the characteristically Christian conception of factical life"

(*GA* 60, 272). Thus, while we live in hope of eternal rest and enjoyment, the present, temporal life remains one of labor and difficulty.

Heidegger questions the suitability of this Greek metaphysical hierarchy to the "phenomenon" of factical life. The *Confessions* clearly reveal to us the interweaving of the authentically Christian problematic—the question of *tentatio*, of the *deflux in multum*, and of the *quaestio mihi factus sum*—with an axiology that is fundamentally Greek and metaphysical in origin (*GA* 60, 280–81). They freely intermingle the contemplation of eternal and unchangeable being, which Heidegger suggests is a way that "Greek philosophy plays itself into Augustine's thought" (*GA* 60, 279)—with the dynamics of factical life. The Christian and the Greek constitute not only different historical epochs but phenomenologically different ways of making God accessible, resulting in different determinations of God's *Gegenständlichkeit*, the way God comes to stand in experience (*GA* 60, 179–80, 292–93). It is one thing to make God accessible as *summum bonum* or *summa pulchritudo*, which is to treat God, in Hellenic and Neoplatonic terms, as the summit of a desire for intuitive vision and unity. But it is a radically different thing to approach God in fear and trembling, with a chaste and pure fear, what Augustine calls a *timor castus*—a loving, even trusting, fear of separation from God—as opposed to the more slavish fear (*timor servilis*) of eternal punishment (*GA* 60, pp. 293–97).[7] Augustine arrived at this distinction by way of resolving the seeming contradiction between the psalmist's cry that the fear of the Lord is pure, enduring forever (Ps. 19:9) and John's reminder that perfect love casts out fear (1 John 4:18) by saying that love casts out servile fear while loving fear lives forever. The God given in chaste fear, on the battlefield of *tentatio*, is the living God, the biblical and Pauline God, who competes for attention throughout Augustine's texts with a Neoplatonic *summum bonum*, a being of peace and light, of rest and beauty: "But on the whole, the explication of the experience of God in Augustine is specifically 'Greek' (in the sense in which indeed our whole philosophy is 'Greek'). It never comes to a radically critical posing of the question and consideration of origins (destruction)" (*GA* 60, 292). And what is true of God is no less true of the "self," treated alternatively by Augustine as spiritual substance and as a land of difficulty, and the "world," which is not only an aggregate of entities for him but a phenomenological region of lure and temptation. Augustine's texts oscillate between metaphysics and facticity, on the verge of a conceptual and categorical revolution of which they are never quite capable, which both invite and require a *Destruktion* that would transform the three great themes of metaphysics—God, the self, and the world—around which Descartes and Kant organized modern philosophy. Today, Heidegger laments, we read Augustine through the lens of modern and especially of Cartesian philosophy, mistaking the factical life of the self that is astir in Augustine for a Cartesian *cogito* born of Descartes's epistemological problematic of doubt and certitude (*GA* 60, 298–99).

The conflation of Greek and Christian thematics in Augustine, perhaps even the inundating of the Christian by the Greek, was authorized and made possible, Heidegger points out, by the reading of Romans 1:20 that prevailed from the patristic period throughout medieval philosophy, according to which the invisible things of God are seen through the visible things he has made. This text was taken to be a Pauline confirmation of the Platonic ascent of the soul from the sensible to the supersensible world (*GA* 60, 281). It is only in Luther, Heidegger contends, that the meaning of this text is properly elucidated. "Only *Luther* in his earliest works has opened a new understanding of primal Christianity (*Urchristentum*)," Heidegger says (*GA* 60, 281–82), an understanding which, it is not too much to say, fundamentally shaped Heidegger's conception of a hermeneutics of facticity, particularly in the mediation of Luther to Heidegger by Kierkegaard, although later on, Heidegger laments, even Luther fell into a scholasticism of a peculiarly Protestant kind.

Luther's conception is most clearly articulated in three theses from the Heidelberg Dissertation of 1518: "No. 19: 'The man who looks upon the invisible things of God as they are perceived in created things does not deserve to be called a theologian.'" Upon which Heidegger comments, "The initial giving (*Vorgabe*) of the object of theology is not attained by way of a metaphysical consideration of the world" (*GA* 60, 282). The second thesis reads thus: "No. 21: 'The theologian of glory calls evil good and good evil, while the theologian of the Cross says what a thing is.'" Upon this, Heidegger says, "The theologian of glory, who amuses himself aesthetically with the wonders of the world, calls the sensible God. The theologian of the cross says what things are" (*GA* 60, 282). The third thesis follows: "No. 22: 'The wisdom that looks upon the invisible things of God from His works, inflates us, blinds us, and hardens our heart'" (*GA* 60, 282).

As Alister McGrath explains, "[t]he 'theologian of glory' expects God to be revealed in strength, glory and majesty, and is simply unable to accept the scene of dereliction on the cross as the self-revelation of God."[8] The theologian of glory looks to sensible things to embody in their beauty the surpassing beauty of God, hoping to find the majesty of God in a majestic mountain and to find the glory of God in a sunrise. This is dangerously close to paganism for Luther, to a Greek and Neoplatonic ascent from the sensible to the supersensible. Above all else, it ignores the distinctively Christian message of the cross. For in the cross, contrary to the expectations of human reason, God reveals himself not by analogy and by an approximate ascent through similitudes, but, *per contaria*, through his opposite, and *per posteriora* (Thesis No. 20), through his back or "rearward" parts (Exod. 33:23). In the cross, God reveals himself not through the order of the natural world, which is a common and natural revelation, but through Christ, through the perversity and disorder of his death, *per passiones et crucem*. In the cross, God is revealed not through the glory of natural manifestations but is revealed in the concealment of death and ignominy.

Thus, God reveals his power through weakness, his heights through lowliness, his wisdom through foolishness. He has revealed his power and justice by concealing it in the humiliation and death of Jesus on the cross. He has chosen for his own the least among men, those whom the world counts as *me onta*, the nothings and nobodies, who are not wise or powerful by the world's standards, and these he employs "to reduce to nothing the things that are" (1 Cor. 1:28). The defining feature of Christianity, that which sets it apart from paganism and a merely natural knowledge of God, is the cross, something that is neither visible to the senses nor understandable to reason but that is accessible only to faith. *Crux sola est nostra theologia*. So he is "worthy to be called a theologian" (*dignus dicitur*), a genuinely Christian theologian, who relies not on reason but faith and who proceeds not from the visible manifestations of God's glory but from the scenes of ignominy and distress that beset the human condition under which God has paradoxically revealed himself precisely by concealing himself from human wisdom.

What Luther calls the *theologia gloriae* lies unmistakably behind what Heidegger calls Augustine's "axiology," that is, his Neoplatonic scale of lower and higher, his metaphysics of ascent to the *summum bonum*, his ordering of human life to the enjoyment of self-sufficient and all-fulfilling goodness and beauty. By the same token, Luther's *theologia crucis* lies no less clearly behind Heidegger's valorization of struggle and difficulty, trial and trouble, and his insistence that what is distinctively *Christian* in Augustine, the still detectable traces of *Urchristentum* in Augustine, is his narrative of the life of *tentatio*, which goes to the essence of what Heidegger means by "facticity" or "factical life."

Indeed, Heidegger sketches the "dimensions" of factical life, let us says its factical spatiality (anticipating the existential spatiality of *Dasein* discussed in § 22–24 of *Being and Time*), in terms of Augustine's account of the "symbolism" of the cross in Sermon 53. When Augustine speaks of "interiority," Heidegger warns, we must avoid every "cosmic-metaphysical reification of the concept of God" (*GA* 60, 290). God is found in the inner man, in the heart, but only so long as we understand the dimensions of interiority—the proper dimensionality of the heart—whose measure is to be taken from the cross. When we turn within, we do not find an inner nook of the world from which everything else is excluded but rather the infinite length and breadth of God's infinity. We do not lose everything else but find everything anew "*in te*." The inner life and spatiality of the heart do not have the sense of a *res extensa* but of a *Vollzugssinn*, an actional or operative sense, a sense that is grasped or understood only in the doing, in *actu exercitu*, in the very act and action of concrete life.

Thus, according to Augustine, the breadth (*Weite, latitudo*) of the inner world, symbolized by the outstretched hands of Jesus nailed to the cross, is the richness and fullness of good works. Its length (*Länge, longitudo*), symbolized by that part of the upright post of the cross extending from the transversal that tends toward the ground, upon which Jesus's body is stretched out, is its patience and perseverance. Its height (*Höhe, altitudo*), symbolized by the upright from the transversal to the sky above (*supernus*), is its expectation of what lies above it, to which the heart must lift itself (*sursum corda*). Finally, its depth (*Tiefe, profundum*), symbolized by that part of the cross which is sunk into the ground, is the hidden grace of God, which itself unseen is that from which what is seen rises up (*GA* 60, 290n25).[9]

Odd as it may sound to secular ears, this Pauline theology of the Cross, of Christ and of him crucified, which so captured Luther (and after him, Kierkegaard), lies behind what Heidegger called in the early Freiburg lectures the "hermeneutics of facticity"; it lies also behind the famous account of *Dasein* as a being of "care" (*Sorge*) in *Being and Time*, from which it issued. Thus is it possible to understand what Heidegger meant when he said, in that remarkable footnote, that the analytic of *Dasein* as a Being of care is "one which has grown upon the author in connection with his attempts to interpret the Augustinian (i.e., Helleno-Christian) anthropology with regard to the foundational principles reached in the ontology of Aristotle" (*SZ*, 199n1; *BT*, 492nvii). To understand the reference to Aristotle we would need to follow a separate lecture course on the *Nicomachean Ethics*, in which Heidegger focused on the Aristotelian demand to hit the mark of *arete*, which is but one, neither overshooting nor undershooting it, as a task of particular "difficulty" (*GA* 60, 108–10), while there are many ways to miss it, which is, accordingly, "easy" to do (*Nicomachean Ethics*, 1106 b 28.).

CIRCUMFESSION: THE PRAYERS AND TEARS OF JACQUES DERRIDA

The issue of Derrida's reading of the Confessions is not a "hermeneutics of facticity" but a deeply personal meditation on the passion and death of his mother, not a war journal but a journal of her death agony. The *Confessions*, Derrida tells us, are the place that he "discovered the prayers and tears of Saint Augustine" (*Circ.*, 12/*Circum.*, 9)—not the dynamics of authentic *Dasein*. He does not write a commentary on the *Confessions* in the third person; rather, he identifies with the *Confessions*, with Augustine, "my compatriot" (*Circ.*, 19/*Circum.*, 18)—he, the son of these tears (*filius istrarum lacrymarum*) (*Circ.*, p. 126/*Circum.*, p. 132), whose mother is dying, like Monica, on the other side of the Mediterranean. He does not write *on* the *Confessions*, but he confesses, in the first person, like Augustine. "[F]or like SA [Saint Augustine] I love only tears, I only love and speak through them" (*Circ.*, 95/*Circum.*, 98). He confesses with tears and prayers—"not only do I pray, as I have never stopped doing all my life" (*Circ.*, 57/*Circum.*, 56)—asking for pardon, addressing You, or God. But what is there for him to confess? He confesses by writing his Judaism and his breach with Judaism, his circumcision and his "de-circumcision," a divided spirit which suffers both the guilt of being Jewish and the guilt of having bid farewell to Judaism. But that cut in his flesh, that divided self, is creative, constituting the passion of his life and work.

He writes of his bodily fluids, of the flow of his tears, of his blood, of semen and menstrual blood, too, and of the running bedsores (*escarres*) of his dying mother, all circulating in the image of circumcision, in a flowing, fluid paratactical prose whose fifty-nine chapters (one for each of his fifty-nine years of life) constitute the flow of a single sentence or *phrase* (*Circ.*, 110–11/*Circum.*, 115). If the Christian Augustine confesses the winding path by which he was drawn to faith in Christ, Derrida, the "little black and very Arab Jew," confesses the cut in his flesh, his circumcision—"Circumcision, that's all I've ever talked about" (*Circ.*, 70/*Circum.*, 70)—about which all his writings on limits, margins, marks, cuts, incisions, inscriptions, the ring of economy and the gift, and so on, turn.

The counterpart to the *theologia crucis* in *Circonfession* is not the robust vitality of *Selbstbekümmerung* but the flowing blood and wounded body of his dying mother, which stands in for the death of every other, in connection with which he cites a line from Celan: "It was blood, it was, that you shed, O Lord" (*Es war Blut, es war, was du vergossen, Herr*) (*Circ.*, 99–100/*Circum.*, 103). He lives with "the terror of an endless crucifixion, a thought for all my well-beloved Catherines of Siena," who wrote about the blood of Christ shed in his circumcision and on the Cross. In his texts, Derrida says, he is always shedding his own blood, tearing at his skin until he hits blood, although he does so by writing about others, so that we will be indebted to them, not him (*Circ.*, 222–23/*Circum.*, 239–40). *Circonfession* is a remarkably Derridean *theologia crucis*—sans the theology, a deconstructivist *theologia crucis*.

So, unlike Heidegger, Derrida's interest is not confined to Book 10, but he is drawn to the preceding autobiographical books, to the narratives of Monica and Augustine's youth. Still, like Heidegger, Derrida is also fascinated by Book 10: *Ecce ubi sum*; See in what a condition I am. *Flete mecum et pro me flete*; Weep with me and weep for me. But when this text is cited, it refers not to the athletic robustness of factical life, but to his dying mother—once a lovely young woman who loved to play card games and stayed up late playing poker the night before Derrida was born—now unable to drink from a cup, the water running down her chin, and to his own condition when he suffers a facial paralysis that is eventually identified as a form of Lyme disease (*Circ.*, 95/*Circum.*, 98, 115, 120). *Tu autem, domine deus meus, exaudi et respice et vide et miserere et sana me*; But do thou O Lord my God hear me and look upon me and see me and heal me—*in cujus oculis mihi quaestio factus sum*—in whose eyes I have become a question to myself (*Confessions*, bk. 10, chap. 33). But for Derrida, the questionability of life does not signify the insecurity of the self, the battle the self wages with itself for authenticity, but rather the longing of love and desire, the question of what I love when I love my God, of what I desire when I love and desire what is "to come" (*à venir*), which is what Derrida calls "the impossible"—"having never loved anything but the impossible" (*Circ.*, 7/*Circum.*, 3).

For Derrida, Augustine's *Confessions* are the occasion of a prayer, of revealing the "secret" of his prayers and tears—"I wonder if those reading me from up there see my tears . . . if they guess that my life was but a long history of prayers" (*Circ.*, 40/*Circum.*, 38–39)—not of an analysis of the formal structure of factical life. Derrida finds in Augustine not the virile militancy of a spiritual battlefield but bodies bent by sorrow and grief, not the brawny bravado of *Eigentlichkeit* but the woman weeping at the foot of the cross, not the combative strength of a Christian soldier but the weakness of a suppliant begging for God's help, not a masculinized *Kampfsphilosophie* but love, not a soul whose mettle is fired by a war with concupiscence but saintly eyes blinded by tears.

For Heidegger, the hermeneutic presupposition of *confiteri*, of the confessional mode, is that the soul is the scene of battle, turmoil, and unrest. But for Derrida, confession reduces us to tears and to asking for pardon, and it is linked with the flow of blood. *Cruor, confiteor*: to confess is to let my blood flow, to draw my blood with a syringe/pen, and to store my confession of faith (*cru*) in a labeled bottle like wine (*cru*) (*Circ.*, 13/*Circum.*, 10). To confess is to mix the outpouring of blood with the outpouring of tears. "I owe it to autobiography to say that I have spent my life teaching so as to return in the end to what mixes prayer and tears with blood" (*Circ.*, 22/*Circum.*, 20). Blood is the color of mortal life, of "desire, history, or event" (*Circ.*, 82/*Circum.*, 80). Circumfession is the confession in writing, *in litteris*, of Derrida's circumcision, the confession of his Jewish/Arab provenance and of his lack of a language, for the Christian/Latin/French in which he writes these confessions is and is not his, and that is brought home by the generous citations of Augustine's lush Latin. I am the last of the Jews (*Circ.*, 145/*Circum.*, 154), he says, like his namesake Elijah, the last of the prophets—a philosopher, who, having left Judaism, revisits or is revisited by his Jewishness, in this age after the death of God. Confession means for him to make a gift without return, like a last will and testament, beyond the circle (*Circ.*, 221/*Circum.*, 238), leaving behind a secret that everyone understands but him.

Monica never makes an appearance in Heidegger's lecture course. Like Kierkegaard, this Heideggerian Augustine seems to have no mother. But *Circonfession* is, from the first page on, all about Monica/Georgette Safar Derrida, dying in her emigrant home, on the other side of the Mediterranean in Nice (having emigrated from what is today Algiers), like Monica dying in Ostia (*Circ.*, 20/*Circum.*, 19). Derrida looks like his mother, favors his mother's side, resembling perhaps an ancestor on the mother's side who emigrated from Portugal to Algeria at the beginning of the nineteenth century (*Circ.*, 232–34/*Circum.*, 253). When he weeps, he never knows who is weeping, he or his mother (*Circ.*, 243/*Circum.*, 263). There is no evading death and dying in *Being and Time*, but that always means *my* death, while *Circonfession* is a journal of the death of Derrida's mother, of the other, of what Mark Taylor calls the "(m)other," and of my death insofar as it concerns the other. In *Circonfession*, at fifty-nine years of age, Derrida says, he is learning how to die, but that is always seen from the point of view of the other. He tries to give himself death, *se donner la mort*, not in the sense of committing suicide but in the sense of seeing himself dead and of seeing others "seeing me lying on my back," gathered around his grave, "and I weep like my own children at the edge of my grave" (*Circ.*, p. 41/*Circum.*, p. 40). He fears for his life, not for himself but for her, from her fear for him, so that he fears too that perhaps, after her death, he will no longer fear death (*Circ.*, 198/*Circum.*, 212).

As Augustine's *Confessions* (though they are addressed to God) do not tell God anything God does not know (bk. 9, chap. 1), so Derrida's circumfession consists not in disclosing the truth, in communicating some secret truth to anyone, to G(eoffrey), God, or us. Derrida has no truth to tell but is making the truth, doing the truth, *facere veritatem*, confessing in writing, *confiteor in litteris*, with prayers and tears, as much religion as literature. But what then is confessed? The "essential truth of avowal" has "nothing to do with truth, but consist[s] . . . in asked for pardon," because to write is to ask pardon (*Circ.*, 47–50/*Circum.*, 46–49). As Augustine is not trying to give God some information that God otherwise lacks but rather "to arouse my feeling of love toward Thee, and that of those who read these pages" (bk. 10, chap. 1), Derrida, who does not know the secret, who has no secret Truth to tell, is trying to arouse his love of life and ours, to transform himself through and through (*Circ.*, 75–76/*Circum.*, 76–77), and to learn how to die (*Circ.*, 193/*Circum.*, 208). He walks around with a secret unknown to himself, in a sealed text, which he is always commenting upon, which others will open and read (*Circ.*, 238–39/*Circum.*, 257–58).

If Heidegger identifies the formal structure of *Vollzugsinn*, Derrida actually carries it out, enacts a confession, performs it, *in litteris*. *Circonfession* is written with the personal passion of the *Confessions*, as a work of "memory and heart" (*Circ.*, 85/*Circum.*, 87). Of his dying mother, Derrida writes, "A little while ago she pronounced my name, Jackie, in echo to the sentence from my sister passing her the receiver, 'hello Jackie,' something she had not been able to do for months and will perhaps do no more, beyond the fact that through her whole life she scarcely knew the other name" (*Circ.*, 80–82/*Circum.*, 83). "Jackie," we learn, is his given name, "Jacques" a pen name, and "Elie" a Hebrew name given to him at birth, a name so secret that it was unknown until recently even to him, a "*given* name that I received without receiving . . . a sign of election (*on élit*)" (*Circ.*, 82/*Circum.*, 84). He thought of calling a notebook on circumcision that he had been keeping the "Book of Elijah," Elijah being the prophet guardian of circumcision. Like Monica weeping for Augustine when he set sail for Europe, Georgette weeps over the nineteen-year-old Jackie setting sail for France (*Circ.*, 16/*Circum.*, 177). He remembers feigning illness one day as a child when, holding his mother's hand, she walked him to school; when later in the afternoon she returns to pick him up, he reproached her for leaving him "in the world, in the hands of others," having forgotten that he was supposed to be sick. "She must have been as beautiful as a photograph" (*Circ.*, 250/*Circum.*, 271). These are secrets of the heart that he communicates to us, *in litteris*, in a personal memoir.

There is pain in *Circonfession*, not the pain of factical life struggling for authenticity but the pain emblematized in circumcision. That, of course, is a pain I do not remember but whose trace is unmistakable, hence a "phantom pain," a pain we think, presumptuously, that the infant does not much mind. We assure and comfort ourselves with the thought, possibly the fantasy, Derrida says, that the orange flower water with which the child is bathed immediately after the rite of circumcision has an anesthetic virtue. The phantom pain I cannot remember, with which I try to identify, is the pain of the mother who is kept in a separate room, in tears, while the rite is enacted; or the pain of the mother, Monica/Georgette, dying on the other side of the Mediterranean. The unmistakable trace of pain left by circumcision is the pain of the other—"a threat which returns every time the other is in pain, if I identify with him, with her, even" (*Circ.*, 66/*Circum.*, 66), whose pain is always a phantom for me, for, like the trace of circumcision, I see it but do not feel it and can only try to remember it.

The lively kinetics and spiritual athleticism of the hermeneutics of facticity that Heidegger finds in the *Confessions* stand in remarkable contrast to the dominant motifs of *Circonfession*: a dying woman confined to bed, her running bedsores, fading memory and speech; and Derrida's facial paralysis, finally diagnosed as Lyme disease, which appears as a filial counterpart to the mother's terminal illness. The cause of Derrida's facial paralysis was at first unknown, an alarming symptom of a stroke perhaps and perhaps the prelude to a more massive stroke and an untimely death. Might Derrida's death overtake and precede his mother's? Would he be dead before her, before he finished these confessions? He sees himself dead before her, while she, her memory gone, does not see his death. *Ecce ubi sum*: a twisted mouth, a disfigured face, a cyclops: "My left eye fixed open like a glass-eyed cyclops" (*Circ.*, 98/*Circum.*, 95), an invisible scar to match the visible *escarres* of the dying mother, an invisible scar to match the visible scar of circumcision, a "scarface . . . the monocular warning light of his [God's] evil" (*Circ.*, 101/*Circum.*, 104; cf. *Confessions*, bk. 7, chap. 5), a punishment perhaps for any of many faults—*Ecce ubi sum*: the dying mother, increasing blindness, distorted speech, inability to recognize her children, living, dead or dying—if that is what is happening to Jackie.

There is a conversion, a *metanoia*, in *Circonfession*, but it is not the self-recovery of authentic Christian freedom from the sway of sin that Heidegger reads in Augustine but a conversion brought about in Derrida from without—"I am no longer the same since the FP [facial paralysis], whose signs seem to have been effaced though I know I'm not the same persona" (*Circ.*, 117/*Circum.*, 123). Derrida is learning how to die and what his death means for others.

One of the surprises that is in store for us in *Circonfession* is Derrida's love of God. "What do I love when I love you," "my God," Augustine asks (*Confessions*, bk. 10, chaps. 6–7). For Heidegger, the name of God is the name of struggle (*Kampf*): to love God is to love difficulty (*Schwierigkeit*), burden (*onus*), and trouble (*molestia*) (*Confessions*, bk. 10, chap. 28). *Vita . . . tota tentatio [est]* (*Confessions*, bk. 10, chap. 32): "God is there," Heidegger says, "in troubling over the life of the self" (*GA* 60, 289). Struggle gives the measure to life, and the life of the soul before God, *coram deo*, raises struggle (*Kampf*) to its highest pitch and to its most exuberant vitality. But for Derrida the name of God is mingled with tears. Where is God? *In memoria mea*. Where in my memory? "Well, I'm remembering God this morning, the name, a quotation, something my mother said . . . to quote the name of God as I heard it perhaps the first time, no doubt in my mother's mouth when she was praying, each time she saw me ill, no doubt dying like her son before me, like her son after me . . . I hear her say, '*grâce à Dieu, Dieu merci*' when the temperature goes down, weeping in pronouncing your name . . . I'm mingling here the name of God with the origin of tears" (*Circ.*, 112–13/*Circum.*, 117–18). For "Jackie," this weepy, pusillanimous little child whom the adults love to tease and reduce to tears, the name of God commingles with tears; for the internationally known philosopher, for "Derrida," the name of God remains the question of all questions. Unlike Heidegger, for whom this name spells the end of questioning, Derrida asks again and again, confesses that he has been asking all his life, *quid ergo amo cum deum [meum] amo*: What do I love when I love my God? "Can I do anything other than translate this question by SA into my own language?" (*Circ.*, 117/*Circum.*, 122), having slightly altered the position of the *meum* in the text of *Confessions* (bk. 10, chap. 6). The emphasis in this very biblical expression "my God" is on the *my*, not in the sense that this is merely some sort of subjective fabrication on his part but in the sense of a God who belongs to him even as he belongs to his God, to this most personal God who knows the secrets of his heart and to whom he confesses; a little like, in the beginning of Genesis, the God "of Abraham" and "of Jacob" had such a personal sense that it needed to be made plain that these are the same God. This preoccupation with Judaism and God is "what my readers won't have known about me," he says, "like my religion about which nobody understands anything" (*Circ.*, 146/*Circum.*, 154).

Even Monica/Georgette, worrying over the faith of the son of these tears, knows nothing of this religion. She had been afraid to ask Jackie whether he still believed in God, even though she might have known that "the constancy of God in my life is called by other names, so that I quite rightly pass for an atheist" (*Circ.*, 146/*Circum.*, 155). God is omnipresent for Derrida, in this "absolved, absolutely private language," not in the form of an eyewitness who sees everything he does nor of a transcendent law regulating every moment of life but in the sense of being "the secret I am excluded from," the "open secret" (*secret de Polichinelle*), which is known to others but not to him. The name of God is the name of the secret that penetrates and suffuses everything he does and writes, where the secret is not a deep and hidden *magnum mysterium* in the sense of a negative theology but rather the secret that there is no secret, that there is no deep Truth to which only a few initiates have access. The secret is that there is no Secret Truth, which is why there is no Truth or Secret to confess but only texts. To be sure, this is no cause for despair for Derrida but rather a source of passion, what he calls elsewhere *la passion du non-savoir*, the passion which arises from non-knowledge, from the un-truth, which does not condemn but enjoins the endless play of interpretation. That is why the secret is known to everyone but him, why it is an open secret, for it is precisely in the ear of the other, or in their counter-signatures to come, that the secret of Derrida will be laid bare. His secret is nothing he knows and nothing he can confess, so that his God "circulate[s] among the unavowables" (*Circ.*, 146–47/*Circum.*, 155–56), God being the name of the secret, of I know not what, of the passion of not knowing that drives writing.

For Heidegger, language is the furnace in which authentic *Dasein* is tried, the chatter of the "they" which distracts and dissipates authentic resolve. But for Derrida, language is a mark of dispossession: "I'm reaching the end without *ever* having read Hebrew" (*Circ.*, 264–65/*Circum.*, 286–87), the notorious convolutions and learned circumlocutions of his texts being, thus, the way he constantly gropes with the unknown grammar of Hebrew in "Christian Latin French," "a language made a present to me by its colonization of Algeria in 1830" (*Circ.*, 263/*Circum.*, 285). Even circumcision, the thing itself, has been relayed to him in the word "*circoncision*," which is Christian/Latin/French; indeed, even that word was dropped among Algerian Jews who, "through fearful acculturation," preferred to speak of their "baptism" and to call bar mitzvah "communion" (*Circ.*, 71–72/*Circum.*, 71–73). Derrida speaks the language of the outside, an outsider's language, the Latin of the *numerus clausus*. He took flight from Hebrew when they tried to make him learn it as a child, even as French could never be his (*Circ.*, 267/*Circum.*, 289). That exile, that loss, engendered his taste for words and letters and became the passion that would make his whole life a *confiteri in litteris*. That is a profoundly different conception of language than is to be found in Heidegger's thought, where language is the language of the *Heimat*, Germany's or Being's, where speaking is empowered by autochthony, by the gathering together of the essential power of the *Volk* or *Sprache* from which one speaks.

In *Being and Time*, Heidegger speaks of a primordial and ontological guilt, of a finitude which it is the whole point of authentic *Dasein* to assume, to appropriate and take over, to make one's own. In the Heideggerian analysis of guilt, the idea is to refine guilt into the one point of authentic resoluteness so that authentic *Dasein* is pointed into the definite, finite, refined finitude of its own singlemost *Seinkönnen*, the *Seelenfünklein* of authentic freedom. Primordial or ontological guilt for Heidegger is thus the scene of freedom, but for Derrida, guilt is the scene of confession. Derrida, too, writes of a guilt for which he can remember no fault: "Scenes of guilt in some sense faultless, without any deliberate fault, situations in which the accusation surprises you," scenes that constitute a paradigm for a whole life, scenes he must not precisely "assume," since they are older than freedom (Levinas) but which he must allow to become productive, for they "play in their Confessions an organizing and abyssal role" (*Circ.*, 278/*Circum.*, 301). This incomprehensible fault is "all Hebrew [not Greek] to me" (*Circ.*, 279/*Circum.*, 302), the fault of being all Hebrew, or not quite all, "for I am perhaps not what remains of Judaism." But then again, "what else am I in truth, who am I if I am not what I inhabit and where I take place, *ich bleibe also Jude*, i.e., today in what remains of Judaism to this world," a fragment of Judaism, a broken shard and remainder (*Circ.*, 279–80/*Circum.*, 302–3). This faultless guilt, which is to be Jewish and then again to have broken with Judaism, is like the scar of circumcision for which he can remember no pain, or like Augustine's notion of original sin, that which we inherit but do not commit (which Kierkegaard, whose lead Heidegger followed, felt compelled to rewrite in *The Concept of Anxiety* so as to give freedom a place), or like Kafka (another prisoner of Prague), or like Isaac (whose fate on Moriah was even more incomprehensible than father Abraham's).

Derrida speaks of the "despair" that stretches from "the innocent child who is by accident charged with a guilt he knows nothing about, the little Jew expelled from Ben Aknoun school" to "the drug-factor incarcerated in Prague, and everything in between" (*Circ.*, 282/*Circum.*, 306). "I always thought," he writes, "the other must have good reason to accuse me" (*Circ.*, 277/*Circum.*, 300), and he did not then see that "it was enough to seek to track down the event by writing backward, never seeing the next step"—about the future, always to come (*à venir*), he is essentially blind—in order to prepare "the moment when things turn round, the moment at which you will be able to convert and see your sacrificer face on," not in order to continue the cycle of persecution but to "make the truth," *facere veritatem*, to confess in writing. His fault is the crime of being Jewish, the guilt of being the hated other, which is compounded by his own unfaithfulness to being Jewish, his breach with, his crime against, Judaism. He is chosen from of old to be Jewish, but he has abandoned the chosen (*élu*) people, the people of *élu/Élie*, abandoned (*aban-donné*) his givenness, himself, so that by marrying outside Judaism and by not circumcising his sons, he too is one of those who persecutes the Jews, who does nothing to save the Jews, in Christian/Latin/French.

Circonfession ends on May 1, 1990, in Laguna Beach, California, not far from Santa Monica, California (Derrida's mother still lay dying in Nice—she would not succumb until December 5, 1991), on the occasion of the "Final Solution" conference at the University of California–Los Angeles. After his address, a "young imbecile," apparently unaware that Derrida is Jewish, asks Derrida what he did to save the Jews during the war. Still, the youngster might be right, the other is always right, for he did not do enough to save one Jew, himself, *for* his Jewishness, this being an alliance mostly honored in the breach, or from his Jewishness, this lack of continuity with his Jewishness also amounting to a lack of rupture. His circumcision signifies his cut from the covenant cut in his flesh, from the community of the covenant, but a cut that is not clean.

Sero te amavi, pulchritudo tam antiqua et tam nova (*Confessions*, bk. 10, chap. 27), Augustine writes: Too late have I loved thee, o beauty so ancient and so new. Too late, Derrida writes, you are too late (*trop tard*), you (*toi*), the counterpart of me (*moi*), for this secret which is withheld. "You have spent your life inviting calling promising, hoping sighing dreaming, convoking invoking provoking, constituting engendering producing, naming assigning demanding, prescribing commanding sacrificing"—so that you, the witness and the counterpart of me, will attest this "secret truth, severed from truth, that you will never have had any witness" (*Circ.*, 290–91/*Circum.*, 314).

The truth is that there is no Truth; the secret is that there is no Secret, no Secret Truth to which we have some secret access or witness. Unlike Heideggerian *Denken*, which is steered by a mighty *Geschick*, a destiny and *moira*, our destiny on Derrida's account is "destinerrance," destiny gone errant, cut off from destiny and the Truth of Being. The cut of circumcision in *Circonfession* comes down to being cut off from truth, *sevrée de la vérité*, from the Truth of Being or of the Book. "You alone, whose life will have been so short, the voyage short, scarcely organized, by you with no lighthouse and no book, you the floating toy at high tide and under the moon, you the crossing between these two phantoms of witnesses that will never be the same," where *toi* and *moi*, the witness and the one to whom witness is given, can never be one, where both the witness and the one to whom one gives witness are both in the blind, where no Truth, no Truth of truth, no Secret Truth can ever be testified to and secured. But this destinerrant condition, the blindness of eyes blinded by tears, these prayers and tears, are for Derrida not a paralyzing and immobilizing despair but the passion of non-knowing, the prayers and tears of a somewhat Jewish, avant-garde Augustine, who has in his own unrepeatable way found a way to repeat the *Confessions* of Augustine and even to repeat, in a slightly postmodern beat, the *theologia crucis*.

NOTES

1. John D. Caputo, *Demythologizing Heidegger* (Bloomington: Indiana University Press, 1993), chaps. 2–3.

2. The following abbreviations are used in this study: *SZ*, Martin Heidegger, *Sein und Zeit*, 15th ed. (Tübingen, Germany: Niemeyer, 1979); *BT*,

Martin Heidegger, *Being and Time*, trans. John Macquarrie and Edward Robinson (New York: Harper & Row, 1962); *GA* 60, *Phänomenologie des religiösen Lebens*, 1, "*Einführung in die Phänomenologie der Religion*" (Wintersemester 1920–21), ed. Matthias Jung and Thomas Regehly; 2, "*Augustinus und der Neuplatonismus*" (Sommersemester, 1921); 3, "*Ausaurbeitung und Entwürfe*," ed. Claudius Strube, *Gesamtausgabe*, B. 60 (Frankfurt: Klostermann, 1995); *SUD*, *Kierkegaard's Writings*, vol. 19, *Sickness unto Death*, trans. Howard Hong and Edna Hong (Princeton, NJ: Princeton University Press, 1980); *Circon.*, *Circonfession: Cinquante-neuf périodes et périphrases*, in *Jacques Derrida*, Geoffrey Bennington and Jacques Derrida (Paris: Éditions du Seuil, 1991); *Circum.*, *Circumfession: Fifty-nine Periods and Periphrases*, in *Jacques Derrida*, Geoffrey Bennington and Jacques Derrida, trans. Geoffrey Bennington (Chicago: University of Chicago Press, 1993). For excellent accounts of the matters discussed in the first part of this article, see Theodore Kisiel, *The Genesis of Heidegger's "Being and Time"* (Berkeley: University of California Press, 1993), and John van Buren, *The Young Heidegger: Rumor of the Hidden King* (Bloomington: Indiana University Press, 1994).

3. As van Buren shows in *Young Heidegger* (162–67), the very term *Destruktion*, first appearing in Heidegger's early Freiburg lectures, in the winter semester 1919–20 course, seems to have been taken from Luther's use of the Latin *destructio*, which describes the "right" attitude a Christian theology should take to that "blind pagan Master Aristotle." The Lutheran destruction became for Heidegger the paradigm of the task of the destruction of Greek and scholastic meta-physics, down to its sources in primal Christianity. See Heidegger, *Gesamtausgabe*, vol. 58, *Grundprobleme der Phänomenologie* (Frankfurt: Klostermann, 1993), 139, 61–62, 205.

4. Indeed, Heidegger was early on interested in the work of theologian Franz Overbeck, who had declared that even by the time of the New Testament, the primitive Christian experience was beginning to be turned over to theological objectification because of contamination by Greek philosophy. See Istvan Féher, "Heidegger's Understanding of the Atheism of Philosophy," *American Catholic Philosophical Quarterly* 69 (1995): 189–228 (appendix 2).

5. "Ecce unde vita humana super terram tota tentatio est." Augustine, *Epistulae*, bk. 95, chap. 2; cf. *GA* 60, 241n1.

6. Van Buren, *Young Heidegger*, 29. It is distinguished from the content-sense or intentional content; and the relational-sense, or meaning of the way we are related to the content. See van Buren, *Young Heidegger*, 29–32.

7. See Augustine, *In Epist. Joannis ad Parthos*, bk. 9, chap. 5, and *In Psalmos*, bk. 19, chap. 10. In a note to the analysis of *Angst* in § 40 of *Being and Time*, Heidegger draws our attention to Augustine's distinction between *timor castus* and *timor servilis* and treats it as a predecessor of the distinction between *Angst* and *Furcht*, on which latter distinction, he says, the most headway has been made by Kierkegaard (*SZ*, 190n; *BT*, p. 492niv). This is a not entirely generous way of saying that he has taken this distinction over, in all of its phenomenological particulars, from Kierkegaard and then reinscribed it within his own project, the "existential analytic." Pure fear, Heidegger says in 1921, is self-fear, a salutary troubling about one's own being, while servile fear is world-fear, a concern directed at things or other persons (*GA* 60, 296–97).

8. Alister E. McGrath, *Luther's Theology of the Cross* (Oxford: Blackwell, 1990), 167. My characterization of this distinction is greatly indebted to McGrath, *Luther's Theology of the Cross*, 148–75. See also van Buren, *Young Heidegger*, 159–67, 187–90, 196–202, 376–82.

9. See Augustine, *Sermones*, bk. 53, chaps. 15–16.

17
Jacques Derrida (1930–2004)

With the death of Jacques Derrida on October 8, 2004, some thirty-seven years after he first burst upon the scene in 1967 with three explosive books of philosophy, the world lost one of its deepest, most original, and most provocative figures. Born of an assimilated French-speaking Jewish family in Algeria on July 15, 1930, he immigrated to France to study philosophy in 1950 and in 1957 made his first visit to the United States, to which he would be linked by the stars. Named after the American child movie star Jackie Coogan—his birth name was "Jackie"—he was to achieve there an astonishing and long-standing celebrity, perhaps even greater than in France.

His death was greeted with both an outpouring of moving eulogies from his admirers and several sharp attacks on his legacy from both liberal and conservative media. On what passes for an American Left these days, the *New York Times* obituary was so mean-spirited and unfair that it elicited a letter of protest that ended up going online and collecting the signatures of thousands of academics, architects, writers, artists, and other intellectuals, while the *Wall Street Journal*, on the other hand, simply put a right-wing hit man on the job. Scott McLemee's pieces in *The Chronicle of Higher Education* stood out as a glaring and thoughtful exception to this media attack.

Why the controversy? Because the genius of Derrida lay in brushing against the grain. He showed the left that Enlightenment "reason" was to a great extent a historical construction, a more scrupulous account of which would have to include a lot more about faith, contingency, and context. He showed the Right that "tradition" was also a construction that was a far more complex and polyvalent mix, a more scrupulous study of which would turn up a lot more than family values and proof that God was on your side. He did this, to boot, in a sometimes playful punning style of writing and of thinking—he was a great and early admirer of James Joyce—that violated the protocols of received academic discourse, a transgression that even the Marxists had avoided. Those who knew Derrida know that he always had the devil in his eyes. Pursuing a program calculated to madden everyone, his care for more scrupulous renderings of reason and of tradition was greeted with unscrupulous attack. This is not without precedent. The same of course could have been said for Socrates, who had the same fatal genius for stirring up the great sleeping Athenian steed; for St. Paul, who was run out of more towns than he could count; and for Kierkegaard, at whose burial there was actually a riot.

The fuss was about something Derrida called "deconstruction," a word that has actually made it into high-popular culture and shows signs of making it into the common vocabulary. What everyone has more or less picked up about deconstruction, even if they have never read a word of it, is its destabilizing effect on our favorite texts and institutions. Derrida exposes a certain coefficient of uncertainty in all of them, which causes all of us, right and left, religious and nonreligious, male and female, considerable discomfort. That was the side of deconstruction that grabbed all the headlines and made it in the 1970s a kind of academic *succès de scandale*. Without reading very closely, it all looked like a joyous nihilism. But what his critics missed (and here not reading him makes a difference!), and what never made it into the headlines, is that the destabilizing agency in his work is not a reckless relativism or an acidic skepticism but rather an affirmation, a love of what in later years he would call the "undeconstructible." The undeconstructible is the subject matter of pure and unconditional affirmation—"*viens, oui, oui*" (come, yes, yes)—something unimaginable and inconceivable by the current standards of imagining and conceiving. The undeconstructible is the stuff of a desire beyond desire, of a desire to affirm that goes beyond a desire to possess, the desire of something for which we can live without reserve. His critics had never heard of this because it was not reported in *Time Magazine*, but they did not hesitate to denounce what they had not read. This was the case with the famous signatories of the letter to Cambridge University who disgracefully declared Derrida unworthy of an honorary degree because he undermined the standards of responsible scholarship—the most elemental tenet of which would surely have been first to read what you criticize in public (a close second being, if you do read it, try to understand it).

It was not surprising that in the last fifteen years Derrida would start talking about religion, telling us about his "religion (without religion)," about his "prayers and tears," and about the Messiah. He would even write a kind of Jewish Confessions called "Circumfession," a haunting and enigmatic journal he kept while his beloved mother lay dying in Nice, a diary *cum* dialogue with St. Augustine, his equally weepy "compatriot." Modern-day Algeria is the ancient homeland (Numidia) of Augustine, and Derrida even lived on a street called the *Rue Saint Augustin*. In this text, the son of these tears (Augustine/Jacques) circumfessed (to God/"you") about his mother (Monica/Georgette), who lay dying on the northern shores of the Mediterranean (Ostia/Nice), to which both families had immigrated. This side of Derrida even makes some admirers nervous, for they would prefer their Derrida straight up, not on what seems to them religious rocks.

His critics failed to see that deconstructing this, that, and everything in the name of the undeconstructible is a lot like what religious people, especially Jews, would call the "critique of idols." Deconstruction, it turns out, is not nihilism; it just has high standards! Deconstruction is satisfied with nothing because it is waiting for the Messiah, which Derrida translated into the philosophical figure of the "to come" (*à venir*), the very figure of the future (*l'avenir*), of hope and expectation. Deconstruction's meditation on the contingency of our beliefs and practices—on democracy, for example—is made in the name of a promise that is astir in them, for example, of a democracy "to come" for which every existing democracy is a but a faint predecessor state.

But if this religious turn made his secularizing admirers nervous, it made religious people still more nervous. For after all, by the standards of the local rabbi or pastor, Derrida "rightly passes for an atheist," which gives secular deconstructors much comfort (but giving comfort is not what deconstruction was sent into the world to do). When asked why he does not say "I am" an atheist (*je suis, c'est moi*), he said it was because he did not *know* if he were, that there are many voices within him that give one another no rest, and he lacks the absolute authority of an authorial "I" to still this inner conflict. So the best he can do is to rightly pass for this or that, and he is very sorry that he cannot do better. That, it seems to me, is an exquisite formula not only for what might be called Derrida's atheism, but also for faith. Rightly passing for this or that, a Christian, say, really is the best we can do. It reminds me of the formula put forward by Kierkegaard's "Johannes Climacus" (more Socratic figures!) who deferred saying that he "is" a Christian but is doing the best he can to "become" one.

Derrida visits upon all of us—Christian and Jew, religious and secular, left and right—the unsettling news of the radical instability of the categories to which we have such ready recourse, and he raises the idea of a still deeper idea of ourselves which (religiously?) confesses its lack of categories. He exposes us to the "secret" that there is no "Secret," no Big Capitalized Secret to which we have been wired up—by scientific reason, by poetic or religious revelation, or by political persuasion. We make use of such materials as have been available to us, forged in the fires of time and circumstance. We do not in some deep way know who we are or what the world is. That is not nihilism but a quasi-religious confession, the beginning of wisdom, the onset of faith and compassion. Derrida exposes the doubt that does not merely insinuate itself into faith but that in fact constitutes faith, for faith is faith precisely in the face of doubt and uncertainty, the passion of non-knowing. Violence on the other hand arises from having a low tolerance for uncertainty so that Derrida shows us why religious violence is bad faith. On Derrida's terms, we do not know the name of what we desire with a desire beyond desire. That means that leading a just life comes down to coping with such non-knowing, negotiating among the several competing names that fluctuate undecidably before us, each pretending to name what we are praying for. For we pray and weep for something that is coming, something I know not what, something nameless that in always slipping away also draws us in its train.

May he rest in peace, he who was sent to us to give us no peace.

Adieu, Jacques.

§4

Impossible Hermeneutics: From Sacred Anarchy to Radical Theology

18 Sacred Anarchy: Fragments of a Postmodern Ethics

RADICALLY DIFFICULT HERMENEUTICS

"Postmodernism," on my reading, is the issue of a crisis in hermeneutics. It is a radicalization of the problem of *hermeneusis* that faces up to the fact that hermeneutics has no metaphysical backup, no Hegelian assurances that the truth is inevitably working itself out, continually being reappropriated again and again. It is a more merciless hermeneutics that does not so much deny "tradition," as its critics charge, as redefine tradition as a highly factical, fortuitous, and almost hopelessly complex accumulation of competing subtraditions, power plays, and incommensurable language games, along with a dash of wisdom here and there. (Whose wisdom? Can we reach a consensus about that? You see the problem.) Postmodernism is less inclined to think that the tradition process is an ongoing retrieval of truth and more inclined to regard it as a repetition forward in the direction of who-knows-what. It is, on my rendering, the outcome of recognizing the inescapability of *hermeneusis*, and its much trumpeted "anti-foundationalism" is mostly a matter of recognizing how slippery the grounds are upon which we (almost) stand. Like Derrida, it likes to slip in this slippery "almost" (*presque*) wherever "philosophy" thinks it stands on solid ground.

Postmodernism is for me still a version of hermeneutics, even though it is the issue of the anti-hermeneutical tendencies of structuralist semiotics and poststructuralism. For the most part, postmodernism pursues in a more merciless way the radical difficulties entailed by the hermeneutic situation. That is why, in associating myself with postmodernism, I always speak of "radical hermeneutics," that is, a radically difficult hermeneutics. I am trying to inhabit a place where, if I get it right, my more Gadamerian critics will think I have made things too difficult and my more postmodern critics will think I have not made things difficult enough. That of course is a very perverse intention on my part. For I will then claim to have it right, and the proof will be that everyone thinks I am wrong (provided of course we could ever agree about what getting it right means).

Now up to a point this sounds like fun. Almost. Until you turn to ethics. Then it is that brows wrinkle and faces grow red. Ethics has to do with violence, and while hermeneutical violence is one thing, the sort of violence that spills blood is not funny. We fail to see the humor of postmodernists who insist on saying that, even when you get to ethics, the ground gives way. So what I want to address here is what ethics looks like from the standpoint of a radically difficult hermeneutics, that is, one which recognizes that we never have to do with uninterpreted facts of the matter, that *hermeneusis* is inescapable. Let's make it harder, more difficult, and let us speak of "undecidability," that you can never still the unrest between undecidables, that things have a way of wavering, trembling, so that we cannot come down with assurance on either side, without the fear and trembling. Now let us make it harder still: consider the case of Auschwitz, of unspeakable horror. What is undecidable about that? Can we not condemn Auschwitz with unequivocal decisiveness, with assurance, with no hermeneutical ambiguity, with no conflict of interpretations?

In what follows, I hope to show that ethics too is an interpretation, a "reading" we give to experience, and I want to follow the lines of one reading in particular, to sketch out one sort of hermeneutics, one sort of ethics in particular, the one I would say that has the most claim upon us. I want to take this particular occasion to make use of certain distinctly biblical motifs, and that calls for a few important precautionary comments. I do not wish to identify myself with every line of thought to be found in the scriptures, every text that can be trotted out against me, because as a "text" I take the scriptures to be an (almost) hopelessly complex maze of competing lines of thought. Nor do I wish to wrap my views in the institutional power of the church—far from it! Nor am I making a "theological" argument, invoking theological authority—far from that too! I want to keep my distance from all such concentrated forms of power.

What I am doing is taking up a certain historical form of life, or life world, which I treat as a certain hermeneutico-phenomenological type or exemplar. Its value to me, here, lies strictly in its hermeneutical, interpretive worth, its persuasiveness, and its power to lay claim to us. I am going to hold this *hermeneusis*—which I am going to call "Jewish," in a sense that will become increasingly generic—over and against another type which I am going to call "Greek," in an equally generic sense, and I am going to see if Jewish hermeneutics upsets the cart of Greek hermeneutics—which will make a lot of difference to ethics, I hope to show. The result of that will be neither Jewish nor Greek but much more like the line that Derrida, when he is discussing Levinas, cites from James Joyce, "Jewgreek is Greekjew." ("Jew" and "Greek" never was a binary scheme in which we should put too much trust).

Then, at the end, I will come back to the question of the fear and trembling, the wavering and the difficulty, because it will, for a while, look like I have made this hermeneutics too easy. For I am invoking one of the most powerful and authoritative books in our tradition, a book that is inextricably intertwined with a very authoritative, patriarchal, hierarchical institution, the church; a book and an institution that are dead set on stilling the flux and putting things to rest. Not a lot of readers of the scriptures are anti-foundationalist; a lot more are fundamentalist. So, at the end, I will try to restore the difficulty that it is the perversity of radical hermeneutics so to cherish.

POSTMODERNISM, ETHICS, AND THE LOSS OF THE ARCHE

A very good postmodern writer—Philippe Lacoue-Labarthe—has put the problem of ethics from the standpoint of a radically difficult hermeneutics in an excellent way. We lack the authority to write an ethics, he says. We lack the name, above all the sacred names that govern the space of ethical life, in whose name it would be possible to judge, to pass judgment. That is our postmodernism. Still, we are all agreed that it is a crime to be a Nazi. So he brings in Auschwitz. (Lacoue-Labarthe is speaking of Heidegger.) That is our ethics.

Our common postmodern problem—we are at least that much of a "community," a community of the groundless ones—is that the authority of ethics has been withdrawn, its foundations have been made to tremble. The problem is that we are all postmoderns, caught in the postmodern fix, at least in the purely descriptive sense where "postmodern" depicts a sociological-historical plurality, an incommensurability of contemporary discourses, a multiplicity of voices. We are all postmoderns, even the most traditional among us, for today "traditionalism" is but another voice, one more view in the marketplace of competing views. I myself use "postmodernism" in an even stronger, normative sense, because I think that this incommensurability tells us the cold truth about ourselves, exposes the slippery slopes on which we stand—that it actually gets something right.

So, like it or not, "sacred names," names with real hieratic authority, the authority to compel submission across the board and to being everybody into line, are wanting. What metaphysics has always called the *arche*, which sets the terms for any *hier-arche*, has simply made its excuses and quietly withdrawn, stepping back from the stage. Overarching metanarratives "lack credulity," Lyotard says (*PC*, xxxiv).[1] That is an interesting way to put it: it is not that we have refuted them—although that could be done easily enough by showing empirically how much more complicated things are—we just do not believe them anymore. We greet them with a smile or a yawn.

That spells particular trouble for ethics, which has always had a metaphysical twist and always depended upon an *arche* and a hierarchy—lest there be an an-archy. Ethics has always relied upon a certain hierarchical sorting out of the true good from the apparent good, of the natural from the unnatural, of the rational from the irrational, of the ought from the is. Ethics has always been marked by the movement of the "meta-," the metaphysics of morals, the transcendence, the movement beyond, the desire to put its finger on the *arche*. That is the old and very Greek desire, the desire to set forth clearly the grounds upon which we stand. But such a ground, or an agreement upon such a ground, is just what we are denied in the postmodern situation. The authority of the grounding, centering *arche* has disappeared, has (been) withdrawn. Like an overdrawn check, it lacks credit, which is why it lacks credulity. Principles always live on credit, and at a certain point someone calls in the loan.

So we cannot quite fulfill our Greek desire. We can never become the Greeks we wish to be. Still, we—western, Euro-American, scientific, adult, still too white, still too male, Catholics—can hardly be anything else than Greek. We have never not been Greek; it belongs to our oldest memory, our most ineradicable vocabulary and grammar. It is in our bones. The categories of Greek ontology have not so much broken up as they have come home to roost. If we have lost our faith in a single all-embracing ontology, we have replaced it with a robust enthusiasm for the multiple, overlapping, sometimes conflicting regional ontologies of the sciences. That does not represent the outright destruction of ontology but its reconfiguration, its redistribution among the plurality of contemporary natural and social sciences.

So we are both hopelessly Greek—committed to the project of science, conceptualization, categorical determination, what is called "reason"—and yet we have no hope of being Greek, of fulfilling our Greek desire for the overarching story that will deliver in one punch both Being and the Good and provide the common measure for our incommensurables. That is one of the double binds of postmodernism, which is both modern, rational, scientific—the "high tech" civilization—and postmodern, lacking a metanarrative. We "want" (desire/lack) a metanarrative.

The situation seems hopeless. We are Greek through and through. We can never "overcome" the Greeks. We can never step outside of or get clear of metaphysics. Even as we can never *be* Greek, establish a metaphysics, really settle down inside of it. We can never become what we always already are; we must necessarily be what it is denied us to be. We can never get as far as ethics, never mount an ethical system, never deliver the ethical *logos* and *arche*. Still we want to agree, we must agree, that it was, after a certain point, a crime to be a Nazi. We want an ethics, even as we lack what we want.

The situation seems dangerous, for where else can the lack of a metanarrative and overarching *arche* lead us than into chaos and anarchy? Does not postmodernism mark off our hopelessness and confusion? Is postmodernism little more than a frank confession that we do not believe in anything, that we are incredulous, not only about metanarratives, but about anything that would "command our respect"? Is postmodernism not the antimetaphysics of the greedy generation, the antiontology of caprice and selfishness, the will to folic about in a world without constraints, where things have neither ontological nor deontological weight. How can the loss of the *arche* result in anything other than irresponsible anarchy and libertinism, the denial that there is anything "out there," any "transcendental signified" that can subdue the will or that the mind must confess to be true? Ethics has always meant a set of constraints—the strain of the ascent to the Platonic Good, or straining our archer's eye to hit the Aristotelian mark, or the constraining of inclinations within the limits of Kantian duty. But if there is no overarching metanarrative, no (agreement about a) metaphysics of upper world and lower world, or of noumenal agents and phenomenal appearances, if there is no transcendental signified around which to order our discourse—which is our postmodern fix—what can constrain, restrain the will?

And if all that is so, if the situation is that far out of control, then how far removed is postmodernism from Nazism? To be sure, the postmodernists in the normative sense, the ones who love this Dionysian whirl, are not Nazis, even though the reputations of de Man and Heidegger are on the line these days, and Nietzsche has always been a dangerous thinker. But what is there within postmodernism in virtue of which it could condemn Nazism? It does not have the resources, the authority, the *arche*, to pronounce a judgment.

Now here is where my postmodernism gets very hermeneutical, where I come back to a certain *hermeneusis* of our experience, one which makes all the difference. Here is where I think everything depends upon a certain hermeneutic cut or choice, a decisiveness within this undecidability. For decisiveness and undecidability are not opposed; on the contrary, undecidability is the condition of possibility for decision and it ensures fear and trembling—like Abraham on the way up the mountain, never *knowing* for sure whether the "call" to sacrifice Isaac was the will of God or a hallucination.

Here is where I make a de-cision, a cut, between two kinds of postmodernism, which I will call "responsible" and "irresponsible" postmodernism, where a lot of weight and a lot of responsibility fall on the word "responsibility." I locate a certain, literal irresponsibility in the tendency within the work of Deleuze and others to affirm the play of difference at the cost of all responsiveness and responsibility. In Deleuze, everything is made to turn upon the distinction between the active and reactive. The result of this that re-sponsibility, re-sponsiveness—and we here today can add re-ligion—are taken to be inherently re-active, even as, at the same time, for this is really just the same thing, spontaneous overflow and discharge are inordinately, phallically valorized.

I would say that what interests me about postmodernism is almost precisely the opposite tendency, let us say, on this point at least, something quite anti-Deleuzian, a much more "responsible" postmodernism, and, accordingly, a more religious one too. Such a concept of postmodernism as I would defend has nothing to do with the freedom to frolic about in ontological weightlessness, or with a blind rage against every form of structure and constraint. It does not seek to discredit the *arche* in the name of anarchical violence. It is, instead, answering a call. It hears an appeal. It is (and this is very anti-Deleuzian) very responsive, very responsible. For it hears and hearkens to the call of that which calls to us from beyond the *arche* or beneath the *arche*. So you see it has a lot to do with ears and hearing, with having the ears to hear, like Abraham, with a certain hermeneutical rendering of what addresses us, what we take to be addressing us.

I would like to say that this is a certain an-archy, but of a very subtle, a very Kierkegaardian, Levinasian sort. For it is turned toward the violence *of* the *arche*, toward what is missed or lost, passed over or unseen, forgotten about or left out, excluded or ground under, erased or violated, cast out or cast down by the *arche*. This is not a negative anarchy, because it is not a negation of the *arche* but an affirmation of the an-archical, an affirmation which remembers the forgotten, which cherishes the remnant, which recovers what is lost, which honors the ruins. It wants to be vigilant about overarching stories and sweeping principles, to their power to sweep away. It is on that account very responsive and responsible to everything that calls to us—calling is a very central metaphoric to it—from "beyond" our principles, to the particulars who are lost in universals, to the unique, the idiosyncratic, the abnormal, the outcast, the different, the lost sheep, the exceptions, to the radically singular. It is a kind of consorting with outcasts, with a cast of strange characters, with those who are different, outside the mainstream. It is not so much that it has another *arche*, the *arche* of what is other, as that it has turned its eye—or its ear—to the other of the *arche*, the other of the law, the other of language itself. Still it holds that there is no transcendental signified, no clean break with the chain of signifiers in virtue of which it is able to attach itself to an ineffable singularity or an ineffable other.

The postmodernism I defend is not the sworn enemy of the law; it does not wish to bury laws or the rule of law. It is not a romanticism that thinks that outside the law is pure freedom, nor a foolishness that fails to understand that the rule of law is a precious way to defend the weak against the strong. In heeding the other of the law, it puts the law in its place, delimiting it while saving it. For the law is as good as the cash it has on line. But the other of the law is what is always at stake, what always has a purchase on us. So this postmodernism has, both in the name of the law and of the other of the law, turned its attention, its "ear," to what the law leaves out and excludes, to what is literally out-lawed, il-legal, an-archical, which likewise means what is ab-normal, insane, ir-rational. The postmodernism of the sort I favor is not irresponsible to the law but deeply marked by an-archic responsibility, by an anarchic imperative, which wants justice to flow over the land like water. If it has its doubts about the sacred names, about every *hierarche*, that is because it has, instead, begun to move toward a sacred an-archy.

Such a post*modernism* is a continuation of modernism under another name, an extension of modernism, of its critique of the violence of authority and tradition. But it is a modernism without the metaphysics of pure subjectivity, without the illusions of liberalism and rationalism, without the meta-narratives either of ahistorical rationality (Kant) or historical reason (Hegel, Marx). It is a modernism that has sensitized itself to the debris of modernism—it is, as we shall shortly see, a kind of ethics of debris—to everything which modernism has ground to dust. It is a modernism that is trying to summon the nerve to live without the metanarrative, that consorts with the out-law, the an-archical. Its paradoxical claim is that such flirting with danger is itself the safest path and the most effective way to ensure the rule of laws. It is true—I agree completely—that "cold hermeneutics" has a warm heart. There are worse things that could be said about it.

So the postmodernism that I will defend here, and the sort you will find in writers like Lyotard, Girard, Blanchot, Levinas, and above all Derrida, is very responsible. And even slightly Jewish: Levinas is very Jewish; Lyotard has written about *les juifs*, and Derrida, well, that is undecidable. Now I, who have owned up to being very Greek, am going to be a little Jewish. Almost. My idea here is to plant a little bug in all this Greek ontology, to inject a little virus in our big Greek computer, to put a little biblical bug in its (our) Greek ear. But I must warn you, my Jewishness is going to be subversive. It will come by way of Jesus, who is very Jewish, but also a little un-Jewish too, at least that is how it turned out. For Jesus is not quite Christian, not quite Jewish, not their synthesis or *Aufhebung*, but on the margins, on the slash. That is why, in what follows, I will call him Yeshua, which is his name in Aramaic, the name he had before they gave him all those titles, when he was still on the slash, between BC and AD, before he was handed over to the Councils and to all those Greeks in love with *logos* and *arche*.

My more or less Greek desire here is thus to produce something slightly different, something slightly un-Greek, which, however, will be all too Greek since I will inevitably—I cannot help myself—adopt the manner and the style of "ethics," which is "philosophy," which the Germans tell us *is* Greek (by which they usually mean that it is *German*). It is very Greek even to worry about "having an ethics." Ethics is a Greek word, a discipline of Greek philosophy, a Greek discipline. Still, what I hope to produce here—if I am lucky, this will depend on chance, a freak, a hybrid, a miscegenation, something tormented and disturbed from within by what is un-Greek, unphilosophical—will be something Jewgreek, Greekjew. In other words, no racial purity here.

I am going to twist and turn with the Greek within me (us), roll around in the dust with the Greeks; all such twisting and turning, wresting and wrestling (*wenden*) is what Heidegger meant by the *Überwindung* of Greek metaphysics, which meant something like "coping." But Heidegger's *Überwindung* does not satisfy me because Heidegger was trying to wrest free something more primordially Greek than Greek ontology, something more purely Greek, archi-Greek. This side of Heidegger is not very postmodern at all, but rather antimodern. I, on the other hand, am not interested in racial purity—even if all that means is "the most metaphysical of all peoples" (that's enough!); I prefer contamination. I do not want to purify the Greeks but to defile them, to bug them. I am not out to find the pure primordial spring, the *Urquel*. I am not trying to get a good running start for a leap (*Sprung*) into the origin (*Ursprung*). I am happy enough to drift downstream to the derivative (*de-rivus*), maybe even to consort with what has been sold down the river. My idea is to follow the exile into the desert, to stay on the track of everything that has been excommunicated from the purity of the great Greek origin.

So my desire is not to write an ethics—that is too much for me, too Greek—or even to write a book, which also exceeds my ability. The best I can hope for is to make a little contribution, to put in my own two cents, to toss in a few loose unscientific ethical fragments. I/we—we who are caught in a postmodern fix—lack the authority to write an ethics, to settle comfortably inside metaphysics, to mount the metaphysical high ground from which to survey good and evil, the authority to pass judgment. Still, it was, after a certain point (one has to make distinctions), a crime to be a Nazi. We have to have an ethics. But I do not want to cast this ethics in such Greek terms, to surrender so unequivocally to my Greek desires.

My idea is to forge ahead, because it is in any case necessary to act and to judge, to decide in the midst of our undecidability. For if we do not, someone else will, maybe someone less cautious, less vigilant, less "philosophical." But the aim will be to stay alert to what this very "philosophy" regularly excludes, occludes, precludes, which it does "systematically," by the very tendency of its discourse.

TEMPLES: STONE AND FLESH

So I begin with something primordially Greek, in which everything Greek (and hence primordial and originary) is gathered together—at least according to Heidegger, who is very Greek, or at least the next best thing (according to Heidegger), very German. I begin with the Greek temple in "The Origin of the Work of Art." For Heidegger has captured something that, just as he says, extends across the subsequent history of philosophy, even of the West, albeit in a diminished or occluded form. We all love Heidegger's temple, the temple at Paestum. There is no denying that. After all, deconstruction has nothing to do with knocking down buildings, especially Greek temples—but with vigilance.

Still, I am not going to play this straight, not walk right into Heidegger's temple. I am going to interrupt Heidegger's discourse, scribble in its margins, deface the marble columns of the temple with graffiti (rather in the manner of Derrida's *Glas*). I want to break Heidegger's spell, interrupt the very strong *pathos* of this discourse (which is, this can be shown, at the same time quite without feeling). I want to contaminate Heidegger's temple, or better, for this is nothing one does by an act of aggression, see if it is not already contaminated, if its Greek beauty has not already been defiled by a Jewish or a Christian contaminant.

I want to throw Heidegger's temple into another relief by shifting the scene back and forth—this could get a little confusing—between a Greek temple and a Jewish one. I will from time to time interrupt Heidegger's hymn of praise, his song of songs to the Greek temple, with another temple, another scene, one which betokens another ethics. After all, my fellow democrats, we ought not fear to interrupt this authoritative voice, this speaker who puts on the airs of Greco-Germanic authority.

I will mix, in quite a disorderly and indiscriminate manner, two scenes, two scenarios, two *hermeneuses*—one Heideggerian-Greek, the other downstream, de-rivative, down the river, Jewish, Christian, ontico-existentiell. This will all be by way of intimating another ethics, the ethics of what the ethics of the temple leaves out, even locks out, quite intentionally. I am trying here to mix two discourses, two life-worlds, two ways to be, two kinds of ethics (*ethos*), two "paradigms," which is more Greek. I apologize for the solemn tone and grave mien of the next few paragraphs; these are very Heideggerian solemnities in which we engage and I am doing my best to match gravity with gravity, to stretch American English to its Greco-Germanic limits. Readers of Derrida will detect a little bit of *glas* sticking like glue to these pages.

The Greek temple rises suddenly from the ground, a majestic stone in a valley cut out of stone. Its long, strong, hard marble columns stand straight and tall, shining in the Mediterranean sun. The temple is regular and well-proportioned, a model of symmetry and grace, "proud and well constituted" Nietzsche would have said. Inside, through the portico, one catches a glimpse of the statue of the god, a tall, towering erect divinity who comes to presence in the marble and dominates the sanctuary. The temple shines brilliantly under the open sky, letting sun and light be what they are. Likewise, it holds its own steadfastly against the raging of the storm, lets the storm manifest itself in all its violence. Rain and wind shatter against its steady, rock-hard rectitude. The temple's unshakable solidity, its stony hardness, lets the fierceness of the storm stand out. "And as he came out of the temple, one of his disciples said to him, 'Look teacher, what wonderful stones and what wonderful buildings!' And Yeshua said to him, 'Do you see all these great buildings? There will not be left here one stone upon another that will not be thrown down' (Mk. 13:1–2; cf. Mt. 24:1–2; Lk. 21:5–10).

Everything Greek is gathered together in the temple, all the Greek paths—"birth and death, disaster and blessing, victory and disgrace, endurance and decline" (32/43). In the temple, as in Greek tragedy, a *battle* (*Kampf*) rages, the primordial struggle in which a decision is to be made about "what is holy and what unholy, what great and what small, what brave and what cowardly, what lofty and what flighty, what master and slave" (cf. Heraclitus, Fragment 53). The temple is a scene of a great and primordial *Kampf*, what Heraclitus (to whom we are referred by the passage on the temple) calls a *polemos*, which is what Heidegger is translating (in the early '30s) by *Kampf*. This *Kampf* establishes what stands up the straightest, is the most erect; it determines what has position (*Stellung*), standing (*Stand*), rank (*Rang*) (66/IM 63).

The master stands straightest, like the god, like the temple itself, whereas the small, cowardly slave slumps, cowers, bent and cringing, like a fallen building, a broken statue, like ruins, human ruins, debris, not very erect. So this *polemos* is very orderly, establishes order, give us *arche* and *hier-arche.* Far from throwing us into turmoil and anarchy, it puts people in their place, establishes class, tolls the bell (*glas*) which signals who comes in first:

> Because being as *logos* is basic gathering, not mass and turmoil in which everything has as much or as little value as everything else, rank (*Rang*) and domination (*Herrschaft*) are implicit in being. If being is to disclose itself, it must itself have and maintain a rank. That is why Heraclitus speaks of the many as dogs and asses.
>
> > [And when they drew near to Jerusalem . . . he sent two of his disciples, and said to them, "Go into the village opposite you, and immediately as you enter it you will find a colt [of an ass] tied, on which no one has ever sat; untie it and bring it . . .And they brought the colt to Yeshua, and threw their garments on it; and he sat upon it (Mk. 11:1-7).]
>
> This attitude was an essential part of Greek being-there. Nowadays a little too much fuss is sometimes made over the Greek *polis.* If one is going to concern oneself over the *polis*, this attitude should not be forgotten, or else the whole idea becomes insignificant and sentimental. What has the higher rank is the stronger . . .
>
> Because being is *logos, harmonia, aletheia, physis, phainesthai*, it does not show itself as one pleases. The true is not for every man but only for the strong.
>
> > [And James and John, the sons of Zebedee came forward to him and said to him . . . "Grant us to sit, one at your right hand, and one at your left, in your glory." But Yeshua said to them, "You do not know what you are asking . . . You know that those who are supposed to rule over the Gentiles lord it over them, and their great men exercise authority over them. But it shall not be so among you; but whoever would be great among you must be your servant and whoever would be first among you must be slave of all. For the Son of man also came not to be served by to serve, and to give his life as a ransom for many." (Mk. 35:41-45)]

The temple separates out people who are god-like and erect, who are allowed inside the temple, from the dogs and asses who can at best look up at it from outside, who slink in its shadows. Everything Greek crosses in the temple, as if the temple were a complicated, concentrated, central intersection. Almost a Greek traffic jam.

Fixed steadfastly between heaven and earth, gods and mortals, the temple lets the Greek world "world," lets the world come to presence in all its worldly glory, and lets the earth recede in all its density and rock hard solidity. The temple building, the marble columns, stand on rock-hard ground, in the midst of a valley that has been carved out of stone. In the temple, sun and air, light and dark, wind and rain, warmth and cold come to be what they are, come to shine, come to presence. In the temple, marble comes to be marble. We experience its earthly texture and solidity, its rich veins of color; we experience it for what it is. Hard, cold, solid, massive, smooth, straight, strong, upright, invulnerable, towering, ageless, without crack or fissure, without the rift of pain without frailty or feeling, its smooth, white marble skin washed clean.

Out of the stony valley juts the temple. Inside the temple sanctuary, inside its hidden parts, the statue of the god stands erect. "A stone is worldless"; yet, out of the stone, a world rises, emerges, stands forth, comes to presence. The Greeks called this *physis*—and *polemos*: an order of presence, an order of rank, of what stands tall and what sinks low.

Now let us change the scenery of this very Greek, very Heideggerian, temple which we have already interrupted, incised with another text. We need an interlude here, some music to play, while the scenery is being replaced, while the cast of characters is switched. Let us use this time to slip back out through the portico, leaving the site of the statue of the god within, to those who are outside, to those who are not allowed to set foot inside, to those who lack *Stellung, Stand*, and *Rang*. Let us slide down the long stiff column of the temple—to the ground. Once again, I beg indulgence for the solemnity of this prose, for I have decided to make trouble for Heidegger, the *magister solemnitatis*.

At the foot of the temple column slumps a broken figure, soiling the surface of the shining marble steps, refuse to be swept away. A loiterer, litter (literally). He does not stand erect, does not emerge into presence, but slumps in the shadows. He crouches against the wall, sheltered against the busy commerce of those whose rank and standing summon them to the temple, protecting himself from the feet of those who rush by the temple on the way to answer the day's calls. He never speaks or goes inside the temple to pray or offer sacrifice. He *is* the sacrifice, the body cut in two in testimony to the covenant cut between gods and mortals—evidently other mortals, not him. He has been left out of the deal. This must be one of Heraclitus's slaves, an ass, a left over, a remnant, one of those whom the original *polemos* has let settle on the bottom, a sediment, which is no doubt why he sits on the ground.

A shaking, filthy hand, a web of bent bones and protruding veins, stretching out from a crumpled heap. A stick man with rags. Not much *physis* here.

When the rain and wind roar, he huddles all the more closely to the wall. The cold rain penetrates him, a numbing cold he cannot bear or withstand, although he has no other choice. The cold and rain let his flesh stand out in all its frail vulnerability.

In the evenings, when the same unseeing faces rush back to the homes from whence they emerged, when the temple guards assume their evening watch and clear the temple steps of refuse, he drags himself off to disappear into the night, who knows where, for he does not have the wherewithal to lay down his head. He cannot walk but only crawl. He cannot stand erect. His is the bent and distorted body of a leper: "Chronic . . . malady capable of producing, when untreated, various deformities and mutilations . . . skin lesions appear as light red or purplish spots [or] as yellow or brown infiltrated nodules. . . . This leads to numbness (usually of the extremities), contractures and ulceration. [But only] mildly infectious." Not much Greek symmetry here. A body out of joint, out of line, unsymmetric, disproportioned, ill-constituted, diseased, uncomely, loathsome, unclean, unwelcome. "[While he was in one of the cities there came a man full of leprosy; and when he saw Yeshua, he fell on his face and besought him, 'Lord, if you will, you can make me clean.' And he stretched out his hand, and touched him, saying, 'I will; be clean.' And immediately the leprosy left him. And he charged him to tell no one; but to go to the priest, and make an offering for your cleansing, as Moses commanded, for a proof to the people" (Lk. 5:12–16)]. He lives off the public places of the *polis*, not in them. He does not have being-in-the-world but being outside. He parasites public space, infiltrating its gaps and empty spaces, depending upon the rain to bathe, or perhaps a public fountain, if he is not chased off. That is his only entrance into the space of the *polis*. You should wear gloves (*glaives*) if you touch him, Nietzsche said, or keep him at a sword's (*gladius*) distance. He does not smell like a flower (*gladiolus*).

A stick-man—made of flesh and bones. Not marble and stone.

Flesh is an altogether different paradigm than the "thing." Flesh is soft and vulnerable; it tears, bleeds, swells, bends, burns, starves, grows cold, exhausted, numb, ulcerous. You cannot ulcerate a marble column. Flesh smells—Nietzsche is right about this: these slave types really do smell bad—especially when it is deprived of rushing water, or when it burns. Flesh is exposure, vulnerability, the ability to be cut and bleed, to swell and fester. And it needs to be sheltered from the rain and the cold, but no less from the eye. Flesh is life, not (only) shining exuberant *physis* but *zoe*, animal life, a living thing, with a digestive tract and organs of reproduction.

> [For I was hungry and you gave me food, I was thirsty and you gave me drink, I was a stranger and you welcomed me. I was naked and you clothed me, I was sick and you visited me, I was in prison and you came to me. The righteous will answer him, "Lord, when did we see thee hungry and feed thee, or thirst and give thee drink? And when did we see thee sick or in prison and visit thee? . . . Truly, I say to you, as you did it to one of the least of these my brethren, you did it to me. (Mt. 25:36–40)]

Flesh is a tissue of sensitivity, of feeling, not an invulnerable monumental structure. It becomes what it is exposed to, is invaded by the elements—heat or cold, light or darkness, storm or gentle breeze. Flesh does not rest securely within itself or stand imperiously under the sky. Flesh is permeable, pervious. Flesh aches—with exhaustion or hunger, from disease or disability. Flesh shivers or sweats, limps or falls, is crippled, bent, disabled. Flesh is pain; it is the possibility of pain. There is no pain outside the flesh.

Enough of these hermeneutic solemnities, these solemn phenomenologies of the temple and the flesh. Let this be enough to show that we have to do with very different "life-worlds," with very different ethics, with very different paradigms. On the one hand, let us say, an ethics of excellence, of *arete*, but of an especially "phainesthetic" sort, filled with a lot of bravado about shining beauty and the order of rank, about who has the highest standing, who is the most erect. Let us say, an ethics of glory. On the other hand, another ethics, an ethics of misery and mercy (not one without the other), an ethics not of glory but of humiliation, not of the strong and erect but of those who have been laid low, not of the great but of the small, not of the straight but of the crippled, not of the beautiful but the ugly, not of great and beautiful buildings but of lepers crouched in their shadows, not of marble but of flesh.

Let us say, an ethics of honor on the one hand, an ethics of the humiliated, on the other. Now one of the things I am claiming is that philosophy, which is Greek, has always had its eye on the ethics of honor. Aristotle, for example, who was a good deal more sensible than Heidegger, and who tried to put moderation in the place of heroic excess, shows how deeply he is marked by this when he defines ethics in terms of honor. Ethics he says ought not to be concerned with honor and glory—Aristotle has good sense—but with that for the sake of which one ought to be honored. That is more sensible; yet that still turns on the same thing, but in a more moderate form; it is still an ethics of honorable Greek gentlemen, not of outcasts. (Heidegger thinks that such moderation is the beginning of the withdrawal of Being.) Foucault captures a good deal of this when he defines Greek ethics in terms of making oneself beautiful. Heidegger offers us an ontological version on this ethics; he wants to make Being beautiful. But his other ethics, the one Heidegger wants to excommunicate, the one to which philosophy—which is Greek—has never been much attracted, is an ethics of the humiliated, of those who systematically lack honor, and this for a variety of reasons—because they lack beauty, or because they are not men, or are not white, or are not Christian (that would stick in our throat), or for any number of reasons. We really are quite imaginative about such matters.

Let us say, an ethics of excellence and an ethics of the outcast, an ethics directed at all those who are systematically left out, who drop to the bottom in the various orders of rank, the slaves not the masters, the women not the men, the black not the white, and so on, wherever a *logos* and a *polemos* shake things down and distribute them into an hierarchy.

This is an ethics of those who come in last, of the losers, and so it is not all that enamored of the image of the Olympic Games. It turns on a different metaphysics, that of the leper, a powerful biblical image that appears in postmodern writing at the beginning of Foucault's *Madness and Civilization*. Leprosy is a signifier for everyone whose afflicted condition fills us with terror, for all who threaten to infect us, to carry us off into an abyss, a signifier far in excess of the medical threat (only "mildly infectious"). There have always been lepers and leprosaria in which to confine them: the mad, homosexuals, blacks, Jews, and, nowadays, the victims of AIDS whose illness has clearly taken on biblical proportions. The leper is everyone whom we want to exclude, everyone we fear, everyone whom we cast out.

In the biblical narratives, Yeshua clearly takes the side of the outcast—"Lord, when did we see thee hungry and feed thee, or thirst and give thee drink?"—and the narrative clearly means to put the mainstream, those who are not hungry, not naked, and not in prison—on the spot. The biblical favor is not bestowed on the *arche*—on the rulers, or the wealthy, or the ones who have the power—but on those who drop through the cracks, those who fall out, or are cast out, on everyone an-archical: lepers, prostitutes, tax collectors, Samaritans, prodigals. He does not identify with the establishment but with the disenfranchised, the remnants, the leftovers.

So you see what I am up to by slipping this "biblical ethics" into Heidegger's texts. I am not trying to write a postmodern *Summa Contra Gentiles*. I am not trying to defend the truth of the Catholic faith against the nations or to invoke the authority of a powerful book and a very powerful, very authoritarian, very hierarchical institution. On the contrary, that is the part of my argument that makes me the most nervous. I am just looking for an un-Greek ethics, for the ethics that is excluded when you exclude everything which is not Greek from the origin. You do not have to "believe" anything at all about Yeshua in a theological sense. You do not have to believe in miracles, for example, that Yeshua had the miraculous power to heal leprosy. The point of that story, as far as a radically difficult hermeneutics is concerned, was not to show forth the glorious power of Yeshua, to demonstrate that he was a divine miracle man (*theios aner*), full of divine *arete*, to produce another aretology. That would be too Greek. The point is to show us where his heart was, what Yeshua meant by the "kingdom" (which maybe is why he tells the leper to keep his cure under his hat)—which was a little more Jewish. You do not have to have the least interest in the Pauline notion that Yeshua died to atone for the sins of mankind. Many early followers of Yeshua never heard of that idea, nor evidently did Yeshua. They just thought that sharp tongued Jewish prophets like the Baptist and Yeshua had a way of getting themselves killed, that the children of Israel, like everyone else's children, had a habit of killing prophets who told them the hard truth about themselves. I am interested in the historical form of life here, the *ethos*, not in theologies or revelation, in the biblical ethic as a "form of life," as "life world," one which is not Greek. Speaking philosophically—and I cannot kick this habit—I am treating Yeshua as a hermeneutic type, a certain exemplar or paradigm.

ETHICS AND SUFFERING

I admit that this is perverse. For I am being very philosophical, very Greek, with this un-Greek exemplar. I am looking for the "ethical point," trying to see what kind of ethics they have downstream, de-rivatively, down the river, outside the early Greek origin, outside philosophy, in the "world" of the New Testament. (This is actually how Heidegger started out, but he got sidetracked.) I use this ethico-religious example "historically," as another and quite different tradition, another life-world, to make a point in which I am more than a little interested, a point about pointed tips and torn flesh, lacerations and cuttings, victims and executions. A postmodern point, a kind of Derridean "spur," about pain. I want to defend a notion of ethics—how Greek can you be?—that takes account of pain and suffering.

Pain is the issue of a fissure, a cut, or a gap. Pain cuts into our flesh, tears into the surface of our bodies. It opens up a wound, rips apart, tears us to shreds, divides and separates. To put a Derridean point on it, you could say that there is a *dif-ferre* in *suf-ferre,* a bearing-apart (*de*) which tears and separates. *Souffrance*—let us say "*sufférance*"—is constituted by the tear of pain.

But that is also the significance of Dionysus, the god torn to shreds, cut up and disseminated. And that is a tip off that the Greeks are a much more complicated phenomenon than the phainesthetic Greeks delivered to us on Heidegger's postcards of shining Greek temples. So let it be known that the Greeks for whom we are making trouble are above all Heidegger's Greeks, not necessarily even Hölderlin's Greeks, and certainly not the tragic Greeks who were capable of tearing out their eyes and of multiple forms of laceration, of unburied brothers and of lovers buried alive. The god torn to shreds: that is both Dionysis *and* Christ, Jew/Greek. Nietzsche said it all; he posed the problem of ethics in which I am interested, when we wrote:

> "Dionysius versus the crucified": there you have the antithesis. It is *not* a difference in regard to their martyrdom—it is a difference in the meaning of it. Life itself, its eternal fruitfulness and recurrence, creates torment, destruction, the will to annihilation. In the other case, suffering—the "Crucified as the innocent one"—counts as an objection to this life, as a formula for its condemnation.—One will see that the problem is that of the meaning of suffering: whether a Christian meaning or a tragic meaning. In the former case, it is supposed to be the path to a holy existence; in the latter case, being is counted as holy enough to justify even a monstrous amount of suffering. The tragic man affirms even the harshest suffering: he is sufficiently strong, rich and capable of deifying to do so. The Christian denies even the happiest lot on earth: he is sufficiently weak, poor, disinherited to suffer from the life in whatever form he meets it. The god on the cross is a curse on life, a signpost to seek redemption from life; Dionysus cut to pieces is a *promise* of life: it will be eternally reborn and return again from destruction.[2]

The god torn to shreds: Dionysus torn limb from limb, the body of Yeshua pierced by thorns, nails, a soldier's sword. These are figures of cuttings, piercings, open wounds. Both Dionysus *and* the crucified; the difference is not in the suffering, as Nietzsche so rightly says, but in the suffering. There is ethics because there is suffering, and the meaning of the suffering is the measure of the ethics.

What is the meaning of Dionysus? Dionysus is a cosmological signifier. The meaning of his suffering is the "natural violence" of the earth's own rhythms, the entirely natural movements of the seasons, of life and death, the rhythm of *physis,* of all and spring, the natural cycle of birth and rebirth of nature, the circle of seed, flower, seed. For Nietzsche, justice is the justice of becoming, of nature's own incessant going over and going under, where being, nature, becoming are altogether, radically innocent. But the cross is not a signifier for natural rhythms, but for an execution; it does not signify justice but injustice. It is not nature's inevitable cycle but a violent disruption of nature.

Now this is where my distinction between the ethics of the temple and the ethics of the leper, of marble and flesh, has been leading. Let us give it one final formulation by distinguishing the Heideggerian "thing" and the "cross." The cross is not a "thing," not a place of gathering and unity, not a thing of shining beauty in which earth and sky, mortals and divinities intersect. The cross is a figure of tearing, of violent wrenching and stretching apart, of naked shame and humiliation, of piercing pain. Crucifixion is not the gentle death of a "mortal," not a moment in the rhythm of *physis*, but a violent execution. That is what Nietzsche and Heidegger have in common. They both pursue a certain cosmology, a philosophy of the worlding of the world, not of the flesh. Still, the case of Nietzsche is more complicated, because he has a powerful, a masterful (he would like that word) discourse on the body. The cross is not a signifier for *physis*—whether it be the frenzied violence of Dionysian *physis* or the gentle worlding of the Heideggerian *physis*—it is a signifier for flesh. If there is an ethics here, an ethics of the cross, it is an ethics of the flesh, of suffering, not of the gentle worlding of the world. (Maybe this gentleness ends up being very violent; maybe this tearing and piercing is more filled with mercy.)

This violent execution on a tree is not gentle dwelling on the earth under the skies but something *unheimlich*, uncanny, out of joint, skewed, violent, weird:

> Now from the sixth hour there was darkness over all the land until the ninth hour. And about the ninth hour Yeshua cried with a loud voice, "Eli, Eli, lama sabachtani? that is, "My God, my God, why hast thou forsaken me?" . . . And Yeshua cried again with a loud voice and yielded up his spirit.
>
> And behold, the curtain of the temple was torn in two, from top to bottom; and the earth shook, and the rocks were split; the tombs were opened, and many bodies of the saints who had fallen asleep were raised, and coming out of the tombs after his resurrection, they went into the holy city and appeared to many. (Mt. 27:45–54)

The sky does not shine with splendor but grows dark in the middle of the day. The great temple is shaken, and its mighty veil is torn. Firm and solid rocks split apart. Dead men rise up from their tombs and walk the streets. This is very *unheimlich*, an almost Kafkaesque scene. This death is not the pruning of limbs but the piercing of flesh, not a natural rhythm but an unjust execution, not the inevitable rise and decline of life, but injustice, victimization, evil. The death of Dionysus is innocent, not evil; the rhythm of spring and fall is innocent not evil.

But murder is everything we mean by evil. Yeshua was the victim of a religious and political establishment that had had enough of his sharp tongue and blistering words, of this subversive way of consorting with lepers, prostitutes, tax collectors—with the many whom Heraclitus called asses and whom Nietzsche said smelled bad. He was the victim of an *arche*, of a power structure, of a *grand récit*, a metanarrative that the powers that be told about themselves. He was the sort of man who made both religious and political authorities nervous, the sort to be silenced by the Vatican, or, as Dostoevsky pointed out, the sort to be executed by the Inquisition, by people who are too much in love with their *arche*.

Shall we say that the cross institutes a "clearing," but a clearing of another, non-Heideggerian order? That in the cross a world is opened up? Or is "clearing" not too thoroughly implicated in phainesthetics? We can at least call it a world, which, as Heidegger points out, is a biblical idea. If it is a clearing, it displaces the Greco-Germanico-Heideggerian clearing of jugs and old bridges, and returns us to the order of the flesh, of suffering, of the victim, the order of justice. It displaces phainesthetics for ethics and institutes the space of ethical discourse, an ethics of victims. It opens up a wholly different space, a different ethics, an ethics of body and blood. This is a very somatic space, a space of wounds and flesh and blood and suffering. The phenomenality of this opening is the opening of a wound, not of open skies. There is no Heideggerian *Verdinglichung* here, but if I may say so, a kind of *Verleiblichung*, an assumption of the full weight of the flesh, of embodiment, of the agony of the body, an assumption of bodily pain, of a body in pain under its own weight.

I do not want to lose my balance here. There are *many* clearings, many ways to clear the open space of factical life, many ways for Being to be. I do not want to smash the jug or burn the bridge in Heidelberg. I do not want to be wholly un-Greek, or anti-Greek, but Jew/Greek. I do not want to ban works of art or level what remains of the beautiful temples at Paestum, or abolish Christian art. I am not attacking art or *aesthesis*. I am attacking phaenesthetic art and phainesthetic ethics. I want to gain a hearing—and this is a strategy (what is not a strategy?)—for other kinds of art, for works of art that precipitate a shudder, that embody the body of pain, which would make all lovers of Pre-Socratic splendor tremble with the agony of the garden and the cross, the agony of factical life. I want here to gain a hearing for an art that would be a hermeneutics of suffering.

THE SPACE OF SUFFERING

Let me say a word or two about the horizons of this hermeneutics. The space of this clearing—if it is a clearing, if that is not too Greek—is curved. The leper lying at the foot of the temple and the body on the cross come to us from on high, even as they have been laid low. Victims are always less than human, beneath us. They have been lowered, reduced, demeaned, degraded: they lie on a lower grade. They have been pushed below the ordinary human horizon by suffering and affliction. They are less than us, not up to us, not as clean or as beautiful, not as smart or as well-off, not as healthy or as erect. Their bodies are bent or maimed, foul or faulty, sick or deformed—or maybe just black or feminine. They are cast out, cast down.

We cannot look them in the eye, face to face in the level space of Gadamerian or Habermasian conversation. That is why it is impossible to help them, even when we reach out to help them, especially then. For that is when we look down on them, condescend to (help) them, which humiliates and lowers them all the more. To cross the space that separates us from the victim with a helping hand is an ethical descent, a slide down from the space of our own comfort and superiority to their lowliness, which only serves to intensify their lowliness. We cannot straighten the curvature of this space by an act of generosity. Our generosity is a function of our superiority. That we minister to their needs humiliates them all the more, even as we can do nothing else.

That is why Nietzsche wanted to protect life from pity and from the priest who brings comfort, for those who bring comfort rob others of a certain chance for nobility. That I think is a delicate point, one which is tightly interwoven with the humiliation that the outcast suffer. It is impossible not to humiliate the person whom one helps—that is the double bind of mercy. But one must beware of turning ethics into the aesthetics of making oneself beautiful. The prisoners of the concentration camps must have been humiliated when the allied soldiers who liberated them saw their destitute condition. That is not to say that they did not want liberation or that their pride forbade them from accepting liberation. The liberation was the condition of the restitution of their pride. At the point that Nietzsche's critique of pity becomes a politics, it becomes dangerous. We can never forget that Nietzsche's politics were elitist and undemocratic, that there is something profoundly corrupt—let us say *decadent*—about a thinker who evaluates human lives in terms of the creative few and the smelly many, for whom those are the terms of the discourse.

The one on the cross is humiliated when they offer him bitter wine to quench his thirst. He is humiliated when they torture him. He is humiliated when they look at him. He hangs in humiliation, for that is the space of the victim.

All of which elevates the claim of the victim upon us. "And I, if I be lifted up, will draw all things to myself." The degradation of the victim, the humiliation and casting down, that is precisely what raises him over us. The victim has been lifted up by the cross, pulled up over us, comes to us from on high. He is higher than us because he is lower than us, elevated because he is reduced, a commanding presence just because he has been reduced by imperial power. The one who has been pushed below the horizon in degradation and humiliation now rises above the horizon with a moral force. The laying low of the victim in a mundane sense, his worldly destitution and nullity, is precisely the source of his moral elevation and authority. That is the perversity of the biblical ethic and the reason why those who are well-born and who come to us from on high in a mundane way are at a biblical disadvantage and are faced with squeezing the camel through the needle's eye.

Now that rising up, that moral elevation is for me the "genealogy of morals"—there is no reason why every "genealogy" should end up robbing things of their authority—the origin of moral beliefs, the motivation which sets ethics in motion. The victim comes to us "from on high," from out of a higher space, and descends upon us, drawing us up toward him, laying claim to us. He comes upon us with a higher authority, with the authority of height itself, from out of the heights of authority itself, if there is any such thing.

CONCLUSION: ETHICS, THE LAW AND THE FLESH

But then, have I not done myself in, undone the very postmodernism with which I began. Did I not define postmodernism in terms of the loss of *arche*, the withdrawal of the sacred names in virtue of which we are authorized to pass judgment? Yet have I not found my *arche*, the *arche* of suffering, fallen back on the authority of those who have been laid low? Have I not simply introduced my own *arche*, the *arche* of suffering and the outcast, and have I not invested it with the authority of a powerful tradition? Have I all along had another *arche* up my sleeve, the *arche* of the other, the *arche* of *an-arche* itself. That would be my undoing. So I must proceed very cautiously here and formulate what I want to say carefully.

The ethics I propose here shifts its attention from the principle to those whom the principle leaves out, from the system to those for whom the system was not designed, from the powers that be to their victims, from offering a vision of the Good to the fate of those who are not captured by that vision or who choose to dissent from it. What then is the fate of principles? What becomes of the archical in the anarchical? They are treated with vigilance, not contempt, as deconstructible, but not as dispensable, like a check about which we are always slightly worried that it is going to bounce (but after all you need to have a checking account). We want to foster an extremely tentative attitude toward principles and laws, a sense for what they exclude, a need to generate them "from below," in fear and trembling, from amid the flow of quotidian experience, to allow them maximum flexibility. Principles do not fall from the sky; they are not implanted in the soul at birth, although that would make things a lot easier.

That is why I think that it is never a question of "applying" principles to individual cases—we can never be assured that we have reached the ethical high ground to survey the "case." The existing individual is not a case, a *casus*, a fall from a universal. That would make the individual a casualty, a catastrophic reversal. Hermeneutics is rather a matter of applying cases to principles: for principles have no weight or substance apart from the cases from which they arise, by which they are nourished—which is the money they have in their account—to which they are always more or less in/adequate. Principles are falls from individuals, fall under cases, are cases and encasements of individuals. They take their place, represent them.

The individual case is the "other" of the principle, what the principle does not capture, which it may even injure. The individual case is the remnant, the residue, the fragment, the debris, even the excrement of the universal. It is what is left over whenever the universal is brought into play, even when the universal is as concrete as possible, even when I say "here now," which is as concrete as I can be: "What, after all, of the remain(s), today, for us, here, now, of a Hegel? For us, here, now: from now on that is what one will not have been able to think without him. For us, here, now: these words are citations, already, always, we will have learned from him [Hegel]."[3] The individual is always, already lost, fallen, other than the principle, the other of the principle, the other of language. So the point behind this postmodern suspicion of principles is to prevent cases from becoming casualties of principles, to make principles respect their other. For this we need more than *phronesis*, for in the postmodern condition the assured frameworks are on the run; the *arche* is lost. Maybe we need some kind of *metaphronesis* for an epoch of anarchy.

This is where we must be careful. Such an ethics turns not on the principle of the other but on the other of principles, what is always otherwise than an *arche*, what the *arche* always already—here, now—leaves out, omits, excludes, violates, grinds up. That is why we cannot say that this is an ethics that turns on the "principle of the other" or the "principle of anarchy," or that it has made the "other" its *arche*. For the *arche* moves about in the element of the universal, whereas the ethical has to do with the singular, with what Kierkegaard called the existing individual. This is an ethics that has steadfastly turned its eye and its ear to the realm of which the universal has lost sight.

(The singular is ineffable, which is why there is no proper name. The singular can only appear—does it appear?—in the gaps and interstices of language, the caesura which are opened up within the linguistic chain, the spaces that are created by the play of signifiers, by the coded reiteration, by the universals. The singular is like a "pregnant silence": it is a silence which must be surrounded on all sides by language otherwise it is not silence at all. The individual has always already slipped away, disappeared, has already deferred and withdrawn, whenever we turn its way. Language always arrives too late and barely catches a glimpse of the back of the singular as it slips out the door. A slippery, self-deferring, withdrawing, elusive, invisible individual: that is the subject matter of ethics, about which Aristotle, who can be counted on to be sensible, warned us not to expect too much precision.)

Once again, and for the last time, some help—an example, an exemplar—from Jewish anarchy:

> Again he entered the synagogue, and a man was there who had a withered hand. And they watched him to see whether he would heal on the Sabbath, so that they might accuse him. And he said to the man who had the withered hand, "Come here." And he said to them, "Is it lawful on the Sabbath to do good or to do harm, to save life or to kill?" But they were silent. And he looked around at them with anger, grieved at their hardness of heart, and said to the man, "Stretch out your hand." He stretched it out, and his hand was restored. The Pharisees went out, and immediately held counsel with the Herodians against him, how to destroy him. (Mk. 3:1–6)

This is an ethics that keeps its eye on the withered hand, not on the law, and that tries to keep the eye of the law on the withered hand. It is an ethics of withered hands, not of the Sabbath; of saving life on the Sabbath, not of saving the Sabbath at the cost of life. All the authority comes from the withered hand, not the law. The law lives on credit, on the promissory notes it makes to heal withered hands. But the law is for the withered hand, not the withered hand for the law.

Everything turns on the withered hand, on leper bodies, on the flesh. That is where the authority comes from, that is its genealogy. The authority is not invested in the principle but in the flesh, and the flesh is always the casualty, the remnant, the litter left behind by the law. The authority to which ethics harkens, to which it responds, is not ours but the other's. Principles do not have authority; they borrow it. They live on credit and have limited credulity. The problem of ethics is not a problem of principles, of legitimating them, of establishing the conditions of possibility for legitimating validity claims. It is a matter rather of keeping an ear cocked for what calls for our response from beyond the principle, from the abyss of illegitimacy, from the ineffable disturbance within language and law that is elicited by its other. Ethics has a good deal less to do with "validity claims," which is the law of the Sabbath, than with being claimed by the withered hand, which is the anarchy of healing on the Sabbath, of lording it over the Sabbath. It has less to do with will-centered rational subjects than with decentered ones, less to do with the autonomy of pure practical reason than with subjects who have been drawn out of themselves into the domain of the other. That is not a very modernist subject, not a very modernist way to think about ethics. So maybe it is postmodern.

Ethics as I conceive it is a kind of communication between flesh and flesh. Ethics means flesh with flesh, flesh to flesh. Ethics means flesh calling out to flesh and flesh answering flesh; flesh stirring as flesh and flesh awakened as flesh. Withered, leprous flesh and healing flesh, withered hand and healing hands.

But this is indirect, not direct communication. Ethics is not magic, not a miracle. We can say "Be clean" but it is another thing to make it happen. We can say we want the land to flow with justice like running waters, but it is, as William Sloane Coffin said (*New York Times Book Review*, February 18, 1990), another thing to build the irrigation system. There is always a medium that stands between the two events of flesh, a medium that establishes a certain contact, no doubt, but which at the same time prevents contact, which leaves something out; a barrier which cannot be laid aside, but also an indispensable means of communication. *Différance* as the condition of im/possibility of the law, a quasi-transcendental (almost).

The medium is the law, the *arche,* the universal, which cannot lay hold of the other, its other, the other of the law, in its bodily presence. The law gropes for the other like a man feeling for a door in the dark. The ethical is not the law; the law is in the dark. The ethical is the flesh. The law is the Sabbath; the ethical is the withered hand. The flesh of the withered hand, the body of the leper, calls out from beyond the law, across the law, its small, trembling voice barely audible in the midst of the noise of the law and of the busy traffic that hurries past the temple. But the ethical is a communication of the flesh with flesh, as response of flesh to flesh. So there is no ethical until a man pushes his way through the temple crowd toward the leper and, reaching out the flesh of his hand, says "be clean." That is the communication of flesh with flesh.

The stirring of the flesh of the other is the awakening of my flesh, of that strange otherness which is me. For we do not belong to ourselves, are not lords even in our own household. I too am a certain kind of temple, a surface for I know not what, a house not of Being but of flesh.

Ethics, as I conceive it, is a kind of communication of flesh with flesh across the *arche* of the law, a communication not of *arche* with *arche*, but of abyss with abyss—*abyssus abyssum invocat*—in a kind of sacred anarchy.

UNDECIDABILITY

But abyss it is, and that brings us back to the *hermeneusis*, to the difficulty. For I do not think that this ethics of the flesh arrests the trembling or stills the waters (or still less allows us to walk on them). The decision, the cut, does not remove the undecidability, the impossibility of a clean cut. There remains, there was never anything more than, a *hermeneusis*. We do not know who or what we are, who are what flesh is, and we cannot quiet the Dionysian laughter, stop the Dionysian dance. Maybe all that calls, all that rumbles within what we have called flesh, is a kind of cosmic dance, a playfulness of the elements going over and going under. Ethics, this ethics of the flesh, of mercy, of calling and responding, is all a matter of ears and hearing, of having the ears to hear, and cannot be exempted from the inescapability of hermeneutics.

To illustrate this point I will conclude these remarks with a little story, a little parable, a slightly Schillebeeckxian retelling of a New Testament episode. Let us go back to the case of Yeshua one last time, this time shortly after his death, back to Simon, in Galilee, fishing and thinking over what had transpired down in Jerusalem just a few weeks ago. The longer Simon sits under the evening sky, the more he is convinced that there was nothing you could do that could not be forgiven. (Hannah Arendt says that Yeshua was the master of forgiveness.) So Simon thinks to himself that perhaps he should go round up the others and talk some of this over with them. Maybe they could go fishing together. Maybe if they could spend an evening together fishing under the stars, if they could hear what Simon had to say, maybe they, too, would agree that Yeshua wasn't gone, that he was still offering them the father's loving forgiveness, that his strangely beautiful stories could still be heard floating softly above the waters of an evening sea.

Still, there was one thing in all this that bothered Simon—here comes the *hermeneusis*—and he would never be able to get it out of his mind, even long after he had gotten Yeshua's followers together again, long after they started calling him "Rocky" as a kind of joke, because he was the rock they always fell back on when they met resistance or their faith faltered. Simon kept thinking of the fish, of their cold scaly flesh, struggling and twisting, fighting to get free from his net. He thought of how impassively he looked on at their struggling, remaining all the while quite indifferent to their fate, for it was their appointed role to be food for Simon and his family. He wondered whether—and this was just a passing thought, but he couldn't quite get it out of his mind—life was not like a great cosmic game, a chain of stronger and weaker, and whether it simply played itself out, without justice or injustice, but with a kind of vast stupidity. He wondered whether the death of Yeshua was like that of the fish; it had nothing to do with guilt or innocence. It is simply the way life plays itself out, like a vast impersonal game, like the game the stars played overhead. Maybe the stars do not care about Yeshua or Simon or the fish. The only thing that helped Simon cope with that abysmal thought was Yeshua's smile.

NOTES

1. Jean-François Lyotard, *The Postmodern Condition: A Report on Knowledge*, trans. Geoffrey Bennington and Brian Massumi (Minneapolis: University of Minnesota Press, 1984). Hereafter referred to as *PC*.
2. Friedrich Nietzsche, *The Will to Power*, trans. Walter Kaufman and R. J. Hollingdale (New York: Vintage Books, 1968), 1052.
3. Jacques Derrida, *Glas*, trans. John P. Leavey and Richard Rand (Lincoln: University of Nebraska Press, 1990), p.1a.

19
In Search of a Sacred Anarchy: An Experiment in Danish Deconstruction

Like Martin Heidegger, like many of us, Calvin Schrag has had a theological point of departure. His earliest work, *Existence and Freedom*, published some forty years ago, undertook one of the first important confrontations of Heidegger and Kierkegaard in English.[1] Schrag understood that a great deal of Continental philosophy originated in the decision made by Kierkegaard to expose philosophy to biblical categories, on the premise that if the categories of Greek philosophy are all we have, then the poor existing individual is lost. It was in no small part from that decision that Heidegger's *Being and Time* emerged, and with that book, much of contemporary Continental thought. Kierkegaard's was the first "deconstruction" of speculative metaphysics, and it has remained paradigmatic for Continental philosophy to this day. Does this mean, I wonder, that we are to include the achievement of Cal Schrag—like that of Kierkegaard, Heidegger, Ricoeur, and Levinas (it is difficult to know where to do the line here)—among those whose work amounts to what Jacques Derrida calls a nondogmatic repetition of religion, "a *thinking* that 'repeats' the possibility of religion without religion"?[2] I simply pose that as a question, for him, for myself, for his readers.

In tribute to the remarkable contribution Calvin Schrag has made to philosophical thinking in America, in gratitude for the lead he has given us in showing us how to think in America within a Continentalist framework, and in the spirit of Schrag's first book, his early *Auseinandersetzung* of Kierkegaard and Heidegger, I would like to conduct a little experiment in what I will call Danish deconstruction. By this lovely little alliteration, Danish deconstruction, I have in mind the concept of deconstruction with constant reference to Kierkegaard. My idea is to put the names of Derrida and Kierkegaard to work in order—to speak oxymoronically—to set forth the plans and stake out the borders of what I will call here a "sacred anarchy," the whole idea for which turns on a hypothesis that I will spell out below, about the communication between God, philosophy's most famous protagonist, and *différance*, philosophy's most famous misspelling.

A KINGDOM OF *DIFFÉRANCE*

I begin with the misspelling, with *différance*. *Différance* is a secular word coined for a secular philosophical world by a philosopher who says of himself "I quite rightly pass for an atheist."[3] Still, for whatever reasons, God and *différance* keep up what must seem to some an unholy communication with each other, with which Derrida has constantly to deal.[4]

Some years ago, in his famous essay "*Différance*," Derrida said that *différance* "everywhere comes to solicit, in the sense that *sollicitare*, in old Latin, means to shake as a whole, to make tremble in entirety." For that reason, he went on to say that *différance* should not be construed as some sort of *primum ens* sent into the world to set things straight, some principle of order and governance: "It governs nothing, reigns over nothing, and nowhere exercises any authority. It is not announced by any capital letter. Not only is there no kingdom of *différance*, but *différance* instigates the subversion of every kingdom. Which makes it obviously threatening and infallibly dreaded by everything within us that desires a kingdom, the past or future presence of a kingdom. And it is always in the name of a kingdom that one may reproach *différance* with wishing to reign, believing that one sees it aggrandize itself with a capital letter."[5] In other words, although many of its admirers have come to expect quite a lot of it, *différance* is not God, and it does not set up court in something like a Kingdom of God. Indeed, far from having the status of God or of any sort of arche, divine or otherwise, far from being a principium or prince which orders and stabilizes, *différance* is downright subversive of such orderliness. Its "natural" tendency, if it had a nature, is to destabilize the stable, to shake the firm, resolutely to oppose every kingdom, every ordered totality. Not only is there no *royaume de différance*, the very idea of *différance*, if it is an idea, is the idea of no more reigning, no more kingdoms, not now, not ever, the idea of subverting kingdoms wherever they appear.

Unless of course, in the best spirit of deconstruction, one might speak, in all perversity, of the possibility of a kingdom of the kingdomless, a kingdom of those who do not reign and have no power, an un-kingly, an-archic kingdom. That is the possibility that interests me, in the spirit of a certain deconstruction, and also in the spirit of what Derrida now calls the "democracy to come" which also suggests a slightly anarchical arche.[6]

Derrida does not mean to say that *différance* breeds outright chaos. He does not favor a simpleminded anarchy that would let lawlessness sweep over the land, although that is just what his most simpleminded and anxious critics take him to say. For that would amount to nothing more than a counterkingdom, a kingdom of lawlessness, where lawlessness rules, where a still greater violence holds sway. Like a simple totalitarianism, a simple anarchy would break the tension between the arche and the anarche; pure life would spell death. That is why, twenty years later, in "Force of Law," and in his more recent writings generally, Derrida has made it plain that deconstruction is not a matter of leveling laws in order to produce a lawless society, but of deconstructing laws in order to produce a just society.[7] To deconstruct the law means to hold the constructedness of the law plainly and constantly in view so as to subject the law to relentless analysis, revision, and repeal, to rewriting and review, and this in view of the fact that there is a structural and necessary gap between the law, which is constructed, and justice, which is undeconstructible, a fundamental tension that must never be relaxed. *Lex mala, lex nulla*: A bad law is no law at all, not if the law is meant to serve justice. Deconstruction resists the closure of the law in the name of what laws close off and exclude, namely, the singularity of the poor existing individual. Deconstruction, which situates itself in that gap, breeds justice, even as it is born and bred of justice; indeed, to invoke one of Derrida's most startling formulations, "deconstruction is justice." That is not an act of self-congratulation but the name of a task. Deconstructing the law means to hold the law in question, to solicit the law, to make the law tremble, while always letting oneself be solicited and troubled by justice, by the need for justice, by the need to let justice come, to let justice flow like water over the land, to let justice rule.

But if justice "rules," then is there not a "kingdom of justice," not in the sense of some locality where justice is to be found, but in the sense of the summons that justice issues, of a call to let justice reign, a demand to stay steadily open to the call of justice, tuned to justice's address? After all, there are kingdoms and there are kingdoms, and "kingdom" is not a "bad name," not evil in itself.[8] Indeed, "kingdom" is nothing in itself, apart from the economy in which it is made to operate.

Could we not say that the rule of justice, the reign or kingdom of justice, constitutes a world or social order in which the sails of the law are trimmed close to the winds of justice? Could there not be a kingdom of *différance* after all, contrary to Derrida's most literal claim, albeit a very strange sort of kingdom, one governed not by a powerful and overarching arche, a positive, princely principium that holds all things mightily in its sway, but, almost the opposite, a kingdom organized around the power of the powerless, by a sustained sense for the exceptional and singular, the different and the left-out, the foreigner and the immigrant, to which the arche is systematically blind? Would this not be something of an an-archic kingdom, a kingdom whose ear is cocked for the different, whose *Stimmung* is tuned to those who stand outside the law? Could there not be a kingdom, not of law but of justice, not of unbending rule but of the holding sway of the outlaws and the losers, the left-out and the lost, which keeps an ear and eye out for poor existing individuals?

In that sense, *différance* would have the effect of subverting every "kingdom of law," every archical kingdom, every rigorous and unbending rule of law, precisely in the name of another kingdom, a "kingdom of justice." The kingdom of justice is (dis)organized around everything singular and outlawed, everything marginal and dispossessed, everything that is null and void before the law, and this just in order to let justice reign. This kingdom of *différance* would constitute an anarchic kingdom of cast-offs and cast-outs, of the ill-born and lowborn, of everyone unroyal and unkingly, uncourtly and disreputable, a kingdom of everyone who amounts to nothing or who is nobody from the point of view of worldly power, a "kingdom of nuisances and nobodies," as John Dominic Crossan puts it.[9] In this very odd kingdom, everything odd and out of step would enjoy special favor, would capture justice's anarchic eye, watched over in the watch that justice keeps for the anarchical who slip beneath the radar of the arche and the law. If the law is blind, then deconstruction takes its stand with the glance that the eye of justice casts upon the singularity to which the law blinds itself, which we might call, in the language of Danish deconstruction, the *Augenblick* of justice.

Now if we take a "prophet" in the biblical sense, not as one who tries to the see the future, which is what the blind Greek prophet and seer has in mind, but as one who speaks for (*pro-phetes*) justice, then the kingdom of justice would have a *prophetic* quality about it. The kingdom of justice calls to us and puts "us" in the accusative, on the spot, called on the carpet about the privileges "we" currently enjoy under the law and in the present order. In prophetic grammar, the "we" is always part of the problem, and the idea behind the prophetic is to reconstitute the "we" as an "us" which recognizes itself as under accusation, *me voici*: here I am, here we are, on the receiving end of a call. That would mean that the present order, which certainly includes the "euphoria of liberal democracy" and of the "new world order," is the very kingdom for which deconstruction is designed to make trouble.[10] In Danish deconstruction, what Kierkegaard called the "present age," the age of presence and the present, is always under the "revolutionary" gun.[11] A prophet is a troublemaker who speaks for justice now, in the present, which is why he usually ends up getting killed, which is another thing that distinguishes Jewish prophets from Greek ones. A prophet is not someone who sees the future but someone who comes to deliver the word that "we" in the present do not want to hear, to tell us what is urgently demanded of us, now, in the present—justice deferred is justice denied.[12] The prophet lets us know what we do not want to know, troubles and solicits us, makes us tremble, decentering the "I," the arche/self, which has a tendency to organize everything around itself and to ensure that everything returns to itself. Like *différance*, the prophetic is an operation of solicitation. It is because of their common commitment to *sollicitare*, to disturbing the peace, to troubling the tranquility of the present order, of the present age, that Derrida can say that deconstruction is "produced in a space where the prophets are not far away."[13] The "present age" is not a fixed date in calendar time, but a floating structure of human existence, like a Heideggerian "existentiale," a structure that, like the poor, you always have with you, that is always already in place, wherever two or three are gathered together. The present age is the structure of the authority of presence and of the prestige of the present, for which there is a standing need of solicitation, that is, of deconstruction, for Danish deconstruction is always the deconstruction of presence, of the power and prestige of the present age.

DIVINE SUBVERSION AND DANISH DECONSTRUCTION

Now I turn to God (a lifelong task), and to my hypothesis.

Suppose we grant all this business about disturbing the prestige of the present. What has any of this to do with God or with a Kingdom of God? Does not *différance* spell trouble for God? Does not *différance* spell the end of religion and the death of God? *Différance* steadfastly resists becoming a "master word or master concept" and accordingly "blocks every relationship to theology," since the discourse on God is a discourse on the master-word *par excellence*, the Lord and master of the universe.[14] Is not God the dream of plenitude, "of being as presence, as Parousia, as life without *différance*," and is not "theology" the very name, the very model, of the logocentric love of presence and the effacement of the trace?[15] Can one imagine a more powerful presence or a more prestigious Parousia, a more permanently present presence than the "God" around which religious power groups itself? Can one imagine anything more supportive of the established order, anything more top-down, more entrenched in the status quo, anything more immobilized, contented, and *nunc stans* than religion and religion's "God"? *Pro deo et patria*: Is that not literally a call to arms in whose ungodly name more blood has been spilled than just about anything else we can imagine? What has founded and grounded top-down orders of power more firmly than such a "God"? How often has the "reign of God" (a very theocratic idea!) meant a reign of terror? What has been more violent than theocracy? What more patriarchal, more hierarchical? What more authoritarian, inquisitorial, misogynistic, colonialist, militaristic, terroristic?

But suppose—and this is our working hypothesis in this experiment in Danish deconstruction—as a regular reader of essays like "*Différance*" and "The Present Age," we raise the possibility of a "God" who belongs not to the order of presence but to the (dis)order of the deconstruction of presence? Suppose God does not belong to the order of manifestation and presence, and hence even of truth, whether truth is taken as *aletheia* or *adequatio rei et intellectus*, but rather withdraws from the world in order to station himself or herself (Godself is the gender-neutral word) with everything that the world despises?[16] Suppose our thought of God is not swept away by ecstatic visions of the supereminent power of the supreme creator of heaven and earth, its arche and telos, but takes its lead from the most powerless remnants and marginalized nobodies, the little *me onta*, the obscure pockets and folds and hovels of the world? Suppose God most especially hovers and makes a home among the homeless, so that God would be the last one to speak *pro deo et patria*?

Suppose further that "religion" tends systematically, structurally, regularly to forget this, to such an extent that religion, which is our doing, not God's, and religion's

God, might almost be defined by its oblivion of "God" so that the first step that would be required, as Meister Eckhart said, is to pray "God" to rid us of God? To which we might add, "I pray 'God' to rid us of religion," since, according to Isaiah (Isa. 1:11–17), Amos (Amos 5:21–24), and Hosea (Hos. 6:6), God is not interested in religion, in cultic sacrifice and ritual, but in justice.[17] Suppose we add the prophets to the list that Derrida composes of those who advocate a religion without religion? Suppose, indeed, that "God" is stationed not on the side of arche and the principium, or of timeless being and unchanging presence, of the true, the good, and the beautiful, but on the side of the an-archic and subversive, as the driving force—the *agens movens*—of a divine subversion? Suppose "God" is situated not inside the churches on the high altars, but among the beggars with outstretched hands on the church steps? Suppose "God" is not to be conceived as the overarching governor of the *ordo universi*, of the kosmos, but as what disorders such orders, deworlds such worlds, and subverts such universes? Suppose "God" is not conceived theocratically and onto-theo-logically, as the rock solid ground upon which the onto-theo-political edifice is erected, but systematically associated with the different, the marginal, the outsider, the left-out, the least among us, the poor existing individuals, the destitute, the *anawim*, those who are plundered and ground under (Amos 8:4)—and hence as subversive and "revolutionary"? Suppose "God" is to be found at the heart of a revolutionary age, not as the stabilizing center of the present age?

Suppose "God" is not identified with infinite power, *omnipotens deus*, but with the powerless? Suppose the sense of "God" is to interrupt and disrupt, to confound, contradict, and confront the established human order, the human, all-too-human way of doing business, the authority of man over man—and over women, animals, and the earth itself—human possessiveness and dominion, to pose, in short, the contradiction of the "world"? Suppose the idea behind the "rule of God" is not to back up human authority but to break it up, to turn the eye of the law to the widow, the orphan, and the stranger, which is the *Augenblick* of justice? Suppose the idea behind calling God a father is not to set up an oppressive patriarchal model but to establish a relativization of worldly power: "Do not call any man on earth father, for you have one Father, and he is in heaven . . . the greatest among you must be your servant" (Matt. 23:8–12).[18] Then repeat that with a difference, a sexual difference, and say that you have one Mother in heaven, and for the same reason.

Suppose we associate God with disseminating tongues and deconstructing towering edifices, with confusion and profusion, the way he interrupted the plans of the Shemites (Gen. 11:1–9), who wanted to build the tower of Babel and who disseminated their language into a profusion of unintelligible tongues so that they could no longer build up a consensus, no longer communicate, and no longer build their transcendental tower?[19]

Suppose we stop thinking about God onto-theo-logically as *prima causa*, as some sort of ontological power source, and onto-theo-politically as the foundation of value and good order, "one nation under God," the backup for the established order, and begin to think of "God" in terms of what is left out and ground under by the whole "economy" of nations, causes, values, orders, and what groans for freedom. Suppose "God" stands for everything that confounds, confuses, contradicts, and scandalizes this economy, these crusts of power and privilege, this order of presence, *not*, I hasten to add, in order to throw us to the wolves but in order to let the lamb lie down with the wolf (Isa. 11:6), not in order to level institutions and civilizations but precisely in order to keep them just, to let justice reign? Suppose, as Jean-Luc Marion suggests, we cross out the name of "God," which parallels Heidegger's crossing out of the name of Being, as well as the deforming *a* in *différance*, in order to save the name of God from *religion's* God, which is an idol, a graven image, an instrument of institutional power, moral melancholy, and confessional divisiveness?[20]

What then?

Then the "Kingdom of God" would begin to look a little like this so called anarchic kingdom of *différance*, and we would find ourselves with a certain analogy that helps get something like Danish deconstruction off the ground: that the Kingdom of God threatens and subverts the "world" (kosmos) just the way the kingdom of *différance* threatens and subverts the order of presence. For the world is the kingdom of this world, the holding sway of the present age, of the *aion*, in the Jewish and Christian scriptures, where the world stands for the business as usual of the powerful and privileged, the oppressive system that builds wealth on the backs of the poor and the outcast, that builds privilege on the backs of the despised and the different.

In Danish deconstruction, *différance*, a defaced and misspelled word, would not lack a certain analogy to the effects produced by crossing out the name of God as suggested by Marion (which Marion then brilliantly crosses with the Cross).[21] Then this kingdom of *différance*, this anarchic kingdom, if there is such a thing, would serve as a certain *reminder* to religion of the Kingdom of God (*basileia tou theou*), the repression of which allows religion to sit down to table with the world and thus constitutes religious power.

I hasten to add that I am not saying that the deconstructor occupies God's point of view. I am not trying surreptitiously to insinuate the divinity of *différance*, surreptitiously to claim that *différance* is to be raised up to the status and stature of the divine or of God (even as I do not say that God can be reduced to *différance*). Derrida has been plain about this. Although the "detours, locutions, and syntax in which I will often have to take recourse will resemble negative theology," still it must be insisted:

> *Différance is not*, does not exist, is not a present-being (*on*) in any form. . . . It derives from no category of being, whether present or absent. And yet those aspects of *différance* which are thereby delineated are not theological, not even in the order of the most negative of negative theologies, which are always concerned with disengaging a superessentiality beyond the finite categories of essence and existence, that is, of presence, and always hastening to recall that God is refused the predicate of existence, only in order to acknowledge his superior, inconceivable, and ineffable mode of being.[22]

There are "syntactical" similarities between the God of negative theology and *différance*, similarities in the rhetorical resources needed to name something which, in each case, *mutatis mutandis*, does not exist, which is not a being, not an entity, not one more thing, not even if it is the highest thing. When Crossan asked, "Why, then, are the syntactics so similar if the semantics are so different?" Hart rightly responded by saying that this has to do with the difference between the ineffability of God's utter "transcendence" and the ineffability of a "transcendental," or better, quasi-transcendental called *différance*.[23] No one should at this late date be tempted to confuse the God of negative theology with *différance*.

THE TASK OF JUSTICE: THE IMPOSSIBLE

On this hypothesis, God is not only the *hyperousia* of negative theology, the *puritas essendi* beyond being, not only the God of eminence and supereminence, but the one who stands with nullity and insignificance, the one who stands steadfastly with the nobodies of the world. The prophetic God is not to be found high above in the realm of Neoplatonic *hyperousia* but down below in the bowels of the earthly kingdom of the *me onta*. The question of confusing *différance* with God, which is resolved by showing that *différance* is not a *hyperousios*, was a characteristic problem of Derrida's early writings. But in Derrida's later writings, the effect of *différance* is not only to prevent closure in the work of *naming* God—the basic resource upon which negative theology draws, which is why negative theology needs deconstruction—but also to address the closures effected by power, to address ethico-political closures. Hitherto the question of deconstruction and theology has been a little too preoccupied with the question of negative theology, while I am proposing here, on my more Danish hypothesis, that this is only half the story. For over and beyond the question of how to speak, or of how not to speak, of God (*comment ne pas parler*), of what we are to call God, there lies the question of what God calls us, what God calls upon us, to do.

In Danish deconstruction, that is to say, in the sphere of poor existing individuals, the name of God is not a name to speculate about, as Johannes Climacus insists, but the name of a *task* which is infinitely difficult to carry out.[24] And that is the rest of this little hypothesis: If the name of God is the name of a disruptive, deconstructive force, then the name of God is the name of a *task* or a *deed*.

The name of "justice" must be added to the list of tasks enumerated by Johannes Climacus, where the simplest things become exceedingly difficult, more difficult even than astronomy and veterinary science, indeed impossible (*the* impossible), once they become a deed, a matter for doing, not speculating.[25] Just like father Abraham, deconstruction would become great not by doing the possible or the necessary but by doing *the* impossible. Deconstruction turns on what Climacus calls "subjective truth," which means that truth is something to do, not to think, which is what Augustine means by *facere veritatem*, one of Derrida's favorite Augustinian lines.[26] In Danish deconstruction, justice is indeed a deed, not a matter for speculation; it is a demand to do *the* impossible, to pursue the impossible justice that contradicts the prevailing order of presence, which calls for something else, for something different, something to come. Justice is the stuff from which the hope of something to come is woven. For justice is not *différance*, but justice is the moral life of *différance*, for *différance* means non-closure and justice is the obligation that is imposed upon us by the different, the marginalized, the excluded, or closed-off. Derrida's "justice" functions not theo-logically or onto-theo-logically, which would mean serving as a backup for the order of presence, but *prophetically*, with a touch of what he nowadays calls the "messianic," which serves to threaten and subvert the order of presence.[27] Indeed, is not the "prophetic imagination," as Walter Brueggeman says, a "subversive imagination," a way of imagining differently, whose aim is the reconfiguration of the present world, the role of the prophets being to "fund" the present with "materials for subversion"?[28] As long as there is God or "justice," there is a "beyond," a higher court of appeal to challenge the present order, the "age" or the "law." Derrida's "justice" occupies the same "place" as God, the place of the displaced, addressing a call from the margins to the centers of power, and it belongs to the same "time," coming from the future, calling for what is to come, *á venir*, for a justice to come, for a kingdom to come. Let the kingdom come.

If justice and God are non-names, impossible names, names for *the* impossible, so that we do not know what we ask for when we call for the rule of God, or for justice's rule, then is justice God or is God justice? That of course is what the prophets have always thought. But from that identification Derrida will always keep a respectful distance. He does not speak or think with the authority of a prophet, or with any authority, and it is an important part of what he says to insist that he does not know, determinately and decisively, what he is saying when he says "justice" or from where the call of justice originates. He will never say, "Hitherto you have been told to do this, but *I tell you* do that," or that he himself has been *sent* to tell us this or that, which are central parts of the prophetic style. Perhaps this Derridean modesty is all the propheticism of which we postmoderns, or late, very late, moderns, are capable. Or perhaps this is the condition of contemporary intellectuals, for while the present age has not been without prophetic voices, from Ghandi to Martin Luther King to Nelson Mandela, they have not been the holders of endowed chairs.

We are all held captive by the "secret," which makes it impossible to resolve the translatability of these sacred names, to translate one in to the other, or both into some metalanguage that adjudicates between the two. We are all alike, Danish and non-Danish, deconstructors or not, caught up in the flux of *différance*, the flux of these names, which name what we love and desire, but whose speculative cognitive contours we cannot quite make out. For seeing is not what they are all about. God and justice are matters for doing, not seeing, in the spirit in which Augustine speaks of "doing the truth," *facere veritatem*.

SACRED ANARCHY

On my little Danish hypothesis, that the name of God is the name of a disruption and a deed, of a disruptive deed, it follows that the deconstruction of religion releases religion's prophetic side. I do not say its prophetic *roots*, for who can claim to know roots and origins, *Ursprung* and arche, the *Ur*-spring from which all things spring, and who knows if things have a root, a single root, one deep root, let alone whether there is just one thing called "religion"? To avoid this foundationalist discourse, let us just say that *différance* keeps religion on its prophetic toes. With a little dash of *différance*, religion can be made to recall that God stands for difference, stands with the differend, which implies the outcast and outsider, and that the name of God is the name of something to do. That has the effect of displacing the notion of a "hierarchy," of a sacred order, a divinely organized order of rank that keeps each thing in its divinely "appointed place" in the "present age," all of which would be from a prophetic point of view an extremely ungodly and unholy idea. In its place, we put the notion of a hier-anarchy, or let us say, a sacred an-archy.

If the idea of God commits us to the notion that something is sacred, and not just to saying it but to doing it, then I am arguing that what is sacred is not the arche but the an-arche, so that if there is anything sacred in deconstruction, it would have to be part of a sacred anarchy, of a blessed rage for a (certain) disorder, pace David Tracy, a disorder in which the last will be first and the first last. Now it is often lamented in these "postmodern times," this "epoch of *différance*," that nothing is sacred. That is true enough, in the sense that our egalitarian sensibilities have led us rightly to distrust sacred cows of any sort and to suspect their privileges, and in that sense the loss of the sacred is not bad news. But the good news delivered to religion by *différance*, one might even say its kerygma, the call it constantly proclaims, is to recall religion to a different sense of the sacred, to the old prophetic sense where the sacred means precisely what is left out of every hierarchical order, what is systemically forgotten, repressed, excluded, ground under. The good that deconstruction can do for religion is to dislodge it from its corporate headquarters, to get it back in the streets and the alleyways of life, to make the order of presence suspect, and to put God on the side of the remnants and leftovers so that the effect of invoking the name of God would be to set off a sacred anarchy.

If one were willing to surrender the deliciously disruptive effect of "sacred anarchy" (*hier-an-arche*), one might, on strictly Levinasian grounds, prefer to speak instead of a "holy" anarchy (which has the advantage, in American English, of sounding a little like "(raising) *holy* hell"). Levinas distinguishes the holy (*saint*) from the sacred (*sacré*), as the separate or transcendent from the immanent, where the world or the earth, a mountain or a homeland, is "sacred." He is trying to make trouble for Heidegger, trying to call him a "pagan." Levinas is more or less right about this, I think, and Heidegger deserves what he is getting from Levinas, because in Heidegger this Hölderlinian economy of gods and mortals, heavens and earth, is all put in the service of poetizing a dangerous Greco-German homeland of Being. But that should not blind us to the power of the "sacred—the power, say, of Native American reverence for the earth, which is a counter to a destructive violence of the technological will to power that Heidegger understands extremely well and Levinas ignores (nothing is simple). The "holy," on the other hand, in Levinas's scheme, is the power of the transcendent, of the other, of the wholly other, and here the paradigm is not Native American religion but the God of Israel, the transcendent Jahweh, whose unnameable Name is/means "I am who I am and choose to be" (and you, Moses, should mind your own business) (Exod. 2:14).

That paradigm of difference, of the "wholly other," of the one who always eludes the order of presence, has to do with the *saint*, not with the *sacré*, and that is what is behind the present experiment. The crucial thing, however, is not to take this transcendence onto-theologically or onto-theo-politically and to make of this transcendence something grandly ousiological, some superbeing that outknows and outdoes and outexists everything here below, and not to mythicize this being into a higher entity, a hyperpresence dwelling in a higher world. The crucial thing is to see that all of the resources of this transcendence are deployed on behalf of the different and with the aim, not of supporting presence with a hyperpresence, but of disturbing presence. On this scheme, and this is the anarcho-prophetico-deconstructive point, in the religion of a deconstructionist, "God" stands not above being as a hyperpresence, but in the middle of being, by identifying with everything the world casts out and leaves out. Indeed, rather than speaking of God's transcendence, it would be better to speak of God's "insistence," in the sense of God's withdrawal from the worldliness of the world, from the world's order of presence, into those pockets or recesses that are formed in the world by the little ones, the nothings and nobodies of the world, what Paul calls *ta me onta*, where God pitches his or her tent.

When, in accordance with our hypothesis we hold the name of God in tandem with *différance*, the name of God falls like a blow upon the order of presence and crosses it out, shocking the powers that be, displacing the complacent, disturbing the established order, putting business as usual into question. The prophetic name of God is subversive and threatening, "infallibly dreaded" (which is the only sense of infallibility I accept), above all by religions and lovers of infallibility. The name, or non-name, of *différance* is a "formal indication," to use the language of the young Heidegger, a syntactical and semantic rule or nonrule, of which the name, or non-name, "God," is a certain deformalization, organizing a specific semantic and practical field in which the effectiveness of *différance* itself is organized, its energies harnessed and deployed, its powers potentiated, the infinite range of its potential effects defined, focused, and unleashed, given a certain finite form. The God of prophetic religion, and the talk and practice that God engenders, communicates with *différance* along the most internal and vital lines. God and *différance* belong together in the most interesting and productive ways, and they need each other. Far from being antagonists, God crossed out and *différance* are collaborators, coconspirators, fellow subversives, and defaced inscriptions.

For after all, *différance* in itself, if there is such a thing, does not exist, is not a thing somewhere that will come to save us, and the kingdom of *différance*, even if there is one, is not a place we can actually go.[29] There is no *différance*. God is one of the ways that *différance* enters the world, by entering the interstices and back alleys of the world, a way of giving it flesh and bones, historical and linguistic actuality, institutional life. It is not by deconstructive analysis, or a new core curriculum, however important both may be, that prophetic transformations are effected, that things are really moved, that hearts are changed (metanoia), but by Martin Luther King or Nelson Mandela, by grass-roots movements which are shoots coming out of the stump of Jesse (Isa. 11:10). Movement is prophetic movement. If it makes Heidegger happy to think that language is the house of Being, by which he mainly means Greco-German poetry, the prophetic is the house of *différance*, or rather the name of its homelessness. That is why *différance* needs God in order to exist, or to impinge upon the order of existence, even as God needs *différance*, in order to slip free of the order of presence and to protect religion against itself. *Différance*, which does not exist, is a condition, a quasi-transcendental condition, without life or substance, actuality or vitality, except insofar as it comes about in traditions and institutions, languages and literatures, practices and programs, one of which—there are many, I am not trying to tie up *différance* or corner the market on *différance*—is prophetic religion.

THE KINGDOM OF GOD

I am not, nor is deconstruction, in the business of inventing a private religion. If anything, I have been speaking like Johannes Climacus in *Philosophical Fragments* about the communication of deconstruction and "the god," without giving it any historical garb. So now I must, like Climacus, here "call the matter by its proper name and clothe the issue in its historical costume."[30] For I have been speaking all along of a determinate, biblical religion, however far from that ideal "Christendom," as Kierkegaard liked to call it, or the churches generally, or Islamic or Jewish fundamentalism may have drifted. My references to *ta me onta* were perfectly transparent allusions to Paul's First Letter to the Corinthians, where Paul flaunts the scandal and the anarchy of the ones who are favored in God's kingdom, the ones upon whom God has set his eye and his favor. God chose everything foolish (*moria*, moronic), Paul says, to solicit the wisdom (sophia) of the wise, which, according to Isaiah (Isa. 29:14), God means to "destroy" (*apolo*), to confound and scandalize. When human rule is displaced, which is what it means to say that God rules, then foolishness is favored over the sophia and philosophia of the present age (*aion*) (1 Cor. 1:18–20). Those whom God calls upon, Paul says, are not wise, not powerful, not well born (*eugeneis*): "God chose what is weak in the world to shame the strong; God chose what is low and despised [*ta agene*] in the world, things that are not (*ta me onta*), to reduce to nothing things that are [*ta onta*]" (1 Cor. 1:27–28). God chose the "outsiders," the people deprived of power, wealth, education, high birth, high culture. Theirs is a "royalty" of outcasts so that, from the point of view of the *aion*, the age or the world, the word "kingdom" is being used ironically, almost mockingly, to refer to those pockets of the lowly and despised that infect and infest the world.[31] For this is a Kingdom of the low-down and despised, the "excluded," the very people who, it could be shown with the right socioeconomic structural analysis, are precisely the victims of the worldly kingdom.

First Corinthians, then, which proceeds from a heightened sense of God, is the almost perfect "inversion" (Nietzsche would say, with a Greco-German sneer, the *Umwertung*) of Greek sophia or *phronesis*, subverting, soliciting, threatening the world's wisdom, making it tremble. In contrast to the smart, moderate man who knows what is best for himself and for the polis generally, to Aristotle's virtuous gentlemanly man of reason, Paul says that God chose people who are fools from the world's point of view, people who do not act in their own best interest, who are of "no account," no Logos, a-Logos. In the kingdom, things turn on what Paul calls the "*Logos tou staurou*" (1 Cor. 1:18), the mad logic, word, or message of the Cross which crosses out the world and, in the process, gets done in by the world, taking a hit from the world, as opposed to the Aristotelian *Logos*, which means staying on top of what is going on around you and knowing how to hit the mark (and hoping to get lucky).

The Aristotelian comparison is especially instructive. Aristotle wanted to cultivate the virtues of the mind, of the intellect or reason (nous, Logos). His *phronimos* "sees" something, has "insight" into the particularities of the case, whereas the Corinthians are to be bowed over, overcome, touched by the needs of one another, which is what should rule in their hearts. That means that the "rule of God" is associated with the rule of that part of the soul that Aristotle called the "a-Logos," whereas for Aristotle the Logos is the divine part and should rule, not the a-Logos, which is the part that should be ruled.

When Paul says that the kingdom is populated with "*ta me onta*" (1 Cor. 1:28), he is almost taunting the Greeks, flaunting one of the most honorable words in Greek philosophy. Being (*to on, ousia*), the central concept of Greek philosophy, has the sense of what really and truly is, what is enduringly and permanently present, as opposed to all that is fleeting and apparent and superficial. Rhetorically, even conceptually, associated with sun, light, and gleaming manifestation, the essence of Greek wisdom is to bend all one's efforts to ascend to the element of Being and to avoid getting caught up in non-Being. The wise man is wired up to Being, knows his way around what is, can sort through what is and what is not, and can always hit the mark of what is. But the Kingdom of God is populated with shadowy semi-beings, with half-real nobodies of no worldly account. By choosing "what is not" (*ta me onta*), God can "cross out," again following Jean-Luc Marion, the difference the Greeks make between Being and non-Being, between wisdom and foolishness. God crosses one sort of "kingdom," a worldly kingdom, a kingdom in the "straight" sense, with another, paradoxical, even ironical kingdom, in which the rule of everything human-all-too-human has been shattered.

I would add still one more gloss to this remarkable passage. Paul cites Isaiah, who says, as we saw above, that God "will destroy" (*apolo* [1 Cor. 1:19]) the wisdom of the wise. In Latin, *apollumi* is *destruere, destructio.* John Van Buren has suggested that Heidegger's *Destruktion*—of which, of course, Derrida's *déconstruction* is a paraphrase and translation—derives from Luther, who spoke of the need for a *destructio* (in Latin) of medieval scholasticism, and Van Buren suggests that Luther may possibly have had this citation of Isaiah from First Corinthians in mind.[32] One could then, by a certain interesting retrojection, render this text of Isaiah, "I will deconstruct the wisdom of the wise," or, more freely, "I will deconstruct the metaphysics of the onto-theo-logians, sayeth the Lord God." The Kingdom of God, then, is the deconstruction of kingdom in the ordinary sense; the Kingdom of God is what things look like when the business as usual of human power is displaced, disordered, disarrayed, anarchized, inverted, crossed out.

The "Kingdom of God" meant a certain style or way to be—a certain structure of existence, a certain existentiale—in which the rule of everything human that was all too human had been broken, a way to be in which human power and authoritarianism are shaken, solicited, broken, displaced, deconstructed. In the Kingdom of God, the *aion* is subjected to another, uncanny, unusual rule, a rule of displacement, in which the oddest things eventuated, in which the oddest results obtained. In the business of the Kingdom of God, God means no more business as usual.

You know you have to do with God and the "Kingdom of God" just when something unreasonable from the world's point of view is demanded of us, just when we are expected to forgo our own interests, just when our most natural tendencies and desires to have things our own way are contradicted and we are told to look like a fool for the Kingdom of God. The "Kingdom of God" lands like a blow to the head, contradicting the world and its wisdom, confronting the kosmos, the ways of this world, the "system."

The "system" was for Jesus, as for Jeremiah (Jer. 7:4), embodied in the "temple," and when Jesus attacked the temple, he was quickly killed. As Daniel Maguire writes: "He [Jesus] was fussing with the system, and scholars now think he may have been killed within hours of his attack on the temple. Jesus was attacking the law and order that preserves unjust privileges and exploitative social arrangements.

Had he and Jeremiah contented themselves with urging private charity and a depoliticized piety, they could have died in their beds at a ripe old age. Neither did, because they were prophets of Israel and agents of the subversive reign of God."[33] The "Kingdom of God" is the contradiction of the "world" (kosmos), which is the order of power and privilege, of greed and self-interest, of the business as usual of the most powerful. Kierkegaard could not have been more biblical and more prophetic when he insisted that Christianity stands in permanent, structural opposition to this world, to the kingdom of this world, and that it is a sign of decadence in Christianity to have sat down to table with the world, to have made peace with that kosmos upon which it is called to make war. He also said that the way to refute Christendom was simply to walk through the streets holding the New Testament over one's head for all to read.

The Kingdom of God is a kingdom of base, ill-born, powerless, despised outsiders, a kingdom of nobodies who are null and void in the eyes of the world, dropouts measured by the world's arche and the world's *aion*, and yet precisely for that reason favored by God, precisely the ones whom God called (*kletos*) and set apart, whom God chose, favored, singling them out for all their singularity and exceptionality. The call that God makes, what God calls for, is justice, *sedaqah*, breaking the rule of power and privilege, which is what the prophets announced when they call for the rule of God, a call that often costs the prophets their life.

CYNICISM AND PHILOSOPHY

To see just how far we are carried by this hypothesis of a sacred anarchy, let us pursue a point made by John Dominic Crossan. Crossan's research into the apocryphal and noncanonical gospels, into lost, outlawed texts that have been marginalized and silenced by the institutionally sanctioned canon, has proven to be itself quite a nuisance to the powers that be. Crossan has been deliciously disturbing the academic and ecclesiastical peace for some time now by telling us a remarkable story about just such a "Kingdom of God," just such a sacred anarchy, as we have begun to sketch here. Crossan has been carefully, even tediously, reconstructing a surprisingly bestselling portrait of a historical Jesus as all-at-once Mediterranean, thoroughly Jewish, and a peasant, indeed, "an illiterate peasant, but with an oral brilliance that few of those trained in literate and scribal disciplines can ever attain," about whom these same institutional and right-wing political powers that be do not want to hear, one that situates Jesus squarely on the prophetic side—and so, by my perverse accounting, deconstruction on Jesus's side—which situates the church and the right wing you know where.[34] The church, after all, as a religious and legal institution, is something to be deconstructed, something that demands the most regular, rhythmic, systematic deconstruction, in order to save it from itself, while justice and God are not deconstructible.

According to Crossan, Jesus included in the "kingdom" just about everybody whom the Greco-Roman world excluded from power and prestige, whoever is "a nothing, a nobody, a nonperson." Jesus waged a "savage attack on family values," which will not bring the sanctimonious Christian right wing much comfort, in which patriarchal power and domestic peace is displaced—"whoever does not hate father and mother"—by the radical egalitarianism and open-endedness "equally accessible to all under God" that defines the Kingdom of God. Jesus said that it is the poor who are blessed and who especially deserve the Kingdom of God. When Matthew (the tax collector) redacts this saying, among the most authentic according to most scholars, to poor "in spirit," he removes the sting of *ptochos*, which means "destitute" rather than merely "poor" (*penes*), and diverts it from economic to interior poverty, whereas Jesus seems to have been saying, in contemporary terms, blessed are the homeless and the street people. Crossan comments: "In any situation of oppression, especially in those oblique, indirect, and systemic ones where injustice wears a mask of normalcy or even of necessity, the only ones who are innocent or blessed are those squeezed out deliberately as human junk from the system's own evil operations."[35] So then Jesus is saying, blessed are the junk, the rubbish, those whom society excretes, its detritus and excretions and so—I am citing a citation in *Glas*—its "shit," which provides an opportunity for a still more irreverent use of "holy" than "holy hell" or "holy anarchy."[36]

The parables of "open commensality," in which a master commands his servants to go out on the streets and bring in anyone they can find, "both bad and good" (Matt. 22:10), to his banquet, are particularly suggestive of the open-endedness and inclusiveness of the kingdom. The invitation is indiscriminate—male or female, free or slave, highborn or lowborn, ritually pure or impure. The "hospitality," as Derrida would say, is "unconditional." Adds Crossan: "Think, for a moment, if beggars came to your door, of the difference between giving them some food to go, of inviting them into your kitchen for a meal, of bringing them in to the dining room to eat in the evening with your family, or of having them come back on Saturday night for supper with a group of your friends."[37] If, as has been argued, table fellowship is a miniature of the larger social network in which the system of socialization is writ small, then this parable of "egalitarian commensality" would have been viewed as particularly threatening. If Jesus dined indiscriminately, then he would be accused of consorting with "tax collectors and sinners," and if women were present, of eating with "whores." The kingdom was structured around radical, disturbing, and extreme egalitarian practices that completely unhinge the binary social scheme of honor and shame upon which Greco-Roman societies turn, destroying the wisdom of the wise. Jesus then would have had nothing to do with the fraternalism and phallo-centrism of the "Christian" conception of philia—something that Derrida discusses in *The Politics of Friendship*—but he would have practiced a "discipleship of equals," which is what would be left of friendship if one withdrew it from this phallocentric scheme of philia.

Crossan's Jesus thus is a revolutionary, not an armed revolutionary, to be sure, but one whose practices of eating and healing hovered on the "borderline between the covert and overt arts of resistance." After his death, a revolutionary "movement" formed, not of armed insurgents and zealots conducting a guerrilla war, but of migrant disciples, traveling in pairs, with no provisions:[38]

> Go, look, I send you out as lambs among wolves. Do not carry money, or bag, or sandals; and do not greet anyone on the road. . . . Whatever house you enter, say, "Peace be to this house." And if a child of peace is there, your greeting will be received. But if not, let your peace return to you. And stay in the same house, eating and drinking whatever they provide, for the worker deserves his wages. Do not go from house to house. . . . Pay attention to the sick and say to them, "God's kingdom has come near to you." (Luke 10:2–11)

These texts, says Crossan, among the oldest we have, closely connecting eating and healing, are not to be confused with Paul's dramatic missionary campaigns to major urban centers in the Greco-Roman world. The disciples move from peasant village to peasant village within Galilee, taking up as guests in a house, accepting no payments beyond food and lodging, in a spirit of egalitarian sharing. They were radical missionaries who traveled without provisions and who strike many scholars today as Jewish Cynics, Jewish versions of those ancient "philosophers" who flaunted common standards of propriety and decency.

The Cynics are not gentlemen but, as Aristotle (who seems to be repeating a familiar epithet) called them, dogs (*kyon*, *canes*), whence the name by which they are known to us today. They are Greek philosophers—the word sticks in Aristotelian throats—who repudiate the aristocratic and hierarchical system of the polis and who do so by leading a countercultural life that flaunts the model of the urbane and gentlemanly *phronimos*. On this point, the Cynics were not unlike those eccentrics, the prophets themselves, who, from Isaiah to John the Baptist, showed a shocking penchant for nudity, for howling and wailing, for life in the wilderness and bizarre diets of locusts and honey.[39]

The Cynics followed "nature," the rule of the gods, of the divine, not "culture" (polis), which is man-made. They lived in the city, but they did so as if they were living in the wild. The rule (*basileia*) of nature, of God, for them is the rule of freedom, that is, freedom from culture, other people, social standing, income, prestige, power, from all the things that Aristotle called "external goods," which formed for Aristotle a "necessary supplement" to arete. They carried only a cloak, a staff, a satchel; they wore uncut hair and bare feet, and lived itinerant, mendicant lives. Their physical poverty constituted a spiritual freedom; they believed that poverty provides freedom, which constitutes the true royalty (Kingdom).[40]

Cynicism overlaps with "Stoicism" as an internal attitude of mind, but it differs radically from Stoicism in externals. The Stoic says, "I have but do not care," while the Cynic says, "I do not have but do not care." Marcus Aurelius could be a Roman Emperor and Stoic, and Seneca could be a millionaire and a Stoic, but they could hardly be Cynics. Comments Crossan: "Cynicism is the Greco-Roman form of that universal philosophy of eschatology or world-negation, one of the great and fundamental options of the human spirit. For wherever there is culture and civilization there can also be counterculture and anticivilization."[41] Now the Cynics bear a striking resemblance to the earliest followers of Jesus, the so-called Q community—something we can say without knowing what Jesus knew of the Cynics, whether he was "just reinventing the Cynic wheel all by himself," or whether he might have encountered Cynics, say, in the nearby town of Sepphoris, and taken a page from their book.[42] Like the Cynics, the disciples too were itinerants who lived like the birds of the air, who scolded society for its falsity, who said outrageous things to shock the establishment, and who set out on journeys with the barest of provisions. But the singular difference between the Cynics and the followers of Jesus—apart from the fact that the Cynics inhabited the cities and the disciples were rural—was that the Cynics went nowhere without their knapsack, which contained a little food and the few things necessary for life. The Cynics stressed their independence, their self-sufficiency, which they achieved by reducing their needs to the minimal point at which they could provide for themselves; they needed nothing because they wanted nothing that they could not provide for themselves. The followers of Jesus, however, took not even a knapsack for the day's food, not to show their independence, but because they trusted that their needs would be provided for by those who would receive them in the next town, by the brethren, which means by God's rule. For the very hospitality with which the brethren receive one another, the agape and caritas, means that there God's rule holds sway. The kingdom has drawn near; it is not off in a distant place. It reigns here, now, in this hospitality, and its mark is agape.[43]

CONCLUSION

I have undertaken this experiment in Danish deconstruction not because I am sick of philosophy (or cynical about it) and have turned to religion, but in order to jolt philosophy off dead center and give it a new start, which is pretty much what I think Kierkegaard did when he decided to shock the categories of Greek philosophy with biblical categories on behalf of poor existing individuals everywhere. I agree with Derrida, and with the poststructuralists generally, that disciplinary borders need to be crossed and new objects of study invented, the difference being that for most postmodern writers, such crossings generally mean crossing over to the turf of art and literature, not of religion, religious poetry, and sacred literature. Derrida himself will tell us, however, that "the original, heterogeneous elements of Judaism and Christianity," before they were assimilated by Greek philosophy, belong to the "other" of Greek philosophy and Western civilization, an other that "haunts" the philosophical tradition, "threatening and unsettling the assured 'identities' of Western philosophy."[44] As Kevin Hart says, Judaism and Christianity—before they are assimilated by Greek philosophy—are part of the process of deconstruction, not part of deconstruction's prey.[45]

The idea behind this experiment in sketching the lines of a sacred anarchy is to expose philosophy to its other, to another of its others, to some other other than *dichtendes Denken*, to the more scandalous other of the prophetic, messianic, and eschatological lines of force that run through the Kingdom. The idea is to let ourselves be solicited by the scandal of what must seem to some an ungodly communication between God and *différance*, which means to let religion's God, and the God of the philosophers, be crossed out by God, where the name of God is the name of a task and a disruption.

The idea is not all that different than the one Calvin Schrag had some forty years ago when he first sketched the lines of communication between existence and freedom.

NOTES

1. Calvin O. Schrag, *Existence and Freedom: Towards an Ontology of Human Finitude* (Evanston, IN: Northwestern University Press, 1961).

2. See Jacques Derrida, *The Gift Death*, trans. David Wills (Chicago: University of Chicago Press, 1995), 49. Hereafter cited as *GD*.

3. See Jacques Derrida, *Circumfession: Fifty-Nine Periods and Periphrases*, in *Jacques Derrida*, ed. Geoffrey Bennington and Jacques Derrida (Chicago: University of Chicago Press, 1993), 155 (hereafter cited as *Circum.*). That is not true, however, of *écriture*, a word that means both "writing" and "Scripture," and the constant rendering of it as "writing" by Derrida's translators tends to efface its theological sense. Most deconstructors are not interested in making deconstruction a study of Scripture, although that is a sense that the theologically tuned will hear. See Kevin Hart, *The Trespass of the Sign* (Cambridge: Cambridge University Press, 1989), 49, who suggests that this oscillation in *écriture* is like the oscillation in *pharmakon* and "*supplément*," and hence that *écriture* is an undecidable. Whatever Derrida's authorial intentions, "Derrida's text cannot help but signify both 'writing' and 'scripture'" (61).

4. I have examined the question of Derrida and religion in more detail in two books: *The Prayers and Tears of Jacques Derrida: Religion without Religion* (Bloomington: Indiana University Press, 1997); and *Deconstruction in a Nutshell: A Conversation with Jacques Derrida* (New York: Fordham University Press, 1997).

5. See Jacques Derrida, *Margins of Philosophy*, trans. Alan Bass (Chicago: University of Chicago Press, 1982), 22. Hereafter cited as *MP*.

6. See Jacques Derrida, *Specters of Marx: The State of the Debt, the Work of Mourning, and the New International*, trans. Peggy Kamuf (New York: Routledge, 1994), 64–65. Hereafter cited as *SoM*,

7. See Jacques Derrida, "The Force of Law: 'The Mystical Foundation of Authority,'" trans. Mary Quaintance, in *Deconstruction and the Possibility of Justice*, ed. Drucilla Cornell, Michel Rosenfeld, and David Gray Carlson(New York: Routledge, 1992), 68–91, 14–15. Hereafter cited as *Fl*.

8. See Jacques Derrida, *Of Grammatology*, trans. Gayatri Spivak (Baltimore: Johns Hopkins University Press, 1974), 42. Hereafter cited as *OG*.

9. John Dominic Crossan, *Jesus: A Revolutionary Biography* (New York: Harper-Collins, 1994), 54. Hereafter cited as *J*.

10. Derrida, *SoM*, 56.

11. Søren Kierkegaard, *Kierkegaard's Works*, vol. 14, *Two Ages: The Age of Revolution and the Present Age*, ed. and trans. Howard V. Hong and Edna H. Hong (Princeton, NJ: Princeton University Press, 1978).

12. Derrida, *Fl*, 26.

13. When Augustine defined "peace" as the tranquility of order, he reflected a world in which Christianity had made its peace with political power and had begun to devise a theory of just war. Christian life after Constantine soon lost its prophetic spirit, which distrusts the tranquility of

the prevailing order and is bent on disturbing the peace, and this in the name of *shalom*. *Shalom* is the peace that comes from "justice" (*sedaqah*) for the poor and the outcast, the peace that comes of God's rule, not the highly hierarchical domestic tranquility prized by the religious and political right wing. By devising a theory of just war, Christianity had unfortunately lost the prophetic spirit that was alive and well in the sayings of Jesus, in Jesus's prophetic discourse on the "Kingdom of God." See Richard Kearney, ed., *Dialogues with Contemporary Thinkers* (Manchester: Manchester University Press, 1984), 119.

14. Jacques Derrida, *Positions*, trans. Alan Bass (Chicago: University of Chicago Press, 1981), 40.

15. Derrida, *OG*, 71.

16. Commenting on Hegel, who is commenting on Moses Mendelssohn, Derrida writes, "Since God does not manifest himself, he is not truth for the Jews, total presence or parousia. He gives orders without appearing" (Jacques Derrida, *Glas*, trans. Richard Rand and John Leavey [Lincoln: University of Nebraska Press, 1986], 51a, cited by Hart, *Trespass of the Sign*, 62). Yahweh then would be what is "essentially other than truth," not Heideggerian lethe, which is the very heart of truth, pace John Sallis, "Deformatives: Essentially Other Than Truth," in *Double Truth*, by John Sallis (Albany: State University of New York Press, 1995).

17. Daniel Maguire, *The Moral Core of Judaism and Christianity* (Minneapolis: Fortress Press, 1993), 189–90.

18. Ibid., 264–65.

19. See Hart, *Trespass of the Sign*, 107; Derrida, "Des tours de Babel," trans. Joseph Graham, in *Difference in Translation* (Ithaca, NY: Cornell University Press, 1985), 209.

20. Jean-Luc Marion, *God without Being: Hors-Texte*, trans. Thomas A. Carlson (Chicago: University of Chicago Press, 1991), 70.

21. Ibid., 70.

22. Derrida, *MP*, 6.

23. See John Dominic Crossan "Difference and Divinity" *Semeia* 23 (1982): 39; Hart, *Trespass of the Sign*, 186.

24. Søren Kierkegaard, *Kierkegaard's Works*, vol. 12, bk. 1, *Concluding Unscientific Postscript to Philosophical Fragments*, ed. and trans. Howard V. Hong and Edna H. Hong (Princeton, NJ: Princeton University Press, 1992), 165.

25. Jacques Derrida, *Given Time, I. Counterfeit Money*. Trans. Peggy Kamuf (Chicago: University of Chicago Press, 1991), 6.

26. Derrida, *Circum.*, 47–48.

27. Derrida, *SoM*, 167–69.

28. Walter Brueggemann, *Texts under Negotiation: The Bible and the Postmodern Imagination* (Minneapolis: Fortress Press, 1994), 90–91. Indeed, Yahweh himself is not above lying (or advising Samuel to lie) in order to plot a coup against Saul's rule, and so Yahweh too subscribes to Nietzsche's famous description of truth as fiction, as a mobile army of metaphors and metonymies (79–83).

29. Derrida, *MP*, 6.

30. Søren Kierkegaard, *Kierkegaard's Works*, vol. 7, *Philosophical Fragments*, ed. and trans. Howard V. Hong and Edna H. Hong (Princeton: Princeton University Press, 1985), 109.

31. A little like Heidegger, who, in a comment on Heraclitus's saying that the *basileia* is in the hands of a child (*paidos*), speaks of a child king, a kingdom in the hands of a child at play, of anarchic arche. See *Der Satz vom Grund*, 3rd ed. (Pfullingen: Gunther Neske, 1965), 188. Hereafter cited as *SC*.

32. John Van Buren, *The Young Heidegger* (Bloomington: Indiana University Press, 1994), 167.

33. Maguire, *Moral Code*, 159–60.

34. Crossan, *J*, 58.

35. Ibid., 64, 60, 62.

36. Derrida, *Glas*, 1a.

37. Crossan, *J*, 68.

38. Ibid., 105. Translation of Luke 10:2–11 is from Crossan.

39. Maguire, *Moral Code*, 183–86.

40. John Dominic Crossan, *The Historical Jesus: The Life of a Mediterranean Jewish Peasant* (San Francisco: Harper), 78–79.

41. Ibid., 117.

42. This hypothesis on the connection between the Cynics and the Q community is argued by F. Gerald Downing, *Christ and the Cynics: Jesus and Other Radical Preachers in First-Century Tradition* (Sheffield: Sheffield University Press, 1988); John Kloppenborg, *The Formation of Q: Trajectories in Ancient Wisdom Collections* (Philadelphia: Fortress Press, 1987); and Leif E. Vaage, *Galilean Upstarts: Jesus's First Followers according to Q* (Valley Forge, PA: Trinity Press, 1994). For an overview of both sides of this debate, see Hans Dieter Betz, "Jesus and the Cynics: Survey and Analysis of a Hypothesis" *Journal of Religion* 74 (October 1994), 453–75. See also Crossan, *J*, 122.

43. Crossan, *J*, 117–22.

44. Kearney, *Dialogues*, 116–17.

45. Hart, *Trespass of the Sign*, 93.

20
The Experience of God and the Axiology of the Impossible

Who would not want to have an experience of God? But if no one has seen God and lived, who would want to risk it? Would this experience be some very extraordinary and death-defying event, like landing on the moon or being abducted by aliens? Or would it rather be a much calmer, cooler, and more calculating affair, like trying to read extremely complex computer data from the Galileo telescope that only a few highly trained experts can understand? What would "experience" mean if one had an experience of God? For that matter, what would "God" mean if God could be experienced?

Rather than engage in any speculative adventure, I will keep close to the phenomenological ground, for phenomenology, which is nothing but the cartography of experience, is what for me comes "after ontotheology."[1] Although I will speak of a certain leap, what I offer here is a careful explication of what is going on here below, in experience. On that basis, then, let me pose a risky hypothesis: I will venture the idea that the very idea of "experience" drives us to the idea of God—which may sound at first a little bit like the dream of an "absolute empiricism" that Derrida discusses at the end of his essay "Violence and Metaphysics"—and, in a strictly parallel way, that the very idea of "God" is of something that (or of someone who) sustains and sharpens what we mean by experience, with the result that the "experience of God" requires a "God of experience." On this hypothesis, then, "God" and "experience" are intersecting, prefitted notions that fit together hand in glove. This is all possible, I will hypothesize, only in virtue of the impossible, of what I call, after Derrida, "the impossible." The impossible will be the bridge, the crucial middle term in my logic, that links "God" and "experience."

I will pursue the hypothesis that the experience of the impossible makes the experience of God possible, or, to put it slightly differently, that we love God because we cannot help but love the impossible. But by "the impossible," I hasten to add, I do not mean a simple contradiction, the simple logical negation of the possible, like (*p* and -*p*), which is a cornerstone of the old ontotheology,[2] but something phenomenological, that is, that which shatters the horizon of expectation and foreseeability. For if every experience occurs within a horizon of possibility, the experience of the impossible is the experience of the shattering of this horizon. I am resisting all a priori logical and ontotheological constraints about the possible and the impossible in order to work my way back into the texture of the phenomenological structure of experience.

THE IMPOSSIBLE

Let us assume as an axiom that only the impossible will do, that anything less will produce what the noted Danish phenomenologist Johannes Climacus calls a "mediocre fellow." Climacus is speaking about the phenomenon of the paradox: "But one must not think ill of the paradox, for the paradox is the passion of thought, and the thinker without the paradox is like the lover without passion: a mediocre fellow. But the ultimate potentiation of every passion is to will its own downfall, and so it is also the ultimate passion of the understanding to will the collision, although in one way or another the collision must become its downfall. This, then, is the ultimate paradox of thought: to want to discover something that thought itself cannot think."[3]

On Climacus's hypothesis, the highest passion of thought is to think something that cannot be thought. To think something less, to confine oneself to thinking within the horizon of what it is possible to think, is to fail to extend thinking beyond itself or push it beyond its normal range. Thinking within the horizon of the possible has all the makings of mediocrity, of that measured, moderate middle ground that wants to minimize risk and maintain present boundaries.

Mediocrity confines itself to practicing the art of the possible. What Climacus here calls the ultimate "potentiation" of a passion, which means raising it to its highest pitch, means at the same time reaching a point of impotency and impossibility (which are at root the same word, *adynaton*) in a kind of phenomenological *coincidentia oppositorum*. The full intensity of experience, the fullest passion, is attained only in extremis, only when a power—which here is "thinking"—is pushed to its limits, indeed beyond its limits, to the breaking point, to the point where it breaks open by colliding against what is beyond its power.

Clearly we can extend Climacus's hypothesis to other passions and other powers and formulate a kind of general theory of impossibility, turning on a certain axiom of impossibility, which might represent a kind of Aristotelianism—a theory of potencies and powers—gone mad, but with a divine madness. Thus the ultimate potentiation of desire would be to discover something that exceeds desire, that desire cannot desire, in a desire beyond desire; to desire something that it is impossible to desire because it is beyond desire's reach. Desire thus is fully extended and reaches its apex only when desire wills or desires its own downfall. When we confine our desire within the horizon of the possible, of the realistically attainable, will that not always result in something less than we truly desire? What can arouse desire more than to be told we cannot have the object of our desire, that it is forbidden or unattainable? Rather than extinguishing desire, does not the very impossibility fire and provoke the desire all the more? Desire is really desire when we desire beyond desire, when the desire of desire is in collision with itself. The highest potentiation of a passion and a power is reached when that power is brought face to face with its own impotency. The impotency and the impossibility provide the condition of possibility of the potentiation. The very condition that blocks the expenditure is what intensifies it. Anything less than the impossible just will not do; anything less will leave the power intact, still standing within the horizon of the same, and will not push it beyond itself or force it to another register. So to put our axiom very precisely we can say that for any x, where x is a power, like thinking or desiring, x reaches its highest potentiation only when it is impossible for x to act. Thus a power is most intensely itself only when it is brought to a standstill, brought to the point that it breaks up or breaks open and is forced beyond itself; it reaches its highest potentiation only when by a kind of discontinuous leap it moves, or is moved, to another sphere or register, beyond its own proper potency.

EXPERIENCE

The axiom of impossibility, the law of the highest potentiation, goes to the heart of what I mean by experience, by the passion and intensity of experience, for an experience must have passion to be worthy of the name. To have an experience is to have a taste for adventure, for venturing and risk, which is meaning of the root *peira*. Thus to be a real "empiricist" means not to sniff along the ground of experience like a hound dog but to search for opportunities, even perilous ones, like piracy (all of which have the same etymology).[4] So experience in the positive and maximal sense, experience that is really worth its salt—and salt is my criterion of experience—is not for mediocre fellows. The easy humdrum drift of everydayness is experience only in the minimal and negative sense that we are not stone dead, fast asleep, dead drunk, or completely unconscious, although sometimes, it seems, we might just as well be. Experience is really experience when we venture where we cannot or should not go; experience happens only if we take a chance, only if we risk going where we cannot go, only if we have the nerve to step where angels fear to tread, precisely where taking another step farther is impossible. (Since the condition of its possibility is its impossibility.)

Having, or rather venturing, an experience, involves a double operation: first we understand full well that it is impossible to go, that we are blocked from moving ahead, that we cannot take another step, that we have reached the limit: then we go. We venture out and take the risk, perilous as it may be. First immobilization, then movement. The movement is mobilized by the immobilization. We take the Kierkegaardian leap into the rush of existence, come what may. First we are frozen with fear and immobility; then we leap. When we go where we cannot go, then we are really moving and something is really happening, over and above the routinized flow of tick-tock time that runs on automatic pilot. The immobilization belongs more to the cognitive domain: we know this can't be done; we have been instructed by the understanding about the limits of what it possible. But then we go. Thus the movement is carried out by a shift to the sphere of praxis and the pragmatic order (which is also related to *peira*), to a certain non-cognitive leap that overcomes the hesitations of the understanding; that is what Augustine calls doing the truth, *facere veritatem*. We know better but we do it anyway against our knowledge, or—to give this a sharper edge—we do it for just that reason. Experience is for leapers and risk takers, for venturers and adventurers, while mediocre fellows would rather stay home and let the clock run out on life, preferring the safety and security of their living rooms to the leap. The impossible is what gives experience its bite, its kick, and draws us out of the circle of sameness, safety, ease, and familiarity.

Seen from a modernist and Kantian point of view, I am adopting a perverse and quite contrarian position. According to my axiom of impossibility, whatever conforms to what Kant calls the "conditions of possibility of experience" is precisely not what I mean by experience, while the mark of experience in the highest sense, *sensu eminentiore*, is the impossible, which defies and exceeds Kant's conditions. Experience has to do precisely with what is not possible, with what violates or breaches the conditions of possibility that have been set forth by the understanding. Seen from a Lyotardian point of view, experience does not mean merely to make a new move in an old game, but to invent a new game altogether. An experience does not move about safely within fixed limits, abiding within prescribed conditions of possibility, playing the game by the existing rules; rather, it ventures forth and crosses the borders, transgressing and trespassing the limits laid down by the understanding, the limits of the possible, of the safe and sane and the "same."

GOD

By "God," I mean the possibility of the impossible, a sense that is both scriptural and phenomenological. I am not speculating about this name[5] in the manner of an ontotheology, but consulting one of its oldest and most venerable uses in the biblical tradition. When the angel Gabriel visits the Virgin Mary and gives her the startling news, Mary first remarks upon the great unlikelihood that the angel is right, to which Gabriel replies with angelic imperturbability not to fear, "for nothing will be impossible with God" (Lk. 1). When Jesus heals the epileptic boy, the disciples wonder why they could not do the same, and Jesus tells them that it is because they have too little faith. "For truly I tell you, if you have faith the size of a mustard seed, you will say to this mountain, 'Move from here to there,' and it will move; and nothing will be impossible for you" (Mt. 17:20–21). Nothing is impossible for God, or for those who being faced squarely with the impossible put their faith in God and let God do the heavy lifting. When Jesus tells the rich man to sell everything he has and give it to the poor, and then adds that it will be harder for a rich man to gain entrance to the kingdom of God than for a camel to pass through the eye of a needle, the disciples are thrown into despair, for who then can be saved? They have reached the point of the impossible; they see there is no way to take a single step forward. Then, having been driven to that point, Jesus says, "For human beings it is impossible, but for God all things are possible" (Mt. 19:26). Including the impossible. What is impossible for us (*para anthropois*) is God's business, for with God (*para theo*) nothing is impossible. That is why Nicholas of Cusa says, and this is another axiom to add to our axiology of the impossible, "since nothing is impossible for God, we should look for Him (in whom impossibility is necessity) in those things which are impossible in this world."[6] Wherever the impossible happens, there is God. The impossible (*adynaton*), then, is a sign of God, like a marker in the road that points us toward God, *à Dieu*, where the road swings off, occasioning a shift from our powers and our possibilities to the powers and possibilities of God, where we pass from the sphere of human rule to the sphere where God rules, which is what the scriptures call the kingdom of God (*basileia tou theou*). The mark of God's kingdom is that there *imposse* becomes *posse*, the *adynaton* becomes *dynaton*. The impossible draws us out of the sphere of the sane and the same, of the "human," into another sphere, where a divine madness rules, which is the rule of God.

It follows that the "experience of God" is closely tied to the "God of experience" and that the love of God is tied to our love of the impossible. "Experience" is the sort of thing that calls for God and the name of "God" is the sort of thing that raises experience to its highest pitch. Anything that falls short of God will not have the bite of experience. By the same token, anything that eludes or has nothing to do with charging experience to the utmost will not be God. In the experience of God, "experience" and "God" are keyed to each other in such an intimate way that experience enters into what we mean by God. To which I should hasten to add, what we mean by God and what we mean by experience, for by tracking experience phenomenologists are always tracking someone's experience, not some transcendental, transhistorical "essence" in the manner of classical Husserlian phenomenology; in that sense, phenomenology is ineluctably hermeneutical, probing the structure of a historical experience.[7] So I am trying to get a sense of what we Westerners mean, we who have a specific scriptural and historical tradition behind us, where there is a taste for time and history, for freedom and decision, in a word, for "experience," for what we mean by experience. The experience of God always comes down to our experience, and our experience is of a God of experience, a God who lends himself to experience.

THE EXPERTS OF THE POSSIBLE

We can put a sharper point on what we mean by this experience of the impossible by contrasting it with what I will call here the experts of the possible, the master practitioners of the art of the possible. The experts of the possible practice what was called by the medieval theologians the "cardinal" virtues, which would be precisely those virtues that are possible "for humans" (*para anthropois*), as Matthew has Jesus say, that is, those virtues that remain within the horizon of the powers of human beings. The cardinal virtues are, as the image goes, the "hinges" (*cardo*) upon which a hale and whole human life swings, if we have a door hinge in mind. But since there are in fact four cardinal virtues—practical wisdom, justice, courage, and moderation—the metaphor seems to suggest the hinges by which the four legs of a table are attached to the tabletop, hence the hinges upon which our moral life is stabilized and firmly planted on the floor. Either way, the cardinal virtues, which go back to Plato and Aristotle, have to do with the life of *arete*, of human excellence. They turn on the figure of what Aristotle called the *phronimos*, the man of "practical wisdom," or "prudent" man (*phronesis* was translated as *prudentia* in the Middle Ages).

Aristotle was the master of those who know what is what about the possible and the actual, the master theoretician of potencies and possibilities, and he thought you could explain anything in those terms, so long as you saw that the actual moved about within the horizon fixed by the potential and stayed as far away as possible from the impossible. That is the central thesis of ontotheology, which tended to keep a metaphysical lid on experience in a way that I am resisting. The *phronimos* is a well-bred, well-educated, well-trained, and in general well-hinged fellow who knows how to conduct the business of life amid its shifting circumstances. He is a man of good habits and insight, the noble, aristocratic sort of fellow who shows up all the time in the novels of Jane Austen and Anthony Trollope. We need not strain to use gender-neutral language here because Aristotle was only talking about men; it did not hit him that women (or slaves) could hit the mark of *arete* just as regularly as men do (which was not true of Austen and Trollope).

The *phronimos* does the good so regularly that it comes to be a kind of second nature for him, a stratum of virtuous conduct layered over his basic human nature so thickly that doing the right thing comes almost as naturally as breathing. The facility in virtuous conduct comes to him by dint of practice, and the practice breeds the "habit," the *hexis*, the natural possession, of hitting the mark, like the skill acquired by an archer who practices every day for many hours. All this practice sharpens his eye so that he can easily sight the mark and hit it. The exact mark is the middle of the target, neither too high nor too low, neither too much nor too little. The mark is the median point of moderation, the well-measured middle mark, right in the center. This moderation does not produce mediocrity but excellence (*arete*), because finding the right mark is rare and hard to do and most people miss it, which is where the mediocrity would lie for Aristotle.

For example, the *phronimos* knows that "courage" does not consist in being stupid, in putting one's body in front of a six-axle truck that is roaring down a street out of control in order to stop it from plowing into a crowd. He also knows that courage does not mean being cowardly under the cover of caution, avoiding a situation we should confront, failing to speak up when a word is required of us. Now this can be very hard to determine and sometimes requires exquisite judgment. When Pius XII held his tongue about Nazi atrocities during World War II, his defenders said he was being prudent and his critics said he was being cowardly. The *phronimos* avoids excess (*hyperbole*), overshooting the mark, and defect (*elipsis*), undershooting the mark. He regularly sees and does what is just right. But this is not a fixed but a moving target, a floating mark that bobs up and down in the flux of changing circumstances, and it takes a practiced eye to spot it, what defines the *phronimos*.

Now when the *phronimos* runs into trouble, that is, when he hits an idiosyncratic and anomalous situation, then far from falling apart, far from willing his own downfall, far from breaking up from the force of the collision, this well-hinged fellow hits full stride and comes into his own precisely as the prudent man that he is. For the *phronimos* has so sharp and practiced an eye, an eye that so regularly sizes up what is to be done and what is not to be done in most situations, that when he hits an irregular and incommensurable circumstance, he has the insight to make a good judgment, to adjudicate just what is demanded here and now by this particular situation, in just these singular circumstances. He is not bowled over by the oddity of the situation but he gets on top of it and reaches a judicious and equitable judgment about just what is demanded, about just what justice requires, or courage. The oddity of the situation does not knock him off his hinges but he stands firm like a table with all four feet firmly fixed on the ground.

From our point of view, the *phronimos* is a self-possessed fellow who does not lose it, whose highest potentiation is to maintain the calm possession of his powers. He is smart enough to know not to tamper with what lies outside his domain of his own possibilities. He wisely remains within the realm of things over which he retains the powers of disposition, over which he rules with a seasoned eye and practiced self-control. He is, in a word, a master of his powers, an expert of the possible. He undertakes the risky business of hitting the mark in unforeseen circumstances, which is why we admire his expertise, but he does not dare venture out into that abyss where he does not rule. The latter is the place where there are no experts, where, according to the scriptures, God rules, with whom all things are possible, including the impossible, where the experts of the possible are forced to yield to the experience of the impossible.

FAITH AND THE UNBELIEVABLE

The expert of the possible is a well-hinged fellow, and who can fail to admire such excellence? He knows what is what and remains in control. But the requirement of a genuine experience involves taking a greater risk than that, venturing into the domain where our powers of self-possession slip away and we are exposed to risk on every side. So in contradistinction to the four virtues of the well-hinged, let us offer the three "virtues" of the unhinged—if that phallocentrism is a word we still want to use at this point (virtues suggest something virile). In the interest of coming up with something that comes after ontotheology, let us propose three cases of the frame of mind of those who will the ultimate potentiation of their powers right on up to the point of the impossible, where the highest potentiation of one's powers lies in willing their downfall.

The *phronimos* is a prudent man, and he does not do foolish things. He knows what his chances are and he carefully deliberates about when a risk is worth taking. This is the sort of fellow one wants as an investment counselor. So when he believes something we can be assured that he has good reasons for believing it, that it is eminently believable. What he believes is credible and his credulity is warranted. His idea is the moderation not the ultimate potentiation of belief, not to believe too much too easily or to believe too little with too much resistance. For he believes in things just insofar as they are warranted and reasonable. But that is to believe something just so far as he can see that it is likely to be so, just where the evidence is the greatest and the amount of actual faith required is the least. Inasmuch as his beliefs are organized around the principle of the possible, which is here the probable or likely, he always prefers the situation that requires the least faith and the most evidence possible. Once the scale of probabilities tips against him, he will abandon his belief and put his confidence elsewhere. So it is not faith that has won the heart of the *phronimos* but evidence, seeing, where faith is a kind of tentative supplement or prosthesis that he employs while waiting for all the evidence to arrive to support his primary thetic act. But clearly this is a fellow with only a moderate faith in faith, with only a moderate heart for the ultimate potentiation of belief, for is not faith most required when things start to look a little unbelievable? Is not faith really faith just insofar as it tends to be impossible to believe? We need faith precisely when the odds are against us, when everyone else thinks it mad to go on, when it starts to look incredible. Faith is faith not in the reasonable and likely, which is less a matter of faith and more a calculus of probabilities; faith is faith in the incredible. That's when we need faith to go on just in order to keep on going.

Let us take the case of an innocent man who has been unjustly accused of wrongdoing. At first his friends believe in his innocence and rally around him in support, especially early on, when they do not know the whole story and the facts are on his side. But as the tide of evidence shifts against the fellow, the more fainthearted among his friends fade away and the crowd of his supporters thins. For they, alas, are disciples of the principle of the possible, and they shy away from the axiom of the impossible. They believe things only insofar as they are believable, that is, reasonable, which is to believe something only insofar as it requires a minimum of belief. That is what Johannes Climacus would call the faith of a mediocre fellow who tries to stick to the golden middle where all the evidence is clustered. But this poor fellow under unjust accusation needs friends precisely at the extreme point, which requires a maximum of belief, where all the evidence is against him, in that darkest midnight hour in which he is condemned as a guilty man by all the world. To go on believing in this fellow then, when in all likelihood he is a guilty man, at that point when it seems unbelievable, that is faith, the ultimate potentiation of the faith one has in a friend, a faith tried and tested in the fire of the impossible. The rest is just happy-hour companionship, the vacillating support of a hail-fellow-well-met who heads for the door at the first sound of trouble.

Faith does not come down to believing things just insofar as they are believable, but believing in what has become unbelievable, when it has become impossible to believe. Only the impossible will do to fire the steel of faith. At that most extreme point, at that darkest hour, when we have run up against the impossibility of believing and going on, just then, we believe. Before that, it was just a poker game and we were playing the odds.

At that point, we reach one of the edges of our experience, a boundary or limit case where our own powers and potentialities reach a breaking point and we realize that we have entered a domain where we have no control, where we do not rule, and we put our faith in God—or something, God knows what, since it is out of our hands. That is one of the ways that the name of "God" enters our "experience." For God to gain admission, for the name of God to come into play, the walls of the possible must be razed and the experts of the possible must have fled the scene. For God is given in the experience of the impossible, when we have reached our limits and conceded that we do not know what to do.

"I believe you, I believe in you, I will stand by you no matter what, even if for all the world you are condemned as guilty. I will believe the unbelievable, right on up to the end. And I commend you to God. I will pray for you and ask God to watch over you. For with God all things are possible, even the impossible." For us, for our limited powers, it is impossible, but it is possible for God. For God makes the crooked straight and makes the lamb lie down with the lion. God watches over the little ones and sets his heart not on the ninety-nine who are in the fold but on the one who is lost, the odd one out. The name of God is the name of one who can make this possible, even if it is impossible. For God is the giver of all good gifts, above all if they are impossible. That is what we mean by God, what the name of God means, and it is this sort of limit-experience—a term that is in a certain sense redundant, that gives the name of God meaning, what we might call its phenomenological content, which is in the truest sense of the word experiential. For to have an experience is to take a risk, to brave the stormy seas of the impossible, to venture out where common sense tells us to stick close to the land and keep the shoreline in sight, to expose ourselves where the odds are against us. We look for God, as Cusa says, where the impossible happens.

The experience of God is to "see" the hand of God in the course that things take, to take the course of experience as guided by God, to find a loving hand, a providential care where others see chance, so that when things happen they happen as a gift, not fortuitously but gratuitously. But the gift is not a gift of chance, a bit of fortuitousness, but a gratuity that is marked by a divine graciousness.

Of course, we must concede that this will always include the possibility that the outcome will be a disaster, that God will have permitted a disaster, God knows why. As Qoheleth points out, God also makes his sun to shine upon the wicked and the just so we none of us know how this will turn out. The disaster may strengthen the hand of those who say our lives are held not in the palm of God's hand but exposed to chance and the play of forces. That is true, but only on the basis of the logic or onto logic of the possible. For the disaster also strengthens the hand of those who believe in God, because faith is faith in the face of the impossible, in the midnight hour where night is its element and it has become impossible to believe, according not to the logic of the possible but to the axiom of the impossible. I will come back to this complication about chance.

HOPING AGAINST HOPE

The experts of the possible have reasonable hopes. Their hope is well founded on the facts so that they can have every reasonable expectation that things will turn out well. The physician says the disease has been caught in its earliest stages and he expects a full recovery. He has treated many such cases before and the outcome is almost always favorable. The future has all the weight of the past behind it; the course of events seems almost inevitable. That is hope with a minimum of hope and a maximum of reasonable expectation.

That is hope in a "future-present," a future I can almost see and taste on the basis of the present, a future that is so strongly predictable that it has practically happened already. I have done everything that is possible, everything that is in my power, to make the future happen just as I planned. One is reminded of the "future" for stockbrokers who bid up the price of stocks on the basis of the expectation of good news—like the expectation that the Federal Reserve Board will lower interest rates—so that when the expected action by the board in fact takes place, nothing happens to the stocks; the future event was already built into the price.

But in the experience of the impossible, all such reasonable calculation breaks down and things look hopeless: the disease has spread too far and has not been caught in time and there is no hope for the patient. But are not those bleak and hopeless times just when hope is required? Is not hope really hope only when things begin to look hopeless and it is mad to hope? Is that not when we need to brave the stormy waters of hope, undertake the risk of hope, which is, we recall, what having an experience means? That at least is the opinion not of the stockbrokers or of Aristotle but of the Apostle Paul, whose favorite example is not the *phronimos* but Abraham, the father of us all. Abraham is remembered not as the father of the stock market or of the *phronimoi* but as the father of faith and hope. Abraham trusted in the promise of the Lord that he would be the father of many generations just when it was hopeless, when his body was as good as dead, and he was nearly a hundred years old, and Sarah's body was barren. Being fully convinced that it was impossible, Abraham continued to hope, even to the point of what Paul calls "hoping against hope" (Rom. 4:18), which is, it seems to me an exquisite formulation of the axiom of impossibility. Hope is hope only when one hopes against hope, only when the situation is hopeless. Hope has the full force of hope only when we have first been led to the point where it is impossible to hope—and then we hope against hope, even as faith is faith in the face of the incredible. Hope is hope when all I can do is to try to keep hope alive even though there is no hope. There is no hope, I know that and I am convinced of that, but still I hope. Only the impossible will do for the highest potentiation of faith and hope. The experts of the possible will have long since slipped out the back door.

But why did Abraham continue to hope even when it was hopeless? Because "God was able to do what he had promised" (Rom. 4:21). For the name of God is the name of the possibility of the impossible. We invoke the name of God in order to "keep hope alive," as Jesse Jackson says—the name of God is the name of hope for Jackson and for Martin Luther King, for Gandhi and Dietrich Bonhoeffer, for Nelson Mandela and Bishop Tutu—to keep the future open, even when every door has been closed. We need hope when we see no way out, no way to go, when we are blocked on every side in an aporia more complete and encompassing than Aristotle ever imagined. The name of God is the name of our hope, the power that steps in for our weakness and hopelessness. For "if God is for us, who is against us?" (Rom. 8:31) Nothing at all—"neither death nor life, nor angels, nor rulers, nor things present, nor things to come, nor powers, nor height nor depth, nor anything else in all creation" will be able to stand between us and our hope (Rom. 8:38–39).

Paul says that "hope that is seen is not hope. For who hopes for what is seen? But if we hope for what we do not see, we wait in patience" (Rom. 8:24–25). If hope has to do precisely with the unseen then, in its highest potentiation, it is concerned not with the unseen but foreseeable, but with the absolutely unforeseeable, which constitute a more radical and "absolute" future than the "future present" of the stockbrokers.

When the future is more or less planned and foreseeable, time becomes a certain approximation process that gradually edges closer and closer to the hoped-for point in the future, making asymptotic progress toward the goal. Then we are filled with rising expectations. But hope that has pushed to its highest potentiation is blinder than that, more open-ended than that, and cannot see its way. Hope cannot imagine what the future holds, or how things will turn around, and when the unexpected happens we are left wondering how that was possible, given that it was impossible. So insofar as the name of God is linked to the experience of the impossible, it also opens up another experience of time and a certain phenomenology of an absolute future.

The name of God is the name of a horizon of absolute expectation, of unconditional hope. More precisely, the name of God is not the horizon but rather the hope that lies beyond the horizon when there is no hope in sight, no hope on the horizon. The name of God opens closed horizons, interrupts the predictability of the future. When we are surrounded on every side by an encompassing horizon that encloses us within hopelessness, when we see nowhere to turn, then we turn to God. When every possibility has been dashed, then the way has been made clear for God, for with God everything is possible, including the impossible. When we reach the limits of our power to hope, then the power of God steps in to lift us out of despair.

What I am suggesting on purely phenomenological grounds is an important part of what we mean by God and hope, what *we* mean, as I have said, we in the West, where there is a taste for time and history, in a word, for "experience." Our experience of God is very much tied to a God of experience where experience has the sense of venture and adventure, of risk and exposure to the future. I do not deny that this experience of God is our experience, and our idea of God, whoever we are, we who are an ambiguous mix of Greek and Jew, who live in the difference between the two.

LOVE IS WITHOUT WHY

Let there be no mistake, the *phronimos* has friends and is an advocate of *philia*. He thinks that when it comes to friendship the best should stick with the best and that true *philia* is possible only among those of equal station, where it can be properly reciprocated, so that men may love women, slaves, and animals only in an increasingly weak and proportionate extension of the term. You need friends to be happy because no mere mortal can make it alone. You need a talent for friendship and you need the good fortune not to be born mean, repulsive, and curmudgeonly so that you drive people away from you. Having a closed circle of friends, of people who mutually will the good of one another and support each other when times are tough, belongs to the circle of good that one draws around oneself in order to be happy. A good wine, a good job, a good investment counselor, and good friends are all part of the good life.

Now of all the "virtues" that least lend themselves to the *phronimos*'s idea of measured moderation, love leads the list, for the only measure of love is love without measure. The fellow who says he loves something—be it a woman or a cause or even his cat—just so far and but too far, neither too little nor too much, all within the limits of reason and moderation, since one never wants to go overboard, is a lover without passion, the very idea of what Climacus means by a mediocre fellow. If upon being pressed whether he loves his spouse or fiancée, this fellow says, after a certain amount of deliberation, "Yes, in certain respects, and up to a certain point, very definitely—but you always have to watch out for number one," then whatever it is the poor fellow feels, it is not love. For love is measured by its measureless expenditure, its unconditionality, its no-holds-barred, until-death-us-do-part commitment and giving.

Love does not calculate the return for its expenditure; it is perfectly true that one loves and desires the return of love for love, but the return is not the condition or precondition of the expenditure. Love is a gift that is given unconditionally.

Love, too, perhaps love above all, is governed by this axiom of the impossible, is potentiated or raised to its highest potentiation by the impossible. For, after all, what is easier than to love those who love us, who sing our praises, who stick by us, who think well of us, and return our love with love? Is that not even a common practice among the Mafia, an organization not widely known for love? Loving those who are lovable and who return our love with love—is that not possible, all too entirely possible? Does it not rank high among the achievement of the experts of the possible?

But does not love begin to reach its higher registers only when it starts to become a little madder, a little more impossible, which would mean when what we love is not so lovable and tends not to return our love? Like loving an aged parent who no longer even knows our name or recognizes us? Or loving an ungrateful child who has no appreciation of the genuine bond that unites children with their parents? Or an ungrateful friend who only shows up when he needs a handout and never shows the least bit of gratitude for all we do for him? We are beginning to move into a space where love is tested and fired by the increasing heat of—what else?—the impossible. We start to hit a point where it is not possible to love these people, where the understanding says, "These people do not deserve our love," which of course is an eminently reasonable thing to say. But then again, must love be deserved—or is love a gift? If love must be deserved or earned, then it is something we owe to the one who earned it, and then it is more like wages for labor than a gift we give without condition.

Is love given unconditionally or do you have to meet certain conditions in order to earn it? Does love always have to have be reasonable, to have a logos, a why, a reason—or is love without why?

But let us raise the stakes still higher, and push love to its highest potentiation. Consider the following hymn to the impossible:

> But I say to you that listen, love your enemies, do good to those who hate you, bless those who curse you, pray for those who abuse you.
>
> If you love those who love you, what credit is it to you? For even sinners love those who love them. If you do good to those who do good to you, what credit

> is that to you? For even sinners do the same. If you lend to those from whom you hope to receive, what credit is that to you? Even sinners lend to sinners, to receive as much again. But love your enemies, do good, and lend, expecting nothing in return. Your reward will be great and you will children of the Most High; for he is kind to the ungrateful and the wicked. Be merciful, just as your Father is merciful. (Luke 6:27–28, 32–36)

These sayings are predicated directly on the axiom of impossibility, turning on the idea that nothing short of the impossible will do, that the impossible makes for the highest potentiation of love, for here we are asked to love the completely unlovable, and to love those who return love with hate.

But that is impossible. To be sure. It is mad; yes, indeed. That is why this love is what it is and why we love this love so much, or at least recognize in it love's highest potentiation, even if we keep a safe distance from it ourselves and would not blame someone who avoided it. Just as thought desires to think what cannot be thought, and faith is asked to believe what is most unbelievable, and hope is called for when it is hopeless, so love is love when love is faced with the most loveless and unlovable hate, when it is mad to love. When your love is like that, then this text from Matthew says you are the children of love, or of God, for God is love: "Beloved, let us love one another, because love is from God; everyone who loves is born of God and knows God. Whoever does not love does not know God, for God is love. . . . God is love and those who abide in love abide in God and God abides in them" (1 John 4:7–8, 16).

There is no name more closely associated in the Christian scriptures with "God" than love.[8] That is what God is, and this comes as close as the New Testament comes to a "definition" of God, as opposed to defining God ontotheologically in terms of possibility and actuality, essence and existence. Even so, it would be at best a quasi-definition because in saying that God is love one is not defining God in the sense of setting forth God's limits and boundaries, but saying that God is unbounded and unlimited and unconditional excess, for love is love only in excess and overflow, not in moderation.

So the experience of God is given in the experience of love. But love is perfect not when love is drawn around a closed circle of friends and intimates, which makes perfect sense and is perfectly possible, but precisely when love is stretched to the breaking point of loving when love is mad and impossible. The God of love and the God of the impossible seem like a nice fit, a kind of prefit.

THANKING OUR LUCKY STARS

Thus to the well-hinged experts of the possible, sane and moderate fellows that they are, whose acts are always well ordered within the horizon of the possible and properly proportioned to their potencies, we oppose the experience of the impossible, which is a kind of divine madness that is intoxicated with excess and the impossible, that does not get going unless it is provoked by the impossible, which is when or where God rules.

God—or perhaps just chance? Now we come back to a point I intimated earlier. With the experience of the impossible, we cannot avoid feeling a little like June bugs with whom children play of a summer's night, or like fish caught in a cosmic net, twisting and flipping about until the air gives out. Here, at this limit point, in extremis, when we are or when someone we love is struck by a potentially fatal disease, a qualitative shift takes place in our experience and we enter another domain where things slip out of our control. Speaking in strictly phenomenological terms, the things that are not under our control, where we have run up against the limits of our powers, are the raw materials of religion, the stuff of which it is made, the occasion upon which the name of God makes its entry.

We would do well to make it clear that in this confrontation with the impossible we are not praying for a magical divine intervention on the course of nature. For a God who, upon being pressed by our prayers, alters natural processes is every bit as ontotheological as the *causa sui* of metaphysical theology, constituting a kind of divine supercause who produces effects that are beyond our human powers. For even after the event, after the death of the beloved, when history or nature has taken its deadly course and God has not intervened to stop the disaster or the disease in its tracks, we are still praying.

For our prayer is a way to affirm that there is meaning in our lives, that behind the meaninglessness and tragic course that is taken by our lives, both personal and collective, there is a mysterious love not blind chance, that our lives have meaning for God in the midst of this tragedy. The impossible is not that, against all the odds, there will be a miraculous intervention from on high, but that there is a meaning here, in this impossible situation, that a meaning is possible where it is impossible that this death or illness, this tragedy or misfortune, could have any meaning, for with God all things are possible.

The prayer of Jesus in Gethsemane is paradigmatic in this regard. Foreseeing the sufferings that lay ahead, he "threw himself on the ground and prayed, that if it were possible [*dynaton estin*], the hour might pass." Then he said, "Abba, Father, for you all things are possible [*panta dynata soi*]; remove this cup from me; yet, not what I want, but what you want" (Mark 14:35–36). First we pray for a specific outcome, for what I want, for with God, all things are possible. Then, in a second motion, we amend that prayer and pray for what God wants, that we will have the strength to believe and hope and love that, come what may, God's mysterious love is unfolding in our lives. We do not pray that God rethink the matter and alter his present plans, but that what is happening in our lives, which it is impossible to comprehend, is sustained by incomprehensible love.

Still, the question persists, do these limit situations necessarily present us with "God" or with what we sometimes call "the gods," by which we just mean chance? At these limit points in our experience, have we come face to face with the gift of God's grace? Or with a fortuitous turn of events? Might the impossible be a mark not of the "kingdom of God" but of the domain of fortune and chance, not of love but of luck?[9] Indeed, if we treat life itself as a gift, is it a gift of God?

Or is it not just the effect of a quirky molecular mutation taken in some far off corner of the universe, just an idiosyncratic turn of events in the great cosmic stupidity as it hurdles its way into entropic dissipation? Here we touch upon the question of the gift and its enigmatic hermeneutic.

In terms of the specific problematic of the impossible, the question is this: Can one desire to think what cannot be thought, or to hope against hope, without implicating oneself in God or religion? With God, nothing is impossible, but might the impossible be possible without God? Is the "highest potentiation" of our powers an independent phenomenological structure that stands with or without God, with or without religion? By confining ourselves to a rigorously phenomenological ground, have we actually pulled the rug out from under religion? Even if the name of God is the name of the possibility of the impossible, might "the possibility of the impossible" go under another name than "God?" Might the name of God be an incognito under which the possibility of the impossible travels? Might the impossible still be possible, even without the God of the Jewish and Christian scriptures, with whom nothing is impossible? Might there be an experience of the impossible that would belong to a certain religion that we can call a religion without religion, which gets along without what the scriptures call a loving father? Might the work that is performed by (in) the "name of God" be carried out in other ways and under other names? Might a certain "religion" survive as a residue of biblical religion in the phenomenological structures it leaves behind (if biblical religion has been left behind, which I doubt)? Are not these structures inscribed deep within our "experience," which is the experience of us Westerners who have been shaped by (among other things) these very scriptures, like it or not?

We concede that our lives are tossed about by the winds of chance and there is no benign design behind it all. We hang on to such happiness as we have by a tenuous gossamer thread, knowing full well that it can be extinguished by the slightest shift in the cosmic winds. Johannes de Silentio said that without faith in God, with whom all things are possible, we can only get as far as infinite resignation; we need faith in God to believe that we will get Isaac back, that there will be a repetition, for after having given Isaac up one would actually be embarrassed to get him back. For faith is not just believing something in "childlike and naive innocence," which though it is a beautiful thing that can "bring the very stones to tears . . . does not dare, in the pain of resignation, to look the impossibility in the eye." That is true, and far be it for me to take on as redoubtable a phenomenologist as Johannes de Silentio. But since I take the results achieved by Johannes Climacus and Johannes de Silentio to be phenomenological, I can conclude that one might use the name of God as a kind of "placeholder" or "incognito" for our hope against hope.

After all, the name of God means the possibility of the impossible. I did not invent that, and it is not up to me to ban that linguistic usage, to try to outlaw it. The name of God is the name of one who can make the impossible possible; the impossible is where we look for God. That is a large part of what the name of God signifies in the biblical tradition, which I am treating here as its phenomenological content, its detachable phenomenological content. For the phenomenon stands with or without the historical religions. Constituting a certain religion with or without the historical religions. (The next question is this: is "the possibility of the impossible" a kind of free-standing phenomenological unit that sometimes goes under the name of "God" in religion? Or is it radically parasitic upon the historical scriptural traditions, from whom we learned it in the first place?)

Things happen in this sphere beyond our control "gratuitously," like a grace, but the gift may well be a gift of chance, a bit of fortuitousness, not the gratuity of a divine graciousness. We believed against all the odds and kept the faith in order to keep the future open but we were prepared for the worst, prepared to go under. Still, we caught a break and our faith and hope were "rewarded." The impersonal course of things took a fortuitous turn. If there is a "gift" here, the gift is not the doing of anyone's generosity and there is no one to thank; if we express our gratitude to the stars we are engaged in a monologue and we are simply purging ourselves of a need to express our gratitude. We thank our lucky stars, but the stars, alas, do not know we are here.

The phenomenological structure of ineradicable faith, hope, and love, the phenomenological structure of this passion for the impossible, remains in place, but without the historical religions, constituting the structure of what Derrida calls a religion without religion. By this Derrida means, and I am following him here, a passion for the experience of the impossible, which is a passion that outstrips the conditions of possibility imposed upon experience by modernist criticism. Modernity is marked by a needless and distortive secularization of our experience, which is why it has come under increasing fire ever since Kierkegaard first gave it a piece of his formidable mind. There is an ineradicable undecidability here between "God" and "the gods," the gift of God and the gift of chance, mysterious love and blind chance, between two different ways to regard the gift and to treat the course of events, whose discernment constitutes the stuff of what I like to call a "more radical hermeneutics." One might well think that a repetition, however impossible, is just the sort of thing that might be brought about by the shifting tides of time and chance, which could bring Isaac back just as easily as they snatched him away, just so long as we do not give up, which is what the scriptural traditions call God.

We got lucky, the gods smiled upon us—or we were blessed by God—and the impossible happened. To be sure, no such hermeneutics, radical or more radical, will be able to provide a general formula for resolving the difference, for there is no higher axiom in virtue of which one could name, identify, or resolve the irresoluble fluctuation in the experience of the impossible. Making a move in this impossible situation is what I mean by radical hermeneutics, which does not set out to resolve this conflict but to identify the precise point of fluctuation at which a resolution, if there is one, would be carried out.

I can—indeed, I would say as a phenomenological matter, I must—love the impossible and think that anything is possible, even the impossible, for only the impossible will do. And if the impossible happens, I thank God, or my lucky stars. I love God because I love the impossible, but I love the impossible in any case. When the impossible happens, I thank what the great patristic phenomenologist Augustine of Hippo called in the most intimate and the most powerful phenomenological terms "*deus meus*," "my God." Speaking strictly as a phenomenologist, I would say that I thank God because with God nothing is impossible, but the question is, as Augustine also said, "what do I love when I love my God?"

Now, by way of a parting gesture, a concluding impudent postscript, let us thicken the plot and complicate the paradox with a final twist that would call for another and extended analysis: suppose one said that nothing turns on how one resolves this fluctuation, that as a phenomenological matter faith is faith, hope is hope, and love is love, so long as each is fired by the experience of the impossible, so that it does not matter whether one makes use of the name of God at all?

Then what difference would there be between standing by the beloved until the end, even though the situation is impossible, in the name of God, for with God nothing is impossible, and standing by the beloved until the end, tout court? I have been arguing that the "experience of the impossible" is the way in which the "experience of God" is given. But might the "experience of God" be no more than a name we have for the experience of the impossible, and the "love of God" be no more than a name we have for our love of the impossible? Perhaps. But now we ask, as long as one hopes against hope and loves beyond love, does that matter? Recalling that the *peira* of experience and praxis share a common root, does not a certain transformation into praxis occur at this point in virtue of which the experience of God and the experience of the impossible are caught up in a cognitive fluctuation that is resolved in the doing, in loving God in spirit and in truth, in spending oneself on behalf of the democracy to come? *Facere veritatem.* Could it be that the experience of God is given in an experience in which the name of God never comes up? Unlike landing on the moon, might one undergo an experience of God and never even know that that is what happened? Would that not correspond rather nicely to what Derrida calls a "gift," where no one suspects that anyone gave anyone anything? Again, would it not correspond to what theology calls God's kenosis, where God slips out of sight in order to let the world come into view, where God withdraws in order to make things possible, all things, including the impossible, for with God nothing is impossible?

NOTES

1. A phenomenology is always concerned with the precise sense of appearing, with the structure of phenomenality, rather than the objective reality of an appearance. Minimally, it would bracket a causal or realist account of experience and adhere closely to a descriptive account, without being in principle committed to a Husserlian theory of "consciousness" and the primacy of the cognitive, as the history of phenomenology after Husserl testifies. In the case of the scriptures, it would concentrate on the "sense" of a faith that can move mountains rather than , worrying about its objective physical or metaphysical possibility, on the sense of the angel Gabriel's "Annunciation to the Virgin Mary" rather than whether the evangelist records an actual historical episode.

2. Given the plurivocity of the word "impossible," it would be arbitrary to restrict the notion of the impossible to the objectivistic sense of a simple logical contradiction, which is but one of its many meanings. Some things, for example, are possible for women that are impossible for men, possible for the wealthy or strong that are impossible for the poor or weak, or possible for God that are impossible for human beings; this last sense plays an important role in this paper.

3. *Kierkegaard's Writings*, 7, *Philosophical Fragments; or, A Fragment of Philosophy and Johannes Climacus, or De Omnibus dubitandum est*, trans and ed. Howard Hong and Edna Hong (Princeton, NJ: Princeton University Press, 1985), 37. Kierkegaard's pseudonyms constitute clear antecedent figures in the history of phemenology: what else are their descriptions of freedom, possibility, anxiety, despair, and so on, than phenomenologies *avant la lettre*?

4. Joseph T. Shipley, *The Origins of English Words* (Baltimore: Johns Hopkins University Press, 1984), "per II I," 304.

5. The name of God is not primarily a matter for philosophical or theological speculation but a historical expression in which a community articulates how "God" has entered into the structure of its everyday life—its births and deaths, joys and sorrows. Its primary sense is found in its use, in a greeting ("God be with you") or a prayer ("O God") before its occurrence in any philosophical treatise. The name of God will flourish as long as there are such communities, and the speculations of the philosophers and theologians about this name will always be parasitic upon these practices. Philosophers have neither the means nor the authority to ban its use; their main role is to respond to the learned despisers of this name. As William F. Nietmann says, in a religious language, the name of God is not something requiring justification or explanation, but something that is invoked in the face of the meaninglessness of life. See his *The Unmaking of God* (Lanham, MD: University Press of America, 1994).

6. *De possest*, No. 59; see the translation of *De posset* in Jasper Hopkins, *A Concise Introduction to the Philosophy of Nicholas of Cusa*, 3rd ed. (Minneapolis: Arthur J. Banning Press, 1986). In *De possest* Nicholas of Cusa is content to show the coincidence of possibility and actuality in God: *possest est, posse/esse, possest*, where God is the actuality of every possibility. But in *On the Vision of God* (*De vision dei*), he ventures further to show that God is also the coincidence of necessity and impossibility, since God by the necessity of his infinite being is capable of what is impossible for us. There he writes, "I thank You, only God, for disclosing to me that there is no other way of approaching You than this way which seems to all men, including the most learned philosophers, altogether inaccessible and impossible. For You have shown me that You cannot be seen elsewhere than where impossibility appears and stands in the way. And You, O Lord, who are the Nourishment of the full-grown, have encouraged me to do violence to myself, because impossibility coincides with necessity." See Jasper Hopkins, *Nicholas of Cusa's Dialectical Mysticism, Text, Translation, and Interpretive Study of De Visione Dei*, 3rd ed. (Minneapolis: Arthur J. Banning Press, 1988), no. 39.

7. I do not think that Ricoeur's attempt to distinguish a phenomenology of essences from a hermeneutic of historical texts and cultures can stand up; see Paul J. Ricoeur, "Experience and Language in Religious Discourse," *Phenomenology and the Theological Turn: The French Debate*, ed. Dominique Janicaud, Jean-François Courtine, Jean-Louis Chrétien, Jean-Luc Marion, Michel Henry, and Paul Ricoeur (New York: Fordham University Press, 2000), 127–46.

8. One can say this without a trace of supercessionism, for in stressing love the New Testament is just being as Jewish as possible, despite the polemics of the new "Way" against the older Jewish traditions. See E. P. Sanders, *Jesus and Judaism* (Philadelphia: Fortress, 1985).

9. The *phronimos*, for example, knows as well as any reader of scripture that not everything is under his control and that he can only be praised or blamed for the things that are up to him. As for the rest, he leaves that up to *moira* or "the gods," which are an essential element (over and above his own virtue) in what he calls *Eudaimonia*. *Eudaimonia*, which we usually translate as "happiness," means have a "good spirit," like a "guardian angel," accompany you through life and protect you from fortune's more outrageous turns. You need the good fortune not to be born stupid, ugly, poor, or dispositionally unlovable, or all of these at once, and to enjoy good luck as life goes on. A good *daimon* bears a resemblance to the loving hand of what the Scriptures call "God" watching out for the least among us, or what Jesus called his *abba* keeping a loving care over us, but within a framework governed not by love but by luck, by the shifting tides of happenstance, catching a break in the cosmic twists and turns.

21 Without Sovereignty, Without Being: Unconditionality, the Coming God, and Derrida's Democracy to Come

Is there something "unconditional" that is nonetheless without "sovereignty"? Is there something that makes an unconditional claim without laying claim to unconditional force or power? Is there something that, even if it were a certain power or force, would be at most a "force without force" or a "power of powerlessness"?

Is there something unconditional that would neither *be* nor be *something*? Does the unconditional resist the very language of being in which we pose this question? Might it be that the unconditional would not really have a seat in being, that the conditions that obtain in being would be no match for the unconditional? Might it be that whatever has being can come to be only under certain conditions while the unconditional would somehow be otherwise than being, a kind of demi-being, almost like a ghost, almost nothing?

But if something unconditional happens, without sovereignty and without being, without force and without power, would it have the wherewithal to transform us, to turn us around, to make us new? Would it, could it, be something truly revolutionary, or would it lie lame and lifeless and ineffective? Could something be revolutionary without having revolutionary power? Could something that is at best a "weak force" (*force faible*) be strong enough to save us?

That is the cluster of questions that Jacques Derrida has been raising of late, questions that strike at the heart of some of our fondest and most unquestioned presuppositions.[1] Deep and probing questions, even matters of ultimate concern, Paul Tillich might have said, in any case very far from the "relativism" with which he is wrongly charged (*Voyous*, 13). But, for all that, these are also highly topical and contemporary questions, as contemporary as September 11, questions that Derrida raises in the midst of the most concrete politics of the day, of the "war on terrorism" and the "rogue states," of national sovereignty, international law, and the United Nations.

SYMBIOSIS: UNAVOWED THEOLOGEMES AND THE COMING GOD

Imagine an analogy—or a symbiosis—among the soul, the state, and the universe. That is a venerable and prestigious premise that goes back as far as Plato's *Republic*, one that has guided our thinking ever since antiquity. Just as there is but one God in Heaven, the Father [*sic*] Almighty, creator of heaven and earth, governing the universe, so the analogy goes there is but one king governing the state (and one father governing the family), and so, finally, is each man [*sic*] the lord of his own actions. We modern democrats congratulate ourselves on having revolutionized this schema, having turned it upside down, by ridding it of its top-down power structure. We have shown the king the door (or even handed him his head) and replaced him with a constitutional democracy, according to which power rises from the bottom up. We have gradually gotten around to giving the vote to every adult citizen, regardless of race or gender, propertied or not. Let there be no mistake: that was no little achievement for which we are grateful and which, even today, is far from finished. We have even gotten around to God and made God a lot more gender sensitive and egalitarian and much less patriarchal. So the revolution has seemed more or less complete, at least in principle.

But the truth is, while we have inverted the old schema, turning it on its head, by giving power to the people, we have not slipped free of its most basic presupposition, that of sovereignty itself, which goes unchallenged. Modern democracies have considered the revolution complete—at least in principle, as one will never be finished making this actually work—if they repopulate the sovereign center with the people, running the lines of power from the bottom up. Consider that, even though they separate church and state, modern democracies, spawned in the "Enlightenment," are run by the light of what Kant called "autonomy." Autonomy means answering only to a law (*nomos*) that you give yourself (*autos*), which for Kant is the only way to be "rational," which means not to allow your reason to be overwhelmed by an alien power. That model is the secularized cousin of a theological image of God Almighty, the brightest light, the most autonomous agent, and the most serene and sovereign freedom of all. Just as Carl Schmitt, the conservative political philosopher, defines the sovereign in terms of his power to suspend the law and to make an exception of himself (*Voyous*, 211–12), so in its most extreme formulations, in the writings of eleventh-century theologian Peter Damian, for example, the omnipotence of God is such that God has the power to suspend the laws of reason, even to the point of changing the past, to make it be that what happened (that the city of Rome was founded) had not happened, were God so minded. So, on this point at least, our modern democracies are continuous with the *ancien régime*, with monarchies and aristocracies and oligarchies and the old ontotheologies, all of which rely upon some version of a completely classical schema of God the Father, of "the theological idea of sovereignty."[2] While they have shifted the rule (*kratia*) from a sovereign one or few to the people (*demos*), no mean achievement, our modern democracies have left the space of sovereignty and autonomy undisturbed. So now mighty nation-states stride the earth where once mighty kings inspired fear and trembling—and having the power to inspire fear and trembling, to terrorize, is built right into the idea of sovereignty (*Voyous*, 214).

Autonomy is a perfect circle, beginning and ending in the self. That is what a sovereign democracy wants to be. Everything begins and ends in the people, in a government of the people, by the people, for the people—under God, who is an even more perfect, powerful, and prestigious circle. A democracy makes a perfect return upon itself (*Voyous*, 31, 34). Whatever goes out from the people comes back to the people, like the "going out" (*exitus*) and "return" (*reditus*) of God in Christian Neoplatonism or Aristotle's prime mover. One nation, under God: after a sovereign God comes the sovereign nation or people. But must a democracy be a sovereignty? Or is the very idea of sovereignty incompatible with a true or radical democracy? Might it be that wherever democracy tries to come, sovereignty would have to go? Do we not require a *new* democratic revolution, not a revolution *to* democracy but a revolution *in* democracy, one that turns the screw of democracy once again and thereby turns it *into* democracy?

However secular modern democracies think they are or have become, the truth is that secularization always presupposes a theology to secularize, so that, for better or for worse, secularism is the continuation of theology by another means. There is always what Derrida calls "some unavowed theologeme" (*Voyous*, 155), a certain bit of undigested theology lodged in the throat of even the most secular societies. Without deciding what is the controlling element in this symbiotic system, it is clear that a certain idea of God is a traveling companion of our understanding of ourselves and a certain understanding of the social system, and that sovereignty is the "heritage of a barely secularized theology."[3] The undecidability here is archaic; it goes all the way down. Are we made in the image of God, or is God made in our image? Are both God and self simply reflections of the dominant social systems, or might it be that social systems give outward expression to a deeper preunderstanding of self and God? How would we know that? Where would we be standing when we pronounced that decision? How would we have gotten clear of the dominant social system, self-understanding, or inherited theological presuppositions long enough to resolve that fluctuation? It is enough to describe the symbiosis without attempting to find its law. So if any effort to radicalize democracy, to carry the revolution one step further, would involve extricating democracy from the politics of sovereignty altogether, then in whatever direction the symbiotic fluids flow, the coming of the democracy to come must be accompanied by a new coming of God, by a new God to come. A radical democratic revolution would not mean jettisoning theology once and for all and a final accomplishment of secularization, but rather a parallel radicalization of theology.

But what would be it like to rid ourselves of the theology, the politics, and the anthropology of sovereignty? What would it be like to refashion theology around a God without sovereignty, to refashion a politics without sovereign nation-states, and to refashion our self-understanding in terms of a self without sovereign ipseity?

These are all limit concepts, imponderables, paradoxes, the very stuff that feeds and nourishes deconstruction, just the sort of aporetic element in which deconstruction thrives. Can we imagine the "coming" of a God without sovereignty, Derrida asks?[4] "Nothing is less sure, of course, than a god without sovereignty, nothing is less sure than his coming, of course" (*Voyous*, 161). To thus imagine God would be as difficult—as impossible—as trying to think of the coming of a self without the ipseity of the self, the *per se* or *a se* subsistence of one who is the lord of one's own domain. Would we not then be flirting with a God who would hardly be God, who would hardly be, a God without being or without being God (*Dieu sans l'Être*) and a self that would not be itself, a self without being a self, *soi sans l'Être*? And would not a nation without national sovereignty be a poor excuse for a nation, a nation without nationhood, *l'etat sans l'Être*, without manhood? God forbid! (*Voyous*, 161).

In *Voyous*, Derrida raises these questions—tackling the whole chain or symbiotic system of sovereignty—in a deeply political context, to which we will return below. Suffice it for the moment to note that the French word *voyou*—perhaps derived from *voie*—means a street runner, a hooligan, or riffraff, and is used to translate an Americanism: *les états voyous* are the "rogue states." Why take on such formidable opponents? Why try to wipe away the entire horizon? Because Derrida thinks the very idea of "sovereignty" is undemocratic. "The abuse of power is constitutive of the idea of sovereignty" (*Voyous*, 145). It is built right into it. For the sovereign asserts the right to act on his own, unilaterally, regardless of the will of the majority. He only answers to laws that he gives himself, which means that he only goes along with the will of the majority if the majority agrees with him. The sovereign reserves the right to make an exception of himself and does not give his will over to the common will, thus withdrawing from the circle of democracy, in order to stand apart. The sovereign does not let go; he does not share (*partager*) his power (*Voyous*, 73–83); he does not make gifts or expenditures without return. That means that the very idea of sovereignty cannot withstand the withering white light of what Derrida has been calling since 1989 the "democracy to come," a democracy all the way down, which is a democracy *without being* (*sans l'Être*), for being does not reach as far as this democracy, which is still to come. That means, as we will see shortly, that any sovereign nation is a rogue!

To speak of the symbiosis of the democracy to come and of the God to come means that they both belong to the same future (*l'avenir*), to the same coming (*venire*), to the same structure of the *à venire*. They are coming together; they will arrive arm in arm, like traveling companions, carried over (*metaphorein*) on the same vehicle.

But why should we bother ourselves with such an impossible democracy, which does not do us the courtesy of even existing, when the problems that beset existing democracies are so pressing? It is not so much that we are bothering with it as that it is bothering with us. For it is calling us, provoking us, disturbing our sleep, keeping democratic hearts up at night. We find ourselves always already in the train of its solicitation, disturbed by a call that calls upon us before we call upon it. If it does not have the structure of being, that is because it has the structure of a call from beyond being to which being, always breathless, cannot catch up. If we dare not say of this democracy that "it is," we cannot avoid saying that "it calls"; we cannot silence its ringing in our ears. It calls because it promises. There is something astir in the word "democracy," something "promised," something we can hardly resist, something "unconditional." Still, if it is irresistible, then is it not an irresistible force? Shall we then say that "democracy" is a word of sovereign force and power, nay, even a word of divine authority? That would be to fall down before the old god, the one that belongs to the order of being and power, whereas Derrida is venturing out onto more uncharted seas, trying to think god otherwise, trying to tell a whole new story about God (*Voyous*, 215–16), about some sort of vulnerable, non-sovereign, suffering God, some sort of "force without force" or some "power of powerlessness," for which we have no concept.

Derrida is dreaming of something unconditional, something for which the current conditions of being are no match, something that belongs to another order, that of the call or the promise. The unconditionality of the democracy to come is thus not that of unconditional force but the unconditionality of a promise that has not compromised with the conditions of being. For Derrida—and this is something residually phenomenological about deconstruction—we today find ourselves always already in the world on the receiving end of an uncompromisable promise that we have inherited. We are constituted by such promises, summoned by their voice. Something, which is not a thing, lays an unconditional *claim* upon us—*uns in Anspruch nehmen*, as Heidegger would say—not as a sovereign power in the order of being that invades and overpowers us, but as a summons that provokes us, a call that incites us, a promise that lures us and awakens our desire. Something of unconditional appeal, without the force of sovereignty. Might not something be—without being—of unconditional import or value, might something not be—without being—the object of an unconditional desire or love? Might it not make an unconditional claim upon us without overpowering us, without belonging to the order of being and power and force? Might it not lay claim to us from beyond being, luring being on—to come?

We are inching closer to the democracy to come, and inching closer to the coming God.

But what might that be like? Let us attempt a risky analogy. Let us assume that the promise belongs to the order of the "good," while force and power are attendant upon "being," running the risk of using very classical terms of the sort that Derrida usually sets out to disturb. On this analogy, we cast Derrida in the Neoplatonic and Levinasian terms of a good beyond being, a good that does not exist because being does not reach as far as the good, a good that is beyond being from excess, where being always and already falls short of the good. It is not so much that the good fails to be as that being fails short of the good; the good does not fail the test of being, but being fails the test of the good. The good rises up like a command from the ashes of being. The good is without being, but this "without" is not the name of a lack but an excess. On this analogy, what Derrida is calling the "unconditional" belongs to the order of the Platonic and Neoplatonic Good, while sovereignty belongs to the order of being.

But that is no more than an analogy, and of limited use, because were it to hold in a more rigorous way, then the democracy to come would not represent a call for a revolution but would simply be a recall, a repetition of the classical doctrine of Plato and Christian Neoplatonism. For the call that in a certain way is certainly coming from Plato, who is our inescapable heritage, is not the call of the Good in the *Republic* (509), where the Good is articulated as an ultimate sovereign power, as a king (*kurios*) in its own kingdom (*basileia*), the very knowledge of which entitles one to rule. Plato's Good is not the power of powerlessness but a power more powerful than power, sovereign and superlative, which imposes an analogical and hierarchical order upon its sensible subordinates, which is the very stuff of sovereignty. The Good is the superpowerful origin of the reason that is right about everything and gets the better of everything (*a raison de tout*). It reigns with all the majesty and dignity of the father of all, of the *arché*. Plato has supplied us with the fundamental vocabulary of the ontotheological politics of sovereignty (Voyous, 193–94). Nor is the call for the democracy to come, which comes along with a coming God, a recall or rehearsal of Christian Neoplatonism. For the "unconditional" for Derrida is not the name of a *hyperousios*, a hyperbeing beyond or higher than being, a Godhead beyond God (*Gottheit über Gott*), not if Derrida "rightly passes for an atheist." Far from being a hyperbeing, what Derrida calls the unconditional call is perfectly capable of being described as a ghost, as a shade or a specter, a demi-being, not real enough to do anything but able only to haunt us with uncanny possibilities, above all, the haunting possibility of the impossible.[5]

What Derrida has in mind by the unconditional is neither a hyperpower nor a hyperbeing, neither the form of the Good nor God the Father Almighty, but the power of powerlessness, the power of a powerless solicitation or promise or provocation, which in Derrida's discourse belongs not to the metaphysically loaded and prestigious category of the "good beyond being" but to the humble sphere of the "perhaps," the *peut-être* threatening to irrupt from within and to disturb the conditions of *être*,[6] the dangerous perhaps of the possibility of the impossible that solicits us from afar. His "unconditional" is constituted not as a being beyond being but as a "call" coming from beyond being to something unconditional or the unconditional call to something beyond being—here the democracy to come. Not a form or a being but a promise without the power to keep its promise, a call without the force to enforce what it calls for, a call whose realization is exposed to all the hazards of the *khora*, which is the opposite end of the kingly line that starts at the top with the Good. Of the democracy—or the God—who is to come we would not say "it is" but "it calls," which is how "it comes." It calls without the worldly wherewithal to enforce its demands or to be enforced, to create the concrete entitative conditions in the world in which its unconditional appeal would be realized. Derrida's unconditional belongs to the order of the call, to the order of the order or command, but not to the order of existing authorities (*exousiai*) or entitative conditions. Nor is its unconditional call a categorical imperative, for it lacks the imperial authority to be an imperative, so it is not of Kantian lineage either.

What then? How can the democracy to come call upon us without power or force or authority? A trace of what Derrida means is found in Levinas's famous example of the impossibility of murder. "Thou shalt not kill" is the first word, that is, it is a command inscribed on the face of the other, and in that sense comes from "on high," but it comes not with the majesty of worldly height or power, or with the authority of a divine command or of a command of pure reason, but with the penury of the most helpless and vulnerable one. It is inscribed on the face of anyone, but most palpably on the face of the helpless victim. Thus, the impossibility of murder is a law in the order of the call, but not, alas, of being where it is an all too banal and common fact. Derrida uses hospitality as an example of unconditionality without sovereignty, where this means the appeal made by the wayfarer, the stranger, the immigrant, for example—who has not the wherewithal to lay down his head, who lacks the power to defend him or herself, whose only defense is defenselessness, the power of powerlessness, the appeal to the good (*Voyous*, 204). The call of hospitality calls unconditionally, however helpless and humble the real conditions under which the call is issued. So too the call of and for the democracy to come, of and for the coming God, is issued from the face of the street people, and in that sense from a certain *voyou*.

But the call is not simply negative, a prohibition of violence or murder, but an affirmative call, the call for something unconditional to happen. When something occurs for which the conditions are already in place, something made possible by these conditions and conventions, then nothing really "happens" in the strong sense. When someone comes who has been invited, who made an exclusive short list, that is not hospitality; hospitality happens only when the uninvited one shows up at our door. Only the impossible can really happen.[7] Only the impossible, only the coming God, can save us. The theological dream in the dream of the democracy to come, the "unavowed theologeme," is the God not of traditional ontotheology, nor of Christian Platonism, nor the Aristotelian First Mover, who like the Platonic Good is the purity of power. Who can deny, Derrida asks, that his notion of a sovereignty to come in which justice and law would have been combined might go under the name of the god mentioned in Heidegger's "*Nur noch ein Gott kann uns retten*," a god to come who will come to somehow save us (*Voyous*, 155–56; *PTT*, 190n14)? Allow me to say, in fear and trembling, that I for one can deny it. I am willing to cast my sole vote in the minority and deny it. For it is only half true. Remember, this is the author's avowal of his "unavowed," his authorial intention to say what is unintended, to identify what lies unconsciously behind his conscious intentions as an author, of which he is, in principle, at best only half conscious. It is half true, for Derrida's use of *venire*, *à venire*, *événement*, bears an important analogy to Heidegger's use of *kommen*, *Zukunft* and *Ereignis*. Hence the very idea of the *à venire* and of the promise it contains, here the promise of the coming God, in Derrida, has a formal parallel in Heidegger's notion of a wait or watch or expectation, in this time of the flight of the gods, in which thinking attends to the traces of the coming god, *der zukommenende, zukünftliche Gott*, by which Heidegger means the transforming historical event of another beginning. Unlike Osama bin Laden, neither Derrida nor Heidegger is expecting to go to heaven; both are waiting upon a historical transformation or revolution in "this world" (*PTT*, 114).

But the other half is not true, for the parallel is strictly formal. That is why Derrida concedes that this is a "fanciful interpretation" of Heidegger, one that would have "shocked Heidegger." So add Derrida's vote to mine; we both deny it; we are beginning to build a majority. The democracy to come "is certainly not what 'he [Heidegger] meant'" and he would have regarded—"wrongly," Derrida adds—the international body that Derrida dreams of as "the absolute technological state," whereas, for Derrida "nothing resembles an 'absolute technological state' less than that which I have spoken about under the terms *faith*, *messianicity*, *democracy to come*, the untenable promise of a *just*, *international institution*, an institution that is strong in justice, *sovereign without sovereignty*, and so on" (*PTT*, 190n14).What then *is* the unavowed theologeme in Derrida in a non-fanciful interpretation? Nothing less than the Godof the "promise," which is after all a very Jewish and prophetic god, and if the "promise" is also a Heideggerian figure it is Jewish before it is Heideggerian, as Marlene Zarader has shown, Jewish being something that Heidegger would never have any part of, that is to say, never avow, never "think."[8] For while Heidegger was interested in calling and promises and being laid claim to, he was not interested in being laid claim to by justice. Or if Heidegger was interested in justice, it was the mystified, mythologized justice of all-gathering *dike* that had nothing to do with suffering flesh.[9] Heidegger was not interested in the justice of the great ungathered and unwashed *demos*, which is precisely what interests Derrida—and the Jewish prophets—the justice due the *voyous*, the street people. Despite his ridiculous romanticizing of the wisdom of *Schwarzwald* farmers, *demos* and *hoi polloi* were definitely not among the words of elemental power in the Greek language upon which Heidegger chose to meditate high up in his *Hütte*. Indeed, the God who would come to save us in Heidegger's myth of Being would come to save us from democracy, past, present, or to come, and the revolution of which Heidegger was dreaming would have been an ultra-right revolution. His god, as he himself pointed out, is the god of the poet, not the biblical god, while Derrida's god is profoundly prophetic.[10] Derrida's "fanciful" interpretation of Heidegger's suspicion of existing democracies depends upon ignoring that Heidegger—who is not convinced that democracy is what is needed in an age of planetary domination (*Voyous*, 157)—entertains a radically reactionary, aestheticizing, and right-wing suspicion of democracy. Heidegger's god will deliver less democracy not more, no more democracy (*plus de démocratie*), which is not to be confused with Derrida's own suspicion that there is more to democracy (*plus de démocratie*) than democracy delivers at present. Derrida's unavowed theologeme is much less Heidegger's god of the poets, God forbid, than the prophetic God.[11]

Still, let us be clear. The unconditional promise by which Derrida is solicited is not to be identified with the covenant made with Abraham and Moses by the Lord God, the One God, blessed be his name, no more than with the philosophemes of Plato or Aristotle,[12] of Kant or Heidegger. Derrida's is a faith without religion or religious institutions, without theocracy and without a church, a faith in the unconditional and the incalculable. But this faith is also what Derrida means by reason (*Voyous*, 211). Reason is a movement back and forth between the incalculable and the calculable, calculating always in the face of the incalculability, keeping calculability open to the incalculable. While the irrational for Kant lay in allowing reason to be overcome by something other, reason for Derrida is precisely defined by its openness to the other, to the event, to the future, its desire for the incalculable and the unconditional, for the promise. Reason is not measured by consensus, as for Habermas, which would always present a certain closure and compromise, but by the promise, which is open-ended. Reason—in a way that is not entirely foreign to the religious idea that the mind is a *capax dei*, a capacity for God or for the infinite—is defined by Derrida by the promise, which is always infinite; by the possibility of the impossible; by something deeply inscribed in language, for example, if it is an example, the promise lodged in the word "democracy." Derrida's idea of reason is marked by faith, by a faith in reason that belongs to an "Enlightenment to come" (*Voyous*, 167), so that the distinction between faith and reason remains porous.

But who is making this promise? Who knows? It is a promise made by who knows whom coming from who knows where and calling to something to come that is who knows what. But then to whom is it made? To us, to those who hear the word, who have inherited it, in whatever language. What is it promising? Who knows? Who knows what the democracies are coming to or what is coming to democracy or what democracy is to come? It is a promise lodged in language itself, a whisper, a hint of things to come, a trace of a coming god, a promise that has us before we have it, a promise that is engaged as soon as we are engaged in language, as soon as we open our mouths. The unconditional promise is nobody's speech act, nor is it a hyperbeing of prestigious power, or a word of God, or a categorical command, but a fragile and powerless solicitation awakened in and by language itself in a khoral night.

Anything as fetching and as haunting as this "democracy to come" would also be what Derrida calls "undeconstructible," and it would relate to existing and highly deconstructible democracies just the way justice, which is unconditional, is related to the force of law, where laws are always positive and conditional. The democracy to come, *s'il y en a*, is not deconstructible, while existing democratic polities and juridical systems, which enjoy the prestige of being and the power of the possible, are deconstructible. The democracy to come, accordingly, is impossible, *the* impossible (*PTT*, 134), which solicits us from afar, demanding the impossible of us, as the object of a desire beyond desire for something unforeseeable to come. That alone should be enough to tell us that "deconstruction" is the least bad word for a profoundly affirmative undertaking to unearth the most deeply buried and unfulfilled promises lodged in our least bad words—words such as "justice" and "democracy," the "gift" and "forgiveness," "friendship" and "hospitality." These are the words that Derrida has analyzed more and more in recent years in what some would say represents an ethico-political turn in deconstruction, although he protests the idea that this is all something new (*Voyous*, 64). But these are also words of such undeniable *biblical* resonance that they bring his unavowed theologeme more and more to the level of an explicit confession or circumfession.

AUTO-IMMUNITY: THE DEMOCRACY TO COME

What does the democracy to come call for? If the call comes from the heart of a promise lodged deep within the word democracy, and if it calls to us democrats who are not yet democrats, what does it say? Like any call of conscience worthy of the name, in Heidegger or Levinas, say, it pronounces us guilty, guilty of being the basis of a nullity, of not yet being democrats, infinitely responsible to respond to the call to be or become democratic, asking us to put off the old way and to turn around. O my democratic friends, there are no democrats.[13] Derrida addresses modern democracies like Kierkegaard—whom he is always following (*PTT*, 135)—addressing Christendom: they are both faced with the task of disabusing their audiences of the illusion that they already are Christian or democrats and that becoming Christian or democratic is just what is being asked of them. So in asking us to turn around, the democracy to come calls for a revolution, one more revolution (at least) beyond the first wave of democratic revolutions. That brings us to politics.

I have used the figure of a symbiotic system because Derrida's reflections in *Voyous* and elsewhere are so much guided by the figure of life itself, of the health (*santé*) of living things, of keeping them safe (*sauf*), in a salutary state (*salut*), hale and whole. It is in keeping with this figure that he says that democracy today is suffering from an autoimmune disease, redeploying a figure he first used in "Faith and Reason."[14] Democracy today is a victim of the "strange illogical logic" by which a living thing destroys the very thing that is meant to fortify (*munis*) it against attack by a foreign body (*Voyous*, 173). The result is that instead of attacking the other, it attacks itself and tolerates or plays host to the presence of the aggressor. So democracies often think that if, as a practical matter, they are to survive, they must make themselves safe from democracy and learn how to tolerate antidemocratic forces within their own bodies. Thus, in order to make the American way of life safe against the threat of terrorists who threaten democracy, Attorney General John Ashcroft wanted to abridge the democratic rights of American citizens (*Voyous*, 64–65), or the rights of prisoners being held in Guantanamo Bay, even as the Rehnquist court has seen fit to profoundly abridge the civil liberties of Americans to keep the streets of democracy safe. When, in 1992, the Algerian government saw that the elections were going to result in the election of an antidemocratic Islamic party that would abolish democracy, it suspended a democratically held election in the name of democracy, which means a place where the people enjoy the right to choose their own leaders (*Voyous*, 54–66). That of course is nothing new. When Salvador Allende was democratically elected in Chile, Henry Kissinger said that the United States was not going to let the interests of democracy (read: the United States) be injured by a lot of damn fools (a loose translation of *demos*) in Chile expressing their democratic will for a socialist president. Everybody knows that you cannot trust democracy, which has a suicidal side that we have to protect it against (*Voyous*, 57). Autoimmunity is thus a kind of *pharmakon* (*PTT*, 124), when the body is poisoned by the very drug that is meant to save it. An absolute democracy could bring a democratic end to democracy; that risk is built right into democracy. The National Socialists were democratically elected. The art of governing democratically is to know when democracy should suppress its own immunities to the undemocratic and attack itself (*autos*)—in the interests of democracy, of course.

Or of America! Of our own self-interest, the interest of our "self" (*autos*), the interests of a "sovereign" nation (under God)? God bless America. But the very idea of a democracy is to divide and share (*partager*) sovereignty among the people. To have faith in democracy is to trust and have faith in the many, to give up the rule of the sovereign one or few and share it among the many, among the "people," come what may. To be true to the idea of democracy demands that we be unselfish, that we give up our attachment to own private will. Democracy cannot be achieved without the anxiety, the fear and the trembling, that accompanies every sacrifice, above all the sacrifice of the self, which is at bottom what every sacrifice must be. So if we were true to this idea of democracy, we would end up with another and more radical idea of *auto*immunity, one that is not simply self-destructive but rather breaks down the "ipseity" of the "self," its mastery and autonomy (*Voyous*, 71), in order to open the self to sharing with "the other."[15] That in turn would require a revolutionary turn in which we would reverse the model that democracy follows from one of autonomy to one of "heteronomy" (*Voyous*, 154), where the one would agree to be governed by the many, the self by the others. The symbiotic effect of undoing the idea of political sovereignty would be to have redescribed the autonomous self in terms of the other in the self, as a self that is not identical with itself, a self that is always already divided within itself, inhabited by the other, a complex of many selves. The self itself then would turn out to be a kind of democratic polity, the unruly rule of the many, a certain kind of "mob rule," a voyoucracy, which is a possible translation of the Greek word *demokratia* (*Voyous*, 97). If we immunize ourselves against the sovereign self, if we are suicidal about this sovereign *sui*, or "sui-sovereignty," democracy will not have to put up with this pseudo-democracy, the self-aborting autoimmunizing fake that passes itself off for democracy today. Autoimmunity then will mean the right to criticize one*self* (*Voyous*, 126).

This is not just abstract theory. This is all about September 11, all about politics today. During the Cold War, things were maximally dangerous but perfectly clear. Two large sovereign superpowers guided by the "MAD" logic of "mutual assured destruction" kept each other more or less in check. Occasionally, most notably in the Cuban missile crisis, we stared into the abyss. But, for the most part, sovereign nations guided by self-interest are not suicidal, and it proved to be in the best interests of each to respect the space of the other. This absurdist logic worked and produced a simulacrum of peace, a lack of war that seemed at times almost as much like war as peace. When the Cold War ended, things became more complicated, but no less dangerous, its place taken by the war on international terrorism, and on what "we" call the "rogue states" that finance, support, and harbor terrorists. Not a war between superpowers, but between the respectable, legitimate states that respect international law (the true and the good) and the evil empire, the axis of evil, the "rogues," the outlaws, the hooligans, who have no respect for law or life, "MAD" now having given way to "WMD" (concealed "weapons of mass destruction").

Or so it seemed. September 11, 2001, shattered that illusion. With the collapse of the Twin Towers, the whole façade of a "war" on rogue "states" also collapsed. Now it is clear that the "enemy" is no longer an identifiable "state" with diplomats and a capital city but elusive bands of faceless, stateless terrorists willing to sacrifice their lives to take out large buildings, the Pentagon, and the White House itself, and to poison or kill countless numbers of innocent people in large cities with suicidal stealth. The classical concepts of war too had fallen. The collapse of the towers exposes the deeper anxiety that simmers beneath the bravado of a "war" on the "rogue states." The second Gulf War was an effective way to prop up that illusion—Derrida wrote this book in 2002, before the war—not to mention to enhance the standing with the people for a president seeking reelection in a coming presidential campaign. But the cold truth is, after the end of the Cold War, the rogue states are not *states* (*Voyous*, 148–51, 212–14; *PTT*, 98, 110–12). They are faceless terrorists hiding who knows where, in disguise, somewhere in Somalia, say, and a thousand other places, and if they get their hands on weapons of mass destruction, ones they can conceal on their person, or in a vehicle, God help us all. We knew where Moscow was, and we could train our missiles on the precise place, but we do not know who or where these people are. But, by the same token, the legitimate states are precisely the ones who assert their sovereign and unilateral right to act in their own interests.

As Bill Clinton said in his 1993 address to the United Nations, the United States will act multilaterally when possible, but unilaterally when necessary (*Voyous*, 147), whether or not we have the authorization of the UN General Assembly or even the Security Council, which we can usually control; whether or not we are in defiance of international law or human rights. But that is *precisely* what one means by an outlaw state, with no respect for international law, that is, a rogue state. Derrida says, "So there are no longer any rogue states and there are only rogue states" (*Voyous*, 150)—that is, the rogues are not *states*, and the states are *rogues* (by exercising sovereignty, the self-styled legitimate states behave like rogues). Being a rogue is built right into being sovereign; it is pretty much what one means by a rogue state (*Voyous*, 214). There are more rogues than you think: the USA first, then the UK, then France, if you just count how many times these sovereign states exercised their veto power in the Security Council on behalf of their national-sovereign-interests. The powers that be, the *exousiai*, that shaped the United Nations saw to it that the UN is another one of those democracies that has immunized itself against democracy. It has done this by establishing a Security Council whose principal function is to ensure the security of the most powerful few against the democratic many in the General Assembly. The Security Council serves to secure the sovereignty of the five permanent members. Why just those five? Because they were winners of the last world war. Might makes right. The *strongest* reason, *la raison du plus fort*, prevails, not the strongest *reason*.

To be sure, the very idea of the democracy to come is not just utopic but aporetic, for simply to submit national sovereignty to the higher authority of an international body would be once again to leave the place of sovereignty standing and to repopulate it, not with a king or nation-state, but with a world-state. This would not dispel the notion of sovereignty but reconstitute a new figure of universal or world sovereignty (*PTT*, 115). We would have dissipated, disseminated, or distributed sovereignty still more widely—from the king to the nation, from the nation to the community of nations—but the end result would be a sovereign mega-state of just the sort that Kant and Hannah Arendt rejected. For Derrida the "democracy to come" would not be a world-state, which would or could be in many ways even more terrifying than anything of which a national sovereignty is capable.[16] No system of law, no legal sovereignty or mega-sovereignty, however widely based, would embody justice or be "the last word" (*PTT*, 115). The democracy to come could never take a purely legal or juridical form, as a system of law (droit), for it would always be without being as a demand of justice. As such, the democracy to come would be a-cosmopolitan or postcosmopolitan, admitting at most of a certain "sovereignty without sovereignty," some kind of force or power—since force or power is what constitutes the law—some sort of *kratia*, in which, *per impossibile*, justice would have the force of law, and the law would be just, not manipulated or ignored at will by the most powerful nations. That is the impossible, the promise inscribed in the word democracy, on which no existing world body can deliver (*PTT*, 119–20). The promise inscribed in the "democracy to come" is bound up with the promise inscribed in the words "united nations," a body to come that would be free of the hegemonic influence of its most powerful members, with a "wholly other" security council (*Voyous*, 161), on which the present world body cannot deliver because of the roguish behavior of the sovereign powers on the security council. But the promise is astir in these words, which at least point us in the right direction, which gives us the right "heading." Derrida in fact thinks that this is very much a "European promise," as Giovanna Borradori puts it.[17] He thinks that there is more to hope for in this regard from Europe than from the United States, which is insufficiently secularized, still too dominated by a pledged allegiance to Judaic and Christian religion, so that its "war on terrorism" is still marked by a religious war of Jewish and Christian doctrine against Islam, a war of "two political theologies," both Abrahamic, a war among the Messianisms of which Jerusalem is the symbolic center. Even though this movement of secularization is still incomplete and relatively unfulfilled in Europe, the Enlightenment ideal of extricating the political order from religious authority is more advanced there and the Enlightenment has made more headway (*PTT*, 116–17).[18]

CONCLUSION: A WHOLLY OTHER STORY ABOUT GOD

The question, is there something that lays claim to us unconditionally but without power or force, is directed at "us," all of us—Americans and Europeans, democrats and theologians, Westerners and non-Westerners—*anyone* who is associated with the cruel logic of sovereignty.

The democracy to come calls for a new revolution, another and still more radically democratic revolution, a revolution in the name of the democracy to come, in which we will break more decisively still with the *ancien régime* of sovereignty itself, dreaming of the incalculable possibility of the impossible, of a democracy without sovereignty. Dreaming of the incalculable, but also calculating, because one must count very carefully and carefully devise ways of counting how the member voices of the democratic assembly will count, who will be allowed to vote, at what age, with what status, and so on (*Voyous*, 63). The revolution that is being called for will also cut deeply into our psyche and our psychology, because it will force us to reconceive the self, that famous liberal individual, in terms of the other one who lays claims to me, even as it will cut into our theology, because it will force us to reimagine God without sovereignty. God forbid!

What is called for in and by the democracy to come is the unconditional gift, which does not seek a return on one's investment, the gift in which the self gives up its power, the power of the "I can," the power of the possible, which is what constitutes a self. What we have asked of the king, we now must ask of ourselves: to give up power, to share and divide it. What is called for is a self that shares its power in a gift without return, a self without ipseity. What is called for is unconditional hospitality to the other, to the stranger and the immigrant, to the tired, the hungry, and the huddled masses. What is called for is a transforming and transfixing revolution in which the self turns itself inside out and lets itself be claimed by the other.

What is called for is to imagine God otherwise, to turn our thinking about God around, almost upside down or inside out: "In speaking of an onto-theology of sovereignty, I refer, under the name of God, of One God, to the determination of a sovereign and hence indivisible omnipotence. But when the name of God would give us something else to think, for example a vulnerable non-sovereignty, suffering and divisible, mortal even, capable of contradicting himself, of regret (a thought which is neither impossible nor without example), that would be a wholly other story and perhaps that of a god who would be deconstructed even in his ipseity" (*Voyous*, 215–16).

What calls, what is calling, what is called for is the God to come, the coming of a God to save us, a God who has no seat of power, no sovereign authority, no ontological prestige, vulnerable and mortal, who has not the wherewithal to lay down his head, whose only power is the power of a powerless but unconditional appeal.

"The democracy to come—*salut*" (*Voyous*, 161).

The God to come—*viens, oui, oui.*

NOTES

This essay was previously published electronically in the *Journal for Cultural and Religious Theory* 4, no. 3 (August 2003), http://www.jcrt.org/archives/04.3/ caputo.pdf. In addition, extracts of the article were previously published in "More Rogues Than You Think: Derrida on the Cruel Logic of Sovereignty," in *France Today: The Journal of French Travel and Culture* 18, no. 7 (September 2003): 21–26.

1. Derrida takes up these issues in several places, most recently in *Philosophy in a Time of Terror: Dialogues with Jürgen Habermas and Jacques Derrida*, ed. with commentary by Giovanna Borradori (Chicago: University of Chicago Press, 2003), hereafter cited in text as *PTT*, and in *Voyous* (Paris: Galilee, 2003), hereafter cited in text as *Voyous*. The English translation is *Rogues: Two Essays on Reason*, trans. Pascale-Anne Brault and Michael Naas (Stanford: Stanford University Press, 2005). For "weak force" (*force faible*), see *Voyous*, 13. See also "The University without Condition," in Jacques Derrida, *Without Alibi*, ed. and trans. Peggy Kamuf (Stanford: Stanford University Press, 2002), 202–37, where Derrida describes a university that, while it does not exist, is structured by the unconditional right to ask any question. It offers resistance, even a "force" of resistance, of dissidence and disobedience, to the order of being—to the powers that be, to sovereign states, to economic powers, and to the powers of the media, the church, the popular culture, and so on (204). But since this unconditionality has never existed, this invincible university is impotent, very vulnerable to the influence of power. The humanities are the privileged place in which this unconditional freedom would be theorized and presented. The freedom, autonomy (213–14), or "immunity" (220) of the university does not make for a sovereign university (235), since sovereignty has to do with power and the real order. The task of the university, then, is neither to acquire external power nor to withdraw into the interior of an inner and unconditional freedom, but to negotiate the difference between the two, to move back and forth between the conditional and the unconditional in such a way as to "resist effectively, by allying itself with extra-academic forces, in order to organize an inventive resistance" to all the figures of sovereignty (236). That also means the "university" is not to be identified with a physical campus but is found wherever the voice of this dangerous perhaps poses the possibility of the impossible. Nor does he think that the philosophers of the future are necessarily to be found in philosophy departments or even in the academy (*PTT*, 106).

2. Derrida, "University," 235. See also *PTT*, 111, 124. Derrida says he doubts that the "value of sovereignty can be completely secularized or detheologized" (*PTT*, 113).

3. Derrida, "University," 207.

4. In a roundtable at the Religion and Postmodernism 3 conference, held at Villanova University in September 2001, Derrida said: "We usually identify God with the almighty, that is, with absolute power. I'm trying now in seminars and in texts, by following a political thread, to deconstruct, so to speak, the ontotheological politics of sovereignty. God is supposed to be absolutely powerful in our tradition. I don't know if it is Christian or not. I'm trying to think of some unconditionality that would not be sovereign, that is, to deconstruct the theological heritage of the concept, the political concept, of sovereignty, without abandoning the unconditionality of gifts, of hospitality, and so on. That means that some unconditionality might be associated not with power but with weakness, with powerlessness. Now some would say this is still Christian. There is in Jesus Christ some weakness, some vulnerability, some powerlessness, but there you see that the powerlessness of course is also a sign of the almighty. I'm trying to think of some divinity dissociated from power, if it is possible. This would have heavy ethical and political consequences, but it would deserve a long, much longer answer" (*Augustine and Postmodernism: Confessions and Circumfession*, eds. John D. Caputo and Michael J. Scanlon [Bloomington: Indiana University Press, 2005], 41–42).

5. This is, of course, the dominant trope of Derrida's *Specters of Marx: The State of the Debt, the Work of Mourning, and the New International*, trans. Peggy Kamuf (New York: Routledge, 1994).

6. Derrida, "University," 234; Jacques Derrida, "As If It Were Possible, 'Within Such Limits' . . . ," in *Negotiations: Interventions and Interviews*, ed. and trans. Peggy Kamuf (Stanford: Stanford University Press, 2002), 343–70.

7. Derrida, "University," 234.

8. Marlene Zarader, *La dette impensée: Heidegger et l'héritage hébraïque* (Paris: Seuil, 1990).

9. I have made this argument in more detail in *Demythologizing Heidegger* (Bloomington: Indiana University Press, 1993). See Martin Heidegger's interview with *Der Spiegel*: "Only a God Can Save Us," trans. Maria Alter and John D. Caputo *Philosophy Today* 20, no. 4 (Winter 1976): 267–84.

10. See appendix to *The Piety of Thinking: Essays by Martin Heidegger*, trans. and ed. James G. Hart (Bloomington: Indiana University Press, 1976), 65; for the prophetic reading of Derrida, see Mark Dooley's interview with Jacques Derrida, "The Becoming Possible of the Impossible," in *A Passion for the Impossible: John D. Caputo in Focus* (Albany: SUNY Press, 2003), 21–34, and John D. Caputo, *The Prayers and Tears of Jacques Derrida: Religion without Religion* (Bloomington: Indiana University Press, 1997).

11. See the four points on which Derrida distinguishes deconstruction from Heideggerian *Destruktion* in *Voyous*, 206–7n2.

12. Inasmuch as it attracts by desire, without the force of moving or efficient causality, the "promise" of the "to come" can in fact be likened to Aristotle's first cause, which is a telos that moves by attracting. But apart from the fact that Aristotle's telos is the highest actuality, what Derrida has in mind would be a telos without a teleol*ogy*, without imposing a teleological order or a final regulative goal to pursue. It moves by way of promoting a kind of endless or atelic restlessness. So it would be at best a telos without telos. If one could imagine a radical object of desire that does not exist and that does not impose a teleological order, then one would have imagined a Derridean correlate to Aristotle's prime unmoved mover, a kind of primary undeconstructible deconstructor. Like Aristotle, and unlike the One God of the great monotheisms, there would be a plurality of such undeconstructibles, as many as there are orders of desire, were there any at all, that is, as many as are desired.

13. In *Politics of Friendship*, trans. George Collins (London: Verso, 1997), Derrida thus adapts the saying attributed to Aristotle by Diogenes Laertius, "Oh my friends, there are no friends."

14. See Jacques Derrida "Faith and Reason," trans. Samuel Weber, in *Acts of Religion*, ed. Gil Anidjar (London: Routledge, 2002), 40–101, and *PTT*, 94–96.

15. Derrida works out this argument (*Voyous*, 63–83) by accepting the spirit but worrying over the letter of Jean-Luc Nancy's revisiting of freedom in *The Experience of Freedom*, trans. Bridget McDonald (Stanford: Stanford University Press, 1993); he comments especially on 70–71.

16. In the wildly popular Christian fundamentalist apocalyptic *Left Behind* series by Tim LaHaye and Jerry B Jenkins, the first and pivotal thing undertaken by the Antichrist, the very antipode of the messianic peace, is the establishment of a world government engineered through a takeover of the United Nations and the disarmament of the member states.

17. See Giovanna Borradori in *PTT*, 169–72, and her helpful commentary in "Deconstructing

Terrorism: Derrida," in *PTT*, 137–72. See also Jacques Derrida, *The Other Heading: Reflections on Today's Europe*, trans. Pascal-Anne Brault and Michael Nass (Bloomington: Indiana University Press, 1992).

18. We should not mistake the sense in which Derrida associates himself with the idea of secularization. He embraces the critical attitude cultivated by the Enlightenment with regard to the political hegemony of *religious doctrines*—the concrete messianism—over the political order. But then he adds parenthetically, "Notice I'm not saying with regard to religion or faith" (*PTT*, 116–17) itself, that is, with regard to the messianic. That is because the very idea of the democracy to come takes the form of a faith in a pure messianicity, the very idea of a to-come, which indicates that his position more precisely stated is postsecular. His idea of a pure *á venir*, a pure messianic, remains residually and deeply Abrahamic; it is not a Buddhist idea, for example, where peace has to do with the excising of desire, recognizing the unreality of the past and the future, and allowing oneself to be saturated with the present.

22
"Lazarus, Come Out": Rebirth and Resurrection

And do not bring us to the time of trial and deliver us from the evil one.

—Matthew 6:13

DEAD MAN WALKING

Once, during the time that Jesus was using Bethany as a base of operations, staying with his close friends Mary and Martha, he had left town for a short spell when Lazarus, the brother of Mary and Martha, became ill. The two sisters, whom Jesus loved, sent him a message to return at once. By the time Jesus got back, however, he found that Lazarus had been dead for four days. At his approach to Bethany, Martha had gone out to meet him on the road into town and as much as rebuked him for having been away at this critical time: "Lord I know that if you had been here, my brother would not have died." Mary, it seems, would not even meet him and came out only after being entreated by Martha and Jesus. Together the three went to the tomb where Lazarus was laid and, as the gospel says very movingly, "Jesus began to weep." He was touched to his heart by the loss of his friend, by the inescapability of death, by the grief that engulfed them all. Then he cried to the tomb, "Lazarus, come out." And in one of the New Testament's most famous scenes, out came the dead man, walking—reborn to a new life by the words of Jesus.

To be sure, the author of the Gospel of John, writing many years later and from an ultra-high Christological perspective, one that tries to make the Jews look bad and the new religion look good, has orchestrated this story into a messianic message to the Jews who rejected Jesus. It was not, according to John, that Jesus was unable to get back in time. Rather, he intentionally stayed away from Bethany for two more days, during which time Lazarus died. In John's redaction, then, Jesus is not subject to the limitations of time and space but purposely manipulates them. As Ernst Kasemann says, "He permits Lazarus to lie in the grave for four days in order that the miracle of his resurrection may be more impressive."[1] Jesus took this delaying action in order to give Lazarus time to die so that he could use this death as a way that the Son of God could be glorified. If so, that was a particularly tough way to treat his dear friends Mary and Martha, not to mention poor Lazarus, lying moldering in his grave, and all in order to glorify himself. One can only imagine that Lazarus must have grown exceedingly anxious the next time Jesus left town.

What event stirs within this story? What event is harbored there and kept safe, sheltered but also concealed?

Exactly what original historical core lies behind this narrative is impossible to say.[2] As we have had occasion to mention more than once, in a theology of the event, we have to make do with archives, not the *arche*. Perhaps Jesus revived the flagging spirits of a man at death's door and was able by the magnetism of his person to persuade Lazarus not to pass through that door but to come back, to "come out." Perhaps Lazarus died in the flesh, but the return of Jesus healed the spirit of Mary and Martha and gave them the strength to go forward, to "come out" of the dark abyss of grief. Jesus and other spiritual masters over the ages undoubtedly move about in the ambiguous ambiance of the psychosomatic and, without being expected to magically "cure diseases" or magically resuscitate corpses, they are indeed able to "heal" whole persons.

The tears of Jesus, his weeping in the face of death and loss, is the most human-and-divine component in the story. He weeps because he is too late, because his friend died before he was able to help. This story takes us back, not to divine omnipotence, but to the powerlessness of God that we identified in the original Genesis creation myths, to the limitations with which God him- and herself is confronted, to the inoriginate and formless void, the *anarche,* that seeps into the very bones and interstices of creation and causes everyone, human and divine, so much trouble. The Genesis myths provide for the limits under which all action, divine and human, takes place.

But if it is hard to say what historical core lay behind stories like this, it is not as difficult to discern the event that they harbor, that they visit upon us. We have said from the start that the kingdom is marked by amazing metamorphoses, stunning reversals and transformations, the radical capacity for reinvention. Now among all such anarchic events in a world that is defined by its unforeseeable irregularities there is none more amazing than the raising of the dead, the transformation from death to life. Rebirth and resurrection—that is what the kingdom is all about. The stories of Jesus are stories of exorcizing evil spirits, healing the lame and leprous, transforming water into wine, and, most amazing of all, of one who raises the dead. Then above even that, he is himself raised.

This singular transformation from death to life contains in a preeminent and paradigmatic figure the very substance of what Jesus is always doing in all of his works and deeds; it describes, in a word, what he is always teaching in all of his sayings. Even as the creative act of Genesis is a movement from a lifeless wild to a world teeming with life, the work of Jesus is to assist in the reversal of death into life. That is what he has been sent by his *Abba* to do; that is what constitutes the coming of the kingdom. Jesus is the locus of divine transformation, the prophetic center of the transformative energy of the kingdom, by coming in contact with which all things are made new, which is what the kingdom means. Thus, in the person of Jesus, the work of the two creation myths is continued and extended—for through him things are remade, refashioned in accord with their original and congenital goodness. Where there is sorrow, he brings joy; where there is illness, health; where there is death, life. "I am the resurrection and the life. Those who believe in me, even though they die, will live." Even as Elohim brought forth life from the lifeless void, Jesus restores life where there is death. He is always about his *Abba*'s work.

What is the event harbored inside the literal narrative? Once again we come back to the difference between religion and magic. In keeping with the distinction I am maintaining between name and event, I do not understand this story to reveal the *arche* of divine superpower that intervenes on natural processes and stands them on their head, reversing the decomposition of a rotting body, which is the literal narrative. Rather, it lays bare, first, the powerlessness of God before grief and sorrow—and "Jesus began to weep"—and our impotence before pain and death and suffering; accordingly, it reveals the finitude, the *an-arche* in which we are all steeped, always and already. Still, it is not a story of death and defeat but of life and rebirth—those who believe in him shall live—in the face of inescapable death, even though they really do die. So this literal story of resuscitation contains the uncontainable miracle of rebirth.

Miracles belong to the sphere of a theology of the event, not to a mythology of magical occurrences. The miracle narratives should not be read as exercises in magic. The whole idea of my poetics of the event is to provide an interpretation of these miracle stories that neither reduces them to supernaturalism nor inflates them into a metaphysical tour de force. They are not magic, but they do disclose something miraculous, the event of the impossible, which can be explicated in terms of a poetics of the impossible. A "miracle" harbors an event of a deeply incarnate kind. A miracle is constituted by its head-turning and astonishing power to make things new, to transform our lives, to give us hope where there was despair, love where there was hate, companionship where there was only solitude. Miracles are figures belonging to the wondrous stories of the Scriptures, but the Scriptures belong to the poetics of the event. They are to be read for their imaginative power to portray the life-transforming character of the kingdom, not literalized as if they were giving eyewitness reports of supernatural occurrences.

The gospels sing songs of the legendary charism of Jesus. Magic, on the other hand, involves being really released from the limits of space and time, being effectively *disincarnated*, actually exempted from bodily constraints and suspending the laws of nature, allowing us to dream away the constraints imposed by finitude. Magic relieves us of our finitude and even of our mortality. A magician can resuscitate corpses or be himself physically resuscitated; he can shrink cancerous tumors, cause physical wounds to mend, pass through solid walls, walk on water, and calm stormy seas. A miracle is an element in a narrative, a component of a poetics of the event, but belief in magic results from the mistake of *not* suspending your narratival disbelief, of taking miraculous narratives literally. A miracle requires the hard work of hoping in the impossible; magic simply waves a wand or a word. Miracles are narratival elements that are crudely mimed by magic, which is a psychical and religious fantasy. In magic, we take a striking narrative that captures our fancy, like the story of Lazarus, and fantastically transcribe it from imaginative to real space, from an event to an entity. Belief in magic results from failing to understand a literary genre, from locking the meaning of a miracle narrative inside its literal content, which would be like investigating whether the sorts of things Stephen King writes about actually occur, or whether there really was someone named "Jane Eyre" who really could have heard someone named Mr. Rochester call the name "Jane" from miles away across the moors, which ruins the story.

A miracle has hermeneutical authenticity on the plane of the event by figuring in a purely narratival and imaginative space a transforming experience in our lives, whereas magic is the superstitious transference of narrativity to reality. Miracle stories teach us something about our real life, even while they occur in poetic space, on stage and screen, in literature and art; whereas magic distorts real life and leaves us holding the straw of illusions when we come back to the prose of our senses. Resurrection is miraculous, but resuscitation is magic. Healing is a miracle, curing real diseases by the wave of a hand or a word is magic. The opposite of a belief in the miraculous is despair and despondency, the tragic sense that we are trapped and everything is hopeless; the opposite of belief in magic is good sense. The miraculous has the structure of what is called in deconstruction *the* impossible; magic is a cruel trick that is simply impossible. Magic is an illusory strong force; a miracle is the genuine but weak force of God.

I am trying to quash the idea of an intellectual somersault in which a metaphysical argument is mounted that shows that there is no trick too great for an omniscient, omnipotent, and beneficent being, not even resuscitating a corpse, since such a super-being who can create *ex nihilo* can do pretty much anything whatsoever that it comes into his or her super-head to do, a notion I rejected earlier on in this book. Just as miracle stories stir the souls of plain folk, such metaphysical demonstrations stir the souls of archi-theologians of divine omnipotence like Peter Damian. Such proofs at once prove too much—they make light of the *tehom* and the *tohu wa-bohu*, the formless void with which we must all cope, starting with Elohim himself, to whom we have attributed a certain limit on his power—even as they prove too little, because they are themselves abstract, unpersuasive, and, if I may say so, impotent arguments, metaphysical paralogisms, logically problematic from top to bottom, a point that Kant demonstrated over two centuries ago.

My purpose is to put the epoche (as in putting the kibosh) on all such magic and mental metaphysical leaps and to pursue a low-flying path that clings closely to the phenomenological surface of the event. My purpose is to release the event by finding the phenomenological "form of life" that stirs in these stories, to identify the sense of time and space, of embodiment, affectivity, and lived meaning that give them such enormous significance for us. Their significance is their head-turning, life-transforming power to make all things new, what I have been calling their "metanoetic" power, which is, I propose, the phenomenological core of what theology calls a miracle, which I am wiring up with what Derrida calls "*the* impossible." So the question I am posing is this: If we are unwilling to reduce Jesus to a divinely sponsored magician, if "rebirth" and "resurrection" do not mean magical resuscitation, what do they mean? What event is sheltered there and kept safe? What does it mean to speak of living even if you die? What is the phenomenological cash value of this transformation? What is the saving power of the kingdom? The question, in short, is not, How is such magic physically or metaphysically possible? but rather, What event do these stories harbor? What do these stories *mean*? Hermeneutics is all. All things flow in a river of meaning.

SALARIES VERSUS SALVATION

Lazarus was gone, irreparably swallowed up by death and irreversible time, or so it seemed. Having arrived back in Bethany too late, Jesus wept. But Mary and Martha had come to expect the impossible. They expected Jesus to turn things around, to reach back, deep into time's clenched jaws, and restore the life of Lazarus, not just on the last day along with everyone else (John 11:24), but that day, that very day in time, in Bethany. They wanted Jesus to save Lazarus from death, from the dreadful days of the last week, which had been a nightmare for the sisters. They wanted, not eternity beyond time, but a new time, one in which Lazarus lived again.

What then is the phenomenal structure of the event of new time that is portrayed in the story, a time cast as a phenomenon of rebirth and resurrection? Clearly, this event is intimately linked with the preceding discussion of the event of forgiveness, which also seeks a new time, a "forgiven" time, in which we are also released from the sting of the past. The new time is to be distinguished from ruined time, from which we seek to be released, "pardoned" in a more comprehensive and sweeping sense from the past even if we are not guilty of wrongdoing, issued a kind of "general pardon" in which we are released, not from sin but from the destructive power of pain and death, in order to be able to go on. Just as sin requires forgiveness and release, suffering requires relief. Ruined time is evil, and we need some way to be delivered from evil, not just when evil is the evil we have done, but when evil is visited upon us from without and through no fault of our own. Lord, rescue us from the forces of the evil one, release us from the ruins of evil, from evil's ruined time.

In order to analyze ruined time, I will reenlist the aid of Levinas, who makes a critical distinction between the "time of the world" and the "time of salvation," which corresponds to our distinction between the time of being and the time of the event. So in the spirit of improving Christian and Jewish relations, I propose to read the story of Lazarus by way of Levinas, to use Levinas to read a story from a gospel of love that does not much love the Jews. The "world," Levinas says, is "the possibility of wages," of a salary (*salaire*), whereas the exigency of suffering and ruined time is for salvation (*salut*). In the time of the world, which is the time of economic calculations and market exchanges, we can be compensated for our time or for the losses we suffer. But in the time of *salvation,* or "messianic" time, there is no question of any counterbalancing economic consideration, but rather of being redeemed or reborn. That is because ruined time is irreparable, and when the loss is incalculable or irreparable, the only repair is rebirth and a new time, which in religious discourse we call *salvation.* In the time they keep in the kingdom, there is no table of equivalences, no scale of compensation, nothing that can repay a loss. In the kingdom, every loss is infinite, so something else must be done. Incalculable suffering is an event of another sort that overflows any possible measure, not an event that bears good news, but an evil that exceeds any measure.[3]

Thus, in the order of the event, what is required—indeed, the only thing that is possible—is "salvation," being saved *from* ruined time *for* a new time. Salvation, rebirth, renewal are events of time, time's most treasured events. They do not mean to be saved *from time* in order to pass one's time in eternity—Lord, we know Lazarus will rise on the last day, but that is not what we need now—but to be given a new time. Rebirth does not mean to escape from time into eternity but to transform *time,* to make time new. Not salvation *from* time, but a time of salvation, time as rebirth and salvation, time as an event. Salvation means a new beginning, a new life, a new influx and incoming of God's own good time, a new day, a future, the coming of the Messiah who saves us and gives us hope, today. So in keeping with the book of days that we have been writing, we are dedicating a chapter here to the new day. Like a death followed by resurrection, which is the figure of a new time.

The need for rebirth holds true for both sin and suffering, for both the evil that we do, which requires forgiveness, and for the evil that is done to us, which requires salvation. In either case, what we want is to be saved from the time of the world, which makes us "do time" for the evil we perpetrate, or which "robs us" of time in sickness, suffering, and "untimely" death. Forgive us our trespasses and deliver us from evil. That is what we pray daily. Deliver us from evil, from the evil one who stalks us, from evil itself, if it has a self, from the evil that we cause and from the evil that befalls us. Levinas is addressing phenomenologically the same problem, *mutatis mutandis,* that concerned Peter Damian in a high-flying metaphysical way: how to reach back across the temporal distance into the past and repair what has gone irreparably wrong.

IRREPARABLE LOSS

By ruined time I mean irreparable loss, and by that I mean irredeemable suffering, suffering lodged irremissibly in the past, suffering and loss beyond repair. The irremissible past is a time of ruin, *mal-heure,* a bad time that seared and scorched the souls of the dead—in Auschwitz or Belfast, in Kosovo or the West Bank, in all the Auschwitzes, Kosovos, and Belfasts recorded in history and unrecorded, from time out of mind—and then slipped away forever, without repeal or compensation, without redemption or any possible remuneration. The time of irreparable loss cannot be worked into an economy or a balance of payments. The sufferings of the irrecuperable past were not undertaken voluntarily in exchange for the reward that follows, like a long period of punishing, grueling physical training in preparation for an athletic event, or of prolonged study for an examination in order to win a degree. This is not the pain of "sacrifice" willingly undertaken in exchange for a higher good, part of the economy of no pain, no gain. Irreparable loss is not even the suffering, involuntarily suffered, that finally issues in an unforeseen and unintended reward, like a childhood passed in stinging poverty that forges strength of character in adulthood. Of this irreparably ruined and irrecuperable time we will never be able to take a long view and say, "It was all worth it." There is nothing that makes it worth it, nothing with which it can be "compensated." This is not the pain that pays off, but the misery of pure loss, of disaster. A child born with AIDS, whose life is short and painful, which no one can justify or compensate, which one can only try to comfort or ameliorate. The innocent victim of a crime, like a child inadvertently caught in a crossfire between warring drug lords on an inner-city street. The child, who is a special emblem of new life, is a special victim of death and the sort of loss that makes theodicy an obscenity. Or the years of confinement, abuse, and humiliation suffered by people who are unjustly imprisoned, which cannot be returned or restored, for which there cannot be any compensation, whatever monetary considerations the government may later offer, whatever honors their advocates might later bestow on them for their courage. Indeed, is not the strongest argument against capital punishment the irreversibility of the state's action when the accused is innocent, which unhappily happens all too often and has occasioned more and more caution among state legislatures in recent years? The lost time, the ruined life, is gone forever, without return, without remuneration. The misery and grief descend upon us with impunity and then vanish like thieves in the night. The damage is done, the forces of destruction make their escape, and we are left without recourse, defenseless against the destruction, abandoned to wanton violence. Lazarus lies cold in his grave, and Jesus, too late, weeps.

We pray to be kept safe from such evil, to be guided around the fiery pits of the evil one who stalks us. For there is no good face to put on the face of faceless evil, of irreparable loss, no theodicy to explain ruined time that is not an obscenity. As Lyotard has said, the Holocaust is pure death, not a "sacrifice" of the Jews in exchange for something higher. The very attempt to offer some sort of rationale or explanation for the Holocaust, to fit it into some larger account or Providential design in which it is but a moment, is an obscenity that defiles the very names of each of its victims, of each one, taken singly, one by one.[4] The decision to name the dead, one by one, by their proper names, on the Vietnam War Memorial is a powerful way to recognize the infinite loss of each one where the death toll is quantitatively staggering, a way to accommodate both the large numbers and the qualitative infinity of each of these little ones. Imagine, then, a memorial that would contain the names of every victim on both sides of every war, of every evil, of every natural disaster, in every place and every time. Imagine a record of all such evils, recorded and unrecorded. Imagine as a counterpart to the Book of Life, a Book of Death.

Irreparable loss escapes the order of economy in a way that is precisely contrary to the gift: rather than an expenditure without return, an unlimited giving, we suffer an uncontainable destruction without repair, unlimited taking away, without compensation, remedy, or redress.

At the end of these remarks, I will point out the implications of this analysis for the possibility of another style of doing history, which is the record of evils done and suffered, a history other than the one that Levinas denounces as totalizing in the Preface to *Totality and Infinity*, a messianic or eschatological history of radical historians, or of what Edith Wyschogrod calls the "heterological" historian.[5] Such a history, which allows itself to be haunted by the voices of the dead, whose unrequited misery and persecution cry out for justice, would be the record of the unrecorded, the archive of the anarchivable and anarchical, the treasury of irreparable loss. It proceeds from the recognition that history and justice come too late for the dead and persecuted. Justice, however swift, is not swift enough to return to the moment of their misery and redress it. History, however sweeping and radical, cannot erase the misery of their lives. That impossibility is what drives the radical historian who would, were it possible, reach back into the past like Damian's God—whose metaphysical madness is always a limit case and an odd inspiration for me in these investigations—and undo the evil done to the dead, bringing them back to life, like Jesus raising Lazarus or the widow's son in the Gospels. But radical history is not God (and even God is not up to what metaphysics calls God). All that history has to offer is fragile memory and meek mourning, a poor substitute for omnipotence, but the only one available, and that is what Walter Benjamin means by a weak messianic force, which is not far from what I am calling the weak force of God.[6]

How, then, are we to console the dead who are long since dead? How console the survivors who live on in inconsolable grief? How are we to repair irreparable loss? That is the impossible demand that is placed upon us, the demand for a time of salvation that would be no less a salvation of time, a remedy or renewal that time builds into itself. Lord, if you had been here, our brother would not have died. Those words of Martha describe a fundamental quality of time ruined and of time forgiven, and hence of time itself.

SOLITUDE AND SUFFERING

The point of maximum intensity is only reached at *the* impossible. How to forgive the unforgivable? How to hope when all is hopeless? How to repair the irreparable? To pursue this impossible question, I invoke Levinas's analysis of suffering in *Existence and Existents*.[7] To be something existent, to be a subject, is to be fashioned from the abyss of *il y a* but then, starting out from there, to be held captive there (*y*), in being, where it has (*il a*) us, from which we need to escape or be saved. That is why Derrida says, commenting on this text, that the existent requires "forgiveness" and this "from the threshold of existence,"[8] a pardoning of our being, not of our deeds, from the prison of being and the solitude of the present. The existent is "fatigued" by the exertion of the act of existing, its fatigued movement being made up of stops (*arrêts*) lurching discontinuously from instant to instant, punctuating the "anonymous flow of existence" (*DEE*, 48/*EE*, 34), tearing or ripping out little commencements or beginnings from the flow without beginning (*TA*, 32/*TO*, 52). The time of suffering is fractured, each instant starting out from itself (*à partir de soi*) all over again, a new beginning, a momentary triumph in constant need of renewal, as in the Cartesian and Malebranchian conceptions of time (*DEE*, 126–29/*EE*, 73–75). Each instant is a stop (*arrêt*), but this stop does not threaten annihilation, but rather an "irremissible," inescapable bonding to being or existence, so that one cannot escape the steady beat, the ticktock, of existence in which the existent is established.

The discontinuity of time is intensified in suffering. The passing of Lazarus is the presence of pain, which causes Jesus to weep and Mary and Martha to cry out for relief. We are caught up in an "event of irremissible engagement, without the possibility of being redeemed" (*sans pouvoir de rachat*) from it (*DEE*, 49/*EE*, 34), which is revealed in a "state of purity" in pain: "In pain [*peine*], sorrow [*douleur*], and suffering [*souffrance*], we once again find, in a state of purity, the definitiveness [*definitive*] that constitutes the tragedy of solitude" (*TA*, 55/*TO*, 68–69). Physical pain represents "in a state of purity" the bond of the subject to itself, the tragedy of solitude, and this because: "[P]hysical suffering in all its degrees entails the impossibility of detaching oneself from the instant of existence. It is the very irremissibility of being. The content of suffering merges with the impossibility of detaching oneself from suffering. . . . In suffering there is an absence of all refuge. It is the fact of being directly exposed to being. It is made of the impossibility of fleeing or retreating. . . . In this sense suffering is the impossibility of nothingness" (*TA*, 55–56/*TO*, 69). In physical suffering I am riveted to being, panicked by the absence of refuge, haunted, not by death but by the impossibility of death, which would be an escape, forced to live on. The painfulness of pain lies in a sense of unremitting assault, of being pinned to existence, backed against the wall of being (*TA*, 59–60/*TO*, 72). It is one thing to stand tall against overwhelming forces and take a beating, like a virile Heideggerian being smashed to pieces (they all love it!). But it is quite another thing to be beaten senseless, reduced to "crying and sobbing" (*le pleur et le sanglot*), turned inside out, reduced from a subject to subjection, my activity thrown in reverse into passivity, which is what happens when suffering "attains its purity."[9]

PARDONING OUR BEING

Enter *l'autrui*. Or, Jesus returns to Bethany.

Death does not relieve the tragedy or "curse" of solitude because it cannot truly "give" (*donne*) the future; death cannot give time (*TA*, 68/*TO*, 79). It shatters the solitude by shattering the subject (*TA*, 63/*TO*, 74), by crushing this solitary being (*TA*, 65/*TO*, 77). There is nothing that death or I can do to transcend my solitude. I cannot give transcendence to myself. I must instead be *for-given* my solitude by the other. The radical breakup of my solitude, the release from solitude—that means to be pardoned (*c'est être pardonné*) (*DEE*, 144/*EE*, 85), particularly in the biblical sense of *released*. The givenness of my being, in which I am steeped, can only be *forgiven by the other*, not forgiven for a wrongdoing, but released from metaphysical solipsism—like the coming of the other in Husserl's *Fifth Cartesian Meditation* (of which this is a transcription), like Jesus coming down the road to Bethany (for which this provides a phenomenology).[10] The other comes and forgives me, not by forgiving my trespasses but by releasing my existence, unchaining not my doing but my being, even as the arrival of Jesus in Bethany releases Mary, Martha, and Lazarus. *The coming of the other is time and forgiveness.* Jesus comes too late to avert physical death, but the event he visits upon them, the comfort he gives them, gives them time, and maybe it also gave Lazarus time, if it rallied his spirits, giving them all a new time, a new birth. In Greek metaphysics, time is a mark of our insufficiency and limitation, a changing image of the plenitude of eternal being. But in Levinas's biblical view, our being is all too sufficient and self-sufficient, all too saturated with presence and replete with itself, and time is "a remedy for the excess of the definitive contact [with being] which the instant effects." Time is salvation (*salut*) from the present, welcoming the other.

The more gravely I am weighed down by the present and the more I am pressed in upon by the present, the sharper and livelier the hope. Hope flourishes most when the situation is most hopeless: "The irreparable is its natural atmosphere. Hope is hope only when it is not permitted. Now what is irreparable in the instant of hope, is that this instant is itself a present [*c'est son présent même*]" (*DEE*, 153/*EE*, 89). What is more "irreparable" than the bond of the present to itself in suffering, when the subject is riveted to itself in pain and loss? Even if the future, the subsequent course of moments, brings relief, consolation, or even "compensation," still "the suffering of the present remains like a cry whose echo will resound forever in the eternity of spaces" (*DEE*, 153–54/*EE*, 89–90).

The moment of suffering cannot be entered into a system of exchange; or, when it is—you can always sue a person or an institution that causes you pain and injury—that occurs only in what Levinas is calling the time of the "world," the "time of economy" (*DEE*, 154/*EE*, 90), the time of the lawyers. That transaction is marked by the breezy lightness of an "I" that presides over our conscious acts and barters with them. The ego is on hand at a *later* moment to collect its "compensation" for the misery of an earlier moment that has, by then, acquired a certain cash value, deciding what it will take "for its trouble." In that way suffering is indemnified instead of "releasing (*détendent*) the torsion of the instant upon itself," letting the intensity of pain be what it is, insisting on or standing in the pain of the *instans*, in order to pass over into a new time. The "profound exigencies" of the pain are nullified because they are bought off by economics. When pain is taken in its irreparability, the ego is contracted to the instant, arrested, mired in the misery, the *malheure*,[11] of the moment, and only then experiences the hopelessness, the no way out, which is really the *only* way out, if the Messiah arrives in time.

"The world is the possibility of wages," Levinas says, the ego willing to strike a bargain. The time of the world dries all our tears, and it enables us to forget "the unforgiven instant and the pain for which nothing can compensate" (*DEE*, 154/*EE*, 90)—by putting them in the bank! But it is precisely this unforgiven, uncompensated quality of suffering that strips away the mask of the ego with which it masquerades in the world and exposes the fraudulent lightness of its mundane transactions. It is just this suffering for which nothing can compensate that constitutes the "torsion" and "exigency" of the moment—what pain and sorrow and suffering of the moment truly demand—which gives it the force or energy to "unleash the future," to open up the future and make a new beginning possible. In the time of the world, Levinas says, the "engagement in existence which is effort is repressed, compensated and amortized"—like a "mortgage"—"instead of being repaired in its very present" (*DEE*, 154/*EE*, 90).

In the kingdom, we require salvation (*exigence du salut*), an an-archic an-economy in which living through irreparable loss releases the event of a new birth. The "world" is through and through "secular" (*laïque*); that is, the world is the place where everything is for sale and everything has a price, where everything is done for a salary or a wage. That is a corruption from which religion itself is hardly immune. Religion is not religious when it is reduced to rewards gained for expenditures made, which is made plain by Derrida's critique of the "celestial economy" that is invoked in the gospel of Matthew against the Pharisees.[12] There the light that illumines the children of the light simply makes for more enlightened investors, buying stocks in goods that will not rust or perish.

Hope transpires in—or unleashes—another time, a time of rebirth, resurrection, and salvation. In this time, it does not suffice to wipe away a tear (Rev. 21:4), or to avenge a death, or to make things "even." Instead, Levinas says, "no tear should be lost" (*DEE*, 155/*EE*, 91). We do not want to wipe away these tears but to preserve them, for they have a saving power, and they are precious beyond any price. Likewise, he says, "no death should take place without resurrection": it is not a question of avenging death, of putting a price on a priceless life in a wrongful death lawsuit, for example, or of counting ourselves even by exchanging death for death in war or capital punishment, say, or of exchanging eternal life for temporal death, but a question of following death with resurrection. The exigency of suffering is not for compensation but for salvation (*salut non salaire*); the exigency of ruined time is to be given a new time. What is required and demanded (*exigence*) is a double gesture in which the subject first undergoes irreparable loss and then, *without losing the loss*, in a precisely *non-indemnifying* movement, *demands repair*, not as a worker demands a wage, but as death demands resurrection or rebirth.[13]

Levinas makes contact with the poetics of the event, the poetics of the impossible that is at work in the time of the kingdom, with the phenomeno-logic of rebirth and resurrection, which requires a transformation that shifts us into another "messianic" time. Messianic time, the time of salvation, applies no less to sin, which requires forgiveness, than to suffering, which requires rebirth. Either way we get a new start, "pardoned" from evil suffered, from which we require release, and from evil committed, from which we require forgiveness. Salvation always means a new time, a new beginning, a fresh start, new life, rebirth, the continuation and multiplication of the original work of creation described by the priestly author where Elohim looked upon all the things he made and declared them good.

MESSIANIC TIME: THE TIME OF SALVATION

My goal is a phenomenological transcription of Jesus's mighty deeds when he called Lazarus from his tomb or raised the widow's son and the daughter of Jairus—a transcription that resists the temptation to turn them into deeds of magic. "[Jesus] cried with a loud voice, 'Lazarus, come out!' The dead man came out, his hands and feet bound with strips of cloth, and his face wrapped in a cloth. Jesus said to them, 'Unbind him, and let him go'" (John 11:43–44). How, then, are we to do the impossible, to repair the irreparable? How are we to change the past, according to the dream of Damian? How to resurrect the dead? How are we to hope if it is hopeless? What hope for life is there in death? But is that not what hope is? Is that not when hope really gets under way, really gets some traction, when all is hopeless? Still, small comfort that, to know that hope is *the* impossible, for how are we to do that? Hope, for Levinas, is not the market-wise ego trading in his most marketable moments precisely for the highest price. "The true object of hope is the Messiah, or salvation" (*DEE*, 156/*EE*, 91), the coming of Jesus down the road to Bethany. I need the Messiah, a paraclete, a consoler, to console me. I need a healer, to lay hands on me and release me from myself. Like Lazarus in the grave, I need the Messiah to lift me up, to call me out of the grave. I need the miracle of the caress, which is the first form in which we can identify the saving event: "The caress of a consoler, the lightness of his strokes in our pain, do not promise the end of suffering, do not announce any compensation, and in their very contact, are not concerned with what is to come *afterwards* in economic time. They concern the very instant of physical pain, which is then no longer condemned to itself, is transported 'elsewhere' [*ailleurs*], by the movement of the caress, and is freed from the vice grip of 'oneself' [*soi-même*], finds 'fresh air,' a dimension and a future" (*DEE*, 156/*EE*, 91). The "doctor," the healer, beyond being an empirical individual, "is an a priori principle of human mortality"[14]—that, at least, before the advent of HMOs, which reassimilate the healer back into economics—even as Jesus, beyond speaking prophetic words, speaks words of healing. A lot of people exercise this healing power without ever having seen the inside of a medical school, while a lot of medical school graduates know very little about healing. The alterity of death, the alien force that menaces the sufferer, far from stripping me down to my authentic *Selbstsein,* pries open my solitude, opening up an "appeal to the Other, to his friendship and medication."[15] The threat of death elicits hope in the Other, in the messianic coming of the Other.

Salvation requires the time of the consoler, who lifts the subject out of himself by way of the caress, whose soft and gentle stroke, whose light embrace, *effleurer,* opens up the self-enclosed subject to the other, allowing an even momentary escape. Blessed are those who mourn for they will be given comfort, and blessed are those who give comfort (Matt. 5:4). The time of the consoler is to divide the self-enclosed instant of mourning in half and share it. If I may be forgiven a repetition, a self-citation, I would put it thus:

> Therapists and clinical psychologists and counsellors of every stripe belong [to] . . . the paradigm of the "healer," people who "drive out devils," usually by "laying on hands." I imagine what is behind such old jewgreek stories is the power of a man or woman of compassion to calm a troubled heart, to take the hand of the troubled one in their hands, literally to lend them a hand, to be on hand. They did not have anything special to say to

> them or the miraculous power to suspend the laws of nature. They did not know anything special. Who does? But they talked with their troubled friends through long nights or lonely days, hand in hand, flesh in flesh. It is not what they said (*le dit*) that matters but the saying (*le dire*)—and the flesh of their hand. That was the miracle of what they did. . . . The hand heals of itself, because it is a hand, because it is flesh. We all have the hands of healers and we can all heal by laying on hands. . . . It is not a question of finding an answer to the night of truth but of sitting up with one another through the night, of dividing the abyss in half in a companionship that is its own meaning.[16]

To divide the abyss in half, to break open the tragic solitude, to divide the instant by sharing it between us, that is the time of the consoler, of the paraclete, of the Messiah, of the one who is to come.

Economic time moves along the circle of the same and so cannot effect a genuine release from the present. Only the Messiah can save us from our *malheure*, our miredness in the misery of the moment and open up another time. Salvation can be effected only from without, from a movement that is initiated *elsewhere*, by a laying on of hands by the other, by the coming of the Messiah who has come to save us, who is defined by, and is interchangeable with, salvation: "That is the Messiah or salvation," that is, the Other, and who thereby opens the ego to the future, to time and the future, which it cannot give itself. The voice that consoles, the hand that gently touches, the vow to be with you through this long night, to stay by your side, the promise, absolute and unconditional, to be there when you awake: *c'est le Messie ou salut*. That is the messianic time and the salvation, the coming of the Messiah for which we pray and weep, *viens, oui, oui*, as Derrida says (prays, weeps), the coming of Jesus for whom Mary and Martha prayed and wept. That is the weak force of God, not the strong force of magician.

The future that thereby opens up, the new time, is more than a "simple future," more than the foreseeable future that we can reasonably expect on the basis of present investments. For pain does not belong to secular time; it cannot be bought off or paid for (*ne rachète pas*). *Pace* the Utilitarians, you cannot justify the misery (*malheure*) of an individual by saying that it purchased the happiness (*bonheure*) of many. *Malheure* and *bonheure* do not constitute an economy; that is a category mistake. The rewards of the future do not wipe out the misfortune of the present. There is no justice—here Levinas means a "retributive" justice—wise enough or swift enough to "repair" the present, which has been irreparably ruined. Such "repair" of the irreparable as there is, is the effect of salvation, is the exigency of salvation. Salvation requires the reparation of the irreparable, beyond retributive justice. Reparation requires *the* impossible. "One should have to return to that instant, or be able to resurrect it" (*DEE*, 156/*EE*, 91). Reparation requires time-travel, a miraculous return to the instant to repair the irreparable, to resuscitate the dead, the way Lazarus was resuscitated. Reparation requires something like the dream of Peter Damian, that Damian be *somehow* right about the alterability of the past, which is the time of *the* impossible! Beyond the wise but calculative justice of Solomon, who knew how to split the difference and was willing to roll the dice, reparation requires the caress of the Messiah himself, for whose appearance we can only hope against hope. Reparation requires messianic *hope*. "To hope, then, is to hope for the reparation of the irreparable. It is to hope for the present" (*DEE*, 156/*EE*, 91). The hope is for *now*. Martha believes that Lazarus will rise on the last day, but that is not what she is asking of Jesus. It is not a question of hoping to escape time, but of hoping for a new time, for a new day and a new birth. Hope is not a hope in an afterlife, for gaining entrance to the "world behind the scenes," the *arrière-monde*, which would be no less worldly or secular for Levinas, for the very reasons pointed out by Derrida in *The Gift of Death*. World-time is any economic time whatever, which includes the "celestial economy." An after-world-time called eternity, "which does not seem to us indispensable," Levinas says (*DEE*, 156/*EE*, 91), belongs to the calculations of the world, not the kingdom. Heavenly rewards are celestial salaries, not the event of salvation. Salvation is situated, not in a heavenly pleasure but in pain of the present, "the very instant of pain." It is effected when pain is not compensated but comforted, healed, released, caressed, in the balm of flesh softly stroking flesh, or simply with words of comfort, or more simply still with wordless companionship; and it transpires, not in eternity, but now, in an hour or two, or a long night of anguish and suffering, or many nights. Is that not the essence of time? "Is not the future above all the resurrection of the present?" (*DEE*, 157/*EE*, 91–92). To hope, is that not to hope in the coming of the Messiah, of the Other, *autrui*, in what Derrida calls the incoming of the other (*l'invention de l'autre*)?[17]

In *Totality and Infinity*, the miracle of resurrection is the miracle of the child, which is a new beginning, a new life—an "event"!—humanity's ongoing internal auto-resurrection. Life is passed on to life, thus enabling life to elude the snares of death, which arrives too late, for life has already moved on to the child and a new life begun with which death will never catch up.[18] The exigency of suffering is the subject's "very need [*besoin*] of time," what Levinas later called the "desire," as opposed to the need, of the time of the other. But it cannot "give itself" this alterity; it cannot give itself time. We require the Messiah to call us forth from the tomb. The subject cannot save itself, even as it cannot effect the movement of time by itself. Neither time nor salvation, neither rebirth nor resurrection, is possible in the solitary ego. Levinas means thus to overturn the Augustinian motif (which made its way into Kierkegaard and Heidegger), when Augustine said, do not go elsewhere (*nolite foras ire*), for God is here, within us. For Levinas, on the contrary, what is here (*ici*) is a prison from which we hope to be released by the coming of the Messiah, who does indeed come from elsewhere (*ailleurs*), from the other (*autrui*), like Jesus hastening back to Bethany.[19] The pardoning extends the saving hand of the healer who heals the subject trapped in the tension and intensity of suffering, of the consoler who gives the subject consolation.[20] And when it is we who are offended, then we occupy the messianic position; we are the ones who have been waited for to come and release the other.

Release us from our trespasses as we release the other. We must offer the dead salvation or resurrection, even as we require rebirth and resurrection. We stand alternately in the position of the trespasser who waits for the Messiah and in the position of the Messiah himself. As if *we* were the Messiah for whom the past was waiting, which is the Benjaminian idea to which we now turn: the present is the messianic time, and we are the ones for whom the past, the dead, were waiting, and we must offer them such salvation as memory provides. The para-logic, or the ethics, of the tear, the poetics of the impossible, does not call for wiping away every tear but for seeing that "no tear is to be lost, no death without resurrection."

HISTORY AND THE DANGEROUS MEMORY OF SUFFERING

The idea of messianic time—of rebirth and salvation—in turn opens up the idea of a messianic history, of a salvation history, not in the sense of a history of salvation, but of history as offering a form of salvation and rebirth, providing another variation on the death of Lazarus, where the historian is cast in the role of the messianic healer.

History always runs the risk of romanticism and nostalgia, of a voyeuristic desire to revisit ancient sites, to observe, invisible and unnoticed, as bygone worlds unfold. That desire feeds the historical novel or film, seducing us into suspending our disbelief so that we may walk again the streets of medieval

Europe, pray again in Gothic cathedrals, dine with the landed gentry of Austen's England, and slip unnoticed into vanished worlds. That knowing relation to the past, as Levinas would say, is too possessive, too much aimed at reappropriating or reconstituting the alterity of the past. A more radical history, one written with prayers and tears, in which justice precedes truth and ethics precedes *episteme,* is constituted by the impossible desire to repair the irreparable. That does not mean to wipe away every tear (Rev. 21:4) but to see to it that no tear is lost—like Benjamin's chronicler who records every event, however minor, or like the biblical God, who keeps watch over every hair on our head (Luke 21:18). A radical salvation history records every loss and remembers every forgotten death, proceeding in the belief that memories are dangerous.[21]

Damian's dream conceals a profound reflection upon history as a response to the sighs of prayers and tears now long gone. We are carried by the wings of historical desire above the constraints that time and being place upon us, to "brush history against the grain," as Benjamin says,[22] across the—alas irreversible—flow of moments, to a moment that is no longer there so as to undo the damage and destruction, to stay the hand of the oppressor. But, as we learn from Levinas, the past is not to be altered or annulled but to be "saved." The time of the consoler, I contend, enters—by an impossible gesture—into the structure of writing history with prayers and tears, driven by the desire to console the dead and grant them resurrection. Note well that we speak of "resurrection," which is miraculous and a weak force, not of "resuscitation," which is a magical trading in strong forces.

The historical act is to record the tears of the dead, to keep them in our heart (*recordare*), even and especially when their deaths are lost and unrecorded. The historian records with the feeble tools of memory—not a passive, reproductive memory, but an active, heartfelt, searching and researching memory, which understands that history is the archive of countless tears and untold deaths. Radical history is a weak messianic power, reflecting what we have been calling the weak force of God. Matthew says that God has counted every hair our head (Matt. 10:30), an operation that I would say very beautifully describes the biblical God, as opposed to the impassive, apathetic, tearless *nous noetikos* of the Athenians, who thought of God in terms of a self-thinking thought. I would assign that divine operation to the desire of the radical historian,[23] who would reach across the uncrossable space of time and comfort those who weep and are persecuted, to tell the stories of the untold dead and thereby to offer them resurrection in the hope that the flames of hope would flare up from their ashes. Radical history is the record of unjust and unrecorded deaths, the archive of those without *arche*, who have vanished without a trace.

In "Diachrony and Representation," Levinas says that I am commanded by the "mortality" of the other, by his very weakness and vulnerability. That is what we are calling here a weak force. I am commanded, he says, "not to remain indifferent to his death, to not let the Other die alone, that is, to answer for the life of the other person"—lest I become an "accomplice" in that death (*TO*, 109). The authority of the Other is his precariousness, his strength is his weakness, his power is his powerlessness, in perfect accord with the poetics of the impossible. But if I am commanded by the "mortality" of the others, then I am no less commanded by their actual death, commanded postmortem, after their death, like Lazarus lying cold in his grave for four days. The command that comes to me from the living Other, "Thou shalt not kill," comes no less from the dead, comes no less from those who have already been killed. The command of the dead comes back to me from the grave and fixes me in its gaze. The blood of the dead cries to us from their graves like the blood of Abel, making us all responsible, making us all the children of Cain.

Benjamin speaks of the "chronicler who narrates (*hererzählt*) events without distinguishing between major and minor ones," who believes that "nothing that has ever happened should be regarded as lost to history."

For a "redeemed mankind," Benjamin says, every moment in the past is deserving of memory and citation.[24] Every moment of the past is to be remembered, the way someone is remembered in our prayers. We must become like saints who remember *everyone* in their prayers, the whole world, even the least of God's creatures. The link between memory, recording, keeping in your heart, devotion, and prayer is never stronger than in this moment of remembering the injustices suffered by the dead. Prayer is not a way to ask God to exert his mighty power to make things different; it is a way to draw strength from our weakness by recalling in our hearts every slain and fallen innocent.

That is why the memories of the historians are dangerous, which is what Johann Baptist Metz calls, in a magnificent expression, "the dangerous memories of suffering," the memories of countless tears and unaccountable untold deaths, the record of unrecorded evils.[25]

The historian has come to supply the voice of these mute dead, to sigh their sighs, to weep their tears, and to offer them the weak force of a resurrection that comes too late. *Sero te amavi.* If the dead constitute those whom Levinas calls the "subjectivity poorly heard in history,"[26] then the historian must make them better heard and amplify their cries. The historian of prayers and tears must in a certain sense rise to the revisionist historian's challenge that Lyotard denounces in *Heidegger and "the jews,"* to let those who were gassed to death step forward and register their complaints, to let the untold dead of nineteenth-century Ireland register their complaints against the English from the grave, to transform them from the *differend* to which the revisionist historian would confine them, into historical plaintiffs, with new voices and new life.

The history denounced in the preface to *Totality and Infinity* was a totalizing or "teleological" history, an economic affair in which the countless deaths were cost-accounted as a good investment in the progress of the world spirit, the high but affordable toll the Spirit must pay for advancing from one *Gestaltung* to the next. The sufferings of the past would eventually bring a good return or "result," and Auschwitz would be but a challenging "example" of a deeper and more sweeping law. Teleological history is one in which many an innocent flower is trodden on the way to *savoir absolue*, very brilliantly explicated in "Result," the central chapter of *The Differend*.[27] Thus instead of opposing eschatology to historiology, one would speak instead of an eschatological history, a salvific or saving history of prayers and tears. This would be a history that goes beyond history, to that *eschaton* beyond or beneath the sweep of world history, in order to take heed of the innocent flowers, the tender shoots that are trampled under the boots of teleology.

Eschatological history deals in the bottomless infinities that are the stuff of a poetics of the impossible, the priceless ones who cannot be counted in quantitative terms, who are the concern of the odd para-logic of the countable and unaccountable that we encounter in the New Testament and with which we began these remarks. Eschatological history would attend to the secrets of the heart that are unknown to the "judgments of history," secrets that are revealed only in the "judgment of God,"[28] in the *kardiognostes*, the God who knows the human heart (Luke 16:15). Rather than entering irreparable loss into a long-term gain, eschatological history would let the loss be a loss and seek, by an impossible gesture, to comfort the dead. The historiographer, Levinas says in *Totality and Infinity*, is a survivor who calculates the contributions of the dead to the living, a historical cost accountant who computes and recapitulates the investments of the past in terms of the return they make in the present. In the time of the scientific historiographers, "particular existences are lost [*se perdent*],"[29] taking a position that perfectly reproduces the one struck by Johannes Climacus against Hegelian world history. But as long as I am alive, as long as I have breath enough to protest, I take a "leave of absence" *(congé)* from world history, I postpone the reckoning against which I will be defenseless in death, when I will not be on hand to explain myself.

To be alive is to safeguard the secret of the self from the calculations of the historiographer, where no hair is uncounted, no tear is lost, no grief allowed to dissipate in the economy of historiographical reckoning. After that, I depend upon salvation by the other.

This work of the radical historian is to offer the dead not compensation but salvation, an impossible salvation, for its caress is not made of flesh but of memory and record, its gentle hand is stretched out to those who no longer receive its touch. As an event, the act of radical historical memory does not effect an entitative change but gives a new meaning. The historian cannot, of course, caress and give hope *to* the dead, save them or release them from the present of their suffering, now long gone. The radical historian can only offer hope and a future *for* the dead, on their behalf, pleading on their behalf for the future, for a new birth, new life, for such resurrection as death allows. That means that historical desire is directed at an opening on the future that would not be the "afterwards [*après*] of economic time," like returning the art stolen from the victims of the Holocaust, but the future of hope. That would come about *as if* we had assisted at the sufferings of the past, *as if* we had been on hand to lend a hand to their grief, like the consoler *qui effleure dans la douleur*, and to offer them a word of consolation. What remains now is to *hope*, and to hope, Levinas says, requires first to be driven into a state where, calculatively speaking, it is hopeless, where the odds are hopelessly against us, to hope against hope, as St. Paul says. Hope is not hope if you can see what you are hoping for on the horizon. We need hope when we cannot see the way out. Hope requires blindness. Hence, the work of the historian is the impossible one of giving comfort to the dead by way of memory and hope for the coming of the messianic time.

By memory we mean not a Hegelian memory that interiorizes, that sucks up the interiority of the dead into the present and makes it our own, but a memory like mourning, which preserves the distance of the dead, their fallen tears, the irreducible loss, then offers hope for the future they will never know. The historian sees to it that their lives are a gift without return, because they cannot return, a gift to the future, so that their memory makes its impossible that the future would ever close, that we would ever give up or give in to the odds against us. The irreparability of the past goes hand in hand with the open-endedness of the future, with the radicality of the *to come*, so that the more intensely we experience the tension and intensity of the past, the more radically we pray and weep, *viens, oui, oui*!

For as Walter Benjamin says, not even the dead are safe from the assaults of the antichrist, whom the Messiah must subdue.

The correlate of the irreparable past is the irrepressible future, the future of the "come," the *viens* of the *à-venir*, the unforeseeable, unprogrammable future, whose unforeseeability is directly proportionate to the irreparability of the past, which was at the least neglected by Benjamin. That is the new time, the time of hope, the time of the gift, beyond calculation and reparation, the future that converts the past into a gift without return, the new life that follows death, like a newborn child. Only the dead can give a gift without return. A genuine gift must be given beyond my death, for an absolute future that will never become present. That is possible for the dead alone. For the dead alone cannot be compensated, cannot draw some secret, unconscious payment for their expenditures. So they alone stand able, by the strange dynamics of the gift, to give a gift without return and reappropriation. Their gift alone outstrips all economy. The future of the gift alone provides for a "resurrection" that, beyond resuscitation, alone grants new life.

Levinas was early on thinking of the time of the other in terms of the *child*, the gift of fecundity. If, with a heart full of despair, one asks, What can come after Auschwitz, or after Kosovo? How is poetry or even life itself possible after Auschwitz or the Middle East? The answer is always the child. The child, who is a paradigm in the kingdom of God—for one must become like a child to enter the kingdom—is no less a paradigm for the historian, for the children are the ones to come in history no less than in the family. History is being written *for* the children, *to* the children; and it is to the children that we call "come," for whom we pray and weep, *viens, oui, oui.* History is written *in* prayers and tears, *with* prayers and tears, *about* prayers and tears, now long gone, praying and weeping over the coming of the Messiah, praying for the time of salvation, for the messianic time which will have recounted unaccountable death.

Suffer the little children—to come.

Come out, Lazarus. It is as if when Lazarus comes out, and they unwrap the strips of cloth by which he is bound, a child steps forth.

Behold the lilies of the field; how beautiful they are, but they only last for a day. How much more beautiful our days, which the Lord God, blessed be his name, has multiplied many times over. Over the next weeks and months, Jesus and the two sisters would have laughed over many a good story about the foibles of Lazarus, his good heart, his love for his sisters and his friends. Gradually they would gather the strength to come out from the dark grave of despair and go on, like the sun that rises every morning, like the new day that never fails to come, like the new tide, the new moon, the new spring—all figures of the new time. Jesus always had the gift, the grace, to see things that way, God's gift, God's grace. That was precisely who Jesus was, and that is what everyone remembered about him.

THE TEARS OF GOD

The figure upon which I seize in the story of Lazarus is that of Jesus weeping, which is the figure of the weakness of God. It is impossible to believe the Johannine contrivance that Jesus purposely stayed away for two days and also to believe that he would then weep. That is just bad storytelling. There is nothing divine about it, but a purely human, all too human love of displaying power. The only thing that explains Jesus's weeping is that he could not get there in time. The divinity is in the weakness, not the power. It is the weeping that is divine, not this high Christological sleight of hand, as if Jesus would be the source of immense human suffering in order to stage a display of divine might. But the weeping is the weakness of God, the tears of God, which is the compassion, the healing, the restoration of lost life. The divinity is the compassion he would have extended to Lazarus, the long night at his bedside, had he gotten there before his death, which is the weak force of God. The divinity is compassion he extended to Mary and Martha in the days after his death, the courage he gave them to go on, the joy he taught them to take in a brother well-loved, now lost, but always loved.

NOTES

1. "In what sense is he flesh, who walks on the water and through closed doors, who cannot be captured by his enemies, who at the well of Samaria is tired and desires a drink, yet has no need of drink and has food different from that which his disciples seek? He cannot be deceived by men, because he knows their innermost thoughts even before they speak. He debates with them from the vantage point of the infinite difference between heaven and earth. He has need neither of the witness of Moses nor of the Baptist. He dissociates himself from the Jews, as if they were not his own people, and he meets his mother as the one who is her Lord. . . . And in the end the Johannine Christ goes victoriously to his death of his own accord" (Ernst Kasemann, *The Testament of Jesus*, trans. Gerhard Krodel [Philadelphia: Fortress Press, 1968], 9).

2. See the interesting account of this story in Bruce Chilton, *Rabbi Jesus: An Intimate Biography* (New York: Doubleday Image Books, 2000), 244–46.

3. That is the point of the three highly anarchical and an-economic "lost and found" stories in the New Testament—the lost sheep, the lost

coin, and the lost son. In the calculations of the kingdom, each one is a singularity of infinite depth, a precious pearl. These "little ones" cannot be bought or sold or compensated for their time. Each individual is a qualitative infinity that outstrips any mere quantitative accounting. God alone, who knows what is in their heart, who has taken careful account of every hair on their head (Luke 21:18), can take account of their unaccountable worth.

4. Jean-François Lyotard, *The Differend: Phrases in Dispute*, trans. Georges Van Den Abbeele (Minneapolis: University of Minnesota Press, 1988), 100–103.

5. Edith Wyschogrod, *An Ethics of Remembering: History, Heterology and Nameless Others* (Chicago: University of Chicago Press, 1998).

6. Cf. John D. Caputo, *The Weakness of God: A Theology of the Event* (Bloomington: Indiana University Press, 2006), chap. 4, "Omnipotence."

7. The works of Emmanuel Levinas will be cited with the following abbreviations (page numbers given for original and translation): *DEE*: *De l'existence à l'existant* (Paris: Fontaine, 1947); *EE*: *Existence and Existents*, trans. Alphonso Lingis (Dordrecht: Kluwer, 1978; Pittsburgh: Duquesne University Press, 2001); *TA*: *Le Temps et l'autre* (Paris: PUF/ Quadrige, 1983), 11; *TO*: *Time and the Other*, trans. Richard Cohen (Pittsburgh: Duquesne University Press, 1987), 33. Levinas is discussing a kind of phenomenology of the first moment of creation in which the existent rises up from the formless anonymity of "existence" or the *il y a*, from the indeterminate sea of being (*il y a de l'être*)—*tehom and tohu wa-bohu*—and seizes upon existence. The victor, the existent, is taken captive by the vanquished in an odd version of the master/slave dialectic. The triumphant existent must now bend all its efforts to "escaping" being—the first piece the young Levinas published, in 1935, was entitled *On Escape* [*De l'évasion*], trans. Bettina Bergo (Stanford: Stanford University Press, 2003)—in order to break its captivity by that in which it has first established itself by its "virile" efforts. Both of these texts have an unfortunate tendency to describe being or existence as "evil," which is a particularly bad choice of words, given the fact that he is supplying a phenomenological version of Genesis in which all things are made good from something that is innocent of good or evil; this point is criticized rather too enthusiastically by Phillip Blond, "Emmanuel Levinas: God and Phenomenology," in *Post-Secular Philosophy: Between Philosophy and Theology*, ed. Phillip Blond (London: Routledge, 1998), 195–228.

8. Jacques Derrida, "Hostipitality," in *Acts of Religion*, ed. Gil Anidjar (London: Routledge, 2002), 390–91.

9. "Where suffering attains its purity, where there is no longer anything between us and it, the supreme responsibility of this extreme assumption turns into supreme irresponsibility, into infancy. Sobbing is this, and precisely through this it announces death. To die is to return to this state of irresponsibility, to be the infantile shaking of sobbing" (*TA*, 60/*TO*, 72). Levinas's phenomenological analysis of suffering is strikingly confirmed for us in Elaine Scarry's well-known book, *The Body in Pain* (New York: Oxford University Press, 1985), which I discuss in *Against Ethics: Contributions to a Poetics of Obligation with Constant Reference to Deconstruction* (Bloomington: Indiana University Press, 1993), 205–6.

10. Derrida, "Hostipitality," 391.

11. Note the mistranslation in *DEE*, 156/*EE*, 91: "Just as the happiness (*bonheure*) of humanity does not justify the misery (*malheure*)"—not "mystery"—"of the individual." This remains uncorrected in the Duquesne reprint (Pittsburgh: Duquesne University Press, 2001), 93.

12. See Jacques Derrida, *The Gift of Death*, trans. David Wills (Chicago: University of Chicago Press, 1995), 97–98; and Jacques Derrida, *Voyous: Deux essais sur la raison* (Galilée, 2003), 14–15, translated in English as *Rogues: Two Essays on Reason*, trans. Pascale-Anne Brault and Michael Naas (Stanford: Stanford University Press, 2005), where Derrida speaks of *salus* without salvation or an economy of redemption.

13. Charles Winquist describes something similar in Tillich's concept of salvation. While Tillich seems to speak of the kingdom of God, eternal life, and judgment as the final conquest of life's ambiguities, we should remember that these are symbols of the quest for an unambiguous life, that he is against literalism, supernaturalism, and magic. There is no revelatory super-knowledge that annuls our finitude. For example, in serious despair over the meaning of life, in which we take a secret pleasure, we experience the seriousness of life and hence the power to affirm life. Despair participates in the power of life. We are blessed/happy in our despair; meaninglessness becomes meaningful in despair, and we affirm a faith in life. Eternal blessedness is the positivity that emerges from negativity. Grace strikes us in despair when we find the courage

to be, to say yes to the finitude of life. A beatific vision, not of God but of the world. The world is divinely ordinary, and life can be lived meaningfully under the conditions of finitude. Theological thinking is unsettling because it unsettles the ordinary, making us think it under the pressure of that than which no greater can be conceived, our ultimate concern and a demand for what does not disappoint. We have the courage to be because we look into the abyss and say yes to life, to its divine ordinariness. See Charles Winquist, *The Surface of the Deep* (Aurora, CO: Davies Group, 2003), 221–23.

14. Emmanuel Levinas, *Totality and Infinity*, trans. Alphonso Lingis (Pittsburgh: Duquesne University Press, 1969), 234.

15. Ibid.

16. Caputo, *Against Ethics*, 243–44.

17. The time of salvation is neither Bergsonian duration, in which the present impinges or "encroaches" (*DEE*, 157/*EE*, 91–92) upon the future by the sheer precipitancy of the *élan vitale*, nor the headlong rush, the *Vorlaufen*, of ecstatic *Dasein*'s anticipatory projection upon its ownmost possibility to be. Neither Bergson nor Heidegger gives the present its moment in the sun, its time and duration, and so neither allows the future to be truly accomplished as a release from the present. The Levinasian notion of resurrection—we live time and the future more deeply as the resurrection of the present—requires the "indispensable interval of nothingness" (*DEE*, 158/*EE*, 93), which separates the instant and allows it to be constituted. The present must first surge up in its discontinuous density, for it is only then that the *exigency* of the present can be nourished and engendered. In just the same way that there is a nourishing of the present in epiousiology, where we are counseled by Jesus to trust, not to worry about what we shall eat or how we shall be clothed, there is a comparable enduring of the hopelessness of the present in all hope. The enchainment to the present needs to be constituted before the need for release is felt. It is not enough to enter the next instant "identical and unforgiven (*impardonné*)," which would be no more than the repetition of the same. This exigency is not a demand for the perseverance of the same but for dénouement—for something that unties the knot by which it is tied to itself—and recommencement, for a new beginning. The exigency is a demand for a "miraculous" beginning, a "beginning again as other" (*DEE*, 159/*EE*, 93), not a beginning from itself (*à partir de soi*), but beginning from the other, from the caress of the other. "Resurrection," Derrida says, commenting on this text, "is the miracle of each instant" (Derrida, "Hostipitality," 392).

18. While the child is a powerful figure of hope, although this should not be taken sentimentally and in isolation from economic analyses that explain why the lives of children are also rendered hopeless, Levinas was rightly criticized by Luce Irigaray as proposing this as the final word on "love" (*eros*), because love mutually engenders life in the lovers, quite apart from the child. See Luce Irigaray, *An Ethics of Sexual Difference*, trans. Carolyn Burke and Gillian C. Gill (Ithaca: Cornell University Press, 1993), 185.

19. Truly to break outside into the "absolute alterity of another instant" is not possible for the solitary subject. "This alterity comes to me only from the other" (*DEE*, 160/*EE*, 93). The ticktock time that flows in "internal time consciousness" is fraudulent for Levinas, amounting only to a repetition of the same in which the instant is "negated" only in order to resurface in the next instant as the same, which is nothing more than simple self-preservation or self-regeneration—as opposed to a new birth. Such internal negation is not true alterity but a self-assertion that deploys the mediation of self-negation. Whether as protention and retention in Husserl, the projection upon death in Heidegger, the dialectical power of the negative in Hegel, or the freedom derived from *le néant* in Jean-Paul Sartre's *pour soi*, such time is nothing but monotony in comparison with that genuine alterity that gives time starting from the other, issuing in a false freedom and a false time, altogether different from the time issuing from pardoning, *pardoner*, from being released by the other (*autrui*) (*DEE*, 161/*EE*, 94).

20. The text of *De l'existence à l'existant* concludes with a shift of focus, a reversal of the terms of the self (*moi*) and the other (*autrui*). Up to that point, the subject is one who suffers and is released by the coming of the other, where the other is "the Messiah or salvation." But in the conclusion of the work it is the other who suffers—the other is "the weak one whereas I am the strong," or "the poor one, 'the widow and the orphan,'" or the other is the enemy and stronger (*DEE*, 162–63/*EE*, 95). In either case, the other is no longer one who alleviates the suffering of the subject. By the same token, the "caress" shifts from the caress *by* the other, by the healer or consoler who alleviates the suffering of the subject, to become the erotic caress, the caress *of* the other by the subject who

reaches out into the infinite mystery and exteriority of the feminine other, groping in a distance that cannot be crossed. The caress is not the one by which the subject is lifted out of its misery and misfortune, but the caress whose loving futility would cross the distance of the other that is maintained in the very proximity of the embrace. In these final pages, alterity, salvation, and pardon are quickly sketched in terms of eros and the ethics of the other, terms that will require the lengthy analyses in *Totality and Infinity* to make sense. But what interests me in these pages is their first appearance in the healing gesture of the other, who comes, like the Messiah, to save the subject from itself.

21. For many years, the "Colonial Williamsburg Foundation" in Virginia attempted a nostalgic reconstruction of eighteenth-century Virginia by leaving out the slaves who made that economy run. The foundation is very good at reconstructing the architecture, paints, and wallpapers of the era, but they wanted to forget the tears.

22. Walter Benjamin, "The Concept of History," IX, in *Walter Benjamin: Selected Writings*, vol. 4, 1938–40, ed. Michael Jennings (Cambridge, MA: Belknap Press of Harvard University Press, 2003), 392.

23. What I am describing here as a radical historian, Edith Wyschogrod describes as a "heterological historian" in *Ethics of Remembering*.

24. Benjamin, "Concept of History," 390.

25. Johann Baptist Metz, *Faith in History and Society*, trans. D. Smith (New York: Crossroad, 1980), 109–15.

26. Levinas, *Totality and Infinity*, 182.

27. Lyotard, *The Differend*, 86–196; Jean-François Lyotard, *Heidegger and "the jews,"* trans. Andreas Michel and Mark Roberts (Minneapolis: University of Minnesota Press, 1990).

28. Levinas, *Totality and Infinity*, 240–47.

29. Ibid., 55.

23
A Prayer for the Impossible: A Catechumen's Guide to Deconstruction

One of the things Derrida means by a text or a tradition is that it keeps "happening" (*arriver*) without ever quite "arriving" at a final, fixed, and finished destination. We cannot simply "derive" (*dériver*) direct instruction from it, but we must instead allow it a certain drift or free play (*dérive*), which allows that tradition to be creative and reinvent itself so that it can be, as Augustine said of God, ever ancient yet ever new. That, as I pointed out, does not scuttle the figure of walking "in the steps" of someone, but it does give it some teeth. I said in the first chapter that I am presenting the New Testament as a "poetics" of the Kingdom of God, a theo-poetics—as opposed to a "theo-logic," an ethics, or a church dogmatics—as a complex of narratives, parables, and paradoxes of which Jesus is the centerpiece. From a work such as that we cannot simply and straightforwardly "derive" a course of action. We need instead to "arrive" at an instantiation, a concretization, a way to translate it into existence, all the while letting it happen (*arriver*) to us, allowing ourselves to come under its spell and be transformed by the event it harbors. For that we require a delicate style of interpretation, a "hermeneutics," which is the role played here by deconstruction, which I am presenting as the hermeneutics of the Kingdom of God.

To that end I want to sketch out in this chapter some features of the slightly Jewish-Augustinian reading I am giving of Derrida, according to which deconstruction can be seen—not without controversy—as a form of prayer. In the view I take of deconstruction, we are constantly praying for something that has already happened but is always arriving, for something remembered but also promised, for something nameless that goes under many names, something that overtakes us and draws us out of ourselves. Among the many names under which deconstruction travels, I number "justice," the "gift," "forgiveness," and "hospitality" as the most important to our present purposes. These I will treat below as incognitos of "*the* impossible."

THE VOCATIVENESS OF EVENTS

I begin with a distinction between events—something that has already happened but is still arriving—and the names or things in which events are expressed. Allow me to illustrate this distinction with an anecdote. I once attended a conference in which a theologian who (like God, he will be nameless), not liking Jacques Derrida very much (I could tell), asked the audience, or rather, quite indignantly intoned as from on high, "Can God be deconstructed?" I ventured a reply—to his surprise, I think, because he did not really expect anyone to answer, he being of the opinion that he had with this question thereby deconstructed deconstruction (by which he meant reduced it to rubble). I allowed that while I hesitated to speak for God, it was certainly true that the *name* of God can and should be deconstructed. Indeed, I would go so far as to say that the long history of "theology" (which, however venerable a name, has like the rest of us to stay on guard against *hybris*) has been an ongoing work of deconstructing the name of God in order to release the event that stirs within that name. On that point we may all be well instructed by the respect shown for this name in the Jewish tradition. Furthermore, although this is another point, one of the difficulties that theologies of any stripe must face is that the event that stirs within the name of God can take place under other names, which complicates the distinction between theism and atheism.

So, then, what is an event? Let us start by saying that events are not names or things but something going on *in* names or things, and it is that special something that commands the particular attention of deconstruction.[1] Think of the event as first of all a simmering potency in a name, a possibility that inhabits the name, what that name is trying to express while never quite succeeding, something that the name recalls but never quite remembers, promises but never quite delivers. When we respond to the event in a name we not only respond to what it "actually" refers to, but we are also being provoked by what it promises or recalls. One of Derrida's favorite examples in this regard is the name "democracy." He once wrote an essay that cited Michel de Montaigne: "Oh my fellow democrats, there are no democrats."[2] The ever-righteous Right, which has a tin ear for Derrida, gets up in arms when Derrida says things like that, and it self-righteously proclaims, again from on high (I think they must carry portable folding pulpits with them), the difference between the Western democracies and, say, the Nazis or the old Soviet Union. But that is rather a flatfooted and unpoetic way to take what Derrida meant. Kierkegaard could very well have stood up in church some Sunday morning and said to his fellow Danes, "Oh my fellow Christians, there are no Christians," by which he was not remarking that the Danes had all recently become Hindus. Anyone who hears what is resonating in the word "democracy" (or "Christianity"), anyone with an ear for its poetics, for what it promises and recalls, knows that no existing democracy, nothing that dares call itself a democracy today, is up to what is called for in that name. When we call something by a name like "democracy," something is being called for, something is being recalled and promised, an event of democracy, that, as the Scriptures might put it, eye has not seen nor ear heard. When we speak of something (say the United States) being "worthy of the name" (say, democracy), we are speaking of the event that name contains. The event that is going on *in* the name is the event of a *call*, of something calling and of something being called for *by* the name. The event has the structure of a call (and a re-call) while the name is a kind of shelter or temporary housing for the event. Let us say that the event belongs to the "vocative" order—the order of what is calling, what is called for, what is recalled, and who is called on—while names and things belong to the "existential" order, the order of what actually exists, of natural languages and real things.

Democracy, or rather the event that is "harbored" (which means both protected and hidden) in the name "democracy," is what is coming, as the "democracy to come." The event is unconditional because it is the promise of something that is never realized under the existing conditions in which things are actually found. This is an idea that Derrida has borrowed not from Plato but from Judaism, which is why he calls it the "pure messianic" form, not an "ideal" form. But be aware that he has in mind a slightly peculiar idea of the "Messiah," found in some rabbinic traditions, where the Messiah never actually shows up, where the Messiah is the name of the pure structure of hope and expectation. In that understanding, if the Messiah did show up he would ruin everything, for then there would be no future, which is a way of saying that history would be over. That point is well illustrated by the history of Christianity, in which, since it is believed that the Messiah has already come, its history consists in waiting for him to come *again*. Originally, Christianity was not supposed to have a history because the Messiah had come. There wasn't even supposed to be such a thing as Christianity. The "history of Christianity" opens only with the delay that came about when Jesus failed to come (again)—the church being the temporary shelter that has been built in the meantime (Plan B). So even if the Messiah has already come, that would not satisfy us, for as long as we live in time and history, among the deconstructibles, we will want him to come *again*! The structure of the "to come," symbolized by the empty chair that is set for Elijah, is a structure of openness to the future, to what may come knocking at our door. On this Jewish analogy, it would be "idolatrous" to identify the event of something like democracy with its present state of affairs—the current conditions under which it is found being like the golden calf—instead of being drawn by the call of that event toward an open-ended future.

But we should not be misled by this stress on the "to come" into thinking that the temporality of the call, or the historicity of the event, is one-sidedly futural, as if we were just dreaming about something that will never be. Remember what we said above about the dangerous memories of the suffering of the dead. Deconstruction is a way to dream, and dreaming is important, as Martin Luther King Jr. made perfectly plain. But deconstruction is not only a dream, and it is not only about the future. As a "call" or solicitation, the event is no less a memory, a call back, a re-call to the past that has given us this name. When we hear the event that is called for in a name like "democracy," we hear an old name and an old promise, a promise first made among the Greeks, to whose language this word belongs, and we are called back to the long history of the efforts that have been made over the centuries to make this name come true. We hear the history of success, but we no less hear what the theologian Johannes Baptist Metz, following the lead of Jewish writer Walter Benjamin, called the *memoria passionis*, the memory of the suffering that has been endured in the name of democracy, in the name of the event that has been promised in that name. That is a notion that is profoundly rich in its implications for Christianity, which is organized around its own *memoria passionis*: the memory of the passion of Jesus, which Metz calls the "dangerous memories of the sufferings of Jesus."[3] Dangerous to whom? To the powers that be, to the long robes of the present order, to a world that wants to close over and close off and repress those memories of past injustice.

By the same token, it also belongs to the vocativeness of the event to be addressed, to be called on, *here and now*, in the present, to be made responsible, to be asked to respond, to what this name calls for. We are reminded of the way the congregation in Sheldon's opening scene was put on the spot by the appearance of someone who should have reminded them of Jesus, when he "called on" them in an uninvited way, and in so doing elicited from them a promise about how they would live in the future. We must be responsible to events, responsive to them, welcome them, and show them hospitality when they show up uninvited at our door. We must, as Gilles Deleuze says, make ourselves worthy of the events that befall us, worthy of the name that harbors these events—names like democracy or Christianity.[4] We are thus not only called forward and called back by the event, but we are also called on. Remember that in the theory of the event, "truth" means what is trying to come true, which points to our responsibility to make it actually come true—let us say, to give it a Pauline twist, to fill up what is missing in the body of this name (Col. 1:24). Benjamin put this point in an odd but striking way. He said that the messianic age is not off in the future but *right now*, that *now* is the messianic age, that we are the messianic people, we are the ones whom the dead were waiting for—to right the wrong of their sufferings.[5] That is not unlike what Abraham Lincoln said at the Gettysburg Cemetery: that we here today must resolve that these dead will not have died in vain—this "will not have," which in grammar is called the "future anterior," being of special importance in deconstruction. That is how things work in the vocative order, where memories can be dangerous and where our dreams for what is promised are also dangerous, as two of the most famous orations in American history confirm (Lincoln's and King's). They endanger the present order, challenging the pretense of the present form of things—the existential order—to pass itself off as the event itself, to actually *be* democracy or justice or truth or Christianity or whatever it pretends to "be," whatever it says it "is," whatever the "powers that be" are trying to get away with. That is why when Derrida once famously described deconstruction as a critique of the "metaphysics of presence," he took the side of the better angels of our nature, even though his detractors thought he was the devil himself. (Actually, for strategic reasons, he is better off on the "devilish" side, angels on the whole being a little too pious for deconstructors.)

Derrida sometimes describes the event by saying that while the event is possible, it represents a very special kind of "perhaps."[6] This is because it is a prayer not for what is straightforwardly possible but for "the possibility of *the* impossible." This is my favorite description of deconstruction; it is the one that Derrida himself calls its "least bad definition."[7] What is "possible" in the straightforward sense is the foreseeable future, the future that we can reasonably anticipate and plan for and that can be called the "future present." That, of course, is of the utmost importance. We can and should foresee and plan for the education of our children and for our own retirement; we should plan our calendar and our time commitments. But by *the* impossible he means something that exceeds the horizon of foreseeability and expectation and not a simple logical contradiction (like p *and* -p). He means the possibility of something more "unconditional," which he calls the "absolute" future, the future that takes us by surprise, the one that lies beyond our horizon of expectation. That is the future of the event, like the way hope is truly hope when it has been pushed up against the impossible and everything looks hopeless.[8]

A PRAYER FOR JUSTICE

I am identifying deconstruction as a kind of passion or prayer for the impossible, or as an affirmation of the "undeconstructible." The first time I find mention of something "undeconstructible" is in a 1989 essay titled "The Force of Law."[9] This essay is the best place to start with the more overtly religion-friendly accenting of deconstruction in Derrida's writings.[10] The law is always deconstructible, Derrida writes, but "justice in itself, if such a thing exists, outside or beyond law, is not deconstructible" ("Force of Law," 14). The deconstructibility of the law, Derrida adds, is not "bad news"—in fact it is a stroke of luck. As readers of St. Paul's Letter to the Romans would be able to see, this suggests a comparison with the distinction between grace and the law, a point that is worked out very nicely in a recent study of Derrida and Paul,[11] even as it suggests the attitude that Jesus had toward the law. On the one hand, the law as such only ensures legality, not justice; when the laws that are in force are unjust, we say that might makes right, that is, real injustice is cloaked with merely legal right. That is how opponents of abortion consider *Roe v. Wade*, and that is how advocates of gun control view the laws protecting gun owners. Both groups think the law lets us get away with murder. On the other hand, justice as such, without the law, is just a dream. Justice in itself is an unconditional demand, but of itself, it has no flesh and bones, no force, no teeth. Deconstruction turns on, is made possible by, and "takes place in the interval between" the undeconstructibility of justice and the deconstructibility of the law ("Force of Law," 15), between something undeconstructible but without force and something forceful but deconstructible.

In the terms I have introduced, "justice" belongs to the vocative order—it is what is called for and what calls on us, what we pray for—while laws belong to the existential order. Laws exist, but justice calls. Laws are deconstructible because laws have been constructed to begin with; laws are "positive," which means historical, regional, variable, repealable, amendable. But laws should always have the event of justice in mind. Laws may or may not be just in fact, and they may very well start out just and become unjust when the circumstances change but the laws do not. Thus there might once have been circumstances in which the personal right to bear arms was justified, although one would expect a Christian to have a very delicate conscience about such things; but to support such laws today, when the dangers to life and limb from the proliferation of such weapons is as plain as the nose on your face, defies comprehension, especially for Christians. That is why the deconstructibility of the law serves the cause of justice, which is not deconstructible. There is no better "example," if that is all it is, of why the word "deconstruction" does not signify something destructive (although it is always risky). If laws were not deconstructible they would soon become monsters that menace justice, the way the National Rifle Association menaces justice today. In Derrida's carefully crafted expression, that "justice in itself, if there is such a thing, is not deconstructible," the qualification "if there is such a thing" (*s'il y en a*) makes all the difference, a messianic difference. Justice in itself does not exist but it is something we demand and something that is demanded of us. Justice is what we call for and something that calls on us, something we solicit and something by which we are solicited, a matter of prayer and solicitation. In the deconstruction of the law, the law is exposed to the call of justice in order to provoke the reinvention of the law, thus offsetting the tendency the law has to close down around itself. Justice aerates the law, turns its soil, keeping it just.

Of a vocative like justice, we should say not "it is" but rather "it calls." Speaking of justice Derrida says in French *il y a*, just as Heidegger, speaking of Being, said in German *es gibt*, both of which get translated into English as "there is," but there is no "is" in the French or German, which is to their advantage. Justice is not a being that exists but an event that "appeals" to us, demanding our response. "There is" justice, *if* there is (*s'il y en a*). When Derrida says "if there is such a thing," he is saying not that he regards justice as a Platonic form that exists outside space and time, or as a pure utopian ideal advanced by Thomas More, but rather that it has the character of a messianic hope and demand, an open-ended appeal, a solicitation that everywhere exceeds the condition that reality itself has attained. It has a more open-ended and unforeseeable quality than a Platonic *eidos*, which is precisely an ideal we see but cannot attain. Laws exist under real and determinate circumstances, under definite conditions that vary from time to time and place to place, while the demand for justice is unconditional. Laws are real but justice is like a "ghost," a specter, that haunts the laws, a good ghost, a caring spirit or guardian angel, whispering words of justice in the ears of the law, incessantly calling for what is yet to be.

We like to say that laws are "blind"—the scales of the law are administered by a blinded figure—meaning that they are universals, applied to everyone equally, allowing no special treatment, providing "equal protection" to everyone, but binding everyone with equal force, no exceptions for the big contributors to a political campaign. But if laws are universals, justice is sensitive to the singularity of the situation, to the idiosyncrasies and differences, and it is positively mad over these little singularities. Once again, the biblical resonance is plain: laws have to do with the ninety-nine, but justice has to do with the one lost sheep, with the one lost coin, with the widow, the orphan, and the stranger. Every time we feel unjustly treated by the law we say, "But this case is different." A body of laws precise enough to cover everything singular, a perfect set of laws, would be like a map that is so exact that it is the same size as the region of which it is the map. A perfect map, a perfect set of laws, would be perfectly useless, a nightmare.

Laws have a strong existential force; there is a whole order of police, courts, and prisons to "enforce" the law. So if you break the law you stand a good chance of feeling the force of its long arm, which happened to both Paul and Jesus. But justice has only a weak or vocative force: in itself it has no institutional apparatus, no police or army, no place to lay its head; its kingdom, you might say, is not of this world. It is only a weak force. So you may very well refuse its call and get away with it; that happens all the time. Sometimes, if you have enough influence with the lawmakers, you can violate the demands of justice under the protection of the law and persecute the just; this happens all the time. The Bush administration does it every day by unjustly making the poor poorer while shrinking the size of the middle class and filling the pockets of the rich with perfectly legal tax breaks (which does not mean there are no honest people among the rich or dishonest ones among the poor). What we want, what we desire, with a desire beyond desire, is a justice with the force of law and laws that answer to the call of justice.

On this point the voice of deconstruction is not far from the voice of the prophets, which calls for justice to flow like water over the land.[12] Indeed, it is a sad commentary on the Christian Right to see how vociferously its call for "law and order" hardly makes any mention of justice. The Christian Right is all for the force of law, for rigorously enforcing laws against illegal immigrants, for keeping order in the streets, and they applaud wooden formulas like "three strikes and you're out" while slandering jurists who value discernment and adjudication as merely pandering to criminals. But it makes little mention of the biblical demands for social justice and it does little to address the injustice suffered by people who are forced to leave their homes and native lands to try to squeeze out a meager living in a foreign land. It turns a deaf ear to the poverty of inner-city life that makes a life of crime an inviting alternative to working for below-subsistence wages and no healthcare. They campaign vigorously for right-wing politicians who grant increasing tax breaks to the wealthy but refuse to raise the minimum wage—in the name of Jesus! The cry of the Christian Right for "law and order" drowns out the words of Deuteronomy (24:12–22), which tell the Israelites to respond to the needs of the widows and orphans and resident aliens, even as the Lord God led them out of Egypt.

Derrida condenses his view of justice into what he calls the three "aporias" of the law. In deconstruction the hermeneutical situation is always aporetic, that is, the situation in which interpretation is called for is sufficiently sharpened only when we appreciate the impossible bind or impasse in which we are caught. It is only when we realize that things are getting impossible that we start to get anywhere. As long as things are clearly "possible," we are cruising along on automatic pilot, nothing special is demanded of us, the oars are up, and we are going with the flow, hardly making any decisions at all. Nothing is happening; the "event" is not in play. Thus, the event of justice stirs within the rule of law in the following three impasses.

1. The *epoché* of the rule. The law provides a rule that must be applied to a situation, but if the rule is applied routinely and mechanically without insight into the particulars of the situation, if the law is reduced to a simple "calculation" or to producing a "programmable" result, then the law will be unjust. "Three strikes and you're out" represents the height of injustice because it prevents the judge and the jury from making a "fresh judgment" and "reinventing" the law, here and now. The truly "responsible interpretation"—responsible to the call or the demands of justice—will be both regulated (have a law) and unregulated ("suspend"—which is what *epoché* means—the

law). The judge and jury must proceed under the law but they must not be reduced to calculating machines. They must respect the difference of this situation, the justice that is called for or demanded, here and now; they must respect the event by which we are solicited in these concrete circumstances. We should never say a law as such is just or that some person as such is just, for there are too many times when each fails to respond to the demands of justice. The most we could hope for is that in this moment, here and now, the event of justice will flash, and once that occurs, it will no longer be just simply to repeat that decision in the next set of circumstances, which may be different.

2. The ghost of the undecidable. A just decision becomes a real decision only when it passes through the "undecidable," that is, through the oscillation between two conflicting decisions—when justice is making a demand on us from both sides, from two different directions—and that oscillation has to be resolved one way or the other. The most famous case of this in biblical literature is the story of the binding of Isaac, which Derrida, following Kierkegaard, has taken up.[13] That is when a decision is most responsible, most responsive to the solicitations of justice; otherwise we can beg off and say we were just following the law. From this we can see that undecidability—pace its vociferous critics—is the condition of possibility of a real decision, not the opposite of one. The opposite of undecidability is not decisiveness but decidability, which means programmability, derivability from a rule. Undecidability ensures that a decision will be the issue of a human "judgment," not the application of a rule, which could be done by a computer: The predecessor of undecidability in the history of ethics is not Nietzsche's theory of fictions but Aristotle's notion of practical reason (*phronesis*), which is the capacity to judge amid shifting and variable circumstances and to bring a schema to bear in an unprecedented situation; *phronesis* is the model for all hermeneutics, for which understanding is always interpretation. While in Aristotle this represents a form of practical "reason," there is also something wonderfully "mad" here—"deconstruction is mad about this kind of justice" ("Force of Law," 25)—with a kind of divinely deconstructive madness, the way one is a mad fool for the Kingdom of God.

3. Urgency. Justice does not wait. However undecidable the situation may be, however much deliberation is required, however true it is that justice does not quite exist, the truth is that justice deferred is justice denied. Justice is always to come, never realized, always soliciting from ahead, but at the same time justice is demanded now. At some point, the transition from deliberation to decision must be made, which inevitably takes the form of what Kierkegaard called a "leap," "acting in the night of non-knowledge and non-rule" ("Force of Law," 26).That does not mean the simple absence of knowledge and rule, thus ensuring a blind and wild choice, but rather the necessity to act inventively, to make a judgment where there are no guard rails or clear precedents, literally, to decide, to make the cut, to respond to the event here soliciting us. We must go as far as we can with calculation, but then beyond calculation make the cut, terminate the interminable, decide the oscillation of the undecidable, make the impossible happen.

That indeed is what deconstruction "is," if it is: "It [deconstruction] is possible as an experience of the impossible, there where, even if it does not exist (or does not yet exist, or never does exist), *there is* [*il y a*] justice. Wherever one can replace, translate, determine the x of justice, one should say: deconstruction is possible, as impossible, to the extent (there) where *there is* (undeconstructible) x, thus to the extent (there) where *there is* (the undeconstructible)" ("Force of Law," 15)" In deconstruction, one sets out in search of, or rather, one is oneself searched out or called on by whatever is unconditional, or undeconstructible, in a given order, and it is precisely in virtue of this undeconstructible *x*, which does not exist, which does not exist yet, which never quite exists, that everything that does exist in that order is deconstructible. Whatever exists, whatever is present, is contingent, historical, constructed under determinate conditions—like the church or the

Sabbath—and as such is inwardly disturbed by the undeconstructible, unconditional impulse that stirs within it—which for the church is the event that occurs in the name of Jesus. To "deconstruct" is on the one hand to analyze and criticize but also, on the other hand, and more importantly, to feel about for what is living and stirring within a thing, that is, feeling for the event that stirs within the deconstructible structure in order to release it, to set it free, to give it a new life, a new being, a future. Is it lawful to do good on the Sabbath? That is why deconstruction is affirmation, doubly so, *oui, oui,* the affirmation of the impossible, of the undeconstructible event whose life it bears within it like an expectant mother, which means a mother who expects and prays for an event.

THE GIFT

We cannot do everything "for the money," for the pay off. There have to be things we do for the sheer love of them, things that are given to us to which we in turn give ourselves, where we break the chain of means-and-ends. That is what is behind the madness that deconstruction shows for the "gift," which is one of Derrida's most well-known and characteristic discussions. The gift is a paradigm of an impossible and aporetic situation, even though it seems for all the world simple enough.[14] A gives x to B, freely and graciously. But consider the chain of consequences that is thereby set off. It is common courtesy for B to respond with gratitude, to say "thank you," for example, while also making a mental note to repay the gift, not right away, of course, which would be obvious and rude, but in a discrete and timely fashion. So the generous gesture on the part of A inevitably moves B to give y to A. Part of B's discretion, too, will be to get a sense of what x (the original gift) is worth, because it would also violate the protocol of gift giving to return the gift with something very cheap, or the opposite, to humiliate A by repaying the gift later on with something very expensive, which makes A look bad. Checking prices online is a handy and discreet way to determine the range in which to shop or at least in which to keep an eye out for something with which one might "casually" return the gift. Of course, the timing of a lot of gift exchanging is more regulated than this, as on birthdays or Christmas, but you still need to carefully gauge the value of the gifts in which you are trading.

Notice what has happened: as soon as the gift is given, the gift begins to annul itself. How so? We started with A trying to give a gift to B, but no sooner has this taken place than B is encumbered with a sense of debt that B sets about trying to discharge. Along with receiving a gift, B received a debt. We speak of "owing a debt of gratitude" to someone, and that is a fair enough description. Instead of merely being given something, B has gone into debt. In contrast, A, who ought to be experiencing a lack now that A is bereft of what A has given away, has added to his reputation for generosity. By giving x to B, A has come out ahead and B has come out behind. That is the very opposite of what A set out to do, and B immediately sets about to restore the equilibrium. The gift is supposed to be an act of "giving," but it has quickly turned into an economy, a matter of "debts" and "repayment," of balance of payments. The idea behind a gift ideally ought to be to give a gift without return, to make an expenditure without the expectation of reciprocation, in a kind of "mad" generosity. But the result is a thinly disguised economy of exchange that coolly calculates the value of the gift and is very much governed by the principle of sufficient reason. What started out as the madness of the gift, a one-way giving without return, has turned into a circle of exchange. Indeed, that is why giving "gifts" to public officials needs to be regulated—because the big-time donors expect a big-time return on their "investment," which is not just a gift. Moreover, we can all think of friends and relatives whose gift giving is intended to buy them favor and influence.

Is there no way out of this circle? Suppose A gives the gift anonymously so that B does not know whom to thank? That will only make things worse, for then B will be blocked from ever discharging this debt while A will congratulate himself for the nobility of his nature, which is such as to give an anonymous gift and not expect a show of gratitude. Or suppose I give my children the gift of an inheritance for which I will not, in principle, be around to receive expressions of gratitude. Still, I know in the quiet of my mind how profoundly grateful my children will be, and I am repaid over and over again by the prospect that they will prosper as a result of my generous benefaction. Indeed, I am sometimes given to wonder if I might not get an excellent portrait of my own good self made for them to hang in a place of prominence as a constant reminder of my boundless beneficence. Then suppose, by contrast, a situation where your gift is met with cold ingratitude—surely that would stop the circle in its tracks. Not so, for then you would congratulate yourself still more, this time for the superiority of your giftgiving nature over the mean-spiritedness of this wretched ingrate on whom you have spent your time and energy. In short, it seems that as soon as anyone is conscious that anything has been given, the circle is set in motion and the gift begins to annul itself.

From this discussion critics of Derrida, like the philosophical theologian Jean-Luc Marion, have concluded that for Derrida the self-annulling character of the gift means that the gift is impossible.[15] But that is to cut Derrida's discussion short, to applaud before the last movement has been played, or to leave at intermission, before the lecture is over, and not stay around for its conclusion. The conclusion is not that the gift is impossible but that the gift is *the* impossible (it belongs to the vocative order), which is why we love it so and why we are mad about the gift with the madness of love itself, which dreams of the impossible. The aporia, *the* impossible, is never the end of action in deconstruction but the start, the condition of possibility of a genuine action, one with teeth in it. So what Derrida actually concludes from the analysis of this aporia is twofold:

First, *know* what the gift is and how the gift works. Know that the gift sets off the circle of return and appreciate the aporetic situation—but still *give*. It is impossible that the gift will not in one way or another be reciprocated, even as it is impossible to purge ourselves of every expectation of a return, for even were such purity of intention possible for our consciousness, there would be no telling what is going on in our unconscious. But still *give*, make the Kierkegaardian leap, seize the madness of the moment, and give, expecting no return—even though there will inevitably be a return. Circles there always are, like the pool but in virtue of the gift the circles are opened up. The circular economies in which we conduct our lives are thereby widened, becoming more open ended and generous, expanding into ever-wider rings of generosity and beneficence.

Second, to this first bit of advice, Derrida adds a second counsel: give economies a chance. Economies, after all, are all that exist, while the gift, if there even is such a thing, is *the* impossible. (Gifts belong to the vocative and poetic order, economies to the colder, less poetic order of the existential and the factual.) But economies are everywhere and all around us—in the workplace, the schools, medicine, the law, the government. Economies are how things happen, how they get done. Not many people can work just for their health (*salut*); people expect a salary (*salaire*) with benefits. But then again, consider what would happen if there were only economies, if nobody did anything except for a buck. Of course, teachers, lawyers, nurses, doctors, and the rest of us expect and deserve a fair wage and a decent salary; but consider what a nightmare it would be if no one did anything except for a return, if no one did anything extra, made a special effort to see that things were done well, if no one went the extra mile. That goes for employers, too—employers especially—who should not expect to exploit their workers in virtue of the deconstruction of the gift! When people on either end of a contract are reduced to working the contract, to doing nothing but what the contract literally demands, the result is a nightmare. Economies are made fertile and productive by the gift by which they are ruptured and interrupted, punctuated, opened up, and expanded. Economies need gifts even as the gift goes beyond what is needed.[16] We might say that every existing gift, every "present" (in French *cadeau*, from the Latin *catena*, meaning "chain"), is deconstructible, which means it sets off a circle (or a chain) of exchange, but the gift in itself, if there is such a thing—in French *le don*, from *donner* (French), *donare* (Latin)—is not deconstructible. Economies are what exist but the gift calls to us from beyond the order of existence and being, soliciting us to go beyond what is, which here means to give, to make an expenditure without reserve, to go where you cannot go. The gift, *if there is such a thing*, is the event, the impossible, the undeconstructible. The gift is what we love and desire with a desire beyond desire, in which we hope with a hope against hope. The gift is given with love, even if we are not loved in return.

Derrida's analysis of the gift has several important implications for Christianity. In the first place, it constitutes a ringing warning against allowing a spiritual capitalism to invade our thinking about the kingdom, against bringing an investment mentality to the kingdom. The saints have often warned us about just such a creeping celestial capitalism, which is very likely to seep into our understanding of the counsels Jesus gives in the Synoptics. Jesus says to practice your piety in secret—to give alms in secret, to pray in secret—because otherwise you will have a reward for your piety here on earth instead of being rewarded later in heaven (Matt. 7:21–28). That would be like selling your stock short, before it reaches its full worth. In our effort to avoid hypocrisy—parading our piety in public—we must also beware of making everything turn on rewards, even long-term celestial rewards. Such piety must always take the form of the gift, if there is such a thing, which ought not to be allowed to degenerate into a bald economy. For the gift is made from love, and love, as Meister Eckhart said, is "without why." Love is its own why; love is for its own sake. It does not demand a further or external reason. When I do something for love of my spouse or child or friend, that is an expenditure made without expectation of return, even though we understand that in fact the circle of return is always there. The force of deconstruction in this context is to preserve the "madness" of the gift giving, the expenditure that is made madly on behalf of the other, and to delimit the rigorous—as in *rigor mortis*—rationality of cost accounting our lives. There is, there ought to be, something that we do in life that is not for a return but just because what we are doing is life itself, something a little mad. That is the gift.

FORGIVENESS

But there is another and perhaps even more poignant point of contact between deconstruction and the New Testament, and that is the question of forgiveness, to which Derrida devoted several lectures and seminars in the last decades of his life.[17] Once again, his approach was aporetic: the only thing that can be truly forgiven is the unforgivable; the only condition under which true forgiveness is possible is when forgiveness is impossible. How is that so? Forgiveness ought to be a matter of the gift, not of an economy. Is there not a graciousness, a gratuity, a giftlike character at play whenever I forgive someone or am myself forgiven? Is that not why we speak of the "grace" of forgiveness? Or is this just a fair deal? Normally the news is filled with stories of violence, rancor, and revenge, but occasionally we read in the newspapers or see on television stories of people who have forgiven someone who has murdered their child or spouse or parent, and we wonder how that is possible.

It is beyond understanding, beyond reason, beyond all accounting, all cost accounting.[18] It is a gift, bearing witness to the possibility of *the* impossible. If you borrow money from the bank and then make all the payments on the loan, the bank says the debt is "forgiven"—but this is strictly bank talk. Banks do not make gifts, and when they do we know they are up to something, trying to sell us some new service they have come up with. Nor do they forgive anything. They are business people and strict in their accounting.

Now the theological traditions, both Christian and Jewish, have tended to behave like bankers when it comes to forgiveness. That is, they spell out the conditions under which forgiveness is possible, typically four in number. Forgiveness requires an expression of sorrow, the intention to make amends, a promise not to repeat the offense, and a willingness to do penance. If someone meets all four conditions then they have *earned* forgiveness. We *owe* it to them the way the bank owes us the deed once the mortgage is paid off. A deal is a deal. But a deal is not a gift, and a gift is not a deal. Then what would it mean to forgive someone? It would have to mean something uneconomic—like a gift—something unconditional, something unaccountable, something mad. But the New Testament turns on just such unaccountables—like loving your enemies. If you love those who love you, what good is that? It makes perfect sense. Even the mafia does that. The unaccountable excess of love is felt when you love your enemies, when you love the unlovable—those whom it is unreasonable to love—which is the madness of the kingdom, which follows the nonprinciple of nonsufficient reason! Just so, the unaccountable excess of forgiveness is felt when we forgive precisely those who do not meet some or all of the four conditions, who are not sorry, do not repent, and do not intend to mend their ways. That is, genuine forgiveness is offered unconditionally, not subject to meeting any or all of these four conditions, exactly the way Jesus prayed for the forgiveness of the Roman soldiers. Just so, we often speak of things that are unforgivable—the Holocaust, say, or the atrocities of American slavery or of apartheid, or the several attempts at genocide we have witnessed in the past century. But would not such unforgivable things be the very subject matter of genuine forgiveness?

E. P. Sanders, the distinguished New Testament scholar, has ventured the hypothesis that, considering how much unfavorable attention the teachings of Jesus drew down on himself, Jesus might just have taught some such unorthodox—or mad—variation on the classical doctrine of Teshuvah. Jesus, it is said, consorted with sinners; the text does not specify with former or reformed sinners, but simply says sinners. It just might be, Sanders thinks, that Jesus was making an offer of unconditional forgiveness, that he did not insist that they first repent or promise to make amends. He may very well have been teaching that in the kingdom where God reigns, they are forgiven unconditionally. Had Jesus done so, he may well have given scandal to more traditional rabbis, who saw forgiveness in terms of its classical conditions and thus who submitted forgiveness to the principle of sufficient reason.[19]

There is still another twist to the aporias of the gift and forgiveness, and perhaps even the most important twist of all. If the visible God is revealed in the visible icon or figure of Jesus in the New Testament, and if the teachings of Jesus turned on forgiveness in an important way, then the God of Jesus is a God of forgiveness. But if forgiveness is a gift and not an economic exchange, that puts in question the classical terms in which we think of the death of Jesus, specifically as "atonement" or as a debt paid to the Father that squares our accounts with God. Is the Father the "Keeper of All Accounts"? Or is the Father not imaged best in the father portrayed in the story of the prodigal son? For if the younger son was prodigal or profligate with his inheritance, was not the father in turn prodigal or prodigious in his love? When the son returned home, this father did not seek to determine the right measure of punishment that would redress the offense and repair his wounded dignity. He did not look to settle the accounts, but rather set aside all such calculation for the excess of love he bore his son! So he threw a party that bent the nose of the older son out of joint; the father looked weak to the older son, whose resentment made him look bad. Is not the highly Anselmian story we have been telling ourselves in atonement theology completely at odds with the figure of the father in this parable told by Jesus? Is not the God of Jesus marked first and foremost by forgiveness? Are the dealings of the Father with the world governed by the principles of economics, of exchanging this for that, or by the nonprinciples, the uneconomics, of love?

HOSPITALITY

There is another point that I have yet to mention in which the excess of the gift in deconstruction makes contact with the text of the New Testament, and that is the attention that Derrida gave to "hospitality" in his later lectures and seminars. Hospitality is another of those words that resonate with the event—words that promise something that they do not quite deliver—representing another case of the "madness" of the messianic.[20] Once again, it all starts out very innocently. What hospitality means seems simple enough: welcoming the other, welcoming the coming of the other into the same, into my house, for example. But when in fact we actually offer hospitality, whom do we typically invite? Our friends, of course, those whose company we enjoy and from whom we can expect reciprocity (the circle of exchange), or else people whose favor we are currying. Either way, we welcome only those who serve our pleasure or our interests, which means tightening the circle of the same, not welcoming the other. One very good proof of this is that we depend on the discretion of those whom we invite not to broadcast it all over creation, lest others—the real others, in this case—discover that they were not invited. So there is a good deal of inhospitality built into our hospitality. We welcome those who are welcome to begin with, not those who are unwelcome. But if hospitality is what we say it is—that is, welcoming the other—then ought it not be a matter of welcoming those who are unwelcome? Should it not be extended beyond our neighbors to strangers? Beyond our friends to our enemies? Beyond the invited to the uninvited? In fact, is not the very act of invitation foreign to the idea of hospitality—genuine or unconditional hospitality—inasmuch as "inviting" is a selection process whereby one puts in place in advance a set of prior conditions under which the hospitality will be exercised? Would not the most radical or unconditional hospitality be a hospitality without invitation, a welcoming of the uninvited? Derrida insists on distinguishing between invitation and visitation: hospitality by invitation is always conditional, a compromised and programmed operation, as opposed to hospitality to the uninvited other—who pays us an unexpected visit—which is unconditional and unprogrammed.[21]

But what is to say that I will not be murdered in my bed by all this hospitality? How am I to distinguish between the guest and an outright enemy, who will do me and mine the worst violence? Am I not duty bound to protect myself and my family from such violence? Is this messianic madness not just madness plain and simple? Derrida's answer to these questions, which are valid questions, is that there would never be any way in principle to eliminate all the risk and still preserve the idea of hospitality.[22] There is even a trace of this undecidability in language itself. The word "hospitality" derives from *hostis* + *posse*. The word means, first, to have a certain "power" (*posse*) of disposition over the place of welcome: I cannot invite a guest to stay in someone else's home. So it means to make my home your home, remembering that it is my home, not yours, which is a crucial part of its tension. Second, "hospitality" means to welcome or admit the *hostis*, which in Latin means the stranger, who is the guest (of a "host" in a "hotel"); but a *hostis* is sometimes the stranger who is alien or "hostile." This very undecidability between friend or enemy is built into the language of hospitality, which leads Derrida to speak of "hostipitality." While Derrida is not encouraging reckless behavior, he is saying that the only way to eliminate the risk built into hospitality is to eliminate hospitality itself by screening the guests so carefully in advance that every trace of welcoming the other has been extinguished. There is always a risk in everything worthwhile. We are always put at risk whenever we welcome someone, just as we are put at risk whenever we love or trust or believe in someone, and the greater the love or hospitality, the greater the risk.

That means that there is always something slightly mad about hospitality, as indeed there is about the gift in all its forms, for what are forgiveness and hospitality if not versions of the gift, of an expenditure without return? But where indeed would one ever expect to find anything so mad? One suggestion I have is the New Testament, in which Jesus said: "When you give a luncheon or a dinner, do not invite your friends or your brothers or your relatives or rich neighbors, in case they may invite you in return, and you would be repaid. But when you give a banquet, invite the poor, the crippled, the lame, and the blind" (Luke 14:12–13).[23] This is followed by the story of the great banquet in which the invited guests make their excuses and fail to show up. Then the offended master rounds up his slaves and instructs them, "Go out at once into the streets and lanes of the town and bring in the poor, the crippled, the blind, and the lame." When told by the slaves that there is still room remaining at his tables, the master tells the slaves to round up even casual passersby and compel them to come in (Luke 14:15–24). In Matthew, the same parable is told except there the feast is a wedding (Matt. 22:1–14), which would surely make for one of the most extraordinary wedding receptions on record! These are parties as mad as any Hatter's party dreamed up by Lewis Carroll, mad with the madness of the Kingdom of God—and the madness of the gift in deconstruction.

That indeed is what is so interesting about the opening scene of Charles Sheldon's *In His Steps*, which very precisely portrays the demands of the madness of hospitality in Derrida's sense. The appearance of Jack Manning, the other one who comes knocking on the doors of the good parishioners of the First Church of Raymond, is a clear case of a visitation that is not an invitation. His appearance calls for welcoming the unwelcomed and receiving the uninvited, who show up at our door dressed in rags. We constantly pray and call for Jesus to come, but the question is—and this, we recall, is part of Derrida's analysis of the messianic—do we *really want* him to come, or is his true appearance always really *uninvited*? Is not Jesus showing up the last thing we really want to have—dressed in rags and laying claim to us in all his neediness, as one of the least among us? Or looking in at what we in the church are doing in his name? Rev. Maxwell's decision that the very essence of Christian life means the madness of turning one's life upside down in response to this visitation bears the mark, down even to the details, of what Derrida calls the messianic madness of hospitality. Christianity would be well advised to consider itself under the permanent promise/threat of just such a *visitation*—quite uninvited—by Jesus, who may at any time show up at the doors of our churches, requiring of us an accounting of what we have made of his memory or asking for a cup of cold water—or perhaps an increase in the minimum wage and basic health insurance.

LOVE

All along, whether we have been talking about justice or the gift, forgiveness or hospitality, the topic will have been love. Derrida once said, "Deconstruction . . . is not negative, even though it has often been interpreted as such despite all sorts of warnings. For me, it always accompanies an affirmative exigency, I would even say that it never proceeds, without love."[24] Deconstruction does not take a single step without love; it always follows "in the steps" of love, following love's call. What does it love? The impossible, the undeconstructible, what is coming, the event. Deconstruction is affirmation, the affirmation of the impossible, of the coming of the event. That is what I called in the preceding chapter the "real beyond the real," the hyper-real, which participates in the structure of the step/not beyond. Every time a "deconstructive critique" is undertaken, every time something is criticized as a fiction or an unjustifiable assumption, such critiques "are always advanced *in the name of the real*, of the irreducible reality of the real, not of the real as the objective, present, perceptible or intelligible *thing* (*res*), but of the real as the coming or the event of the other." But what, then, is the "real"? "The real is this nonnegative impossible, this im-possible coming or invention of the event whose thought is not an onto-phenomenology. It is a thought of the event (singularity of the other, in its unanticipatible coming, *hic et nunc*)."[25]

That is a particularly Parisian way of putting the following perfectly clear point. The "real" is precisely what eludes or withdraws from us whenever we think we have gotten it in our grips, whenever we imagine we see it (phenomenology) or can claim "there it is" (ontology) or think we can anticipate it (hermeneutic fore-structures). It is the element, the event, *in* experience that makes experience possible—because when we run into what is real, something is really happening—precisely by never being itself directly experienced. The "real" is the ultrareal in every *res*, the thing that slips away, the secret that will not yield to our advances or embrace, like an elusive lover whose play only deepens our desire. The real is what we are trying to make come true, even while it resists our comprehension, our grasp or grip: "Nothing is more 'realist,' in this sense, than a deconstruction. It is *ce qui arrive* (he who/that which arrives or happens)."[26]

What is more real, more nonsubjective, than that which resists the very grasp of the subject? Deconstruction is not realism, not because it is in love with illusion, but because it desires what is more than the real rather than settling for what is less, for the real is always deconstructible. What do we desire more than that which withdraws, that which is always already withdrawn and whose approach is always coming, always already coming, that which is never present but always drawing us on, drawing us out by withdrawing itself, soliciting and inviting us, luring us? That is what we love and pray for.

Then what is love (an ancient and venerable question!) and why does Derrida dare the formulation that deconstruction never proceeds without love? Is this not a little too edifying for a tough character like Derrida? Is his talk of love a sign that Derrida is getting soft? Is this deconstruction in its dotage? Not one bit. Remember what Jacques Lacan (who, to my knowledge, has never been accused of being too soft or smarmy) says: *les non-dupes errent*.[27] Those who think that they are too smart and too sophisticated to talk about love are just the ones to be misled. Or keep in mind Kierkegaard quoting St. Paul: love believes all things but love is not deceived! So let us hear Derrida out and not leave at intermission. On his accounting, the thing itself always slips away, which is what he, following Levinas, calls the "wholly other" that we love, what we want, in fact, to protect and "keep safe." In a manner that reminds us of nothing so much as "negative theology," he says that the thing itself is safe (*sauf*) if, and only if, it is safely secreted away, if what presents itself as the real is everything save (*sauf*) the thing itself, which safely slips away. That is what Levinas means when he says that love "is a relation with that which always slips away" (*une relation avec ce qui dérobe à jamais*).[28] For Derrida, in much the same sense as Levinas, love means to "surrender to the impossible," *se rendre*, to render oneself over to, to give up one's arms, and give oneself back to the impossible: "To surrender to the other, and this is the impossible, would amount to giving oneself over in going toward the other, to coming toward the other but without crossing the threshold, and to respecting, to loving even the invisibility that keeps the other inaccessible."[29] The "(loved) other," *l'autre (aimé)* must remain other, must be kept safe as other, and we must lay down our arms (*rendre les armes*) and surrender. By sacrificing or giving up the assault of "realism" on the world, we allow the thing itself to slip away—just to keep it safe and to show it our love—which is, of course, very close to Augustine saying that if you understand it, then what you understand is not God. If it is God, it eludes your grasp and always slips away.

It is, of course, not enough to keep hanging one award after another on deconstruction's wall—awards for justice, the gift, forgiveness, hospitality, and even love itself—for the question will always remain: what would love or justice or hospitality require, here and now, in the concrete? While insisting there will never be criteria that will enable us to program or "derive" an answer to this question, we have at least prepared the ground for getting down to cases by first getting a sense of what deconstruction is up to, by getting a feel for its spirit, which I have characterized as a spirit of prayers and tears, of madness and excess, for justice and the gift, and which on numerous issues presents a striking contemporary counterpart to the madness of the Kingdom of God and therefore does excellent service as its hermeneut. But before finally posing the question, "What would Jesus deconstruct?" as to its particulars, we have one more duty, which is to pause over the "Jesus" in this question and pursue the particular weight this name bears.

NOTES

1. I am also making use here of the sense of "event" in Gilles Deleuze, *The Logic of Sense*, trans. Mark Lester with Charles Stivale, ed. Constantin V. Boundas (New York: Columbia University Press, 1969).

2. Jacques Derrida, *Politics of Friendship*, trans. George Collins (New York: Verso, 1997), 1–25.

3. Johannes Baptist Metz, *Faith in History and Society*, trans. David Smith (New York: Seabury, 1980), 88–99.

4. Deleuze, *Logic of Sense*, 149.

5. Walter Benjamin, "The Concept of History," in *Walter Benjamin: Selected Writings, 1938–40*, vol. 4, ed. Michael Jennings (Cambridge, MA: Harvard University Press, 2003), 389–400.

6. Jacques Derrida, "As If It Were Possible, 'Within Such Limits' . . ." in *Negotiations: Interventions and Interviews: 1971–2001*, trans. Elizabeth Rottenberg (Stanford: Stanford University Press, 2002), 343–70.

7. Jacques Derrida, "Afterwards or, at least, less than a letter about a letter less," www.hydra.umn.edu/derrida/after2.html; "*Sauf le nom* (Post-Scriptum)," trans. John Leavey Jr., in *On the Name*, by Jacques Derrida, ed. Thomas Dutoit (Stanford, CA: Stanford University Press, 1995), 43.

8. See Mark Dooley's interview of Jacques Derrida, "The Becoming Possible of the Impossible," in *A Passion for the Impossible: John D. Caputo in Focus*, ed. Mark Dooley (Albany: State University of New York Press, 2003), 21–33, where Derrida uses this phrase as a marker for God. It also goes a long way toward marking off what we in the West mean by "religion," that is, as a certain covenant with the impossible, a point I explore in depth in *The Prayers and Tears of Jacques Derrida: Religion without Religion* (Bloomington: Indiana University Press, 1997).

9. Jacques Derrida, "The Force of Law: 'The Mystical Foundation of Authority,'" trans. Mary Quantaince, in *Deconstruction and the Possibility of Justice*, ed. Drucilla Cornell, Michel Rosenfeld, and David Gray Carlson (New York: Routledge, 1992), 3–69. All references to this essay appear in the text. I strongly recommend the first half of this essay, pp. 3–29, as one of the best ways into deconstruction that I know; the second half is a difficult interpretation of a strange essay by Walter Benjamin.

10. For purposes of economy I am omitting Derrida's earlier work, which only seems to look less friendly to theology. That omission is unforgivable, which on Derridean grounds invites your forgiveness. Let me say this much here and then beseech the reader who really cares to read further, especially *Of Grammatology*, corrected edition, trans. Gayatri Spivak (Baltimore: Johns Hopkins University Press, 1997), at least through p. 164. Derrida follows Ferdinand de Saussure's revolutionary notion of structural linguistics. Saussure pruned the study of language of the

classical and ornate terms of "ideas" in the "soul" (metaphysics) or in "consciousness" (psychology) that are "expressed" in "words" and correspond to "reality" and proposed a simpler, more streamlined and scientific approach. Think of Saussure (a Genevan) as being like John Calvin and John Knox in sixteenth-century Geneva coming up with a leaner, meaner version of Christianity! He used a scientific and functional model of "signifiers" as "arbitrary" (it does not matter whether you say *roi* or "king") and "differential" (just so long as we can discern the difference between *roi* and *loi* or "king" and "sing"), which work in virtue of the "space" (or differential) between them. A language is a coded string of signifiers constituted by their differences from one another, a point that can be seen intuitively by consulting a dictionary, in which words are defined by other words. A "speaker" is not some interior thinking thing who outwardly "expresses" already constituted "ideas" but a place where particular linguistic utterances (*parole*) called "events" occur—that is one of the sources of this word in French philosophy—in virtue of the rules of the linguistic system (*langue*). Personal consciousness is displaced and preceded by an impersonal differential system or "structure." Saussure, like Marx and Freud, thought it is an illusion to consider people as pure autonomous agents, which is criticized as "humanism," by which he did not mean "acting humanely." Think of "humanism" as a kind of linguistic Pelagianism, the heresy of thinking too much of pure human autonomy and not recognizing that human beings come into the world always already marked—not by inherited sin but by inherited social, linguistic, and historical systems or structures.

Derrida criticized Saussure on two points: (1) The privileging of speech over writing. While we learn to speak before we learn to write, on the strictly scientific terms set by Saussure, that is merely a psychological, not a structural, point. The one no less than the other is a form of arbitrary differential "spacing," without regard to whether it occurs in a written or a spoken medium. Speech is just a way of writing with air; an instance of "archi-writing" (or *différance*). (2) The "structure" (*langue*) is not a closed system but an open one. There is not a finite set of rules (langue) that precontains in principle every possible sentence that any given speaker could ever come up with (*parole*) that anticipates every possible "event." For example, no one can set an a priori limit to the metaphors that can be constructed or to the chance "events" that occur in puns, creative misuse, misunderstanding, and so on. Think of James Joyce or the Internet, which "disseminates" in a way that is very close to what Derrida means by linguistic "dissemination." Language is a system, not a Hegelian or "totalizing" system, but an open-ended one, like the World Wide Web. "Deconstruction" does not "destroy" something but loosens it up, opening it up to invention, novelty, and innovation, not absolute novelty, but the novelty that comes from innovating on the existing system. When Derrida emphasized the "unprogrammable"—and "undecidable," a word borrowed from mathematician Kurt Gödel that has been scandalously misrepresented—he meant this innovative open-endedness of the system.

Derrida summarized these two innovations under the neologism *différance*—spelled with an "a"—a graphic (written) misspelling that in French is phonically undetectable (that is, a homonym). In coining this word, Derrida was (1) indicating that language is constituted by spacing or differences; (2) contesting the privilege of speech and marking its graphic (or differential) character; (3) pointing how signifiers stand in for and so "defer" the presence of a thing; and (4) trying to perform in the concrete the inventiveness of language whose theory he was defending. *Différance* is a word that exhibits what words do, which is impossible, because if *différance* caught on, as it did, it would just become one more word in the language, not a word for what language does. So *différance* was an early example of *the* impossible.

Because of these criticisms of Saussure, Derrida is better described as a "poststructuralist," a term that has been drowned out by "postmodernism," which has a looser cultural significance going back to architecture. Derrida rejects both terms and embraces the "modern" Enlightenment project of social and political emancipation. Unlike Lyotard, he has no objection to a "metanarrative of emancipation" and advocates a New Enlightenment free of the illusions of the old one. Derrida went beyond his early interest in language—as well as in the phenomenology of Husserl, which would also need to be analyzed—to form a wider philosophical point of view. The criticism of the priority of speech over writing is ripe with social, political, and theological import—like the war between Judaism and Christianity. "The Jews" are people of the dead letter, of the written contract, legalists, an eye for an eye, a tooth for a tooth; but the Christians live with the breath of the spirit, by the word of honor, by love and the gift (see Shakespeare's *The Merchant of Venice*). The privilege of speech over writing is part of a more basic system as old as Western culture itself: life over death, soul over body, spirit over matter, eternity over time, man over woman, original over copy, human over animal, being over becoming, and so on.

Such hierarchies constitute what Derrida famously condensed into the phrase the "metaphysics of presence," a binary system privileging "presence" over "absence" (Derrida, *Of Grammatology*, 49). On this schema, men are full presence and women are defined as missing something. Against this, Derrida argued, first, that the superior member of a binary pair is subverted by its inferior member, the way speech turns out to be a form of "writing" (with air) or the "master" both depends on and becomes dependent on the "slave" in Hegel. That is what Derrida called "reversal." But second, both members of the pair are variations on a third that is prior to each (the movement of "displacement"). For example, neither speech nor writing should be privileged since both are a form of differential spacing (= *différance*) prior to both. Or again, in the New Testament, first a strategic reversal privileges the poor and warns woe to the rich, then displacement occurs because we are all children of God. Moreover, "ethical difference" has been a central part of the lexicon of deconstruction ever since 1964, when Derrida took up Levinas's "ethics of the other," belying the too simple schema of an "early" Derrida concerned with literature and a "later" Derrida concerned with ethics and politics. Derrida is not undermining all distinctions but showing that distinctions are better thought of differentially, as occupying different points along a continuous line, where elements of one thing blend and bleed into others, and demonstrating that the "black-and-white," either/or way of thinking in terms of binary oppositions—where one thing is simply the lack of the other—is invidious and loaded with traps. We cannot understand men or women if we do not first understand what is womanly about men and manly about women (reversal); both "man" and "woman" are traps that prevent the invention of new forms of gendered existence that shatter traditional stereotypes (displacement). That gives a church with a long history of patriarchy—not to mention unresolved tensions between "Christian and Jew" or "Christian and Muslim"—something to think about. For a start on all this, see Jacques Derrida, *Deconstruction in a Nutshell: A Conversation with Jacques Derrida*, edited with a commentary by John D. Caputo (New York: Fordham University Press, 1997), and James K. A. Smith, *Jacques Derrida: Live Theory* (New York: Continuum, 2005).

11. Theodore W. Jennings Jr., *Reading Derrida/Thinking Paul* (Stanford, CA: Stanford University Press, 2006).

12. See Richard Kearney, "Deconstruction and the Other," in *Debates in Continental Philosophy: Richard Kearney in Conversation with Contemporary Thinkers* (New York: Fordham University Press, 2004), 139–56. Kearney conducts a brilliant interview with Derrida, which is a superb place to start the reading of Derrida's work.

13. Jacques Derrida, *The Gift of Death*, trans. David Wills (Chicago: University of Chicago Press, 1995), chaps. 3–4.

14. The following discussion of the gift is based on Jacques Derrida, *Given Time, I: Counterfeit Money*, trans. Peggy Kamuf (Chicago: University of Chicago Press, 1991), chap. 1; see esp. pp. 6–7, 9–10, 30–31.

15. See the interesting exchange between Marion and Derrida in *God, the Gift, and Postmodernism*, ed. John D. Caputo and Michael J. Scanlon (Bloomington: Indiana University Press, 1999), 42–47, 54–78.

16. The sort of gift Derrida has in mind happens to teachers who influence students they no longer remember, by having said things they do not remember saying.

17. See Jacques Derrida, *Cosmopolitanism and Forgiveness*, trans. Mark Dooley and Michael Hughes (New York: Routledge, 1997).

18. For a good example of evangelical madness, see HBO's 2007 film *Longford*. It is a marvelous presentation of the true story of a deeply Christian man, Frank Pakenham, the seventh earl of Longford, whose belief in forgiveness ruined his public career when he took up the cause of child-killer Myra Hindley. Jim Broadbent is a superb Longford.

19. See E. P. Sanders, *Jesus and Judaism* (Philadelphia: Fortress, 1985) for a superb account of Jesus's position on forgiving sin, which I am following here.

20. Jacques Derrida, "Hostipitality," in *Acts of Religion*, ed. Gil Anidjar (New York: Routledge, 2002), 362.

21. Ibid.

22. Richard Kearney, Jacques Derrida, and I debated this point in Caputo and Scanlon, *God, the Gift, and Postmodernism*, 130–36.

23. Kierkegaard is especially protective of the paradox here: do not try to write this off as an "act of charity" with charity-house food. The

Scriptures are explicit: this is a "banquet" and everything is the best. See Howard Hong and Edna Hong, trans. and eds., *Kierkegaard's Writings*, vol. 16, *Works of Love* (Princeton, NJ: Princeton University Press, 1995), 81–84.

24. Jacques Derrida, *Points . . . Interviews, 1974–1994*, ed. Elisabeth Weber, trans. Peggy Kamuf et al. (Stanford: Stanford University Press, 1995), 83.

25. Jacques Derrida, "Hospitality, Justice, and Responsibility," in *Questioning Ethics: Contemporary Debates in Philosophy*, ed. Richard Kearney and Mark Dooley (New York: Routledge, 1999), 77–79.

26. Ibid.

27. *"Les non dupes errent," Séminaire oral du 14 Mai 1974, Seminaries de Jacques Lacan: 1973–74*, available online at http://perso.orange.fr/espace.freud/topos/psycha/psysem/nondup/nondup 13.htm.

28. Emmanuel Levinas, *Ethics and Infinity*, trans. Richard Cohen (Pittsburgh: Duquesne University Press, 1985), 67.

29. Derrida, *On the Name*, 74.

24
God, Perhaps: The Fear of One Small Word

Peut-être—il faut toujours dire peut-être pour . . .[1]
See, I am sending you out like sheep into the midst of wolves;
so be as wise as serpents and innocent as doves.
—Matthew 10:16

I dream of learning how to say "perhaps." I have the same dream, night after night, of a *tolle, lege* experience, in which I open a book—I cannot make out the title—always to the same sentence, "*Peut-être—il faut toujours dire peut-être pour . . .*" In the morning I cannot remember the rest of the sentence.

I am dreaming of a new species of theologians, of theologians to come, theologians of the "perhaps," a new society of friends of a dangerous "perhaps." I would like to think we are, perhaps, already a little like these theologians we see coming and that they will be a little like us.[2] But, of course, since we cannot see them coming and do not know what they will be like, we can only call, "come."

"PERHAPS"

There is every reason for philosophers and theologians to fear this one small word, "perhaps."[3] It seems the very antithesis of what we want from them. We expect philosophers and theologians to help us decide, but "perhaps" is the language of indecision and of the suspension of judgment. We expect knowledge and precision from philosophy but "perhaps" is vague and evasive, an admission that we just don't know. We expect faith from the theologians but "perhaps" means we are uncertain, skeptical, too timid to say anything definite. "Perhaps" is the abdication of faith, decision, ethics, judgment and knowledge, of philosophy and theology, a retreat to the safety of the indecisive and uncommitted. "Perhaps" is the motto of the aesthete in *Either/Or*: if you do it, you will regret it; if you don't do it, you will regret it. So, play it safe and stay out of it.[4]

Unless, perhaps, there is "another experience of the perhaps."[5] Unless "perhaps" has another role and belongs to another order, otherwise than the business as usual of philosophy and theology, otherwise than logic, ontologic, and onto-theo-logic.[6] That is the premise of the present study. I pursue the possibility that "perhaps" belongs to another "regime" than that of mere opinion and hazy indecision,[7] that it enjoys an "irreducible modality" all its own. I am in search of a "perhaps" that is not a category of logic but proves to be of a more subtle disposition, one uniquely accommodated to address the "event," one that is indeed "the only *possible* thought of the event."[8]

"See, I am sending you out like sheep into the midst of wolves; so be as wise as serpents and innocent as doves" (Matt. 10:16).

In an undertaking as uncertain as this, I call upon the animals of Jesus to be my companions. Animal that I am, I am following (*je suis*) an alternate zoology, a zoo-theological order of beasts who distrust sovereigns that is proposed by Jesus and Derrida,[9] and my candidate for such a strange beast is "perhaps." Accordingly, my advocacy of the weak force of "perhaps" must be as innocent as a dove and as shrewd and sly as a snake, able to brave the wolves of philosophy and theology and their love of monarchy and sovereignty and principial order. I am issuing a call for a new species of theologians, weak theologians who must be, just as Jesus says, as wise, shrewd, and prudent as serpents, the wise ones (*phronimoi*) of the "perhaps"—even as they must be as harmless (*akeraioi*) as the doves. This is a combination so odd as even to merit a pink "perhaps" from the Jesus Seminar, which is exceedingly high praise for the seminar. Even the Jesus Seminar is forced to admit that this is such a strange saying that Jesus might have actually said it—perhaps, in the pink, almost ruby rubric red.

The "perhaps" of which I speak here does not belong to the "strong" or sovereign order of presence, power, principle, essence, actuality, knowledge, or belief. The "perhaps," "powerless in its very power," does not belong to the "dominant thinking about the possible in philosophy."[10] "Perhaps" does not mean the onto-possible, the future present, where it is only a matter of time until it rolls around at some later date. It does not belong to the system of categories organized around the binary pairing of necessary and contingent, presence and absence, being and non-being, knowledge and ignorance, belief and unbelief, certainty and uncertainty, actuality and potentiality, substance and accident, theism and atheism. Nor is this "perhaps" a simple compromise between these binaries, a safe middle ground that would maintain a strategic neutrality while still remaining within that order. It belongs to a different register altogether, not the presential order of ontology but a weaker, more dovelike order, what Derrida amusingly (but he is dead serious) calls the order of "hauntology," which means the order of the event which haunts ontology.[11] The event spooks the black-or-white to-be-or-not-to-be of metaphysics and so it unnerves the onto-theologians. The haunting specter of "perhaps" provokes a more radical opening in the present.[12] It prevents the present from closing down upon itself, from being identical with itself, leaving it structurally exposed to the future, not the future present but the very structure of the to-come (*à venir*). The event (*événement*) is the advent of what is coming, the coming (*venir*) of what we cannot see coming (*voir venir*), the coming of the future (*l'avenir*), which always comes as a surprise and includes the best and the worst.[13] "Perhaps" twists free (sly as a serpent) from the grip of thinking in terms of the power of the actual, of the prestige of the present, and opens thinking to the weak force of the to-come. I hold my ground on the groundless ground of "perhaps" in order to stay alive to the chance of the event.

"Perhaps" is the only way to say yes to the future.[14] Yes, yes, perhaps. Yes, yes, to the "perhaps." That is an act of faith (*foi*) that exceeds the simple binarity of belief (*croyance*) and unbelief, an affirmation more elusive than any positive position, deeper than any positively posited belief. "Perhaps" is thus a non-knowing that exceeds simple ignorance as faith exceeds simple blindness, because it is responding to what solicits us from afar, sensing what might be coming, desiring something beyond desire. The weak force of "perhaps" is more resolute than any simple credo, a knight of faith more unflinching than any firm belief, more ready for the ordeal, for the test. "Perhaps" is not a simple indecision between presence and absence but an exposure to the promise of what is neither present nor absent. "Perhaps" is not the safety of indecision but a radical risk, for nothing guarantees that things will turn out well, that what is coming will not be a disaster. "Perhaps" is not paralysis but the fluid milieu of undecidability in which every radical decision is made, by which I mean a decision that is not merely programmed or dictated by the circumstances.

"Perhaps" is not a simple disinterest but a word of desire for something, I know not what, something I desire with a "desire beyond desire."[15] "Perhaps" does not mean the diffidence of maybe-maybe-not but the hope harbored in what happens. Perhaps, I hope, perchance, there is a chance, a ghost of a chance, in what is happening.

"Perhaps" is not to be confused with the "possible" as the counter-part of the actual, with a merely logical possibility or empirical unpredictability.[16] To think "perhaps" is to follow the tracks of a more radical possibilizing, of the weak force of a more unpredictable implausible chance that comes quietly on the wings of a dove. To say "perhaps" is to expose ourselves to a possibility that for all the world seems impossible, that may also turn out to be a disaster. To say "perhaps" is to abandon the shield of safety provided by power, presence, principle, and predictability, by actuality and the real. "Perhaps" risks exposure to a spooky, irreal, inexistent insistence, where insistence exceeds existence and existence can never catch up to what insists.

"Perhaps" gives us access to something that eludes the rule of knowledge as certainty and method because it belongs to another register. "Perhaps" is a principle without principle, an anarchic and unmonarchical *arche*, issuing in an odd sort of affirmative, grammatological and "aphoristic energy."[17] It is not a failed way to know but another way to gain access to what is otherwise than knowledge, to what comes otherwise than by knowing. The un-certainty of "perhaps" does not constitute a defect, a failure to attain certainty, but a release from the rule of the certain, an emancipation from the block that certainty throws up against thinking or desiring otherwise. "Perhaps" galvanizes another kind of thinking. "Perhaps" does not signify a simple lack of purpose but a way to stay on the tracks of something unknown, something structurally to come. "Perhaps" is a surmise of the promise, a relation without relation with what is given only as a promise, given while held back. "Perhaps" bends in the winds of what insists without existence, of what withdraws from presence, pointing like the arrow of a weathervane in the direction of the promise, of the flickering possibility of what neither is nor is not. "Perhaps" shelters things from the harsh light of the concept or the program that prevents the event. Instead of constituting a failure of exact knowledge or of determinate decision, "perhaps" represents a greater rigor and a more resolute adhering to what solicits us, a refusal to allow the prima facie claims of the present to take hold, a refusal to be taken in by an accident of birth. Its weakened vision makes for a more resolute listening and heightened attentiveness, which keeps on the tracks of an ever-vanishing trace.

Because it seeks access to the inaccessible, to the unprogrammable, to the uncertain, to the "event," "perhaps" affirms a more obscure and radical faith (*foi*) not a well-defined and positive belief (*croyance*).[18] The positionality of a positive belief shuts down the open-endedness of the affirmation of the future, provoking the formation of schools, camps, cabals, manifestos, doxa, orthodoxies, heresiologies, excommunicative communities, all closed circles, whose seeming decisiveness is in fact a way of avoiding responsibility, in full flight from a deeper and more unnerving responsibility, all for fear of one small word. "Perhaps" does not refuse to make a leap of faith. It recognizes that what passes for a "leap of faith" in "orthodoxy" is an assertion, an assertiveness, that is trying to make contact with the certain, vainly trying to contract a more abysmal affirmation into a creedal assent. Creeds dissimulate a more disconcerting leap, a more disseminated and open-ended faith in something insistent yet indiscernible. The faithful are of little faith; they fear the faith of this small word "perhaps," the faithful being an assembly of believers in beliefs whose contingency they do not quite confront. "Perhaps" harbors a deeper faith while looking for all the world like doubt, like a lamb amid wolves.

"Perhaps" sounds like the soul of indecision, like a lame excuse for an answer, a refusal to take a stand, the safest course possible. I, on the other hand, think it is risky business, a venture into the abyss, a wild and disproportionate risk, exposing us to an excess, opening us to the best while exposing us to the worst, deprived of the mighty armor of metaphysics. "Perhaps" sounds like mere propositional indecisiveness, maybe this or maybe that, who knows which? But I am interested not in the propositional but the expositional, not in what we propose but in that to which we are exposed, in what poses itself before us, imposes itself upon us, posing and presupposing a possibility that leaves us groping for words.

"Perhaps" is not a refusal to engage with reality but a response to the solicitation of the real beyond the real, not the real as the *res*, present and objective, but the real as the insistence of the ultra-real or hyper-real that insinuates itself into what passes itself off for reality.[19] "Perhaps" belongs not to the logic of the present but to the hyperlogic of the *super, epekeina, hyper, über, au-delà.*[20] "Perhaps" unhinges us from the real, making the impossible possible. "Perhaps" is not a refusal to answer but the depths of responsibility, a recognition of the extent to which the question exceeds us and puts us in question. "Perhaps" opens a door that is (perhaps) better kept shut, raises a possibility we would prefer not to think about, opens a question we would rather keep closed, makes a motion that the powers that be want to table.

"Perhaps" sounds like it has renounced all truth and has consigned itself to a regime of opinion. But in truth the society of the friends of "perhaps" is also the society of the true friends of truth, not because they are *in* the truth, which means inside the secure confines of certainty and dogma, but in the sense of befriending it, seeking it, loving it, exposing themselves to its unforeseeable and dangerous coming, to the risk of the "perhaps." They do not claim to be the truth but to be its friends. These friends of truth are "anchorites," solitaries, outside the commonly received opinions of the community, which means they are dreaming of a community without community.[21]

"Perhaps" sounds neutral, like an anemic inability to affirm or deny, whereas in truth it represents what Keats called a "negative capability," an ability to sustain uncertainty and to venture into the unknown.[22] "Perhaps" sustains our openness to the obscurity of what is going on beneath the surface of what is happening. Those who insist on certainty seize upon the actual and close off an obscure but fertile event. They lack the negative capability of thinking "perhaps not."

The decisiveness of "is" and "is not" keeps the real in check, sweeping the border of the present for illegal entrants, putting a lid on actuality, the fragility and rigidity of which is exposed by "perhaps." "Perhaps" is not a retreat to subjectivity or to some safe inner sanctum in which we are relieved of the need for commitment. It is an unnerving relationship to the real, to the real beyond the real, to the open-endedness of the real. "Perhaps" is attuned to what Heidegger called the quiet power of the possible, where the power of the possible consists in the power of the impossible. "Perhaps" does not withdraw but reaches out; it does not refuse the real but reaches out to its outer limit, to the possibility of the impossible, opening itself to the coming of something, I know not what. *Je ne sais quoi. Il faut croire.*[23]

"Perhaps" is not cowardice compared to the "courage to be" (Tillich), but the courage required for what Nietzsche calls the "dangerous" perhaps, the courage for the open-ended, for the fear and trembling before the uncontainable, for the unforeseeable, a way to conquer our ontological agoraphobia, our "khora-phobia." "Perhaps" is not an empty wish or idle fantasy that takes a shortcut that skips the hard work of reality, but a desire beyond desire for something coming, for something that I cannot see coming. "Perhaps" says it is possible when it is impossible, believes when it is incredible, still hopes even after hope is lost. "Perhaps" is a steely, indefatigable, resolute openness to what seems to have been closed off—while looking for all the world like a sleepy indifference. Perhaps is sly as a serpent, innocent as a dove, a lamb among wolves.

GOD, PERHAPS

One clue to what is going on in the present study is as follows: "'Perhaps'—one must (*il faut*) always say *perhaps* for God. There is a future for God and there is no God except to the degree that some event is possible which, as event, exceeds calculation, rules, program, anticipations, and so forth. God, as the experience of absolute alterity, is unpresentable, but God is the chance of the event and the condition of history."[24] One must, it is absolutely necessary, always say "perhaps" for God: God, perhaps (*peut-être*). Whenever and wherever there is a chance for the event, that is God, perhaps. God can happen anywhere. But history has no future, and God has no future; indeed there is no history or God at all, unless there is a chance for the event. If there is a chance for the event, if the event can happen anywhere, that is God, perhaps. If there is a chance for history, that is God, perhaps.

As the observant reader may have noticed, I have (as is my wont) begun with the words of Jacques Derrida. Perhaps. I admit to having introduced a slight alteration in the text (sly as a snake), a small point, really (harmless as a dove): I have substituted "God" where Derrida said "justice." I assume full responsibility for such audacity. I do not want to blame Derrida for everything I do in this game of jacks. I take it upon myself to show that God, like justice, has to do with a dangerous "perhaps," fully conscious that this will disconcert the philosophers and theologians among my readers. The philosophers want autonomy, not subservience to God, and theologians want the surety of being saved, not "perhaps." So what good can "God, perhaps" do for either cause?

My claim is that a genuine grammar of assent is found in a grammatology of "perhaps," which is the best suited to meet the needs of a coming theology, of a theology of the event, that is, of a weak theology that comes on the wings of doves. Theology in the strong standard version belongs to the sovereign order of power and presence and favors a grammar of great omni-nouns and hyper-verbs. It strides confidently within the assured and strident categories of theism and atheism, belief and unbelief, existence and nonexistence, existence and hyper-existence, nature and super-nature, presence and super-presence, visible and invisible, changing and unchanging, absolute and relative, true and false. Weak theology, on the other, is content with a little adverb like "perhaps," which can do no more than interrupt or intercept, deflect or modify other, more prestigious substantive and verbal things, introducing modalities, conditions, degrees, and exceptions, focusing on the "how," not the "what," on little prepositions, not big propositions. Weak theology operates in the spooky, shadowy order of the event, where the event is best addressed, and perhaps only addressed, in the fluctuating shadows and spectral grammar of "perhaps." "Perhaps" provides the grammar of an archi-assent, the grammatology of faith in the event, reinventing theology in the register of a theo-grammatology. "Perhaps" is the watchword of the theologians to come, a messianic sign of their coming.

When I say "God, perhaps" I am proposing the subject matter of a weak theology but I am not advocating agnostic indecisiveness. "Perhaps" is indeed a Janus head, but it is not an attempt to have it both ways, to escape between the horns, to split the difference, to sit on the fence. On the one hand, I am trying to open thinking and practice to God, to the event that is playing itself out under the name of God, to what we desire in and under that name, to the truth of God. I am taking the name of God seriously. I am praying, to God, which sends the philosophers rushing for the exits. I am trying to expose, or to maintain our exposure, or to give a word to our inescapable exposure, to the insistent claim that is made upon us in that name.

But, on the other hand, in saying "perhaps," I am not allowing the claim made by the event to be contracted to that name, to be identified with that name, to be "identified" as "God." At the point at which the event is identified, it is undermined. I am suspending the name (of) "God" in scare quotes. That sends the (strong) theologians heading for the exits, because they are looking for something to save them, to keep them safe. They are not afraid of sheep or doves, but they have a terrible fear of wolves and snakes. Once I say I know the name of the event, once I can say, this is God, the event is God, then the event ceases to be an event and becomes something that I have added to my repertoire, brought within the horizon of my experience, knowledge, belief, identification, and expectation, whereas the event is precisely what always and already, structurally, exceeds my horizons. What I mean by the event is the surprise, what literally over-takes me, shattering my horizon of expectation. God is *a* name for the event, but the very idea of an event prevents us from saying the event *is* God, because the very idea of the event is that I cannot see it coming. For the event, names are always lacking, even the name of God. But that is not because the event is a *hyperousios*, the unnamable hyperpresence of mystical theology, with which deconstruction is sometimes confused, but because the event is still coming, is structurally to-come, *à venir*, while I am always saying, praying "come," *viens*. That is the very idea of a religion without religion, as opposed to the strong religion that reposes on the power of principles and propositions, the prestige of proper names, of properly sacred names, of sacred proper names found in sacred books.

The event that is harbored within the name of "God" does not belong to experience in the usual phenomenological or Kantian sense of the sphere of possible experience, which is the order of presence, and that is because it lies on the border of that experience, slyly eluding its horizon of expectation, which it is capable of shattering. To shatter the horizon of possible experience is to be impossible, to belong to an impossible experience, to belong to an experience of "the" impossible. That in turn introduces a new or second sense of experience, the experience proper to the event, whose grammar is the grammar of the "perhaps," which does not refer to the merely possible but to the possibility of the impossible. The second sense moves from the impossibility of experience to the experience of the impossible. The possibility of the impossible is one of God's most venerable biblical names, the proper referent, if there is such a thing, of "perhaps," maybe even of God, perhaps.

"Perhaps" provides not the logic but the grammatologic of the "weakness of God," where the might of God Almighty turns out to be the subjunctive might of "maybe" or "might be," whose reach extends all the way to the impossible.[25] "Perhaps" provides a grammatical, rhetorical, poetic, strategic, syntactic, and semantic alternative to the militant logic of omnipotence, to the imperial logic of onto-logic and theo-logic. Onto-theologic trades in the hard and fast, the dogmatic, the decisive scission that cuts off being from non-being, which occludes the may-being of "perhaps." "Perhaps" is the weak force of a possibility (of the impossible) not the strong force of actuality, the weakness of a solicitation not the strength of a command, the faintness of a suggestion not the power of an imperative, the fragility of a call not the audacity of an order. The discursive form that can accommodate itself to "perhaps" is not a logic but a "poetics," so a grammatology is a poetics of "perhaps." "Perhaps" is like a sheep among wolves, or like a dove charged with keeping the low profile of a snake.

To gain some sense of what I mean when I say "God, perhaps," let us contrast it with what it could quite legitimately mean within classical ("strong") theology. There saying "perhaps" of God is a function of the sovereignty of God, of the unlimited possibilities of Almighty God, all that the Almighty is able to do, all the Almighty may be, which is quite a lot, considering that with God nothing is impossible. If God is the God who is, who already is all that God is able to be, the plenitude of being, the hyper-plenitude of overflowing being, then God will always be God. The "I am who am" (Exod. 3:14) as it is understood in medieval theology will provide metaphysical support for the biblical God who will always be faithful to his people. The lion of Athens can lay down with the lamb of Jerusalem, as the rock of ages, the immutable, unshakeable warrantor of a promise. The biblical God who always will be there for us in the future is the God who always was and always is there in the first place, *per omnia saecula saeculorum*. God is the God who will be just because God is the God Who Is, in the classical and rather Greek, or Greco-Latin terms of Aquinas, *ipsum esse per se subsistens*. God is now, always was and always will be, and will always be faithful to his promises, his word, can always ultimately be counted upon in the future, and in so doing and so being God brings peace to our hearts.[26]

But when I say "God, perhaps," I am inscribing the Tetragrammaton in a general grammatology, inscribing God in spacing and timing *without remainder.* I am signing on to the futural, to becoming, while confessing that this becoming is not underwritten by some divine steadfastness or providential warranty, as it is in Hegel. My "perhaps" is not an appositional appendix, an appresentation added to a prior presence. My "perhaps," "maybe," *peut-être* cuts deeply into the name of God so much that the name (of) "God" takes place in the very element of the *peut-être* itself, of the "event" of the promise, which is no less a threat, of the maybe, which is also a maybe not. We are not the least assured that God will be there, not the least assured that God may be at all, not the least assured that the "name" of God offers anything more than a hope, a prayer, a faith in something coming, something I know not what, a hope that may turn out in fact to be a nightmare, a monster, which happens time and time again when people act "in the name of God."

The name of God is the name of a hope, which means of a promise/threat that also licenses murder. If we made a list of all the names in the name of which murder is committed, the name of God would, perhaps, head the list, in close competition with "truth" and "justice." Every promise is inscribed in *khora*, in the groundless ground of the trace, of the play of differences, of spacing-and-timing. That means that every promise is structurally inhabited by a threat. We rely upon promises in the face of a threat even as a threat can be posed only if something is promised, and "perhaps" means there is no guarantee about how things will turn out. In face of *khora* we can only hope against hope, since it is only when things are impossible that real hope is possible. Then what? Then we must, as Derrida says, go where we cannot go; know that the gift is impossible, then *give.* That means that the name of God is the name of a call in which we are called upon to respond, which we may or may not do, whether or not we think there is anyone or anything out there making such a call. The name of God is the name of a deed, of what is to be done, something that may or may not be done, something that demands to be done with or without God, something that may be done under other names, something structurally to-come where what happens rests upon our response and may end up being a disaster.

The poetics of "perhaps," of the possibility of the im/possible, implies that the conditions under which we trust also undermine our trust, so that trust is trust in a radical "perhaps," a God who may or may not be, who may or may not be trusted, which is after all what "perhaps" must surely mean, even as a trust in what is completely trustworthy is little or no trust at all but a surety. *Khora* is nothing human but neither is it a monster, and this because "she" does not belong to the order of presence, but serves only as a nickname for the spacing of *différance*, the play of traces within which anything—void or plenum, fear or hope, good or evil, ground or abyss, monster or angel—is inscribed. Without *khora* there is no "perhaps," no maybe/maybe not—and hence, to refer back to ethics, no risk in opening the door to a stranger. *Khora* is not a monster, not a thing at all, good or bad, but the spacing of *peut-être*, the slash between maybe/maybe not, the distance between these binaries, which means these binaries are provisional inscriptions, contingent unities of meaning, constitutable and substitutable in *différance*.[27] Our hopes and fears are linked to each other, and neither the one nor the other can break loose from its radical hermeneutic concatenation with the other, break free, break out into the open and declare itself triumphant. We pray and weep, hope and fear, within the play of traces, hoping against hope, which is, I would say, the very being of may-being, the very *être* of the *peut-être* harbored in and by the name of God. When I say "God, perhaps," this God is not receiving secret funding from the God Who Is.

I have in mind the unconventional idea that God, like Zarathustra's great star, is not really and truly God without us, that the insistence of God requires our existence and so depends on us. The divine life is incarnated in us, and God's weakness requires that we do all the heavy lifting. God insists, while we exist. I treat the name of God as the name of an inexistence, an insistence, a call that is visited upon us and demands our response, so that God and the divine omnipotence are more radically emptied into the world. "God, perhaps" means that the name of God is the name of the chance of the event, one of the names, one of the events, which are innumerable and impossible.

The name (of) "God" harbors the omnipresent beckoning of the "perhaps," like a spirit that insists and insinuates itself into everything, that breathes where it will, the possibility of the impossibility that inheres in still and small things. God does not exist; God is a spirit that calls, a spirit that can happen anywhere and haunts everything, insistently. I have found it necessary to deny existence in order to make room for insistence. I have found it necessary to deny omnipotence in order to make room for an omni-potentializing, to make the way clear for an omni-possibilizing, or impossibilizing, an insistent "perhaps" that insinuates itself in all things, great and small. I have found it necessary to deny omnipotence in order to re-invent the omnipresence of an omni-"perhaps."

Far from being a full-scale retreat into the safety of agnosticism, "God, perhaps" names a new theology with the courage of an eerie non-conviction, that calls for a new species of theologians, for venturers upon the turbulent seas of a perilous "perhaps," equipped only with the thinnest of protection, like a sheep amid wolves, theologians of risk, whose subject matter is the irreducible danger of life. This is all contracted in the small word "perhaps," which inspires fear even among sovereigns, for fear that the being of God lies in may-being.[28]

INSISTENCE AND EXISTENCE

When I speak of the "insistence of God" I mean that God does not exist or subsist but that God insists, while it is the world that exists. God's insistence requires God's inexistence. The world's existence requires God's insistence. The name of God is the name of an insistent call or solicitation that is visited upon the world, and whether God comes to exist depends upon whether we resist or assist this insistence. The insistence of God means that God insists upon existing. If I say that God's essence lies in God's insistence, I mean that while metaphysics turns on the distinction between essence and existence, what I am calling here a "poetics" of the "perhaps" turns on the distinction between insistence and existence. God is an insistent claim or provocation, while the business of existence is up to us—existence here meaning response or responding, assuming responsibility to convert what is being called for in the name of God into a deed. So where metaphysics theorizes the distinction between of essence and existence, a poetics describes the "chiasm," the "intertwining," of God's insistence with our existence.[29]

In a chiasm, each depends upon the other, neither one without the other. God needs us to be God, and we need God to be human. The insistence of God needs us for strength, even as we draw strength from God's weakness. God's insistence needs our existence to make any difference. Our existence needs God's insistence in order to have a difference to make. God comes to exist in our response; our deeds constitute the "effects" the name of God has in the world. But we should be very careful not to attach any metaphysical baggage to such talk or confuse ourselves with God. A theology of the event is not supposed to end up in pantheism or reinventing "panentheism," which is a fetching idea and close to my heart, but in the end a bit too far-fetched, still more metaphysics. A theology of the event is instead a poetics, a post- or quasi-phenomenological undertaking trying to avoid the traps and trappings of metaphysics. A poetics that takes up the name of God is a theopoetics. On the whole it is better just to say that God insists and to leave the existing to us, where the question of "existing" is a matter of human responsibility. The chiasm shows up in expressions like "the people of God," but God is God and people are people. God insists; people exist.

But if God is "weak," how can God be insistent? If the insistence of God is so insistent, why speak of the insistence of "God, perhaps?" What is the link between "insistence" and "perhaps?" Is not "perhaps" the very lack of insistence? Perhaps what? Why "perhaps?" I have several things in mind in saying "God, perhaps" when I speak of the insistence of God, but for a start I single out only the three most important. The first has to do with insistence itself—something is calling, or rather something is getting itself called, in and under the name of God, of "God—perhaps," inasmuch as the caller in the call is structurally inaccessible, unidentifiable.[30] It may not be God. It belongs to the very nature of responsibility that the caller of the call is unknowable, unnamable. That is the only way to assume real responsibility. Once we claim to know "this is God," "this is the Law," "this is Nature," then we can always plead that we are just obeying orders, just doing our duty, and thereby avoid responsibility. The call, I will say here, always takes place in the middle voice, meaning we go too far if we presume to identify the caller. If we are called upon in a radical way, we don't get to call out the caller.

The second reason I am saying "God, perhaps" has to do with existence, since it is altogether possible that what is insisted upon will be resisted; a solicitation can be ignored, and a call can go unanswered. The call is after all only a call and as such structurally "weak." It has the force without force of "justice," not the real force of law; there are no police to enforce it. The response is up to us and we may, perhaps, respond, which means that perhaps we may not. God may, perhaps, make a difference. Thirdly, when the insistence of God is translated into existence and made to make a difference, the difference God makes may, perhaps, be a disaster. In the case of the name of God, justice may flow like water over the land or perhaps what will flow will be the blood of injustice, the worst violence, which happens time and again with names like "God." The name of God, like "justice" or "love," is a high-velocity word, a speeding projectile. As such it elicits the best and the worst, and so it is invoked for better or for worse.

"Perhaps" spooks everything insisting and existing. "Perhaps" haunts everything inside and outside "theology" or "philosophy," ethics and politics—the list goes on. That is why "perhaps" is indissolubly linked with prayer, which emerges from the tension between the insistence or inexistence of God and existence. In a certain sense, I keep writing one book after another about prayer, which seems to be my only topic. The insistence of God refers to the insistence with which God calls upon us, while prayer means calling upon a God who calls. The insistence of God means that the being (*l'être*) of God is may-being (*peut-être*), the "maybe" or "perhaps" of an ambiguous promise/threat, which may be leading us into grace or into the worst evil, and prayer means we are trying to hang on. I will say more about prayer below, but here at the start let me warn the reader that when

I use the word "prayer," this has nothing to do with the pieties of religion. Indeed I fear it will bring small comfort to the theologians of piety, peace, and quiet. I am thinking of expressions like "being left without a prayer," meaning we have no chance, the odds are long, the chance is slim, the situation is dangerous and impossible. I am thinking of "hanging on by a prayer," of someone reduced to pleading, praying, which is the root of the word in Latin, *precari,* to plead, to beg, to entreat. The English word "precarious" means what is "obtained by entreaty, hence uncertain." To "serve at the pleasure" of a leader means one's position is literally "precarious," dependent on the favor of the leader, which is why those who profess unorthodox things that displease the leader need "tenure," from *tenere,* "holding on" (for dear life, by a prayer).

As a matter of grammar, grammatology, and weak theology, they only pray whose situation is precarious, who are surrounded on all sides by uncertainty, who are at the mercy of events, at the mercy of "perhaps"—and who is not? Our physical life is precarious, at the mercy of the natural elements that sometimes rise up against us and upon whose favor we depend. Our lives are lived at the pleasure of a little planet which has provided us with a favorable environment, unless or until it does not. Events are merciful, perhaps, *merci,* unless they are not, which means we all live lives of prayer, praying for mercy, living off their promise, fretful of their threat, dependent upon their good graces—even if we never go near a house of prayer. They pray who are in an uncertain situation—and who is not?—unable to see what is coming, hounded by the wolves of unforeseeable forces, praying for the grace of an event. They pray who appreciate the precariousness of life, the fragility of what we love or desire, which is made all the more precious by its precariousness. In the most rigorous linguistic and etymological sense of the word, the only sensible response to being surrounded by wolves is to pray for an event, for the grace of an event, for an event of grace. When you pray, be as harmless as a dove and as wise as a serpent. Prayer requires a *phronimos*—this is Matthew's word—of the *peut-être,* which is Derrida's word. Praying in a precarious situation is all a basic matter of phenomenology and etymology and it does not necessarily have anything to do with theology. The theologians arrive at a scene that has already been constituted in human experience. Prayer is older than theology and it is not the private property of the long robes who make a profitable living out of saying "Lord, Lord." My interest in theology stems from an interest in something much older than theology, older than the hoariest theologian, something that can do with or without theology, and would be at best the business of a new species of theologians.

I would understand it if, at this point, the orthodox theologians feel rejected, if they get up and leave, before my lecture has even started, rejecting out of hand the very idea that this is theology at all. I share their suspicion. Indeed, such a suspicion of what I am doing is the condition under which I do it, under which I conduct what I am calling a "radical" theology. I would publish this book under protest if the orthodox theologians did not protest it. If this "theology" were not suspect, if it did not threaten a walkout by the pious, I would not be associated with it. What I call theology is possible only under the condition that it might not—perhaps—be theology, that it might be impossible for it to be theology, that it might be impossible, plain and simple. If it could sail smoothly and identifiably, without running up against the impossible, it would not be what I am talking about. So I can only pray for the patience of the orthodox. But they are right, and I readily admit it, the Bible would never have broken all the records for book sales if Exodus 3:14 read, "I am, perhaps, who I am, but then again I might not be. It might turn out that, after all, I am not who I say I am, or that I am not who you think I am."

The insistence of God in a thin theology is not for the risk-averse—but then again how can the risk-averse pray? As with God, so with theology, so with prayer: one must always remember to say "perhaps." The fortunes of one are tied to the others, all chiasmically intertwined. When Derrida started talking about "the possibility of the impossible" there must have been echoes of the Bible they made him read as a child bouncing around in his head.[31] The impossible just might be possible, perhaps. Is that not our constant prayer? Is that not why we pray? Is there any other reason to pray? Is that not God, perhaps? Is that not the sort of thing that is always going on with "God," in one way or the other, what is happening in the name (of) "God," what is always being insisted upon in and by this name? That is my question, my thesis, my hypothesis, my presupposition, my concern, my faith, my wager, my prayer.

Think of this book as a prayer, a prayer to be faithful to God, perhaps, where "perhaps" is the element of prayer. I believe in prayer. I am a man of prayer. I am praying all the time. I am dead serious about this, but I cannot conceal a smile as I say it.[32] I am always praying and weeping, but I am also smiling throughout, laughing through my tears. I am saying this, I shamelessly admit it, in part to win over the pious, to make peace with them and offer them something "edifying," at the sound of which the theologians of peace and piety will bow their heads in devout assent, as is their wont whenever someone says, "let us pray." But I will not conceal the fact that my prayer is slightly impious, for I admit I am saying that to pray is to pray to God, perhaps, which is the part I fear will empty the pews. I am praying for the chance of an event, for the possibility of the impossible. Pray I say, pray to God, perhaps, but pray, with or without God, with or without religion, with or without a book of prayer, because prayer is for the precariousness, and who among us is not in a precarious situation? I invoke prayer and grace and the name of God, all of which is highly reassuring to the pious, but I also fear I am going to lose their confidence. No matter; I must take the risk. I can do no other. For it is always necessary to say "perhaps" when it comes to God, to let a certain cloud of unknowing and uncertainty settle over sacred names, like grace and prayer, theology and God, over all the divine names, omni-names too powerful and intimidating to be trusted by doves and sheep.

There is no God except insofar there is a chance of an event, which we cannot see coming, the unforeseeable come-what-may which may be the grace of a new beginning. Unless it is a disaster. There may be grace or there may be dragons and monsters. The "may be" is the problem. God, who is the possibility of the impossible, may happen anywhere, may arrive unannounced, a knock on the door in the middle of the night, and that may be trouble. No one, especially not God, is guaranteeing anything. It's not in his nature! It may be in his "essence," which is a dogma of metaphysics, but it is not in his "insistence," which is why I restrict myself to a poetics and maintain that theology has to clear its head of metaphysics. Hence, in this essay, "perhaps" will serve as a dim but guiding light, a slightly anarchic quasi-principle, a principle without principle, whose flickering lead we are asked to follow with fear and trembling. We are called upon to be the *phronimoi* of the "perhaps," on the off chance that this may be theology, perhaps.

If the faithful stick around and hear me out to the bitter end, they will overhear that my faith is placed in what is going on *in* the name (of) "God" and of "theology," which is the insistence of the event, or the chance of the event, and the corresponding faith that God can happen anywhere. My faith is deeper than faith in God and cannot be contracted to faith in God. What corresponds to insistence is a deep and structural faith; what corresponds to existence is a belief that some being is or is not there. My faith is faith in faith itself—it's faith all the way down, and there is no bottom—which is what is involved in having faith in the event. Insistence is a pure trembling, a specter, almost nothing, like a spirit. There's no one out there, no hyper-entity, to ensure it will all turn out well in the end. According to my hermeneutic principle—which is never to avoid the difficulty in life[33]—the event that is going on in theology only emerges once we set loose this dangerous and problematic "perhaps," which sets loose the trouble with God, the auto-problematizing character of God, problematizing both insistence and existence, opening up a chasm, a chiasm, a chaosmos.

Amen. *Ite, missa est.* Go, it is ended, but I pray you, do not go in peace. Remember always to say "perhaps."

NOTES

1. Jacques Derrida, Force de loi: Le "Fondement mystique de l'autorité" (Paris: Galilée, 1994), 60–61; Jacques Derrida,"Force of Law: 'The Mystical Foundation of Authority,'" trans. Mary Quantaince, in *Acts of Religion*, ed. Gil Anidjar (New York: Routledge, 2002), 257.("Perhaps—one must always say perhaps for . . .")

2. Jacques Derrida, *Politics of Friendship*, trans. George Collins (New York: Verso, 1997), 34, 41, 43.

3. The expression "the fear of one small word" is a riff on the use that Slavoj Žižek makes of a line from G. K. Chesterton, who is speaking of our fear of "four words: He was made Man." See Slavoj Žižek and John Milbank, *The Monstrosity of Christ: Paradox or Dialectic*, ed. Creston Davis (Cambridge, MA: MIT Press, 2009), 25. Chesterton meant the Incarnation, and he really meant it. Žižek says these four words really mean the death of God. I am saying that they are really both too strong-minded, too orthodox, both afraid of just one small word.

4. Søren Kierkegaard, "The Rotation of Crops," in *Kierkegaard's Writings*, trans. and ed. Howard Hong and Edna Hong, vol. 3, *Either/Or, Part I* (Princeton, NJ: Princeton University Press, 1987), 281–300.

5. Jacques Derrida, *Paper Machine*, trans. Rachel Bowlby (Stanford: Stanford University Press, 2005), 74.

6. For an excellent introduction to the workings of this other order of the "perhaps," see Rodolphe Gasché, "Perhaps—A Modality," in *Of Minimal Things: Studies on the Notion of Relation*, by Rodolphe Gasché (Stanford: Stanford University Press, 1999), 173–91. Gasché explores the logic, or grammatologic, of "perhaps" in connection with its use by Martin Heidegger as a way to stay on the way to the Way, the Tao, which for Heidegger means staying *unterwegs*, on the way to the secret reserve of language. See also Colby Dickinson, "The Logic of the 'As If' and the Non-existence of God: An Inquiry into the Nature of Belief in the Work of Jacques Derrida," *Derrida Today* 4, no. 1 (2011): 86–106 (although we should remember the distance Derrida preserves between deconstruction and a "regulative ideal").

7. Derrida, *Politics of Friendship*, 43.

8. Ibid., 29.

9. On the thematics of the animal in Derrida, see Jacques Derrida, *The Animal That Therefore I Am*, ed. Marie-Louise Mallet, trans. David Wills (New York: Fordham University Press, 2008), and Jacques Derrida, *The Beast and the Sovereign*, vols. 1–2, trans. Geoffrey Bennington (Chicago: University of Chicago Press, 2009–11). On the assessment by the Jesus Seminar, see Robert W. Funk, Roy W. Hoover, and the Jesus Seminar, trans. and commentary, *The Five Gospels: The Search for the Authentic Words of Jesus* (New York: Macmillan, 1993), 169–70.

10. Derrida, *Paper Machine*, 90.

11. In my articulation of the figure of "insistence," I will draw throughout upon the motif of "specter" and "hauntology" found in Jacques Derrida, *Specters of Marx: The State of the Debt, the Work of Mourning, and the New International*, trans. Peggy Kamuf (New York: Routledge, 1994).

12. Derrida, *Paper Machine*, 89–90.

13. See Jacques Derrida, "Faith and Knowledge," no. 21, in Anidjar, *Acts of Religion*, 56.

14. Derrida, *Paper Machine*, 74.

15. Jacques Derrida, *Given Time, I: Counterfeit Money*, trans. Peggy Kamuf (Chicago: University of Chicago Press, 1991), 30.

16. If in logic "impossible" means the logical contradiction of the possible, then the impossible is more than impossible. If the possible is merely the logically possible, then "perhaps" is more than possible. See Jacques Derrida, *On the Name*, ed. Thomas Detroit (Stanford: Stanford University Press, 1995), 43.

17. Jacques Derrida, *Of Grammatology*, corrected ed., trans. Gayatri Spivak (Baltimore: Johns Hopkins University Press, 1997), 18.

18. I will rely upon and elaborate throughout Derrida's distinction between *foi* and *croyance*, found in "Faith and Knowledge," no. 11, p. 47, and in many other later texts.

19. Derrida, *Paper Machine*, 96.

20. Derrida, *On the Name*, 64.

21. Derrida, *Politics of Friendship*, 35, 42–43.

22. John Keats, *The Complete Poetical Works and Letters of John Keats—Cambridge Edition* (repr., Whitefish, MT: Kessinger, 2010), 277.

23. Jacques Derrida, *Memoirs d'aveugle: L'autoportrait et autres ruines* (Paris: Éditions de la Réunion des musées nationaux, 1990), 129; Jacques Derrida, *Memoirs of the Blind: The Self-Portrait and Other Ruins*, trans. Pascale-Anne Brault and Michael Naas (Chicago: University of Chicago Press, 1993), 130.

24. Jacques Derrida, "Force of Law," 257 (translation modified).

25. As a matter of terminological usage, Derrida himself prefers the English "perhaps" to "maybe." That is because "perhaps" suggests happenstance and chance, and hence is closer to what he means by the "event," while "maybe" is more closely linked to the being and potentiality of metaphysics. But I have not given up entirely on "maybe" and I especially appreciate the ambiance of "might" (strong) and "might be" (weak, subjunctive). See Jacques Derrida, "Perhaps or Maybe," *Pli: Warwick Journal of Philosophy* 6 (1997): 1–18.

26. This is the question I raise with Richard Kearney about what he calls the "God Who May Be" versus what I am calling "God, perhaps." See John D. Caputo, "God, Perhaps: The Diacritical Hermeneutics of God in the Work of Richard Kearney," in "Philosophical Thresholds: Crossings of Life and World," ed. Cynthia Willett and Leonard Lawlor, SPEP supplement, *Philosophy Today* 55 (2011), 56–65, and Kearney's reply, "Eros, Diacritical Hermeneutics and the 'Maybe,'" also in the SPEP supplement. Some of the present discussion is borrowed from these pages.

27. See the exchange I have with James Olthuis about the makeup of *khora* in Neal Deroo and Marko Zlomsic, eds., *Cross and Khora: Deconstruction and Christianity in the Work of John D. Caputo* (Eugene, OR: Pickwick, 2010), 174–96, and with Richard Kearney in Mark Dooley, ed., *A Passion for the Impossible: John D. Caputo in Focus* (Albany: SUNY Press, 2003), 107–28.

28. As Derrida points out, the trace of such an idea is already inscribed in the old theology, in the dangerous tradition of Giordano Bruno, Nicolaus Cusanus, and Jakob Böhme. "They define God as 'perhaps.' God is the perhaps." Jacques Derrida, "Deconstructions: The Impossible," in *French Theory in America*, ed. Slyvère Lotringer and Sande Cohen (New York: Routledge, 2001), 31.

29. The chiasmic intertwining of Cixous and Derrida that constitutes their lifelong friendship is described by them as their mutual "insistence," she in him, he in her, his texts in hers, her texts in his. See Hélène Cixous, *Insister of Jacques Derrida*, trans. Peggy Kamuf (Stanford: Stanford University Press, 2007), 52.

30. This goes back to Heidegger, *Being and Time*, trans. John Macquarrie and Edward Robinson (New York: Harper & Row, 1962), 319 (§ 57): the caller refuses to make itself known, to identify itself, and this indefiniteness is not a defect but belongs to its positive constitution.

31. The first time I find him doing so is also one of the best: Jacques Derrida, "Psyche: Invention of the Other," *Psyche: Inventions of the Other*, vol. 1, trans. Peggy Kamuf and Elizabeth Rottenberg (Stanford: Stanford University Press, 2007), 1–47.

32. For one thing, as Johannes Climacus says, prayer as the infinite pathos of existence is incommensurate with any outward expression and always has something comic about it. I always think of the paintings of saints with an unctuous look on their face, their eyes cast heavenward, by which I was surrounded while growing up. Howard Hong and Edna Hong, trans. and eds., *Kierkegaard's Writings*, vol. 7.1, *Concluding Unscientific Postscript to Philosophical Fragments* (Princeton, NJ: Princeton University Press, 1992), 90–91.

33. Remaining loyal to the difficulty of life is the motif of Erick Jansson and Jack D. Caputo, *Radical Hermeneutics: Repetition, Deconstruction and the Hermeneutic Project* (Bloomington: Indiana University Press, 1987). The radical theology of the present book may be thought of as the outcome of this radical hermeneutics, although it is of course one that I did not see coming. I am always feeling around for a non-foundational sense of "radical," for a radical risk or groundlessness as opposed to a single absolute ground or foundation.

INDEX

B. KEITH PUTT is Professor of Philosophy at Samford University in Birmingham, Alabama. He is editor (with Clayton Crockett and Jeffrey W. Robbins) of *The Future of Continental Philosophy of Religion* (Indiana University Press). His primary interests lie in the areas of Continental philosophy and philosophy of religion, specifically the radical hermeneutics and radical theology of John D. Caputo.

JOHN D. CAPUTO is Thomas J. Watson Professor Emeritus of Religion and Humanities at Syracuse University and the David R. Cook Professor of Philosophy Emeritus at Villanova University. He is author of many books, including *The Weakness of God: A Theology of the Event* (Indiana University Press), *The Insistence of God: A Theology of Perhaps* (Indiana University Press), *Hoping Against Hope: Confessions of a Postmodern Pilgrim*, and *Truth: Philosophy in Transit.*

CPSIA information can be obtained
at www.ICGtesting.com
Printed in the USA
BVHW011216280219
541296BV00049B/1390/P